The first**writer**.com

Writers' Handbook
2015

The first**writer**.com

Writers' Handbook
2015

EDITOR
J. PAUL DYSON

Published in 2014 by JP&A Dyson
Copyright JP&A Dyson

http://www.firstwriter.com

ISBN 978-1-909935-05-1

Registered with the IP Rights Office
Copyright Registration Service
Ref: 3009962426

Foreword

The firstwriter.com Writers' Handbook returns for its 2015 edition with over 1,200 listings of literary agents, publishers, and magazines, updated in firstwriter.com's online databases between 2012 and 2014, including revised and updated listings from the previous edition and 30% new entries.

The 2014 version of the handbook was bought by writers across the United States, Canada, and Europe; and in the United Kingdom it became the number one bestselling writing and publishing directory on Amazon.co.uk within just a few weeks of its launch. The 2015 edition continues this international outlook, giving writers all over the English-speaking world access to the global publishing markets.

Readers of this edition can also benefit from insights from Andrew Lownie, of the Andrew Lownie Literary Agency Ltd, who offers tips and advice on how best to approach literary agents.

The handbook also provides free online access to the entire current firstwriter.com databases, including over 850 literary agencies, over 1,600 book publishers, over 1,800 magazines, and constantly updated listings of current writing competitions, with typically more than 50 added each month.

For details on how to claim your free access please see the back of this book.

Included in the subscription

A subscription to the full website is not only free with this book, but comes packed with all the following features:

Advanced search features

- Save searches and save time – set up to 15 search parameters specific to your work, save them, and then access the search results with a single click whenever you log in. You can even save multiple different searches if you have different types of work you are looking to place.
- Add personal notes to listings, visible only to you and fully searchable – helping you to organise your actions.
- Set reminders on listings to notify you when to submit your work, when to follow up, when to expect a reply, or any other custom action.
- Track which listings you've viewed and when, to help you organise your search – any listings which have changed since you last viewed them will be highlighted for your attention!

Daily email updates

As a subscriber you will be able to take advantage of our email alert service, meaning you can specify your particular interests and we'll send you automatic email updates when we change or add a listing that matches them. So if you're interested in agents dealing in romantic fiction in the United States you can have us send you emails with the latest updates about them – keeping you up to date without even having to log in.

User feedback

Our agent, publisher, and magazine databases all include a user feedback feature that allows our subscribers to leave feedback on each listing – giving you not only the chance to have your say about the markets you contact, but giving a unique authors' perspective on the listings.

Save on copyright protection fees

If you're sending your work away to publishers, competitions, or literary agents, it's vital that you first protect your copyright. As a subscriber to firstwriter.com you can do this through our site and save 10% on the copyright registration fees normally payable for protecting your work internationally through the Intellectual Property Rights Office (http://www.Copyright RegistrationService.com).

firstwriter.magazine

firstwriter.magazine showcases the best in new poetry and fiction from around the world. If you're interested in writing and want to get published, the most important thing you can do is read contemporary writing that's getting into print now. Our magazine helps you do that.

Half price competitions

As well as saving money on copyright registration, subscribers to firstwriter.com can also make further savings by entering writing competitions at a special reduced rate. Subscribers can enter the firstwriter.com International Poetry Competition and International Short Story Contest for half price.

Monthly newsletter

When you subscribe to firstwriter.com you also receive our monthly email newsletter – described by one publishing company as "the best in the business" – including articles, news, and interviews for writers. And the best part is that you can continue to receive the newsletter even after you stop your paid subscription – at no cost!

For details on how to claim your free access please see the back of this book.

Contents

*Claim your FREE access to **www.firstwriter.com**: See p.379*

Magazines

Free Access

Glossary of Terms

This section explains common terms used in this handbook, and in the publishing industry more generally.

Academic

Listings in this book will be marked as targeting the academic market only if they publish material of an academic nature; e.g. academic theses, scientific papers, etc. The term is not used to indicate publications that publish general material aimed at people who happen to be in academia, or who are described as academic by virtue of being educated.

Adult

In publishing, "adult" simply refers to books that are aimed at adults, as opposed to books that are aimed at children, or young adults, etc. It is not a euphemism for pornographic or erotic content. Nor does it necessarily refer to content which is unsuitable for children; it is just not targeted at them. In this book, most ordinary mainstream publishers will be described as "adult", unless their books are specifically targeted at other groups (such as children, professionals, etc.).

Agented

An *agented* submission is one which is submitted by a literary agent. If a publisher accepts only *agented* submissions then you will need a literary agent to submit the work on your behalf.

Author bio

A brief description of you and your life – normally in relation to your writing activity, but if intended for publication (particularly in magazines) may be broader in scope. May be similar to *Curriculum Vitae* (CV) or résumé, depending on context.

Bio

See *Author bio*.

Curriculum Vitae

A brief description of you, your qualifications, and accomplishments – normally in this context in relation to writing (any previous publications, or awards, etc.), but in the case of nonfiction proposals may also include relevant experience that qualifies you to write on the subject. Commonly abbreviated to "CV". May also be referred to as a résumé. May be similar to *Author bio*, depending on context.

CV

See *Curriculum Vitae*.

International Reply Coupon

When submitting material overseas you may be required to enclose *International Reply Coupons*, which will enable the recipient to send a response and/or return your material at your cost. Not applicable/available in all countries, so check with your local Post Office for more information.

IRC

See *International Reply Coupon*.

Manuscript

Your complete piece of work – be it a novel, short story, or article, etc. – will be referred to as your manuscript. Commonly abbreviated to "ms" (singular) or "mss" (plural).

MS
See *Manuscript*.

MSS
See *Manuscript*.

Professional
Listings in this book will be marked as targeting the professional market if they publish material serving a particular profession: e.g. legal journals, medical journals, etc. The term is not used to indicate publications that publish general material aimed at a notional "professional class".

Proposal
A proposal is normally requested for nonfiction projects (where the book may not yet have been completed, or even begun). Proposals can consist of a number of components, such as an outline, table of contents, CV, marketing information, etc. but the exact requirements will vary from one publisher to another.

Query
Many agents and publishers will prefer to receive a query in the first instance, rather than your full *manuscript*. A query will typically consist of a cover letter accompanied by a *synopsis* and/or sample chapter(s). Specific requirements will vary, however, so always check on a case by case basis.

SAE
See *Stamped Addressed Envelope*. Can also be referred to as SASE.

SASE
Self-Addressed Stamped Envelope.

Variation of SAE. See *Stamped Addressed Envelope*.

Stamped Addressed Envelope
Commonly abbreviated to "SAE". Can also be referred to as Self-Addressed Stamped Envelope, or SASE. When supplying an SAE, ensure that the envelope and postage is adequate for a reply or the return of your material, as required. If you are submitting overseas, remember that postage from your own country will not be accepted, and you may need to provide an *International Reply Coupon*.

Synopsis
A short outline of your story. This should cover all the main characters and events, including the ending. It is not the kind of "teaser" found on a book's back cover. The length of synopsis required can vary, but is generally between one and three pages.

TOC
Table of Contents. These are often requested as part of nonfiction proposals.

Unagented
An unagented submission is one which is not submitted through a literary agent. If a publisher accepts unagented submissions then you can approach them directly.

Unsolicited mss
A manuscript which has not been requested. Many agents and publishers will not accept unsolicited mss, but this does not necessarily mean they are closed to approaches – many will prefer to receive a short *query* in the first instance. If they like the idea, they will request the full work, which will then be a solicited manuscript.

Youth
The term "Youth" in this book is used to indicate the Young Adult market.

Formatting Your Manuscript

Before submitting a manuscript to an agent, magazine, or publisher, it's important that you get the formatting right. There are industry norms covering everything from the size of your margins to the font you choose – get them wrong and you'll be marking yourself out as an amateur. Get them right, and agents and editors will be far more likely to take you seriously.

Fonts

Don't be tempted to "make your book stand out" by using fancy fonts. It *will* stand out, but not for any reason you'd want. Your entire manuscript should be in a monospaced font like Courier (not a proportional font, like Times Roman) at 12 points. (A monospaced font is one where each character takes up the same amount of space; a proportional font is where the letter "i" takes up less space than the letter "m".)

This goes for your text, your headings, your title, your name – everything. Your objective is to produce a manuscript that looks like it has been produced on a simple typewriter.

Italics / bold

Your job as the author is to indicate words that require emphasis, not to pick particular styles of font. This will be determined by the house style of the publisher in question. You indicate emphasis by underlining text; the publisher will decide whether they will use bold or italic to achieve this emphasis – you shouldn't use either in your text.

Margins

You should have a one inch (2.5 centimetre) margin around your entire page: top, bottom, left, and right.

Spacing

In terms of line spacing, your entire manuscript should be double spaced. Your word processor should provide an option for this, so you don't have to insert blank lines manually.

While line spacing should be double, spaces after punctuation should be single. If you're in the habit of putting two spaces after full stops this is the time to get out of that habit, and remove them from your manuscript. You're just creating extra work for the editor who will have to strip them all out.

Do not put blank lines between paragraphs. Start every paragraph (even those at the start of chapters) with an indent equivalent to five spaces. If you want a scene break then create a line with the "#" character centred in the middle. You don't need blank lines above or below this line.

Word count

You will need to provide an estimated word count on the front page of your manuscript. Tempting as it will be to simply use the word processor's word counting function to tell you exactly how many words there are in your manuscript, this is not what you should do. Instead, you should work out the maximum number of characters on a line, divide this number by six, and then multiply by the total number of lines in your manuscript.

Once you have got your estimated word count you need to round it to an approximate value. How you round will depend on the overall length of your manuscript:

- up to 1,500 words: round to the nearest 100;
- 1,500–10,000 words: round to the nearest 500;
- 10,000–25,000 words: round to the nearest 1,000;
- Over 25,000 words: round to the nearest 5,000.

The reason an agent or editor will need to know your word count is so that they can estimate how many pages it will make. Since actual pages include varying amounts of white space due to breaks in paragraphs, sections of speech, etc. the formula above will actually provide a better idea of how many pages will be required than an exact word count would.

And – perhaps more importantly – providing an exact word count will highlight you immediately as an amateur.

Layout of the front page

On the first page of the manuscript, place your name, address, and any other relevant contact details (such as phone number, email address, etc.) in the top left-hand corner. In the top right-hand corner write your approximate word count.

If you have registered your work for copyright protection, place the reference number two single lines (one double line) beneath your contact details. Since your manuscript will only be seen by agents or editors, not the public, this should be done as discreetly as possible, and you should refrain from using any official seal you may have been granted permissions to use. (For information on registering for copyright protection see "Protecting Your Copyright", below.)

Place your title halfway down the front page. Your title should be centred and would normally be in capital letters. You can make it bold or underlined if you want, but it should be the same size as the rest of the text.

From your title, go down two single lines (or one double line) and insert your byline. This should be centred and start with the word "By", followed by the name you are writing under. This can be your name or a pen name, but should be the name you want the work published under. However, make sure that the name in the top left-hand corner is your real, legal name.

From your byline, go down four single lines (or two double lines) and begin your manuscript.

Layout of the text

Print on only one side of the paper, even if your printer can print on both sides.

In the top right-hand corner of all pages except the first should be your running head. This should be comprised of the surname used in your byline; a keyword from your title, and the page number, e.g. "Myname / Mynovel Page 5".

Text should be left-aligned, *not* justified. This means that you should have a ragged right-hand edge to the text, with lines ending at different points. Make sure you don't have any sort of hyphenation function switched on in your word processor: if a word is too long to fit on a line it should be taken over to the next.

Start each new chapter a third of the way down the page with the centred chapter number / title, underlined. Drop down four single lines (two double lines) to the main text.

At the end of the manuscript you do not need to indicate the ending in any way: you don't need to write "The End", or "Ends", etc. The only exception to this is if your manuscript happens to end at the bottom of a page, in which case you can handwrite the word "End" at the bottom of the last page, after you have printed it out.

Protecting Your Copyright

Protecting your copyright is by no means a requirement before submitting your work, but you may feel that it is a prudent step that you would like to take before allowing strangers to see your material.

These days, you can register your work for copyright protection quickly and easily online. The Intellectual Property Rights Office operates a website called the "Copyright Registration Service" which allows you to do this:

- *http://www.CopyrightRegistrationService.com*

This website can be used for material created in any nation signed up to the Berne Convention. This includes the United States, United Kingdom, Canada, Australia, Ireland, New Zealand, and most other countries. There are around 180 countries in the world, and over 160 of them are part of the Berne Convention.

Provided you created your work in one of the Berne Convention nations, your work should be protected by copyright in all other Berne Convention nations. You can therefore protect your copyright around most of the world with a single registration, and because the process is entirely online you can have your work protected in a matter of minutes, without having to print and post a copy of your manuscript.

Some Tips on Approaching an Agent

Andrew Lownie, of the Andrew Lownie Literary Agency Ltd, offers some advice on how best to present yourself to an agent.

Authors are often angry, frustrated or shocked by the responses or lack of responses from agents, and it might be useful to give some background and advice which might help with pitching to agents.

Your book is special to you, and may one day be to other people, but at the moment it is just another submission. Authors need to remember that agents are inundated with submissions. Most have full lists already and need to concentrate on their existing clients. Of course agents are looking for new talent, but the chances of selling books from the slush pile are small.

Some agents claim they have never sold anything from the slush pile, though I take it very seriously, and personally look at almost twenty thousand submissions each year. Given each submission may be over forty pages long, that is a lot of reading to fit around the reading of my existing clients' work, such as the fifty delivered manuscripts each year, and the normal work of the agency.

The most promising submissions – some eight a week – once read by me are passed to one of my specialist readers where the average charge for a reading will be about £40, which I pay; my bill for reading each year is over £15,000. Sometimes I will obtain several reports and spend years with authors reworking proposals and still fail to sell the book. Out of all those submissions, I will only take on around a dozen authors a year, and of those I might place eight.

The decision whether or not to look more carefully at a submission is made quickly, so authors may benefit from the following tips:

Address the agent correctly. I often receive proposals meant for other agencies, Mr Brown, Mr Mooney, Ms Lownie, the Andrew Lownie Litter Agency, the Andrew Lownie Literacy Agency. Sometimes the email claims to be addressed to me exclusively but refers to another agent in the body of the text.

Make sure the agent actually handles what you are offering. Well over half my submissions are for genres which, in all the reference books and on my website, I categorically say I don't represent. I don't know any agency which handles poetry and short stories so best to try publishers direct in those genres.

There are a number of annual reference books that list the leading literary agents, such as *The firstwriter.com Writers' Handbook*, the *Writers' and Artists' Yearbook* and *Guardian Media Guide*. Many agencies now have web-sites giving a good sense of what they handle and their success rates There are countless websites, such as *http://www.firstwriter.com*, giving information about submitting to agencies and publishers and numerous writing magazines, such as *Writer's News* and *Writing Monthly*, with tips not just on writing books but also placing material.

Pitch by email rather than phone as it's the writing which will sell you. If leaving a phone message, explain why you have phoned. You are unlikely to receive a return call to Australia if you simply say "Steve called".

Try and personalise your email. It is easy enough now agencies have websites to find out the authors they handle. Look at the acknowledgements page of books which are comparable and try the agent who handled the book. Any email submission which I see has been copied to hundreds of other agencies is immediately discarded. A submission which shows the author has done research on the agency and comes with a recommendation is always taken seriously.

Follow instructions. If agencies have a preferred format then follow it and customise your proposal. The format is generally the one that they find works with publishers and helps everyone assess the proposal most effectively. Don't insist they read the whole manuscript.

In the agency we initially ask for a short synopsis and the first three chapters for fiction. For nonfiction we ask for:

- one page mini-synopsis highlighting with bullet points what makes the book new and special with proposed word count and delivery date;
- one page on your qualifications to write the book;
- one page with a few lines on the five most recent competing and comparable books, giving author, title, publisher and date of publication together with a note on how the books relate to the author's own book;
- one page on sources used;
- one page on any specialist marketing outlets such as websites, organisations or magazines; and
- a sample chapter.

We then ask for a half page synopsis per chapter – roughly ten pages – if we are interested and want to take it further.

If the book is categorically rejected then don't respond pointing out the agent has made a "mistake". Move on to the next agency. It is a subjective business and agents turn down proposals – even perfectly publishable ones – for all sorts of specific reasons, even if they don't always give you those reasons.

Agents understand that authors need to make multiple submissions to agencies but dislike "beauty parades". It is not flattering nor encouraging to be told you are simply one of a hundred approaches. Time is limited, and if an agent suspects the author may go elsewhere then they will simply say "no" at the beginning. Keep quiet about multiple submissions and only send a few at a time so you can adapt your submission in the light of the responses you receive.

Agencies are keen to find and nurture talent but they are inundated with submissions. Remember they are businesses, not the Citizens Advice Bureau; manuscript evaluation services; or a branch of Social Services. Don't expect them to recommend other agencies within or outside their areas of expertise.

Presentation is important. Check spelling and punctuation. Don't underline or use exclamation marks.

Submissions should be sent by email, preferably as Microsoft Word files or similar, not least as this is how we will submit. Gone are the days of photocopied proposals and scripts being posted. Remember that often more than thirty people in a publishing company may be asked to assess the submission so it needs to be circulated easily. My agency no longer accepts submissions by post.

Be clear in your covering letter. The concept of the book should be apparent in the opening sentence.

Don't boast – the agent will be the judge of the quality of the material – but do highlight in a covering note what you think makes your book different and special.

Not every idea makes a book. It might solely work as a television programme and long article.

And remember, if you receive lots of rejections, that not every book is sufficiently commercial for an agent or trade publisher. There are now plenty of opportunities to self-publish without being ripped off.

The Andrew Lownie Literary Agency Ltd, founded in 1988, is one of the UK's leading boutique literary agencies, with some two hundred nonfiction and fiction authors handled respectively by Andrew Lownie and David Haviland. It prides itself on its personal attention to its clients and specialises both in launching new writers and taking established writers to a new level of recognition. Andrew Lownie remains the top selling agent worldwide, according to Publishers Marketplace, and was short-listed for Literary Agent of the Year at the 2013 and 2014 Bookseller Awards.

Books represented have included: The Cambridge Guide to Literature in English; The Oxford Classical Dictionary; The Penguin Companion to the European Union; Norma Major's history of Chequers; the memoirs of Sir John Mills, Alan Whicker, Gloria Hunniford, David Hasselhoff, Emily Lloyd, Kerry Katona and Patrick MacNee; the best-selling fostering series by Cathy Glass and Casey Watson; Sam Faiers' Living Life the Essex Way; Daniel Tammet's international best-seller Born on a Blue Day; Laurence Gardner'sThe Magdalene Legacy and The Shadow of Solomon, the literary estates of Joyce Cary and Julian MacLaren-Ross; the historians Juliet Barker, Roger Crowley, Tom Devine, Robert Hutchinson, Sean McMeekin, Linda Porter, Geoff Roberts ,Desmond Seward, David Stafford and Christian Wolmar; the wine writer Michael Schuster; crime writers, such as Mei Trow and David Roberts, and thriller writers such as Duncan Falconer.

US Literary Agents

For the most up-to-date listings of these and hundreds of other literary agents, visit http://www.firstwriter.com/Agents

*To claim your **free** access to the site, please see the back of this book.*

A+B Works

Email: query@aplusbworks.com
Website: http://www.aplusbworks.com

Handles: Fiction; Nonfiction; *Areas:* Women's Interests; *Markets:* Adult; Children's; Youth

Specialises in young adult and middle grade fiction, women's fiction, and select narrative nonfiction. No thrillers, literary fiction, erotica, cook books, picture books, poetry, short fiction, or screenplays. Query by email only. Response not guaranteed. Accepts very few new clients.

Dominick Abel Literary Agency, Inc

146 W. 82nd Street, #1B, New York, NY 10024
Tel: +1 (212) 877-0710
Fax: +1 (212) 595-3133
Email: dominick@dalainc.com

Handles: Fiction; Nonfiction; *Markets:* Adult

Handles adult fiction and nonfiction. 100 clients. Not accepting submissions as at September 2013.

Above the Line Agency

468 N. Camden Drive, #200, Beverly Hills, CA 90210
Tel: +1 (310) 859-6115
Fax: +1 (310) 859-6119
Website: http://www.abovethelineagency.com

Handles: Scripts; *Areas:* Film; TV; *Markets:* Adult; Children's

Send query via online web system only. Represents writers and directors; feature films, movies of the week, animation.

Bret Adams Ltd

448 West 44th Street, New York, NY 10036
Tel: +1 (212) 765-5630
Email: bretadamsltd@bretadamsltd.net
Website: http://www.bretadamsltd.net

Handles: Scripts; *Areas:* Film; Theatre; TV; *Markets:* Adult

Handles projects for theatre, film, and TV only. No books. No unsolicited submissions. Accepts approaches by referral only.

Adams Literary

7845 Colony Road, C4 #215, Charlotte, NC 28226
Tel: +1 (704) 542-1440
Fax: +1 (704) 542-1450
Email: submissions@adamsliterary.com
Website: http://www.adamsliterary.com

Handles: Fiction; *Markets:* Children's; Youth

Handles books for children, from picture books to teen novels. No unsolicited MSS. Send query with complete ms via webform, or by email if you encounter problems with the webform. See website for full submission guidelines.

The Agency Group, Ltd
142 West 57th Street, Sixth Floor, New York, NY 10019
Tel: +1 (310) 385-2800
Fax: +1 (310) 385-1220
Email: marcgerald@theagencygroup.com
Website: http://www.theagencygroup.com

Handles: Fiction; Nonfiction; *Areas:* Anthropology; Archaeology; Architecture; Arts; Autobiography; Biography; Business; Cookery; Crime; Culture; Design; Entertainment; Finance; Health; Historical; How-to; Humour; Legal; Lifestyle; Medicine; Music; Nature; Politics; Psychology; Self-Help; Sport; *Markets:* Adult

Multimedia agency representing recording artists, celebrities, and with a literary agency operating out of the New York office. Takes on new clients by referral only.

Agency for the Performing Arts (APA)
405 S. Beverly Dr , Beverly Hills, CA 90212
Tel: +1 (310) 888-4200
Fax: +1 (310) 888-4242
Website: http://www.apa-agency.com

Handles: Fiction; Nonfiction; Scripts; *Areas:* Film; Theatre; TV; *Markets:* Adult

Handles nonfiction, novels, scripts for film, theatre, and TV, as well as musicians and other performing artists.

Aimee Entertainment Agency
15840 Ventura Blvd., Ste. 215, Encino, CA 91436
Tel: +1 (818) 783-3831
Fax: +1 (818) 783-4447

Email: info@onlinemediapublications.com
Website: http://www.aimeeentertainment.com

Handles: Fiction; Scripts; *Areas:* Film; *Markets:* Adult

Handles film scripts and book-length works.

Ambassador Speakers Bureau & Literary Agency
PO Box 50358, Nashville, TN 37205
Tel: +1 (615) 370-4700
Fax: +1 (615) 661-4344
Email: info@ambassadorspeakers.com
Website: http://www.ambassadorspeakers.com

Handles: Fiction; Nonfiction; *Areas:* Adventure; Autobiography; Biography; Culture; Current Affairs; Finance; Health; Historical; How-to; Legal; Lifestyle; Medicine; Politics; Religious; Self-Help; Women's Interests; *Markets:* Adult; *Treatments:* Contemporary; Literary; Mainstream

Represents select authors and writers who are published by religious and general market publishers in the US and Europe.No short stories, children's books, screenplays, or poetry. Send query by email with short description. Submit work on invitation only.

Anonymous Content
588 Broadway, Suite 308, New York, NY 10012
Tel: +1 (212) 925-0055
Fax: +1 (212) 925-5030
Email: litmanagement@anonymouscontent.com
Website: http://www.anonymouscontent.com

Handles: Scripts; *Areas:* Film; TV; *Markets:* Adult

Works in the areas of film, TV, adverts, and music videos.

Robert Astle & Associates Literary Management, Inc.
419 Lafayette Street, New York, NY 10003

Tel: +1 (212) 277-8014
Fax: +1 (212) 228-6149
Email: robert@astleliterary.com
Website: http://www.astleliterary.com

Handles: Fiction; Nonfiction; *Areas:* Arts; Autobiography; Biography; Culture; Drama; Historical; Humour; Media; Mystery; Politics; Sport; Suspense; Theatre; Thrillers; Travel; Women's Interests; *Markets:* Adult; Children's; Youth; *Treatments:* Commercial; Literary; Mainstream

See website for submission guidelines. States that email submissions are preferred and provides details of format email should take, but also provides web form for submission and asks authors to make their approach via it. No attachments or mass emails.

Audrey A. Wolf Literary Agency

2510 Virginia Avenue NW, #702N, Washington, DC 20037
Email: audreyrwolf@gmail.com

Handles: Nonfiction; *Areas:* Autobiography; Biography; Business; Current Affairs; Finance; Health; Historical; Lifestyle; Politics; Self-Help; Sport; *Markets:* Adult

Send query by post or email, including synopsis up to two pages long showing the full structure of the book: beginning, middle, and end. Also include chapter outline.

Avenue A Literary LLC

419 Lafayette Street, 2nd Floor, New York, NY 10003
Tel: +1 (212) 624-5859
Fax: +1 (212) 228-6149
Email: submissions@avenuealiterary.com
Website:
http://www.avenuealiterary.com/93.html

Handles: Fiction; Nonfiction; *Markets:* Adult; Youth; *Treatments:* Commercial; Literary

Actively seeking new authors of fiction and nonfiction. Send query of about 400 words by email only, with plot synopsis and author bio (including any publishing history). All

information must be in the body of your email. Emails with attachments will not be read. No hard copy submissions.

Barbara Hogenson Agency

165 West End Ave., Suite 19-C, New York, NY 10023
Tel: +1 (212) 874-8084
Fax: +1 (212) 362-3011
Email: Bhogenson@aol.com

Handles: Fiction; Nonfiction; Scripts; *Areas:* Theatre; *Markets:* Adult

Represents fiction, nonfiction, and stage plays. Send query by email only. No unsolicited MSS.

Barer Literary, LLC

20 West 20th Street, Suite 601, New York, NY 10011
Tel: +1 (212) 691-3513
Fax: +1 (212) 691-3540
Email: submissions@barerliterary.com
Website: http://www.barerliterary.com

Handles: Fiction; Nonfiction; *Areas:* Biography; Culture; Historical; Short Stories; Women's Interests; *Markets:* Adult; *Treatments:* Contemporary; Literary; Mainstream

Send query with SASE and sample of the work. Material will not be returned without the proper postage. No reponse will be given to queries by phone or fax. Queries by email are accepted, provided they do not include attachments. Handles a wide range of fiction and nonfiction, but no Health/Fitness, Business/Investing/Finance, Sports, Mind/Body/Spirit, Reference, Thrillers/Suspense, Military, Romance, Children's Books/Picture Books, Screenplays. No longer seeking Young Adult.

Bidnick & Company

Email: bidnick@comcast.net

Handles: Nonfiction; *Areas:* Cookery; *Markets:* Adult

Handles cookbooks and narrative nonfiction. Send query by email only.

Vicky Bijur Literary Agency
333 West End Avenue, Apt. 5B, New York, NY 10023
Email: queries@vickybijuragency.com
Website: http://www.vickybijuragency.com

Handles: Fiction; Nonfiction; *Areas:* Biography; Cookery; Health; Historical; Politics; Psychology; Science; Self-Help; Sociology; *Markets:* Adult

Send query by email or by post with SASE. For fiction include synopsis and first chapter (pasted into the body of the email if submitting electronically). For nonfiction include proposal. No attachments or queries by phone or fax. No children's books, poetry, science fiction, fantasy, horror, or romance.

Brandt & Hochman Literary Agents, Inc.
1501 Broadway, Suite 2310, New York, NY 10036
Tel: +1 (212) 840-5760
Fax: +1 (212) 840-5776
Email: ghochman@bromasite.com
Website: http://brandthochman.com

Handles: Fiction; Nonfiction; *Areas:* Arts; Autobiography; Culture; Current Affairs; Health; Historical; Lifestyle; Mystery; Science; Thrillers; *Markets:* Adult; Children's; Youth; *Treatments:* Commercial; Literary; Popular

Send query by post with SASE or by email with query letter up to two pages long, including overview and author details and writing credits. See website for full submission guidelines and for details of individual agents' interests and direct contact details, then approach one agent specifically. No screenplays or textbooks. Response to email queries not guaranteed.

The Helen Brann Agency, Inc.
94 Curtis Road, Bridgewater, CT 06752
Fax: +1 (860) 355-2572

Email: helenbrannagency@earthlink.net

Handles: Fiction; Nonfiction; *Markets:* Adult

Send query with SASE. Works mostly with established writers and referrals.

Paul Bresnick Literary Agency, LLC
115 West 29th Street, 10th Floor, New York, NY 10001
Tel: +1 (212) 239-3166
Fax: +1 (212) 239-3165
Email: query@bresnickagency.com
Website: http://bresnickagency.com

Handles: Fiction; Nonfiction; *Areas:* Autobiography; Biography; Crime; Culture; Health; Historical; Humour; Lifestyle; Psychology; Sport; Travel; *Markets:* Adult; *Treatments:* Popular

Send query by email only, with two sample chapters (fiction) or proposal (nonfiction).

Brown Literary Agency
410 7th Street NW, Naples, FL 34120-2039
Tel: +1 (239) 455-7190
Email: broagent@aol.com
Website: http://www.brownliteraryagency.com

Handles: Fiction; *Areas:* Erotic; Historical; Humour; Mystery; Romance; Suspense; Thrillers; Women's Interests; *Markets:* Adult; Youth; *Treatments:* Contemporary

Handles romantic fiction for women only. Within these categories will consider romantic suspense, humour, contemporary, historical, and paranormal. Send query by email only with synopsis and one chapter.

Tracy Brown Literary Agency
P.O. Box 88, Scarsdale, NY 10583
Tel: +1 (914) 400-4147
Fax: +1 (914) 931-1746
Email: tracy@brownlit.com

Handles: Fiction; Nonfiction; *Areas:* Biography; Current Affairs; Health;

Historical; Humour; Nature; Psychology; Sport; Travel; Women's Interests; *Markets:* Adult; *Treatments:* Contemporary; Literary; Mainstream; Serious

Send query with author bio, outline/proposal, synopsis, and one sample chapter. Queries accepted by email but not by fax. No Young Adult, Science Fiction, or Romance.

Marcus Bryan & Associates Inc.

1500 Skokie Boulevard, Suite 310, Northbrook, IL 60068
Tel: +1 (847) 412-9394
Fax: +1 (847) 412-9394
Email: mba3308@aol.com
Website: http://marcusbryan.com

Handles: Fiction; Scripts; *Markets:* Adult

Note: Not accepting new clients as at July 2013. Check website for current status.

Accepts query letters from book authors and screenwriters.

Sheree Bykofsky Associates, Inc.

4326 Harbor Beach Boulevard, PO Box 706, Brigantine, NJ 08203
Email: submitbee@aol.com
Website: http://www.shereebee.com

Handles: Fiction; Nonfiction; Reference; *Areas:* Biography; Business; Cookery; Culture; Current Affairs; Film; Hobbies; Humour; Lifestyle; Mystery; Psychology; Self-Help; Spiritual; Women's Interests; *Markets:* Adult; *Treatments:* Commercial; Literary

Send query by email only. Include one page query, and for fiction a one page synopsis, and first page of manuscript, all in the body of the email. No attachments. Always looking for a bestseller in any category, but generally not interested in poetry, thrillers, westerns, romances, occult, science fiction, fantasy, children's or young adult.

Maria Carvainis Agency, Inc.

1270 Avenue of the Americas, Suite 2320, New York, NY 10020
Tel: +1 (212) 245-6365
Fax: +1 (212) 245-7196
Email: mca@mariacarvainisagency.com
Website: http://mariacarvainisagency.com

Handles: Fiction; Nonfiction; *Areas:* Autobiography; Biography; Business; Culture; Finance; Historical; Mystery; Psychology; Science; Suspense; Technology; Thrillers; Women's Interests; *Markets:* Adult; Children's; Youth; *Treatments:* Contemporary; Literary; Mainstream; Popular

Send query with synopsis, two sample chapters, and details of any previous writing credits, by post or by email. If sending by post and return of the material is required, include SASE; otherwise include email address for response, usually within 5-10 days. If submitting by email, all documents must be Word or PDF. No screenplays, children's picture books, science fiction, or poetry.

Castiglia Literary Agency

1155 Camino Del Mar, Suite 510, Del Mar, CA 92014
Tel: +1 (858) 755-8761
Fax: +1 (858) 755-7063
Email: CastigliaAgency-query@yahoo.com
Website: http://www.castigliaagency.com

Handles: Fiction; Nonfiction; *Areas:* Architecture; Biography; Business; Cookery; Crime; Culture; Current Affairs; Design; Finance; Health; Lifestyle; Mystery; Science; Sci-Fi; Thrillers; *Markets:* Adult; Youth; *Treatments:* Contemporary; Literary; Mainstream

Send one-page query by email, including brief description / synopsis and background / short bio of author. See website for full guidelines.

Elyse Cheney Literary Associates, LLC

78 Fifth Avenue, 3rd Floor, New York, NY 10011

Tel: +1 (212) 277-8007
Fax: +1 (212) 614-0728
Email: submissions@cheneyliterary.com
Website: http://www.cheneyliterary.com

Handles: Fiction; Nonfiction; *Areas:*
Autobiography; Biography; Business;
Culture; Current Affairs; Finance; Historical;
Horror; Literature; Politics; Romance;
Science; Sport; Suspense; Thrillers;
Women's Interests; *Markets:* Adult;
Treatments: Commercial; Contemporary;
Literary

Send query only by post with SASE, or by
email (no attachments).

Linda Chester & Associates
630 Fifth Avenue, Suite 2000, Rockefeller
Center, New York, NY 10111
Tel: +1 (212) 218-3350
Fax: +1 (212) 218-3343
Email: submissions@lindachester.com
Website: http://www.lindachester.com

Handles: Fiction; Nonfiction; *Markets:*
Adult; *Treatments:* Commercial; Literary

Send query by email only with short bio and
first five pages pasted directly into the body
of the email. Response within 4 weeks if
interested only. No submissions by post.

The Chudney Agency
72 North State Road, Suite 501, Briarcliff
Manor , NY 10510
Tel: +1 (914) 488-5008
Email: mail@thechudneyagency.com
Website: http://www.thechudneyagency.com

Handles: Fiction; *Areas:* Historical;
Mystery; Suspense; *Markets:* Children's;
Youth; *Treatments:* Commercial; Literary;
Mainstream

Handles children's and young adult books.
Send query only in first instance. Happy to
accept queries by email. Submit material
upon invitation only. See website for full
guidelines.

Cine/Lit Representation
PO Box 802918, Santa Clarita, CA 91380-
2918
Tel: +1 (661) 513-0268
Fax: +1 (661) 513-0915
Email: makier@msn.com

Handles: Fiction; Nonfiction; *Areas:*
Adventure; Biography; Culture; Horror;
Mystery; Nature; Thrillers; Travel; *Markets:*
Adult; *Treatments:* Mainstream; Popular

Handles nonfiction and novels. Send query
with SASE. No romance, westerns, or
science fiction.

W.M. Clark Associates
186 Fifth Avenue, 2nd Floor, New York, NY
10010
Tel: +1 (212) 675-2784
Fax: +1 (347) 649-9262
Email: general@wmclark.com
Website: http://www.wmclark.com

Handles: Fiction; Nonfiction; *Areas:*
Architecture; Arts; Autobiography;
Biography; Culture; Current Affairs; Design;
Film; Historical; Music; Philosophy;
Religious; Science; Sociology; Technology;
Theatre; Translations; *Markets:* Adult;
Treatments: Contemporary; Literary;
Mainstream

Query through online form on website only.
No simultaneous submissions or screenplays.

The Collective
8383 Wilshire Boulevard, Suite 1050,
Beverly Hills, CA 90211
Tel: +1 (323) 370-1500
Website: http://www.thecollective-la.com

Handles: Scripts; *Areas:* Film; TV; *Markets:*
Adult

A full-service entertainment management,
media and content production company, with
offices in Beverly Hills, New York,
Nashville, and San Francisco. Handles
scripts for film and TV.

Frances Collin Literary Agent

PO Box 33, Wayne, PA 19087-0033
Tel: +1 (610) 254-0555
Fax: +1 (610) 254-5029
Email: queries@francescollin.com
Website: http://www.francescollin.com

Handles: Fiction; Nonfiction; *Areas:*
Autobiography; Biography; Culture;
Fantasy; Historical; Nature; Sci-Fi; Travel;
Women's Interests; *Markets:* Adult;
Treatments: Literary

Send query by email (no attachments) or by
post with SASE or IRCs if outside the US.
No queries by phone or fax.

Don Congdon Associates, Inc.

110 William St. Suite 2202, New York, NY
10038
Tel: +1 (212) 645-1229
Fax: +1 (212) 727-2688
Email: dca@doncongdon.com
Website: http://doncongdon.com

Handles: Fiction; Nonfiction; *Areas:*
Adventure; Anthropology; Archaeology;
Autobiography; Biography; Cookery; Crime;
Culture; Current Affairs; Film; Health;
Historical; Humour; Legal; Lifestyle;
Literature; Medicine; Military; Music;
Mystery; Nature; Politics; Psychology;
Science; Technology; Theatre; Thrillers;
Travel; Women's Interests; *Markets:* Adult;
Treatments: Literary; Mainstream

Send query by email (no attachments) or by
post with SASE. Include one-page synopsis,
relevant background info, and first chapter,
all within the body of the email if submitting
by email. Include the word "Query" in the
subject line. See website for full guidelines.
No unsolicited MSS.

CowlesRyan Agency

Email: katherine@cowlesryan.com
Website: http://www.cowlesryan.com

Handles: Fiction; Nonfiction; *Areas:* Arts;
Autobiography; Biography; Cookery;
Culture; Current Affairs; Historical;
Literature; Mystery; Nature; Psychology;
Science; Self-Help; Spiritual; *Markets:*

Adult; Children's; *Treatments:* Commercial;
Contemporary; Literary; Mainstream;
Popular; Satirical

We specialise in quality fiction and nonfiction. Our primary areas of interest include
literary and selected commercial fiction,
history, journalism, culture, biography,
memoir, science, natural history, spirituality,
cooking, gardening, building and design, and
young adult and children's books. We also
work with institutions and organisations to
develop books and book programs. We do
not represent authors in a number of
categories, e.g. romance and westerns, and
we do not represent screenplays. See website
for full submission guidelines.

Crawford Literary Agency

92 Evans Road, Barnstead, NH 03218
Tel: +1 (603) 269-5851
Fax: +1 (603) 269-2533
Email: crawfordlit@att.net

Handles: Fiction; Nonfiction; *Areas:*
Adventure; Crime; Entertainment; How-to;
Legal; Media; Medicine; Psychology;
Romance; Self-Help; Suspense; Thrillers;
Women's Interests; *Markets:* Adult;
Treatments: Commercial

No poetry or short stories. Send query with
SASE.

Creative Trust, Inc.

5141 Virginia Way, Suite 320, Brentwood,
TN 37027
Tel: +1 (615) 297-5010
Fax: +1 (615) 297-5020
Email: info@creativetrust.com
Website: http://www.creativetrust.com

Handles: Fiction; Scripts; *Areas:* Film;
Markets: Adult

Literary division founded in 2001 to handle
authors with particular potential in cross-
media development, including movie scripts,
graphic novels, etc. Accepts queries by email
from previously published authors only. No
attachments.

Criterion Group, Inc.

4842 Sylmar Avenue , Sherman Oaks, CA
91423
Tel: +1 (818) 995-1485
Fax: +1 (818) 995-1085
Email: info@criterion-group.com
Website: http://www.criterion-group.com

Handles: Scripts; *Areas:* Film; Theatre;
Markets: Adult

**Note: Reports that this agency is not
accepting scripts as at July 19, 2013.
Check website for current status.**

Handles film and stage scripts. Send query
by post only. No unsolicited material
accepted.

The Croce Agency

PO Box 3161, Fort Lee, NJ 07024
Tel: +1 (201) 248-3175
Email: submissions@thecroceagency.com
Website: http://www.thecroceagency.com

Handles: Fiction; Nonfiction; *Areas:*
Autobiography; Biography; Historical;
Mystery; Science; Suspense; Thrillers;
Travel; Women's Interests; *Markets:* Adult;
Treatments: Commercial; Literary;
Mainstream

**Note: not accepting submissions as at
February 2013. Check website for current
situation.**

Represents character-driven upmarket fiction
and plot-driven commercial fiction
(including chick lit). Also represents
narrative nonfiction. Searching for strong,
unique writing with commercial appeal, even
it falls outside their usual categories of work.

Actively seeking submissions, which must
be made by email and include: brief
synopsis; word count; stage of completion;
explanation of what makes your book
unique; first chapter (if written); author
credentials.

The Culinary Entertainment Agency (CEA)

53 W 36, #706, New York, NY 10018

Tel: +1 (212) 380-1264
Email: info@the-cea.com
Website: http://www.the-cea.com

Handles: Nonfiction; *Areas:* Cookery;
Lifestyle; *Markets:* Adult

Literary agency focused on the cooking and
lifestyle markets. Accepts new clients by
referral only.

Curtis Brown Ltd

10 Astor Place, New York, NY 10003
Tel: +1 (212) 473-5400
Fax: +1 (212) 598-0917
Email: gc@cbltd.com
Website: http://www.curtisbrown.com

Handles: Fiction; Nonfiction; *Markets:*
Adult; Children's; Youth

Handles material for adults and children in
all genres. Send query with SASE, synopsis,
CV and a sample chapter. No unsolicited
MSS. No scripts.

Daniel Literary Group

1701 Kingsbury Drive, Suite 100, Nashville,
TN 37215
Tel: +1 (615) 730-8207
Email:
submissions@danielliterarygroup.com
Website: http://www.danielliterarygroup.com

Handles: Nonfiction; *Markets:* Adult

Specialises in nonfiction and is closed to
submissions of fiction. No Children's
literature, Romance, Science fiction,
Screenplays, Poetry, or Short stories. Query
by email only, including brief synopsis, key
selling points, author biography, and
publishing history, all pasted into the body of
the email. No attachments, or queries by post
or telephone. Response not guranteed if
guidelines are not adhered to.

DeFiore and Company

47 East 19th Street, 3rd Floor, New York,
NY 10003
Tel: +1 (212) 925-7744
Fax: +1 (212) 925-9803

Email: submissions@defioreandco.com
Website: http://www.defioreandco.com

Handles: Fiction; Nonfiction; *Areas:* Arts;
Biography; Culture; Current Affairs;
Historical; Lifestyle; Literature; Medicine;
Military; Music; Nature; Philosophy;
Politics; Psychology; Romance; Science;
Short Stories; Sociology; Technology;
Thrillers; *Markets:* Adult; Children's; Youth;
Treatments: Commercial; Literary;
Mainstream

Always looking for exciting, fresh, new
talent, and currently accepting queries for
both fiction and nonfiction. Send query with
summary, description of why you're writing
the book, any specific credentials, and (for
fiction) first five pages. Send by email (with
all material in the body of the text; no
attachments; and the word "Query" in the
subject line) or post with SASE. See website
for specific agent interests and methods of
approach. No scripts for film, TV, or theatre.

Sandra Dijkstra Literary Agency

PMB 515, 1155 Camino Del Mar, Del Mar,
CA 92014
Tel: +1 (858) 755-3115
Fax: +1 (858) 794-2822
Email: queries@dijkstraagency.com
Website: http://www.dijkstraagency.com

Handles: Fiction; Nonfiction; *Areas:*
Autobiography; Business; Cookery; Culture;
Current Affairs; Design; Fantasy; Health;
Historical; Humour; Lifestyle; Music;
Mystery; Politics; Religious; Romance;
Science; Sci-Fi; Self-Help; Short Stories;
Sociology; Sport; Thrillers; Travel;
Women's Interests; *Markets:* Adult;
Children's; Youth; *Treatments:* Commercial;
Contemporary; Literary

Check author bios on website and submit
query by email to one agent only. For fiction,
include a one-page synopsis, brief bio, and
first 10-15 pages. For nonfiction, include
overview, chapter outline, brief bio, and first
10-15 pages. All material must be in the
body of the email. No attachments. See
website for full submission guidelines.

Donadio & Olson, Inc.

121 W. 27th Street, Suite 704, New York,
NY 10001
Tel: +1 (212) 691-8077
Fax: +1 (212) 633-2837
Email: mail@donadio.com
Website: http://donadio.com

Handles: Fiction; Nonfiction; *Areas:* Arts;
Biography; Culture; Historical; Literature;
Nature; Science; *Markets:* Adult; Youth;
Treatments: Commercial; Literary;
Mainstream

Handles literary fiction and nonfiction in a
range of subjects, particularly literary
history, biography, and cultural
phenomenology.

Jim Donovan Literary

5635 SMU Boulevard, Suite 201, Dallas, TX
75206
Email: jdliterary@sbcglobal.net

Handles: Fiction; Nonfiction; Reference;
Areas: Adventure; Autobiography;
Biography; Business; Crime; Culture;
Current Affairs; Finance; Health; Historical;
How-to; Legal; Lifestyle; Medicine;
Military; Music; Mystery; Nature; Politics;
Sport; Suspense; Thrillers; Women's
Interests; *Markets:* Adult; *Treatments:*
Commercial; Contemporary; Literary;
Mainstream; Popular

Send query with SASE or by email. For
fiction, include first 30-50 pages and a 2-5
page outline. Handles mainly nonfiction, and
specialises in commercial fiction and
nonfiction. No poetry, children's, short
stories, or inspirational.

Dunham Literary, Inc.

110 William Street, Suite 2202, New York,
NY 10038
Tel: +1 (212) 929-0994
Fax: +1 (212) 929-0904
Email: query@dunhamlit.com
Website: http://www.dunhamlit.com

Handles: Fiction; Nonfiction; *Areas:*
Autobiography; Biography; Culture; Current
Affairs; Fantasy; Historical; Lifestyle;

Music; Nature; Politics; Science; Sci-Fi; Spiritual; Technology; Travel; Women's Interests; *Markets:* Adult; Children's; Youth; *Treatments:* Literary

Handles quality fiction and nonfiction for adults and children. Send query by email or by post with SASE. See website for full guidelines. No genre romance, Westerns, poetry, or approaches by phone or fax. No email attachments.

Dunow, Carlson & Lerner Agency

27 West 20th Street, Suite 1107, New York, NY 10011
Tel: +1 (212) 645-7606
Email: mail@dclagency.com
Website: http://www.dclagency.com

Handles: Fiction; Nonfiction; *Areas:* Autobiography; Culture; *Markets:* Adult; Youth; *Treatments:* Commercial; Literary

Send query by post with SASE or by email. No attachments. Does not respond to all email queries.

Eames Literary Services, LLC

4117 Hillsboro Road, Suite 251, Nashville, TN 37215
Fax: +1 (615) 463-9361
Email: info@eamesliterary.com
Website: http://www.eamesliterary.com

Handles: Fiction; Nonfiction; *Areas:* Religious; *Markets:* Adult; Youth

Handles adult and young adult fiction and nonfiction that supports a Christian perspective on life. Send query by email with book proposal; author bio (including publishing history); plot synopsis or chapter summary; and 2-3 chapters of sample content (attached as a Microsoft Word document). Incomplete enquiries will not be responded to. No queries by post.

East West Literary Agency LLC

1158 26th Street, Suite 462, Santa Monica, CA 90403

Tel: +1 (310) 573-9303
Fax: +1 (310) 453-9008
Email: rpfeffer@eastwestliteraryagency.com
Website: http://eastwestliteraryagency.com

Handles: Fiction; Nonfiction; *Markets:* Adult; Children's; Youth; *Treatments:* Niche

Specialises in children's books of all genres: from concept, novelty and picture books toh young adult literature. Represents both authors and illustrators.

Accepts queries via email only and by referral only. See website for current details. As at June 7, 2012, website states that they will be open to queries from "the first of the year" -- however there is no indication as to which year is being referred to.

Ebeling & Associates

PO Box 790267, Pala, HI 96779
Tel: +1 (808) 579-6414
Fax: +1 (808) 579-9294
Email: ebothat@yahoo.com
Website: http://www.ebelingagency.com

Handles: Nonfiction; *Areas:* Business; Health; Self-Help; *Markets:* Adult

Accepts queries and proposals by email only. Write "Inquiry for Author Representation" in subject line and outline your book in up to 200 words in the body of the email. Attach proposal as Word or PDF document. See website for proposal requirements. Submissions by post are not accepted. No fiction, poetry, children's, illustrated books, religion, history, culture, biography, or memoir.

Judith Ehrlich Literary Management

880 Third Avenue, 8th Floor, New York, NY 10022
Tel: +1 (646) 505-1570
Email: jehrlich@judithehrlichliterary.com
Website: http://www.judithehrlichliterary.com

Handles: Fiction; Nonfiction; *Areas:* Arts; Autobiography; Biography; Business; Culture; Current Affairs; Fantasy; Health;

Historical; How-to; Humour; Legal; Lifestyle; Medicine; Mystery; Politics; Psychology; Romance; Science; Self-Help; Sociology; Sport; Thrillers; Women's Interests; *Markets:* Adult; Children's; Youth; *Treatments:* Commercial; Literary; Mainstream

Send query by email only. No attachments. For nonfiction give details of your book, your qualifications for writing it, and any existing platform. For fiction include synopsis, writing credentials, and 7-10 sample pages, pasted into the body of the email. See website for full guidelines and individual agent details and email addresses. Response not guaranteed.

Einstein Thompson Agency

27 West 20th Street, Suite 1003, New York, NY 10011
Tel: +1 (212) 221-8797
Fax: +1 (212) 221-8722
Email: submissions@einsteinthompson.com
Website: http://www.einsteinthompson.com

Handles: Fiction; Nonfiction; *Areas:* Autobiography; Cookery; Crime; Culture; Health; Historical; Humour; Politics; Psychology; Science; Sport; Women's Interests; *Markets:* Adult; Children's; Youth; *Treatments:* Commercial; Literary; Popular

Accepts submissions by email only. See contact section of website for full submission guidelines.

Ethan Ellenberg Literary Agency

548 Broadway, #5E, New York, NY 10012
Tel: +1 (212) 431-4554
Fax: +1 (212) 941-4652
Email: agent@ethanellenberg.com
Website: http://www.ethanellenberg.com

Handles: Fiction; Nonfiction; *Areas:* Adventure; Autobiography; Biography; Cookery; Crime; Culture; Current Affairs; Fantasy; Health; Historical; Mystery; New Age; Psychology; Romance; Science; Sci-Fi; Spiritual; Thrillers; Women's Interests; *Markets:* Adult; Children's; *Treatments:* Commercial; Literary

Actively looking for established and new writers in a wide range of genres. Send query by email (no attachments; paste material into the body of the email) or by post with SASE. For fiction send synopsis and first 50 pages. For nonfiction send proposal, author bio, and sample chapters. For picture books send complete MS. No poetry, short stories, scripts, or queries by fax.

We have been in business for over 17 years. We are a member of the AAR. We accept unsolicited submissions and, of course, do not charge reading fees.

Nicholas Ellison, Inc.

55 Fifth Avenue, 15th Floor, New York, NY 10003
Tel: +1 (212) 206-5600
Fax: +1 (212) 436-8718
Email: nellison@sjga.com
Website: http://www.greenburger.com

Handles: Fiction; Nonfiction; *Markets:* Adult; *Treatments:* Literary; Mainstream

Represents primarily fiction, along with a select list of nonfiction. Send queries by email including brief descriptiona and any relevant credentials in the body of the email, and attach at least 50 pages along with any other relevant material. Assume rejection if no response within 6 weeks.

Ann Elmo Agency, Inc.

305 Seventh Avenue, #1101, New York, NY 10001
Tel: +1 (212) 661-2880
Fax: +1 (212) 661-2883
Email: aalitagent@aol.com

Handles: Fiction; Nonfiction; *Areas:* Biography; Culture; Current Affairs; Gothic; Health; Historical; How-to; Romance; Science; Thrillers; Women's Interests; *Markets:* Adult; Family; *Treatments:* Contemporary; Mainstream

No unsolicited mss.

Energy Entertainment

9107 Wilshire Boulevard, 6th Floor, Los

Angeles, CA 90069
Email: info@energyentertainment.net
Website:
http://www.energyentertainment.net

Handles: Scripts; *Areas:* Film; TV; *Markets:*
Adult

Agency specialising in discovering new and
edgy screenwriters. No unsolicited MSS or
calls; send query only.

Elaine P. English, Attorney & Literary Agent

4710 41st Street, NW, Suite D, Wahington,
DC 20016
Tel: +1 (202) 362-5190
Fax: +1 (202) 362-5192
Email: queries@elaineenglish.com
Website: http://www.elaineenglish.com

Handles: Fiction; *Areas:* Erotic; Fantasy;
Gothic; Historical; Humour; Mystery;
Romance; Women's Interests; *Markets:*
Adult; *Treatments:* Commercial;
Contemporary; Dark; Light; Serious;
Traditional

Handles women's fiction, mysteries, and
thrillers. Handles romance ranging from
historical to contemporary, funny to erotic,
and paranormal. No memoirs, science
fiction, fantasy (unless romance fantasy),
children's, young adult, horror, thrillers,
short stories, screenplays, or nonfiction.
Send query by email in first instance – see
website for full guidelines. No attachments
or unsolicited materials.

The Epstein Literary Agency

P.O. Box 484 Kensington, Kensington, MD
Tel: +1 (781) 718-4025
Email: kate@epsteinliterary.com
Website: http://www.epsteinliterary.com

Handles: Nonfiction; Reference; *Areas:*
Crafts; How-to; *Markets:* Adult; Children's;
Family; Youth

My agency was founded in 2005; my
expertise comes from four years as an editor
at Adams Media, where I handled many of

the subject areas I am currently seeking to
handle as an agent.

What I look for more than anything else is
distinction – how will the book grab the
reader in three seconds? It's better to grab
many people and only please some of them
than to try to please everyone and grab no
one.

I follow AAR guidelines.

Currently open to crafts titles only. See
website for full details.

Felicia Eth Literary Representation

555 Bryant Street, Suite 350, Palo Alto, CA
94301
Tel: +1 (650) 375-1276
Fax: +1 (650)401-8892
Email: feliciaeth@aol.com

Handles: Fiction; Nonfiction; *Areas:*
Anthropology; Autobiography; Biography;
Business; Crime; Culture; Current Affairs;
Finance; Health; Historical; Legal; Lifestyle;
Medicine; Politics; Psychology; Science;
Sociology; Technology; Women's Interests;
Markets: Adult; *Treatments:* Commercial;
Contemporary; Literary; Mainstream

Send query with SASE and outline.
Particularly interested in intelligent
nonfiction and quality commercial fiction.
No crime fiction (true crime only).

Mary Evans, Inc.

242 East Fifth Street, New York, NY 10003
Tel: +1 (212) 979-0880
Fax: +1 (212) 979-5344
Email: info@maryevansinc.com
Website: http://www.maryevansinc.com

Handles: Fiction; Nonfiction; *Markets:*
Adult; *Treatments:* Commercial; Literary

Works mainly with established authors; most
new clients by referral. Send query with
SASE by post only. No queries by fax.

Farris Literary Agency, Inc.

PO Box 570069, Dallas, Texas 75357-0069
Tel: +1 (972) 203-8804
Email: farris1@airmail.net
Website: http://www.farrisliterary.com

Handles: Fiction; Nonfiction; Scripts; *Areas:*
Adventure; Autobiography; Biography;
Business; Crime; Culture; Current Affairs;
Entertainment; Finance; Health; Historical;
How-to; Humour; Legal; Lifestyle; Military;
Music; Mystery; Politics; Religious;
Romance; Self-Help; Spiritual; Sport;
Suspense; Thrillers; Travel; Women's
Interests; *Markets:* Adult; *Treatments:*
Mainstream; Satirical

**NOTE: As at April 2, 2013, only accepting
submissions by referral or writers'
conferences. Check website for current
status.**

Send query by post with SASE, or by email.
Include title, description of project, author
bio, and (for fiction) the genre and word
count, or (for nonfiction) the type of book
and your qualifications for writing it. No
science fiction, fantasy, gay and lesbian,
erotica, young adult, children's, or email
attachments.

FinePrint Literary Management

115 West 29th Street, 3rd Floor, New York,
NY 10001
Tel: +1 (212) 279-1282
Email: peter@fineprintlit.com
Website: http://www.fineprintlit.com

Handles: Fiction; Nonfiction; Reference;
Areas: Autobiography; Beauty and Fashion;
Biography; Business; Cookery; Crime;
Culture; Entertainment; Fantasy; Health;
Historical; Horror; How-to; Humour;
Lifestyle; Military; Music; Mystery; Nature;
Religious; Romance; Science; Sci-Fi; Self-
Help; Spiritual; Suspense; Technology;
Thrillers; Travel; Women's Interests;
Markets: Adult; Children's; Youth;
Treatments: Contemporary; Dark; Literary;
Serious

Consult agent profiles on website for

individual interests and approach appropriate
agent for your work. Send query by email
(no attachments) with proposal and sample
chapters for nonfiction, or synopsis and first
two chapters for fiction.

The James Fitzgerald Agency

118 Waverly Pl., #1B, New York, NY 10011
Tel: +1 (212) 308-1122
Email: submissions@jfitzagency.com
Website: http://www.jfitzagency.com

Handles: Fiction; Nonfiction; *Areas:*
Culture; *Markets:* Adult

Primarily represents books reflecting the
popular culture of the day, in fiction,
nonfiction, graphic and packaged books. No
poetry or screenplays. All information must
be submitted in English, even if the
manuscript is in Spanish. See website for
detailed submission guidelines.

Fletcher & Company

78 Fifth Avenue, Third Floor, New York,
NY 10011
Tel: +1 (212) 614-0778
Fax: +1 (212) 614-0728
Email: info@fletcherandco.com
Website: http://www.fletcherandco.com

Handles: Fiction; Nonfiction; *Areas:*
Autobiography; Biography; Business;
Current Affairs; Health; Historical; Humour;
Lifestyle; Science; Sport; Travel; *Markets:*
Adult; Youth; *Treatments:* Commercial;
Literary

Full-service literary agency representing
writers of nonfiction and commercial and
literary fiction. Send query with brief
synopsis by post with SASE, or by email (no
attachments). No genre fiction. Query only
one agent at a time and allow 4-6 weeks
before following up.

Folio Literary Management, LLC

630 9th Avenue, Suite 1101 , New York, NY
10036
Email: jeff@foliolit.com
Website: http://www.foliolit.com

Handles: Fiction; Nonfiction; Reference; *Areas:* Autobiography; Business; Cookery; Crime; Culture; Entertainment; Fantasy; Health; Historical; Horror; How-to; Humour; Lifestyle; Media; Military; Music; Mystery; Politics; Psychology; Religious; Romance; Science; Sci-Fi; Self-Help; Spiritual; Sport; Suspense; Technology; Thrillers; Women's Interests; *Markets:* Adult; Children's; Youth; *Treatments:* Commercial; Contemporary; Dark; Literary; Popular; Serious

Read agent bios on website and decide which agent to approach. Do not submit to multiple agents simultaneously. Each agent has different submission requirements: consult website for details. No unsolicited MSS or multiple submissions.

Foundry Literary + Media

33 West 17th Street, PH, New York, NY 10011
Tel: +1 (212) 929-5064
Fax: +1 (212) 929-5471
Email: info@foundrymedia.com
Website: http://www.foundrymedia.com

Handles: Fiction; Nonfiction; *Areas:* Adventure; Autobiography; Biography; Business; Culture; Current Affairs; Health; Historical; How-to; Humour; Lifestyle; Music; Psychology; Religious; Science; Sci-Fi; Sport; Thrillers; Travel; Women's Interests; *Markets:* Adult; Children's; Youth; *Treatments:* Commercial; Literary; Niche; Popular

Queries should be addressed to a specific agent (see website) and sent by email or by post with SASE, according to requirements of individual agent (se website). For fiction queries, send letter with synopsis, First Three Chapters of Manuscript, and Author Bio. For nonfiction approaches send letter with Sample Chapters, Table of Contents, and Author Bio.

Fox Chase Agency, Inc.

701 Lee Road, Suite 102, Chesterbrook Corporate Center, Chesterbrook, PA 19087

Handles: Fiction; Nonfiction; *Markets:* Adult

Handles novels and nonfiction. Send query with SASE.

Jeanne Fredericks Literary Agency, Inc.

221 Benedict Hill Road, New Canaan, CT 06840
Tel: +1 (203) 972-3011
Fax: +1 (203) 972-3011
Email: jeanne.fredericks@gmail.com
Website: http://jeannefredericks.com

Handles: Nonfiction; Reference; *Areas:* Antiques; Arts; Biography; Business; Cookery; Crafts; Design; Finance; Gardening; Health; Historical; How-to; Legal; Leisure; Lifestyle; Medicine; Nature; Photography; Psychology; Science; Self-Help; Sport; Travel; Women's Interests; *Markets:* Adult

Send query by email (no attachments) or post with SASE. Specialises in adult nonfiction by authorities in their fields. No fiction, true crime, juvenile, textbooks, poetry, essays, screenplays, short stories, science fiction, pop culture, guides to computers and software, politics, horror, pornography, books on overly depressing or violent topics, romance, teacher's manuals, or memoirs. See website for full guidelines.

Fresh Books Literary Agency

231 Diana Street, Placerville, CA 95667
Email: matt@fresh-books.com
Website: http://www.fresh-books.com

Handles: Nonfiction; Reference; *Areas:* Business; Design; Finance; Health; How-to; Humour; Lifestyle; Photography; Science; Self-Help; Technology; *Markets:* Adult

Handles narrative non-fiction, lifestyle and reference titles on subjects such as science and technology, health and fitness, computers, photography, careers, education, parenting, personal finance, recreation, cooking, gardening, etc. No fiction, children's books, screenplays, or poetry. Send query by email. No attachments. Send further material upon request only.

Fredrica S. Friedman and Co. Inc.

136 East 57th Street, 14th Floor, New York, NY 10022
Tel: +1 (212) 829-9600
Fax: +1 (212) 829-9669
Email: submissions@fredricafriedman.com
Website: http://www.fredricafriedman.com

Handles: Fiction; Nonfiction; *Areas:* Arts; Autobiography; Biography; Business; Cookery; Crime; Culture; Current Affairs; Design; Film; Finance; Health; Historical; How-to; Humour; Lifestyle; Music; Photography; Politics; Psychology; Self-Help; Sociology; Women's Interests; *Markets:* Adult; *Treatments:* Literary

Send query with synopsis by email. For fiction, include one-page sample. All material must be in the body of the email – no attachments. No poetry, plays, screenplays, children's books, sci-fi/fantasy, or horror.

Full Throttle Literary Agency

P.O.Box 5, Greenwich, Ohio 44837
Tel: +1 (419) 752-0444
Email: fullthrottlelit@aol.com
Website: http://www.fullthrottleliterary.com

Handles: Fiction; Scripts; *Areas:* Adventure; Drama; Film; Horror; Humour; Mystery; Short Stories; Suspense; Thrillers; Westerns; *Markets:* Adult; Children's; Family; *Treatments:* Contemporary; Light; Mainstream; Traditional

We are an independent agency that specializes in fiction material. Accepting new clients for manuscripts,screenplays and short stories. No e-mail queries. Send query through regular mail along with S.A.S.E. and short bio.

The Gage Group

Suite 505 , 14724 Ventura Blvd, Sherman Oaks, CA 91403
Tel: +1 (818) 905-3800
Fax: +1 (818) 905-3322
Email: Literary.GageGroupLA@gmail.com

Handles: Scripts; *Areas:* Film; Theatre; TV;

Markets: Adult

Send query by post with SASE, or by email. Prefers to receive submissions by post. Willing to consider scripts on all subjects. No queries by fax.

Nancy Gallt Literary Agency

273 Charlton Avenue, South Orange , NJ 07079
Tel: +1 (973) 761-6358
Fax: +1 (973) 761-6318
Email: nancy@nancygallt.com
Website: http://www.nancygallt.com

Handles: Fiction; *Markets:* Children's; Youth

Handles children's books only. Use submission form on website or submit by post with SASE and appropriate postage if return of material required. All online submissions must go through the submission form on the website.

Don Gastwirth & Associates

265 College Street, New Haven, CT 06510
Tel: +1 (203) 562-7600
Fax: +1 (203) 562-4300
Email: Donlit@snet.net

Handles: Fiction; Nonfiction; *Areas:* Business; Crime; Culture; Current Affairs; Historical; Military; Music; Mystery; Nature; Psychology; Thrillers; Translations; *Markets:* Academic; Adult

Highly selective agency which rarely takes on clients who are not referred to the agency by an industry professional.

Gelfman Schneider Literary Agents, Inc.

850 Seventh Avenue, Suite 903, New York, NY 10019
Tel: +1 (212) 245-1993
Email: mail@gelfmanschneider.com
Website: http://www.gelfmanschneider.com

Handles: Fiction; Nonfiction; *Areas:* Autobiography; Culture; Current Affairs; Historical; Mystery; Politics; Science;

Suspense; Thrillers; Women's Interests; *Markets:* Adult; *Treatments:* Commercial; Literary; Mainstream; Popular

Different agents within the agency have different submission guidelines. See website for full details. No screenplays, or poetry.

The Gernert Company

136 East 57th Street, New York, NY 10022
Tel: +1 (212) 838-7777
Fax: +1 (212) 838-6020
Email: info@thegernertco.com
Website: http://www.thegernertco.com

Handles: Fiction; Nonfiction; *Areas:* Adventure; Arts; Autobiography; Biography; Crafts; Current Affairs; Fantasy; Historical; Politics; Science; Sci-Fi; Sociology; Sport; Thrillers; *Markets:* Academic; Adult; Children's; Youth; *Treatments:* Commercial; Literary; Popular

Send query describing work by post with SASE or email with author info and sample chapter. If querying by email, send to generic email and indicate which agent you would like to query. No queries by fax. Response only if interested.

Barry Goldblatt Literary Agency, Inc.

320 7th Avenue, #266, Brooklyn, NY 11215
Email: query@bgliterary.com
Website: http://www.bgliterary.com

Handles: Fiction; *Markets:* Children's; Youth

Handles books for young people; from picture books to middle grade and young adult. Send query by email including the word "Query" in the subject line and synopsis and first five pages in the body of the email. No attachments. Emails with attachments will be ignored. See website for full details.

The Susan Golomb Literary Agency

540 President Street, 3rd Floor, Brooklyn, NY 11215

Email: susan@sgolombagency.com

Handles: Fiction; Nonfiction; *Areas:* Anthropology; Archaeology; Autobiography; Biography; Business; Culture; Current Affairs; Finance; Health; Historical; Humour; Legal; Military; Nature; Politics; Psychology; Science; Sociology; Technology; Thrillers; Women's Interests; *Markets:* Adult; Youth; *Treatments:* Literary; Mainstream; Satirical

Send query by email or by post with SASE, including synopsis / proposal, author bio, and one sample chapter. No genre fiction.

Irene Goodman Literary Agency

27 W. 24 Street, Suite 700B, New York, NY 10010
Tel: +1 (212) 604-0330
Fax: +1 (212) 675-1381
Email: irene@irenegoodman.com
Website: http://www.irenegoodman.com

Handles: Fiction; Nonfiction; *Areas:* Autobiography; Cookery; Culture; Fantasy; Historical; Lifestyle; Mystery; Romance; Sociology; Suspense; Thrillers; Women's Interests; *Markets:* Adult; Youth; *Treatments:* Commercial; Literary; Popular

Select specific agent to approach based on details given on website (specific agent email addresses on website). Send query by email only with synopsis, bio, and first ten pages in the body of the email. No poetry, inspirational fiction, screenplays, or children's picture books. Response only if interested. See website for further details.

Ashley Grayson Literary Agency

1342 18th Street, San Pedro, CA 90732
Tel: +1 (310) 548-4672
Email: graysonagent@earthlink.net

Handles: Fiction; Nonfiction; *Areas:* Business; Crime; Culture; Fantasy; Finance; Health; Historical; Lifestyle; Mystery; Romance; Science; Sci-Fi; Self-Help; Spiritual; Sport; Technology; *Markets:* Adult; Children's; Youth; *Treatments:*

Commercial; Literary

Accepts nonfiction proposals from authors aho are recognised within their field, and queries from published authors. Only accepts queries from unpublished authors if they already have an offer from a reputable publisher, have an industry recommendation, or have met the agents at a conference and had an ms requested. Self-published or print on demand published does not count as published for these purposes. Send query by email. No attachments.

Kathryn Green Literary Agency, LLC

250 West 57th Street, Suite 2302, New York, NY 10107
Tel: +1 (212) 245-2445
Fax: +1 (212) 245-2040
Email: query@kgreenagency.com

Handles: Fiction; Nonfiction; *Areas:* Autobiography; Biography; Business; Cookery; Crime; Culture; Current Affairs; Design; Finance; Health; Historical; How-to; Humour; Lifestyle; Psychology; Romance; Self-Help; Sport; Suspense; Thrillers; Women's Interests; *Markets:* Adult; Youth; *Treatments:* Contemporary; Literary; Mainstream; Satirical

Send query by email. Do not send samples unless requested. No science fiction, fantasy, or queries by fax.

Sanford J. Greenburger Associates, Inc

15th Floor, 55 Fifth Avenue, New York, NY 10003
Tel: +1 (212) 206-5600
Fax: +1 (212) 463-8718
Email: queryHL@sjga.com
Website: http://www.greenburger.com

Handles: Fiction; Nonfiction; Reference; *Areas:* Arts; Autobiography; Biography; Business; Entertainment; Fantasy; Health; Historical; Humour; Lifestyle; Music; Mystery; Nature; Politics; Psychology; Romance; Science; Sci-Fi; Self-Help; Sociology; Sport; Thrillers; Women's Interests; *Markets:* Adult; Children's; Youth;

Treatments: Commercial; Literary; Popular

Check website for specific agent interests, guidelines, and contact details. Most will not accept submissions by post. Aims to respond to queries within 6-8 weeks.

Blanche C. Gregory Inc.

2 Tudor City Place, New York, NY 10017
Tel: +1 (212) 697-0828
Email: info@bcgliteraryagency.com
Website: http://www.bcgliteraryagency.com

Handles: Fiction; Nonfiction; *Markets:* Adult; Children's

Specialises in adult fiction and nonfiction, but will also consider children's literature. Send query describing your background with SASE and synopsis. No stage, film or TV scripts, or queries by fax or email.

Greyhaus Literary Agency

3021 20th St. Pl. SW, Puyallup, WA 98373
Email: scott@greyhausagency.com
Website: http://www.greyhausagency.com

Handles: Fiction; *Areas:* Historical; Romance; Suspense; Women's Interests; *Markets:* Adult; *Treatments:* Contemporary; Traditional

ONLY focuses on traditional romance and traditional women's fiction.

Opens to submissions on May 20, 2013.

We only focus on Romance Writers in the following sub-genres: Contemporary, Mainstream Paranormal/Time Travel, Regency, Historical, Inspirational, Romantic Suspense. Send query by email or through submission form on website. Only considers writers with completed manuscript ready for publication. No Fantasy, Single Title Inspirational, YA or Middle Grade, Picture Books, Memoirs, Biographies, Erotica, Urban Fantasy, Science Fiction, Screenplays, Poetry, Authors interested in only e-publishing or self-publishing, or Works that have already been published.

Jill Grosjean Literary Agency

1390 Millstone Road, Sag Harbor, NY
11963-2214
Tel: +1 (631) 725-7419
Fax: +1 (631) 725-8632
Email: JillLit310@aol.com

Handles: Fiction; *Areas:* Crime; Gardening;
Historical; Humour; Mystery; Nature;
Romance; Suspense; Thrillers; Travel;
Women's Interests; *Markets:* Adult; Literary

Prefers email queries. No attachments.
Particularly interested in literary novels and
mysteries. Editorial assistance offered.

Laura Gross Literary Agency

PO Box 610326, Newton Highlands, MA
02461
Tel: +1 (617) 964-2977
Fax: +1 (617) 964-3023
Email: query@lg-la.com
Website: http://lauragrossliteraryagency.com

Handles: Fiction; Nonfiction; *Areas:*
Autobiography; Biography; Culture; Current
Affairs; Health; Historical; Legal; Lifestyle;
Medicine; Mystery; Politics; Psychology;
Sport; Suspense; Thrillers; Women's
Interests; *Markets:* Adult; *Treatments:*
Literary; Mainstream

Submit query using online web form,
including your book's genre and a synopsis
or plot summary. No sample chapters in first
instance.

The Mitchell J. Hamilburg Agency

149 South Barrington Avenue #732, Los
Angeles, CA 90049-2930
Tel: +1 (310) 471-4024
Fax: +1 (310) 471-9588

Handles: Fiction; Nonfiction; Poetry; *Areas:*
Adventure; Anthropology; Architecture;
Autobiography; Biography; Business;
Cookery; Crime; Current Affairs; Fantasy;
Finance; Gardening; Health; Historical;
Horror; Humour; Leisure; Lifestyle;
Military; Mystery; Nature; New Age;
Politics; Psychology; Religious; Romance;
Science; Sci-Fi; Self-Help; Short Stories;
Sociology; Spiritual; Sport; Suspense;
Thrillers; Travel; Women's Interests;
Markets: Adult; Children's; *Treatments:*
Experimental; Literary; Mainstream

Send query with SASE, outline, and 2
sample chapters.

Heacock Hill Literary Agency, LLC

1020 Hollywood Way, #439, Burbank, CA
91505
Tel: +1 (818) 951-6788
Email: Agent@HeacockHill.com
Website:
http://www.heacockliteraryagency.com

Handles: Fiction; Nonfiction; *Areas:*
Anthropology; Arts; Business; Crafts;
Culture; Gardening; Health; Lifestyle;
Nature; Politics; Science; Spiritual; *Markets:*
Adult; Children's; Youth

Fiction: Juvenile, middle grade children's,
picture books, young adult. No juvenile
nonfiction. No adult fiction at this time.
Please check website for updates. Open to all
kinds of adult nonfiction, particularly those
outlined above. Query by email only. See
website for full details.

Hidden Value Group

1240 E. Ontario Ave, STE #102-148,
Corona, CA 92881
Tel: +1 (951) 549-8891
Fax: +1 (951) 549-8891
Email: bookquery@hiddenvaluegroup.com
Website: http://www.hiddenvaluegroup.com

Handles: Fiction; Nonfiction; *Areas:*
Adventure; Autobiography; Biography;
Business; Crime; Criticism; Fantasy;
Finance; Historical; How-to; Lifestyle;
Literature; Psychology; Religious; Self-Help;
Thrillers; Westerns; Women's Interests;
Markets: Adult; Youth; *Treatments:* Literary

Represents previously published Christian
authors (not including self-published
authors). Send one-page summary,
marketing information, author bio, and two
or three sample chapters by email or by post

with SASE. Cannot guarantee a response to all email queries. No poetry or short stories.

Hill Nadell Literary Agency

8899 Beverly Bl., Suite 805, Los Angeles, CA 90048
Tel: +1 (310) 860-9605
Fax: +1 (310) 860-9672
Email: queries@hillnadell.com
Website: http://www.hillnadell.com

Handles: Fiction; Nonfiction; *Areas:* Autobiography; Biography; Cookery; Culture; Current Affairs; Health; Historical; Legal; Nature; Politics; Science; Thrillers; Women's Interests; *Markets:* Adult; Youth; *Treatments:* Literary; Mainstream

Handles current affairs, food, memoirs and other narrative nonfiction, fiction, thrillers, upmarket women's fiction, literary fiction, genre fiction, graphic novels, and occasional young adult novels. No scripts or screenplays. Accepts queries both by post and by email. See website for full submission guidelines.

Hudson Agency

3 Travis Lane, Montrose, NY 10548
Tel: +1 (914) 737-1475
Fax: +1 (914) 736-3064
Email: hudsonagency@optonline.net
Website: http://www.hudsonagency.net

Handles: Scripts; *Areas:* Crime; Drama; Fantasy; Film; Humour; Mystery; Romance; TV; Westerns; *Markets:* Adult; Children's; Family; Youth; *Treatments:* Contemporary

Send query with SASE. Most new clients taken on by recommendation from industry professionals.

Andrea Hurst Literary Management

PO Box 1467, Coupeville, WA 98239
Email: info@andreahurst.com
Website: http://www.andreahurst.com

Handles: Fiction; Nonfiction; *Areas:* Adventure; Autobiography; Business; Cookery; Crime; Current Affairs; Fantasy;

Historical; How-to; Humour; Politics; Psychology; Religious; Romance; Science; Sci-Fi; Self-Help; Thrillers; Westerns; Women's Interests; *Markets:* Adult; Youth; *Treatments:* Commercial; Contemporary

Check website for submission guidelines. Different genres handled by different agents, so check website for correct agent to query. Query only one agent. Queries accepted by email only (email addresses for each agent available on website). Do not include any attachments, proposals, sample chapters, etc.

International Transactions, Inc.

PO Box 97, Gila, NM 88038-0097
Tel: +1 (845) 373-9696
Fax: +1 (845)373-7868
Email: info@intltrans.com
Website: http://www.intltrans.com

Handles: Fiction; Nonfiction; *Areas:* Adventure; Arts; Biography; Crime; Historical; Medicine; Mystery; Short Stories; Thrillers; Women's Interests; *Markets:* Academic; Adult; Youth; *Treatments:* Contemporary; Literary; Mainstream

Send query with outline or synopsis by email. No fiction enquiries from unpublished authors. No queries by fax, or material which is too influenced by TV or other successful novels. See website for full submission guidelines.

J de S Associates Inc

9 Shagbark Road, Wilson Point, South Norwalk, CT 06854
Tel: +1 (203) 838-7571
Fax: +1 (203) 866-2713
Email: jdespoel@aol.com
Website: http://www.jdesassociates.com

Handles: Fiction; *Areas:* Autobiography; Biography; Business; Crime; Culture; Current Affairs; Finance; Health; Historical; How-to; Legal; Lifestyle; Medicine; Military; Mystery; New Age; Politics; Self-Help; Sociology; Sport; Suspense; Thrillers; Translations; Westerns; *Markets:* Adult; Children's; Youth; *Treatments:* Literary; Mainstream

Welcomes brief queries by post and by email, but no samples or other material unless requested.

Jill Grinberg Literary Management LLC

16 Court Street, Suite 3306, Brooklyn, NY 11241
Tel: +1 (212) 620-5883
Fax: +1 (212) 627-4725
Email: info@jillgrinbergliterary.com
Website: http://www.jillgrinbergliterary.com

Handles: Fiction; Nonfiction; *Areas:* Autobiography; Biography; Business; Culture; Current Affairs; Fantasy; Finance; Health; Historical; Legal; Medicine; Politics; Psychology; Romance; Science; Sci-Fi; Spiritual; Technology; Travel; Women's Interests; *Markets:* Adult; Children's; Youth; *Treatments:* Commercial; Literary

Send query with synopsis and first 50 pages for fiction, or proposal and author bio for nonfiction. No queries by fax or email.

Ken Sherman & Associates

1275 N. Hayworth, Suite 103, Los Angeles, CA 90046
Tel: +1 (310) 273-8840
Fax: +1 (310) 271-2875
Email: ken@kenshermanassociates.com
Website:
http://www.kenshermanassociates.com

Handles: Fiction; Nonfiction; Scripts; *Areas:* Film; TV; *Markets:* Adult

Handles fiction, nonfiction, and writers for film and TV. Query by referral only.

Virginia Kidd Agency, Inc

P.O. Box 278, Milford, PA 18337
Tel: +1 (570) 296-6205
Fax: +1 (570) 296-7266
Website: http://www.vk-agency.com

Handles: Fiction; *Areas:* Fantasy; Historical; Mystery; Sci-Fi; Suspense; Women's Interests; *Markets:* Adult; *Treatments:* Mainstream

Specialises in science fiction and fantasy. Currently accepting queries from published authors only. No approaches from unpublished authors.

Kimberley Cameron & Associates (Formerly Reece Halsey North)

1550 Tiburon Blvd #704, Tiberon, CA 94920
Tel: +1 (415) 789-9191
Fax: +1 (415) 789-9177
Email: info@kimberleycameron.com
Website: http://www.kimberleycameron.com

Handles: Fiction; Nonfiction; *Areas:* Mystery; Thrillers; *Markets:* Adult; Family; *Treatments:* Contemporary; Literary; Mainstream

Send query by email only with "Author Submission" in the subject line, and one-page synopsis and writing sample of up to 50 pages as separate Word file attachments. No screenplays, Children's Literature, poetry, novels in a foreign language, or teleplays. Approach one agent specifically – direct email address available for each agent on website.

The Knight Agency

Email: submissions@knightagency.net
Website: http://www.knightagency.net

Handles: Fiction; *Areas:* Autobiography; Business; Culture; Entertainment; Fantasy; Finance; Health; How-to; Lifestyle; Media; Mystery; Psychology; Romance; Sci-Fi; Self-Help; Suspense; Thrillers; Women's Interests; *Markets:* Adult; Youth; *Treatments:* Commercial; Literary

Send one-page query by email, providing details of your awards and affiliations, an explanation of what makes your book unique, and a synopsis. No paper or phone queries. Any unsolicited material will not be returned.

Not accepting Screen Plays, Short Story Collections, Poetry Collections, Essay Collections, Photography, Film Treatments, Picture Books (excluding graphic novels),

Children's Books (excluding young adult and middle grade), Biographies, Nonfiction Historical Treatments.

Linda Konner Literary Agency

10 West 15 Street, Suite 1918, New York, NY 10011
Tel: +1 (212) 691-3419
Email: ldkonner@cs.com
Website:
http://www.lindakonnerliteraryagency.com

Handles: Nonfiction; Reference; *Areas:* Biography; Business; Cookery; Culture; Entertainment; Finance; Health; How-to; Lifestyle; Psychology; Science; Self-Help; Women's Interests; *Markets:* Adult; *Treatments:* Popular

Send one-two page query by email or by post with SASE, synopsis, and author bio. Attachments from unknown senders will be deleted unread. Nonfiction only. Books must be written by or with established experts in their field. No Fiction, Memoir, Religion, Spiritual/Christian, Children's/young adult, Games/puzzles, Humour, History, Politics, or unsolicited MSS. See website for full guidelines.

Elaine Koster Literary Agency LLC

55 Central Park West Suite 6, New York, NY 10023
Tel: +1 (212) 362-9488
Fax: +1 (212) 712-0164
Email: ElaineKost@aol.com

Handles: Fiction; Nonfiction; *Areas:* Biography; Business; Cookery; Culture; Current Affairs; Finance; Health; Historical; How-to; Mystery; Nature; Psychology; Self-Help; Spiritual; Thrillers; Women's Interests; *Markets:* Adult; *Treatments:* Literary; Mainstream

Send query with SASE. No science fiction, children's, screenplays, simultaneous submissions, or queries by fax or email.

Barbara S. Kouts, Literary Agent

PO Box 560, Bellport, NY 11713
Tel: +1 (631) 286-1278
Fax: +1 (631) 286-1538
Email: bkouts@aol.com

Handles: Fiction; *Areas:* Autobiography; Biography; Crime; Current Affairs; Health; Historical; Lifestyle; Mystery; Nature; Psychology; Suspense; Thrillers; Women's Interests; *Markets:* Adult; Children's; *Treatments:* Literary

Send query with SASE. Postal queries only. Particularly interested in adult fiction and nonfiction and children's books.

Edite Kroll Literary Agency, Inc.

20 Cross Street, Saco, ME 04072
Tel: +1 (207) 283-8797
Fax: +1 (207) 283-8799
Email: ekroll@maine.rr.com

Handles: Fiction; Nonfiction; *Areas:* Autobiography; Biography; Culture; Current Affairs; Health; Humour; Legal; Medicine; Politics; Psychology; Religious; Self-Help; Women's Interests; *Markets:* Academic; Adult; Children's; Youth; *Treatments:* Literary

Handles mainly nonfiction so very selective about fiction. Particularly interested in international feminists and women writers and artists. No genre books such as mysteries, romance, or thrillers; no diet, cookery, etc.; no photography books, coffee table books, or commercial fiction. Send query by email, fax, or by post with SASE, including synopsis, author bio, and one or two sample chapters. For picture books, send complete MS. No queries by phone.

Larsen Pomada Literary Agents

1029 Jones Street, San Francisco, CA 94109-5023
Tel: +1 (415) 673-0939
Fax: +1 (415) 673-0367
Email: larsenpoma@aol.com

Website: http://www.Larsen-Pomada.com

Handles: Fiction; Nonfiction; *Areas:*
Anthropology; Architecture; Arts;
Autobiography; Biography; Business;
Cookery; Crime; Culture; Current Affairs;
Design; Fantasy; Film; Finance; Health;
Historical; How-to; Humour; Legal;
Lifestyle; Medicine; Music; Mystery;
Nature; New Age; Politics; Psychology;
Religious; Romance; Science; Self-Help;
Sociology; Sport; Suspense; Thrillers;
Travel; Women's Interests; *Markets:* Adult;
Children's; *Treatments:* Commercial;
Literary; Mainstream; Satirical

See website for detailed submission
guidelines.

LaunchBooks Literary Agency
566 Sweet Pea Place, Encinitas, CA 92024
Tel: +1 (760) 944-9909
Email: david@launchbooks.com
Website: http://www.launchbooks.com

Handles: Fiction; Nonfiction; *Areas:*
Adventure; Business; Culture; Current
Affairs; Historical; Humour; Nature;
Politics; Science; Sociology; Sport;
Technology; *Markets:* Adult; *Treatments:*
Contemporary; Mainstream; Popular

Handles mainly nonfiction, but will also
consider fun, engaging, contemporary novels
that appeal to a broad audience. Send query
or proposal with sample chapters by email.

Sarah Lazin Books
121 West 27th Street, Suite 704, New York,
NY 10001
Tel: +1 (212) 989-5757
Fax: +1 (212) 989-1393
Email: slazin@lazinbooks.com
Website: http://lazinbooks.com

Handles: Fiction; Nonfiction; *Areas:*
Autobiography; Biography; Culture; Current
Affairs; Historical; Music; Politics; *Markets:*
Adult

Accepting queries via referral only. No
queries by email.

Lenhoff & Lenhoff
830 Palm Avenue, West Hollywood, CA
90069
Tel: +1 (310) 855-2411
Fax: +1 (310) 855-2412
Email: charles@lenhoff.com
Website: http://www.lenhoff.com

Handles: Scripts; *Areas:* Film; *Markets:*
Adult

No unsolicited material. Approach via
conference or referral only.

Lescher & Lescher
346 East 84th Street, New York, NY 10028
Tel: +1 (212) 396-1999
Fax: +1 (212) 396-1991
Email: cl@lescherltd.com

Handles: Fiction; Nonfiction; *Areas:*
Autobiography; Biography; Cookery;
Culture; Current Affairs; Historical; Legal;
Mystery; Suspense; *Markets:* Adult;
Treatments: Commercial; Literary

Send query by post with SASE or by email.
No screenplays, science fiction, or romance.

Levine Greenberg Literary Agency, Inc.
307 Seventh Ave., Suite 2407, New York,
NY 10001
Tel: +1 (212) 337-0934
Fax: +1 (212) 337-0948
Email: submit@levinegreenberg.com
Website: http://www.levinegreenberg.com

Handles: Fiction; Nonfiction; *Areas:* Arts;
Autobiography; Biography; Business;
Cookery; Crafts; Crime; Culture; Finance;
Gardening; Health; Historical; Hobbies;
Humour; Leisure; Lifestyle; Mystery;
Nature; New Age; Politics; Psychology;
Religious; Romance; Science; Self-Help;
Sociology; Spiritual; Sport; Suspense;
Technology; Thrillers; Travel; Women's
Interests; *Markets:* Adult; Children's; Youth;
Treatments: Literary; Mainstream; Popular

No queries by mail. Send query using online
form at website, or send email attaching no
more than 50 pages. See website for detailed

submission guidelines. No response to submissions by post.

Lippincott Massie McQuilkin

27 West 20th Street, Suite 305, New York, NY 10011
Tel: +1 (212) 352-2055
Fax: +1 (212) 352-2059
Email: info@lmqlit.com
Website: http://www.lmqlit.com

Handles: Fiction; Nonfiction; *Areas:* Autobiography; Biography; Crime; Culture; Current Affairs; Historical; Humour; Politics; Psychology; Science; Sociology; *Markets:* Adult; *Treatments:* Commercial; Literary

Send query by email only, including outline, relevant author bio, and stating which agent you want to review your project.

The Literary Group

330 W 38th Street, Suite 408, New York, NY 10018
Tel: +1 (646) 442-5896
Fax: +1 (646) 792-3969
Email: js@theliterarygroup.com
Website: http://www.theliterarygroup.com

Handles: Fiction; Nonfiction; *Areas:* Autobiography; Biography; Cookery; Crime; Current Affairs; Fantasy; Health; Historical; Horror; Humour; Lifestyle; Military; Mystery; Nature; Psychology; Religious; Romance; Science; Sport; Suspense; Thrillers; Women's Interests; *Markets:* Adult

Send query by email or by post with SASE, writing credentials, 2 page synopsis, and 50-page writing sample. Response only if interested. Asks for a 30-day exclusivity period, beginning from the date the material is received.

Literary Management Group, Inc.

PO Box 40965, Nashville, TN 37204
Tel: +1 (615) 812-4445
Email: BruceBarbour@LiteraryManagementGroup.com

Website: http://literarymanagementgroup.com

Handles: Fiction; Nonfiction; *Areas:* Autobiography; Biography; Business; Lifestyle; Religious; Spiritual; *Markets:* Adult

Handles Christian books (defined as books which are consistent with the historical, orthodox teachings of the Christian fathers). Handles adult nonfiction and fiction only. No children's or illustrated books, poetry, memoirs, YA Fiction or text/academic books. Download proposal from website then complete and send with sample chapters.

Sterling Lord Literistic, Inc.

65 Bleecker Street, New York, NY 10012
Tel: +1 (212) 780-6050
Fax: +1 (212) 780-6095
Email: sterling@sll.com
Website: http://www.sll.com

Handles: Fiction; Nonfiction; *Areas:* Autobiography; Biography; Business; Culture; Current Affairs; Health; Historical; Lifestyle; Science; Self-Help; Women's Interests; *Markets:* Adult; Children's; Youth; *Treatments:* Commercial; Literary

Send query with SASE, synopsis, brief author bio, and first three chapters. Literary value considered above all else. No response to unsolicited email queries.

Lyons Literary LLC

540 President Street, Third Floor, Brooklyn, NY 11215
Tel: +1 (212) 851-8428
Fax: +1 (212) 851-8405
Email: info@lyonsliterary.com
Website: http://www.lyonsliterary.com

Handles: Fiction; Nonfiction; *Areas:* Autobiography; Biography; Cookery; Crime; Current Affairs; Entertainment; Fantasy; Health; Historical; Hobbies; How-to; Humour; Legal; Leisure; Lifestyle; Literature; Men's Interests; Military; Music; Mystery; Politics; Science; Sport; Suspense; Thrillers; Travel; TV; Women's Interests;

Markets: Adult; *Treatments:* Literary

A full service literary agency in New York dedicated to providing detailed and substantive guidance to its clients throughout the publication process. The agency provides comprehensive assistance to an exclusive client list in all areas related to their intellectual property, including editorial guidance, submission and sale of works in the domestic market to both large and small publishers, contract negotiations, foreign language sales, film and television licenses, marketing and publicity strategies, and career planning.

This agency only accepts electronic queries sent electronically via the agency's website submission form. Queries sent in any other manner (including by post) will not receive a response.

Gina Maccoby Agency

PO Box 60, Chappaqua, NY 10514
Tel: +1 (914) 238-5630
Email: query@maccobylit.com

Handles: Fiction; Nonfiction; *Areas:* Autobiography; Biography; Culture; Current Affairs; Entertainment; Health; Historical; Lifestyle; Mystery; Nature; Politics; Self-Help; Thrillers; Women's Interests; *Markets:* Adult; Children's; Youth; *Treatments:* Literary; Mainstream

Send query by post with SASE, or by email with "Query" in the subject line. No attachments. Response not guaranteed.

MacGregor Literary

2373 N.W. 185th Avenue, Suite 165, Hillsboro, OR 97124-7076
Tel: +1 (503) 277-8308
Email: submissions@macgregorliterary.com
Website: http://www.macgregorliterary.com

Handles: Fiction; Nonfiction; *Areas:* Autobiography; Biography; Business; Crime; Culture; Current Affairs; Finance; Historical; How-to; Humour; Lifestyle; Mystery; Religious; Romance; Self-Help; Short Stories; Sport; Suspense; Thrillers; Women's Interests; *Markets:* Academic; Adult;

Treatments: Contemporary; Mainstream

Handles work in a variety of genres, but all from a Christian perspective. Not accepting unpublished authors, except through conferences and referrals from current clients. Unsolicited MSS will not be returned, even if an SASE is provided.

Kirsten Manges Literary Agency, LLC

115 West 29th Street, 3rd Floor, New York, NY 10001
Email: kirsten@mangeslit.com
Website: http://www.mangeslit.com

Handles: Fiction; Nonfiction; *Areas:* Autobiography; Cookery; Culture; Health; Historical; Psychology; Science; Spiritual; Sport; Technology; Travel; Women's Interests; *Markets:* Adult; Youth; *Treatments:* Commercial; Literary

Send query by email or by post with SASE. Particularly interested in women's issues.

Carol Mann Agency

55 Fifth Avenue, New York, NY 10003
Tel: +1 (212) 206-5635
Fax: +1 (212) 674-4809
Email: submissions@carolmannagency.com
Website: http://www.carolmannagency.com

Handles: Fiction; Nonfiction; *Areas:* Anthropology; Archaeology; Architecture; Arts; Autobiography; Biography; Business; Culture; Current Affairs; Design; Finance; Health; Historical; Humour; Legal; Lifestyle; Medicine; Music; Nature; Politics; Psychology; Religious; Self-Help; Sociology; Spiritual; Sport; Women's Interests; *Markets:* Adult; Youth; *Treatments:* Commercial; Literary

Send query by email only, including synopsis, brief bio, and (in the case of fiction and memoir) first 25 pages. No submissions by post, or phone calls. Allow 3-4 weeks for response.

Manus & Associates Literary Agency, Inc.

425 Sherman Avenue, Suite 200, Palo Alto, CA 94306
Tel: +1 (650) 470-5151
Fax: +1 (650) 470-5159
Email: ManusLit@ManusLit.com
Website: http://www.ManusLit.com

Handles: Fiction; Nonfiction; *Areas:* Autobiography; Biography; Business; Culture; Current Affairs; Finance; Health; How-to; Lifestyle; Mystery; Nature; Psychology; Romance; Science; Self-Help; Suspense; Thrillers; Women's Interests; *Markets:* Adult; *Treatments:* Literary; Mainstream

Send query letter describing your project and giving pertinent biographical info only by fax or email, or send query letter by post with SASE and include complete proposal (nonfiction), or first 30 pages (fiction). When querying by email use one of the direct personal emails of a specific agent as given on the website, not the generic inbox shown on this page. Approach only one agent. No horror, romance, science fiction, fantasy, western, young adult, children's, poetry, cookbooks, or magazine articles. See website for full guidelines.

Denise Marcil Literary Agency, Inc.

110 William Street, Suite 2202, New York, NY 10038
Tel: +1 (212) 337-3402
Email: dmla@denisemarcilagency.com
Website:
http://www.denisemarcilagency.com

Handles: Fiction; Nonfiction; Reference; *Areas:* Biography; Business; Health; Lifestyle; Self-Help; Spiritual; Suspense; Thrillers; Women's Interests; *Markets:* Adult; *Treatments:* Contemporary; Popular

Send query by email or by post with SASE. No science fiction, children's books, or political nonfiction. No queries by fax.

Elaine Markson Literary Agency

450 Seventh Ave, Suite 1408, New York, NY 10123
Tel: +1 (212) 243-8480
Fax: +1 (212) 691-9014
Email: gary@marksonagency.com
Website: http://www.marksonagency.com

Handles: Fiction; Nonfiction; *Markets:* Adult; *Treatments:* Literary

Most new clients obtained through recommendation.

The Martell Agency

1350 Avenue of the Americas, Suite 1205, New York, NY 10019
Tel: +1 (212) 317-2672
Email: submissions@themartellagency.com
Website: http://www.themartellagency.com

Handles: Fiction; Nonfiction; *Areas:* Autobiography; Business; Finance; Health; Historical; Medicine; Mystery; Psychology; Self-Help; Suspense; Thrillers; Women's Interests; *Markets:* Adult; *Treatments:* Commercial

Send query by post or by email, including summary, short bio, any information, if appropriate, as to why you are qualified to write on the subject of your book, any publishing credits, the year of publication and the publisher. No original screenplays or poetry.

Martin Literary Management

7683 SE 27th Street, #307, Mercer Island, WA 98040
Tel: +1 (206) 466-1773
Fax: +1 (206) 466-1774
Email:
Sharlene@martinliterarymanagement.com
Website:
http://www.martinliterarymanagement.com

Handles: Fiction; Nonfiction; *Areas:* Autobiography; Biography; Business; Crime; Current Affairs; Entertainment; Health; How-to; Lifestyle; Media; Self-Help; Women's Interests; *Markets:* Adult; Children's; Youth; *Treatments:* Commercial;

Literary; Mainstream; Popular; Positive; Traditional

This agency has strong ties to film/TV. Actively seeking nonfiction that is highly commercial and that can be adapted to film. Please review our website carefully to make sure we're a good match for your work. How to contact: Completely electronic: emails and MS Word only. No attachments on queries. Place letter in body of email. See submission requirements on website. Do not send materials unless requested. We give very serious consideration to the material requested. We are actively seeing new submissions. We only ask to see materials that we intend to offer representation for – IF the work is saleable. Therefore, in exchange for that close evaluation, we require a two week exclusive consideration period, whereby your agree if we offer representation, you are already certain you are willing to accept pending our contract.

No adult fiction. Principal agent handles adult nonfiction only. See website for submission guidelines and separate email address for submissions of picture books, middle grade, and young adult fiction and nonfiction.

The Marton Agency, Inc.
1 Union Square West, Suite 815, New York, NY 10003-3303
Tel: +1 (212) 255-1908
Fax: +1 (212) 691-9061
Email: info@martonagency.com
Website: http://www.martonagency.com

Handles: Scripts; *Areas:* Theatre; Translations; *Markets:* Adult

International literary rights agency, specialising in foreign-language licensing.

Margret McBride Literary Agency
PO Box 9128, La Jolla, CA 92037
Tel: +1 (858) 454-1550
Fax: +1 (858) 459-0550
Email: staff@mcbridelit.com
Website: http://www.mcbrideliterary.com

Handles: Fiction; Nonfiction; *Areas:* Business; Health; Self-Help; *Markets:* Adult; *Treatments:* Commercial

Represents commercial fiction and nonfiction, business, health, and self-help. No poetry or romance. As at December 2013 accepting submission by referral only. See website for current status and detailed submission guidelines.

McIntosh & Otis, Inc
353 Lexington Avenue, New York, NY 10016
Tel: +1 (212) 687-7400
Fax: +1 (212) 687-6894
Email: info@mcintoshandotis.com
Website: http://www.mcintoshandotis.com

Handles: Fiction; Nonfiction; *Areas:* Adventure; Culture; Current Affairs; Fantasy; Historical; Horror; Humour; Music; Mystery; Nature; Psychology; Romance; Sci-Fi; Self-Help; Spiritual; Sport; Suspense; Thrillers; Travel; Women's Interests; *Markets:* Adult; Children's; Youth; *Treatments:* Commercial; Contemporary; Literary; Mainstream; Popular

Prefers submissions by email. See website for specific agent interests and email addresses, and query appropriate agent. Also accepts submissions by post, see website for full details.

Doris S. Michaels Literary Agency, Inc.
1841 Broadway, Suite 903, New York, NY 10023
Tel: +1 (212) 265-9474
Fax: +1 (212) 265-9480
Email: query@dsmagency.com
Website: http://www.dsmagency.com

Handles: Fiction; Nonfiction; *Areas:* Autobiography; Biography; Business; Current Affairs; Health; Historical; Lifestyle; Music; Psychology; Self-Help; Sociology; Sport; Women's Interests; *Markets:* Adult; *Treatments:* Commercial; Literary

Note: Not taking on new clients as at November 2013. Check website for

current status.

Specialises in business and self-help books from top professionals in their fields, but also handles other nonfiction and fiction. Send query by email only, including synopsis in one to two paragraphs and a paragraph about you, after having consulted submission guidelines on website. No romance, coffee table books, art books, trivia, pop culture, humour, westerns, occult/supernatural, horror, poetry, textbooks, children's books, picture books, film scripts, articles, cartoons or professional manuals. No email attachments or postal queries. Unsolicited MSS are returned unopened. No response unless interested.

Monteiro Rose Dravis Agency, Inc.

4370 Tujunga AVE, Suite 145, Studio City, CA 91604
Tel: +1 (818) 501-1177
Fax: +1 (818) 501-1194
Email: monrose@monteiro-rose.com
Website: http://www.monteiro-rose.com

Handles: Scripts; *Areas:* Adventure; Crime; Drama; Film; Historical; Humour; Mystery; Romance; Sci-Fi; Suspense; Thrillers; TV; *Markets:* Adult; Children's; Family; Youth; *Treatments:* Contemporary; Mainstream

Handles for TV, film, and animation. No unsolicited mss. Accepts new clients by referral only.

Moore Literary Agency

10 State Street #309, Newburyport, MA 01950
Tel: +1 (978) 465-9015
Fax: +1 (978) 465-8817
Email: cmoore@moorelit.com

Handles: Nonfiction; *Areas:* Technology; *Markets:* Adult; Professional

Handles nonfiction books on computers and technology only. Accepts queries by email, but proposals by post with SASE only. No queries by fax.

Patricia Moosbrugger Literary Agency

Denver, CO
Email: submissions@pmagency.net
Website: http://www.pmagency.net

Handles: Fiction; Nonfiction; *Areas:* Literature; *Markets:* Adult; Youth

Send query by email with brief synopsis.

Howard Morhaim Literary Agency

30 Pierrepont Street, Brooklyn, NY 11201
Tel: +1 (718) 222-8400
Fax: +1 (718) 222-5056
Email: kmckean@morhaimliterary.com
Website: http://morhaimliterary.com

Handles: Fiction; Nonfiction; *Areas:* Culture; Fantasy; Health; Romance; Sci-Fi; Sport; Women's Interests; *Markets:* Adult; Youth; *Treatments:* Contemporary; Literary

Send query by email only with outline / proposal for nonfiction, or three sample chapters for fiction. Attachments are accepted. No thrillers, mysteries, crime, politics, true crime, mind/body/spirit, or children's picture books.

William Morris Endeavor Entertainment

1325 Avenue of the Americas, New York, NY 10019
Tel: +1 (212) 586-5100
Fax: +1 (212) 246-3583
Email: jrw@wmeentertainment.com
Website: http://www.wma.com

Handles: Fiction; Nonfiction; Scripts; *Areas:* Film; TV; *Markets:* Adult

Send query with publishing history, synopsis, and SASE.

The Jean V. Naggar Literary Agency

216 East 75th Street, New York, NY 10021
Tel: +1 (212) 794-1082
Email: jvnla@jvnla.com

Website: http://www.jvnla.com

Handles: Fiction; Nonfiction; *Areas:* Adventure; Autobiography; Biography; Culture; Current Affairs; Fantasy; Gothic; Health; Historical; Horror; Humour; Lifestyle; Music; Mystery; Psychology; Romance; Science; Suspense; Thrillers; *Markets:* Adult; Children's; Youth; *Treatments:* Commercial; Dark; Literary; Mainstream; Popular

Accepts queries via online submission system only. See website for more details.

Nappaland Literary Agency

PO Box 1674, Loveland, CO 80539-1674
Fax: +1 (970) 635-9869
Email: Literary@nappaland.com
Website: http://www.nappaland.com/literary

Handles: Fiction; Nonfiction; *Areas:* Culture; Historical; Humour; Lifestyle; Religious; Suspense; Women's Interests; *Markets:* Adult; Youth; *Treatments:* Literary

Deliberately small boutique-sized agency. Send query letter only by email during specific submission windows (see website). No children's books, memoirs, screenplays, poetry, or anything about cats.

New Leaf Literary & Media, Inc.

110 West 40th Street, Suite 410, New York, NY 10018
Tel: +1 (646) 248-7989
Fax: +1 (646) 861-4654
Email: query@newleafliterary.com
Website: http://www.newleafliterary.com

Handles: Fiction; Nonfiction; *Areas:* Culture; Entertainment; Erotic; Fantasy; Historical; Romance; Sci-Fi; Technology; Thrillers; Women's Interests; *Markets:* Adult; Children's; Youth; *Treatments:* Mainstream

Send query by email only, with the word "Query" along with the specific agent's name in the subject line. Do not query more than one agent. Include up to five double-spaced sample pages in the body of the email

-- no attachments. Response only if interested.

Niad Management

15021 Ventura Blvd. #860, Sherman Oaks, CA 91403
Tel: +1 (818) 774-0051
Fax: +1 (818) 774-1740
Email: queries@niadmanagement.com
Website: http://www.niadmanagement.com

Handles: Fiction; Nonfiction; Scripts; *Areas:* Adventure; Autobiography; Biography; Crime; Culture; Drama; Film; Humour; Mystery; Romance; Sport; Suspense; Theatre; Thrillers; TV; *Markets:* Adult; Youth; *Treatments:* Contemporary; Literary; Mainstream

Manages mainly Hollywood writers, actors, and directors, although does also handle a very small number of books. Send query by email or by post with SASE. Responds only if interested.

Nine Muses and Apollo, Inc.

525 Broadway, Suite 201, New York, NY 10012
Tel: +1 (212) 431-2665

Handles: Nonfiction; *Markets:* Adult

Adult nonfiction only. No children's or young adult. Send query with SASE, outline, and two sample chapters. No simultaneous submissions.

Northern Lights Literary Services

762 State Road 458, Bedford, IN 47421
Email: queries@northernlightsls.com
Website: http://www.northernlightsls.com

Handles: Fiction; Nonfiction; *Areas:* Biography; Business; Health; Historical; How-to; Lifestyle; Medicine; Mystery; New Age; Psychology; Romance; Self-Help; Suspense; Women's Interests; *Markets:* Adult

Our goal is to provide personalized service to clients and create a bond that will endure throughout your career. We seriously consider each query we receive and will accept hardworking new authors who are willing to develop their talents and skills.

Encourages email queries but responds only if interested (within 5 working days). No horror or books for children.

Harold Ober Associates

425 Madison Avenue, New York, NY 10017
Tel: +1 (212) 759-8600
Fax: +1 (212) 759-9428
Email: phyllis@haroldober.com
Website: http://www.haroldober.com

Handles: Fiction; Nonfiction; *Markets:* Adult; Children's

Send query addressed to a specific agent by post only, including first five pages and SASE for reply. No plays, screenplays, or queries by fax.

Objective Entertainment

609 Greenwich St. 6th Floor, New York, NY 10014
Tel: +1 (212) 431-5454
Fax: +1 (917) 464-6394
Email: IK@objectiveent.com
Website: http://www.objectiveent.com

Handles: Fiction; Nonfiction; Scripts; *Areas:* Autobiography; Biography; Business; Cookery; Culture; Current Affairs; Fantasy; Film; Lifestyle; Music; Mystery; Politics; Sci-Fi; Sport; Thrillers; TV; Women's Interests; *Markets:* Adult; Children's; Youth; *Treatments:* Commercial; Literary

We represent over 100 celebrities, musicians, authors and bestselling writers.

Paradigm Talent and Literary Agency

360 Park Avenue South, 16th Floor, New York, NY 10010
Tel: +1 (212) 897-6400
Fax: +1 (212) 764-8941
Email: books@paradigmagency.com
Website: http://www.paradigmla.com

Handles: Fiction; Nonfiction; Scripts; *Areas:* Film; Theatre; TV; *Markets:* Adult

Talent agency with offices in Los Angeles, New York City, Monterey, California and Nashville, Tennessee, representing actors, musical artists, directors, writers and producers. Handles scripts and all areas of fiction and nonfiction. Send query by email with first ten pages of the work in the body of the email. Response only if interested.

The Park Literary Group LLC

270 Lafayette Street, Suite 1504, New York, NY 10012
Tel: +1 (212) 691-3500
Fax: +1 (212) 691-3540
Email: queries@parkliterary.com
Website: http://www.parkliterary.com

Handles: Fiction; Nonfiction; *Areas:* Adventure; Arts; Autobiography; Culture; Historical; Mystery; Politics; Science; Thrillers; Travel; *Markets:* Adult; *Treatments:* Commercial; Literary

Send query by email or by post with SASE. For fiction include short synopsis and first three chapters in the body of the email only (no attachments), and for nonfiction include proposal and sample chapter(s). No poetry or screenplays. Response only if interested.

The Richard Parks Agency

P.O. Box 693, Salem, NY 12865
Tel: +1 (518) 854-9466
Fax: +1 (518) 854-9466
Email: rp@richardparksagency.com
Website: http://www.richardparksagency.com

Handles: Fiction; Nonfiction; *Areas:* Adventure; Anthropology; Archaeology; Arts; Autobiography; Biography; Business; Cookery; Crafts; Culture; Current Affairs; Film; Finance; Gardening; Health; Historical; Hobbies; How-to; Humour; Legal; Lifestyle; Medicine; Military; Music; Nature; Politics; Psychology; Science; Self-Help; Sociology; Technology; Theatre; Travel; Women's Interests; *Markets:* Adult; *Treatments:* Commercial; Literary

Send query by post only, including SASE. No children's books, poetry, plays, screenplays, unsolicited MSS, or queries by fax or email. Fiction considered by referral only.

Kathi J. Paton Literary Agency

PO Box 2236, Radio City Station, New York, NY 10101-2236
Tel: +1 (212) 265-6586
Email: kjplitbiz@optonline.net

Handles: Fiction; Nonfiction; *Areas:* Biography; Business; Culture; Current Affairs; Finance; Health; Historical; Humour; Lifestyle; Politics; Religious; Science; Sport; Technology; *Markets:* Adult; *Treatments:* Literary; Mainstream; Popular

Send query with brief description by email only. No attachments or referrals to websites. Specialises in adult nonfiction. No science fiction, fantasy, horror, category romance, juvenile, young adult or self-published books. Response only if interested.

Pavilion Literary Management

660 Massachusetts Avenue, Suite 4, Boston, MA 02118
Tel: +1 (617) 792-5218
Email: jeff@pavilionliterary.com
Website: http://www.pavilionliterary.com

Handles: Fiction; Nonfiction; *Areas:* Adventure; Autobiography; Fantasy; Historical; Mystery; Science; Thrillers; *Markets:* Adult; Children's; Youth; *Treatments:* Popular

Only accepting approaches for fiction work by previously published authors or client referral. Send query by email specifying fiction or nonfiction and title of work in the subject line. No attachments. See website for full details.

Barry Perelman Agency

415 Washington Boulevard, Suite 902, Marina del Rey, CA 90292
Tel: +1 (310) 659-1122
Fax: +1 (310) 659-1122

Handles: Scripts; *Areas:* Adventure; Biography; Drama; Film; Historical; Horror; Mystery; Romance; Science; Thrillers; TV; *Markets:* Adult; *Treatments:* Contemporary

Handles motion pictures. Send query with SASE.

L. Perkins Associates

5800 Arlington Ave, Riverdale, NY 10471
Tel: +1 (718) 543-5344
Fax: +1 (718) 543-5354
Email: submissions@lperkinsagency.com
Website: http://lperkinsagency.com

Handles: Fiction; Nonfiction; *Areas:* Biography; Cookery; Culture; Erotic; Fantasy; Film; Historical; Horror; Humour; Music; Mystery; Psychology; Science; Sci-Fi; Theatre; Thrillers; *Markets:* Adult; Youth; *Treatments:* Commercial; Dark; Literary; Popular

Send query by email with synopsis, bio, and first five pages of your novel / proposal in the body of the email. No email attachments and no queries by post or any other means apart from email. Pitch only one book at a time, and to only one agent. Specific agent email addresses are available at website, or use general address provided below. No screenplays, short story collections, or poetry.

James Peter Associates, Inc.

PO Box 358, New Canaan, CT 06840
Tel: +1 (203) 972-1070
Fax: +1 (203) 972-1759
Email: gene_brissie@msn.com
Website: http://www.jamespeterassociates.com

Handles: Nonfiction; Reference; *Areas:* Autobiography; Biography; Business; Cookery; Culture; Film; Finance; Health; Historical; Humour; Leisure; Nature; Politics; Sport; Travel; TV; *Markets:* Adult

Send query with brief outline of project, CV and writing samples. Prefers to read material exclusively. Specialises in business, popular culture, history, health, biography, general, reference, and politics. No poetry, fiction, children's books, young adult, or unsolicited MSS.

Pinder Lane & Garon-Brooke Associates Ltd

159 West 53rd Street, Suite 14-E, New York, NY 10019
Tel: +1 (212) 489-0880
Fax: +1 (212) 489-7104
Email: pinderlanegaronbrooke@gmail.com
Website: http://www.pinderlane.com

Handles: Fiction; Nonfiction; *Areas:* Arts; Autobiography; Biography; Business; Cookery; Crime; Culture; Current Affairs; Entertainment; Erotic; Fantasy; Film; Health; Historical; Horror; Humour; Music; Mystery; Photography; Politics; Romance; Sci-Fi; Self-Help; Spiritual; Sport; Theatre; Thrillers; Travel; Westerns; Women's Interests; *Markets:* Adult; Children's; Youth; *Treatments:* Mainstream

Send query by email or by post with SASE, including brief synopsis and first three chapters only. No film, TV, or theatre scripts, or unsolicited MSS.

Pippin Properties, Inc

155 East 38th Street, Suite 2H, New York, NY 10016
Tel: +1 (212) 338-9310
Fax: +1 (212) 338-9579
Email: info@pippinproperties.com
Website: http://www.pippinproperties.com

Handles: Fiction; *Markets:* Adult; Children's; Youth

Devoted primarily to picture books, middle-grade, and young adult novels, but also represents adult projects on occasion. Send query by email with synopsis, background/publishing history, and any other relevant details.

Alièka Pistek Literary Agency, LLC

302A West 12th St., #124, New York, NY 10014
Email: alicka@apliterary.com
Website: http://www.apliterary.com

Handles: Fiction; Nonfiction; *Areas:* Biography; Current Affairs; Historical; Mystery; Romance; Science; Suspense; Thrillers; Travel; *Markets:* Adult; *Treatments:* Commercial; Literary

Accepts submissions by email only. Send query with bio and proposal/synopsis, and for fiction first three chapters, up to 50 pages max. Mark romance submissions as such in the subject line as these are treated as a special category. No fantasy, science fiction, or westerns.

The Poynor Group

13454 Yorktown Drive, Bowie, MD 20715
Tel: +1 (301)805-6788
Email: jpoynor@aol.com

Handles: Fiction; Nonfiction; *Areas:* Autobiography; Biography; Business; Cookery; Culture; Finance; Health; Medicine; Mystery; Religious; Romance; Suspense; *Markets:* Adult; Children's; Youth

Send query by post with SASE, or by email.

Linn Prentis Literary

c/o Trodayne Northern, Acquisitions Director, for: Amy Hayden, Acquisitions, Linn Prentis Literary, PO Box 674, New York, NY 10035
Tel: +1 (212) 875-8557
Fax: +1 (425) 489-2809
Email: ahayden@linnprentis.com
Website: http://www.linnprentis.com

Handles: Fiction; Nonfiction; *Areas:* Autobiography; Fantasy; Mystery; Sci-Fi; Women's Interests; *Markets:* Adult; Youth; *Treatments:* Contemporary; Literary; Mainstream

Particularly interested in science fiction and fantasy, but willing to consider any fiction of interest. Send query by email or by post with SASE, including synopsis and first ten pages. No books for small children, or queries by fax or phone.

Aaron M. Priest Literary Agency

708 Third Avenue, 23rd Floor, New York, NY 10017-4201
Tel: +1 (212) 818-0344
Fax: +1 (212) 573-9417
Email: querypriest@aaronpriest.com
Website: http://www.aaronpriest.com

Handles: Fiction; Nonfiction; *Areas:* Autobiography; Biography; Culture; Historical; Horror; How-to; Politics; Suspense; Thrillers; Translations; Women's Interests; *Markets:* Adult; Youth; *Treatments:* Commercial; Literary

Send one-page query by email, describing your work and your background. No attachments, but you may paste the first chapter into the body of the email. Query one agent only. See website for specific agent interests and email addresses. No poetry, screenplays, sci-fi, or horror.

Queen Literary Agency, Inc.

420 West End Avenue, Suite 8A, New York, NY 10024
Tel: +1 (212) 974-8333
Fax: +1 (212) 974-8347
Email: submissions@queenliterary.com
Website: http://www.queenliterary.com

Handles: Fiction; Nonfiction; *Areas:* Business; Cookery; Historical; Mystery; Psychology; Science; Sport; Thrillers; *Markets:* Adult; *Treatments:* Commercial; Literary

Founded by a former publishing executive, most recently head of IMG WORLDWIDE'S literary division. Handles a wide range of nonfiction titles, with a particular interest in business books, food writing, science and popular psychology, as well as books by well-known chefs, radio and television personalities and sports figures. Also handles commercial and literary fiction, including historical fiction, mysteries, and thrillers.

Susan Rabiner, Literary Agent, Inc.

315 West 39th Street, Suite 1501, New York, NY 10018
Tel: +1 (212) 279-0316
Fax: +1 (212) 279-0932
Email: susan@rabiner.net
Website: http://www.rabiner.net

Handles: Fiction; Nonfiction; *Areas:* Arts; Autobiography; Entertainment; Finance; Historical; Humour; Politics; Science; Sport; *Markets:* Adult

Send query by email only. Response within two weeks if interested. See website for details and email addresses of individual agents.

Lynne Rabinoff Agency

72-11 Austin Street, No. 201, Forest Hills, NY 11375
Tel: +1 (718) 459-6894
Email: lynne@lynnerabinoff.com

Handles: Nonfiction; *Areas:* Anthropology; Archaeology; Autobiography; Biography; Business; Culture; Current Affairs; Finance; Historical; Legal; Military; Politics; Psychology; Religious; Science; Technology; Women's Interests; *Markets:* Adult

Particularly interested in politics, history, current affairs, and religion. Send query by email or by post with SASE, including proposal, sample chapter, and author bio. No queries by fax.

Raines & Raines

103 Kenyon Road, Medusa, NY 12120
Tel: +1 (518) 239-8311
Fax: +1 (518) 239-6029

Handles: Fiction; Nonfiction; *Areas:* Adventure; Autobiography; Biography; Crime; Fantasy; Finance; Historical; Military; Mystery; Psychology; Sci-Fi; Suspense; Thrillers; Westerns; *Markets:* Adult

Handles nonfiction in all areas, and fiction in the areas specified above. Send query with SASE.

Rees Literary Agency

14 Beacon St., Suite 710, Boston, MA 02108
Tel: +1 (617) 227-9014
Fax: +1 (617) 227-8762
Email: reesagency@reesagency.com
Website: http://www.reesagency.com

Handles: Fiction; *Areas:* Autobiography; Biography; Business; Historical; Psychology; Science; Self-Help; *Markets:* Adult; *Treatments:* Commercial; Literary

See website for specific agents' interests and submission requirements.

Regal Literary Inc.

The Capitol Building, 236 West 26th St., #801, New York, NY 10001
Tel: +1 (212) 684-7900
Fax: +1 (212) 684-7906
Email: submissions@regal-literary.com
Website: http://www.regal-literary.com

Handles: Fiction; Nonfiction; *Areas:* Biography; Historical; Photography; Science; Short Stories; Thrillers; *Markets:* Adult; *Treatments:* Literary

Literary agency with offices in New York and London. Send one-page query by email or by post with SASE, outline, and author bio/qualifications. For fiction, include first ten pages or one story from a collection. No romance, science fiction, poetry, or screenplays. Writers based in the UK/Europe should contact the London office (see website for details).

Renee Zuckerbrot Literary Agency

115 West 29th Street, 10th floor, New York, NY 10001
Tel: +1 (212) 967-0072
Fax: +1 (212) 967-0073
Email: Submissions@rzagency.com
Website: http://rzagency.com

Handles: Fiction; Nonfiction; *Areas:*
Culture; Historical; Literature; Mystery; Science; Short Stories; Thrillers; Women's Interests; *Markets:* Adult; *Treatments:* Commercial; Literary

Send query including the reason that you decided to contact this agency, synopsis, publication history, brief bio, contact information, and excerpt/sample chapter as a Word document attachment (for novels, should be the first chapter). See website for full details. No screenplays, genre romance or westerns, New Age, or how-to books. No unsolicited MSS, or queries by fax.

The Amy Rennert Agency, Inc.

1550 Tiburon Boulevard #302, Tiburon, CA 94920
Email: queries@amyrennert.com
Website: http://www.amyrennert.com

Handles: Fiction; Nonfiction; *Areas:* Autobiography; Biography; Business; Finance; Health; Historical; Lifestyle; Literature; Mystery; Spiritual; Sport; *Markets:* Adult; *Treatments:* Literary

Prefers query by email, with cover letter in body of email and a Word file attachment containing proposal and first chapter (nonfiction) or first 10-20 pages (fiction). For picture books, send cover letter in the body of the email and attach file with the text. Include phone number. Response only if interested. If querying by post do not include return postage as manuscripts will not be returned.

Ann Rittenberg Literary Agency

15 Maiden Lane, Suite 206, New York, NY 10038
Email: info@rittlit.com
Website: http://www.rittlit.com

Handles: Fiction; Nonfiction; *Areas:* Autobiography; Biography; Culture; Historical; Sociology; Women's Interests; *Markets:* Adult; *Treatments:* Literary

Send three sample chapters with outline by email (pasted into the body of the email) or by post with SASE. Email queries receive a response only if interested. No Screenplays, Genre fiction, Poetry, or Self-help. No queries by fax.

Riverside Literary Agency

41 Simon Keets Road, Leyden, MA 01337
Tel: +1 (413) 772-0067
Fax: +1 (413) 772-0969
Email: rivlit@sover.net

Handles: Fiction; Nonfiction; *Markets:* Adult

Send query with outline by email or by post with SASE. Usually obtains new clients by referral.

RLR Associates

Literary Department, 7 West 51st Street, New York, NY 10019
Tel: +1 (212) 541-8641
Fax: +1 (212) 262-7084
Email: sgould@rlrassociates.net
Website: http://www.rlrliterary.net

Handles: Fiction; Nonfiction; *Areas:* Adventure; Anthropology; Arts; Biography; Business; Cookery; Crime; Culture; Current Affairs; Health; Historical; Horror; Humour; Music; Mystery; Nature; Photography; Politics; Psychology; Religious; Science; Self-Help; Short Stories; Sociology; Sport; Thrillers; Translations; Travel; Women's Interests; *Markets:* Academic; Adult; Children's; Family; *Treatments:* Commercial; Experimental; Literary; Mainstream

Represents literary and commercial fiction, genre fiction, and narrative nonfiction. Particularly interested in history, pop culture, humour, food and beverage, biography, and sports. Also represents all types of children's literature. Send query or proposal by post or by email. For fiction, include writing sample (normally the first few chapters). If no response after three months, assume rejection.

Michael D. Robins & Associates

141 Duesenberg Drive, Suite 7-B, Westlake

Village, CA 91362
Tel: +1 (818) 343-1755
Fax: +1 (818) 575-9832
Email: mdr2@msn.com

Handles: Fiction; Nonfiction; Scripts; *Areas:* Film; Theatre; TV; *Markets:* Adult

Send query with SASE, or query by fax or email.

Linda Roghaar Literary Agency, Inc.

133 High Point Drive, Amherst, MA 01002
Tel: +1 (413) 256-1921
Fax: +1 (413) 256-2636
Email: contact@lindaroghaar.com
Website: http://www.LindaRoghaar.com

Handles: Fiction; Nonfiction; *Areas:* Anthropology; Biography; Culture; Historical; Nature; Religious; Self-Help; Women's Interests; *Markets:* Adult

Send query by email (mentioning "query" in the subject line) or by post with SASE. For fiction, include the first five pages. Specialises in nonfiction. No romance, science fiction, or horror. Scripts handled through sub-agents.

Andy Ross Agency

767 Santa Ray Avenue, Oakland, CA 94610
Tel: +1 (510) 238-8965
Email: andyrossagency@hotmail.com
Website: http://www.andyrossagency.com

Handles: Fiction; Nonfiction; *Areas:* Culture; Current Affairs; Historical; Religious; Science; *Markets:* Adult; Children's; Youth; *Treatments:* Commercial; Contemporary; Literary

We encourage queries for material in our fields of interest.

The agent has worked in the book business for 36 years, all of his working life. He was owner and general manager of Cody's Books in Berkeley, California from 1977-2006. Cody's has been recognised as one of America's great independent book stores.

During this period, the agent was the primary trade book buyer. This experience has given him a unique understanding of the retail book market, of publishing trends and, most importantly and uniquely, the hand selling of books to book buyers.

The agent is past president of the Northern California Booksellers Association, a board member and officer of the American Booksellers Association and a national spokesperson for issues concerning independent businesses. He has had signifcant profiles in the Wall Street Journal, Time Magazine, and the San Francisco Chronicle.

Queries by email only. See website for full guidelines.

Jane Rotrosen Agency

318 East 51st Street, New York, NY 10022
Tel: +1 (212) 593-4330
Fax: +1 (212) 935-6985
Email: acirillo@janerotrosen.com
Website: http://www.janerotrosen.com

Handles: Fiction; Nonfiction; *Areas:* Autobiography; Historical; Mystery; Romance; Suspense; Thrillers; Women's Interests; *Markets:* Adult; Youth; *Treatments:* Commercial; Mainstream

Send query by email to one of the agent email addresses provided on the agency bios page of the website, or by post with SASE, describing your work and giving relevant biographical details and publishing history, along with synopsis and the first three chapters in the case of fiction, or proposal in the case of nonfiction. Submissions without an SASE will be recycled without response. Attachments to a blank email will not be opened. See website for full guidelines and individual agent details.

The Rudy Agency

825 Wildlife Lane, Estes Park, CO 80517
Tel: +1 (970) 577-8500
Fax: +1 (970) 577-8600
Email: mak@rudyagency.com
Website: http://www.rudyagency.com

Handles: Fiction; Nonfiction; *Areas:* Autobiography; Biography; Business; Culture; Health; Historical; Medicine; Military; Science; Technology; *Markets:* Adult

Concentrates on adult nonfiction in the areas listed above. Not accepting fiction submissions, except historical fiction. No poetry, children's or young adult, religion books, parenting how-to books, or screenplays. Send query letter only in first instance, by email or by fax.

Marly Rusoff & Associates, Inc.

PO Box 524, Bronxville, NY 10708
Tel: +1 (914) 961-7939
Email: mra_queries3@rusoffagency.com
Website: http://www.rusoffagency.com

Handles: Fiction; Nonfiction; *Areas:* Architecture; Arts; Autobiography; Biography; Business; Culture; Design; Finance; Health; Historical; Medicine; Psychology; *Markets:* Adult; *Treatments:* Commercial; Literary

Send 1-2 page query by post or email, including synopsis and relevant author info and page or word count. Queries sent by email should include the word "query" in the subject line. Changes email address regularly to avoid spam, so check website before querying and notify firstwriter.com via the "Report an Error" button if address has changed from that displayed. May not respond if not interested. No PDFs, CDs, or directions to view material on websites.

The Sagalyn Literary Agency

1250 Connecticut Ave NW, 7th Floor, Washington, DC 20036
Email: query@sagalyn.com
Website: http://www.sagalyn.com

Handles: Fiction; Nonfiction; Historical; Science; *Markets:* Adult; *Treatments:* Mainstream

Some fiction, but mainly upmarket nonfiction. No romance, westerns, science fiction, poetry, children's books, or screenplays. Query by email only, but no attachments. Visit website for details on submissions.

Salkind Literary Agency

734 Indiana Street, Lawrence, KS 66044
Tel: +1 (785) 371-0101
Fax: +1 (516) 706-2369
Email: neil@studiob.com
Website: http://www.salkindagency.com

Handles: Fiction; Nonfiction; *Areas:* Adventure; Arts; Autobiography; Biography; Business; Cookery; Crafts; Crime; Culture; Current Affairs; Fantasy; Finance; Health; Historical; How-to; Humour; Lifestyle; Mystery; Photography; Politics; Psychology; Religious; Science; Sci-Fi; Self-Help; Spiritual; Suspense; Technology; Thrillers; Travel; Women's Interests; *Markets:* Academic; Adult

Handles general nonfiction trade, fiction, and textbook authors. Query by email or telephone.

Schiavone Literary Agency

236 Trails End, West Palm Beach, FL 33413-2135
Tel: +1 (561) 966-9294
Fax: +1 (561) 966-9294
Email: profschia@aol.com

Handles: Fiction; Nonfiction; *Areas:* Biography; Business; Cookery; Crime; Culture; Fantasy; Finance; Health; Historical; Mystery; Politics; Religious; Romance; Science; Sci-Fi; Spiritual; Sport; Suspense; Thrillers; Travel; *Markets:* Academic; Adult; Children's; Family; Youth; *Treatments:* Literary; Mainstream

Send one-page query letter only by email or by post with SASE. No proposals, sample chapters, etc. unless requested. No poetry, short stories, anthologies or children's picture books, unsolicited MSS, or email attachments. No previously published or self-published material. Prefers to work with authors already published by major New York publishing houses.

Jonathan Scott, Inc

933 West Van Buren, Suite 510, Chicago, IL 60680
Tel: +1 (312) 339-7300
Email: jon_malysiak@yahoo.com
Website: http://www.jonathanscott.us

Handles: Nonfiction; *Areas:* Autobiography; Business; Cookery; Health; Historical; Sport; Travel; *Markets:* Adult

Handles nonfiction only. No fiction. Send query by email outlining your book idea and/or a proposal. Hard copy proposals will not be read.

Scovil Galen Ghosh Literary Agency, Inc.

276 Fifth Avenue, Suite 708, New York, NY 10001
Tel: +1 (212) 679-8686
Fax: +1 (212) 679-6710
Email: info@sgglit.com
Website: http://www.sgglit.com

Handles: Fiction; Nonfiction; *Areas:* Adventure; Arts; Autobiography; Biography; Cookery; Culture; Health; Historical; Nature; Psychology; Religious; Science; Sociology; Women's Interests; *Markets:* Adult; Children's; Youth; *Treatments:* Commercial; Literary

Send query letter only in first instance. Prefers contact by email, but no attachments. If contacting by post include letter only, with email address for response rather than an SASE.

Scribe Agency LLC

5508 Joylynne Drive, Madison, WI 53716
Email: submissions@scribeagency.com
Website: http://www.scribeagency.com

Handles: Fiction; *Areas:* Fantasy; Literature; Sci-Fi; Short Stories; *Markets:* Adult; *Treatments:* Commercial; Literary; Mainstream

Handles science fiction, fantasy, and literary fiction. No nonfiction, humour, cozy mysteries, faith-based fiction, screenplays, poetry, or works based on another's ideas.

Send query in body of email, with synopsis and first three chapters as Word docs, RTFs, or PDFs. No hard copy approaches. If unable to submit material electronically, send email query in first instance.

Secret Agent Man

PO Box 1078, Lake Forest, CA 92609-1078
Tel: +1 (949) 463-1638
Fax: +1 (949) 831-4648
Email: query@secretagentman.net
Website: http://www.secretagentman.net

Handles: Fiction; Nonfiction; *Areas:* Crime; Mystery; Religious; Suspense; Thrillers; Westerns; *Markets:* Adult

Send query by email only (no postal submissions) with the word "Query" in the subject line, sample consecutive chapter(s), synopsis and/or outline. No first contact by phone. Not interested in vampire; sci-fi; fantasy; horror; cold war, military or political thrillers; children's or young adult; short stories; screenplays; poetry collections; romance; or historical. Christian nonfiction should be based on Biblical theology, not speculative.

Lynn Seligman, Literary Agent

400 Highland Avenue, Upper Montclair, NJ 07043
Tel: +1 (973) 783-3631

Handles: Fiction; Nonfiction; *Areas:* Anthropology; Arts; Biography; Business; Cookery; Crime; Culture; Current Affairs; Design; Fantasy; Film; Finance; Health; Historical; Horror; How-to; Humour; Lifestyle; Music; Mystery; Nature; Photography; Politics; Psychology; Romance; Science; Sci-Fi; Self-Help; Sociology; Women's Interests; *Markets:* Adult; *Treatments:* Contemporary; Literary; Mainstream

Send query with SASE.

The Seven Bridges Group

5000 Birch Street, Suite 3000, Newport Beach, CA 92660
Tel: +1 (949) 260-2099

Fax: +1 (650) 249-1612
Email: travis.bell@sevenbridgesgroup.com
Website: http://www.sevenbridgesgroup.com

Handles: Fiction; Scripts; *Areas:* Adventure; Autobiography; Biography; Crime; Culture; Current Affairs; Drama; Entertainment; Literature; Men's Interests; Military; Music; Politics; Short Stories; Sport; Suspense; Travel; TV; Westerns; Women's Interests; *Markets:* Adult; Family; Professional; *Treatments:* Commercial; Contemporary; In-depth; Light; Literary; Mainstream; Niche; Popular; Traditional

No upfront fees will be incurred by writer (Client).

Signature Literary Agency

101 W. 23rd St, Suite 346, New York, NY 10011
Tel: +1 (201) 435-8334
Fax: +1 (202) 478-1623
Email: ellen@signaturelit.com
Website: http://www.signaturelit.com

Handles: Fiction; Nonfiction; Reference; *Areas:* Beauty and Fashion; Biography; Crime; Criticism; Culture; Current Affairs; Historical; Military; Politics; Science; Technology; Thrillers; Women's Interests; *Markets:* Adult; Children's; Youth; *Treatments:* Commercial; Literary; Popular

Agency established in Washington DC. The principal agent formerly worked at the Graybill and English Literary Agency. She has a law degree from George Washington University and extensive editorial experience.

Send query by email to specific agent (see website for individual contact details and "wishlists").

Offices in both New York and Washington DC.

SLW Literary Agency

4100 Ridgeland Avenue, Northbrook, IL 60062
Tel: +1 (847) 509-0999
Fax: +1 (847) 509-0996

Email: shariwenk@gmail.com

Handles: Nonfiction; *Areas:* Sport; *Markets:* Adult

Handles sports celebrities and sports writers only.

Valerie Smith, Literary Agent
1746 Route 44/55 RR, Box 160, Modena, NY 12548

Handles: Fiction; Nonfiction; *Areas:* Cookery; Fantasy; Historical; How-to; Mystery; Sci-Fi; Self-Help; Suspense; Women's Interests; *Markets:* Adult; Youth; *Treatments:* Contemporary; Literary; Mainstream

Send query with SASE, synopsis, author bio, and three sample chapters, by post only. No unsolicited MSS, or queries by fax or email. Strong ties to science fiction, fantasy, and young adult.

Spectrum Literary Agency
320 Central Park West, Suite 1-D, New York, NY 10025
Tel: +1 (212) 362-4323
Fax: +1 (212) 362-4562
Email: ruddigore1@aol.com
Website: http://www.spectrumliteraryagency.com

Handles: Fiction; Nonfiction; *Areas:* Fantasy; Historical; Mystery; Romance; Sci-Fi; Suspense; *Markets:* Adult; *Treatments:* Contemporary; Mainstream

Send query with SASE describing your book and providing background information, publishing credits, and relevant qualifications. The first 10 pages of the work may also be included. Response within three months. No unsolicited MSS or queries by fax, email, or phone.

Spencerhill Associates
PO Box 374, Chatham, NY 12037
Tel: +1 (518) 392-9293
Fax: +1 (518) 392-9554
Email:

submission@spencerhillassociates.com
Website: http://spencerhillassociates.com

Handles: Fiction; Nonfiction; *Areas:* Erotic; Fantasy; Mystery; Romance; Thrillers; *Markets:* Adult; Youth; *Treatments:* Commercial; Literary

Handles commercial, general-interest fiction, romance including historical romance, paranormal romance, urban fantasy, erotic fiction, category romance, literary fiction, thrillers and mysteries, young adult, and nonfiction. No children's. Send query by email with synopsis and first three chapters attached in .doc / .rtf / .txt format. See website for full details.

Philip G. Spitzer Literary Agency, Inc.
50 Talmage Farm Lane, East Hampton, NY 11937
Tel: +1 (631) 329-3650
Fax: +1 (631) 329-3651
Email: Luc.Hunt@spitzeragency.com
Website: http://spitzeragency.com

Handles: Fiction; Nonfiction; *Areas:* Biography; Current Affairs; Historical; Mystery; Politics; Short Stories; Sport; Suspense; Thrillers; Travel; *Markets:* Adult; *Treatments:* Literary

Full client list, but will consider queries regarding work you believe is absolutely right for the agency. Send query by email or by post.

Stone Manners Salners Agency
9911 West Pico Boulevard, Suite 1400, Los Angeles, CA 90048
Tel: +1 (323) 655-1313 / +1 (212) 505-1400
Email: info@smsagency.com
Website: http://www.smsagency.com

Handles: Scripts; *Areas:* Film; TV; *Markets:* Adult

Handles movie and TV scripts. Send query by email or post with SASE. No queries by fax.

Robin Straus Agency, Inc.

229 East 79th Street, Suite 5A, New York, NY 10075
Tel: +1 (212) 472-3282
Fax: +1 (212) 472-3833
Email: info@robinstrausagency.com
Website: http://www.robinstrausagency.com

Handles: Fiction; Nonfiction; *Areas:* Autobiography; Biography; Cookery; Culture; Current Affairs; Historical; Lifestyle; Nature; Psychology; Science; Women's Interests; *Markets:* Adult; *Treatments:* Commercial; Literary

Send query with SASE, bio, synopsis or outline, submission history, and market information. You may also include the opening chapter. Approaches by email are accepted, but all material must be in the body of the email. No attachments. No juvenile, young adult, science fiction/fantasy, horror, romance, westerns, poetry or screenplays. No response to approaches without SASE. No metered postage. If no response after 6 weeks, assume rejection.

Pam Strickler Author Management

134 Main Street, New Paltz, NY 12561
Email: pamstrickleragency@gmail.com

Handles: Fiction; *Areas:* Historical; Romance; Women's Interests; *Markets:* Adult

Send query by email only, including one-page letter giving brief description of plot, plus first ten pages, all pasted into the body of the email. Attachments are deleted unread. Hardcopy queries or manuscripts destroyed unread. No unsolicited MSS, children's books, or nonfiction.

Rebecca Strong International Literary Agency

235 West 108th Street, #35, New York, NY 10025
Tel: +1 (212) 865-1569
Email: info@rsila.com
Website: http://www.rsila.com

Handles: Fiction; Nonfiction; *Areas:* Autobiography; Biography; Business; Health; Historical; Science; Travel; *Markets:* Adult

Deliberately small agency focused on building careers rather than dealing with individual projects. Handles general fiction and nonfiction in the areas specified above. No poetry, screenplays, or unsolicited MSS. Generally represents writers with prior publishing experience only (for writers of fiction this includes publication in literary magazines and anthologies). Accepts query letters by email only. Include the words "Submission query" clearly in the subject line. If submitting fiction, include one or two complete chapters only.

The Strothman Agency

197 Eighth Street, Flagship Wharf – 611 , Charlestown, MA 02129
Tel: +1 (617) 742-2011
Fax: +1 (617) 742-2014
Email: strothmanagency@gmail.com
Website: http://www.strothmanagency.com

Handles: Fiction; Nonfiction; *Areas:* Arts; Autobiography; Business; Culture; Current Affairs; Historical; Nature; Science; Travel; *Markets:* Adult; Children's; Youth

Send query by email only. Postal approaches will be recycled or returned unread. Include query, details about yourself, a synopsis, and (for fiction) 2-10 sample pages. All material must be in the body of the email – no attachments. No romance, science fiction, picture books, or poetry.

Stuart Krichevsky Literary Agency, Inc.

381 Park Avenue South, Suite 428, New York, NY 10016
Tel: +1 (212) 725-5288
Fax: +1 (212) 725-5275
Email: query@skagency.com
Website: http://www.skagency.com

Handles: Fiction; Nonfiction; *Areas:* Adventure; Autobiography; Biography; Business; Culture; Current Affairs; Fantasy; Historical; Nature; Politics; Science; Sci-Fi;

Technology; *Markets:* Adult; Youth;
Treatments: Commercial; Literary

Send query by email with first few pages of
your manuscript (up to 10) pasted into body
of the email (no attachments). See website
for complete submission guidelines and
appropriate submission addresses for each
agent.

The Stuart Agency
260 West 52 Street, Suite. 24-C, New York,
NY 10019
Tel: +1 (212) 586-2711
Fax: +1 (212) 977-1488
Email: andrew@stuartagency.com
Website: http://www.stuartagency.com

Handles: Fiction; Nonfiction; *Areas:*
Autobiography; Business; Current Affairs;
Health; Historical; Lifestyle; Psychology;
Religious; Science; Sport; *Markets:* Adult;
Treatments: Commercial; Literary

Send query using submission form on
website.

Susanna Lea Associates
331 West 20th Street, New York, NY 10011
Tel: +1 (646) 638-1435
Fax: +1 (646) 486-0322
Email: us-submission@susannalea.com
Website:
http://www.susannaleaassociates.com

Handles: Fiction; Nonfiction; *Markets:*
Adult

Agency based in France with US office in
New York and UK office in London. No
poetry, plays, screenplays, science fiction,
educational text books, short stories,
illustrated works, or queries by fax. Submit
by email. See website for specific email
addresses for US, UK, and French
submissions. Include query letter, brief
synopsis, first three chapters and/or proposal.

The Swetky Agency and Associates
2150 Balboa Way #29, St. George, Utah
84770

Tel: +1 (435) 313-8006
Email: fayeswetky@amsaw.org
Website:
http://www.amsaw.org/swetkyagency/

Handles: Fiction; Nonfiction; Scripts; *Areas:*
Adventure; Anthropology; Archaeology;
Architecture; Arts; Autobiography; Business;
Cookery; Crime; Criticism; Culture; Current
Affairs; Design; Erotic; Fantasy; Film;
Finance; Gardening; Gothic; Health;
Historical; How-to; Humour; Legal; Leisure;
Literature; Medicine; Military; Mystery;
Nature; Philosophy; Photography; Politics;
Psychology; Religious; Romance; Science;
Sci-Fi; Self-Help; Short Stories; Sociology;
Sport; Suspense; Technology; Theatre;
Thrillers; Translations; Travel; TV;
Westerns; Women's Interests; *Markets:*
Adult; Children's; Youth; *Treatments:*
Contemporary; Experimental; Literary;
Mainstream

Submit query using submission form on
website only. Do not send any portion of
your work until requested to do so. Follow
guidelines on website precisely. Failure to do
so results in automatic rejection. Willing to
consider anything marketable, except short
stories, poetry and children's picture books
(but accepts children's fiction and
nonfiction).

Talcott Notch Literary
2 Broad Street, Second Floor, Suites 1,2 &
10, Milford, Connecticut 06460
Tel: +1 (203) 876-4959
Fax: +1 (203) 876-9517
Email: editorial@talcottnotch.net
Website: http://www.talcottnotch.net

Handles: Fiction; Nonfiction; *Areas:*
Autobiography; Business; Cookery; Crafts;
Crime; Fantasy; Gardening; Historical;
Horror; Lifestyle; Mystery; Nature; Science;
Sci-Fi; Suspense; Technology; Thrillers;
Women's Interests; *Markets:* Adult;
Children's; Family; Youth; *Treatments:*
Mainstream

Rapidly growing literary agency seeking
fresh voices in fiction and expert nonfiction
authors. Our President has over fifteen years
in the publishing industry. Send query by

email or by post with SASE, including outline or synopsis and first ten pages. No email attachments. See website for full guidelines.

Patricia Teal Literary Agency

2036 Vista Del Rosa, Fullerton, CA 92831-1336
Tel: +1 (714) 738-8333
Fax: +1 (714) 738-8333

Handles: Fiction; Nonfiction; *Areas:* Biography; Crime; Health; Historical; How-to; Lifestyle; Mystery; Nature; Psychology; Romance; Self-Help; Women's Interests; *Markets:* Adult; *Treatments:* Commercial; Contemporary; Mainstream

Deals with published authors only. Send query with SASE in first instance. Specialises in women's fiction, and commercial how-to and self-help. No short stories, poetry, articles, regency romance, science fiction, fantasy, or queries by fax or email.

Tessler Literary Agency

27 West 20th Street, Suite 1003, New York, NY 10011
Tel: +1 (212) 242-0466
Fax: +1 (212) 242-2366
Website: http://www.tessleragency.com

Handles: Fiction; Nonfiction; *Areas:* Autobiography; Biography; Business; Cookery; Historical; Psychology; Science; Travel; Women's Interests; *Markets:* Adult; *Treatments:* Commercial; Literary; Popular

Welcomes appropriate queries. Handles quality nonfiction and literary and commercial fiction. No genre fiction or children's fiction. Send query via form on website only.

Tom Lee

716 Kishwaukee Street #D, Rockford, IL 61104
Tel: +1 (815) 505-9147 or +1 (815) 708-7123
Fax: +1 (815) 964-3061
Email: chicagocatorange@yahoo.com

Handles: Fiction; Poetry; Scripts; *Areas:* Adventure; Anthropology; Antiques; Archaeology; Arts; Autobiography; Crime; Drama; Erotic; Fantasy; Film; Historical; Horror; Literature; Mystery; Religious; Sci-Fi; Short Stories; Theatre; Thrillers; *Markets:* Adult; Professional; *Treatments:* Commercial; Dark; Experimental; In-depth; Literary; Mainstream; Progressive; Serious

Want writers who have educated capability in handling their material. Meet the structural and syntactical demands of the publishers and producers, and must be easy to work with, know the industries, and not be playing the self-possessed, eccentric artiste, so to say.

Scott Treimel NY

434 Lafayette Street, New York, NY 10003
Tel: +1 (212) 505-8353
Email: general@scotttreimelny.com
Website: http://www.scotttreimelny.com

Handles: Fiction; Nonfiction; *Markets:* Children's; Youth

Children's books only – from concept / board books to teen fiction. Accepts submissions only by referral from contacts, and from attendees at conferences.

TriadaUS Literary Agency, Inc.

P.O.Box 561, Sewickley, PA 15143
Tel: +1 (412) 401-3376
Email: uwe@triadaus.com
Website: http://www.triadaus.com

Handles: Fiction; Nonfiction; *Areas:* Adventure; Autobiography; Biography; Cookery; Crime; Culture; Current Affairs; Health; How-to; Mystery; Psychology; Romance; Sci-Fi; Self-Help; Sport; Thrillers; Travel; *Markets:* Adult; Children's; Youth; *Treatments:* Commercial; Literary

Actively seeking established and new writers in a wide range of genres. Will only respond to approaches following the guidelines outlined on the website. Only responds to postal queries that include an SASE. Prefers email approaches, but no attachments.

Trident Media Group, LLC

41 Madison Avenue, 36th Fl., New York,
NY 10010
Tel: +1 (212) 333-1511
Email: info@tridentmediagroup.com
Website: http://www.tridentmediagroup.com

Handles: Fiction; Nonfiction; *Areas:*
Adventure; Autobiography; Biography;
Business; Crime; Culture; Current Affairs;
Film; Health; Historical; Humour; Lifestyle;
Music; Mystery; Politics; Romance; Science;
Sport; Suspense; Thrillers; Women's
Interests; *Markets:* Adult; Children's; Youth;
Treatments: Commercial; Literary

Send query using form on website. Check
website for details and interests of specific
agents and approach one agent only. Do not
approach more than one agent at a time. No
unsolicited MSS.

2M Literary Agency Ltd

33 West 17 Street, PH, New York, NY
10011
Tel: +1 (212) 741-1509
Fax: +1 (212) 691-4460
Email: morel@2mcommunications.com
Website:
http://www.2mcommunications.com

Handles: Nonfiction; *Areas:* Autobiography;
Beauty and Fashion; Business; Cookery;
Crime; Culture; Film; Health; Lifestyle;
Medicine; Music; Politics; Psychology;
Science; Sport; *Markets:* Adult; Family;
Treatments: Contemporary; Mainstream;
Niche; Popular; Progressive; Traditional

Only accepts queries from established
ghostwriters, collaborators, and editors with
experience in the fields of business; film;
music and television; health and fitness;
medicine and psychology; parenting;
politics; science; sport; true crime; or the
world of food.

Veritas Literary Agency

601 Van Ness Avenue, Opera Plaza Suite E,
San Francisco, CA 94102
Tel: +1 (415) 647-6964
Fax: +1 (415) 647-6965
Email: submissions@veritasliterary.com

Website: http://www.veritasliterary.com

Handles: Fiction; Nonfiction; *Areas:*
Business; Crime; Culture; Erotic; Fantasy;
Health; Historical; Lifestyle; Mystery;
Nature; Science; Sci-Fi; Self-Help; Thrillers;
Women's Interests; *Markets:* Adult;
Children's; Youth; *Treatments:* Commercial;
Literary

Send query or proposal by email only.
Submit further information on request only.
For fiction, include cover letter listing
previously published work, one-page
summary and first two chapters. For
nonfiction, include author bio, overview,
chapter-by-chapter summary, and analysis of
competing titles.

Beth Vesel Literary Agency

80 Fifth Avenue, Suite 1101, New York, NY
10011
Tel: +1 (212) 924-4252
Fax: +1 (212) 675-1381
Email: kezia@bvlit.com

Handles: Fiction; Nonfiction; *Areas:*
Autobiography; Biography; Business; Crime;
Criticism; Culture; Finance; Health; How-to;
Medicine; Psychology; Thrillers; Women's
Interests; *Markets:* Adult; *Treatments:*
Literary; Serious

Handles serious nonfiction (sophisticated
memoirs, cultural criticism, psychology,
women's issues) and fiction (particularly
literary psychological thrillers). Send query
with SASE.

Wales Literary Agency, Inc

PO Box 9426, Seattle, WA 98109
Tel: +1 (206) 284-7114
Email: waleslit@waleslit.com
Website: http://www.waleslit.com

Handles: Fiction; Nonfiction; *Areas:*
Culture; Politics; *Markets:* Adult;
Treatments: Progressive

Represents quality works of fiction and
narrative nonfiction. The Agency is
especially interested in story-driven
narratives, new voices, and progressive

cultural and political points of view. No self-help, how-to, children's books, romance, genre in general (including mysteries), or screenplays. Send query by post with SASE, or by email (must be no longer than one page and must not include attachments), explaining who you are, what your book is about, and why other readers might be interested. No unsolicited MSS, or queries by fax or phone.

Watkins / Loomis Agency, Inc.

PO Box 20925, New York, NY 10025
Tel: +1 (212) 532-0080
Fax: +1 (646) 383-2449
Email: assistant@watkinsloomis.com
Website: http://www.watkinsloomis.com

Handles: Fiction; Nonfiction; *Areas:* Autobiography; Biography; Culture; Current Affairs; Historical; Nature; Politics; Short Stories; Technology; Travel; *Markets:* Adult; Youth; *Treatments:* Contemporary; Literary; Popular

Specialises in literary fiction, memoir, biography, essay, travel, and political journalism. No unsolicited MSS and does not guarantee a response to queries.

Waxman Leavell Literary Agency

443 Park Ave South, #1004, New York, NY 10016
Tel: +1 (212) 675-5556
Fax: +1 (212) 675-1381
Email: scottsubmit@waxmanleavell.com
Website: http://www.waxmanleavell.com

Handles: Fiction; Nonfiction; *Areas:* Adventure; Autobiography; Biography; Business; Culture; Entertainment; Fantasy; Historical; Humour; Military; Mystery; Romance; Sci-Fi; Sport; Thrillers; Women's Interests; *Markets:* Adult; Children's; Youth; *Treatments:* Commercial; Contemporary; Literary

Send query by email to one of the agent-specific addresses on the website. Do not query more than one agent at a time. For details of what each agent is looking for, see details on website. No attachments, but for

fiction include 5-10 pages in the body of the email.

Irene Webb Literary

551 W. Cordova Road #238, Santa Fe, NM 87505
Tel: +1 (505) 988-1817
Email: webblit@gmail.com
Website: http://www.irenewebb.com

Handles: Fiction; Nonfiction; *Areas:* Autobiography; Crime; Culture; Health; Horror; Mystery; Nature; Self-Help; Spiritual; Thrillers; Women's Interests; *Markets:* Adult; Youth; *Treatments:* Commercial; Literary

Not accepting new clients as at June 4, 2012. Check website for current status.

Send query by email only, with the word "Query" and the title of your work in the subject field.

Weed Literary LLC

Email: info@weedliterary.com

Handles: Fiction; *Areas:* Women's Interests; *Markets:* Adult

Agency specialising in upmarket women's fiction. No picture books, romance, YA, middle-grade, or nonfiction. No submissions by post. Send query by email only. See website for more information.

The Wendy Weil Agency, Inc.

232 Madison Avenue, Suite 1300, New York, NY 10016
Tel: +1 (212) 685-0030
Fax: +1 (212) 685-0765
Email: wweil@wendyweil.com
Website: http://www.wendyweil.com

Handles: Fiction; Nonfiction; *Areas:* Arts; Autobiography; Culture; Current Affairs; Health; Historical; Lifestyle; Mystery; Science; Thrillers; *Markets:* Adult; *Treatments:* Commercial; Literary

Note: The status of this agency is uncertain. The principal agent died in

2012, but the website is still up and still shows the same information as prior to her death. The two remaining agents are reported to have moved to another agency with the intention of taking their clients with them, while the agency itself has been sold to a third party.

Send query by post (up to two pages, plus synopsis and SASE) or by email (response not guaranteed). Response in 4-6 weeks. No screenplays or textbooks.

The Weingel-Fidel Agency

310 East 46th Street, Suite 21-E, New York, NY 10017
Tel: +1 (212) 599-2959
Email: lwf@theweingel-fidelagency.com

Handles: Fiction; Nonfiction; *Areas:* Arts; Autobiography; Biography; Music; Psychology; Science; Sociology; Technology; Women's Interests; *Markets:* Adult; *Treatments:* Commercial; Literary; Mainstream

Accepts new clients by referral only – approach only via an existing client or industry contact. Specialises in commercial and literary fiction and nonfiction. Particularly interested in investigative journalism. No genre fiction, science fiction, fantasy, or self-help.

Wernick & Pratt Agency

1207 North Avenue , Beacon, NY 12508
Email: info@wernickpratt.com
Website: http://www.wernickpratt.com

Handles: Fiction; Nonfiction; *Markets:* Children's; Youth; *Treatments:* Commercial; Literary

Handles children's books of all genres, from picture books to young adult literature. Particularly interested in authors who also illustrate their picture books; humorous young chapter books; literary and commercial middle grade / young adult books.

Not interested in picture book manuscripts of more than 750 words, mood pieces, work

specifically targeted to the educational market, or fiction about the American Revolution, Civil War, or World War II (unless told from a very unique perspective). Accepts queries by email only. See website for full guidelines. Response only if interested.

Whimsy Literary Agency, LLC

310 East 12th Street, Suite 2C, New York, NY 10003
Tel: +1 (212) 674-7162
Email: whimsynyc@aol.com
Website: http://whimsyliteraryagency.com

Handles: Nonfiction; *Areas:* Beauty and Fashion; Business; Cookery; Culture; Entertainment; Health; How-to; Humour; Politics; Psychology; Religious; Self-Help; Spiritual; *Markets:* Adult; *Treatments:* Commercial

No unsolicited mss. Send query by email in first instance.

Writers House, LLC.

21 West 26th Street, New York, NY 10010
Tel: +1 (212) 685-2400
Fax: +1 (212) 685-1781
Email: Azuckerman@writershouse.com
Website: http://writershouse.com

Handles: Fiction; Nonfiction; *Areas:* Autobiography; Biography; Business; Cookery; Fantasy; Finance; Historical; How-to; Lifestyle; Psychology; Science; Sci-Fi; Self-Help; Women's Interests; *Markets:* Adult; Children's; Youth; *Treatments:* Commercial; Literary

Handles adult and juvenile fiction and nonfiction, commercial and literary, including picture books. Send query letter of no more than two pages with SASE, synopsis, and CV. No scripts, professional, poetry, or scholarly. Does not guarantee a response to electronic queries. Policies of individual agents vary. Do not query more than one agent at a time. See website for full details.

Yates & Yates

1100 Town and Country Road, Suite 1300,
Orange, CA 92868
Tel: +1 (714) 480-4000
Fax: +1 (714) 480-4001
Email: email@yates2.com
Website: http://www.yates2.com

Handles: Fiction; Nonfiction; *Areas:*
Autobiography; Biography; Business;
Current Affairs; Legal; Politics; Religious;
Sport; Thrillers; Women's Interests;
Markets: Adult; *Treatments:* Literary

Literary agency based in California. Takes a
holistic approach, combining agency
representation, expert legal advice,
marketing guidance, career coaching,
creative counseling, and business
management consulting.

The Zack Company, Inc

PMB 525, 4653 Carmel Mountain Rd, Ste
308, San Diego, CA 92130-6650
Website: http://www.zackcompany.com

Handles: Fiction; Nonfiction; Reference;
Areas: Adventure; Autobiography;
Biography; Business; Cookery; Crime;
Current Affairs; Entertainment; Erotic;
Fantasy; Film; Finance; Gardening; Health;
Historical; Horror; Humour; Lifestyle;
Medicine; Military; Music; Mystery; Nature;
Politics; Religious; Romance; Science; Sci-
Fi; Self-Help; Spiritual; Sport; Suspense;
Technology; Thrillers; Translations; TV;
Women's Interests; *Markets:* Adult;
Treatments: Commercial; Literary; Popular

IMPORTANT: This agency objects to
being listed on firstwriter.com and has in the
past threatened to reject any submission from
a writer who found his details through this
site. We therefore suggest that if you
approach this agency you do not state where
you found its contact details.

The agent has also stated that his
requirements change frequently, so it is
important to check the agency website before
approaching. Fully consult the agency's
requirements for material and queries before
approaching.

While external reports indicate that this
agency is legitimate and has made confirmed
sales to royalty-paying publishers, please
note that it appears to have been formerly
listed as "not recommended" on another site.
It no longer appears to be part of the AAR. It
also offers Editorial Services, which we
believe would contravene the AAR canon of
ethics, which state "the practice of literary
agents charging clients or potential clients
for reading and evaluating literary works
(including outlines, proposals, and partial or
complete manuscripts) is subject to serious
abuse that reflects adversely on our
profession".

See website at *http://www.zackcompany.com*
for full guidelines on querying. Please note
that approaches are not accepted to the
former submissions email address
(submissions@zackcompany.com).
Electronic approaches must be made via the
form on the website.

Karen Gantz Zahler Literary Agency

860 Fifth Ave Suite 7J, New York, NY
10021
Tel: +1 (212) 734-3619
Email: karen@karengantzlit.com
Website: http://www.karengantzlit.com

Handles: Fiction; Nonfiction; *Areas:*
Autobiography; Cookery; Design;
Entertainment; Historical; Lifestyle; Politics;
Psychology; Religious; Sociology; Spiritual;
Markets: Adult

Considers all genres but specialises in
nonfiction. Send query and summary by
email only.

Helen Zimmermann Literary Agency

3 Emmy Lane, New Paltz, NY 12561
Tel: +1 (845) 256-0977
Fax: +1 (845) 256-0979
Email: Submit@ZimmAgency.com
Website: http://www.zimmagency.com

Handles: Fiction; Nonfiction; *Areas:*
Autobiography; Cookery; Culture; Health;
Historical; How-to; Humour; Lifestyle;

Music; Mystery; Nature; Sport; Suspense; Women's Interests; *Markets:* Adult; *Treatments:* Literary

Particularly interested in health and wellness, relationships, popular culture, women's issues, lifestyle, sports, and music. No poetry, science fiction, horror, or romance. Prefers email queries, but no attachments unless requested. Send pitch letter – for fiction include summary, bio, and first chapter in the body of the email.

UK Literary Agents

For the most up-to-date listings of these and hundreds of other literary agents, visit http://www.firstwriter.com/Agents

*To claim your **free** access to the site, please see the back of this book.*

A & B Personal Management Ltd

PO Box 64671, London, NW3 9LH
Tel: +44 (0) 20 7794 3255
Email: billellis@aandb.co.uk

Handles: Fiction; Nonfiction; Scripts; *Areas:* Film; Theatre; TV; *Markets:* Adult

Handles full-length mss and scripts for film, TV, and theatre. No unsolicited mss. Query by email or by phone in first instance.

Sheila Ableman Literary Agency

36 Duncan House, Fellows Road, London, NW3 3LZ
Tel: +44 (0) 20 7586 2339
Email: sheila@sheilaableman.co.uk
Website: http://www.sheilaableman.com

Handles: Nonfiction; *Areas:* Autobiography; Biography; Historical; Science; TV; *Markets:* Adult; *Treatments:* Commercial; Popular

Send query with SAE, publishing history, brief CV, one-page synopsis, and two sample chapters. Specialises in TV tie-ins and celebrity ghost writing. No poetry, children's books, gardening, or sport.

The Agency (London) Ltd

24 Pottery Lane, Holland Park, London, W11 4LZ
Tel: +44 (0) 20 7727 1346
Fax: +44 (0) 20 7727 9037
Email: recp@theagency.co.uk
Website: http://www.theagency.co.uk

Handles: Fiction; Nonfiction; Scripts; *Areas:* Film; Radio; Theatre; TV; *Markets:* Adult; Children's

Represents writers and authors for film, television, radio and the theatre. Also represents directors, producers, composers, and film and television rights in books. The list ranges from major established talent to the new, up and coming in all these areas. **Handles adult fiction and nonfiction for existing clients only**. Does not consider adult fiction or nonfiction from writers who are not already clients. No unsolicited MSS. Only considers unsolicited material if it has been recommended by a producer, development executive or course tutor. If this is the case send CV, covering letter and details of your referee to the relevant agent, or to the address below. Do not email more than one agent at a time. No unsolicited children's material.

Aitken Alexander Associates

18–21 Cavaye Place, London, SW10 9PT
Tel: +44 (0) 20 7373 8672

Fax: +44 (0) 20 7373 6002
Email: reception@aitkenalexander.co.uk
Website: http://www.aitkenalexander.co.uk

Handles: Fiction; Nonfiction; *Markets:*
Adult

Send query letter through online submissions
system only, with synopsis up to one page,
and 30 consecutive pages. No illustrated
children's books, poetry or screenplays. No
submissions or queries by post.

The Ampersand Agency Ltd

Ryman's Cottages, Little Tew, Chipping
Norton, Oxfordshire OX7 4JJ
Tel: +44 (0) 1608 683677 / 683898
Fax: +44 (0) 1608 683449
Email: amd@theampersandagency.co.uk
Website:
http://www.theampersandagency.co.uk

Handles: Fiction; Nonfiction; *Areas:*
Autobiography; Biography; Crime; Current
Affairs; Fantasy; Historical; Horror; Sci-Fi;
Thrillers; Women's Interests; *Markets:*
Adult; Youth; *Treatments:* Commercial;
Contemporary; Literary

We handle literary and commercial fiction
and nonfiction, including contemporary and
historical novels, crime, thrillers, biography,
women's fiction, history, and memoirs. Send
query by post or email with brief bio,
outline, and first two chapters. Also accepts
science fiction, fantasy, horror, and Young
Adult material to separate email address
listed on website. No scripts except those by
existing clients, no poetry or illustrated
children's books. No unpublished American
writers, because in our experience British
and European publishers aren't interested
unless there is an American publisher on
board. And we'd like to make it clear that
American stamps are no use outside
America!

Darley Anderson Children's

Estelle House, 11 Eustace Road, London,
SW6 1JB
Tel: +44 (0) 20 7386 2674
Fax: +44 (0) 20 7386 5571
Email: childrens@darleyanderson.com

Website:
http://www.darleyandersonchildrens.com

Handles: Fiction; Nonfiction; *Markets:*
Children's

Handles fiction and nonfiction for children.
Send query by email or by post with SAE,
short synopsis, and first three consecutive
chapters. For picture books, send complete
text or picture book. Prefers to read material
exclusively, but will accept simultaneous
submissions if notice given on cover letter.

Anne Clark Literary Agency

PO Box 1221 , Harlton, Cambridge , CB23
1WW
Tel: +44 (0) 1223 262160
Email:
submissions@anneclarkliteraryagency.co.uk
Website:
http://www.anneclarkliteraryagency.co.uk

Handles: Fiction; *Markets:* Children's;
Youth

Handles fiction and picture books for
children and young adults. Send query by
email only with first 20 pages, or complete
ms for picture books. No submissions by
post. See website for full guidelines.

AP Watt at United Agents LLP

12-26 Lexington Street, London, W1F 0LE
Tel: +44 (0) 20 3214 0800
Fax: +44 (0) 20 3214 0801
Email: info@unitedagents.co.uk
Website: http://www.apwatt.co.uk

Handles: Fiction; Nonfiction; Scripts; *Areas:*
Autobiography; Biography; Business;
Cookery; Crime; Film; Gardening; Health;
Historical; Medicine; Music; Politics;
Psychology; Romance; Science; Sport;
Technology; Thrillers; Translations; Travel;
TV; *Markets:* Adult; Children's; *Treatments:*
Commercial; Literary

No poetry, academic, specialist, or
unsolicited MSS. Send query letter by post
or by email for the attention of a specific
agent, including full plot synopsis. See

website for details of agents and their interests.

Artellus Limited

30 Dorset House, Gloucester Place, London, NW1 5AD
Tel: +44 (0) 20 7935 6972
Fax: +44 (0) 20 8609 0347
Email: leslie@artellusltd.co.uk
Website: http://www.artellusltd.co.uk

Handles: Fiction; Nonfiction; *Areas:* Arts; Beauty and Fashion; Biography; Crime; Culture; Current Affairs; Entertainment; Fantasy; Historical; Military; Science; Sci-Fi; *Markets:* Adult; Youth; *Treatments:* Contemporary; Literary

Welcomes submissions from new fiction and nonfiction writers. Send first three chapters and synopsis in first instance. No film or TV scripts. If you would prefer to submit electronically send query by email in advance.

Author Literary Agents

53 Talbot Road, Highgate, London, N6 4QX
Tel: +44 (0) 20 8341 0442
Fax: +44 (0) 20 8341 0442
Email: a@authors.co.uk

Handles: Fiction; Nonfiction; Scripts; *Areas:* Thrillers; *Markets:* Adult; Children's

Send query with SAE, one-page outline and first chapter, scene, or writing sample. Handles fiction, nonfiction, novels, thrillers, graphic novels, children's books, and media entertainment concepts. Handles material for book publishers, screen producers, and graphic media ideas.

AVAnti Productions & Management

Unit 6, 31 St. Aubyns, Brighton, BN3 2TH
Tel: +44 (0) 07999 193311
Email: avantiproductions@live.co.uk
Website: http://www.avantiproductions.co.uk

Handles: Fiction; Nonfiction; Poetry; Scripts; *Areas:* Adventure; Anthropology; Antiques; Archaeology; Arts; Business;

Crafts; Crime; Criticism; Culture; Current Affairs; Drama; Entertainment; Fantasy; Film; Gothic; Historical; Humour; Literature; Media; Men's Interests; Music; Mystery; Philosophy; Photography; Psychology; Radio; Religious; Romance; Sci-Fi; Short Stories; Sociology; Spiritual; Suspense; Theatre; Thrillers; Translations; Travel; TV; Westerns; Women's Interests; *Markets:* Academic; Children's; Family; Professional; *Treatments:* Contemporary; Literary; Niche; Positive; Satirical; Traditional

Talent and literary representation – also, a film and theatre production company.

Bell Lomax Moreton Agency

Ground Floor, Watergate House, 13-15 York Buildings, London, WC2N 6JU
Tel: +44 (0) 20 7930 4447
Fax: +44 (0) 20 7839 2667
Email: info@bell-lomax.co.uk
Website: http://www.bell-lomax.co.uk

Handles: Fiction; Nonfiction; *Areas:* Biography; Business; Sport; *Markets:* Adult; Children's

No unsolicited MSS without preliminary letter. No scripts.

Lorella Belli Literary Agency (LBLA)

54 Hartford House, 35 Tavistock Crescent, Notting Hill, London, W11 1AY
Tel: +44 (0) 20 7727 8547
Fax: +44 (0) 870 787 4194
Email: info@lorellabelliagency.com
Website: http://www.lorellabelliagency.com

Handles: Fiction; Nonfiction; *Markets:* Adult; *Treatments:* Literary

Send query by post or by email in first instance. No attachments. Particularly interested in multicultural / international writing, and books relating to Italy, or written in Italian; first novelists, and journalists. Welcomes queries from new authors and will suggest revisions where appropriate. No poetry, children's, original scripts, academic, SF, or fantasy.

Berlin Associates

7 Tyers Gate, London , SE1 3HX
Tel: +44 (0) 20 7836 1112
Fax: +44 (0) 20 7632 5296
Email: submissions@berlinassociates.com
Website: http://www.berlinassociates.com

Handles: Scripts; *Areas:* Film; Radio;
Theatre; TV; *Markets:* Adult

Most clients through recommendation or
invitation, but accepts queries by email with
CV, experience, and outline of work you
would like to submit.

The Blair Partnership

Middlesex House, 4th Floor, 34-42
Cleveland Street , London, W1T 4JE
Tel: +44 (0) 20 7504 2520
Fax: +44 (0) 20 7504 2521
Email:
submissions@theblairpartnership.com
Website: http://www.theblairpartnership.com

Handles: Fiction; Nonfiction; *Markets:*
Adult; Children's; Family; Youth

Open to all genres of fiction and nonfiction.
Send query by email with one-page synopsis
and first ten pages, including some detail
about yourself.

Blake Friedmann Literary Agency Ltd

First Floor, Selous House, 5-12 Mandela
Street, London, NW1 0DU
Tel: +44 (0) 20 7387 0842
Fax: +44 (0) 20 7691 9626
Email: info@blakefriedmann.co.uk
Website: http://www.blakefriedmann.co.uk

Handles: Fiction; Nonfiction; Scripts; *Areas:*
Biography; Film; Radio; Thrillers; Travel;
TV; Women's Interests; *Markets:* Adult;
Youth; *Treatments:* Commercial; Literary

Send query by email to a specific agent best
suited to your work. See website for full
submission guidelines, details of agents, and
individual agent contact details.

No poetry or plays. Short stories and
journalism for existing clients only.

Media department currently only accepting
submissions from writers with produced
credits.

Reply not guaranteed.

Luigi Bonomi Associates Ltd

91 Great Russell Street, London, WC1 3PS
Tel: +44 (0) 20 7637 1234
Fax: +44 (0) 20 7637 2111
Email: info@lbabooks.com
Website: http://www.lbabooks.com

Handles: Fiction; Nonfiction; *Areas:* Crime;
Health; Historical; Lifestyle; Science;
Thrillers; TV; Women's Interests; *Markets:*
Adult; Youth; *Treatments:* Commercial;
Literary

Keen to find new authors. Send query with
synopsis and first three chapters by post with
SAE (if return of material required) or email
address for response, or by email (Word or
PDF attachments only). See website for
specific agents' interests and email
addresses. No scripts, poetry, children's,
science fiction, or fantasy.

Bookseeker Agency

PO Box 7535, Perth, PH2 1AF
Tel: +44 (0) 1738 620688
Email: bookseeker@blueyonder.co.uk
Website: http://bookseekeragency.com

Handles: Fiction; Poetry; *Markets:* Adult

Handles poetry and general creative writing.
No nonfiction. Send query by post or email
outlining what you have written and your
current projects, along with synopsis and
sample chapter (novels) or half a dozen
poems.

The Bright Literary Academy

Studio 102, 250 York Road, London, SW11
1RJ
Tel: +44 (0) 20 7326 9140
Email: literarysubmissions@
brightgroupinternational.com
Website:
http://www.brightgroupinternational.com

Handles: Fiction; *Areas:* Autobiography; Entertainment; Literature; Mystery; Sci-Fi; Self-Help; Short Stories; Thrillers; TV; Women's Interests; *Markets:* Children's; Youth; *Treatments:* Commercial; Contemporary; Mainstream; Positive

A boutique literary agency representing the most fabulous new talent to grace the publishing industry in recent years. Born out of the success of a leading illustration agency with an outstanding global client list this agency aims to produce sensational material across all genres of children's publishing, including novelty, picture books, fiction and adult autobiographies, in order to become a one-stop-shop for publishers looking for something extra special to fit into their lists.

Prides itself on nurturing the creativity of its authors and illustrators so that they can concentrate on their craft rather than negotiate their contracts. As a creative agency we develop seeds of ideas into something extraordinary, before searching for the right publisher with which to develop them further to create incredible and unforgettable books.

We are fortunate enough to have a never-ending source of remarkable material at our fingertips and a stable of exceptional creators who are all united by one common goal – a deep passion and dedication to children's books and literature in all its shapes and forms.

Alan Brodie Representation Ltd

Paddock Suite, The Courtyard, 55 Charterhouse Street, London, EC1M 6HA
Tel: +44 (0) 20 7253 6226
Fax: +44 (0) 20 7183 7999
Email: ABR@alanbrodie.com
Website: http://www.alanbrodie.com

Handles: Scripts; *Areas:* Film; Radio; Theatre; TV; *Markets:* Adult

Handles scripts only. No books. Approach with preliminary letter, recommendation from industry professional, CV, and SAE. Do not send a sample of work unless requested. No fiction, nonfiction, or poetry.

Jenny Brown Associates

33 Argyle Place, Edinburgh, Scotland EH9 1JT
Tel: +44 (0) 1312 295334
Email: info@jennybrownassociates.com
Website: http://www.jennybrownassociates.com

Handles: Fiction; Nonfiction; *Areas:* Biography; Crime; Culture; Finance; Historical; Humour; Music; Romance; Science; Sport; Thrillers; Women's Interests; *Markets:* Adult; Children's; *Treatments:* Commercial; Literary; Popular

Strongly prefers queries by email. Approach by post only if not possible to do so by email. Send query with market information, bio, synopsis and first 50 pages in one document (fiction) or sample chapter and info on market and your background (nonfiction). No academic, poetry, short stories, science fiction, or fantasy. Responds only if interested. If no response in 8 weeks assume rejection. See website for individual agent interests and email addresses.

Felicity Bryan

2a North Parade Avenue, Banbury Road, Oxford, OX2 6LX
Tel: +44 (0) 1865 513816
Fax: +44 (0) 1865 310055
Email: submissions@felicitybryan.com
Website: http://www.felicitybryan.com

Handles: Fiction; Nonfiction; *Areas:* Biography; Current Affairs; Historical; Science; *Markets:* Adult; Children's; Youth; *Treatments:* Commercial; Literary

Particularly interested in commercial and literary fiction and nonfiction for the adult market, children's fiction for 8+, and Young Adult. Send query by post with sufficient return postage, or by email with Word or PDF attachments. See website for detailed submission guidelines. No adult science fiction, horror, fantasy, light romance, self-help, memoir, film and TV scripts, plays, poetry or picture/illustrated books.

Brie Burkeman & Serafina Clarke Ltd

14 Neville Court, Abbey Road, London, NW8 9DD
Tel: +44 (0) 870 199 5002
Fax: +44 (0) 870 199 1029
Email: info@burkemanandclarke.com

Handles: Fiction; Nonfiction; Scripts; *Areas:* Film; Theatre; *Markets:* Adult; Children's; *Treatments:* Commercial; Literary

Not accepting unsolicited submissions as at June 26, 2012. Check website for current situation.

No academic, text, poetry, short stories, musicals or short films. For scripts, full length only. No reading fee but preliminary letter preferred. Return postage essential. Unsolicited email attachments will be deleted without opening.

Also independent film and television consultant to literary agents.

Do **not** send submissions via email – these will be deleted automatically without opening.

Submissions by email with attachments will be automatically deleted. When sending material, return postage is essential.

Juliet Burton Literary Agency

2 Clifton Avenue, London, W12 9DR
Tel: +44 (0) 20 8762 0148
Fax: +44 (0) 20 8743 8765
Email: juliet.burton@btinternet.com

Handles: Fiction; Nonfiction; *Areas:* Crime; Women's Interests; *Markets:* Adult

Send query with SAE, synopsis, and two sample chapters. No poetry, plays, film scripts, children's, articles, academic material, science fiction, fantasy, unsolicited MSS, or email submissions.

Capel & Land Ltd

29 Wardour Street, London, W1D 6PS
Tel: +44 (0) 20 7734 2414
Fax: +44 (0) 20 7734 8101

Email: georgina@capelland.co.uk
Website: http://www.capelland.com

Handles: Fiction; Nonfiction; *Areas:* Biography; Film; Historical; Radio; TV; *Markets:* Adult; *Treatments:* Commercial; Literary

Handles general fiction and nonfiction. Send query outlining writing history (for nonfiction, what qualifies you to write your book), with synopsis around 500 words and first three chapters, plus SAE or email address for reply. Submissions are not returned. Mark envelope for the attention of the Submissions Department. Response only if interested, normally within 6 weeks.

CardenWright Literary Agency

27 Khyber Road, London, SW11 2PZ
Tel: +44 (0) 20 7771 0012
Email: gen@cardenwright.com
Website: http://www.cardenwright.com

Handles: Fiction; Nonfiction; Scripts; *Areas:* Theatre; *Markets:* Adult; Youth; *Treatments:* Commercial; Literary

Handles commercial and literary fiction and nonfiction, plus theatre scripts. Will consider teenage / young adult. No poetry, screenplays, or children's books. See website for submission guidelines.

Celia Catchpole

56 Gilpin Avenue, London, SW14 8QY
Tel: +44 (0) 20 8255 4835
Email: catchpolesubmissions@googlemail.com
Website: http://www.celiacatchpole.co.uk

Handles: Fiction; *Markets:* Children's

Works on children's books with both artists and writers. Send query by email with sample pasted directly into the body of the email (no attachments). See website for full guidelines.

Mic Cheetham Literary Agency

50 Albemarle Street, London, W1S 4BD

Tel: +44 (0) 20 7495 2002
Fax: +44 (0) 20 7399 2801
Email: info@miccheetham.com
Website: http://www.miccheetham.com

Handles: Fiction; Nonfiction; *Areas:* Crime;
Fantasy; Historical; Sci-Fi; Thrillers;
Markets: Adult; *Treatments:* Commercial;
Literary; Mainstream

Send query with SAE, first three chapters,
and publishing history. Focuses on fiction,
and is not elitist about genre or literary
fiction, providing it combines good writing,
great storytelling, intelligence, imagination,
and (as a bonus) anarchic wit. Film and TV
scripts handled for existing clients only. No
poetry, children's, illustrated books, or
unsolicited MSS. Do not send manuscripts
by email. Approach in writing in the first
instance (no email scripts accepted).

Teresa Chris Literary Agency Ltd

43 Musard Road, London, W6 8NR
Tel: +44 (0) 20 7386 0633
Email: teresachris@litagency.co.uk
Website:
http://www.teresachrisliteraryagency.co.uk

Handles: Fiction; Nonfiction; *Areas:*
Biography; Cookery; Crafts; Crime;
Gardening; Historical; Lifestyle; Women's
Interests; *Markets:* Adult; *Treatments:*
Commercial; Literary

Welcomes submissions. Overseas authors
may approach by email, otherwise hard copy
submissions preferred. For fiction, send
query with SAE, first three chapters, and
one-page synopsis. For nonfiction, send
overview with two sample chapters.
Specialises in crime fiction and commercial
women's fiction. No poetry, short stories,
fantasy, science fiction, horror, children's
fiction or young adult.

Mary Clemmey Literary Agency

6 Dunollie Road, London, NW5 2XP
Tel: +44 (0) 20 7267 1290
Fax: +44 (0) 20 7813 9757
Email: mcwords@googlemail.com

Handles: Fiction; Nonfiction; Scripts; *Areas:*
Film; Radio; Theatre; TV; *Markets:* Adult

Send query with SAE and description of
work only. Handles high-quality work with
an international market. No children's books,
science fiction, fantasy, or unsolicited MSS
or submissions by email. Scripts handled for
existing clients only. Do not submit a script
or idea for a script unless you are already a
client.

Jonathan Clowes Ltd

10 Iron Bridge House, Bridge Approach,
London, NW1 8BD
Tel: +44 (0) 20 7722 7674
Fax: +44 (0) 20 7722 7677
Email: olivia@jonathanclowes.co.uk
Website: http://www.jonathanclowes.co.uk

Handles: Fiction; Nonfiction; Scripts; *Areas:*
Film; Radio; Theatre; TV; *Markets:* Adult;
Treatments: Commercial; Literary

Send query with synopsis and three chapters
(or equivalent sample) by email. No science
fiction, poetry, short stories, academic. Only
considers film/TV clients with previous
success in TV/film/theatre. If no response
within six weeks, assume rejection.

Rosica Colin Ltd

1 Clareville Grove Mews, London, SW7
5AH
Tel: +44 (0) 20 7370 1080
Fax: +44 (0) 20 7244 6441

Handles: Fiction; Nonfiction; Scripts; *Areas:*
Autobiography; Beauty and Fashion;
Biography; Cookery; Crime; Current Affairs;
Erotic; Fantasy; Film; Gardening; Health;
Historical; Horror; Humour; Leisure;
Lifestyle; Men's Interests; Military;
Mystery; Nature; Psychology; Radio;
Religious; Romance; Science; Sport;
Suspense; Theatre; Thrillers; Travel; TV;
Women's Interests; *Markets:* Academic;
Adult; Children's; *Treatments:* Literary

Send query with SAE, CV, synopsis, and list
of other agents and publishers where MSS
has already been sent. Considers any full-
length mss (except science fiction and

poetry), plus scripts, but few new writers taken on. Responds in 3-4 months to full mss – synopsis preferred in first instance.

Conville & Walsh Ltd

5th Floor, Haymarket House, 28-29 Haymarket, London, SW1Y 4SP
Tel: +44 (0) 20 7393 4200
Email: submissions@convilleandwalsh.com
Website: http://www.convilleandwalsh.com

Handles: Fiction; Nonfiction; *Areas:* Biography; Crime; Current Affairs; Historical; Humour; Leisure; Lifestyle; Men's Interests; Military; Mystery; Psychology; Science; Sport; Suspense; Thrillers; Travel; Women's Interests; *Markets:* Adult; Children's; Youth; *Treatments:* Literary

See website for agent profiles and submit to one particular agent only. Send submissions by email as Word .doc files, or by post. For fiction, please submit the first three sample chapters of the completed manuscript (or about 50 pages) with a one to two page synopsis. For nonfiction, send 30-page proposal. No poetry or scripts. See website for full guidelines.

Jane Conway-Gordon Ltd

38 Cromwell Grove, London, W6 7RG
Tel: +44 (0) 20 7371 6939
Email: jane@conway-gordon.co.uk

Handles: Fiction; Nonfiction; *Markets:* Adult

Handles fiction and general nonfiction. Send query with SAE (essential) in first instance. Associate agencies in America, Europe, and Japan. No poetry, short stories, children's, or science fiction.

Coombs Moylett Literary Agency

120 New Kings Road, London, SW6 4LZ
Email: lisa@coombsmoylett.com
Website: http://www.coombsmoylett.com

Handles: Fiction; *Areas:* Crime; Historical; Mystery; Suspense; Thrillers; Women's

Interests; *Markets:* Adult; *Treatments:* Commercial; Contemporary; Literary

Send query with synopsis and first three chapters by post. No submissions by fax, but accepts email queries. No nonfiction, poetry, plays or scripts for film and TV.

Please note that this agency also offers editorial services for which writers are charged. Caution should be exercised in relation to these services, particularly if they are pushed as a condition of representation.

The Creative Rights Agency

17 Prior Street, London, SE10 8SF
Tel: +44 (0) 20 8149 3955
Email: info@creativerightsagency.co.uk
Website: http://www.creativerightsagency.co.uk

Handles: Fiction; Nonfiction; *Areas:* Autobiography; Culture; Men's Interests; Sport; *Markets:* Adult; *Treatments:* Contemporary

Specialises in men's interests. Send query by email with sample chapters, synopsis, and author bio.

Creative Authors Ltd

11A Woodlawn Street, Whitstable, Kent CT5 1HQ
Tel: +44 (0) 01227 770947
Email: write@creativeauthors.co.uk
Website: http://www.creativeauthors.co.uk

Handles: Fiction; Nonfiction; *Areas:* Arts; Autobiography; Biography; Business; Cookery; Crafts; Crime; Culture; Health; Historical; Humour; Nature; Women's Interests; *Markets:* Adult; Children's; *Treatments:* Commercial; Literary

As at March 2014 not accepting new fiction clients. See website for current situation.

We are a dynamic literary agency – established to provide an attentive and unique platform for writers and scriptwriters and representing a growing list of clients. We're on the lookout for fresh talent and books with strong commercial potential. No unsolicited MSS, but considers queries by email. No paper submissions. Do not telephone regarding submissions.

Rupert Crew Ltd

6 Windsor Road, London, N3 3SS
Tel: +44 (0) 20 8346 3000
Fax: +44 (0) 20 8346 3009
Email: info@rupertcrew.co.uk
Website: http://www.rupertcrew.co.uk

Handles: Fiction; Nonfiction; *Markets:* Adult

Send query with SAE, synopsis, and first two or three consecutive chapters. International representation, handling volume and subsidiary rights in fiction and nonfiction properties. No Short Stories, Science Fiction, Fantasy, Horror, Poetry or original scripts for Theatre, Television and Film. Email address for correspondence only. No response by post and no return of material with insufficient return postage.

Curtis Brown Group Ltd

Haymarket House, 28/29 Haymarket, London, SW1Y 4SP
Tel: +44 (0) 20 7393 4400
Fax: +44 (0) 20 7393 4401
Email: cb@curtisbrown.co.uk
Website:
http://www.curtisbrowncreative.co.uk

Handles: Fiction; Nonfiction; Scripts; *Areas:* Biography; Crime; Fantasy; Film; Historical; Radio; Science; Suspense; Theatre; Thrillers; TV; *Markets:* Adult; Children's; Youth; *Treatments:* Literary; Mainstream; Popular

Renowned and long established London agency. Handles general fiction and nonfiction, and scripts. Also represents directors, designers, and presenters. No longer accepts submissions by post or email – all submissions must be made using online submissions manager. Also offers services such as writing courses for which authors are charged.

David Luxton Associates

23 Hillcourt Avenue, London, N12 8EY
Tel: +44 (0) 20 8922 3942
Email: david@davidluxtonassociates.co.uk
Website:
http://www.davidluxtonassociates.co.uk

Handles: Nonfiction; *Areas:* Biography; Culture; Historical; Sport; *Markets:* Adult

Send query by email with brief outline. No unsolicited MSS or sample chapters. Handles little in the way of fiction or children's books. No screenplays or scripts.

Caroline Davidson Literary Agency

5 Queen Anne's Gardens, London, W4 1TU
Tel: +44 (0) 20 8995 5768
Fax: +44 (0) 20 8994 2770
Email: enquiries@cdla.co.uk
Website: http://www.cdla.co.uk

Handles: Fiction; Nonfiction; Reference; *Areas:* Archaeology; Architecture; Arts; Biography; Cookery; Culture; Design; Gardening; Health; Historical; Lifestyle; Medicine; Nature; Politics; Psychology; Science; *Markets:* Adult

Send query with CV, SAE, outline and history of work, and (for fiction) the first 50 pages of novel with 3-sentence description. For nonfiction, include table of contents, detailed chapter-by-chapter synopsis, description of sources and / or research for the book, market and competition analysis, and (if possible) one or two sample chapters.

Submissions without adequate return postage are neither returned or considered. No Chick lit, romance, erotica, Crime and thrillers, Science fiction, fantasy, Poetry, Individual short stories, Children's, Young Adult, Misery memoirs or fictionalised autobiography. Completed and polished first novels positively welcomed. See website for more details. No submissions by fax and only in exceptional circumstances accepts submissions by email.

See website for full details.

Felix de Wolfe

103 Kingsway, London, WC2B 6QX
Tel: +44 (0) 20 7242 5066
Fax: +44 (0) 20 7242 8119
Email: info@felixdewolfe.com
Website: http://www.felixdewolfe.com

Handles: Fiction; Scripts; *Areas:* Film;
Theatre; TV; *Markets:* Adult

Send query letter with SAE, short synopsis,
and CV by post only, unless alternative
arrangements have been made with the
agency in advance. Quality fiction and
scripts only. No nonfiction, children's books,
or unsolicited MSS.

Diamond Kahn and Woods (DKW) Literary Agency Ltd

Top Floor, 66 Onslow Gardens, London,
N10 3JX
Tel: +44 (0) 20 3514 6544
Email:
submissions.bryony@dkwlitagency.co.uk
Website: http://dkwlitagency.co.uk

Handles: Fiction; Nonfiction; *Areas:*
Adventure; Archaeology; Biography; Crime;
Culture; Fantasy; Gothic; Historical; Sci-Fi;
Sociology; Suspense; Thrillers; *Markets:*
Adult; Children's; Youth; *Treatments:*
Commercial; Contemporary; Literary

Send submissions by email. See website for
specific agent interests and contact details.

Diane Banks Associates Literary Agency

Email: submissions@dianebanks.co.uk
Website: http://www.dianebanks.co.uk

Handles: Fiction; Nonfiction; *Areas:*
Autobiography; Beauty and Fashion;
Business; Crime; Culture; Current Affairs;
Entertainment; Health; Historical; Lifestyle;
Psychology; Science; Self-Help; Thrillers;
Women's Interests; *Markets:* Adult; Youth;
Treatments: Commercial; Literary; Popular

Send query with author bio, synopsis, and
three sample chapters by email as Word or
Open Document attachments. No poetry,

plays, scripts, academic books, short stories
or children's books, with the exception of
young adult fiction. Hard copy submissions
are not accepted will not be read or returned.

Dorian Literary Agency (DLA)

32 Western Road, St Marychurch, Torquay,
Devon TQ1 4RL
Tel: +44 (0) 1803 320934
Email: doriandot@compuserve.com

Handles: Fiction; *Areas:* Crime; Fantasy;
Historical; Horror; Romance; Sci-Fi;
Thrillers; Women's Interests; *Markets:*
Adult; *Treatments:* Popular

**Principal agent passed away in October,
2013 – continues to be listed as a member
of the AAA, but a user reports
submissions being returned by solicitors
advising that no new submissions are
being accepted.**

Concentrates on popular genre fiction. Send
query by post with SAE or email address for
response, including outline and up to three
sample chapters. No queries or submissions
by fax, telephone, or email. No poetry,
scripts, short stories, nonfiction, children's,
young adult, or comic material.

Toby Eady Associates Ltd

Third Floor, 9 Orme Court, London, W2
4RL
Tel: +44 (0) 20 7792 0092
Fax: +44 (0) 20 7792 0879
Email:
submissions@tobyeadyassociates.co.uk
Website:
http://www.tobyeadyassociates.co.uk

Handles: Fiction; Nonfiction; *Markets:*
Adult

Send first 50 pages of your fiction or
nonfiction work by email, with a synopsis,
and a letter including biographical
information. If submitting by post, include
SAE for return of material, if required. No
film / TV scripts or poetry. Particular interest
in China, Middle East, India, and Africa.

Eddison Pearson Ltd
West Hill House, 6 Swains Lane, London,
N6 6QS
Tel: +44 (0) 20 7700 7763
Fax: +44 (0) 20 7700 7866
Email: enquiries@eddisonpearson.com
Website: http://www.eddisonpearson.com

Handles: Fiction; Nonfiction; Poetry;
Markets: Children's; Youth; *Treatments:*
Literary

Send query by email only (or even blank
email) for auto-response containing up-to-
date submission guidelines and email address
for submissions. No unsolicited MSS. No
longer accepts submissions or enquiries by
post. Send query with first two chapters by
email only to address provided in auto-
response. Response in 6-10 weeks. If no
response after 10 weeks send email query.

Edwards Fuglewicz
49 Great Ormond Street, London, WC1N
3HZ
Tel: +44 (0) 20 7405 6725
Fax: +44 (0) 20 7405 6726
Email: info@efla.co.uk

Handles: Fiction; Nonfiction; *Areas:*
Biography; Crime; Culture; Historical;
Humour; Mystery; Romance; Thrillers;
Markets: Adult; *Treatments:* Commercial;
Literary

Handles literary and commercial fiction, and
nonfiction. No children's, science fiction,
horror, or email submissions.

Elise Dillsworth Agency (EDA)
9 Grosvenor Road, London, N10 2DR
Email:
submissions@elisedillsworthagency.com
Website: http://elisedillsworthagency.com

Handles: Fiction; Nonfiction;
Autobiography; Biography; *Markets:* Adult;
Treatments: Commercial; Literary

Represents writers from around the world.
Looking for literary and commercial fiction,
and nonfiction (especially memoir and
autobiography). No science fiction, fantasy,

or children's. Send query by email or by post
with SAE or email address for response.
Include synopsis up to two pages and first
three chapters, up to about 50 pages, as
Word or PDF attachments. See website for
full guidelines. Response in 6-8 weeks.

Elizabeth Roy Literary Agency
White Cottage, Greatford, Stamford,
Lincolnshire PE9 4PR
Tel: +44 (0) 1778 560672
Website:
http://www.elizabethroyliteraryagency.co.uk

Handles: Fiction; Nonfiction; *Markets:*
Children's

Handles fiction and nonfiction for children.
Send query by post with return postage,
synopsis, and sample chapters.

Faith Evans Associates
27 Park Avenue North, London, N8 7RU
Tel: +44 (0) 20 8340 9920
Fax: +44 (0) 20 8340 9410
Email: faith@faith-evans.co.uk

Handles: Fiction; Nonfiction; *Markets:*
Adult

Small agency accepting new clients by
personal recommendation only. No scripts,
phone calls, or unsolicited MSS.

The Feldstein Agency
123-125 Main Street, 2nd Floor, Bangor,
Northern Ireland BT20 4AE
Tel: +44 (0) 2891 472823
Email: paul@thefeldsteinagency.co.uk
Website:
http://www.thefeldsteinagency.co.uk

Handles: Fiction; Nonfiction; *Areas:*
Adventure; Autobiography; Biography;
Business; Cookery; Crime; Criticism;
Current Affairs; Historical; Humour;
Leisure; Lifestyle; Media; Military; Music;
Mystery; Philosophy; Politics; Sociology;
Sport; Thrillers; Travel; Women's Interests;
Markets: Adult; *Treatments:* Commercial;
Literary

Handles adult fiction and nonfiction only. No children's, young adult, romance, science fiction, fantasy, poetry, or short stories. Send query by email with 1-2 pages synopsis. No reading fees or evaluation fees. The only instance in which an author would be charged a fee is for ghost-writing.

Film Rights Ltd in association with Laurence Fitch Ltd

Suite 306 Belsize Business Centre, 258 Belsize Road, London, NW6 4BT
Tel: +44 (0) 20 7316 1837
Fax: +44 (0) 20 7624 3629
Email: information@filmrights.ltd.uk
Website: http://filmrights.ltd.uk

Handles: Fiction; Scripts; *Areas:* Film; Horror; Radio; Theatre; TV; *Markets:* Adult; Children's

Represents films, plays, and novels, for adults and children.

Jill Foster Ltd (JFL)

48 Charlotte Street, London, W1T 2NS
Tel: +44 (0) 20 3137 8182
Email: agents@jflagency.com
Website: http://www.jflagency.com

Handles: Scripts; *Areas:* Drama; Film; Humour; Radio; Theatre; TV; *Markets:* Adult

Handles scripts only (for television, film, theatre and radio). Considers approaches from established writers with broadcast experience year-round, but only accepts submissions from new writers during specific reading periods held twice a year – consult website for details.

Fox & Howard Literary Agency

39 Eland Road, London, SW11 5JX
Tel: +44 (0) 20 7352 8691
Email: fandhagency@googlemail.com
Website: http://www.foxandhoward.co.uk

Handles: Nonfiction; Reference; *Areas:* Biography; Business; Culture; Health; Historical; Lifestyle; Psychology; Self-Help;

Spiritual; *Markets:* Adult

Closed to submissions as at May 2014. Please check website for current status and use Report an Error function above if it has changed.

Send query with synopsis and SAE for response. Small agency specialising in nonfiction that works closely with its authors. No unsolicited MSS.

Fraser Ross Associates

6 Wellington Place, Edinburgh, Scotland EH6 7EQ
Tel: +44 (0) 1316 574412
Email: lindsey.fraser@tiscali.co.uk
Website: http://www.fraserross.co.uk

Handles: Fiction; *Markets:* Adult; Children's; *Treatments:* Literary; Mainstream

Send query with SAE, first three chapters, and CV. For picture books, send complete MS. No poetry, scripts, short stories, academic, or adult fantasy or science fiction. No submissions on disk or by email.

Furniss Lawton

James Grant Group Ltd, 94 Strand on the Green, Chiswick, London, W4 3NN
Tel: +44 (0) 20 8987 6804
Email: info@furnisslawton.co.uk
Website: http://furnisslawton.co.uk

Handles: Fiction; Nonfiction; *Areas:* Autobiography; Biography; Business; Cookery; Crime; Fantasy; Historical; Psychology; Science; Suspense; Thrillers; Women's Interests; *Markets:* Adult; Children's; Youth; *Treatments:* Commercial; Literary

Send query with synopsis and first 5,000 words / three chapters by post only. Include SAE if return of manuscript is required.

Noel Gay

19 Denmark Street, London, WC2H 8NA
Tel: +44 (0) 20 7836 3941
Email: info@noelgay.com

Website: http://www.noelgay.com

Handles: Scripts; *Markets:* Adult

Agency representing writers, directors, performers, presenters, comedians, etc. Send query with SASE.

Eric Glass Ltd
25 Ladbroke Crescent, London, W11 1PS
Tel: +44 (0) 20 7229 9500
Fax: +44 (0) 20 7229 6220
Email: eglassltd@aol.com

Handles: Fiction; Nonfiction; Scripts; *Areas:* Film; Theatre; TV; *Markets:* Adult

Send query with SAE. No children's books, short stories, poetry, or unsolicited MSS.

David Godwin Associates
55 Monmouth Street, London, WC2H 9DG
Tel: +44 (0) 20 7240 9992
Fax: +44 (0) 20 7395 6110
Email:
assistant@davidgodwinassociates.co.uk
Website:
http://www.davidgodwinassociates.co.uk

Handles: Fiction; Nonfiction; *Areas:* Biography; *Markets:* Adult; Children's; Youth; *Treatments:* Literary

Handles nonfiction (including biography) and fiction (general and literary). Send query by post with SAE, brief synopsis, and first three chapters / 50 pages. Submissions without correct return postage will be recycled. Accepts submissions for children's (9+) and young adult books by email to address specified on website (see submissions page). No reference, science fiction, fantasy, self-help, poetry or collections of short stories.

Graham Maw Christie Literary Agency
19 Thornhill Crescent, London, N1 1BJ
Tel: +44 (0) 20 7609 1326
Email:
submissions@grahammawchristie.com

Website:
http://www.grahammawchristie.com

Handles: Nonfiction; Reference; *Areas:* Autobiography; Biography; Business; Crafts; Culture; Health; Historical; How-to; Humour; Lifestyle; Psychology; Self-Help; Spiritual; TV; *Markets:* Adult

Send query with one-page summary, a paragraph on the contents of each chapter, your qualifications for writing it, market analysis, and what you could do to help promote your book. Accepts approaches by email. No fiction, children's books, or poetry.

Christine Green Authors' Agent
6 Whitehorse Mews, Westminster Bridge Road, London, SE1 7QD
Tel: +44 (0) 20 7401 8844
Fax: +44 (0) 20 7401 8860
Email: info@christinegreen.co.uk
Website: http://www.christinegreen.co.uk

Handles: Fiction; Nonfiction; *Markets:* Adult; *Treatments:* Literary

Send query with SAE/IPOs, synopsis, and first three chapters. No poetry, scripts, children's books, science fiction, fantasy, simultaneous submissions, or unsolicited MSS. No submissions by fax, email, or on disk.

Louise Greenberg Books Ltd
The End House, Church Crescent, London, N3 1BG
Tel: +44 (0) 20 8349 1179
Fax: +44 (0) 20 8343 4559
Email: louisegreenberg@msn.com

Handles: Fiction; Nonfiction; *Markets:* Adult; *Treatments:* Literary; Serious

Handles full-length literary fiction and serious nonfiction only. All approaches must be accompanied by SAE. No approaches by telephone.

Greene & Heaton Ltd

37 Goldhawk Road, London, W12 8QQ
Tel: +44 (0) 20 8749 0315
Fax: +44 (0) 20 8749 0318
Email: submissions@greeneheaton.co.uk
Website: http://www.greeneheaton.co.uk

Handles: Fiction; Nonfiction; *Areas:* Arts;
Autobiography; Biography; Cookery; Crime;
Culture; Current Affairs; Gardening; Health;
Historical; Humour; Philosophy; Politics;
Romance; Science; Sci-Fi; Thrillers; Travel;
Markets: Adult; Children's; *Treatments:*
Commercial; Contemporary; Literary;
Traditional

Send query by email or by post with SAE,
including synopsis and three chapters or
approximately 50 pages. No response to
unsolicited MSS with no SAE or inadequate
means of return postage provided. No
response to email submissions unless
interested. Handles all types of fiction and
nonfiction, but no scripts.

The Greenhouse Literary Agency

Stanley House, St Chad's Place, London,
WC1X 9HH
Tel: +44 (0) 20 7841 3959
Email:
submissions@greenhouseliterary.com
Website: http://www.greenhouseliterary.com

Handles: Fiction; *Markets:* Children's;
Youth

Transatlantic agency with offices in the US
and London. Handles children's and young
adult fiction only. Picture books by existing
clients only. Send query by email with first
chapter or first five pages (whichever is
shorter) pasted into the body of the email. No
attachments or hard copy submissions.

Gregory & Company, Authors' Agents

3 Barb Mews, London, W6 7PA
Tel: +44 (0) 20 7610 4676
Fax: +44 (0) 20 7610 4686
Email:
maryjones@gregoryandcompany.co.uk

Website:
http://www.gregoryandcompany.co.uk

Handles: Fiction; *Areas:* Crime; Historical;
Thrillers; *Markets:* Adult; *Treatments:*
Commercial

Particularly interested in Crime, Family
Sagas, Historical Fiction, Thrillers and
Upmarket Commercial Fiction.
Send query with CV, one-page synopsis,
future writing plans, and first ten pages, by
post with SAE, or by email. No unsolicited
MSS, Business Books, Children's, Young
Adult Fiction, Plays, Screenplays, Poetry,
Science Fiction, Future Fiction, Fantasy, Self
Help, Lifestyle books, Short Stories,
Spiritual, New Age, Philosophy,
Supernatural, Paranormal, Horror, or True
Crime.

David Grossman Literary Agency Ltd

118b Holland Park Avenue, London, W11
4UA
Tel: +44 (0) 20 7221 2770
Fax: +44 (0) 20 7221 1445
Email: david@dglal.co.uk

Handles: Fiction; Nonfiction; *Markets:*
Adult

Send preliminary letter before making a
submission. No approaches or submissions
by fax or email. Usually works with
published fiction writers, but well-written
and original work from beginners
considered. No poetry, scripts, technical
books for students, or unsolicited MSS.

Gunn Media Associates

50 Albemarle Street, London, W1S 4BD
Tel: +44 (0) 20 7529 3745
Email: ali@gunnmedia.co.uk
Website: http://www.gunnmedia.co.uk

Handles: Fiction; Nonfiction; *Markets:*
Adult; *Treatments:* Commercial; Literary

Handles commercial fiction and nonfiction,
including literary.

Hardman & Swainson

4 Kelmscott Road, London, SW11 6QY
Tel: +44 (0) 20 7223 5176
Email: submissions@hardmanswainson.com
Website: http://www.hardmanswainson.com

Handles: Fiction; Nonfiction; *Areas:*
Autobiography; Crime; Philosophy; Science;
Thrillers; *Markets:* Adult; Youth;
Treatments: Commercial; Literary; Popular

Agency launched June 2012 by former
colleagues at an established agency.
Welcomes submissions of fiction across all
genres and nonfiction. Prefers email
submissions but will accept postal
submissions with SAE if return required. See
website for full submission guidelines.

Antony Harwood Limited

103 Walton Street, Oxford, OX2 6EB
Tel: +44 (0) 1865 559615
Fax: +44 (0) 1865 310660
Email: mail@antonyharwood.com
Website: http://www.antonyharwood.com

Handles: Fiction; Nonfiction; *Areas:*
Adventure; Anthropology; Antiques;
Archaeology; Architecture; Arts;
Autobiography; Beauty and Fashion;
Biography; Business; Cookery; Crafts;
Crime; Criticism; Culture; Current Affairs;
Design; Drama; Entertainment; Erotic;
Fantasy; Film; Finance; Gardening; Gothic;
Health; Historical; Hobbies; Horror; How-to;
Humour; Legal; Leisure; Lifestyle;
Literature; Media; Medicine; Men's
Interests; Military; Music; Mystery; Nature;
New Age; Philosophy; Photography;
Politics; Psychology; Radio; Religious;
Romance; Science; Sci-Fi; Self-Help; Short
Stories; Sociology; Spiritual; Sport;
Suspense; Technology; Theatre; Thrillers;
Translations; Travel; TV; Westerns;
Women's Interests; *Markets:* Adult;
Children's; Youth

Handles fiction and nonfiction in every genre
and category, except for screenwriting and
poetry. Send brief outline by email, or by
post with SASE.

A M Heath & Company Limited, Author's Agents

6 Warwick Court, Holborn, London, WC1R
5DJ
Tel: +44 (0) 20 7242 2811
Fax: +44 (0) 20 7242 2711
Email: enquiries@amheath.com
Website: http://www.amheath.com

Handles: Fiction; Nonfiction; *Areas:* Crime;
Psychology; Suspense; Thrillers; *Markets:*
Adult; Children's; *Treatments:* Commercial;
Literary

Handles general commercial and literary
fiction and nonfiction. Send query with
synopsis and first 10,000 words via online
submission system only. No paper
submissions. Aims to respond within six
weeks.

Rupert Heath Literary Agency

50 Albemarle Street, London, W1S 4BD
Tel: +44 (0) 20 7060 3385
Email: emailagency@rupertheath.com
Website: http://www.rupertheath.com

Handles: Fiction; Nonfiction; *Areas:* Arts;
Autobiography; Biography; Cookery; Crime;
Culture; Current Affairs; Historical;
Lifestyle; Nature; Politics; Science;
Thrillers; Women's Interests; *Markets:*
Adult; *Treatments:* Commercial; Literary;
Popular

Send query giving some information about
yourself and the work you would like to
submit. Prefers queries by email. Response
only if interested.

hhb agency ltd

6 Warwick Court, London, WC1R 5DJ
Tel: +44 (0) 20 7405 5525
Email: heather@hhbagency.com
Website: http://www.hhbagency.com

Handles: Fiction; Nonfiction; *Areas:*
Adventure; Autobiography; Biography;
Business; Cookery; Crime; Culture;
Entertainment; Historical; Humour; Politics;
Travel; TV; Women's Interests; *Markets:*
Adult; *Treatments:* Commercial;
Contemporary; Literary; Popular

Query by email or telephone before submitting any material. No scripts or unsolicited MSS. Specialises in food and cookery.

David Higham Associates Ltd
5-8 Lower John Street, Golden Square, London, W1F 9HA
Tel: +44 (0) 20 7434 5900
Fax: +44 (0) 20 7437 1072
Email: dha@davidhigham.co.uk
Website: http://www.davidhigham.co.uk

Handles: Fiction; Nonfiction; Scripts; *Areas:* Biography; Current Affairs; Historical; *Markets:* Adult; Children's

For adult fiction and nonfiction contact "Adult Submissions Department" by post only with SASE, covering letter, CV, and synopsis (fiction)/proposal (nonfiction) and first two or three chapters. For children's fiction prefers submissions by email to the specific children's submission address given on the website, with covering letter, synopsis, CV, and first two or three chapters (or complete MS if a picture book). See website for complete guidelines. Scripts by referral only.

Vanessa Holt Ltd
59 Crescent Road, Leigh-on-Sea, Essex SS9 2PF
Tel: +44 (0) 1702 473787

Handles: Fiction; Nonfiction; *Areas:* Crime; *Markets:* Adult; Children's; *Treatments:* Commercial; Literary

General fiction and nonfiction. Specialises in crime fiction and books with potential for sales overseas and / or to TV. No scripts, poetry, academic, technical, illustrated children's, or unsolicited MSS. Query by post or phone only.

Valerie Hoskins Associates
20 Charlotte Street, London, W1T 2NA
Tel: +44 (0) 20 7637 4490
Fax: +44 (0) 20 7637 4493
Email: info@vhassociates.co.uk
Website: http://www.vhassociates.co.uk

Handles: Scripts; *Areas:* Film; Radio; TV; *Markets:* Adult

Preliminary introductory letter essential. Particularly interested in feature films, animation, and TV. No unsolicited scripts.

Amanda Howard Associates Ltd
74 Clerkenwell Road, London, EC1M 5QA
Tel: +44 (0) 20 7250 1760
Email: mail@amandahowardassociates.co.uk
Website: http://www.amandahowardassociates.co.uk

Handles: Nonfiction; Scripts; *Areas:* Autobiography; How-to; Humour; *Markets:* Adult; *Treatments:* Popular

Handles actors, writers, creatives, and voice-over artsts. Send query with return postage, CV/bio, and 10-page writing sample. No poetry.

Independent Talent Group Ltd
Oxford House, 76 Oxford Street, London, W1D 1BS
Tel: +44 (0) 20 7636 6565
Fax: +44 (0) 20 7323 0101
Email: laurarourke@independenttalent.com
Website: http://www.independenttalent.com

Handles: Scripts; *Areas:* Film; Radio; Theatre; TV; *Markets:* Adult

Specialises in scripts and works in association with agencies in Los Angeles and New York. No unsolicited MSS. Materials submitted will not be returned.

Intercontinental Literary Agency
Centric House, 390-391 Strand, London, WC2R 0LT
Tel: +44 (0) 20 7379 6611
Fax: +44 (0) 20 7379 6790
Email: ila@ila-agency.co.uk
Website: http://www.ila-agency.co.uk

Handles: Fiction; Nonfiction; *Areas:* Translations; *Markets:* Adult; Children's

Handles translation rights only for, among others, the authors of LAW Ltd, London; Harold Matson Co. Inc., New York; PFD, London. Submissions accepted via client agencies and publishers only – no submissions from writers seeking agents.

Janet Fillingham Associates

52 Lowther Road , London, SW13 9NU
Tel: +44 (0) 20 8748 5594
Fax: +44 (0) 20 8748 7374
Email: info@janetfillingham.com
Website: http://www.janetfillingham.com

Handles: Scripts; *Areas:* Film; Theatre; TV; *Markets:* Adult; Children's; Youth

Represents writers and directors for stage, film and TV, as well as librettists, lyricists and composers in musical theatre. Does not represent books. Prospective clients may register via website.

Johnson & Alcock

Clerkenwell House, 45/47 Clerkenwell Green, London, EC1R 0HT
Tel: +44 (0) 20 7251 0125
Fax: +44 (0) 20 7251 2172
Email: info@johnsonandalcock.co.uk
Website: http://www.johnsonandalcock.com

Handles: Fiction; Nonfiction; Poetry; *Areas:* Autobiography; Biography; Culture; Current Affairs; Design; Film; Health; Historical; Lifestyle; Music; Sci-Fi; Self-Help; Sport; *Markets:* Adult; Children's; Youth; *Treatments:* Commercial; Literary

For children's fiction, ages 9+ only. Send query by post with SASE, synopsis and approximately first 50 pages. Accepts email submission, but replies only if interested. Email submissions should go to specific agents. See website for list of agents and full submission guidelines. No poetry, screenplays, children's books 0-7, or board or picture books.

Michelle Kass Associates

85 Charing Cross Road, London, WC2H 0AA
Tel: +44 (0) 20 7439 1624

Fax: +44 (0) 20 7734 3394
Email: office@michellekass.co.uk

Handles: Fiction; Scripts; *Areas:* Film; Literature; TV; *Markets:* Adult; *Treatments:* Literary

Approach by telephone in first instance.

Frances Kelly

111 Clifton Road, Kingston upon Thames, Surrey KT2 6PL
Tel: +44 (0) 20 8549 7830
Fax: +44 (0) 20 8547 0051

Handles: Nonfiction; Reference; *Areas:* Arts; Biography; Business; Cookery; Finance; Health; Historical; Lifestyle; Medicine; Self-Help; *Markets:* Academic; Adult; Professional

Send query with SAE, CV, and synopsis or brief description of work. Scripts handled for existing clients only. No unsolicited MSS.

Ki Agency Ltd

48-56 Bayham Place, London, NW1 0EU
Tel: +44 (0) 20 3214 8287
Email: meg@ki-agency.co.uk
Website: http://www.ki-agency.co.uk

Handles: Fiction; Scripts; *Areas:* Film; Theatre; TV; *Markets:* Adult

Represents novelists and scriptwriters in all media. No nonfiction, children's, or poetry. Accepts unsolicited mss by post or by email.

Kilburn Literary Agency

Belsize Road, Kilburn, London, NW6 4BT
Email: info@kilburnlit.com
Website: http://kilburnlit.com

Handles: Fiction; Nonfiction; Scripts; *Areas:* Adventure; Arts; Autobiography; Biography; Business; Health; Literature; Medicine; Mystery; Politics; Psychology; Religious; Romance; Science; Short Stories; Sociology; Spiritual; Thrillers; Women's Interests; *Markets:* Adult; Youth; *Treatments:* Commercial; Contemporary; Literary; Mainstream; Popular; Positive

We are an agency founded in 2013 and offer a window of opportunity while we build up our list.

All submissions and queries must be by e-mail initially.

We are international in outlook.

Barbara Levy Literary Agency

64 Greenhill, Hampstead High Street, London, NW3 5TZ
Tel: +44 (0) 20 7435 9046
Fax: +44 (0) 20 7431 2063
Email: blevysubmissions@gmail.com

Handles: Fiction; Nonfiction; *Markets:* Adult

Send query with synopsis by email or by post with SAE.

Limelight Management

10 Filmer Mews, 75 Filmer Road , London, SW6 7JF
Tel: +44 (0) 20 7384 9950
Fax: +44 (0) 20 7384 9955
Email: mail@limelightmanagement.com
Website:
http://www.limelightmanagement.com

Handles: Fiction; Nonfiction; *Areas:* Lifestyle; *Markets:* Adult; *Treatments:* Commercial; Literary

Particularly interested in lifestyle nonfiction, and commercial and literary fiction for the adult market. For nonfiction send query with 3-4 page outline. For fiction send query with synopsis and first three or four consecutive chapters. Accepts queries by email, but no large attachments – emails with large attachments will be deleted unread. No scripts. See website for full submission guidelines.

Lindsay Literary Agency

East Worldham House, East Worldham, Alton GU34 3AT
Tel: +44 (0) 0142 083143
Email: info@lindsayliteraryagency.co.uk

Website:
http://www.lindsayliteraryagency.co.uk

Handles: Fiction; Nonfiction; *Markets:* Adult; Children's; *Treatments:* Literary; Serious

Send query by post with SASE or by email, including single-page synopsis and first three chapters.

London Independent Books

26 Chalcot Crescent, London, NW1 8YD
Tel: +44 (0) 20 7706 0486
Fax: +44 (0) 20 7724 3122

Handles: Fiction; Nonfiction; *Areas:* Fantasy; Travel; *Markets:* Adult; Youth; *Treatments:* Commercial

Send query with synopsis, SASE, and first two chapters. All fiction and nonfiction subjects considered if treatment is strong and saleable, but no computer books, young children's, or unsolicited MSS. Particularly interested in boats, commercial fiction, fantasy, teen fiction, and travel. Scripts handled for existing clients only.

Andrew Lownie Literary Agency Ltd

36 Great Smith Street, London, SW1P 3BU
Tel: +44 (0) 20 7222 7574
Fax: +44 (0) 20 7222 7576
Email: mail@andrewlownie.co.uk
Website: http://www.andrewlownie.co.uk

Handles: Fiction; Nonfiction; *Areas:* Autobiography; Biography; Crime; Culture; Current Affairs; Fantasy; Finance; Health; Historical; Horror; How-to; Lifestyle; Literature; Media; Medicine; Men's Interests; Military; Music; Mystery; Politics; Psychology; Romance; Science; Sci-Fi; Self-Help; Sport; Suspense; Technology; Thrillers; Translations; Westerns; *Markets:* Academic; Adult; Family; Professional; *Treatments:* Commercial; Mainstream; Popular; Serious; Traditional

This agency, founded in 1988, is now one of the UK's leading boutique literary agencies with some two hundred nonfiction and fiction authors and is actively building its fiction list through its new agent (see website for specific contact address for fiction submissions). It prides itself on its personal attention to its clients and specialises both in launching new writers and taking established writers to a new level of recognition.

Lucy Luck Associates

18-21 Cavaye Place, London, SW10 9PT
Tel: +44 (0) 20 7373 8672
Email: lucy@lucyluck.com
Website: http://www.lucyluck.com

Handles: Fiction; Nonfiction; *Markets:* Adult

Send query by post, email, or using form on website to provide cover letter and first 30-50 pages, plus SAE if required. No scripts, childrens books, or illustrated books.

Lutyens and Rubinstein

21 Kensington Park Road, London, W11 2EU
Tel: +44 (0) 20 7792 4855
Email: submissions@lutyensrubinstein.co.uk
Website: http://www.lutyensrubinstein.co.uk

Handles: Fiction; Nonfiction; *Markets:* Adult; *Treatments:* Commercial; Literary

Send up to 5,000 words or first three chapters by email with covering letter and short synopsis. No scripts, or unsolicited submissions by hand or by post.

Madeleine Milburn Literary Agency

42A Great Percy Street, Bloomsbury, London, WC1X 9QR
Tel: +44 (0) 20 3602 6425
Fax: +44 (0) 20 3602 6425
Email: submissions@madeleinemilburn.com
Website: http://madeleinemilburn.co.uk

Handles: Fiction; Nonfiction; Scripts; *Areas:* Autobiography; Crime; Film; Mystery; Suspense; Thrillers; TV; Women's Interests; *Markets:* Adult; Children's; Youth; *Treatments:* Literary

Send query by email only, with synopsis and first three chapters as Word or PDF attachments. See website for full submission guidelines. Film and TV scripts for established clients only.

Andrew Mann Ltd

39 – 41 North Road, London, N7 9DP
Tel: +44 (0) 20 7609 6218
Email: info@andrewmann.co.uk
Website: http://www.andrewmann.co.uk

Handles: Fiction; Nonfiction; Scripts; *Areas:* Film; Radio; Theatre; TV; *Markets:* Adult; Children's

Send query by email, or by post if absolutely necessary. No poetry, spiritual or new age philosophy, short stories or misery memoirs. Not currently accepting submissions for film or theatre. See website for full submission guidelines.

Marjacq Scripts Ltd

Box 412, 19/21 Crawford St, London, W1H 1PJ
Tel: +44 (0) 20 7935 9499
Fax: +44 (0) 20 7935 9115
Email: subs@marjacq.com
Website: http://www.marjacq.com

Handles: Fiction; Nonfiction; Scripts; *Areas:* Film; Radio; TV; *Markets:* Adult; Children's; *Treatments:* Commercial; Literary

For books, send query with synopsis and three sample chapters. For scripts, send short treatment and entire screenplay. All queries must include an SAE for response, if sent by post. If sent by email send only Word or PDF documents less than 2MB. Also handles games developers. See website for full details. No poetry, short stories, or stage plays. Do not send queries without including samples of the actual work.

The Marsh Agency

50 Albemarle Street, London, W1S 4BD
Tel: +44 (0) 20 7493 4361
Fax: +44 (0) 20 7495 8961
Email: steph@marsh-agency.co.uk

Website: http://www.marsh-agency.co.uk

Handles: Fiction; Nonfiction; *Markets:* Adult; Youth; *Treatments:* Literary

Use online submission system to send brief query letter with contact details, relevant information, details of any previously published work, and any experience which relates to the book's subject matter; an outline of the plot and main characters for fiction, or a summary of the work and chapter outlines for nonfiction. Include three consecutive chapters up to 100 pages, and your CV. See website for full guidelines and online submission system. No TV, film, radio or theatre scripts, poetry, or children's/picture books. Does not handle US authors as a primary English Language Agent. Do not call or email until at least 8 weeks have elapsed from submission date.

MBA Literary Agents Ltd
62 Grafton Way, London, W1T 5DW
Tel: +44 (0) 20 7387 2076
Fax: +44 (0) 20 7387 2042
Email: submissions@mbalit.co.uk
Website: http://www.mbalit.co.uk

Handles: Fiction; Nonfiction; Scripts; *Areas:* Arts; Biography; Crafts; Film; Health; Historical; Lifestyle; Radio; Self-Help; Theatre; TV; *Markets:* Adult; Children's; Youth; *Treatments:* Commercial; Literary

For books, send query with synopsis and first three chapters. For scripts, send query with synopsis, CV, and finished script. Prefers submissions by email, but will also accept submissions by post. See website for full submission guidelines. Works in conjunction with agents in most countries.

Duncan McAra
28 Beresford Gardens, Edinburgh, Scotland EH5 3ES
Tel: +44 (0) 131 552 1558
Email: duncanmcara@mac.com

Handles: Fiction; Nonfiction; *Areas:* Archaeology; Architecture; Arts; Biography; Historical; Military; Travel; *Markets:* Adult; *Treatments:* Literary

Also interested in books of Scottish interest. Send query letter with SAE in first instance.

McKernan Agency
Studio 50, Out of the Blue Drill Hall, 36 Dalmeny Street, Edinburgh, EH6 8RG
Tel: +44 (0) 1315 571771
Email: info@mckernanagency.co.uk
Website: http://www.mckernanagency.co.uk

Handles: Fiction; Nonfiction; *Areas:* Autobiography; Biography; Crime; Current Affairs; Historical; *Markets:* Adult; Children's; Family; Youth; *Treatments:* Literary

Handles high quality literary fiction including historical and crime and high quality nonfiction, including memoirs, biography, history, current affairs etc. Also considers fiction for older children. Submit through online webform only. No submissions by post or email.

Bill McLean Personal Management Ltd
23B Deodar Road, London, SW15 2NP
Tel: +44 (0) 20 8789 8191

Handles: Scripts; *Areas:* Film; Radio; Theatre; TV; *Markets:* Adult

Query initially by letter or phone call. Handles scripts for all media. No books or unsolicited MSS.

Judith Murdoch Literary Agency
19 Chalcot Square, London, NW1 8YA
Tel: +44 (0) 20 7722 4197
Email: jmlitag@btinternet.com
Website: http://www.judithmurdoch.co.uk

Handles: Fiction; *Areas:* Crime; Women's Interests; *Markets:* Adult; *Treatments:* Commercial; Literary; Popular

Send query by post with SAE or email address for response, brief synopsis, and and two sample chapters. Provides editorial advice. No poetry, short stories, children's books, science fiction, fantasy, email submissions, or unsolicited MSS.

MNLA (Maggie Noach Literary Agency)

7 Peacock Yard, Iliffe Street, London, SE17 3LH
Tel: +44 (0) 20 7708 3073
Email: info@mnla.co.uk
Website: http://www.mnla.co.uk

Handles: Fiction; Nonfiction; *Areas:* Biography; Historical; Travel; *Markets:* Adult; Children's

Note: As at June 2013 not accepting submissions. Check website for current situation.

Deals with UK residents only. Send query with SAE, outline, and two or three sample chapters. No email attachments or fax queries. Very few new clients taken on. Deals in general adult nonfiction and non-illustrated children's books for ages 8 and upwards. No poetry, scripts, short stories, cookery, gardening, mind, body, and spirit, scientific, academic, specialist nonfiction, or unsolicited MSS.

Andrew Nurnberg Associates, Ltd

20-23 Greville Street, London, EC1N 8SS
Tel: +44 (0) 20 3327 0400
Fax: +44 (0) 20 7430 0801
Email: submissions@andrewnurnberg.com
Website: http://www.andrewnurnberg.com

Handles: Fiction; Nonfiction; *Markets:* Adult; Children's

Handles adult fiction and nonfiction, and children's fiction. No poetry, or scripts for film, TV, radio or theatre. Send query with one-page synopsis and first three chapters by post with SAE (if return required) or by email as .doc or .pdf attachments up to 3MB only.

John Pawsey

8 Snowshill Court, Giffard Park, Milton Keynes, MK14 5QG

Tel: +44 (0) 1908 611841
Email: john.pawsey@virgin.net

Handles: Nonfiction; *Areas:* Biography; Sport; *Markets:* Adult

Send query with SAE for response. No fiction, poetry, scripts, journalism, academic, or children's books. Particularly interested in sport and biography. No email submissions.

PBJ and JBJ Management

22 Rathbone Street, London, W1T 1LA
Tel: +44 (0) 20 7287 1112
Fax: +44 (0) 20 7637 0899
Email: general@pbjmanagement.co.uk
Website: http://www.pbjmgt.co.uk

Handles: Scripts; *Areas:* Drama; Film; Humour; Radio; Theatre; TV; *Markets:* Adult

Handles scripts for film, TV, theatre, and radio. Send complete MS with cover letter and CV, if you have one. Send one script only. No submissions by email. Particularly interested in comedy and comedy drama.

Maggie Pearlstine Associates Ltd

31 Ashley Gardens, Ambrosden Avenue, London, SW1P 1QE
Tel: +44 (0) 20 7828 4212
Fax: +44 (0) 20 7834 5546
Email: maggie@pearlstine.co.uk

Handles: Fiction; Nonfiction; *Areas:* Biography; Current Affairs; Health; Historical; *Markets:* Adult

Small, selective agency, not currently taking on new clients.

Jonathan Pegg Literary Agency

32 Batoum Gardens, London, W6 7QD
Tel: +44 (0) 20 7603 6830
Fax: +44 (0) 20 7348 0629
Email: submissions@jonathanpegg.com
Website: http://www.jonathanpegg.com

Handles: Fiction; Nonfiction; *Areas:* Arts;

Autobiography; Biography; Culture; Current Affairs; Historical; Lifestyle; Nature; Psychology; Science; *Markets:* Adult; *Treatments:* Commercial; Literary; Popular

Established by the agent after twelve years at Curtis Brown. The agency's main areas of interest are:
Fiction: literary fiction, thrillers and quality commercial in general
Non-Fiction: current affairs, memoir and biography, history, popular science, nature, arts and culture, lifestyle, popular psychology

Rights:
Aside from the UK market, the agency will work in association with translation, US, TV & film agents according to each client's best interests.

If you're looking for an agent:
I accept submissions by email. Please include a 1-page mini-synopsis, a half-page cv, a longer synopsis (for non-fiction) and the first three chapters, or around 50 pages to a natural break. Please ensure it is via 'word document' attachments, 1.5 line spacing.

See website for full submission guidelines.

The Peters Fraser & Dunlop Group Ltd (PFD)

Drury House, 34-43 Russell Street, London, WC2B 5HA
Tel: +44 (0) 20 7344 1000
Fax: +44 (0) 20 7836 9523
Email: info@pfd.co.uk
Website: http://www.pfd.co.uk

Handles: Fiction; Nonfiction; Scripts; *Areas:* Film; Radio; Theatre; TV; *Markets:* Adult; Children's

Send query with SAE, CV, synopsis and three sample chapters. Currently not accepting children's and illustrators submissions, or fantasy or science fiction. Submissions by post only. No fax or email submissions. Film, stage, and TV department is accepting new writers by referral only. No unsolicited scripts or pitches.

Shelley Power Literary Agency Ltd

35 Rutland Court, New Church Road, Hove, BN3 4AF
Tel: +44 (0) 1273 728730
Email: sp@shelleypower.co.uk

Handles: Fiction; Nonfiction; *Markets:* Adult

Send query by email or by post with return postage. No attachments. No poetry, short stories, scripts, or children's books.

Redhammer

186 Bickenhall Mansions, Bickenhall Street, London, W1U 6BX
Tel: +44 (0) 20 7486 3465
Fax: +44 (0) 20 7000 1249
Email: info@redhammer.biz
Website: http://www.redhammer.info

Handles: Nonfiction; *Areas:* Autobiography; Current Affairs; Health; Lifestyle; Science; *Markets:* Adult

Specialises in mid-list authors who are already experienced in the mainstream publishing world. No radio scripts, theatre scripts, or unsolicited MSS. Previously published authors may send query via form on website. Unpublished authors are advised that this is probably not the best initial agency for novice writers to approach. Does not encourage writers to send unsolicited submissions, but if you do you are advised to keep a copy as submissions will not be returned, nor correspondence entered into.

Regal Literary

6 Steeles Mews North, London, NW3 4RJ
Email: uk@regal-literary.com
Website: http://www.regal-literary.com

Handles: Fiction; Nonfiction; *Areas:* Biography; Historical; Photography; Science; Thrillers; *Markets:* Adult; *Treatments:* Literary

Literary agency with offices in New York and London. Handles literary fiction, thrillers, narrative nonfiction (history, biography, science, etc.) and photography.

No romance, science fiction, poetry, or screenplays. Send query by email or by post with SASE and details of the book and author. For fiction, include first ten pages or one short story from a collection. See website for full details.

Richford Becklow Literary Agency

Tel: +44 (0)7510 023823
Email: enquiries@richfordbecklow.co.uk
Website: http://www.richfordbecklow.com

Handles: Fiction; Nonfiction; *Areas:* Arts; Autobiography; Biography; Cookery; Crime; Fantasy; Gardening; Gothic; Historical; Horror; Lifestyle; Literature; Romance; Sci-Fi; Self-Help; Women's Interests; *Markets:* Adult; Youth; *Treatments:* Commercial; Contemporary; Literary; Satirical; Serious

Company founded in 2011 by an experienced agent, previously at the longest established literary agency in the world. Interested in fiction and nonfiction. Email submissions only. Does not accept postal submissions and cannot currently offer to represent American authors. No picture book texts for babies and toddlers, or erotica. See website for full submission guidelines.

Robert Dudley Agency

135A Bridge Street, Ashford, Kent TN25 5DP
Email: info@robertdudleyagency.co.uk
Website:
http://www.robertdudleyagency.co.uk

Handles: Nonfiction; *Areas:* Adventure; Biography; Business; Current Affairs; Historical; Medicine; Military; Sport; Technology; Travel; *Markets:* Adult; *Treatments:* Popular

Specialises in nonfiction. No fiction submissions. Send query outlining your idea by post or by email in first instance. See website for full guidelines.

Robin Jones Literary Agency

6b Marmora Road, London, SE22 0RX
Tel: +44 (0) 20 8693 6062

Email: robijones@gmail.com

Handles: Fiction; Nonfiction; *Markets:* Adult; *Treatments:* Commercial; Literary

London-based literary agency founded in 2007 by an agent who has previously worked at four other agencies, and was the UK scout for international publishers in 11 countries.

Rochelle Stevens & Co.

2 Terretts Place, Upper Street, London, N1 1QZ
Tel: +44 (0) 20 7359 3900
Email: books@rochellestevens.com
Website: http://www.rochellestevens.com

Handles: Fiction; Nonfiction; Scripts; *Areas:* Film; Radio; Theatre; TV; *Markets:* Adult; Children's; *Treatments:* Commercial; Literary

Handles script writers and writers of fiction, nonfiction, and children's books. Accepts unsolicited email approaches relating to books only; for scripts submit by post. See website for full submission guidelines.

Uli Rushby-Smith Literary Agency

72 Plimsoll Road, London, N4 2EE
Tel: +44 (0) 20 7354 2718
Fax: +44 (0) 20 7354 2718

Handles: Fiction; Nonfiction; *Markets:* Adult; Children's; *Treatments:* Commercial; Literary

Send query with SAE, outline, and two or three sample chapters. Film and TV rights handled in conjunction with a sub-agent. No disks, poetry, picture books, films, or plays.

The Sayle Literary Agency

1 Petersfield, Cambridge, CB1 1BB
Tel: +44 (0) 1223 303035
Fax: +44 (0) 1223 301638
Email: info@sayleliteraryagency.com
Website:
http://www.sayleliteraryagency.com

Handles: Fiction; Nonfiction; *Areas:*

Biography; Crime; Current Affairs; Historical; Music; Science; Travel; *Markets:* Adult; *Treatments:* Literary

Send query with CV, synopsis, and three sample chapters. No text books, technical, legal, medical, children's, plays, poetry, unsolicited MSS, or approaches by email. Do not include SAE as all material submitted is recycled. If no response after three months assume rejection.

Sayle Screen Ltd

11 Jubilee Place, London, SW3 3TD
Tel: +44 (0) 20 7823 3883
Fax: +44 (0) 20 7823 3363
Email: info@saylescreen.com
Website: http://www.saylescreen.com

Handles: Scripts; *Areas:* Film; Radio; Theatre; TV; *Markets:* Adult

Only considers material which has been recommended by a producer, development executive or course tutor. In this case send query by email with cover letter and details of your referee to the relevant agent. Query only one agent at a time.

The Science Factory

Scheideweg 34C, Hamburg, Germany 20253
Tel: +44 (0) 20 7193 7296 (Skype)
Email: info@sciencefactory.co.uk
Website: http://www.sciencefactory.co.uk

Handles: Fiction; Nonfiction; *Areas:* Autobiography; Biography; Current Affairs; Historical; Medicine; Politics; Science; Technology; Travel; *Markets:* Adult

Specialises in science, technology, medicine, and natural history, but will also consider other areas of nonfiction. Novelists handled only occasionally, and if there is some special relevance to the agency (e.g. a thriller about scientists, or a novel of ideas). See website for full submission guidelines.

Please note that the agency address is in Germany, but the country is listed as United Kingdom, as the company is registered in the United Kingdom.

Linda Seifert Management

48-56 Bayham Place, London, NW1 0EU
Tel: +44 (0) 20 3214 8293
Email: contact@lindaseifert.com
Website: http://www.lindaseifert.com

Handles: Scripts; *Areas:* Film; TV; *Markets:* Adult; Children's

A London-based management company representing screenwriters and directors for film and television. Our outstanding client list ranges from the highly established to the new and exciting emerging talent of tomorrow. Represents UK-based writers and directors only. Accepts submissions by post only. No novels or short stories. See website for full submission guidelines.

Sheil Land Associates Ltd

52 Doughty Street, London, WC1N 2LS
Tel: +44 (0) 20 7405 9351
Fax: +44 (0) 20 7831 2127
Email: info@sheilland.co.uk
Website: http://www.sheilland.co.uk

Handles: Fiction; Nonfiction; Scripts; *Areas:* Autobiography; Biography; Cookery; Crime; Drama; Fantasy; Film; Gardening; Historical; Humour; Lifestyle; Military; Mystery; Politics; Psychology; Radio; Romance; Science; Sci-Fi; Self-Help; Theatre; Thrillers; Travel; TV; Women's Interests; *Markets:* Adult; Children's; Youth; *Treatments:* Commercial; Contemporary; Literary

Send query with synopsis, CV, and first three chapters, addressed to "The Submissions Dept". Welcome approaches from new clients either to start or develop their careers. Do not include SAE or return postage as all submissions are recycled.

Caroline Sheldon Literary Agency

71 Hillgate Place, London, W8 7SS
Tel: +44 (0) 20 7727 9102
Email: carolinesheldon@carolinesheldon.co.uk
Website: http://www.carolinesheldon.co.uk

Handles: Fiction; Nonfiction; *Areas:*

Autobiography; Women's Interests;
Markets: Adult; Children's; *Treatments:*
Commercial; Literary

Send query by email only, attaching synopsis
up to two pages and first three chapters, as
Word documents. Do not query both agents.
See website for both email addresses and
appropriate subject line to include. Handles
fiction and human-interest nonfiction for
adults, and fiction for children, including
full-length and picture books.

Jeffrey Simmons

15 Penn House, Mallory Street, London,
NW8 8SX
Tel: +44 (0) 20 7224 8917
Email: jasimmons@unicombox.co.uk

Handles: Fiction; Nonfiction; *Areas:*
Autobiography; Biography; Crime; Current
Affairs; Entertainment; Film; Historical;
Legal; Politics; Psychology; Sport; Theatre;
Markets: Adult; *Treatments:* Commercial;
Literary

Send query with brief bio, synopsis, history
of any prior publication, and list of any
publishers or agents to have already seen the
MSS. Particularly interested in personality
books of all kinds and fiction from young
writers (under 40) with a future. No
children's books, science fiction, fantasy,
cookery, crafts, gardening, or hobbies. Film
scripts handled for existing book clients
only.

Sinclair-Stevenson

3 South Terrace, London, SW7 2TB
Tel: +44 (0) 20 7581 2550
Fax: +44 (0) 20 7581 2550

Handles: Fiction; Nonfiction; *Areas:* Arts;
Biography; Current Affairs; Historical;
Travel; *Markets:* Adult

Send query with synopsis and SAE. No
children's books, scripts, academic, science
fiction, or fantasy.

Robert Smith Literary Agency Ltd

12 Bridge Wharf, 156 Caledonian Road,
London, N1 9UU
Tel: +44 (0) 20 7278 2444
Fax: +44 (0) 20 7833 5680
Email:
robertsmith.literaryagency@virgin.net
Website:
http://www.robertsmithliteraryagency.com

Handles: Nonfiction; *Areas:* Autobiography;
Biography; Crime; Culture; Current Affairs;
Health; Historical; Humour; Lifestyle;
Military; *Markets:* Adult; *Treatments:*
Mainstream

Send query with synopsis initially and
sample chapter if available, by post or by
email. No poetry, fiction, scripts, children's
books, academic, or unsolicited MSS. Will
suggest revision. See website for full
guidelines.

Standen Literary Agency

4 Winton Avenue, London, N11 2AT
Tel: +44 (0) 20 8245 2606
Fax: +44 (0) 20 8245 2606
Email:
submissions@standenliteraryagency.com
Website:
http://www.standenliteraryagency.com

Handles: Fiction; Nonfiction; *Markets:*
Adult; Children's; Youth; *Treatments:*
Commercial; Literary

Based in London. For fiction, send synopsis
and first three chapters by email only.
Responds if interested only. If no response in
12 weeks assume rejection. For nonfiction,
query in first instance.

Abner Stein

10 Roland Gardens, London, SW7 3PH
Tel: +44 (0) 20 7373 0456
Fax: +44 (0) 20 7370 6316
Email: arabella@abnerstein.co.uk
Website: http://www.abnerstein.co.uk

Handles: Fiction; Nonfiction; *Markets:*
Adult; Children's

Note: Not accepting submissions as at October 2013.

Send query with outline. No scripts, scientific, technical, or unsolicited MSS. Mainly represents US agents and authors.

Shirley Stewart Literary Agency

3rd Floor, 21 Denmark Street, London, WC2H 8NA
Tel: +44 (0) 20 7836 4440
Fax: +44 (0) 20 7836 3482
Email: shirleystewart@btinternet.com

Handles: Fiction; Nonfiction; *Markets:* Adult; *Treatments:* Literary

Paricularly interested in literary fiction and general nonfiction. Send query with SAE and two or three sample chapters. Unsolicited material considered, but no submissions by fax or on disk. No poetry, scripts, children's books, science fiction, or fantasy.

Susanna Lea Associates (UK)

34 Lexington Street, London, W1F 0LH
Tel: +44 (0) 20 7287 7757
Fax: +44 (0) 20 7287 7775
Email: uk-submission@susannalea.com
Website: http://www.susannalea.com

Handles: Fiction; Nonfiction; *Markets:* Adult

Literary agency with offices in Paris, London, and New York. Always on the lookout for exciting new talent. No poetry, plays, screen plays, science fiction, educational text books, short stories or illustrated works. Accepts queries by email only. Include cover letter, synopsis, and first three chapters or proposal. Response not guaranteed.

The Susijn Agency

3rd Floor, 64 Great Titchfield Street, London, W1W 7QH
Tel: +44 (0) 20 7580 6341
Fax: +44 (0) 20 7580 8626
Email: submissions@thesusijnagency.com
Website: http://www.thesusijnagency.com

Handles: Fiction; Nonfiction; *Markets:* Adult; *Treatments:* Literary

Send query with synopsis and three sample chapters only by post or by email. Include SASE if return of material required. Response in 6-8 weeks. Specialises in selling rights worldwide and also represents non-English language authors and publishers for US, UK, and translation rights worldwide. No self-help, science-fiction, fantasy, romance, sagas, computer, illustrated, business, or screenplays.

SYLA – Susan Yearwood Literary Agency

2 Knebworth House, Londesborough Road, Stoke Newington, London N16 8RL
Tel: +44 (0) 20 7503 0954
Email: submissions@susanyearwood.com
Website: http://www.susanyearwood.com

Handles: Fiction; Nonfiction; *Areas:* Autobiography; Biography; Crime; Thrillers; Women's Interests; *Markets:* Adult; Children's; Youth; *Treatments:* Commercial; Literary

Send query by email, including synopsis and first thirty pages in one Word file attachment. No poetry or screenwriting, or submissions by post.

The Tennyson Agency

10 Cleveland Avenue, Wimbledon Chase, London, SW20 9EW
Tel: +44 (0) 20 8543 5939
Email: enquiries@tenagy.co.uk
Website: http://www.tenagy.co.uk

Handles: Scripts; *Areas:* Drama; Film; Radio; Theatre; TV; *Markets:* Adult

Mainly deals in scripts for film, TV, theatre, and radio, along with related material on an ad-hoc basis. Handles writers in the European Union only. Send query with CV and outline of work. Prefers queries by email. No nonfiction, poetry, short stories, science fiction and fantasy or children's writing, or unsolicited MSS.

Thomas Moore Literary Agency

London,
Email: thomasj.moore@me.com

Handles: Fiction; Nonfiction; Poetry; Reference; Scripts; *Areas:* Arts; Cookery; Crafts; Culture; Design; Drama; Entertainment; Film; Gardening; Historical; How-to; Lifestyle; Literature; Media; Music; Nature; Philosophy; Photography; Radio; Romance; Short Stories; Theatre; Translations; Travel; TV; *Markets:* Academic; Adult; Children's; Family; Professional; Youth; *Treatments:* Commercial; Contemporary; Cynical; Dark; Experimental; In-depth; Light; Literary; Mainstream; Niche; Popular; Positive; Progressive; Satirical; Serious; Traditional

Discovering, fostering and promoting talented writers. We currently have an open submissions and are looking to work with writers who are breaking new ground and challenging what modern literature is.

We will only read manuscripts that are accompanied by a short synopsis and an in depth biography of the Client. Clients must be based in the UK.

Jane Turnbull

Barn Cottage, Veryan, Truro TR2 5QA
Tel: +44 (0) 20 7727 9409 / +44 (0) 1872 501317
Email: jane@janeturnbull.co.uk
Website: http://www.janeturnbull.co.uk

Handles: Fiction; Nonfiction; *Areas:* Biography; Current Affairs; Entertainment; Gardening; Historical; Humour; Lifestyle; Nature; TV; *Markets:* Adult

Agency with offices in London and Cornwall. New clients always welcome and a few taken on every year. Send query by post to Cornwall office with short description of your book or idea. No unsolicited MSS.

United Agents

12–26 Lexington Street, London, W1F 0LE
Tel: +44 (0) 20 3214 0800

Fax: +44 (0) 20 3214 0802
Email: info@unitedagents.co.uk
Website: http://unitedagents.co.uk

Handles: Fiction; Nonfiction; Scripts; *Areas:* Biography; Film; Radio; Theatre; TV; *Markets:* Adult; Children's; Youth

Do not approach the book department generally. Consult website and view details of each agent before selecting a specific agent to approach personally. Accepts submissions by email only. Submissions by post will not be returned or responded to.

Wade & Doherty Literary Agency

33 Cormorant Lodge, Thomas More Street, London, E1W 1AU
Tel: +44 (0) 20 7488 4171
Fax: +44 (0) 20 7488 4172
Email: rw@rwla.com
Website: http://www.rwla.com

Handles: Fiction; Nonfiction; *Markets:* Adult; Youth

New full-length proposals for adult and young adult fiction and nonfiction always welcome. Send query with detailed 1–6 page synopsis, brief biography, and first 10,000 words via email as Word documents (.doc) or PDF; or by post with SAE if return required. We much prefer to correspond by email. Actively seeking new writers across the literary spectrum. No poetry, children's, short stories, scripts or plays.

Cecily Ware Literary Agents

19C John Spencer Square, London, N1 2LZ
Tel: +44 (0) 20 7359 3787
Fax: +44 (0) 20 7226 9828
Email: info@cecilyware.com
Website: http://www.cecilyware.com

Handles: Scripts; *Areas:* Drama; Film; Humour; TV; *Markets:* Adult; Children's

Handles film and TV scripts only. No books or theatre scripts. Submit complete script with covering letter, CV, and SAE. No email submissions or return of material without SAE and correct postage.

Watson, Little Ltd

48-56 Bayham Place , London, NW1 0EU
Tel: +44 (0) 20 7388 7529
Fax: +44 (0) 20 7388 8501
Email: office@watsonlittle.com
Website: http://www.watsonlittle.com

Handles: Fiction; Nonfiction; *Areas:*
Business; Crime; Film; Historical; Humour;
Leisure; Music; Psychology; Science; Self-
Help; Sport; Technology; Women's
Interests; *Markets:* Adult; Children's; Youth;
Treatments: Commercial; Literary; Popular

Send query with synopsis, sample chapters,
and return postage if return / response by
post required; otherwise response is by
email. No scripts, poetry, short stories,
purely academic writers, emails, or
unsolicited MSS.

Whispering Buffalo Literary Agency Ltd

97 Chesson Road, London, W14 9QS
Tel: +44 (0) 20 7565 4737
Email: info@whisperingbuffalo.com
Website: http://www.whisperingbuffalo.com

Handles: Fiction; Nonfiction; *Areas:*
Adventure; Anthropology; Arts;
Autobiography; Beauty and Fashion; Design;
Entertainment; Film; Health; Humour;
Lifestyle; Music; Nature; Politics; Romance;
Sci-Fi; Self-Help; Thrillers; *Markets:* Adult;
Children's; Youth; *Treatments:* Commercial;
Literary

Handles commercial/literary
fiction/nonfiction and children's/YA fiction
with special interest in book to film
adaptations. No TV, film, radio or theatre
scripts, or poetry or academic. Address all
material for the attention of the submissions
department. For fiction, send query with
SAE, CV, synopsis, and three sample
chapters. For nonfiction, send proposal and
sample chapter. Also accepts email
submissions in .doc format only, but prefers
hard-copy approaches. Response to email
approaches only if interested.

Eve White: Literary Agent

54 Gloucester Street, London, SW1V 4EG

Tel: +44 (0) 20 7630 1155
Email: eve@evewhite.co.uk
Website: http://www.evewhite.co.uk

Handles: Fiction; Nonfiction; *Markets:*
Adult; Children's; *Treatments:* Commercial;
Literary

**Important! Check and follow website
submission guidelines before contacting!**

**DO NOT send submissions to email
address below – see website for
submission email addresses.**

**QUERIES ONLY to the email address
above.**

This agency requests that you go to their
website for up-to-date submission procedure.

Commercial and literary fiction, nonfiction,
children's fiction and picture books ages 7+
(home 15%, overseas 20%). No reading fee.
No poetry, short stories, screenplays, or
science fiction/fantasy for adults. Does not
consider approaches from US writers. See
website for detailed submission guidelines.
Submission by email only.

Dinah Wiener Ltd

12 Cornwall Grove, Chiswick, London, W4
2LB
Tel: +44 (0) 20 8994 6011
Fax: +44 (0) 20 8994 6044
Email: dinah@dwla.co.uk

Handles: Fiction; Nonfiction; *Areas:*
Autobiography; Biography; Cookery;
Science; *Markets:* Adult

Send preliminary query letter with SAE. No
poetry, scripts, or children's books.

William Morris Endeavor (WME) London

Centre Point, 103 New Oxford Street,
London, WC1A 1DD
Tel: +44 (0) 20 7534 6800
Fax: +44 (0) 20 7534 6900
Email:
ldnsubmissions@wmeentertainment.com
Website: http://www.wmeauthors.co.uk

Handles: Fiction; Nonfiction; *Areas:* Autobiography; Biography; Crime; Culture; Historical; Thrillers; *Markets:* Adult; Youth; *Treatments:* Commercial; Literary

London office of a worldwide theatrical and literary agency, with offices in New York, Beverly Hills, Nashville, Miami, and Shanghai, as well as associates in Sydney. No unsolicited scripts for film, TV, or theatre. No self-help, poetry or picture books. Send query by email, using link on website. See website for full guidelines.

Writers House UK
25 Gerrard Street, London, W1D 6JL
Email: akowal@writershouse.com
Website: http://www.writershouse.com

Handles: Fiction; Nonfiction; *Areas:* Autobiography; Biography; Business; Cookery; Fantasy; Finance; Historical; How-to; Lifestyle; Psychology; Science; Sci-Fi; Self-Help; Women's Interests; *Markets:* Adult; Children's; Youth; *Treatments:* Commercial; Literary

UK branch of established US agency with offices in New York and California.

The Wylie Agency (UK) Ltd
17 Bedford Square, London, WC2B 3JA
Tel: +44 (0) 20 7908 5900
Fax: +44 (0) 20 7908 5901
Email: mail@wylieagency.co.uk
Website: http://www.wylieagency.co.uk

Handles: Fiction; Nonfiction; *Markets:* Adult

Send query by post or email before submitting. All submissions must include adequate return postage. No scripts, children's books, or unsolicited MSS.

Canadian Literary Agents

For the most up-to-date listings of these and hundreds of other literary agents, visit http://www.firstwriter.com/Agents

*To claim your **free** access to the site, please see the back of this book.*

Abela Literature

39 King St, Box 20039 Brunswick Square, Saint John, New Brunswick E2L 5B2
Email: submissions@abela-lit.com
Website: http://www.abela-lit.com

Handles: Fiction; *Areas:* Adventure; Crime; Drama; Fantasy; Gothic; Historical; Horror; Literature; Mystery; Sci-Fi; Suspense; Thrillers; Westerns; *Markets:* Adult; Family; *Treatments:* Literary; Popular; Traditional

Happy to work with both first time and previously published authors. We are not currently looking for any nonfiction projects, but would be interested in queries for manuscripts in a variety of fiction categories.

The Helen Heller Agency

4-216 Heath Street West, Toronto, ON M5P 1N7
Tel: +1 (416) 489-0396
Email: info@helenhelleragency.com
Website: http://www.helenhelleragency.com

Handles: Fiction; Nonfiction; *Markets:* Adult; Youth

Handles adult and young adult nonfiction and fiction. No children's, screenplays, or genre fiction (sci-fi / fantasy etc.). Send query by email or by post with SASE, including brief synopsis and any relevant publishing history.

Robert Lecker Agency

4055 Melrose Avenue, Montréal, Québec H4A 2S5
Tel: +1 (514) 830-4818
Fax: +1 (514) 483-1644
Email: leckerlink@aol.com
Website: http://www.leckeragency.com

Handles: Fiction; Nonfiction; *Areas:* Adventure; Autobiography; Biography; Cookery; Crime; Culture; Entertainment; Erotic; Film; Historical; How-to; Literature; Music; Mystery; Science; Suspense; Theatre; Thrillers; Travel; *Markets:* Academic; Adult; *Treatments:* Contemporary; Literary; Mainstream

Specialises in books about entertainment, music, popular culture, popular science, intellectual and cultural history, food, and travel, but willing to consider any original and well presented material. Particularly interested in books written by academics that can attract a broad range of readers. Send query by email before sending any other material.

P.S. Literary Agency

20033-520 Kerr Street, Oakville, Ontario L6K 3C7
Tel: +1 (416) 907-8325
Email: query@psliterary.com
Website: http://www.PSLiterary.com

Handles: Fiction; Nonfiction; *Areas:* Autobiography; Business; Current Affairs; Health; Historical; Humour; Literature; Mystery; Politics; Psychology; Romance; Science; Sport; Suspense; Thrillers; Women's Interests; *Markets:* Adult; Children's; Youth; *Treatments:* Commercial; Contemporary; Literary; Mainstream; Popular

A literary agency representing both fiction and nonfiction for adults, young adults, and children. Does not handle poetry or screenplays. Send one-page query by email only. No attachments. See website for full submission guidelines.

P. Stathonikos Agency

146 Springbluff Heights SW, Calgary, Alberta T3H 5E5
Tel: +1 (403) 245-2087
Fax: +1 (403) 245-2087
Email: pastath@telus.net

Handles: Fiction; Nonfiction; *Markets:* Children's; Youth

Handles children's books and some young adult. Send query by email or by post with SASE. No romance, fantasy, historical fiction, plays, movie scripts, poetry, or queries by fax.

Westwood Creative Artists

94 Harbord Street, Toronto , Ontario M5S 1G6
Tel: +1 (416) 964-3302
Fax: +1 (416) 975-9209
Email: wca_office@wcaltd.com
Website: http://www.wcaltd.com

Handles: Fiction; Nonfiction; *Areas:* Autobiography; Biography; Current Affairs; Historical; Mystery; Science; Thrillers; *Markets:* Adult; Children's; Youth; *Treatments:* Commercial; Literary

Send query by email with your credentials, a synopsis, and short sample up to ten pages in the body of the email. No attachments.

Irish Literary Agents

For the most up-to-date listings of these and hundreds of other literary agents, visit http://www.firstwriter.com/Agents

*To claim your **free** access to the site, please see the back of this book.*

Author Rights Agency
20 Victoria Road, Rathgar, Dublin, 6
Tel: +353 1 4922112
Email:
submissions@authorrightsagency.com
Website: http://www.authorrightsagency.com

Handles: Fiction; Nonfiction; *Areas:* Crime; Fantasy; Historical; Sci-Fi; Women's Interests; *Markets:* Adult; Children's; Youth; *Treatments:* Contemporary; Literary

Welcomes submissions in English, particularly from Irish and American writers. Send query by email only with synopsis, ideally one page long, and writing sample up to 10 pages or about 3,000 words, as a Word or RTF attachment. Do not include in the body of the email, or send full manuscripts. See website for full guidelines. No phone calls.

Marianne Gunn O'Connor Literary Agency
Morrison Chambers, Suite 17, 32 Nassau Street,, Dublin, 2
Tel: 353 1 677 9100
Fax: 353 1 677 9101
Email: mgoclitagency@eircom.net

Handles: Fiction; Nonfiction; *Areas:* Biography; Health; *Markets:* Adult; Children's; *Treatments:* Commercial; Literary

Send query with half-page synopsis by email.

The Lisa Richards Agency
108 Upper Leeson Street, Dublin, 4
Tel: +353 1 637 5000
Fax: +353 1 667 1256
Email: info@lisarichards.ie
Website: http://www.lisarichards.ie

Handles: Fiction; Nonfiction; Scripts; *Areas:* Autobiography; Biography; Culture; Historical; Humour; Lifestyle; Self-Help; Sport; Theatre; *Markets:* Adult; Children's; *Treatments:* Commercial; Literary; Popular

Send query by email or by post with SASE, including three or four sample chapters in the case of fiction, or proposal and sample chapter for nonfiction. No horror, science fiction, screenplays, or children's picture books.

Australian Literary Agents

For the most up-to-date listings of these and hundreds of other literary agents, visit http://www.firstwriter.com/Agents

*To claim your **free** access to the site, please see the back of this book.*

The Mary Cunnane Agency Pty Ltd

PO Box 336, Bermagui, NSW 2546
Tel: +61 (0) 2 6493 3880
Fax: +61 (0) 2 6493 3881
Email: mary@cunnaneagency.com
Website: http://www.cunnaneagency.com

Handles: Fiction; Nonfiction; *Markets:* Adult

Make initial query by post, phone, or email. If querying by email, copy in both agents. Does not handle North American writers. No science fiction, fantasy, romance novels, new age/spiritual books, or children's books.

Literary Agents Subject Index

This section lists literary agents by their subject matter, with directions to the section of the book where the full listing can be found.

You can create your own customised lists of literary agents using different combinations of these subject areas, plus over a dozen other criteria, instantly online at http://www.firstwriter.com.

*To claim your **free** access to the site, please see the back of this book.*

Adventure
Abela Literature (*Can*)
Ambassador Speakers Bureau & Literary Agency (*US*)
AVAnti Productions & Management (*UK*)
Cine/Lit Representation (*US*)
Don Congdon Associates, Inc. (*US*)
Crawford Literary Agency (*US*)
Diamond Kahn and Woods (DKW) Literary Agency Ltd (*UK*)
Jim Donovan Literary (*US*)
Ethan Ellenberg Literary Agency (*US*)
Farris Literary Agency, Inc. (*US*)
The Feldstein Agency (*UK*)
Foundry Literary + Media (*US*)
Full Throttle Literary Agency (*US*)
The Gernert Company (*US*)
The Mitchell J. Hamilburg Agency (*US*)
Antony Harwood Limited (*UK*)
hhb agency ltd (*UK*)
Hidden Value Group (*US*)
Andrea Hurst Literary Management (*US*)
International Transactions, Inc. (*US*)
Kilburn Literary Agency (*UK*)
LaunchBooks Literary Agency (*US*)
Robert Lecker Agency (*Can*)
McIntosh & Otis, Inc (*US*)
Monteiro Rose Dravis Agency, Inc. (*US*)
The Jean V. Naggar Literary Agency (*US*)
Niad Management (*US*)
The Park Literary Group LLC (*US*)
The Richard Parks Agency (*US*)
Pavilion Literary Management (*US*)
Barry Perelman Agency (*US*)
Raines & Raines (*US*)
RLR Associates (*US*)
Robert Dudley Agency (*UK*)
Salkind Literary Agency (*US*)
Scovil Galen Ghosh Literary Agency, Inc. (*US*)
The Seven Bridges Group (*US*)
Stuart Krichevsky Literary Agency, Inc. (*US*)
The Swetky Agency and Associates (*US*)
Tom Lee (*US*)
TriadaUS Literary Agency, Inc. (*US*)
Trident Media Group, LLC (*US*)
Waxman Leavell Literary Agency (*US*)
Whispering Buffalo Literary Agency Ltd (*UK*)
The Zack Company, Inc (*US*)

Anthropology
The Agency Group, Ltd (*US*)
AVAnti Productions & Management (*UK*)
Don Congdon Associates, Inc. (*US*)
Felicia Eth Literary Representation (*US*)
The Susan Golomb Literary Agency (*US*)
The Mitchell J. Hamilburg Agency (*US*)
Antony Harwood Limited (*UK*)
Heacock Hill Literary Agency, LLC (*US*)
Larsen Pomada Literary Agents (*US*)
Carol Mann Agency (*US*)
The Richard Parks Agency (*US*)
Lynne Rabinoff Agency (*US*)
RLR Associates (*US*)
Linda Roghaar Literary Agency, Inc. (*US*)
Lynn Seligman, Literary Agent (*US*)
The Swetky Agency and Associates (*US*)
Tom Lee (*US*)
Whispering Buffalo Literary Agency Ltd (*UK*)

Irene Goodman Literary Agency (*US*)
Graham Maw Christie Literary Agency (*UK*)
Kathryn Green Literary Agency, LLC (*US*)
Sanford J. Greenburger Associates, Inc (*US*)
Greene & Heaton Ltd (*UK*)
Laura Gross Literary Agency (*US*)
The Mitchell J. Hamilburg Agency (*US*)
Hardman & Swainson (*UK*)
Antony Harwood Limited (*UK*)
Rupert Heath Literary Agency (*UK*)
hhb agency ltd (*UK*)
Hidden Value Group (*US*)
Hill Nadell Literary Agency (*US*)
Amanda Howard Associates Ltd (*UK*)
Andrea Hurst Literary Management (*US*)
J de S Associates Inc (*US*)
Jill Grinberg Literary Management LLC (*US*)
Johnson & Alcock (*UK*)
Kilburn Literary Agency (*UK*)
The Knight Agency (*US*)
Barbara S. Kouts, Literary Agent (*US*)
Edite Kroll Literary Agency, Inc. (*US*)
Larsen Pomada Literary Agents (*US*)
Sarah Lazin Books (*US*)
Robert Lecker Agency (*Can*)
Lescher & Lescher (*US*)
Levine Greenberg Literary Agency, Inc. (*US*)
Lippincott Massie McQuilkin (*US*)
The Literary Group (*US*)
Literary Management Group, Inc. (*US*)
Sterling Lord Literistic, Inc. (*US*)
Andrew Lownie Literary Agency Ltd (*UK*)
Lyons Literary LLC (*US*)
Gina Maccoby Agency (*US*)
MacGregor Literary (*US*)
Madeleine Milburn Literary Agency (*UK*)
Kirsten Manges Literary Agency, LLC (*US*)
Carol Mann Agency (*US*)
Manus & Associates Literary Agency, Inc. (*US*)
The Martell Agency (*US*)
Martin Literary Management (*US*)
McKernan Agency (*UK*)
Doris S. Michaels Literary Agency, Inc. (*US*)
The Jean V. Naggar Literary Agency (*US*)
Niad Management (*US*)
Objective Entertainment (*US*)
P.S. Literary Agency (*Can*)
The Park Literary Group LLC (*US*)
The Richard Parks Agency (*US*)
Pavilion Literary Management (*US*)
Jonathan Pegg Literary Agency (*UK*)
James Peter Associates, Inc. (*US*)
Pinder Lane & Garon-Brooke Associates Ltd (*US*)
The Poynor Group (*US*)
Linn Prentis Literary (*US*)
Aaron M. Priest Literary Agency (*US*)
Susan Rabiner, Literary Agent, Inc. (*US*)
Lynne Rabinoff Agency (*US*)
Raines & Raines (*US*)
Redhammer (*UK*)
Rees Literary Agency (*US*)
The Amy Rennert Agency, Inc. (*US*)

The Lisa Richards Agency (*Ire*)
Richford Becklow Literary Agency (*UK*)
Ann Rittenberg Literary Agency (*US*)
Jane Rotrosen Agency (*US*)
The Rudy Agency (*US*)
Marly Rusoff & Associates, Inc. (*US*)
Salkind Literary Agency (*US*)
The Science Factory (*UK*)
Jonathan Scott, Inc (*US*)
Scovil Galen Ghosh Literary Agency, Inc. (*US*)
The Seven Bridges Group (*US*)
Sheil Land Associates Ltd (*UK*)
Caroline Sheldon Literary Agency (*UK*)
Jeffrey Simmons (*UK*)
Robert Smith Literary Agency Ltd (*UK*)
Robin Straus Agency, Inc. (*US*)
Rebecca Strong International Literary Agency (*US*)
The Strothman Agency (*US*)
Stuart Krichevsky Literary Agency, Inc. (*US*)
The Stuart Agency (*US*)
The Swetky Agency and Associates (*US*)
SYLA – Susan Yearwood Literary Agency (*UK*)
Talcott Notch Literary (*US*)
Tessler Literary Agency (*US*)
Tom Lee (*US*)
TriadaUS Literary Agency, Inc. (*US*)
Trident Media Group, LLC (*US*)
2M Literary Agency Ltd (*US*)
Beth Vesel Literary Agency (*US*)
Watkins / Loomis Agency, Inc. (*US*)
Waxman Leavell Literary Agency (*US*)
Irene Webb Literary (*US*)
The Wendy Weil Agency, Inc. (*US*)
The Weingel-Fidel Agency (*US*)
Westwood Creative Artists (*Can*)
Whispering Buffalo Literary Agency Ltd (*UK*)
Dinah Wiener Ltd (*UK*)
William Morris Endeavor (WME) London (*UK*)
Writers House UK (*UK*)
Writers House, LLC. (*US*)
Yates & Yates (*US*)
The Zack Company, Inc (*US*)
Karen Gantz Zahler Literary Agency (*US*)
Helen Zimmermann Literary Agency (*US*)
Beauty and Fashion
Artellus Limited (*UK*)
Rosica Colin Ltd (*UK*)
Diane Banks Associates Literary Agency (*UK*)
FinePrint Literary Management (*US*)
Antony Harwood Limited (*UK*)
Signature Literary Agency (*US*)
2M Literary Agency Ltd (*US*)
Whimsy Literary Agency, LLC (*US*)
Whispering Buffalo Literary Agency Ltd (*UK*)
Biography
Sheila Ableman Literary Agency (*UK*)
The Agency Group, Ltd (*US*)
Ambassador Speakers Bureau & Literary Agency (*US*)
The Ampersand Agency Ltd (*UK*)
AP Watt at United Agents LLP (*UK*)
Artellus Limited (*UK*)

Robert Astle & Associates Literary Management, Inc. (*US*)
Audrey A. Wolf Literary Agency (*US*)
Barer Literary, LLC (*US*)
Bell Lomax Moreton Agency (*UK*)
Vicky Bijur Literary Agency (*US*)
Blake Friedmann Literary Agency Ltd (*UK*)
Paul Bresnick Literary Agency, LLC (*US*)
Jenny Brown Associates (*UK*)
Tracy Brown Literary Agency (*US*)
Felicity Bryan (*UK*)
Sheree Bykofsky Associates, Inc. (*US*)
Capel & Land Ltd (*UK*)
Maria Carvainis Agency, Inc. (*US*)
Castiglia Literary Agency (*US*)
Elyse Cheney Literary Associates, LLC (*US*)
Teresa Chris Literary Agency Ltd (*UK*)
Cine/Lit Representation (*US*)
W.M. Clark Associates (*US*)
Rosica Colin Ltd (*UK*)
Frances Collin Literary Agent (*US*)
Don Congdon Associates, Inc. (*US*)
Conville & Walsh Ltd (*UK*)
CowlesRyan Agency (*US*)
Creative Authors Ltd (*UK*)
The Croce Agency (*US*)
Curtis Brown Group Ltd (*UK*)
David Luxton Associates (*UK*)
Caroline Davidson Literary Agency (*UK*)
DeFiore and Company (*US*)
Diamond Kahn and Woods (DKW) Literary Agency Ltd (*UK*)
Donadio & Olson, Inc. (*US*)
Jim Donovan Literary (*US*)
Dunham Literary, Inc. (*US*)
Edwards Fuglewicz (*UK*)
Judith Ehrlich Literary Management (*US*)
Elise Dillsworth Agency (EDA) (*UK*)
Ethan Ellenberg Literary Agency (*US*)
Ann Elmo Agency, Inc. (*US*)
Felicia Eth Literary Representation (*US*)
Farris Literary Agency, Inc. (*US*)
The Feldstein Agency (*UK*)
FinePrint Literary Management (*US*)
Fletcher & Company (*US*)
Foundry Literary + Media (*US*)
Fox & Howard Literary Agency (*UK*)
Jeanne Fredericks Literary Agency, Inc. (*US*)
Fredrica S. Friedman and Co. Inc. (*US*)
Furniss Lawton (*UK*)
The Gernert Company (*US*)
David Godwin Associates (*UK*)
The Susan Golomb Literary Agency (*US*)
Graham Maw Christie Literary Agency (*UK*)
Kathryn Green Literary Agency, LLC (*US*)
Sanford J. Greenburger Associates, Inc (*US*)
Greene & Heaton Ltd (*UK*)
Laura Gross Literary Agency (*US*)
Marianne Gunn O'Connor Literary Agency (*Ire*)
The Mitchell J. Hamilburg Agency (*US*)
Antony Harwood Limited (*UK*)
Rupert Heath Literary Agency (*UK*)
hhb agency ltd (*UK*)

Hidden Value Group (*US*)
David Higham Associates Ltd (*UK*)
Hill Nadell Literary Agency (*US*)
International Transactions, Inc. (*US*)
J de S Associates Inc (*US*)
Jill Grinberg Literary Management LLC (*US*)
Johnson & Alcock (*UK*)
Frances Kelly (*UK*)
Kilburn Literary Agency (*UK*)
Linda Konner Literary Agency (*US*)
Elaine Koster Literary Agency LLC (*US*)
Barbara S. Kouts, Literary Agent (*US*)
Edite Kroll Literary Agency, Inc. (*US*)
Larsen Pomada Literary Agents (*US*)
Sarah Lazin Books (*US*)
Robert Lecker Agency (*Can*)
Lescher & Lescher (*US*)
Levine Greenberg Literary Agency, Inc. (*US*)
Lippincott Massie McQuilkin (*US*)
The Literary Group (*US*)
Literary Management Group, Inc. (*US*)
Sterling Lord Literistic, Inc. (*US*)
Andrew Lownie Literary Agency Ltd (*UK*)
Lyons Literary LLC (*US*)
Gina Maccoby Agency (*US*)
MacGregor Literary (*US*)
Carol Mann Agency (*US*)
Manus & Associates Literary Agency, Inc. (*US*)
Denise Marcil Literary Agency, Inc. (*US*)
Martin Literary Management (*US*)
MBA Literary Agents Ltd (*UK*)
Duncan McAra (*UK*)
McKernan Agency (*UK*)
Doris S. Michaels Literary Agency, Inc. (*US*)
The Jean V. Naggar Literary Agency (*US*)
Niad Management (*US*)
MNLA (Maggie Noach Literary Agency) (*UK*)
Northern Lights Literary Services (*US*)
Objective Entertainment (*US*)
The Richard Parks Agency (*US*)
Kathi J. Paton Literary Agency (*US*)
John Pawsey (*UK*)
Maggie Pearlstine Associates Ltd (*UK*)
Jonathan Pegg Literary Agency (*UK*)
Barry Perelman Agency (*US*)
L. Perkins Associates (*US*)
James Peter Associates, Inc. (*US*)
Pinder Lane & Garon-Brooke Associates Ltd (*US*)
Alièka Pistek Literary Agency, LLC (*US*)
The Poynor Group (*US*)
Aaron M. Priest Literary Agency (*US*)
Lynne Rabinoff Agency (*US*)
Raines & Raines (*US*)
Rees Literary Agency (*US*)
Regal Literary (*UK*)
Regal Literary Inc. (*US*)
The Amy Rennert Agency, Inc. (*US*)
The Lisa Richards Agency (*Ire*)
Richford Becklow Literary Agency (*UK*)
Ann Rittenberg Literary Agency (*US*)
RLR Associates (*US*)
Robert Dudley Agency (*UK*)

Linda Roghaar Literary Agency, Inc. (*US*)
The Rudy Agency (*US*)
Marly Rusoff & Associates, Inc. (*US*)
Salkind Literary Agency (*US*)
The Sayle Literary Agency (*UK*)
Schiavone Literary Agency (*US*)
The Science Factory (*UK*)
Scovil Galen Ghosh Literary Agency, Inc. (*US*)
Lynn Seligman, Literary Agent (*US*)
The Seven Bridges Group (*US*)
Sheil Land Associates Ltd (*UK*)
Signature Literary Agency (*US*)
Jeffrey Simmons (*UK*)
Sinclair-Stevenson (*UK*)
Robert Smith Literary Agency Ltd (*UK*)
Philip G. Spitzer Literary Agency, Inc. (*US*)
Robin Straus Agency, Inc. (*US*)
Rebecca Strong International Literary Agency (*US*)
Stuart Krichevsky Literary Agency, Inc. (*US*)
SYLA – Susan Yearwood Literary Agency (*UK*)
Patricia Teal Literary Agency (*US*)
Tessler Literary Agency (*US*)
TriadaUS Literary Agency, Inc. (*US*)
Trident Media Group, LLC (*US*)
Jane Turnbull (*UK*)
United Agents (*UK*)
Beth Vesel Literary Agency (*US*)
Watkins / Loomis Agency, Inc. (*US*)
Waxman Leavell Literary Agency (*US*)
The Weingel-Fidel Agency (*US*)
Westwood Creative Artists (*Can*)
Dinah Wiener Ltd (*UK*)
William Morris Endeavor (WME) London (*UK*)
Writers House UK (*UK*)
Writers House, LLC. (*US*)
Yates & Yates (*US*)
The Zack Company, Inc (*US*)
Business
The Agency Group, Ltd (*US*)
AP Watt at United Agents LLP (*UK*)
Audrey A. Wolf Literary Agency (*US*)
AVAnti Productions & Management (*UK*)
Bell Lomax Moreton Agency (*UK*)
Sheree Bykofsky Associates, Inc. (*US*)
Maria Carvainis Agency, Inc. (*US*)
Castiglia Literary Agency (*US*)
Elyse Cheney Literary Associates, LLC (*US*)
Creative Authors Ltd (*UK*)
Diane Banks Associates Literary Agency (*UK*)
Sandra Dijkstra Literary Agency (*US*)
Jim Donovan Literary (*US*)
Ebeling & Associates (*US*)
Judith Ehrlich Literary Management (*US*)
Felicia Eth Literary Representation (*US*)
Farris Literary Agency, Inc. (*US*)
The Feldstein Agency (*UK*)
FinePrint Literary Management (*US*)
Fletcher & Company (*US*)
Folio Literary Management, LLC (*US*)
Foundry Literary + Media (*US*)
Fox & Howard Literary Agency (*UK*)
Jeanne Fredericks Literary Agency, Inc. (*US*)

Fresh Books Literary Agency (*US*)
Fredrica S. Friedman and Co. Inc. (*US*)
Furniss Lawton (*UK*)
Don Gastwirth & Associates (*US*)
The Susan Golomb Literary Agency (*US*)
Graham Maw Christie Literary Agency (*UK*)
Ashley Grayson Literary Agency (*US*)
Kathryn Green Literary Agency, LLC (*US*)
Sanford J. Greenburger Associates, Inc (*US*)
The Mitchell J. Hamilburg Agency (*US*)
Antony Harwood Limited (*UK*)
Heacock Hill Literary Agency, LLC (*US*)
hhb agency ltd (*UK*)
Hidden Value Group (*US*)
Andrea Hurst Literary Management (*US*)
J de S Associates Inc (*US*)
Jill Grinberg Literary Management LLC (*US*)
Frances Kelly (*UK*)
Kilburn Literary Agency (*UK*)
The Knight Agency (*US*)
Linda Konner Literary Agency (*US*)
Elaine Koster Literary Agency LLC (*US*)
Larsen Pomada Literary Agents (*US*)
LaunchBooks Literary Agency (*US*)
Levine Greenberg Literary Agency, Inc. (*US*)
Literary Management Group, Inc. (*US*)
Sterling Lord Literistic, Inc. (*US*)
MacGregor Literary (*US*)
Carol Mann Agency (*US*)
Manus & Associates Literary Agency, Inc. (*US*)
Denise Marcil Literary Agency, Inc. (*US*)
The Martell Agency (*US*)
Martin Literary Management (*US*)
Margret McBride Literary Agency (*US*)
Doris S. Michaels Literary Agency, Inc. (*US*)
Northern Lights Literary Services (*US*)
Objective Entertainment (*US*)
P.S. Literary Agency (*Can*)
The Richard Parks Agency (*US*)
Kathi J. Paton Literary Agency (*US*)
James Peter Associates, Inc. (*US*)
Pinder Lane & Garon-Brooke Associates Ltd (*US*)
The Poynor Group (*US*)
Queen Literary Agency, Inc. (*US*)
Lynne Rabinoff Agency (*US*)
Rees Literary Agency (*US*)
The Amy Rennert Agency, Inc. (*US*)
RLR Associates (*US*)
Robert Dudley Agency (*UK*)
The Rudy Agency (*US*)
Marly Rusoff & Associates, Inc. (*US*)
Salkind Literary Agency (*US*)
Schiavone Literary Agency (*US*)
Jonathan Scott, Inc (*US*)
Lynn Seligman, Literary Agent (*US*)
Rebecca Strong International Literary Agency (*US*)
The Strothman Agency (*US*)
Stuart Krichevsky Literary Agency, Inc. (*US*)
The Stuart Agency (*US*)
The Swetky Agency and Associates (*US*)
Talcott Notch Literary (*US*)

Tessler Literary Agency (*US*)
Trident Media Group, LLC (*US*)
2M Literary Agency Ltd (*US*)
Veritas Literary Agency (*US*)
Beth Vesel Literary Agency (*US*)
Watson, Little Ltd (*UK*)
Waxman Leavell Literary Agency (*US*)
Whimsy Literary Agency, LLC (*US*)
Writers House UK (*UK*)
Writers House, LLC. (*US*)
Yates & Yates (*US*)
The Zack Company, Inc (*US*)

Cookery
The Agency Group, Ltd (*US*)
AP Watt at United Agents LLP (*UK*)
Bidnick & Company (*US*)
Vicky Bijur Literary Agency (*US*)
Sheree Bykofsky Associates, Inc. (*US*)
Castiglia Literary Agency (*US*)
Teresa Chris Literary Agency Ltd (*UK*)
Rosica Colin Ltd (*UK*)
Don Congdon Associates, Inc. (*US*)
CowlesRyan Agency (*US*)
Creative Authors Ltd (*UK*)
The Culinary Entertainment Agency (CEA) (*US*)
Caroline Davidson Literary Agency (*UK*)
Sandra Dijkstra Literary Agency (*US*)
Einstein Thompson Agency (*US*)
Ethan Ellenberg Literary Agency (*US*)
The Feldstein Agency (*UK*)
FinePrint Literary Management (*US*)
Folio Literary Management, LLC (*US*)
Jeanne Fredericks Literary Agency, Inc. (*US*)
Fredrica S. Friedman and Co. Inc. (*US*)
Furniss Lawton (*UK*)
Irene Goodman Literary Agency (*US*)
Kathryn Green Literary Agency, LLC (*US*)
Greene & Heaton Ltd (*UK*)
The Mitchell J. Hamilburg Agency (*US*)
Antony Harwood Limited (*UK*)
Rupert Heath Literary Agency (*UK*)
hhb agency ltd (*UK*)
Hill Nadell Literary Agency (*US*)
Andrea Hurst Literary Management (*US*)
Frances Kelly (*UK*)
Linda Konner Literary Agency (*US*)
Elaine Koster Literary Agency LLC (*US*)
Larsen Pomada Literary Agents (*US*)
Robert Lecker Agency (*Can*)
Lescher & Lescher (*US*)
Levine Greenberg Literary Agency, Inc. (*US*)
The Literary Group (*US*)
Lyons Literary LLC (*US*)
Kirsten Manges Literary Agency, LLC (*US*)
Objective Entertainment (*US*)
The Richard Parks Agency (*US*)
L. Perkins Associates (*US*)
James Peter Associates, Inc. (*US*)
Pinder Lane & Garon-Brooke Associates Ltd (*US*)
The Poynor Group (*US*)
Queen Literary Agency, Inc. (*US*)
Richford Becklow Literary Agency (*UK*)

RLR Associates (*US*)
Salkind Literary Agency (*US*)
Schiavone Literary Agency (*US*)
Jonathan Scott, Inc (*US*)
Scovil Galen Ghosh Literary Agency, Inc. (*US*)
Lynn Seligman, Literary Agent (*US*)
Sheil Land Associates Ltd (*UK*)
Valerie Smith, Literary Agent (*US*)
Robin Straus Agency, Inc. (*US*)
The Swetky Agency and Associates (*US*)
Talcott Notch Literary (*US*)
Tessler Literary Agency (*US*)
Thomas Moore Literary Agency (*UK*)
TriadaUS Literary Agency, Inc. (*US*)
2M Literary Agency Ltd (*US*)
Whimsy Literary Agency, LLC (*US*)
Dinah Wiener Ltd (*UK*)
Writers House UK (*UK*)
Writers House, LLC. (*US*)
The Zack Company, Inc (*US*)
Karen Gantz Zahler Literary Agency (*US*)
Helen Zimmermann Literary Agency (*US*)

Crafts
AVAnti Productions & Management (*UK*)
Teresa Chris Literary Agency Ltd (*UK*)
Creative Authors Ltd (*UK*)
The Epstein Literary Agency (*US*)
Jeanne Fredericks Literary Agency, Inc. (*US*)
The Gernert Company (*US*)
Graham Maw Christie Literary Agency (*UK*)
Antony Harwood Limited (*UK*)
Heacock Hill Literary Agency, LLC (*US*)
Levine Greenberg Literary Agency, Inc. (*US*)
MBA Literary Agents Ltd (*UK*)
The Richard Parks Agency (*US*)
Salkind Literary Agency (*US*)
Talcott Notch Literary (*US*)
Thomas Moore Literary Agency (*UK*)

Crime
Abela Literature (*Can*)
The Agency Group, Ltd (*US*)
The Ampersand Agency Ltd (*UK*)
AP Watt at United Agents LLP (*UK*)
Artellus Limited (*UK*)
Author Rights Agency (*Ire*)
AVAnti Productions & Management (*UK*)
Luigi Bonomi Associates Ltd (*UK*)
Paul Bresnick Literary Agency, LLC (*US*)
Jenny Brown Associates (*UK*)
Juliet Burton Literary Agency (*UK*)
Castiglia Literary Agency (*US*)
Mic Cheetham Literary Agency (*UK*)
Teresa Chris Literary Agency Ltd (*UK*)
Rosica Colin Ltd (*UK*)
Don Congdon Associates, Inc. (*US*)
Conville & Walsh Ltd (*UK*)
Coombs Moylett Literary Agency (*UK*)
Crawford Literary Agency (*US*)
Creative Authors Ltd (*UK*)
Curtis Brown Group Ltd (*UK*)
Diamond Kahn and Woods (DKW) Literary Agency Ltd (*UK*)
Diane Banks Associates Literary Agency (*UK*)

Jim Donovan Literary (*US*)
Dorian Literary Agency (DLA) (*UK*)
Edwards Fuglewicz (*UK*)
Einstein Thompson Agency (*US*)
Ethan Ellenberg Literary Agency (*US*)
Felicia Eth Literary Representation (*US*)
Farris Literary Agency, Inc. (*US*)
The Feldstein Agency (*UK*)
FinePrint Literary Management (*US*)
Folio Literary Management, LLC (*US*)
Fredrica S. Friedman and Co. Inc. (*US*)
Furniss Lawton (*UK*)
Don Gastwirth & Associates (*US*)
Ashley Grayson Literary Agency (*US*)
Kathryn Green Literary Agency, LLC (*US*)
Greene & Heaton Ltd (*UK*)
Gregory & Company, Authors' Agents (*UK*)
Jill Grosjean Literary Agency (*US*)
The Mitchell J. Hamilburg Agency (*US*)
Hardman & Swainson (*UK*)
Antony Harwood Limited (*UK*)
A M Heath & Company Limited, Author's
Agents (*UK*)
Rupert Heath Literary Agency (*UK*)
hhb agency ltd (*UK*)
Hidden Value Group (*US*)
Vanessa Holt Ltd (*UK*)
Hudson Agency (*US*)
Andrea Hurst Literary Management (*US*)
International Transactions, Inc. (*US*)
J de S Associates Inc (*US*)
Barbara S. Kouts, Literary Agent (*US*)
Larsen Pomada Literary Agents (*US*)
Robert Lecker Agency (*Can*)
Levine Greenberg Literary Agency, Inc. (*US*)
Lippincott Massie McQuilkin (*US*)
The Literary Group (*US*)
Andrew Lownie Literary Agency Ltd (*UK*)
Lyons Literary LLC (*US*)
MacGregor Literary (*US*)
Madeleine Milburn Literary Agency (*UK*)
Martin Literary Management (*US*)
McKernan Agency (*UK*)
Monteiro Rose Dravis Agency, Inc. (*US*)
Judith Murdoch Literary Agency (*UK*)
Niad Management (*US*)
Pinder Lane & Garon-Brooke Associates Ltd
(*US*)
Raines & Raines (*US*)
Richford Becklow Literary Agency (*UK*)
RLR Associates (*US*)
Salkind Literary Agency (*US*)
The Sayle Literary Agency (*UK*)
Schiavone Literary Agency (*US*)
Secret Agent Man (*US*)
Lynn Seligman, Literary Agent (*US*)
The Seven Bridges Group (*US*)
Sheil Land Associates Ltd (*UK*)
Signature Literary Agency (*US*)
Jeffrey Simmons (*UK*)
Robert Smith Literary Agency Ltd (*UK*)
The Swetky Agency and Associates (*US*)
SYLA – Susan Yearwood Literary Agency (*UK*)

Talcott Notch Literary (*US*)
Patricia Teal Literary Agency (*US*)
Tom Lee (*US*)
TriadaUS Literary Agency, Inc. (*US*)
Trident Media Group, LLC (*US*)
2M Literary Agency Ltd (*US*)
Veritas Literary Agency (*US*)
Beth Vesel Literary Agency (*US*)
Watson, Little Ltd (*UK*)
Irene Webb Literary (*US*)
William Morris Endeavor (WME) London (*UK*)
The Zack Company, Inc (*US*)

Criticism
AVAnti Productions & Management (*UK*)
The Feldstein Agency (*UK*)
Antony Harwood Limited (*UK*)
Hidden Value Group (*US*)
Signature Literary Agency (*US*)
The Swetky Agency and Associates (*US*)
Beth Vesel Literary Agency (*US*)

Culture
The Agency Group, Ltd (*US*)
Ambassador Speakers Bureau & Literary
Agency (*US*)
Artellus Limited (*UK*)
Robert Astle & Associates Literary
Management, Inc. (*US*)
AVAnti Productions & Management (*UK*)
Barer Literary, LLC (*US*)
Brandt & Hochman Literary Agents, Inc. (*US*)
Paul Bresnick Literary Agency, LLC (*US*)
Jenny Brown Associates (*UK*)
Sheree Bykofsky Associates, Inc. (*US*)
Maria Carvainis Agency, Inc. (*US*)
Castiglia Literary Agency (*US*)
Elyse Cheney Literary Associates, LLC (*US*)
Cine/Lit Representation (*US*)
W.M. Clark Associates (*US*)
Frances Collin Literary Agent (*US*)
Don Congdon Associates, Inc. (*US*)
CowlesRyan Agency (*US*)
The Creative Rights Agency (*UK*)
Creative Authors Ltd (*UK*)
David Luxton Associates (*UK*)
Caroline Davidson Literary Agency (*UK*)
DeFiore and Company (*US*)
Diamond Kahn and Woods (DKW) Literary
Agency Ltd (*UK*)
Diane Banks Associates Literary Agency (*UK*)
Sandra Dijkstra Literary Agency (*US*)
Donadio & Olson, Inc. (*US*)
Jim Donovan Literary (*US*)
Dunham Literary, Inc. (*US*)
Dunow, Carlson & Lerner Agency (*US*)
Edwards Fuglewicz (*UK*)
Judith Ehrlich Literary Management (*US*)
Einstein Thompson Agency (*US*)
Ethan Ellenberg Literary Agency (*US*)
Ann Elmo Agency, Inc. (*US*)
Felicia Eth Literary Representation (*US*)
Farris Literary Agency, Inc. (*US*)
FinePrint Literary Management (*US*)
The James Fitzgerald Agency (*US*)

Current Affairs

Kathryn Green Literary Agency, LLC (*US*)
Greene & Heaton Ltd (*UK*)
Laura Gross Literary Agency (*US*)
The Mitchell J. Hamilburg Agency (*US*)
Antony Harwood Limited (*UK*)
Rupert Heath Literary Agency (*UK*)
David Higham Associates Ltd (*UK*)
Hill Nadell Literary Agency (*US*)
Andrea Hurst Literary Management (*US*)
J de S Associates Inc (*US*)
Jill Grinberg Literary Management LLC (*US*)
Johnson & Alcock (*UK*)
Elaine Koster Literary Agency LLC (*US*)
Barbara S. Kouts, Literary Agent (*US*)
Edite Kroll Literary Agency, Inc. (*US*)
Larsen Pomada Literary Agents (*US*)
LaunchBooks Literary Agency (*US*)
Sarah Lazin Books (*US*)
Lescher & Lescher (*US*)
Lippincott Massie McQuilkin (*US*)
The Literary Group (*US*)
Sterling Lord Literistic, Inc. (*US*)
Andrew Lownie Literary Agency Ltd (*UK*)
Lyons Literary LLC (*US*)
Gina Maccoby Agency (*US*)
MacGregor Literary (*US*)
Carol Mann Agency (*US*)
Manus & Associates Literary Agency, Inc. (*US*)
Martin Literary Management (*US*)
McIntosh & Otis, Inc (*US*)
McKernan Agency (*UK*)
Doris S. Michaels Literary Agency, Inc. (*US*)
The Jean V. Naggar Literary Agency (*US*)
Objective Entertainment (*US*)
P.S. Literary Agency (*Can*)
The Richard Parks Agency (*US*)
Kathi J. Paton Literary Agency (*US*)
Maggie Pearlstine Associates Ltd (*UK*)
Jonathan Pegg Literary Agency (*UK*)
Pinder Lane & Garon-Brooke Associates Ltd (*US*)
Alièka Pistek Literary Agency, LLC (*US*)
Lynne Rabinoff Agency (*US*)
Redhammer (*UK*)
RLR Associates (*US*)
Robert Dudley Agency (*UK*)
Andy Ross Agency (*US*)
Salkind Literary Agency (*US*)
The Sayle Literary Agency (*UK*)
The Science Factory (*UK*)
Lynn Seligman, Literary Agent (*US*)
The Seven Bridges Group (*US*)
Signature Literary Agency (*US*)
Jeffrey Simmons (*UK*)
Sinclair-Stevenson (*UK*)
Robert Smith Literary Agency Ltd (*UK*)
Philip G. Spitzer Literary Agency, Inc. (*US*)
Robin Straus Agency, Inc. (*US*)
The Strothman Agency (*US*)
Stuart Krichevsky Literary Agency, Inc. (*US*)
The Stuart Agency (*US*)
The Swetky Agency and Associates (*US*)
TriadaUS Literary Agency, Inc. (*US*)

Trident Media Group, LLC (*US*)
Jane Turnbull (*UK*)
Watkins / Loomis Agency, Inc. (*US*)
The Wendy Weil Agency, Inc. (*US*)
Westwood Creative Artists (*Can*)
Yates & Yates (*US*)
The Zack Company, Inc (*US*)
Design
The Agency Group, Ltd (*US*)
Castiglia Literary Agency (*US*)
W.M. Clark Associates (*US*)
Caroline Davidson Literary Agency (*UK*)
Sandra Dijkstra Literary Agency (*US*)
Jeanne Fredericks Literary Agency, Inc. (*US*)
Fresh Books Literary Agency (*US*)
Fredrica S. Friedman and Co. Inc. (*US*)
Kathryn Green Literary Agency, LLC (*US*)
Antony Harwood Limited (*UK*)
Johnson & Alcock (*UK*)
Larsen Pomada Literary Agents (*US*)
Carol Mann Agency (*US*)
Marly Rusoff & Associates, Inc. (*US*)
Lynn Seligman, Literary Agent (*US*)
The Swetky Agency and Associates (*US*)
Thomas Moore Literary Agency (*UK*)
Whispering Buffalo Literary Agency Ltd (*UK*)
Karen Gantz Zahler Literary Agency (*US*)
Drama
Abela Literature (*Can*)
Robert Astle & Associates Literary Management, Inc. (*US*)
AVAnti Productions & Management (*UK*)
Jill Foster Ltd (JFL) (*UK*)
Full Throttle Literary Agency (*US*)
Antony Harwood Limited (*UK*)
Hudson Agency (*US*)
Monteiro Rose Dravis Agency, Inc. (*US*)
Niad Management (*US*)
PBJ and JBJ Management (*UK*)
Barry Perelman Agency (*US*)
The Seven Bridges Group (*US*)
Sheil Land Associates Ltd (*UK*)
The Tennyson Agency (*UK*)
Thomas Moore Literary Agency (*UK*)
Tom Lee (*US*)
Cecily Ware Literary Agents (*UK*)
Entertainment
The Agency Group, Ltd (*US*)
Artellus Limited (*UK*)
AVAnti Productions & Management (*UK*)
The Bright Literary Academy (*UK*)
Crawford Literary Agency (*US*)
Diane Banks Associates Literary Agency (*UK*)
Farris Literary Agency, Inc. (*US*)
FinePrint Literary Management (*US*)
Folio Literary Management, LLC (*US*)
Sanford J. Greenburger Associates, Inc (*US*)
Antony Harwood Limited (*UK*)
hhb agency ltd (*UK*)
The Knight Agency (*US*)
Linda Konner Literary Agency (*US*)
Robert Lecker Agency (*Can*)
Lyons Literary LLC (*US*)

Gina Maccoby Agency (*US*)
Martin Literary Management (*US*)
New Leaf Literary & Media, Inc. (*US*)
Pinder Lane & Garon-Brooke Associates Ltd (*US*)
Susan Rabiner, Literary Agent, Inc. (*US*)
The Seven Bridges Group (*US*)
Jeffrey Simmons (*UK*)
Thomas Moore Literary Agency (*UK*)
Jane Turnbull (*UK*)
Waxman Leavell Literary Agency (*US*)
Whimsy Literary Agency, LLC (*US*)
Whispering Buffalo Literary Agency Ltd (*UK*)
The Zack Company, Inc (*US*)
Karen Gantz Zahler Literary Agency (*US*)

Erotic
Brown Literary Agency (*US*)
Rosica Colin Ltd (*UK*)
Elaine P. English, Attorney & Literary Agent (*US*)
Antony Harwood Limited (*UK*)
Robert Lecker Agency (*Can*)
New Leaf Literary & Media, Inc. (*US*)
L. Perkins Associates (*US*)
Pinder Lane & Garon-Brooke Associates Ltd (*US*)
Spencerhill Associates (*US*)
The Swetky Agency and Associates (*US*)
Tom Lee (*US*)
Veritas Literary Agency (*US*)
The Zack Company, Inc (*US*)

Fantasy
Abela Literature (*Can*)
The Ampersand Agency Ltd (*UK*)
Artellus Limited (*UK*)
Author Rights Agency (*Ire*)
AVAnti Productions & Management (*UK*)
Mic Cheetham Literary Agency (*UK*)
Rosica Colin Ltd (*UK*)
Frances Collin Literary Agent (*US*)
Curtis Brown Group Ltd (*UK*)
Diamond Kahn and Woods (DKW) Literary Agency Ltd (*UK*)
Sandra Dijkstra Literary Agency (*US*)
Dorian Literary Agency (DLA) (*UK*)
Dunham Literary, Inc. (*US*)
Judith Ehrlich Literary Management (*US*)
Ethan Ellenberg Literary Agency (*US*)
Elaine P. English, Attorney & Literary Agent (*US*)
FinePrint Literary Management (*US*)
Folio Literary Management, LLC (*US*)
Furniss Lawton (*UK*)
The Gernert Company (*US*)
Irene Goodman Literary Agency (*US*)
Ashley Grayson Literary Agency (*US*)
Sanford J. Greenburger Associates, Inc (*US*)
The Mitchell J. Hamilburg Agency (*US*)
Antony Harwood Limited (*UK*)
Hidden Value Group (*US*)
Hudson Agency (*US*)
Andrea Hurst Literary Management (*US*)
Jill Grinberg Literary Management LLC (*US*)

Virginia Kidd Agency, Inc (*US*)
The Knight Agency (*US*)
Larsen Pomada Literary Agents (*US*)
The Literary Group (*US*)
London Independent Books (*UK*)
Andrew Lownie Literary Agency Ltd (*UK*)
Lyons Literary LLC (*US*)
McIntosh & Otis, Inc (*US*)
Howard Morhaim Literary Agency (*US*)
The Jean V. Naggar Literary Agency (*US*)
New Leaf Literary & Media, Inc. (*US*)
Objective Entertainment (*US*)
Pavilion Literary Management (*US*)
L. Perkins Associates (*US*)
Pinder Lane & Garon-Brooke Associates Ltd (*US*)
Linn Prentis Literary (*US*)
Raines & Raines (*US*)
Richford Becklow Literary Agency (*UK*)
Salkind Literary Agency (*US*)
Schiavone Literary Agency (*US*)
Scribe Agency LLC (*US*)
Lynn Seligman, Literary Agent (*US*)
Sheil Land Associates Ltd (*UK*)
Valerie Smith, Literary Agent (*US*)
Spectrum Literary Agency (*US*)
Spencerhill Associates (*US*)
Stuart Krichevsky Literary Agency, Inc. (*US*)
The Swetky Agency and Associates (*US*)
Talcott Notch Literary (*US*)
Tom Lee (*US*)
Veritas Literary Agency (*US*)
Waxman Leavell Literary Agency (*US*)
Writers House UK (*UK*)
Writers House, LLC. (*US*)
The Zack Company, Inc (*US*)

Fiction
A & B Personal Management Ltd (*UK*)
A+B Works (*US*)
Dominick Abel Literary Agency, Inc (*US*)
Abela Literature (*Can*)
Adams Literary (*US*)
The Agency (London) Ltd (*UK*)
The Agency Group, Ltd (*US*)
Agency for the Performing Arts (APA) (*US*)
Aimee Entertainment Agency (*US*)
Aitken Alexander Associates (*UK*)
Ambassador Speakers Bureau & Literary Agency (*US*)
The Ampersand Agency Ltd (*UK*)
Darley Anderson Children's (*UK*)
Anne Clark Literary Agency (*UK*)
AP Watt at United Agents LLP (*UK*)
Artellus Limited (*UK*)
Robert Astle & Associates Literary Management, Inc. (*US*)
Author Literary Agents (*UK*)
Author Rights Agency (*Ire*)
AVAnti Productions & Management (*UK*)
Avenue A Literary LLC (*US*)
Barbara Hogenson Agency (*US*)
Barer Literary, LLC (*US*)
Bell Lomax Moreton Agency (*UK*)

Lorella Belli Literary Agency (LBLA) (*UK*)
Vicky Bijur Literary Agency (*US*)
The Blair Partnership (*UK*)
Blake Friedmann Literary Agency Ltd (*UK*)
Luigi Bonomi Associates Ltd (*UK*)
Bookseeker Agency (*UK*)
Brandt & Hochman Literary Agents, Inc. (*US*)
The Helen Brann Agency, Inc. (*US*)
Paul Bresnick Literary Agency, LLC (*US*)
The Bright Literary Academy (*UK*)
Jenny Brown Associates (*UK*)
Brown Literary Agency (*US*)
Tracy Brown Literary Agency (*US*)
Felicity Bryan (*UK*)
Marcus Bryan & Associates Inc. (*US*)
Brie Burkeman & Serafina Clarke Ltd (*UK*)
Juliet Burton Literary Agency (*UK*)
Sheree Bykofsky Associates, Inc. (*US*)
Capel & Land Ltd (*UK*)
CardenWright Literary Agency (*UK*)
Maria Carvainis Agency, Inc. (*US*)
Castiglia Literary Agency (*US*)
Celia Catchpole (*UK*)
Mic Cheetham Literary Agency (*UK*)
Elyse Cheney Literary Associates, LLC (*US*)
Linda Chester & Associates (*US*)
Teresa Chris Literary Agency Ltd (*UK*)
The Chudney Agency (*US*)
Cine/Lit Representation (*US*)
W.M. Clark Associates (*US*)
Mary Clemmey Literary Agency (*UK*)
Jonathan Clowes Ltd (*UK*)
Rosica Colin Ltd (*UK*)
Frances Collin Literary Agent (*US*)
Don Congdon Associates, Inc. (*US*)
Conville & Walsh Ltd (*UK*)
Jane Conway-Gordon Ltd (*UK*)
Coombs Moylett Literary Agency (*UK*)
CowlesRyan Agency (*US*)
Crawford Literary Agency (*US*)
The Creative Rights Agency (*UK*)
Creative Authors Ltd (*UK*)
Creative Trust, Inc. (*US*)
Rupert Crew Ltd (*UK*)
The Croce Agency (*US*)
The Mary Cunnane Agency Pty Ltd (*Aus*)
Curtis Brown Ltd (*US*)
Curtis Brown Group Ltd (*UK*)
Caroline Davidson Literary Agency (*UK*)
DeFiore and Company (*US*)
Felix de Wolfe (*UK*)
Diamond Kahn and Woods (DKW) Literary
Agency Ltd (*UK*)
Diane Banks Associates Literary Agency (*UK*)
Sandra Dijkstra Literary Agency (*US*)
Donadio & Olson, Inc. (*US*)
Jim Donovan Literary (*US*)
Dorian Literary Agency (DLA) (*UK*)
Dunham Literary, Inc. (*US*)
Dunow, Carlson & Lerner Agency (*US*)
Toby Eady Associates Ltd (*UK*)
Eames Literary Services, LLC (*US*)
East West Literary Agency LLC (*US*)

Eddison Pearson Ltd (*UK*)
Edwards Fuglewicz (*UK*)
Judith Ehrlich Literary Management (*US*)
Einstein Thompson Agency (*US*)
Elise Dillsworth Agency (EDA) (*UK*)
Elizabeth Roy Literary Agency (*UK*)
Ethan Ellenberg Literary Agency (*US*)
Nicholas Ellison, Inc. (*US*)
Ann Elmo Agency, Inc. (*US*)
Elaine P. English, Attorney & Literary Agent
(*US*)
Felicia Eth Literary Representation (*US*)
Faith Evans Associates (*UK*)
Mary Evans, Inc. (*US*)
Farris Literary Agency, Inc. (*US*)
The Feldstein Agency (*UK*)
Film Rights Ltd in association with Laurence
Fitch Ltd (*UK*)
FinePrint Literary Management (*US*)
The James Fitzgerald Agency (*US*)
Fletcher & Company (*US*)
Folio Literary Management, LLC (*US*)
Foundry Literary + Media (*US*)
Fox Chase Agency, Inc. (*US*)
Fraser Ross Associates (*UK*)
Fredrica S. Friedman and Co. Inc. (*US*)
Full Throttle Literary Agency (*US*)
Furniss Lawton (*UK*)
Nancy Gallt Literary Agency (*US*)
Don Gastwirth & Associates (*US*)
Gelfman Schneider Literary Agents, Inc. (*US*)
The Gernert Company (*US*)
Eric Glass Ltd (*UK*)
David Godwin Associates (*UK*)
Barry Goldblatt Literary Agency, Inc. (*US*)
The Susan Golomb Literary Agency (*US*)
Irene Goodman Literary Agency (*US*)
Ashley Grayson Literary Agency (*US*)
Christine Green Authors' Agent (*UK*)
Kathryn Green Literary Agency, LLC (*US*)
Louise Greenberg Books Ltd (*UK*)
Sanford J. Greenburger Associates, Inc (*US*)
Greene & Heaton Ltd (*UK*)
The Greenhouse Literary Agency (*UK*)
Gregory & Company, Authors' Agents (*UK*)
Blanche C. Gregory Inc. (*US*)
Greyhaus Literary Agency (*US*)
Jill Grosjean Literary Agency (*US*)
Laura Gross Literary Agency (*US*)
David Grossman Literary Agency Ltd (*UK*)
Marianne Gunn O'Connor Literary Agency (*Ire*)
Gunn Media Associates (*UK*)
The Mitchell J. Hamilburg Agency (*US*)
Hardman & Swainson (*UK*)
Antony Harwood Limited (*UK*)
Heacock Hill Literary Agency, LLC (*US*)
A M Heath & Company Limited, Author's
Agents (*UK*)
Rupert Heath Literary Agency (*UK*)
The Helen Heller Agency (*Can*)
hhb agency ltd (*UK*)
Hidden Value Group (*US*)
David Higham Associates Ltd (*UK*)

The Swetky Agency and Associates (*US*)
The Tennyson Agency (*UK*)
Thomas Moore Literary Agency (*UK*)
Tom Lee (*US*)
Trident Media Group, LLC (*US*)
2M Literary Agency Ltd (*US*)
United Agents (*UK*)
Cecily Ware Literary Agents (*UK*)
Watson, Little Ltd (*UK*)
Whispering Buffalo Literary Agency Ltd (*UK*)
The Zack Company, Inc (*US*)

Finance
The Agency Group, Ltd (*US*)
Ambassador Speakers Bureau & Literary
Agency (*US*)
Audrey A. Wolf Literary Agency (*US*)
Jenny Brown Associates (*UK*)
Maria Carvainis Agency, Inc. (*US*)
Castiglia Literary Agency (*US*)
Elyse Cheney Literary Associates, LLC (*US*)
Jim Donovan Literary (*US*)
Felicia Eth Literary Representation (*US*)
Farris Literary Agency, Inc. (*US*)
Jeanne Fredericks Literary Agency, Inc. (*US*)
Fresh Books Literary Agency (*US*)
Fredrica S. Friedman and Co. Inc. (*US*)
The Susan Golomb Literary Agency (*US*)
Ashley Grayson Literary Agency (*US*)
Kathryn Green Literary Agency, LLC (*US*)
The Mitchell J. Hamilburg Agency (*US*)
Antony Harwood Limited (*UK*)
Hidden Value Group (*US*)
J de S Associates Inc (*US*)
Jill Grinberg Literary Management LLC (*US*)
Frances Kelly (*UK*)
The Knight Agency (*US*)
Linda Konner Literary Agency (*US*)
Elaine Koster Literary Agency LLC (*US*)
Larsen Pomada Literary Agents (*US*)
Levine Greenberg Literary Agency, Inc. (*US*)
Andrew Lownie Literary Agency Ltd (*UK*)
MacGregor Literary (*US*)
Carol Mann Agency (*US*)
Manus & Associates Literary Agency, Inc. (*US*)
The Martell Agency (*US*)
The Richard Parks Agency (*US*)
Kathi J. Paton Literary Agency (*US*)
James Peter Associates, Inc. (*US*)
The Poynor Group (*US*)
Susan Rabiner, Literary Agent, Inc. (*US*)
Lynne Rabinoff Agency (*US*)
Raines & Raines (*US*)
The Amy Rennert Agency, Inc. (*US*)
Marly Rusoff & Associates, Inc. (*US*)
Salkind Literary Agency (*US*)
Schiavone Literary Agency (*US*)
Lynn Seligman, Literary Agent (*US*)
The Swetky Agency and Associates (*US*)
Beth Vesel Literary Agency (*US*)
Writers House UK (*UK*)
Writers House, LLC. (*US*)
The Zack Company, Inc (*US*)

Gardening
AP Watt at United Agents LLP (*UK*)
Teresa Chris Literary Agency Ltd (*UK*)
Rosica Colin Ltd (*UK*)
Caroline Davidson Literary Agency (*UK*)
Jeanne Fredericks Literary Agency, Inc. (*US*)
Greene & Heaton Ltd (*UK*)
Jill Grosjean Literary Agency (*US*)
The Mitchell J. Hamilburg Agency (*US*)
Antony Harwood Limited (*UK*)
Heacock Hill Literary Agency, LLC (*US*)
Levine Greenberg Literary Agency, Inc. (*US*)
The Richard Parks Agency (*US*)
Richford Becklow Literary Agency (*UK*)
Sheil Land Associates Ltd (*UK*)
The Swetky Agency and Associates (*US*)
Talcott Notch Literary (*US*)
Thomas Moore Literary Agency (*UK*)
Jane Turnbull (*UK*)
The Zack Company, Inc (*US*)

Gothic
Abela Literature (*Can*)
AVAnti Productions & Management (*UK*)
Diamond Kahn and Woods (DKW) Literary
Agency Ltd (*UK*)
Ann Elmo Agency, Inc. (*US*)
Elaine P. English, Attorney & Literary Agent
(*US*)
Antony Harwood Limited (*UK*)
The Jean V. Naggar Literary Agency (*US*)
Richford Becklow Literary Agency (*UK*)
The Swetky Agency and Associates (*US*)

Health
The Agency Group, Ltd (*US*)
Ambassador Speakers Bureau & Literary
Agency (*US*)
AP Watt at United Agents LLP (*UK*)
Audrey A. Wolf Literary Agency (*US*)
Vicky Bijur Literary Agency (*US*)
Luigi Bonomi Associates Ltd (*UK*)
Brandt & Hochman Literary Agents, Inc. (*US*)
Paul Bresnick Literary Agency, LLC (*US*)
Tracy Brown Literary Agency (*US*)
Castiglia Literary Agency (*US*)
Rosica Colin Ltd (*UK*)
Don Congdon Associates, Inc. (*US*)
Creative Authors Ltd (*UK*)
Caroline Davidson Literary Agency (*UK*)
Diane Banks Associates Literary Agency (*UK*)
Sandra Dijkstra Literary Agency (*US*)
Jim Donovan Literary (*US*)
Ebeling & Associates (*US*)
Judith Ehrlich Literary Management (*US*)
Einstein Thompson Agency (*US*)
Ethan Ellenberg Literary Agency (*US*)
Ann Elmo Agency, Inc. (*US*)
Felicia Eth Literary Representation (*US*)
Farris Literary Agency, Inc. (*US*)
FinePrint Literary Management (*US*)
Fletcher & Company (*US*)
Folio Literary Management, LLC (*US*)
Foundry Literary + Media (*US*)
Fox & Howard Literary Agency (*UK*)

Jeanne Fredericks Literary Agency, Inc. (*US*)
Fresh Books Literary Agency (*US*)
Fredrica S. Friedman and Co. Inc. (*US*)
The Susan Golomb Literary Agency (*US*)
Graham Maw Christie Literary Agency (*UK*)
Ashley Grayson Literary Agency (*US*)
Kathryn Green Literary Agency, LLC (*US*)
Sanford J. Greenburger Associates, Inc (*US*)
Greene & Heaton Ltd (*UK*)
Laura Gross Literary Agency (*US*)
Marianne Gunn O'Connor Literary Agency (*Ire*)
The Mitchell J. Hamilburg Agency (*US*)
Antony Harwood Limited (*UK*)
Heacock Hill Literary Agency, LLC (*US*)
Hill Nadell Literary Agency (*US*)
J de S Associates Inc (*US*)
Jill Grinberg Literary Management LLC (*US*)
Johnson & Alcock (*UK*)
Frances Kelly (*UK*)
Kilburn Literary Agency (*UK*)
The Knight Agency (*US*)
Linda Konner Literary Agency (*US*)
Elaine Koster Literary Agency LLC (*US*)
Barbara S. Kouts, Literary Agent (*US*)
Edite Kroll Literary Agency, Inc. (*US*)
Larsen Pomada Literary Agents (*US*)
Levine Greenberg Literary Agency, Inc. (*US*)
The Literary Group (*US*)
Sterling Lord Literistic, Inc. (*US*)
Andrew Lownie Literary Agency Ltd (*UK*)
Lyons Literary LLC (*US*)
Gina Maccoby Agency (*US*)
Kirsten Manges Literary Agency, LLC (*US*)
Carol Mann Agency (*US*)
Manus & Associates Literary Agency, Inc. (*US*)
Denise Marcil Literary Agency, Inc. (*US*)
The Martell Agency (*US*)
Martin Literary Management (*US*)
MBA Literary Agents Ltd (*UK*)
Margret McBride Literary Agency (*US*)
Doris S. Michaels Literary Agency, Inc. (*US*)
Howard Morhaim Literary Agency (*US*)
The Jean V. Naggar Literary Agency (*US*)
Northern Lights Literary Services (*US*)
P.S. Literary Agency (*Can*)
The Richard Parks Agency (*US*)
Kathi J. Paton Literary Agency (*US*)
Maggie Pearlstine Associates Ltd (*UK*)
James Peter Associates, Inc. (*US*)
Pinder Lane & Garon-Brooke Associates Ltd (*US*)
The Poynor Group (*US*)
Redhammer (*UK*)
The Amy Rennert Agency, Inc. (*US*)
RLR Associates (*US*)
The Rudy Agency (*US*)
Marly Rusoff & Associates, Inc. (*US*)
Salkind Literary Agency (*US*)
Schiavone Literary Agency (*US*)
Jonathan Scott, Inc (*US*)
Scovil Galen Ghosh Literary Agency, Inc. (*US*)
Lynn Seligman, Literary Agent (*US*)
Robert Smith Literary Agency Ltd (*UK*)

Rebecca Strong International Literary Agency (*US*)
The Stuart Agency (*US*)
The Swetky Agency and Associates (*US*)
Patricia Teal Literary Agency (*US*)
TriadaUS Literary Agency, Inc. (*US*)
Trident Media Group, LLC (*US*)
2M Literary Agency Ltd (*US*)
Veritas Literary Agency (*US*)
Beth Vesel Literary Agency (*US*)
Irene Webb Literary (*US*)
The Wendy Weil Agency, Inc. (*US*)
Whimsy Literary Agency, LLC (*US*)
Whispering Buffalo Literary Agency Ltd (*UK*)
The Zack Company, Inc (*US*)
Helen Zimmermann Literary Agency (*US*)

Historical

Abela Literature (*Can*)
Sheila Ableman Literary Agency (*UK*)
The Agency Group, Ltd (*US*)
Ambassador Speakers Bureau & Literary Agency (*US*)
The Ampersand Agency Ltd (*UK*)
AP Watt at United Agents LLP (*UK*)
Artellus Limited (*UK*)
Robert Astle & Associates Literary Management, Inc. (*US*)
Audrey A. Wolf Literary Agency (*US*)
Author Rights Agency (*Ire*)
AVAnti Productions & Management (*UK*)
Barer Literary, LLC (*US*)
Vicky Bijur Literary Agency (*US*)
Luigi Bonomi Associates Ltd (*UK*)
Brandt & Hochman Literary Agents, Inc. (*US*)
Paul Bresnick Literary Agency, LLC (*US*)
Jenny Brown Associates (*UK*)
Brown Literary Agency (*US*)
Tracy Brown Literary Agency (*US*)
Felicity Bryan (*UK*)
Capel & Land Ltd (*UK*)
Maria Carvainis Agency, Inc. (*US*)
Mic Cheetham Literary Agency (*UK*)
Elyse Cheney Literary Associates, LLC (*US*)
Teresa Chris Literary Agency Ltd (*UK*)
The Chudney Agency (*US*)
W.M. Clark Associates (*US*)
Rosica Colin Ltd (*UK*)
Frances Collin Literary Agent (*US*)
Don Congdon Associates, Inc. (*US*)
Conville & Walsh Ltd (*UK*)
Coombs Moylett Literary Agency (*UK*)
CowlesRyan Agency (*US*)
Creative Authors Ltd (*UK*)
The Croce Agency (*US*)
Curtis Brown Group Ltd (*UK*)
David Luxton Associates (*UK*)
Caroline Davidson Literary Agency (*UK*)
DeFiore and Company (*US*)
Diamond Kahn and Woods (DKW) Literary Agency Ltd (*UK*)
Diane Banks Associates Literary Agency (*UK*)
Sandra Dijkstra Literary Agency (*US*)
Donadio & Olson, Inc. (*US*)

Jim Donovan Literary (US)
Dorian Literary Agency (DLA) (UK)
Dunham Literary, Inc. (US)
Edwards Fuglewicz (UK)
Judith Ehrlich Literary Management (US)
Einstein Thompson Agency (US)
Ethan Ellenberg Literary Agency (US)
Ann Elmo Agency, Inc. (US)
Elaine P. English, Attorney & Literary Agent (US)
Felicia Eth Literary Representation (US)
Farris Literary Agency, Inc. (US)
The Feldstein Agency (UK)
FinePrint Literary Management (US)
Fletcher & Company (US)
Folio Literary Management, LLC (US)
Foundry Literary + Media (US)
Fox & Howard Literary Agency (UK)
Jeanne Fredericks Literary Agency, Inc. (US)
Fredrica S. Friedman and Co. Inc. (US)
Furniss Lawton (UK)
Don Gastwirth & Associates (US)
Gelfman Schneider Literary Agents, Inc. (US)
The Gernert Company (US)
The Susan Golomb Literary Agency (US)
Irene Goodman Literary Agency (US)
Graham Maw Christie Literary Agency (UK)
Ashley Grayson Literary Agency (US)
Kathryn Green Literary Agency, LLC (US)
Sanford J. Greenburger Associates, Inc (US)
Greene & Heaton Ltd (UK)
Gregory & Company, Authors' Agents (UK)
Greyhaus Literary Agency (US)
Jill Grosjean Literary Agency (US)
Laura Gross Literary Agency (US)
The Mitchell J. Hamilburg Agency (US)
Antony Harwood Limited (UK)
Rupert Heath Literary Agency (UK)
hhb agency ltd (UK)
Hidden Value Group (US)
David Higham Associates Ltd (UK)
Hill Nadell Literary Agency (US)
Andrea Hurst Literary Management (US)
International Transactions, Inc. (US)
J de S Associates Inc (US)
Jill Grinberg Literary Management LLC (US)
Johnson & Alcock (UK)
Frances Kelly (UK)
Virginia Kidd Agency, Inc (US)
Elaine Koster Literary Agency LLC (US)
Barbara S. Kouts, Literary Agent (US)
Larsen Pomada Literary Agents (US)
LaunchBooks Literary Agency (US)
Sarah Lazin Books (US)
Robert Lecker Agency (Can)
Lescher & Lescher (US)
Levine Greenberg Literary Agency, Inc. (US)
Lippincott Massie McQuilkin (US)
The Literary Group (US)
Sterling Lord Literistic, Inc. (US)
Andrew Lownie Literary Agency Ltd (UK)
Lyons Literary LLC (US)
Gina Maccoby Agency (US)

MacGregor Literary (US)
Kirsten Manges Literary Agency, LLC (US)
Carol Mann Agency (US)
The Martell Agency (US)
MBA Literary Agents Ltd (UK)
Duncan McAra (UK)
McIntosh & Otis, Inc (US)
McKernan Agency (UK)
Doris S. Michaels Literary Agency, Inc. (US)
Monteiro Rose Dravis Agency, Inc. (US)
The Jean V. Naggar Literary Agency (US)
Nappaland Literary Agency (US)
New Leaf Literary & Media, Inc. (US)
MNLA (Maggie Noach Literary Agency) (UK)
Northern Lights Literary Services (US)
P.S. Literary Agency (Can)
The Park Literary Group LLC (US)
The Richard Parks Agency (US)
Kathi J. Paton Literary Agency (US)
Pavilion Literary Management (US)
Maggie Pearlstine Associates Ltd (UK)
Jonathan Pegg Literary Agency (UK)
Barry Perelman Agency (US)
L. Perkins Associates (US)
James Peter Associates, Inc. (US)
Pinder Lane & Garon-Brooke Associates Ltd (US)
Alièka Pistek Literary Agency, LLC (US)
Aaron M. Priest Literary Agency (US)
Queen Literary Agency, Inc. (US)
Susan Rabiner, Literary Agent, Inc. (US)
Lynne Rabinoff Agency (US)
Raines & Raines (US)
Rees Literary Agency (US)
Regal Literary (UK)
Regal Literary Inc. (US)
Renee Zuckerbrot Literary Agency (US)
The Amy Rennert Agency, Inc. (US)
The Lisa Richards Agency (Ire)
Richford Becklow Literary Agency (UK)
Ann Rittenberg Literary Agency (US)
RLR Associates (US)
Robert Dudley Agency (UK)
Linda Roghaar Literary Agency, Inc. (US)
Andy Ross Agency (US)
Jane Rotrosen Agency (US)
The Rudy Agency (US)
Marly Rusoff & Associates, Inc. (US)
The Sagalyn Literary Agency (US)
Salkind Literary Agency (US)
The Sayle Literary Agency (UK)
Schiavone Literary Agency (US)
The Science Factory (UK)
Jonathan Scott, Inc (US)
Scovil Galen Ghosh Literary Agency, Inc. (US)
Lynn Seligman, Literary Agent (US)
Sheil Land Associates Ltd (UK)
Signature Literary Agency (US)
Jeffrey Simmons (UK)
Sinclair-Stevenson (UK)
Robert Smith Literary Agency Ltd (UK)
Valerie Smith, Literary Agent (US)
Spectrum Literary Agency (US)

Philip G. Spitzer Literary Agency, Inc. (*US*)
Robin Straus Agency, Inc. (*US*)
Pam Strickler Author Management (*US*)
Rebecca Strong International Literary Agency
(*US*)
The Strothman Agency (*US*)
Stuart Krichevsky Literary Agency, Inc. (*US*)
The Stuart Agency (*US*)
The Swetky Agency and Associates (*US*)
Talcott Notch Literary (*US*)
Patricia Teal Literary Agency (*US*)
Tessler Literary Agency (*US*)
Thomas Moore Literary Agency (*UK*)
Tom Lee (*US*)
Trident Media Group, LLC (*US*)
Jane Turnbull (*UK*)
Veritas Literary Agency (*US*)
Watkins / Loomis Agency, Inc. (*US*)
Watson, Little Ltd (*UK*)
Waxman Leavell Literary Agency (*US*)
The Wendy Weil Agency, Inc. (*US*)
Westwood Creative Artists (*Can*)
William Morris Endeavor (WME) London (*UK*)
Writers House UK (*UK*)
Writers House, LLC. (*US*)
The Zack Company, Inc (*US*)
Karen Gantz Zahler Literary Agency (*US*)
Helen Zimmermann Literary Agency (*US*)
Hobbies
Sheree Bykofsky Associates, Inc. (*US*)
Antony Harwood Limited (*UK*)
Levine Greenberg Literary Agency, Inc. (*US*)
Lyons Literary LLC (*US*)
The Richard Parks Agency (*US*)
Horror
Abela Literature (*Can*)
The Ampersand Agency Ltd (*UK*)
Elyse Cheney Literary Associates, LLC (*US*)
Cine/Lit Representation (*US*)
Rosica Colin Ltd (*UK*)
Dorian Literary Agency (DLA) (*UK*)
Film Rights Ltd in association with Laurence
Fitch Ltd (*UK*)
FinePrint Literary Management (*US*)
Folio Literary Management, LLC (*US*)
Full Throttle Literary Agency (*US*)
The Mitchell J. Hamilburg Agency (*US*)
Antony Harwood Limited (*UK*)
The Literary Group (*US*)
Andrew Lownie Literary Agency Ltd (*UK*)
McIntosh & Otis, Inc (*US*)
The Jean V. Naggar Literary Agency (*US*)
Barry Perelman Agency (*US*)
L. Perkins Associates (*US*)
Pinder Lane & Garon-Brooke Associates Ltd
(*US*)
Aaron M. Priest Literary Agency (*US*)
Richford Becklow Literary Agency (*UK*)
RLR Associates (*US*)
Lynn Seligman, Literary Agent (*US*)
Talcott Notch Literary (*US*)
Tom Lee (*US*)
Irene Webb Literary (*US*)

The Zack Company, Inc (*US*)
How-to
The Agency Group, Ltd (*US*)
Ambassador Speakers Bureau & Literary
Agency (*US*)
Crawford Literary Agency (*US*)
Jim Donovan Literary (*US*)
Judith Ehrlich Literary Management (*US*)
Ann Elmo Agency, Inc. (*US*)
The Epstein Literary Agency (*US*)
Farris Literary Agency, Inc. (*US*)
FinePrint Literary Management (*US*)
Folio Literary Management, LLC (*US*)
Foundry Literary + Media (*US*)
Jeanne Fredericks Literary Agency, Inc. (*US*)
Fresh Books Literary Agency (*US*)
Fredrica S. Friedman and Co. Inc. (*US*)
Graham Maw Christie Literary Agency (*UK*)
Kathryn Green Literary Agency, LLC (*US*)
Antony Harwood Limited (*UK*)
Hidden Value Group (*US*)
Amanda Howard Associates Ltd (*UK*)
Andrea Hurst Literary Management (*US*)
J de S Associates Inc (*US*)
The Knight Agency (*US*)
Linda Konner Literary Agency (*US*)
Elaine Koster Literary Agency LLC (*US*)
Larsen Pomada Literary Agents (*US*)
Robert Lecker Agency (*Can*)
Andrew Lownie Literary Agency Ltd (*UK*)
Lyons Literary LLC (*US*)
MacGregor Literary (*US*)
Manus & Associates Literary Agency, Inc. (*US*)
Martin Literary Management (*US*)
Northern Lights Literary Services (*US*)
The Richard Parks Agency (*US*)
Aaron M. Priest Literary Agency (*US*)
Salkind Literary Agency (*US*)
Lynn Seligman, Literary Agent (*US*)
Valerie Smith, Literary Agent (*US*)
The Swetky Agency and Associates (*US*)
Patricia Teal Literary Agency (*US*)
Thomas Moore Literary Agency (*UK*)
TriadaUS Literary Agency, Inc. (*US*)
Beth Vesel Literary Agency (*US*)
Whimsy Literary Agency, LLC (*US*)
Writers House UK (*UK*)
Writers House, LLC. (*US*)
Helen Zimmermann Literary Agency (*US*)
Humour
The Agency Group, Ltd (*US*)
Robert Astle & Associates Literary
Management, Inc. (*US*)
AVAnti Productions & Management (*UK*)
Paul Bresnick Literary Agency, LLC (*US*)
Jenny Brown Associates (*UK*)
Brown Literary Agency (*US*)
Tracy Brown Literary Agency (*US*)
Sheree Bykofsky Associates, Inc. (*US*)
Rosica Colin Ltd (*UK*)
Don Congdon Associates, Inc. (*US*)
Conville & Walsh Ltd (*UK*)
Creative Authors Ltd (*UK*)

Sandra Dijkstra Literary Agency (*US*)
Edwards Fuglewicz (*UK*)
Judith Ehrlich Literary Management (*US*)
Einstein Thompson Agency (*US*)
Elaine P. English, Attorney & Literary Agent (*US*)
Farris Literary Agency, Inc. (*US*)
The Feldstein Agency (*UK*)
FinePrint Literary Management (*US*)
Fletcher & Company (*US*)
Folio Literary Management, LLC (*US*)
Jill Foster Ltd (JFL) (*UK*)
Foundry Literary + Media (*US*)
Fresh Books Literary Agency (*US*)
Fredrica S. Friedman and Co. Inc. (*US*)
Full Throttle Literary Agency (*US*)
The Susan Golomb Literary Agency (*US*)
Graham Maw Christie Literary Agency (*UK*)
Kathryn Green Literary Agency, LLC (*US*)
Sanford J. Greenburger Associates, Inc (*US*)
Greene & Heaton Ltd (*UK*)
Jill Grosjean Literary Agency (*US*)
The Mitchell J. Hamilburg Agency (*US*)
Antony Harwood Limited (*UK*)
hhb agency ltd (*UK*)
Amanda Howard Associates Ltd (*UK*)
Hudson Agency (*US*)
Andrea Hurst Literary Management (*US*)
Edite Kroll Literary Agency, Inc. (*US*)
Larsen Pomada Literary Agents (*US*)
LaunchBooks Literary Agency (*US*)
Levine Greenberg Literary Agency, Inc. (*US*)
Lippincott Massie McQuilkin (*US*)
The Literary Group (*US*)
Lyons Literary LLC (*US*)
MacGregor Literary (*US*)
Carol Mann Agency (*US*)
McIntosh & Otis, Inc (*US*)
Monteiro Rose Dravis Agency, Inc. (*US*)
The Jean V. Naggar Literary Agency (*US*)
Nappaland Literary Agency (*US*)
Niad Management (*US*)
P.S. Literary Agency (*Can*)
The Richard Parks Agency (*US*)
Kathi J. Paton Literary Agency (*US*)
PBJ and JBJ Management (*UK*)
L. Perkins Associates (*US*)
James Peter Associates, Inc. (*US*)
Pinder Lane & Garon-Brooke Associates Ltd (*US*)
Susan Rabiner, Literary Agent, Inc. (*US*)
The Lisa Richards Agency (*Ire*)
RLR Associates (*US*)
Salkind Literary Agency (*US*)
Lynn Seligman, Literary Agent (*US*)
Sheil Land Associates Ltd (*UK*)
Robert Smith Literary Agency Ltd (*UK*)
The Swetky Agency and Associates (*US*)
Trident Media Group, LLC (*US*)
Jane Turnbull (*UK*)
Cecily Ware Literary Agents (*UK*)
Watson, Little Ltd (*UK*)
Waxman Leavell Literary Agency (*US*)

Whimsy Literary Agency, LLC (*US*)
Whispering Buffalo Literary Agency Ltd (*UK*)
The Zack Company, Inc (*US*)
Helen Zimmermann Literary Agency (*US*)
Legal
The Agency Group, Ltd (*US*)
Ambassador Speakers Bureau & Literary Agency (*US*)
Don Congdon Associates, Inc. (*US*)
Crawford Literary Agency (*US*)
Jim Donovan Literary (*US*)
Judith Ehrlich Literary Management (*US*)
Felicia Eth Literary Representation (*US*)
Farris Literary Agency, Inc. (*US*)
Jeanne Fredericks Literary Agency, Inc. (*US*)
The Susan Golomb Literary Agency (*US*)
Laura Gross Literary Agency (*US*)
Antony Harwood Limited (*UK*)
Hill Nadell Literary Agency (*US*)
J de S Associates Inc (*US*)
Jill Grinberg Literary Management LLC (*US*)
Edite Kroll Literary Agency, Inc. (*US*)
Larsen Pomada Literary Agents (*US*)
Lescher & Lescher (*US*)
Lyons Literary LLC (*US*)
Carol Mann Agency (*US*)
The Richard Parks Agency (*US*)
Lynne Rabinoff Agency (*US*)
Jeffrey Simmons (*UK*)
The Swetky Agency and Associates (*US*)
Yates & Yates (*US*)
Leisure
Rosica Colin Ltd (*UK*)
Conville & Walsh Ltd (*UK*)
The Feldstein Agency (*UK*)
Jeanne Fredericks Literary Agency, Inc. (*US*)
The Mitchell J. Hamilburg Agency (*US*)
Antony Harwood Limited (*UK*)
Levine Greenberg Literary Agency, Inc. (*US*)
Lyons Literary LLC (*US*)
James Peter Associates, Inc. (*US*)
The Swetky Agency and Associates (*US*)
Watson, Little Ltd (*UK*)
Lifestyle
The Agency Group, Ltd (*US*)
Ambassador Speakers Bureau & Literary Agency (*US*)
Audrey A. Wolf Literary Agency (*US*)
Luigi Bonomi Associates Ltd (*UK*)
Brandt & Hochman Literary Agents, Inc. (*US*)
Paul Bresnick Literary Agency, LLC (*US*)
Sheree Bykofsky Associates, Inc. (*US*)
Castiglia Literary Agency (*US*)
Teresa Chris Literary Agency Ltd (*UK*)
Rosica Colin Ltd (*UK*)
Don Congdon Associates, Inc. (*US*)
Conville & Walsh Ltd (*UK*)
The Culinary Entertainment Agency (CEA) (*US*)
Caroline Davidson Literary Agency (*UK*)
DeFiore and Company (*US*)
Diane Banks Associates Literary Agency (*UK*)
Sandra Dijkstra Literary Agency (*US*)
Jim Donovan Literary (*US*)

Dunham Literary, Inc. (*US*)
Judith Ehrlich Literary Management (*US*)
Felicia Eth Literary Representation (*US*)
Farris Literary Agency, Inc. (*US*)
The Feldstein Agency (*UK*)
FinePrint Literary Management (*US*)
Fletcher & Company (*US*)
Folio Literary Management, LLC (*US*)
Foundry Literary + Media (*US*)
Fox & Howard Literary Agency (*UK*)
Jeanne Fredericks Literary Agency, Inc. (*US*)
Fresh Books Literary Agency (*US*)
Fredrica S. Friedman and Co. Inc. (*US*)
Irene Goodman Literary Agency (*US*)
Graham Maw Christie Literary Agency (*UK*)
Ashley Grayson Literary Agency (*US*)
Kathryn Green Literary Agency, LLC (*US*)
Sanford J. Greenburger Associates, Inc (*US*)
Laura Gross Literary Agency (*US*)
The Mitchell J. Hamilburg Agency (*US*)
Antony Harwood Limited (*UK*)
Heacock Hill Literary Agency, LLC (*US*)
Rupert Heath Literary Agency (*UK*)
Hidden Value Group (*US*)
J de S Associates Inc (*US*)
Johnson & Alcock (*UK*)
Frances Kelly (*UK*)
The Knight Agency (*US*)
Linda Konner Literary Agency (*US*)
Barbara S. Kouts, Literary Agent (*US*)
Larsen Pomada Literary Agents (*US*)
Levine Greenberg Literary Agency, Inc. (*US*)
Limelight Management (*UK*)
The Literary Group (*US*)
Literary Management Group, Inc. (*US*)
Sterling Lord Literistic, Inc. (*US*)
Andrew Lownie Literary Agency Ltd (*UK*)
Lyons Literary LLC (*US*)
Gina Maccoby Agency (*US*)
MacGregor Literary (*US*)
Carol Mann Agency (*US*)
Manus & Associates Literary Agency, Inc. (*US*)
Denise Marcil Literary Agency, Inc. (*US*)
Martin Literary Management (*US*)
MBA Literary Agents Ltd (*UK*)
Doris S. Michaels Literary Agency, Inc. (*US*)
The Jean V. Naggar Literary Agency (*US*)
Nappaland Literary Agency (*US*)
Northern Lights Literary Services (*US*)
Objective Entertainment (*US*)
The Richard Parks Agency (*US*)
Kathi J. Paton Literary Agency (*US*)
Jonathan Pegg Literary Agency (*UK*)
Redhammer (*UK*)
The Amy Rennert Agency, Inc. (*US*)
The Lisa Richards Agency (*Ire*)
Richford Becklow Literary Agency (*UK*)
Salkind Literary Agency (*US*)
Lynn Seligman, Literary Agent (*US*)
Sheil Land Associates Ltd (*UK*)
Robert Smith Literary Agency Ltd (*UK*)
Robin Straus Agency, Inc. (*US*)
The Stuart Agency (*US*)

Talcott Notch Literary (*US*)
Patricia Teal Literary Agency (*US*)
Thomas Moore Literary Agency (*UK*)
Trident Media Group, LLC (*US*)
Jane Turnbull (*UK*)
2M Literary Agency Ltd (*US*)
Veritas Literary Agency (*US*)
The Wendy Weil Agency, Inc. (*US*)
Whispering Buffalo Literary Agency Ltd (*UK*)
Writers House UK (*UK*)
Writers House, LLC. (*US*)
The Zack Company, Inc (*US*)
Karen Gantz Zahler Literary Agency (*US*)
Helen Zimmermann Literary Agency (*US*)

Literature

Abela Literature (*Can*)
AVAnti Productions & Management (*UK*)
The Bright Literary Academy (*UK*)
Elyse Cheney Literary Associates, LLC (*US*)
Don Congdon Associates, Inc. (*US*)
CowlesRyan Agency (*US*)
DeFiore and Company (*US*)
Donadio & Olson, Inc. (*US*)
Antony Harwood Limited (*UK*)
Hidden Value Group (*US*)
Michelle Kass Associates (*UK*)
Kilburn Literary Agency (*UK*)
Robert Lecker Agency (*Can*)
Andrew Lownie Literary Agency Ltd (*UK*)
Lyons Literary LLC (*US*)
Patricia Moosbrugger Literary Agency (*US*)
P.S. Literary Agency (*Can*)
Renee Zuckerbrot Literary Agency (*US*)
The Amy Rennert Agency, Inc. (*US*)
Richford Becklow Literary Agency (*UK*)
Scribe Agency LLC (*US*)
The Seven Bridges Group (*US*)
The Swetky Agency and Associates (*US*)
Thomas Moore Literary Agency (*UK*)
Tom Lee (*US*)

Media

Robert Astle & Associates Literary
Management, Inc. (*US*)
AVAnti Productions & Management (*UK*)
Crawford Literary Agency (*US*)
The Feldstein Agency (*UK*)
Folio Literary Management, LLC (*US*)
Antony Harwood Limited (*UK*)
The Knight Agency (*US*)
Andrew Lownie Literary Agency Ltd (*UK*)
Martin Literary Management (*US*)
Thomas Moore Literary Agency (*UK*)

Medicine

The Agency Group, Ltd (*US*)
Ambassador Speakers Bureau & Literary
Agency (*US*)
AP Watt at United Agents LLP (*UK*)
Don Congdon Associates, Inc. (*US*)
Crawford Literary Agency (*US*)
Caroline Davidson Literary Agency (*UK*)
DeFiore and Company (*US*)
Jim Donovan Literary (*US*)
Judith Ehrlich Literary Management (*US*)

Felicia Eth Literary Representation (*US*)
Jeanne Fredericks Literary Agency, Inc. (*US*)
Laura Gross Literary Agency (*US*)
Antony Harwood Limited (*UK*)
International Transactions, Inc. (*US*)
J de S Associates Inc (*US*)
Jill Grinberg Literary Management LLC (*US*)
Frances Kelly (*UK*)
Kilburn Literary Agency (*UK*)
Edite Kroll Literary Agency, Inc. (*US*)
Larsen Pomada Literary Agents (*US*)
Andrew Lownie Literary Agency Ltd (*UK*)
Carol Mann Agency (*US*)
The Martell Agency (*US*)
Northern Lights Literary Services (*US*)
The Richard Parks Agency (*US*)
The Poynor Group (*US*)
Robert Dudley Agency (*UK*)
The Rudy Agency (*US*)
Marly Rusoff & Associates, Inc. (*US*)
The Science Factory (*UK*)
The Swetky Agency and Associates (*US*)
2M Literary Agency Ltd (*US*)
Beth Vesel Literary Agency (*US*)
The Zack Company, Inc (*US*)
Men's Interests
AVAnti Productions & Management (*UK*)
Rosica Colin Ltd (*UK*)
Conville & Walsh Ltd (*UK*)
The Creative Rights Agency (*UK*)
Antony Harwood Limited (*UK*)
Andrew Lownie Literary Agency Ltd (*UK*)
Lyons Literary LLC (*US*)
The Seven Bridges Group (*US*)
Military
Artellus Limited (*UK*)
Rosica Colin Ltd (*UK*)
Don Congdon Associates, Inc. (*US*)
Conville & Walsh Ltd (*UK*)
DeFiore and Company (*US*)
Jim Donovan Literary (*US*)
Farris Literary Agency, Inc. (*US*)
The Feldstein Agency (*UK*)
FinePrint Literary Management (*US*)
Folio Literary Management, LLC (*US*)
Don Gastwirth & Associates (*US*)
The Susan Golomb Literary Agency (*US*)
The Mitchell J. Hamilburg Agency (*US*)
Antony Harwood Limited (*UK*)
J de S Associates Inc (*US*)
The Literary Group (*US*)
Andrew Lownie Literary Agency Ltd (*UK*)
Lyons Literary LLC (*US*)
Duncan McAra (*UK*)
The Richard Parks Agency (*US*)
Lynne Rabinoff Agency (*US*)
Raines & Raines (*US*)
Robert Dudley Agency (*UK*)
The Rudy Agency (*US*)
The Seven Bridges Group (*US*)
Sheil Land Associates Ltd (*UK*)
Signature Literary Agency (*US*)
Robert Smith Literary Agency Ltd (*UK*)

The Swetky Agency and Associates (*US*)
Waxman Leavell Literary Agency (*US*)
The Zack Company, Inc (*US*)
Music
The Agency Group, Ltd (*US*)
AP Watt at United Agents LLP (*UK*)
AVAnti Productions & Management (*UK*)
Jenny Brown Associates (*UK*)
W.M. Clark Associates (*US*)
Don Congdon Associates, Inc. (*US*)
DeFiore and Company (*US*)
Sandra Dijkstra Literary Agency (*US*)
Jim Donovan Literary (*US*)
Dunham Literary, Inc. (*US*)
Farris Literary Agency, Inc. (*US*)
The Feldstein Agency (*UK*)
FinePrint Literary Management (*US*)
Folio Literary Management, LLC (*US*)
Foundry Literary + Media (*US*)
Fredrica S. Friedman and Co. Inc. (*US*)
Don Gastwirth & Associates (*US*)
Sanford J. Greenburger Associates, Inc (*US*)
Antony Harwood Limited (*UK*)
Johnson & Alcock (*UK*)
Larsen Pomada Literary Agents (*US*)
Sarah Lazin Books (*US*)
Robert Lecker Agency (*Can*)
Andrew Lownie Literary Agency Ltd (*UK*)
Lyons Literary LLC (*US*)
Carol Mann Agency (*US*)
McIntosh & Otis, Inc (*US*)
Doris S. Michaels Literary Agency, Inc. (*US*)
The Jean V. Naggar Literary Agency (*US*)
Objective Entertainment (*US*)
The Richard Parks Agency (*US*)
L. Perkins Associates (*US*)
Pinder Lane & Garon-Brooke Associates Ltd
(*US*)
RLR Associates (*US*)
The Sayle Literary Agency (*UK*)
Lynn Seligman, Literary Agent (*US*)
The Seven Bridges Group (*US*)
Thomas Moore Literary Agency (*UK*)
Trident Media Group, LLC (*US*)
2M Literary Agency Ltd (*US*)
Watson, Little Ltd (*UK*)
The Weingel-Fidel Agency (*US*)
Whispering Buffalo Literary Agency Ltd (*UK*)
The Zack Company, Inc (*US*)
Helen Zimmermann Literary Agency (*US*)
Mystery
Abela Literature (*Can*)
Robert Astle & Associates Literary
Management, Inc. (*US*)
AVAnti Productions & Management (*UK*)
Brandt & Hochman Literary Agents, Inc. (*US*)
The Bright Literary Academy (*UK*)
Brown Literary Agency (*US*)
Sheree Bykofsky Associates, Inc. (*US*)
Maria Carvainis Agency, Inc. (*US*)
Castiglia Literary Agency (*US*)
The Chudney Agency (*US*)
Cine/Lit Representation (*US*)

Rosica Colin Ltd (*UK*)
Don Congdon Associates, Inc. (*US*)
Conville & Walsh Ltd (*UK*)
Coombs Moylett Literary Agency (*UK*)
CowlesRyan Agency (*US*)
The Croce Agency (*US*)
Sandra Dijkstra Literary Agency (*US*)
Jim Donovan Literary (*US*)
Edwards Fuglewicz (*UK*)
Judith Ehrlich Literary Management (*US*)
Ethan Ellenberg Literary Agency (*US*)
Elaine P. English, Attorney & Literary Agent (*US*)
Farris Literary Agency, Inc. (*US*)
The Feldstein Agency (*UK*)
FinePrint Literary Management (*US*)
Folio Literary Management, LLC (*US*)
Full Throttle Literary Agency (*US*)
Don Gastwirth & Associates (*US*)
Gelfman Schneider Literary Agents, Inc. (*US*)
Irene Goodman Literary Agency (*US*)
Ashley Grayson Literary Agency (*US*)
Sanford J. Greenburger Associates, Inc (*US*)
Jill Grosjean Literary Agency (*US*)
Laura Gross Literary Agency (*US*)
The Mitchell J. Hamilburg Agency (*US*)
Antony Harwood Limited (*UK*)
Hudson Agency (*US*)
International Transactions, Inc. (*US*)
J de S Associates Inc (*US*)
Virginia Kidd Agency, Inc (*US*)
Kilburn Literary Agency (*UK*)
Kimberley Cameron & Associates (Formerly Reece Halsey North) (*US*)
The Knight Agency (*US*)
Elaine Koster Literary Agency LLC (*US*)
Barbara S. Kouts, Literary Agent (*US*)
Larsen Pomada Literary Agents (*US*)
Robert Lecker Agency (*Can*)
Lescher & Lescher (*US*)
Levine Greenberg Literary Agency, Inc. (*US*)
The Literary Group (*US*)
Andrew Lownie Literary Agency Ltd (*UK*)
Lyons Literary LLC (*US*)
Gina Maccoby Agency (*US*)
MacGregor Literary (*US*)
Madeleine Milburn Literary Agency (*UK*)
Manus & Associates Literary Agency, Inc. (*US*)
The Martell Agency (*US*)
McIntosh & Otis, Inc (*US*)
Monteiro Rose Dravis Agency, Inc. (*US*)
The Jean V. Naggar Literary Agency (*US*)
Niad Management (*US*)
Northern Lights Literary Services (*US*)
Objective Entertainment (*US*)
P.S. Literary Agency (*Can*)
The Park Literary Group LLC (*US*)
Pavilion Literary Management (*US*)
Barry Perelman Agency (*US*)
L. Perkins Associates (*US*)
Pinder Lane & Garon-Brooke Associates Ltd (*US*)
Aliéka Pistek Literary Agency, LLC (*US*)

The Poynor Group (*US*)
Linn Prentis Literary (*US*)
Queen Literary Agency, Inc. (*US*)
Raines & Raines (*US*)
Renee Zuckerbrot Literary Agency (*US*)
The Amy Rennert Agency, Inc. (*US*)
RLR Associates (*US*)
Jane Rotrosen Agency (*US*)
Salkind Literary Agency (*US*)
Schiavone Literary Agency (*US*)
Secret Agent Man (*US*)
Lynn Seligman, Literary Agent (*US*)
Sheil Land Associates Ltd (*UK*)
Valerie Smith, Literary Agent (*US*)
Spectrum Literary Agency (*US*)
Spencerhill Associates (*US*)
Philip G. Spitzer Literary Agency, Inc. (*US*)
The Swetky Agency and Associates (*US*)
Talcott Notch Literary (*US*)
Patricia Teal Literary Agency (*US*)
Tom Lee (*US*)
TriadaUS Literary Agency, Inc. (*US*)
Trident Media Group, LLC (*US*)
Veritas Literary Agency (*US*)
Waxman Leavell Literary Agency (*US*)
Irene Webb Literary (*US*)
The Wendy Weil Agency, Inc. (*US*)
Westwood Creative Artists (*Can*)
The Zack Company, Inc (*US*)
Helen Zimmermann Literary Agency (*US*)

Nature
The Agency Group, Ltd (*US*)
Tracy Brown Literary Agency (*US*)
Cine/Lit Representation (*US*)
Rosica Colin Ltd (*UK*)
Frances Collin Literary Agent (*US*)
Don Congdon Associates, Inc. (*US*)
CowlesRyan Agency (*US*)
Creative Authors Ltd (*UK*)
Caroline Davidson Literary Agency (*UK*)
DeFiore and Company (*US*)
Donadio & Olson, Inc. (*US*)
Jim Donovan Literary (*US*)
Dunham Literary, Inc. (*US*)
FinePrint Literary Management (*US*)
Jeanne Fredericks Literary Agency, Inc. (*US*)
Don Gastwirth & Associates (*US*)
The Susan Golomb Literary Agency (*US*)
Sanford J. Greenburger Associates, Inc (*US*)
Jill Grosjean Literary Agency (*US*)
The Mitchell J. Hamilburg Agency (*US*)
Antony Harwood Limited (*UK*)
Heacock Hill Literary Agency, LLC (*US*)
Rupert Heath Literary Agency (*UK*)
Hill Nadell Literary Agency (*US*)
Elaine Koster Literary Agency LLC (*US*)
Barbara S. Kouts, Literary Agent (*US*)
Larsen Pomada Literary Agents (*US*)
LaunchBooks Literary Agency (*US*)
Levine Greenberg Literary Agency, Inc. (*US*)
The Literary Group (*US*)
Gina Maccoby Agency (*US*)
Carol Mann Agency (*US*)

Manus & Associates Literary Agency, Inc. (*US*)
McIntosh & Otis, Inc (*US*)
The Richard Parks Agency (*US*)
Jonathan Pegg Literary Agency (*UK*)
James Peter Associates, Inc. (*US*)
RLR Associates (*US*)
Linda Roghaar Literary Agency, Inc. (*US*)
Scovil Galen Ghosh Literary Agency, Inc. (*US*)
Lynn Seligman, Literary Agent (*US*)
Robin Straus Agency, Inc. (*US*)
The Strothman Agency (*US*)
Stuart Krichevsky Literary Agency, Inc. (*US*)
The Swetky Agency and Associates (*US*)
Talcott Notch Literary (*US*)
Patricia Teal Literary Agency (*US*)
Thomas Moore Literary Agency (*UK*)
Jane Turnbull (*UK*)
Veritas Literary Agency (*US*)
Watkins / Loomis Agency, Inc. (*US*)
Irene Webb Literary (*US*)
Whispering Buffalo Literary Agency Ltd (*UK*)
The Zack Company, Inc (*US*)
Helen Zimmermann Literary Agency (*US*)

New Age
Ethan Ellenberg Literary Agency (*US*)
The Mitchell J. Hamilburg Agency (*US*)
Antony Harwood Limited (*UK*)
J de S Associates Inc (*US*)
Larsen Pomada Literary Agents (*US*)
Levine Greenberg Literary Agency, Inc. (*US*)
Northern Lights Literary Services (*US*)

Nonfiction
A & B Personal Management Ltd (*UK*)
A+B Works (*US*)
Dominick Abel Literary Agency, Inc (*US*)
Sheila Ableman Literary Agency (*UK*)
The Agency (London) Ltd (*UK*)
The Agency Group, Ltd (*US*)
Agency for the Performing Arts (APA) (*US*)
Aitken Alexander Associates (*UK*)
Ambassador Speakers Bureau & Literary
Agency (*US*)
The Ampersand Agency Ltd (*UK*)
Darley Anderson Children's (*UK*)
AP Watt at United Agents LLP (*UK*)
Artellus Limited (*UK*)
Robert Astle & Associates Literary
Management, Inc. (*US*)
Audrey A. Wolf Literary Agency (*US*)
Author Literary Agents (*UK*)
Author Rights Agency (*Ire*)
AVAnti Productions & Management (*UK*)
Avenue A Literary LLC (*US*)
Barbara Hogenson Agency (*US*)
Barer Literary, LLC (*US*)
Bell Lomax Moreton Agency (*UK*)
Lorella Belli Literary Agency (LBLA) (*UK*)
Bidnick & Company (*US*)
Vicky Bijur Literary Agency (*US*)
The Blair Partnership (*UK*)
Blake Friedmann Literary Agency Ltd (*UK*)
Luigi Bonomi Associates Ltd (*UK*)
Brandt & Hochman Literary Agents, Inc. (*US*)

The Helen Brann Agency, Inc. (*US*)
Paul Bresnick Literary Agency, LLC (*US*)
Jenny Brown Associates (*UK*)
Tracy Brown Literary Agency (*US*)
Felicity Bryan (*UK*)
Brie Burkeman & Serafina Clarke Ltd (*UK*)
Juliet Burton Literary Agency (*UK*)
Sheree Bykofsky Associates, Inc. (*US*)
Capel & Land Ltd (*UK*)
CardenWright Literary Agency (*UK*)
Maria Carvainis Agency, Inc. (*US*)
Castiglia Literary Agency (*US*)
Mic Cheetham Literary Agency (*UK*)
Elyse Cheney Literary Associates, LLC (*US*)
Linda Chester & Associates (*US*)
Teresa Chris Literary Agency Ltd (*UK*)
Cine/Lit Representation (*US*)
W.M. Clark Associates (*US*)
Mary Clemmey Literary Agency (*UK*)
Jonathan Clowes Ltd (*UK*)
Rosica Colin Ltd (*UK*)
Frances Collin Literary Agent (*US*)
Don Congdon Associates, Inc. (*US*)
Conville & Walsh Ltd (*UK*)
Jane Conway-Gordon Ltd (*UK*)
CowlesRyan Agency (*US*)
Crawford Literary Agency (*US*)
The Creative Rights Agency (*UK*)
Creative Authors Ltd (*UK*)
Rupert Crew Ltd (*UK*)
The Croce Agency (*US*)
The Culinary Entertainment Agency (CEA) (*US*)
The Mary Cunnane Agency Pty Ltd (*Aus*)
Curtis Brown Ltd (*US*)
Curtis Brown Group Ltd (*UK*)
Daniel Literary Group (*US*)
David Luxton Associates (*UK*)
Caroline Davidson Literary Agency (*UK*)
DeFiore and Company (*US*)
Diamond Kahn and Woods (DKW) Literary
Agency Ltd (*UK*)
Diane Banks Associates Literary Agency (*UK*)
Sandra Dijkstra Literary Agency (*US*)
Donadio & Olson, Inc. (*US*)
Jim Donovan Literary (*US*)
Dunham Literary, Inc. (*US*)
Dunow, Carlson & Lerner Agency (*US*)
Toby Eady Associates Ltd (*UK*)
Eames Literary Services, LLC (*US*)
East West Literary Agency LLC (*US*)
Ebeling & Associates (*US*)
Eddison Pearson Ltd (*UK*)
Edwards Fuglewicz (*UK*)
Judith Ehrlich Literary Management (*US*)
Einstein Thompson Agency (*US*)
Elise Dillsworth Agency (EDA) (*UK*)
Elizabeth Roy Literary Agency (*UK*)
Ethan Ellenberg Literary Agency (*US*)
Nicholas Ellison, Inc. (*US*)
Ann Elmo Agency, Inc. (*US*)
The Epstein Literary Agency (*US*)
Felicia Eth Literary Representation (*US*)
Faith Evans Associates (*UK*)

Mary Evans, Inc. (*US*)
Farris Literary Agency, Inc. (*US*)
The Feldstein Agency (*UK*)
FinePrint Literary Management (*US*)
The James Fitzgerald Agency (*US*)
Fletcher & Company (*US*)
Folio Literary Management, LLC (*US*)
Foundry Literary + Media (*US*)
Fox Chase Agency, Inc. (*US*)
Fox & Howard Literary Agency (*UK*)
Jeanne Fredericks Literary Agency, Inc. (*US*)
Fresh Books Literary Agency (*US*)
Fredrica S. Friedman and Co. Inc. (*US*)
Furniss Lawton (*UK*)
Don Gastwirth & Associates (*US*)
Gelfman Schneider Literary Agents, Inc. (*US*)
The Gernert Company (*US*)
Eric Glass Ltd (*UK*)
David Godwin Associates (*UK*)
The Susan Golomb Literary Agency (*US*)
Irene Goodman Literary Agency (*US*)
Graham Maw Christie Literary Agency (*UK*)
Ashley Grayson Literary Agency (*US*)
Christine Green Authors' Agent (*UK*)
Kathryn Green Literary Agency, LLC (*US*)
Louise Greenberg Books Ltd (*UK*)
Sanford J. Greenburger Associates, Inc (*US*)
Greene & Heaton Ltd (*UK*)
Blanche C. Gregory Inc. (*US*)
Laura Gross Literary Agency (*US*)
David Grossman Literary Agency Ltd (*UK*)
Marianne Gunn O'Connor Literary Agency (*Ire*)
Gunn Media Associates (*UK*)
The Mitchell J. Hamilburg Agency (*US*)
Hardman & Swainson (*UK*)
Antony Harwood Limited (*UK*)
Heacock Hill Literary Agency, LLC (*US*)
A M Heath & Company Limited, Author's Agents (*UK*)
Rupert Heath Literary Agency (*UK*)
The Helen Heller Agency (*Can*)
hhb agency ltd (*UK*)
Hidden Value Group (*US*)
David Higham Associates Ltd (*UK*)
Hill Nadell Literary Agency (*US*)
Vanessa Holt Ltd (*UK*)
Amanda Howard Associates Ltd (*UK*)
Andrea Hurst Literary Management (*US*)
Intercontinental Literary Agency (*UK*)
International Transactions, Inc. (*US*)
Jill Grinberg Literary Management LLC (*US*)
Johnson & Alcock (*UK*)
Frances Kelly (*UK*)
Ken Sherman & Associates (*US*)
Kilburn Literary Agency (*UK*)
Kimberley Cameron & Associates (Formerly Reece Halsey North) (*US*)
Linda Konner Literary Agency (*US*)
Elaine Koster Literary Agency LLC (*US*)
Edite Kroll Literary Agency, Inc. (*US*)
Larsen Pomada Literary Agents (*US*)
LaunchBooks Literary Agency (*US*)
Sarah Lazin Books (*US*)

Robert Lecker Agency (*Can*)
Lescher & Lescher (*US*)
Levine Greenberg Literary Agency, Inc. (*US*)
Barbara Levy Literary Agency (*UK*)
Limelight Management (*UK*)
Lindsay Literary Agency (*UK*)
Lippincott Massie McQuilkin (*US*)
The Literary Group (*US*)
Literary Management Group, Inc. (*US*)
London Independent Books (*UK*)
Sterling Lord Literistic, Inc. (*US*)
Andrew Lownie Literary Agency Ltd (*UK*)
Lucy Luck Associates (*UK*)
Lutyens and Rubinstein (*UK*)
Lyons Literary LLC (*US*)
Gina Maccoby Agency (*US*)
MacGregor Literary (*US*)
Madeleine Milburn Literary Agency (*UK*)
Kirsten Manges Literary Agency, LLC (*US*)
Carol Mann Agency (*US*)
Andrew Mann Ltd (*UK*)
Manus & Associates Literary Agency, Inc. (*US*)
Denise Marcil Literary Agency, Inc. (*US*)
Marjacq Scripts Ltd (*UK*)
Elaine Markson Literary Agency (*US*)
The Marsh Agency (*UK*)
The Martell Agency (*US*)
Martin Literary Management (*US*)
MBA Literary Agents Ltd (*UK*)
Duncan McAra (*UK*)
Margret McBride Literary Agency (*US*)
McIntosh & Otis, Inc (*US*)
McKernan Agency (*UK*)
Doris S. Michaels Literary Agency, Inc. (*US*)
Moore Literary Agency (*US*)
Patricia Moosbrugger Literary Agency (*US*)
Howard Morhaim Literary Agency (*US*)
William Morris Endeavor Entertainment (*US*)
The Jean V. Naggar Literary Agency (*US*)
Nappaland Literary Agency (*US*)
New Leaf Literary & Media, Inc. (*US*)
Niad Management (*US*)
Nine Muses and Apollo, Inc. (*US*)
MNLA (Maggie Noach Literary Agency) (*UK*)
Northern Lights Literary Services (*US*)
Andrew Nurnberg Associates, Ltd (*UK*)
Harold Ober Associates (*US*)
Objective Entertainment (*US*)
P.S. Literary Agency (*Can*)
Paradigm Talent and Literary Agency (*US*)
The Park Literary Group LLC (*US*)
The Richard Parks Agency (*US*)
Kathi J. Paton Literary Agency (*US*)
Pavilion Literary Management (*US*)
John Pawsey (*UK*)
Maggie Pearlstine Associates Ltd (*UK*)
Jonathan Pegg Literary Agency (*UK*)
L. Perkins Associates (*US*)
James Peter Associates, Inc. (*US*)
The Peters Fraser & Dunlop Group Ltd (PFD) (*UK*)
Pinder Lane & Garon-Brooke Associates Ltd (*US*)

Alièka Pistek Literary Agency, LLC (*US*)
Shelley Power Literary Agency Ltd (*UK*)
The Poynor Group (*US*)
Linn Prentis Literary (*US*)
Aaron M. Priest Literary Agency (*US*)
Queen Literary Agency, Inc. (*US*)
Susan Rabiner, Literary Agent, Inc. (*US*)
Lynne Rabinoff Agency (*US*)
Raines & Raines (*US*)
Redhammer (*UK*)
Regal Literary (*UK*)
Regal Literary Inc. (*US*)
Renee Zuckerbrot Literary Agency (*US*)
The Amy Rennert Agency, Inc. (*US*)
The Lisa Richards Agency (*Ire*)
Richford Becklow Literary Agency (*UK*)
Ann Rittenberg Literary Agency (*US*)
Riverside Literary Agency (*US*)
RLR Associates (*US*)
Robert Dudley Agency (*UK*)
Robin Jones Literary Agency (*UK*)
Michael D. Robins & Associates (*US*)
Rochelle Stevens & Co. (*UK*)
Linda Roghaar Literary Agency, Inc. (*US*)
Andy Ross Agency (*US*)
Jane Rotrosen Agency (*US*)
The Rudy Agency (*US*)
Uli Rushby-Smith Literary Agency (*UK*)
Marly Rusoff & Associates, Inc. (*US*)
The Sagalyn Literary Agency (*US*)
Salkind Literary Agency (*US*)
The Sayle Literary Agency (*UK*)
Schiavone Literary Agency (*US*)
The Science Factory (*UK*)
Jonathan Scott, Inc (*US*)
Scovil Galen Ghosh Literary Agency, Inc. (*US*)
Secret Agent Man (*US*)
Lynn Seligman, Literary Agent (*US*)
Sheil Land Associates Ltd (*UK*)
Caroline Sheldon Literary Agency (*UK*)
Signature Literary Agency (*US*)
Jeffrey Simmons (*UK*)
Sinclair-Stevenson (*UK*)
SLW Literary Agency (*US*)
Robert Smith Literary Agency Ltd (*UK*)
Valerie Smith, Literary Agent (*US*)
Spectrum Literary Agency (*US*)
Spencerhill Associates (*US*)
Philip G. Spitzer Literary Agency, Inc. (*US*)
Standen Literary Agency (*UK*)
P. Stathonikos Agency (*Can*)
Abner Stein (*UK*)
Shirley Stewart Literary Agency (*UK*)
Robin Straus Agency, Inc. (*US*)
Rebecca Strong International Literary Agency (*US*)
The Strothman Agency (*US*)
Stuart Krichevsky Literary Agency, Inc. (*US*)
The Stuart Agency (*US*)
Susanna Lea Associates (*US*)
Susanna Lea Associates (UK) (*UK*)
The Susijn Agency (*UK*)
The Swetky Agency and Associates (*US*)

SYLA – Susan Yearwood Literary Agency (*UK*)
Talcott Notch Literary (*US*)
Patricia Teal Literary Agency (*US*)
Tessler Literary Agency (*US*)
Thomas Moore Literary Agency (*UK*)
Scott Treimel NY (*US*)
TriadaUS Literary Agency, Inc. (*US*)
Trident Media Group, LLC (*US*)
Jane Turnbull (*UK*)
2M Literary Agency Ltd (*US*)
United Agents (*UK*)
Veritas Literary Agency (*US*)
Beth Vesel Literary Agency (*US*)
Wade & Doherty Literary Agency (*UK*)
Wales Literary Agency, Inc (*US*)
Watkins / Loomis Agency, Inc. (*US*)
Watson, Little Ltd (*UK*)
Waxman Leavell Literary Agency (*US*)
Irene Webb Literary (*US*)
The Wendy Weil Agency, Inc. (*US*)
The Weingel-Fidel Agency (*US*)
Wernick & Pratt Agency (*US*)
Westwood Creative Artists (*Can*)
Whimsy Literary Agency, LLC (*US*)
Whispering Buffalo Literary Agency Ltd (*UK*)
Eve White: Literary Agent (*UK*)
Dinah Wiener Ltd (*UK*)
William Morris Endeavor (WME) London (*UK*)
Writers House UK (*UK*)
Writers House, LLC. (*US*)
The Wylie Agency (UK) Ltd (*UK*)
Yates & Yates (*US*)
The Zack Company, Inc (*US*)
Karen Gantz Zahler Literary Agency (*US*)
Helen Zimmermann Literary Agency (*US*)

Philosophy
AVAnti Productions & Management (*UK*)
W.M. Clark Associates (*US*)
DeFiore and Company (*US*)
The Feldstein Agency (*UK*)
Greene & Heaton Ltd (*UK*)
Hardman & Swainson (*UK*)
Antony Harwood Limited (*UK*)
The Swetky Agency and Associates (*US*)
Thomas Moore Literary Agency (*UK*)

Photography
AVAnti Productions & Management (*UK*)
Jeanne Fredericks Literary Agency, Inc. (*US*)
Fresh Books Literary Agency (*US*)
Fredrica S. Friedman and Co. Inc. (*US*)
Antony Harwood Limited (*UK*)
Pinder Lane & Garon-Brooke Associates Ltd (*US*)
Regal Literary (*UK*)
Regal Literary Inc. (*US*)
RLR Associates (*US*)
Salkind Literary Agency (*US*)
Lynn Seligman, Literary Agent (*US*)
The Swetky Agency and Associates (*US*)
Thomas Moore Literary Agency (*UK*)

Poetry
AVAnti Productions & Management (*UK*)
Bookseeker Agency (*UK*)

Eddison Pearson Ltd (*UK*)
The Mitchell J. Hamilburg Agency (*US*)
Johnson & Alcock (*UK*)
Thomas Moore Literary Agency (*UK*)
Tom Lee (*US*)
Politics
The Agency Group, Ltd (*US*)
Ambassador Speakers Bureau & Literary Agency (*US*)
AP Watt at United Agents LLP (*UK*)
Robert Astle & Associates Literary Management, Inc. (*US*)
Audrey A. Wolf Literary Agency (*US*)
Vicky Bijur Literary Agency (*US*)
Elyse Cheney Literary Associates, LLC (*US*)
Don Congdon Associates, Inc. (*US*)
Caroline Davidson Literary Agency (*UK*)
DeFiore and Company (*US*)
Sandra Dijkstra Literary Agency (*US*)
Jim Donovan Literary (*US*)
Dunham Literary, Inc. (*US*)
Judith Ehrlich Literary Management (*US*)
Einstein Thompson Agency (*US*)
Felicia Eth Literary Representation (*US*)
Farris Literary Agency, Inc. (*US*)
The Feldstein Agency (*UK*)
Folio Literary Management, LLC (*US*)
Fredrica S. Friedman and Co. Inc. (*US*)
Gelfman Schneider Literary Agents, Inc. (*US*)
The Gernert Company (*US*)
The Susan Golomb Literary Agency (*US*)
Sanford J. Greenburger Associates, Inc (*US*)
Greene & Heaton Ltd (*UK*)
Laura Gross Literary Agency (*US*)
The Mitchell J. Hamilburg Agency (*US*)
Antony Harwood Limited (*UK*)
Heacock Hill Literary Agency, LLC (*US*)
Rupert Heath Literary Agency (*UK*)
hhb agency ltd (*UK*)
Hill Nadell Literary Agency (*US*)
Andrea Hurst Literary Management (*US*)
J de S Associates Inc (*US*)
Jill Grinberg Literary Management LLC (*US*)
Kilburn Literary Agency (*UK*)
Edite Kroll Literary Agency, Inc. (*US*)
Larsen Pomada Literary Agents (*US*)
LaunchBooks Literary Agency (*US*)
Sarah Lazin Books (*US*)
Levine Greenberg Literary Agency, Inc. (*US*)
Lippincott Massie McQuilkin (*US*)
Andrew Lownie Literary Agency Ltd (*UK*)
Lyons Literary LLC (*US*)
Gina Maccoby Agency (*US*)
Carol Mann Agency (*US*)
Objective Entertainment (*US*)
P.S. Literary Agency (*Can*)
The Park Literary Group LLC (*US*)
The Richard Parks Agency (*US*)
Kathi J. Paton Literary Agency (*US*)
James Peter Associates, Inc. (*US*)
Pinder Lane & Garon-Brooke Associates Ltd (*US*)
Aaron M. Priest Literary Agency (*US*)

Susan Rabiner, Literary Agent, Inc. (*US*)
Lynne Rabinoff Agency (*US*)
RLR Associates (*US*)
Salkind Literary Agency (*US*)
Schiavone Literary Agency (*US*)
The Science Factory (*UK*)
Lynn Seligman, Literary Agent (*US*)
The Seven Bridges Group (*US*)
Sheil Land Associates Ltd (*UK*)
Signature Literary Agency (*US*)
Jeffrey Simmons (*UK*)
Philip G. Spitzer Literary Agency, Inc. (*US*)
Stuart Krichevsky Literary Agency, Inc. (*US*)
The Swetky Agency and Associates (*US*)
Trident Media Group, LLC (*US*)
2M Literary Agency Ltd (*US*)
Wales Literary Agency, Inc (*US*)
Watkins / Loomis Agency, Inc. (*US*)
Whimsy Literary Agency, LLC (*US*)
Whispering Buffalo Literary Agency Ltd (*UK*)
Yates & Yates (*US*)
The Zack Company, Inc (*US*)
Karen Gantz Zahler Literary Agency (*US*)
Psychology
The Agency Group, Ltd (*US*)
AP Watt at United Agents LLP (*UK*)
AVAnti Productions & Management (*UK*)
Vicky Bijur Literary Agency (*US*)
Paul Bresnick Literary Agency, LLC (*US*)
Tracy Brown Literary Agency (*US*)
Sheree Bykofsky Associates, Inc. (*US*)
Maria Carvainis Agency, Inc. (*US*)
Rosica Colin Ltd (*UK*)
Don Congdon Associates, Inc. (*US*)
Conville & Walsh Ltd (*UK*)
CowlesRyan Agency (*US*)
Crawford Literary Agency (*US*)
Caroline Davidson Literary Agency (*UK*)
DeFiore and Company (*US*)
Diane Banks Associates Literary Agency (*UK*)
Judith Ehrlich Literary Management (*US*)
Einstein Thompson Agency (*US*)
Ethan Ellenberg Literary Agency (*US*)
Felicia Eth Literary Representation (*US*)
Folio Literary Management, LLC (*US*)
Foundry Literary + Media (*US*)
Fox & Howard Literary Agency (*UK*)
Jeanne Fredericks Literary Agency, Inc. (*US*)
Fredrica S. Friedman and Co. Inc. (*US*)
Furniss Lawton (*UK*)
Don Gastwirth & Associates (*US*)
The Susan Golomb Literary Agency (*US*)
Graham Maw Christie Literary Agency (*UK*)
Kathryn Green Literary Agency, LLC (*US*)
Sanford J. Greenburger Associates, Inc (*US*)
Laura Gross Literary Agency (*US*)
The Mitchell J. Hamilburg Agency (*US*)
Antony Harwood Limited (*UK*)
A M Heath & Company Limited, Author's Agents (*UK*)
Hidden Value Group (*US*)
Andrea Hurst Literary Management (*US*)
Jill Grinberg Literary Management LLC (*US*)

Kilburn Literary Agency (*UK*)
The Knight Agency (*US*)
Linda Konner Literary Agency (*US*)
Elaine Koster Literary Agency LLC (*US*)
Barbara S. Kouts, Literary Agent (*US*)
Edite Kroll Literary Agency, Inc. (*US*)
Larsen Pomada Literary Agents (*US*)
Levine Greenberg Literary Agency, Inc. (*US*)
Lippincott Massie McQuilkin (*US*)
The Literary Group (*US*)
Andrew Lownie Literary Agency Ltd (*UK*)
Kirsten Manges Literary Agency, LLC (*US*)
Carol Mann Agency (*US*)
Manus & Associates Literary Agency, Inc. (*US*)
The Martell Agency (*US*)
McIntosh & Otis, Inc (*US*)
Doris S. Michaels Literary Agency, Inc. (*US*)
The Jean V. Naggar Literary Agency (*US*)
Northern Lights Literary Services (*US*)
P.S. Literary Agency (*Can*)
The Richard Parks Agency (*US*)
Jonathan Pegg Literary Agency (*UK*)
L. Perkins Associates (*US*)
Queen Literary Agency, Inc. (*US*)
Lynne Rabinoff Agency (*US*)
Raines & Raines (*US*)
Rees Literary Agency (*US*)
RLR Associates (*US*)
Marly Rusoff & Associates, Inc. (*US*)
Salkind Literary Agency (*US*)
Scovil Galen Ghosh Literary Agency, Inc. (*US*)
Lynn Seligman, Literary Agent (*US*)
Sheil Land Associates Ltd (*UK*)
Jeffrey Simmons (*UK*)
Robin Straus Agency, Inc. (*US*)
The Stuart Agency (*US*)
The Swetky Agency and Associates (*US*)
Patricia Teal Literary Agency (*US*)
Tessler Literary Agency (*US*)
TriadaUS Literary Agency, Inc. (*US*)
2M Literary Agency Ltd (*US*)
Beth Vesel Literary Agency (*US*)
Watson, Little Ltd (*UK*)
The Weingel-Fidel Agency (*US*)
Whimsy Literary Agency, LLC (*US*)
Writers House UK (*UK*)
Writers House, LLC. (*US*)
Karen Gantz Zahler Literary Agency (*US*)
Radio
The Agency (London) Ltd (*UK*)
AVAnti Productions & Management (*UK*)
Berlin Associates (*UK*)
Blake Friedmann Literary Agency Ltd (*UK*)
Alan Brodie Representation Ltd (*UK*)
Capel & Land Ltd (*UK*)
Mary Clemmey Literary Agency (*UK*)
Jonathan Clowes Ltd (*UK*)
Rosica Colin Ltd (*UK*)
Curtis Brown Group Ltd (*UK*)
Film Rights Ltd in association with Laurence
Fitch Ltd (*UK*)
Jill Foster Ltd (JFL) (*UK*)
Antony Harwood Limited (*UK*)

Valerie Hoskins Associates (*UK*)
Independent Talent Group Ltd (*UK*)
Andrew Mann Ltd (*UK*)
Marjacq Scripts Ltd (*UK*)
MBA Literary Agents Ltd (*UK*)
Bill McLean Personal Management Ltd (*UK*)
PBJ and JBJ Management (*UK*)
The Peters Fraser & Dunlop Group Ltd (PFD)
(*UK*)
Rochelle Stevens & Co. (*UK*)
Sayle Screen Ltd (*UK*)
Sheil Land Associates Ltd (*UK*)
The Tennyson Agency (*UK*)
Thomas Moore Literary Agency (*UK*)
United Agents (*UK*)
Reference
Sheree Bykofsky Associates, Inc. (*US*)
Caroline Davidson Literary Agency (*UK*)
Jim Donovan Literary (*US*)
The Epstein Literary Agency (*US*)
FinePrint Literary Management (*US*)
Folio Literary Management, LLC (*US*)
Fox & Howard Literary Agency (*UK*)
Jeanne Fredericks Literary Agency, Inc. (*US*)
Fresh Books Literary Agency (*US*)
Graham Maw Christie Literary Agency (*UK*)
Sanford J. Greenburger Associates, Inc (*US*)
Frances Kelly (*UK*)
Linda Konner Literary Agency (*US*)
Denise Marcil Literary Agency, Inc. (*US*)
James Peter Associates, Inc. (*US*)
Signature Literary Agency (*US*)
Thomas Moore Literary Agency (*UK*)
The Zack Company, Inc (*US*)
Religious
Ambassador Speakers Bureau & Literary
Agency (*US*)
AVAnti Productions & Management (*UK*)
W.M. Clark Associates (*US*)
Rosica Colin Ltd (*UK*)
Sandra Dijkstra Literary Agency (*US*)
Eames Literary Services, LLC (*US*)
Farris Literary Agency, Inc. (*US*)
FinePrint Literary Management (*US*)
Folio Literary Management, LLC (*US*)
Foundry Literary + Media (*US*)
The Mitchell J. Hamilburg Agency (*US*)
Antony Harwood Limited (*UK*)
Hidden Value Group (*US*)
Andrea Hurst Literary Management (*US*)
Kilburn Literary Agency (*UK*)
Edite Kroll Literary Agency, Inc. (*US*)
Larsen Pomada Literary Agents (*US*)
Levine Greenberg Literary Agency, Inc. (*US*)
The Literary Group (*US*)
Literary Management Group, Inc. (*US*)
MacGregor Literary (*US*)
Carol Mann Agency (*US*)
Nappaland Literary Agency (*US*)
Kathi J. Paton Literary Agency (*US*)
The Poynor Group (*US*)
Lynne Rabinoff Agency (*US*)
RLR Associates (*US*)

Claim your FREE access to **www.firstwriter.com**: *See p.379*

The Mitchell J. Hamilburg Agency (*US*)
Hardman & Swainson (*UK*)
Antony Harwood Limited (*UK*)
Heacock Hill Literary Agency, LLC (*US*)
Rupert Heath Literary Agency (*UK*)
Hill Nadell Literary Agency (*US*)
Andrea Hurst Literary Management (*US*)
Jill Grinberg Literary Management LLC (*US*)
Kilburn Literary Agency (*UK*)
Linda Konner Literary Agency (*US*)
Larsen Pomada Literary Agents (*US*)
LaunchBooks Literary Agency (*US*)
Robert Lecker Agency (*Can*)
Levine Greenberg Literary Agency, Inc. (*US*)
Lippincott Massie McQuilkin (*US*)
The Literary Group (*US*)
Sterling Lord Literistic, Inc. (*US*)
Andrew Lownie Literary Agency Ltd (*UK*)
Lyons Literary LLC (*US*)
Kirsten Manges Literary Agency, LLC (*US*)
Manus & Associates Literary Agency, Inc. (*US*)
The Jean V. Naggar Literary Agency (*US*)
P.S. Literary Agency (*Can*)
The Park Literary Group LLC (*US*)
The Richard Parks Agency (*US*)
Kathi J. Paton Literary Agency (*US*)
Pavilion Literary Management (*US*)
Jonathan Pegg Literary Agency (*UK*)
Barry Perelman Agency (*US*)
L. Perkins Associates (*US*)
Aliěka Pistek Literary Agency, LLC (*US*)
Queen Literary Agency, Inc. (*US*)
Susan Rabiner, Literary Agent, Inc. (*US*)
Lynne Rabinoff Agency (*US*)
Redhammer (*UK*)
Rees Literary Agency (*US*)
Regal Literary (*UK*)
Regal Literary Inc. (*US*)
Renee Zuckerbrot Literary Agency (*US*)
RLR Associates (*US*)
Andy Ross Agency (*US*)
The Rudy Agency (*US*)
The Sagalyn Literary Agency (*US*)
Salkind Literary Agency (*US*)
The Sayle Literary Agency (*UK*)
Schiavone Literary Agency (*US*)
The Science Factory (*UK*)
Scovil Galen Ghosh Literary Agency, Inc. (*US*)
Lynn Seligman, Literary Agent (*US*)
Sheil Land Associates Ltd (*UK*)
Signature Literary Agency (*US*)
Robin Straus Agency, Inc. (*US*)
Rebecca Strong International Literary Agency (*US*)
The Strothman Agency (*US*)
Stuart Krichevsky Literary Agency, Inc. (*US*)
The Stuart Agency (*US*)
The Swetky Agency and Associates (*US*)
Talcott Notch Literary (*US*)
Tessler Literary Agency (*US*)
Trident Media Group, LLC (*US*)
2M Literary Agency Ltd (*US*)
Veritas Literary Agency (*US*)

Watson, Little Ltd (*UK*)
The Wendy Weil Agency, Inc. (*US*)
The Weingel-Fidel Agency (*US*)
Westwood Creative Artists (*Can*)
Dinah Wiener Ltd (*UK*)
Writers House UK (*UK*)
Writers House, LLC. (*US*)
The Zack Company, Inc (*US*)

Sci-Fi

Abela Literature (*Can*)
The Ampersand Agency Ltd (*UK*)
Artellus Limited (*UK*)
Author Rights Agency (*Ire*)
AVAnti Productions & Management (*UK*)
The Bright Literary Academy (*UK*)
Castiglia Literary Agency (*US*)
Mic Cheetham Literary Agency (*UK*)
Frances Collin Literary Agent (*US*)
Diamond Kahn and Woods (DKW) Literary Agency Ltd (*UK*)
Sandra Dijkstra Literary Agency (*US*)
Dorian Literary Agency (DLA) (*UK*)
Dunham Literary, Inc. (*US*)
Ethan Ellenberg Literary Agency (*US*)
FinePrint Literary Management (*US*)
Folio Literary Management, LLC (*US*)
Foundry Literary + Media (*US*)
The Gernert Company (*US*)
Ashley Grayson Literary Agency (*US*)
Sanford J. Greenburger Associates, Inc (*US*)
Greene & Heaton Ltd (*UK*)
The Mitchell J. Hamilburg Agency (*US*)
Antony Harwood Limited (*UK*)
Andrea Hurst Literary Management (*US*)
Jill Grinberg Literary Management LLC (*US*)
Johnson & Alcock (*UK*)
Virginia Kidd Agency, Inc (*US*)
The Knight Agency (*US*)
Andrew Lownie Literary Agency Ltd (*UK*)
McIntosh & Otis, Inc (*US*)
Monteiro Rose Dravis Agency, Inc. (*US*)
Howard Morhaim Literary Agency (*US*)
New Leaf Literary & Media, Inc. (*US*)
Objective Entertainment (*US*)
L. Perkins Associates (*US*)
Pinder Lane & Garon-Brooke Associates Ltd (*US*)
Linn Prentis Literary (*US*)
Raines & Raines (*US*)
Richford Becklow Literary Agency (*UK*)
Salkind Literary Agency (*US*)
Schiavone Literary Agency (*US*)
Scribe Agency LLC (*US*)
Lynn Seligman, Literary Agent (*US*)
Sheil Land Associates Ltd (*UK*)
Valerie Smith, Literary Agent (*US*)
Spectrum Literary Agency (*US*)
Stuart Krichevsky Literary Agency, Inc. (*US*)
The Swetky Agency and Associates (*US*)
Talcott Notch Literary (*US*)
Tom Lee (*US*)
TriadaUS Literary Agency, Inc. (*US*)
Veritas Literary Agency (*US*)

Waxman Leavell Literary Agency (*US*)
Whispering Buffalo Literary Agency Ltd (*UK*)
Writers House UK (*UK*)
Writers House, LLC. (*US*)
The Zack Company, Inc (*US*)
Scripts
A & B Personal Management Ltd (*UK*)
Above the Line Agency (*US*)
Bret Adams Ltd (*US*)
The Agency (London) Ltd (*UK*)
Agency for the Performing Arts (APA) (*US*)
Aimee Entertainment Agency (*US*)
Anonymous Content (*US*)
AP Watt at United Agents LLP (*UK*)
Author Literary Agents (*UK*)
AVAnti Productions & Management (*UK*)
Barbara Hogenson Agency (*US*)
Berlin Associates (*UK*)
Blake Friedmann Literary Agency Ltd (*UK*)
Alan Brodie Representation Ltd (*UK*)
Marcus Bryan & Associates Inc. (*US*)
Brie Burkeman & Serafina Clarke Ltd (*UK*)
CardenWright Literary Agency (*UK*)
Mary Clemmey Literary Agency (*UK*)
Jonathan Clowes Ltd (*UK*)
Rosica Colin Ltd (*UK*)
The Collective (*US*)
Creative Trust, Inc. (*US*)
Criterion Group, Inc. (*US*)
Curtis Brown Group Ltd (*UK*)
Felix de Wolfe (*UK*)
Energy Entertainment (*US*)
Farris Literary Agency, Inc. (*US*)
Film Rights Ltd in association with Laurence
Fitch Ltd (*UK*)
Jill Foster Ltd (JFL) (*UK*)
Full Throttle Literary Agency (*US*)
The Gage Group (*US*)
Noel Gay (*UK*)
Eric Glass Ltd (*UK*)
David Higham Associates Ltd (*UK*)
Valerie Hoskins Associates (*UK*)
Amanda Howard Associates Ltd (*UK*)
Hudson Agency (*US*)
Independent Talent Group Ltd (*UK*)
Janet Fillingham Associates (*UK*)
Michelle Kass Associates (*UK*)
Ken Sherman & Associates (*US*)
Ki Agency Ltd (*UK*)
Kilburn Literary Agency (*UK*)
Lenhoff & Lenhoff (*US*)
Madeleine Milburn Literary Agency (*UK*)
Andrew Mann Ltd (*UK*)
Marjacq Scripts Ltd (*UK*)
The Marton Agency, Inc. (*US*)
MBA Literary Agents Ltd (*UK*)
Bill McLean Personal Management Ltd (*UK*)
Monteiro Rose Dravis Agency, Inc. (*US*)
William Morris Endeavor Entertainment (*US*)
Niad Management (*US*)
Objective Entertainment (*US*)
Paradigm Talent and Literary Agency (*US*)
PBJ and JBJ Management (*UK*)

Barry Perelman Agency (*US*)
The Peters Fraser & Dunlop Group Ltd (PFD)
(*UK*)
The Lisa Richards Agency (*Ire*)
Michael D. Robins & Associates (*US*)
Rochelle Stevens & Co. (*UK*)
Sayle Screen Ltd (*UK*)
Linda Seifert Management (*UK*)
The Seven Bridges Group (*US*)
Sheil Land Associates Ltd (*UK*)
Stone Manners Salners Agency (*US*)
The Swetky Agency and Associates (*US*)
The Tennyson Agency (*UK*)
Thomas Moore Literary Agency (*UK*)
Tom Lee (*US*)
United Agents (*UK*)
Cecily Ware Literary Agents (*UK*)
Self-Help
The Agency Group, Ltd (*US*)
Ambassador Speakers Bureau & Literary
Agency (*US*)
Audrey A. Wolf Literary Agency (*US*)
Vicky Bijur Literary Agency (*US*)
The Bright Literary Academy (*UK*)
Sheree Bykofsky Associates, Inc. (*US*)
CowlesRyan Agency (*US*)
Crawford Literary Agency (*US*)
Diane Banks Associates Literary Agency (*UK*)
Sandra Dijkstra Literary Agency (*US*)
Ebeling & Associates (*US*)
Judith Ehrlich Literary Management (*US*)
Farris Literary Agency, Inc. (*US*)
FinePrint Literary Management (*US*)
Folio Literary Management, LLC (*US*)
Fox & Howard Literary Agency (*UK*)
Jeanne Fredericks Literary Agency, Inc. (*US*)
Fresh Books Literary Agency (*US*)
Fredrica S. Friedman and Co. Inc. (*US*)
Graham Maw Christie Literary Agency (*UK*)
Ashley Grayson Literary Agency (*US*)
Kathryn Green Literary Agency, LLC (*US*)
Sanford J. Greenburger Associates, Inc (*US*)
The Mitchell J. Hamilburg Agency (*US*)
Antony Harwood Limited (*UK*)
Hidden Value Group (*US*)
Andrea Hurst Literary Management (*US*)
J de S Associates Inc (*US*)
Johnson & Alcock (*UK*)
Frances Kelly (*UK*)
The Knight Agency (*US*)
Linda Konner Literary Agency (*US*)
Elaine Koster Literary Agency LLC (*US*)
Edite Kroll Literary Agency, Inc. (*US*)
Larsen Pomada Literary Agents (*US*)
Levine Greenberg Literary Agency, Inc. (*US*)
Sterling Lord Literistic, Inc. (*US*)
Andrew Lownie Literary Agency Ltd (*UK*)
Gina Maccoby Agency (*US*)
MacGregor Literary (*US*)
Carol Mann Agency (*US*)
Manus & Associates Literary Agency, Inc. (*US*)
Denise Marcil Literary Agency, Inc. (*US*)
The Martell Agency (*US*)

Martin Literary Management (*US*)
MBA Literary Agents Ltd (*UK*)
Margret McBride Literary Agency (*US*)
McIntosh & Otis, Inc (*US*)
Doris S. Michaels Literary Agency, Inc. (*US*)
Northern Lights Literary Services (*US*)
The Richard Parks Agency (*US*)
Pinder Lane & Garon-Brooke Associates Ltd (*US*)
Rees Literary Agency (*US*)
The Lisa Richards Agency (*Ire*)
Richford Becklow Literary Agency (*UK*)
RLR Associates (*US*)
Linda Roghaar Literary Agency, Inc. (*US*)
Salkind Literary Agency (*US*)
Lynn Seligman, Literary Agent (*US*)
Sheil Land Associates Ltd (*UK*)
Valerie Smith, Literary Agent (*US*)
The Swetky Agency and Associates (*US*)
Patricia Teal Literary Agency (*US*)
TriadaUS Literary Agency, Inc. (*US*)
Veritas Literary Agency (*US*)
Watson, Little Ltd (*UK*)
Irene Webb Literary (*US*)
Whimsy Literary Agency, LLC (*US*)
Whispering Buffalo Literary Agency Ltd (*UK*)
Writers House UK (*UK*)
Writers House, LLC. (*US*)
The Zack Company, Inc (*US*)
Short Stories
AVAnti Productions & Management (*UK*)
Barer Literary, LLC (*US*)
The Bright Literary Academy (*UK*)
DeFiore and Company (*US*)
Sandra Dijkstra Literary Agency (*US*)
Full Throttle Literary Agency (*US*)
The Mitchell J. Hamilburg Agency (*US*)
Antony Harwood Limited (*UK*)
International Transactions, Inc. (*US*)
Kilburn Literary Agency (*UK*)
MacGregor Literary (*US*)
Regal Literary Inc. (*US*)
Renee Zuckerbrot Literary Agency (*US*)
RLR Associates (*US*)
Scribe Agency LLC (*US*)
The Seven Bridges Group (*US*)
Philip G. Spitzer Literary Agency, Inc. (*US*)
The Swetky Agency and Associates (*US*)
Thomas Moore Literary Agency (*UK*)
Tom Lee (*US*)
Watkins / Loomis Agency, Inc. (*US*)
Sociology
AVAnti Productions & Management (*UK*)
Vicky Bijur Literary Agency (*US*)
W.M. Clark Associates (*US*)
DeFiore and Company (*US*)
Diamond Kahn and Woods (DKW) Literary Agency Ltd (*UK*)
Sandra Dijkstra Literary Agency (*US*)
Judith Ehrlich Literary Management (*US*)
Felicia Eth Literary Representation (*US*)
The Feldstein Agency (*UK*)
Fredrica S. Friedman and Co. Inc. (*US*)

The Gernert Company (*US*)
The Susan Golomb Literary Agency (*US*)
Irene Goodman Literary Agency (*US*)
Sanford J. Greenburger Associates, Inc (*US*)
The Mitchell J. Hamilburg Agency (*US*)
Antony Harwood Limited (*UK*)
J de S Associates Inc (*US*)
Kilburn Literary Agency (*UK*)
Larsen Pomada Literary Agents (*US*)
LaunchBooks Literary Agency (*US*)
Levine Greenberg Literary Agency, Inc. (*US*)
Lippincott Massie McQuilkin (*US*)
Carol Mann Agency (*US*)
Doris S. Michaels Literary Agency, Inc. (*US*)
The Richard Parks Agency (*US*)
Ann Rittenberg Literary Agency (*US*)
RLR Associates (*US*)
Scovil Galen Ghosh Literary Agency, Inc. (*US*)
Lynn Seligman, Literary Agent (*US*)
The Swetky Agency and Associates (*US*)
The Weingel-Fidel Agency (*US*)
Karen Gantz Zahler Literary Agency (*US*)
Spiritual
AVAnti Productions & Management (*UK*)
Sheree Bykofsky Associates, Inc. (*US*)
CowlesRyan Agency (*US*)
Dunham Literary, Inc. (*US*)
Ethan Ellenberg Literary Agency (*US*)
Farris Literary Agency, Inc. (*US*)
FinePrint Literary Management (*US*)
Folio Literary Management, LLC (*US*)
Fox & Howard Literary Agency (*UK*)
Graham Maw Christie Literary Agency (*UK*)
Ashley Grayson Literary Agency (*US*)
The Mitchell J. Hamilburg Agency (*US*)
Antony Harwood Limited (*UK*)
Heacock Hill Literary Agency, LLC (*US*)
Jill Grinberg Literary Management LLC (*US*)
Kilburn Literary Agency (*UK*)
Elaine Koster Literary Agency LLC (*US*)
Levine Greenberg Literary Agency, Inc. (*US*)
Literary Management Group, Inc. (*US*)
Kirsten Manges Literary Agency, LLC (*US*)
Carol Mann Agency (*US*)
Denise Marcil Literary Agency, Inc. (*US*)
McIntosh & Otis, Inc (*US*)
Pinder Lane & Garon-Brooke Associates Ltd (*US*)
The Amy Rennert Agency, Inc. (*US*)
Salkind Literary Agency (*US*)
Schiavone Literary Agency (*US*)
Irene Webb Literary (*US*)
Whimsy Literary Agency, LLC (*US*)
The Zack Company, Inc (*US*)
Karen Gantz Zahler Literary Agency (*US*)
Sport
The Agency Group, Ltd (*US*)
AP Watt at United Agents LLP (*UK*)
Robert Astle & Associates Literary Management, Inc. (*US*)
Audrey A. Wolf Literary Agency (*US*)
Bell Lomax Moreton Agency (*UK*)
Paul Bresnick Literary Agency, LLC (*US*)

Jenny Brown Associates (*UK*)
Tracy Brown Literary Agency (*US*)
Elyse Cheney Literary Associates, LLC (*US*)
Rosica Colin Ltd (*UK*)
Conville & Walsh Ltd (*UK*)
The Creative Rights Agency (*UK*)
David Luxton Associates (*UK*)
Sandra Dijkstra Literary Agency (*US*)
Jim Donovan Literary (*US*)
Judith Ehrlich Literary Management (*US*)
Einstein Thompson Agency (*US*)
Farris Literary Agency, Inc. (*US*)
The Feldstein Agency (*UK*)
Fletcher & Company (*US*)
Folio Literary Management, LLC (*US*)
Foundry Literary + Media (*US*)
Jeanne Fredericks Literary Agency, Inc. (*US*)
The Gernert Company (*US*)
Ashley Grayson Literary Agency (*US*)
Kathryn Green Literary Agency, LLC (*US*)
Sanford J. Greenburger Associates, Inc (*US*)
Laura Gross Literary Agency (*US*)
The Mitchell J. Hamilburg Agency (*US*)
Antony Harwood Limited (*UK*)
J de S Associates Inc (*US*)
Johnson & Alcock (*UK*)
Larsen Pomada Literary Agents (*US*)
LaunchBooks Literary Agency (*US*)
Levine Greenberg Literary Agency, Inc. (*US*)
The Literary Group (*US*)
Andrew Lownie Literary Agency Ltd (*UK*)
Lyons Literary LLC (*US*)
MacGregor Literary (*US*)
Kirsten Manges Literary Agency, LLC (*US*)
Carol Mann Agency (*US*)
McIntosh & Otis, Inc (*US*)
Doris S. Michaels Literary Agency, Inc. (*US*)
Howard Morhaim Literary Agency (*US*)
Niad Management (*US*)
Objective Entertainment (*US*)
P.S. Literary Agency (*Can*)
Kathi J. Paton Literary Agency (*US*)
John Pawsey (*UK*)
James Peter Associates, Inc. (*US*)
Pinder Lane & Garon-Brooke Associates Ltd (*US*)
Queen Literary Agency, Inc. (*US*)
Susan Rabiner, Literary Agent, Inc. (*US*)
The Amy Rennert Agency, Inc. (*US*)
The Lisa Richards Agency (*Ire*)
RLR Associates (*US*)
Robert Dudley Agency (*UK*)
Schiavone Literary Agency (*US*)
Jonathan Scott, Inc (*US*)
The Seven Bridges Group (*US*)
Jeffrey Simmons (*UK*)
SLW Literary Agency (*US*)
Philip G. Spitzer Literary Agency, Inc. (*US*)
The Stuart Agency (*US*)
The Swetky Agency and Associates (*US*)
TriadaUS Literary Agency, Inc. (*US*)
Trident Media Group, LLC (*US*)
2M Literary Agency Ltd (*US*)

Watson, Little Ltd (*UK*)
Waxman Leavell Literary Agency (*US*)
Yates & Yates (*US*)
The Zack Company, Inc (*US*)
Helen Zimmermann Literary Agency (*US*)
Suspense
Abela Literature (*Can*)
Robert Astle & Associates Literary Management, Inc. (*US*)
AVAnti Productions & Management (*UK*)
Brown Literary Agency (*US*)
Maria Carvainis Agency, Inc. (*US*)
Elyse Cheney Literary Associates, LLC (*US*)
The Chudney Agency (*US*)
Rosica Colin Ltd (*UK*)
Conville & Walsh Ltd (*UK*)
Coombs Moylett Literary Agency (*UK*)
Crawford Literary Agency (*US*)
The Croce Agency (*US*)
Curtis Brown Group Ltd (*UK*)
Diamond Kahn and Woods (DKW) Literary Agency Ltd (*UK*)
Jim Donovan Literary (*US*)
Farris Literary Agency, Inc. (*US*)
FinePrint Literary Management (*US*)
Folio Literary Management, LLC (*US*)
Full Throttle Literary Agency (*US*)
Furniss Lawton (*UK*)
Gelfman Schneider Literary Agents, Inc. (*US*)
Irene Goodman Literary Agency (*US*)
Kathryn Green Literary Agency, LLC (*US*)
Greyhaus Literary Agency (*US*)
Jill Grosjean Literary Agency (*US*)
Laura Gross Literary Agency (*US*)
The Mitchell J. Hamilburg Agency (*US*)
Antony Harwood Limited (*UK*)
A M Heath & Company Limited, Author's Agents (*UK*)
J de S Associates Inc (*US*)
Virginia Kidd Agency, Inc (*US*)
The Knight Agency (*US*)
Barbara S. Kouts, Literary Agent (*US*)
Larsen Pomada Literary Agents (*US*)
Robert Lecker Agency (*Can*)
Lescher & Lescher (*US*)
Levine Greenberg Literary Agency, Inc. (*US*)
The Literary Group (*US*)
Andrew Lownie Literary Agency Ltd (*UK*)
Lyons Literary LLC (*US*)
MacGregor Literary (*US*)
Madeleine Milburn Literary Agency (*UK*)
Manus & Associates Literary Agency, Inc. (*US*)
Denise Marcil Literary Agency, Inc. (*US*)
The Martell Agency (*US*)
McIntosh & Otis, Inc (*US*)
Monteiro Rose Dravis Agency, Inc. (*US*)
The Jean V. Naggar Literary Agency (*US*)
Nappaland Literary Agency (*US*)
Niad Management (*US*)
Northern Lights Literary Services (*US*)
P.S. Literary Agency (*Can*)
Alièka Pistek Literary Agency, LLC (*US*)
The Poynor Group (*US*)

Aaron M. Priest Literary Agency (*US*)
Raines & Raines (*US*)
Jane Rotrosen Agency (*US*)
Salkind Literary Agency (*US*)
Schiavone Literary Agency (*US*)
Secret Agent Man (*US*)
The Seven Bridges Group (*US*)
Valerie Smith, Literary Agent (*US*)
Spectrum Literary Agency (*US*)
Philip G. Spitzer Literary Agency, Inc. (*US*)
The Swetky Agency and Associates (*US*)
Talcott Notch Literary (*US*)
Trident Media Group, LLC (*US*)
The Zack Company, Inc (*US*)
Helen Zimmermann Literary Agency (*US*)

Technology

AP Watt at United Agents LLP (*UK*)
Maria Carvainis Agency, Inc. (*US*)
W.M. Clark Associates (*US*)
Don Congdon Associates, Inc. (*US*)
DeFiore and Company (*US*)
Dunham Literary, Inc. (*US*)
Felicia Eth Literary Representation (*US*)
FinePrint Literary Management (*US*)
Folio Literary Management, LLC (*US*)
Fresh Books Literary Agency (*US*)
The Susan Golomb Literary Agency (*US*)
Ashley Grayson Literary Agency (*US*)
Antony Harwood Limited (*UK*)
Jill Grinberg Literary Management LLC (*US*)
LaunchBooks Literary Agency (*US*)
Levine Greenberg Literary Agency, Inc. (*US*)
Andrew Lownie Literary Agency Ltd (*UK*)
Kirsten Manges Literary Agency, LLC (*US*)
Moore Literary Agency (*US*)
New Leaf Literary & Media, Inc. (*US*)
The Richard Parks Agency (*US*)
Kathi J. Paton Literary Agency (*US*)
Lynne Rabinoff Agency (*US*)
Robert Dudley Agency (*UK*)
The Rudy Agency (*US*)
Salkind Literary Agency (*US*)
The Science Factory (*UK*)
Signature Literary Agency (*US*)
Stuart Krichevsky Literary Agency, Inc. (*US*)
The Swetky Agency and Associates (*US*)
Talcott Notch Literary (*US*)
Watkins / Loomis Agency, Inc. (*US*)
Watson, Little Ltd (*UK*)
The Weingel-Fidel Agency (*US*)
The Zack Company, Inc (*US*)

Theatre

A & B Personal Management Ltd (*UK*)
Bret Adams Ltd (*US*)
The Agency (London) Ltd (*UK*)
Agency for the Performing Arts (APA) (*US*)
Robert Astle & Associates Literary
Management, Inc. (*US*)
AVAnti Productions & Management (*UK*)
Barbara Hogenson Agency (*US*)
Berlin Associates (*UK*)
Alan Brodie Representation Ltd (*UK*)
Brie Burkeman & Serafina Clarke Ltd (*UK*)

CardenWright Literary Agency (*UK*)
W.M. Clark Associates (*US*)
Mary Clemmey Literary Agency (*UK*)
Jonathan Clowes Ltd (*UK*)
Rosica Colin Ltd (*UK*)
Don Congdon Associates, Inc. (*US*)
Criterion Group, Inc. (*US*)
Curtis Brown Group Ltd (*UK*)
Felix de Wolfe (*UK*)
Film Rights Ltd in association with Laurence
Fitch Ltd (*UK*)
Jill Foster Ltd (JFL) (*UK*)
The Gage Group (*US*)
Eric Glass Ltd (*UK*)
Antony Harwood Limited (*UK*)
Independent Talent Group Ltd (*UK*)
Janet Fillingham Associates (*UK*)
Ki Agency Ltd (*UK*)
Robert Lecker Agency (*Can*)
Andrew Mann Ltd (*UK*)
The Marton Agency, Inc. (*US*)
MBA Literary Agents Ltd (*UK*)
Bill McLean Personal Management Ltd (*UK*)
Niad Management (*US*)
Paradigm Talent and Literary Agency (*US*)
The Richard Parks Agency (*US*)
PBJ and JBJ Management (*UK*)
L. Perkins Associates (*US*)
The Peters Fraser & Dunlop Group Ltd (PFD)
(*UK*)
Pinder Lane & Garon-Brooke Associates Ltd
(*US*)
The Lisa Richards Agency (*Ire*)
Michael D. Robins & Associates (*US*)
Rochelle Stevens & Co. (*UK*)
Sayle Screen Ltd (*UK*)
Sheil Land Associates Ltd (*UK*)
Jeffrey Simmons (*UK*)
The Swetky Agency and Associates (*US*)
The Tennyson Agency (*UK*)
Thomas Moore Literary Agency (*UK*)
Tom Lee (*US*)
United Agents (*UK*)

Thrillers

Abela Literature (*Can*)
The Ampersand Agency Ltd (*UK*)
AP Watt at United Agents LLP (*UK*)
Robert Astle & Associates Literary
Management, Inc. (*US*)
Author Literary Agents (*UK*)
AVAnti Productions & Management (*UK*)
Blake Friedmann Literary Agency Ltd (*UK*)
Luigi Bonomi Associates Ltd (*UK*)
Brandt & Hochman Literary Agents, Inc. (*US*)
The Bright Literary Academy (*UK*)
Jenny Brown Associates (*UK*)
Brown Literary Agency (*US*)
Maria Carvainis Agency, Inc. (*US*)
Castiglia Literary Agency (*US*)
Mic Cheetham Literary Agency (*UK*)
Elyse Cheney Literary Associates, LLC (*US*)
Cine/Lit Representation (*US*)
Rosica Colin Ltd (*UK*)

Don Congdon Associates, Inc. (*US*)
Conville & Walsh Ltd (*UK*)
Coombs Moylett Literary Agency (*UK*)
Crawford Literary Agency (*US*)
The Croce Agency (*US*)
Curtis Brown Group Ltd (*UK*)
DeFiore and Company (*US*)
Diamond Kahn and Woods (DKW) Literary Agency Ltd (*UK*)
Diane Banks Associates Literary Agency (*UK*)
Sandra Dijkstra Literary Agency (*US*)
Jim Donovan Literary (*US*)
Dorian Literary Agency (DLA) (*UK*)
Edwards Fuglewicz (*UK*)
Judith Ehrlich Literary Management (*US*)
Ethan Ellenberg Literary Agency (*US*)
Ann Elmo Agency, Inc. (*US*)
Farris Literary Agency, Inc. (*US*)
The Feldstein Agency (*UK*)
FinePrint Literary Management (*US*)
Folio Literary Management, LLC (*US*)
Foundry Literary + Media (*US*)
Full Throttle Literary Agency (*US*)
Furniss Lawton (*UK*)
Don Gastwirth & Associates (*US*)
Gelfman Schneider Literary Agents, Inc. (*US*)
The Gernert Company (*US*)
The Susan Golomb Literary Agency (*US*)
Irene Goodman Literary Agency (*US*)
Kathryn Green Literary Agency, LLC (*US*)
Sanford J. Greenburger Associates, Inc (*US*)
Greene & Heaton Ltd (*UK*)
Gregory & Company, Authors' Agents (*UK*)
Jill Grosjean Literary Agency (*US*)
Laura Gross Literary Agency (*US*)
The Mitchell J. Hamilburg Agency (*US*)
Hardman & Swainson (*UK*)
Antony Harwood Limited (*UK*)
A M Heath & Company Limited, Author's Agents (*UK*)
Rupert Heath Literary Agency (*UK*)
Hidden Value Group (*US*)
Hill Nadell Literary Agency (*US*)
Andrea Hurst Literary Management (*US*)
International Transactions, Inc. (*US*)
J de S Associates Inc (*US*)
Kilburn Literary Agency (*UK*)
Kimberley Cameron & Associates (Formerly Reece Halsey North) (*US*)
The Knight Agency (*US*)
Elaine Koster Literary Agency LLC (*US*)
Barbara S. Kouts, Literary Agent (*US*)
Larsen Pomada Literary Agents (*US*)
Robert Lecker Agency (*Can*)
Levine Greenberg Literary Agency, Inc. (*US*)
The Literary Group (*US*)
Andrew Lownie Literary Agency Ltd (*UK*)
Lyons Literary LLC (*US*)
Gina Maccoby Agency (*US*)
MacGregor Literary (*US*)
Madeleine Milburn Literary Agency (*UK*)
Manus & Associates Literary Agency, Inc. (*US*)
Denise Marcil Literary Agency, Inc. (*US*)

The Martell Agency (*US*)
McIntosh & Otis, Inc (*US*)
Monteiro Rose Dravis Agency, Inc. (*US*)
The Jean V. Naggar Literary Agency (*US*)
New Leaf Literary & Media, Inc. (*US*)
Niad Management (*US*)
Objective Entertainment (*US*)
P.S. Literary Agency (*Can*)
The Park Literary Group LLC (*US*)
Pavilion Literary Management (*US*)
Barry Perelman Agency (*US*)
L. Perkins Associates (*US*)
Pinder Lane & Garon-Brooke Associates Ltd (*US*)
Alièka Pistek Literary Agency, LLC (*US*)
Aaron M. Priest Literary Agency (*US*)
Queen Literary Agency, Inc. (*US*)
Raines & Raines (*US*)
Regal Literary (*UK*)
Regal Literary Inc. (*US*)
Renee Zuckerbrot Literary Agency (*US*)
RLR Associates (*US*)
Jane Rotrosen Agency (*US*)
Salkind Literary Agency (*US*)
Schiavone Literary Agency (*US*)
Secret Agent Man (*US*)
Sheil Land Associates Ltd (*UK*)
Signature Literary Agency (*US*)
Spencerhill Associates (*US*)
Philip G. Spitzer Literary Agency, Inc. (*US*)
The Swetky Agency and Associates (*US*)
SYLA – Susan Yearwood Literary Agency (*UK*)
Talcott Notch Literary (*US*)
Tom Lee (*US*)
TriadaUS Literary Agency, Inc. (*US*)
Trident Media Group, LLC (*US*)
Veritas Literary Agency (*US*)
Beth Vesel Literary Agency (*US*)
Waxman Leavell Literary Agency (*US*)
Irene Webb Literary (*US*)
The Wendy Weil Agency, Inc. (*US*)
Westwood Creative Artists (*Can*)
Whispering Buffalo Literary Agency Ltd (*UK*)
William Morris Endeavor (WME) London (*UK*)
Yates & Yates (*US*)
The Zack Company, Inc (*US*)

Translations
AP Watt at United Agents LLP (*UK*)
AVAnti Productions & Management (*UK*)
W.M. Clark Associates (*US*)
Don Gastwirth & Associates (*US*)
Antony Harwood Limited (*UK*)
Intercontinental Literary Agency (*UK*)
J de S Associates Inc (*US*)
Andrew Lownie Literary Agency Ltd (*UK*)
The Marton Agency, Inc. (*US*)
Aaron M. Priest Literary Agency (*US*)
RLR Associates (*US*)
The Swetky Agency and Associates (*US*)
Thomas Moore Literary Agency (*UK*)
The Zack Company, Inc (*US*)

Travel
AP Watt at United Agents LLP (*UK*)

Robert Astle & Associates Literary Management, Inc. (*US*)
AVAnti Productions & Management (*UK*)
Blake Friedmann Literary Agency Ltd (*UK*)
Paul Bresnick Literary Agency, LLC (*US*)
Tracy Brown Literary Agency (*US*)
Cine/Lit Representation (*US*)
Rosica Colin Ltd (*UK*)
Frances Collin Literary Agent (*US*)
Don Congdon Associates, Inc. (*US*)
Conville & Walsh Ltd (*UK*)
The Croce Agency (*US*)
Sandra Dijkstra Literary Agency (*US*)
Dunham Literary, Inc. (*US*)
Farris Literary Agency, Inc. (*US*)
The Feldstein Agency (*UK*)
FinePrint Literary Management (*US*)
Fletcher & Company (*US*)
Foundry Literary + Media (*US*)
Jeanne Fredericks Literary Agency, Inc. (*US*)
Greene & Heaton Ltd (*UK*)
Jill Grosjean Literary Agency (*US*)
The Mitchell J. Hamilburg Agency (*US*)
Antony Harwood Limited (*UK*)
hhb agency ltd (*UK*)
Jill Grinberg Literary Management LLC (*US*)
Larsen Pomada Literary Agents (*US*)
Robert Lecker Agency (*Can*)
Levine Greenberg Literary Agency, Inc. (*US*)
London Independent Books (*UK*)
Lyons Literary LLC (*US*)
Kirsten Manges Literary Agency, LLC (*US*)
Duncan McAra (*UK*)
McIntosh & Otis, Inc (*US*)
MNLA (Maggie Noach Literary Agency) (*UK*)
The Park Literary Group LLC (*US*)
The Richard Parks Agency (*US*)
James Peter Associates, Inc. (*US*)
Pinder Lane & Garon-Brooke Associates Ltd (*US*)
Alièka Pistek Literary Agency, LLC (*US*)
RLR Associates (*US*)
Robert Dudley Agency (*UK*)
Salkind Literary Agency (*US*)
The Sayle Literary Agency (*UK*)
Schiavone Literary Agency (*US*)
The Science Factory (*UK*)
Jonathan Scott, Inc (*US*)
The Seven Bridges Group (*US*)
Sheil Land Associates Ltd (*UK*)
Sinclair-Stevenson (*UK*)
Philip G. Spitzer Literary Agency, Inc. (*US*)
Rebecca Strong International Literary Agency (*US*)
The Strothman Agency (*US*)
The Swetky Agency and Associates (*US*)
Tessler Literary Agency (*US*)
Thomas Moore Literary Agency (*UK*)
TriadaUS Literary Agency, Inc. (*US*)
Watkins / Loomis Agency, Inc. (*US*)
TV
A & B Personal Management Ltd (*UK*)
Sheila Ableman Literary Agency (*UK*)

Above the Line Agency (*US*)
Bret Adams Ltd (*US*)
The Agency (London) Ltd (*UK*)
Agency for the Performing Arts (APA) (*US*)
Anonymous Content (*US*)
AP Watt at United Agents LLP (*UK*)
AVAnti Productions & Management (*UK*)
Berlin Associates (*UK*)
Blake Friedmann Literary Agency Ltd (*UK*)
Luigi Bonomi Associates Ltd (*UK*)
The Bright Literary Academy (*UK*)
Alan Brodie Representation Ltd (*UK*)
Capel & Land Ltd (*UK*)
Mary Clemmey Literary Agency (*UK*)
Jonathan Clowes Ltd (*UK*)
Rosica Colin Ltd (*UK*)
The Collective (*US*)
Curtis Brown Group Ltd (*UK*)
Felix de Wolfe (*UK*)
Energy Entertainment (*US*)
Film Rights Ltd in association with Laurence Fitch Ltd (*UK*)
Jill Foster Ltd (JFL) (*UK*)
The Gage Group (*US*)
Eric Glass Ltd (*UK*)
Graham Maw Christie Literary Agency (*UK*)
Antony Harwood Limited (*UK*)
hhb agency ltd (*UK*)
Valerie Hoskins Associates (*UK*)
Hudson Agency (*US*)
Independent Talent Group Ltd (*UK*)
Janet Fillingham Associates (*UK*)
Michelle Kass Associates (*UK*)
Ken Sherman & Associates (*US*)
Ki Agency Ltd (*UK*)
Lyons Literary LLC (*US*)
Madeleine Milburn Literary Agency (*UK*)
Andrew Mann Ltd (*UK*)
Marjacq Scripts Ltd (*UK*)
MBA Literary Agents Ltd (*UK*)
Bill McLean Personal Management Ltd (*UK*)
Monteiro Rose Dravis Agency, Inc. (*US*)
William Morris Endeavor Entertainment (*US*)
Niad Management (*US*)
Objective Entertainment (*US*)
Paradigm Talent and Literary Agency (*US*)
PBJ and JBJ Management (*UK*)
Barry Perelman Agency (*US*)
James Peter Associates, Inc. (*US*)
The Peters Fraser & Dunlop Group Ltd (PFD) (*UK*)
Michael D. Robins & Associates (*US*)
Rochelle Stevens & Co. (*UK*)
Sayle Screen Ltd (*UK*)
Linda Seifert Management (*UK*)
The Seven Bridges Group (*US*)
Sheil Land Associates Ltd (*UK*)
Stone Manners Salners Agency (*US*)
The Swetky Agency and Associates (*US*)
The Tennyson Agency (*UK*)
Thomas Moore Literary Agency (*UK*)
Jane Turnbull (*UK*)
United Agents (*UK*)

Cecily Ware Literary Agents (*UK*)
The Zack Company, Inc (*US*)
Westerns
Abela Literature (*Can*)
AVAnti Productions & Management (*UK*)
Full Throttle Literary Agency (*US*)
Antony Harwood Limited (*UK*)
Hidden Value Group (*US*)
Hudson Agency (*US*)
Andrea Hurst Literary Management (*US*)
J de S Associates Inc (*US*)
Andrew Lownie Literary Agency Ltd (*UK*)
Pinder Lane & Garon-Brooke Associates Ltd
(*US*)
Raines & Raines (*US*)
Secret Agent Man (*US*)
The Seven Bridges Group (*US*)
The Swetky Agency and Associates (*US*)
Women's Interests
A+B Works (*US*)
Ambassador Speakers Bureau & Literary
Agency (*US*)
The Ampersand Agency Ltd (*UK*)
Robert Astle & Associates Literary
Management, Inc. (*US*)
Author Rights Agency (*Ire*)
AVAnti Productions & Management (*UK*)
Barer Literary, LLC (*US*)
Blake Friedmann Literary Agency Ltd (*UK*)
Luigi Bonomi Associates Ltd (*UK*)
The Bright Literary Academy (*UK*)
Jenny Brown Associates (*UK*)
Brown Literary Agency (*US*)
Tracy Brown Literary Agency (*US*)
Juliet Burton Literary Agency (*UK*)
Sheree Bykofsky Associates, Inc. (*US*)
Maria Carvainis Agency, Inc. (*US*)
Elyse Cheney Literary Associates, LLC (*US*)
Teresa Chris Literary Agency Ltd (*UK*)
Rosica Colin Ltd (*UK*)
Frances Collin Literary Agent (*US*)
Don Congdon Associates, Inc. (*US*)
Conville & Walsh Ltd (*UK*)
Coombs Moylett Literary Agency (*UK*)
Crawford Literary Agency (*US*)
Creative Authors Ltd (*UK*)
The Croce Agency (*US*)
Diane Banks Associates Literary Agency (*UK*)
Sandra Dijkstra Literary Agency (*US*)
Jim Donovan Literary (*US*)
Dorian Literary Agency (DLA) (*UK*)
Dunham Literary, Inc. (*US*)
Judith Ehrlich Literary Management (*US*)
Einstein Thompson Agency (*US*)
Ethan Ellenberg Literary Agency (*US*)
Ann Elmo Agency, Inc. (*US*)
Elaine P. English, Attorney & Literary Agent
(*US*)
Felicia Eth Literary Representation (*US*)
Farris Literary Agency, Inc. (*US*)
The Feldstein Agency (*UK*)
FinePrint Literary Management (*US*)
Folio Literary Management, LLC (*US*)

Foundry Literary + Media (*US*)
Jeanne Fredericks Literary Agency, Inc. (*US*)
Fredrica S. Friedman and Co. Inc. (*US*)
Furniss Lawton (*UK*)
Gelfman Schneider Literary Agents, Inc. (*US*)
The Susan Golomb Literary Agency (*US*)
Irene Goodman Literary Agency (*US*)
Kathryn Green Literary Agency, LLC (*US*)
Sanford J. Greenburger Associates, Inc (*US*)
Greyhaus Literary Agency (*US*)
Jill Grosjean Literary Agency (*US*)
Laura Gross Literary Agency (*US*)
The Mitchell J. Hamilburg Agency (*US*)
Antony Harwood Limited (*UK*)
Rupert Heath Literary Agency (*UK*)
hhb agency ltd (*UK*)
Hidden Value Group (*US*)
Hill Nadell Literary Agency (*US*)
Andrea Hurst Literary Management (*US*)
International Transactions, Inc. (*US*)
Jill Grinberg Literary Management LLC (*US*)
Virginia Kidd Agency, Inc (*US*)
Kilburn Literary Agency (*UK*)
The Knight Agency (*US*)
Linda Konner Literary Agency (*US*)
Elaine Koster Literary Agency LLC (*US*)
Barbara S. Kouts, Literary Agent (*US*)
Edite Kroll Literary Agency, Inc. (*US*)
Larsen Pomada Literary Agents (*US*)
Levine Greenberg Literary Agency, Inc. (*US*)
The Literary Group (*US*)
Sterling Lord Literistic, Inc. (*US*)
Lyons Literary LLC (*US*)
Gina Maccoby Agency (*US*)
MacGregor Literary (*US*)
Madeleine Milburn Literary Agency (*UK*)
Kirsten Manges Literary Agency, LLC (*US*)
Carol Mann Agency (*US*)
Manus & Associates Literary Agency, Inc. (*US*)
Denise Marcil Literary Agency, Inc. (*US*)
The Martell Agency (*US*)
Martin Literary Management (*US*)
McIntosh & Otis, Inc (*US*)
Doris S. Michaels Literary Agency, Inc. (*US*)
Howard Morhaim Literary Agency (*US*)
Judith Murdoch Literary Agency (*UK*)
Nappaland Literary Agency (*US*)
New Leaf Literary & Media, Inc. (*US*)
Northern Lights Literary Services (*US*)
Objective Entertainment (*US*)
P.S. Literary Agency (*Can*)
The Richard Parks Agency (*US*)
Pinder Lane & Garon-Brooke Associates Ltd
(*US*)
Linn Prentis Literary (*US*)
Aaron M. Priest Literary Agency (*US*)
Lynne Rabinoff Agency (*US*)
Renee Zuckerbrot Literary Agency (*US*)
Richford Becklow Literary Agency (*UK*)
Ann Rittenberg Literary Agency (*US*)
RLR Associates (*US*)
Linda Roghaar Literary Agency, Inc. (*US*)
Jane Rotrosen Agency (*US*)

US Publishers

For the most up-to-date listings of these and hundreds of other publishers, visit http://www.firstwriter.com/publishers

*To claim your **free** access to the site, please see the back of this book.*

ABC-CLIO / Greenwood

Acquisitions Department/Greenwood
ABC-CLIO
PO Box 1911
Santa Barbara, CA 93116-1911
Tel: +1 (800) 368-6868
Email: ccasey@abc-clio.com
Website: http://www.abc-clio.com

Publishes: Nonfiction; Reference; *Areas:* Biography; Historical; Military; Religious; Sociology; *Markets:* Academic; Adult

Contact: Cathleen Casey

Publisher of general nonfiction and reference covering history, humanities, and general interest topics across the secondary and higher education curriculum. No fiction, poetry, or drama. Welcomes proposals in appropriate areas. See website for specific imprint / editor contact details.

Alexander Hamilton Institute

Business Management Daily
PO Box 9070
McLean, VA 22102-0070
Tel: +1 (800) 543-2055
Fax: +1 (703) 905-8040
Email:
Editor@BusinessManagementDaily.com
Website: http://www.legalworkplace.com

Publishes: Nonfiction; *Areas:* Business;

Legal; *Markets:* Professional

Publishes material for executives, upper management, and HR managers.

Alice James Books

238 Main St.
Farmington, ME 04936
Tel: +1 (207) 778-7071
Fax: +1 (207) 778-7766
Email: info@alicejamesbooks.org
Website: http://alicejamesbooks.org

Publishes: Poetry; *Markets:* Adult

Poetry press accepting submissions through its various competitions only. Competitions include large cash prizes and reasonable entry fees.

Alondra Press

4119 Wildacres Drive
Houston, TX 77072
Email: lark@alondrapress.com
Website: http://www.alondrapress.com

Publishes: Fiction; Nonfiction; *Areas:* Anthropology; Archaeology; Historical; Philosophy; Psychology; Translations; *Markets:* Adult; *Treatments:* Literary

Contact: Fiction: "Editor"; Nonfiction: Armando Benitez, Solomon Tager, or Henry Hollenbaugh

Send query by email, with synopsis up to 300 words and sample or full manuscript. See website for full guidelines.

Amadeus Press

33 Plymouth Street, Suite 302
Montclair, NJ 07042
Email: jcerullo@halleonard.com
Website: http://www.amadeuspress.com

Publishes: Nonfiction; *Areas:* Music; *Markets:* Adult

Contact: John Cerullo

Publishes books on classical music and opera. Send query with outline or table of contents, one or two sample chapters, sample illustrations, and your schedule for completion. Prefers contact early in the project, but cannot guarantee a response. See website for full details.

American Press

60 State Street #700
Boston, MA 02109
Tel: +1 (617) 247- 0022
Email: americanpress@flash.net
Website:
http://www.americanpresspublishers.com

Publishes: Nonfiction; *Areas:* Anthropology; Architecture; Arts; Business; Drama; Finance; Health; Historical; Legal; Music; Philosophy; Politics; Psychology; Religious; Science; Sociology; Sport; Technology; Theatre; *Markets:* Academic; Professional

Welcomes proposals for academic and professional titles in all subject areas. Accepts textbooks, handbooks, laboratory manuals, workbooks, study guides, journal research, reference books, DVDs, CDs and software programs and materials for college level courses. See website for more details.

Anaiah Press, LLC

7780 49th St. N #129
Pinellas Park, FL 33781
Email: submissions@anaiahpress.com
Website: http://www.anaiahpress.com

Publishes: Fiction; Nonfiction; *Areas:* Adventure; Drama; Fantasy; Historical; Horror; Humour; Lifestyle; Literature; Mystery; New Age; Religious; Romance; Science; Sci-Fi; Spiritual; Suspense; Thrillers; Women's Interests; *Markets:* Adult; Children's; Family; Youth; *Treatments:* Contemporary; Literary; Mainstream; Positive; Traditional

Contact: Eden Plantz

A Christian digital-first publishing house dedicated to presenting quality faith-based fiction and nonfiction books to the public. Our goal is to provide our authors with the close-knit, hands-on experience of working with a small press, while making sure they don't have to sacrifice quality editing, cover art, and marketing.

Our first books will be released in digital formats beginning in Summer 2014.

Currently, we do not accept proposals for works yet to be written. Please, only query us if your manuscript is complete.

As a Christian press, we publish books with a strong inspirational theme and/ or a message of faith. We do not accept manuscripts with the following:

-- Anti-Christian propaganda/ themes
-- Gratuitous sex
-- Messages of religious or social intolerance

We do respond personally to every query received. Please allow 6-8 weeks for a response.

Simultaneous submissions are fine, but we do ask that out of professional courtesy, you let us know if you receive an offer from another publisher or agent.

Arcade Publishing

307 West 36th Street, 11th Floor
New York, NY 10018
Tel: +1 (212) 643-6816
Fax: +1 (212) 643-6819
Email:
arcadesubmissions@skyhorsepublishing.com

Website: http://www.arcadepub.com

Publishes: Fiction; Nonfiction; *Areas:* Adventure; Arts; Autobiography; Business; Cookery; Current Affairs; Historical; Military; Nature; Science; Travel; *Markets:* Adult; *Treatments:* Literary

Send query by email with a brief cover letter; one-to-two page synopsis; annotated chapter outline; market analysis, including competitive research; 1-2 sample chapters; author bio, including list of all previous publishing credits.

Aunt Lute Books

PO Box 410687
San Francisco, CA 94141
Tel: +1 (415) 826-1300
Fax: +1 (415) 826-8300
Email: books@auntlute.com
Website: http://auntlute.com

Publishes: Fiction; Nonfiction; Poetry; *Areas:* Women's Interests; *Markets:* Adult

Contact: Acquisitions Editor

A multicultural women's press. Particularly interested in works by women of colour. No therapy or self-help. Poetry only considered as part of a larger work. Send query by post only, with table of contents and two sample chapters (or approximately 50 pages), plus SASE if return of work is required. See website for full submission guidelines.

Aurora Publishing, Inc

3655 Torrance Blvd., Suite 430
Torrance, CA 90503
Tel: +1 (310) 540-2800
Email: info@aurora-publishing.com
Website: http://www.aurora-publishing.com

Publishes: Fiction; *Areas:* Adventure; Translations; *Markets:* Adult; Children's; Youth

Publishes Japanese manga graphic novels translated into English, and also original American manga for US and worldwide consumption. Keen to develop manga for a more mature audience.

Azro Press

PMB 342
1704 Llano St B
Santa Fe, NM 87505
Tel: +1 (505) 989-3272
Fax: +1 (505) 989-3832
Email: books@azropress.com
Website: http://www.azropress.com

Publishes: Fiction; Nonfiction; *Markets:* Children's

Publishes picture books and illustrated easy reader books for young children. Currently focusing on books written and illustrated by residents of the Southwest. Books need not be about the Southwest, but may be at an advantage if they are. See website for full guidelines.

Baywood Publishing Company, Inc.

26 Austin Avenue
P0 Box 337
Amityville, NY 11701
Tel: +1 (631) 691-1270
Fax: +1 (631) 691-1770
Email: info@baywood.com
Website: http://www.baywood.com

Publishes: Nonfiction; *Areas:* Anthropology; Archaeology; Health; Nature; Psychology; Science; Sociology; Technology; Women's Interests; *Markets:* Academic; Professional

Scholarly professional publisher accepting proposals for publications in counseling, death & bereavement, psychology, and gerontology, health policy and technical communication. See website for full instructions on submitting a proposal.

Behrman House

11 Edison Place
Springfield, NJ 07081
Tel: +1 (973) 379-7200
Fax: +1 (973) 379-7280
Email: customersupport@behrmanhouse.com
Website: http://www.behrmanhouse.com

Publishes: Nonfiction; *Areas:* Historical; Philosophy; Religious; *Markets:* Academic; Adult

Publishes books of Jewish content for the classroom and general readership. Send query with SASE, two sample chapters, table of contents, and market info. No submissions by email.

Betterway Home Books
4700 East Galbraith Road
Cincinnati, OH 45236
Website: http://www.betterwaybooks.com

Publishes: Nonfiction; *Areas:* Architecture; Design; How-to; Lifestyle; *Markets:* Adult

Publishes books on homemaking: repair, improvement, organisation, etc. Send query with SASE, proposal package, outline, and one sample chapter.

Bick Publishing House
16 Marion Road
Branford, CT 06405
Tel: +1 (203) 208-5253
Fax: +1 (203) 208-5253
Email: bickpubhse@aol.com
Website: http://www.bickpubhouse.com

Publishes: Fiction; Nonfiction; *Areas:* Arts; Health; Philosophy; Psychology; Science; Sci-Fi; Self-Help; *Markets:* Adult; Youth

Publishes Life Sciences and Self-Help Books for Teens; Young Adult: Psychology, Science and Philosophy; Science Fiction for Teens; Adult Health and Recovery; Meditation; Living with Disabilities; Wildlife Rehabilitation. See website for submission guidelines. No submissions by email.

Birdsong Books
1322 Bayview Road
Middletown, DE 19709
Tel: +1 (302) 378-7274
Fax: +1 (302) 378-0339
Email: birdsong@birdsongbooks.com
Website: http://www.birdsongbooks.com

Publishes: Nonfiction; *Areas:* Nature; Science; *Markets:* Children's

Publishes natural science picture books for children, concentrating on North American animals and habitats. See website for manuscript submission guidelines.

Black Lawrence Press
Email: editors@blacklawrencepress.com
Website: http://blacklawrence.homestead.com

Publishes: Fiction; Nonfiction; Poetry; *Areas:* Autobiography; Biography; Culture; Literature; Short Stories; Translations; *Markets:* Adult; *Treatments:* Contemporary; Literary

Idependent press specialising in books of contemporary literature and creative nonfiction, including novels, memoirs, short story collections, poetry, biographies, and cultural studies. Also publishes occasional translations from German and French. Submit online via website submission system.

Blind Eye Books
1141 Grant Street
Bellingham, WA 98225
Email: editor@blindeyebooks.com
Website: http://www.blindeyebooks.com

Publishes: Fiction; *Areas:* Fantasy; Romance; Sci-Fi; *Markets:* Adult

Contact: Nicole Kimberling, Editor

Publishes science fiction, fantasy and paranormal romance novels featuring gay or lesbian protagonists. No short story collections, poetry, erotica, horror or nonfiction. Manuscripts should generally be between 70,000 and 150,000 words. Send complete ms by post, unless from overseas, in which case email editor for electronic submission guidelines. See website for full details.

Blue Dolphin Publishing
P.O. Box 8
Nevada City, CA 95959
Tel: +1 (530) 477-1503
Fax: +1 (530) 477-8342
Email:
bdolphin@bluedolphinpublishing.com
Website:
http://www.bluedolphinpublishing.com

Publishes: Fiction; Nonfiction; Poetry;
Areas: Biography; Health; Lifestyle;
Philosophy; Politics; Psychology; Religious;
Self-Help; Sociology; Spiritual; Women's
Interests; *Markets:* Adult; Children's; Youth

Contact: Paul and Nancy Clemens

Include cover letter, synopsis, table of
contents, sample chapters, author resume,
and SASE. See website for full guidelines.
Response in 3-6 months.

Blurbeo
509 7th St
Sultan, WA 98294
Email: alleywolf@gmail.com
Website: http://www.blurbeo.com

Publishes: Fiction; *Areas:* Adventure;
Anthropology; Crime; Drama;
Entertainment; Horror; Humour; Lifestyle;
Literature; Men's Interests; Military;
Mystery; Religious; Romance; Sci-Fi; Short
Stories; Spiritual; Suspense; Thrillers;
Women's Interests; *Markets:* Adult;
Children's; Family; Youth; *Treatments:*
Mainstream

Contact: Chris Vaughn

A small whiteboard video company that
assists authors with promoting their books
through the power of video. Founded by an
author for authors, Blurbeo is now accepting
manuscripts for publication

We are currently seeking works of fiction in
the following genres:

Holiday themed short fiction
Thriller/Action Adventure
Horror
Romance short fiction
YA fiction, short and long

Writers interested in submitting work should
do so via email and should follow the
directions closely. Please put your name and
the word "submission" in the email's subject
line. Your email should include a brief letter
of interest and author bio. Please attached the
first 2,000 words or the first 2 chapters of
your story.

Please allow up to 3 weeks for a response as
there are multiple submissions being sent in.
We will attempt to respond to all who
contact us.

Why publish with us? Simple! We not only
offer a 20% royalty to our authors but we
also include our deluxe video promotion
package absolutely FREE. That way you can
get a jump start on promoting your book!
20% Royalties on sales of digital and print
copies
10% Royalties on all merchandise sales (T-
shirts, poster, etc)
FREE deluxe video package
120 second promotional whiteboard video
Promotion on Blurbeo, Youtube, Vimeo, and
more
Internet radio advertising services
Author-2-Author interview
Dedicated author support (Your success is
our success)

We will never ask our authors to pay fees for
any part of the publishing process, and no
publisher should.

Bold Strokes Books
PO Box 249
Valley Falls, NY 12185
Tel: +1 (518) 677-5127
Fax: +1 (518) 677-5291
Email: submissions@boldstrokesbooks.com
Website: http://www.boldstrokesbooks.com

Publishes: Fiction; Nonfiction; *Areas:*
Adventure; Crime; Erotic; Fantasy;
Historical; Horror; Mystery; Romance; Sci-
Fi; *Markets:* Adult; Youth

Contact: Len Barot, Selections Director

Publishes LesbianGayBiTransQueer general and genre fiction, and nonfiction. Accepts unsolicited mss by email with one-page synopsis. See website for full guidelines.

The Bold Strummer Ltd

110-C Imperial Avenue
PO Box 2037
Westport, CT 06880
Tel: +1 (203) 227-8588
Fax: +1 (203) 227-8775
Email: theboldstrummer@msn.com
Website: http://www.boldstrummerltd.com

Publishes: Nonfiction; *Areas:* How-to; Music; *Markets:* Adult

Publishes books and music for and about the guitar.

Bracket Books

PO Box 286098
New York, NY 10128-9991
Email: info@bracketbooks.com
Website: http://bracketbooks.com

Publishes: Fiction; Nonfiction; *Areas:* Culture; Photography; *Markets:* Adult; Family; *Treatments:* Commercial; Contemporary; Literary; Mainstream

Contact: Sam Majors

Based in New York, New York. The company was established to fill a niche, a publishing void that grows larger as traditional print publishers continue to consolidate, struggle to maintain their narrow profit margins, and hold onto outmoded methods of distribution and old-fashioned book marketing techniques. Our business model embraces digital distribution and online marketing, and although we love to design and devour books that are produced in a printed form, we understand that the key to succeeding in the book industry in the coming decades won't be price points or corporate alliances; the key will be, as it always has been, matching the right author with the right audience, and doing so in an efficient, intelligent way.

Although we publish fiction, our focus is

non-fiction, and we'll be releasing approximately four non-fiction titles for each fiction title we publish. At this time, we do not publish coffee table books, art books, or children's books, and we cannot imagine ever being interested in publishing poetry or plays. We are primarily interested in books about the art of photography or about photographers, but we will also publish fiction that is connected, in an important way, to pop culture, particularly to movements in film or genres of popular music (think, for instance, of Michael Chabon's The Amazing Adventures of Kavalier & Clay).

Bristol Publishing Enterprises

2714 McCone Avenue
Hayward, CA 94545
Tel: +1 (800) 346-4889
Fax: +1 (800) 346-7064
Email: orders@bristolpublishing.com
Website: http://www.bristolpublishing.com

Publishes: Nonfiction; *Areas:* Cookery; Hobbies; *Markets:* Adult

Publishes books on cookery. Send query with outline, author CV, and sample chapter or other writing sample.

Bronze Man Books

Millikin University
1184 W. Main St.
Decatur, Illinois 62522
Tel: +1 (217) 424-6264
Email: rbrooks@millikin.edu
Website: http://www.bronzemanbooks.com

Publishes: Fiction; Poetry; Scripts; *Areas:* Drama; Short Stories; *Markets:* Adult; *Treatments:* Literary

Contact: Dr. Randy Brooks

Publishes 1-2 chapbooks per year of various genres (poetry, prose, drama, etc.). Always open to proposals. Poetry chapbooks should consist of 18-30 poems with a connecting theme or notion; fiction chapbooks should be 32-72 pages and may be short story collections or one or two longer works. Send proposal by email or by post with SASE in first instance. See website for more details.

Bullitt Publishing

Email: submissions@bullittpublishing.com
Website: http://bullittpublishing.com

Publishes: Fiction; *Areas:* Romance; *Markets:* Adult; *Treatments:* Contemporary

Publishes contemporary romance. Submissions by email only – see website for full guidelines.

Burford Books

101 E State Street #301
Ithaca, NY 14850
Tel: +1 (607) 319-4373
Fax: +1 (866) 212-7750
Email: info@burfordbooks.com
Website: http://www.burfordbooks.com

Publishes: Nonfiction; *Areas:* Adventure; Cookery; Gardening; Leisure; Military; Nature; Sport; Travel; *Markets:* Adult

Publishes books on the outdoors, in the widest sense. Send query by email in the first instance. See website for full guidelines.

By Light Unseen Media

PO Box 1233
Pepperell, MA 01463-3233
Email: vyrdolak@bylightunseenmedia.com
Website:
http://www.bylightunseenmedia.com

Publishes: Fiction; Nonfiction; Culture; Fantasy; Historical; Horror; Sci-Fi; *Markets:* Adult; Youth

Publishes vampire fiction and nonfiction.

Fiction should be full-length novels 75,000 to 150,000 words in length. No short story collections. Interested in dramatic fiction with a realistic tone. All work must be entirely the author's work (not using any elements of other, established worlds). No slayers, hunters, etc.

Nonfiction of 50,000 words to 150,000 words exploring vampires in folklore, cultural tradition, occult theory and as a modern social subgroup or counter-culture are also sought.

Accepts approaches by post or email. See website for full guidelines.

Cadence Jazz Books

Cadence Building
Redwood, NY 13679
Tel: +1 (315) 287-2852
Email: orders@cadencebuilding.com
Website: http://www.cadencejazzbooks.com

Publishes: Nonfiction; Reference; *Areas:* Autobiography; Biography; Music; *Markets:* Academic; Adult

Publisher of jazz discographies, reference works, biographies and autobiographies. Send query with SASE, outline, and sample chapters.

Canterbury House Publishing, Ltd

7350 S. Tamiami Trail
Sarasota, FL 34231
Tel: +1 (941) 312-6912
Website:
http://www.canterburyhousepublishing.com

Publishes: Fiction; Nonfiction; *Areas:* Autobiography; Mystery; Romance; Suspense; *Markets:* Adult

Publishes manuscripts that have a strong Southeastern US regional setting. Gives preference to stories along the southern Appalachian trail. Seeks fiction with an unusual protagonist that could be part of a romance/suspense or mystery series. Will consider memoirs or inspirational novels wuth strong regional appeal. No spy thrillers, explicit material, or books for children or young adults. Make contact via web form in first instance, requesting editorial email address. See website for full guidelines. Also provides ebook formatting services.

Cardoza Publishing

5473 S. Eastern Ave
Las Vegas, NV 89119
Tel: +1 (702) 870-7200
Fax: +1 (702) 822-6500
Email: info@cardozabooks.com
Website: http://www.cardozapub.com

Publishes: Nonfiction; *Areas:* Hobbies;
Leisure; *Markets:* Adult; Professional

Publishes books on games, gambling, chess
and backgammon. Send proposal by post
with SASE or by email with entire
manuscript if available. Include suggested
table of contents, overview, comparison of
similar titles, and reasons why the book is
unique and should be published. Also
include list qualifications and credentials
relevant to the writing of the proposed book.

Carstens Publications, Inc.

108 Phil Hardin Road
Newton, NJ 07860
Tel: +1 (973) 383-3355
Fax: +1 (973) 383-4064
Email: carstens@carstens-publications.com
Website: http://www.carstens-
publications.com

Publishes: Nonfiction; *Areas:* Hobbies;
How-to; Photography; *Markets:* Adult

Publishes books for model train and plane
enthusiasts. Send query with SASE.

The Catholic University of America Press

240 Leahy Hall
620 Michigan Avenue NE
Washington, DC 20064
Email: Lipscombe@cua.edu
Website: http://cuapress.cua.edu

Publishes: Nonfiction; *Areas:* Historical;
Literature; Philosophy; Politics; Religious;
Sociology; *Markets:* Academic; Professional

Contact: Trevor Lipscombe, Director

Publishes books disseminating scholarship in
the areas of theology, philosophy, church
history, and medieval studies. Send query

with outline, CV, sample chapter, and
publishing history.

Cedar Fort

2373 W. 700
S. Springville, UT 84663
Tel: +1 (801) 489-4084
Email: submissions@cedarfort.com
Website: http://www.cedarfort.com

Publishes: Fiction; Nonfiction; *Areas:*
Historical; Religious; Self-Help; Short
Stories; Spiritual; *Markets:* Adult;
Children's; Youth; *Treatments:* Positive

Publishes books with strong moral or
religious values that inspire readers to be
better people. No poetry. Rarely publishes
biographies, autobiographies, or memoirs,
and is very selective about children's books.
See website for full submission guidelines.

Centerstream Publishing

Email: Centerstrm@aol.com
Website: http://www.centerstream-usa.com

Publishes: Nonfiction; Reference; *Areas:*
Biography; How-to; Music; *Markets:* Adult

Publishes music books on instruments,
instructional, reference, and biographies.

Changeling Press LLC

PO Box 1046
Martinsburg, WV 25402
Email: Submissions@ChangelingPress.com
Website: http://www.changelingpress.com

Publishes: Fiction; *Areas:* Adventure;
Erotic; Fantasy; Romance; Sci-Fi; *Markets:*
Adult; *Treatments:* Dark; Positive

Contact: Margaret Riley

Publishes Paranormal, Dark Fantasy, Urban
Fantasy, Sci-Fi, Futuristic, BDSM, and
Action/Adventure romantic love stories in
print and as ebooks. Accepts multiple
submissions but not simultaneous
submissions. Stories should be between
10,000 and 28,000 words and have a happy

ending. Submit by email only. See website for full submission guidelines.

Channel Lake, Inc.
P.O. Box 1771
New York, NY 10156-1771
Tel: +1 (347) 329-5576
Fax: +1 (866) 794-5507
Email: info@channellake.com
Website: http://www.channellake.com

Publishes: Nonfiction; *Areas:* Travel; *Markets:* Adult

Publishes travel guides and books of local interest, mainly for sale in the specific local area to tourists and holidaymakers. Send query for full guidelines in first instance.

Chemical Publishing Company
PO Box 676
Revere, MA, 02151
Tel: +1 (888) 439-3976
Email: info@chemical-publishing.com
Website: http://www.chemical-publishing.com

Publishes: Nonfiction; Reference; *Areas:* Business; Medicine; Science; Technology; *Markets:* Academic; Professional

Publishes technical chemistry titles for professionals and academics on graduate courses. See website for more details. Considers both proposals and completed mss.

Chicago Review Press
814 North Franklin Street
Chicago, Illinois 60610
Tel: +1 (312) 337-0747
Fax: +1 (312) 337-5110
Email: frontdesk@chicagoreviewpress.com
Website: http://www.chicagoreviewpress.com

Publishes: Fiction; Nonfiction; *Areas:* Autobiography; Biography; Crafts; Culture; Film; Gardening; Historical; Lifestyle; Music; Politics; Science; Sport; Travel; Women's Interests; *Markets:* Adult; Children's; Youth

Publishes nonfiction through all imprints, and fiction through specific imprint listed above. Also publishes children's and young adult titles, but no picture books. See website for full submission guidelines.

Church Growth Institute
PO Box 7
Elkton, MD 21922-0007
Tel: +1 (434) 525-0022
Fax: +1 (434) 525-0608
Email: info@churchgrowth.org
Website: http://www.churchgrowth.org

Publishes: Nonfiction; *Areas:* How-to; Religious; *Markets:* Adult; Professional

Publishes how-to books for religious professionals and individuals. Send query by post or by email.

City Lights Publishers
Editorial Department
261 Columbus Avenue
San Francisco, CA 94133
Tel: +1 (415) 362-1901
Email: staff@citylights.com
Website: http://www.citylights.com/publishing

Publishes: Fiction; Nonfiction; Poetry; *Areas:* Autobiography; Politics; Sociology; Translations; *Markets:* Adult

Independent publisher of fiction, essays, memoirs, translations, poetry, and books on social and political issues. No New Age, self-help, children's literature, how-to guides, or genre works such as romance, westerns, or science fiction. Send query by post only with SASE, including a description of you and your book, a sample of 10-20 pages, and also an outline and table of contents for nonfiction. See website for full guidelines. No unsolicited mss, or queries by email or in person.

Clear Light Books
823 Don Diego
Santa Fe, NM 87505
Tel: +1 (505) 989-9590
Fax: +1 (505) 989-9519
Email: market@clearlightbooks.com
Website: http://clearlightbooks.com

Publishes: Nonfiction; *Areas:* Cookery;
Culture; Historical; Philosophy; Religious;
Markets: Adult; Children's

Publishes books on American Indian culture,
religion, and history; Southwestern
Americana; and Eastern philosophy and
religion. Also publishes cookbooks and
children's books relevant to these areas. See
website for full submission guidelines.

Coffee House Press
79 Thirteenth Ave NE, Suite 110
Minneapolis, MN 55413
Tel: +1 (612) 338-0125
Fax: +1 (612) 338-4004
Email: info@coffeehousepress.org
Website: http://www.coffeehousepress.org

Publishes: Fiction; Nonfiction; Poetry;
Areas: Autobiography; Short Stories;
Markets: Adult; *Treatments:* Literary

Contact: Anitra Budd, Managing Editor

Publishes literary novels, full-length short
story collections, poetry, and a small number
of essay collections and memoirs. No
submissions for anthologies, or genre fiction
such as mysteries, Gothic romances,
Westerns, science fiction, or books for
children. Not accepting poetry as at June 6,
2012 (see website for current situation).
Strongly discourages approaches by post –
unless you are unable to, use the online
submission system available via website.
Reading periods are March 1 – April 30 and
September 1 – October 31 annually. See
website for full details.

The College Board
The College Board National Office
45 Columbus Avenue
New York, NY 10023-6917
Tel: +1 (212) 713-8000

Website: http://www.collegeboard.com

Publishes: Nonfiction; *Areas:* How-to;
Markets: Academic

Publishes books aimed at providing guidance
to students who are about to make the move
to college. Send query with SASE, sample
chapters, and outline.

Consortium Publishing
640 Weaver Hill Road
West Greenwich, Rhode Island 02817-2261
Tel: +1 (401) 387-9838
Fax: +1 (401) 392-1926
Email: ConsortiumPub@msn.com
Website:
http://consortiumpublishing.tripod.com

Publishes: Nonfiction; *Areas:* Music;
Psychology; Science; Self-Help; *Markets:*
Academic; Children's

Publishes university and college text books,
laboratory manuals, workbooks and other
items used in college courses in various
subject matter areas, including Chemistry,
Counseling and Self-Help, Child
Development and Early Childhood
Education, English and Technical Writing,
and Music. See website for more details.
Send query with SASE, proposal, outline,
table of contents, and sample chapter.

Corwin
2455 Teller Road
Thousand Oaks, CA 91320
Tel: +1 (800) 233-9936
Fax: +1 (805) 499-9734
Email: lisa.shaw@corwin.com
Website: http://www.corwin.com

Publishes: Nonfiction; *Areas:* Literature;
Science; Technology; *Markets:* Professional

Publishes books for educational
professionals. See website for full guidelines
and specific editor email addresses.

The Countryman Press
PO Box 748
Woodstock, VT 05091

Tel: +1 (802) 457-4826
Email: countrymanpress@wwnorton.com
Website: http://www.countrymanpress.com

Publishes: Nonfiction; *Areas:*
Autobiography; Cookery; Crafts; Culture;
Historical; Hobbies; Leisure; Lifestyle;
Mystery; Nature; Photography; Travel;
Markets: Adult

Sends query with SASE, outlining you and
your work, and including a book proposal.
See website for full guidelines.

The Creative Company
PO Box 227
Mankato, MN 56002
Tel: +1 (800) 445-6209
Fax: +1 (507) 388-2746
Email: info@thecreativecompany.us
Website: http://www.thecreativecompany.us

Publishes: Fiction; Nonfiction; *Areas:* Arts;
Biography; Crafts; Culture; Health;
Historical; Hobbies; Music; Nature;
Religious; Science; Sociology; Sport;
Markets: Children's; Youth

Publishes picture books and nonfiction
aimed at children and young adults. Accepts
nonfiction submissions only – no fiction.
Send query with synopsis and two sample
chapters.

Cross-Cultural Communications Publications
239 Wynsum Avenue
Merrick, NY 11566-4725
Tel: +1 (516) 868-5635
Email: info@cross-
culturalcommunications.com
Website: http://www.cross-
culturalcommunications.com

Publishes: Fiction; Nonfiction; Poetry;
Areas: Autobiography; Culture; Historical;
Literature; Translations; *Markets:* Adult

Publishes cross-culture fiction, nonfiction,
and poetry. Most interested in poetry in
translation. Send query with SASE, or for
bilingual poetry submit a sample of 3-6 short
poems in their original language

accompanied by translation, with brief bio of
author and translator.

Crossway
1300 Crescent Street
Wheaton, IL 60187
Tel: +1 (630) 682-4300
Fax: +1 (630) 682-4785
Email: info@crossway.org
Website: http://www.crossway.org

Publishes: Nonfiction; *Areas:* Religious;
Markets: Adult

Publishes books written from an evangelical
Christian perspective. Send query by email
in the first instance.

Cup of Tea Books
Email: weditor@pagespringpublishing.com
Website: http://cupofteabooks.com

Publishes: Fiction; *Areas:* Mystery;
Romance; Women's Interests; *Markets:*
Adult; *Treatments:* Commercial

Publishes fiction for women, including cozy
mysteries, upmarket commercial fiction, and
romance. Send query by email with synopsis
and the first thirty pages in the body of the
email. Include title and the word
"Submission" in the subject line. Aims to
respond within four weeks – follow up if no
response in that time. No submissions or
queries by post.

Cycle Publishing / Van der Plas Publications
1282 7th Avenue
San Francisco, CA 94122
Tel: +1 (415) 665-8214
Fax: +1 (415) 753-8572
Email: rvdp@cyclepublishing.com
Website: http://www.cyclepublishing.com

Publishes: Nonfiction; *Areas:* Hobbies;
Leisure; Sport; *Markets:* Adult

Mainly focuses on books on cycling, but has
also published books on other sports, such as
golf and baseball.

Digital Manga, Inc.

ATTN: SUBMISSIONS
1487 West 178th Street, Suite 300
Gardena, CA 90248
Tel: +1 (310) 817-8010
Fax: +1 (310) 817-8018
Email: contact@emanga.com
Website: http://www.emanga.com

Publishes: Fiction; *Markets:* Adult

Accepts submissions of completed manga works only. Does not publish literary books or Western-style comics. Unable to match writers with artists at this time. Completed works must contain at least 90 pages of material and may be black and white or full colour. Send material by post or provide link to place of publication online. See website for full guidelines.

Divertir Publishing LLC

PO Box 232
North Salem, NH 03073
Email: query@divertirpublishing.com
Website: http://divertirpublishing.com

Publishes: Fiction; Nonfiction; Poetry; *Areas:* Crafts; Current Affairs; Fantasy; Historical; Hobbies; Humour; Mystery; Politics; Religious; Romance; Sci-Fi; Self-Help; Short Stories; Spiritual; Suspense; *Markets:* Adult; *Treatments:* Contemporary; Satirical

Publishes full-length fiction, short fiction, poetry, and nonfiction. No erotica or material which is disrespectful to the opinions of others. Accepts queries and submissions by email only. See website for full guidelines.

DK Publishing

375 Hudson Street
New York, NY 10014
Tel: +1 (646) 674-4000
Email: ecommerce@us.penguingroup.com
Website: http://www.dk.com

Publishes: Nonfiction; *Markets:* Children's

Publishes highly visual nonfiction for children. Assumes no responsibility for unsolicited mss and prefers approaches through an established literary agent.

Dover Publications, Inc.

Attn: Editorial Department
31 East 2nd Street
Mincola, NY 11501
Tel: +1 (516) 294-7000
Fax: +1 (516) 873-1401
Website: http://store.doverpublications.com

Publishes: Nonfiction; *Areas:* Antiques; Architecture; Arts; Crafts; Literature; Music; Science; *Markets:* Adult; Children's

No original fiction, music, or poetry. Welcomes submissions in other areas, but cannot return material and responds only if interested. Send query by post with outline, table of contents, and one sample chapter, if available.

Down East Books

ATTN: Books
PO Box 679
Camden, ME 04843
Email: submissions@downeast.com
Website: http://www.downeast.com

Publishes: Fiction; Nonfiction; *Areas:* Culture; Historical; Leisure; Nature; Sport; *Markets:* Adult; Children's; Family; Youth; *Treatments:* Contemporary; Mainstream

Publishes regional books focusing on New England, and in particular Maine. Publishes mainly nonfiction, but also publishes a handful of adult and juvenile fiction titles per year. Accepts queries by post or by email, but prefers email queries. Send one-page letter describing you and your project, and optionally the first two pages (up to 1,000 words). No unsolicited mss. See website for full guidelines.

Down The Shore Publishing

Attn: Acquisitions Editor
PO Box 100
West Creek, NJ 08092
Fax: +1 (609) 597-0422
Email: info@down-the-shore.com
Website: http://www.down-the-shore.com

Publishes: Fiction; Nonfiction; Poetry; *Areas:* Historical; Nature; Short Stories; *Markets:* Adult

Small regional publisher focusing on New Jersey, the Jersey Shore, the mid-Atlantic, and seashore and coastal subjects. Specialises in regional histories; pictorial, coffee table books; literary anthologies; and natural history titles appropriate to the market. Rarely publishes fiction, and does not generally publish poetry unless as part of an anthology. Willing to consider any exceptional work appropriate to the market, however. See website for more details.

Dragonfairy Press

Email: info@dragonfairypress.com
Website: http://www.dragonfairypress.com

Publishes: Fiction; *Areas:* Fantasy; Romance; Sci-Fi; *Markets:* Adult; Youth

Please follow submission instructions on website. We want manuscripts that stretch beyond the world as we know it. That means fantasy and science fiction, including their various subgenres, such as urban fantasy, paranormal romance/erotica, cyberpunk, supernatural horror, and others. Don't worry about sex, gore, or foul language. While we certainly do not require these, we don't shy away from them either. Although we don't expect manuscripts to be publication-ready, we strongly recommend that your manuscript be clean enough (and in our manuscript format) to minimize distractions as we read. We look for strong writing and well-paced stories.

Dzanc Books

1334 Woodbourne Street
Westland, MI 48186
Email: info@dzancbooks.org
Website: http://www.dzancbooks.org

Publishes: Fiction; *Areas:* Literature; Short Stories; *Markets:* Adult; *Treatments:* Literary

Non-profit publisher of literary fiction that need not fill a particular market niche. No young adult fiction or literary nonfiction. For novels, send first one or two chapters up to 35 pages maximum via online submission manager. Accepts short stories through short story contest only ($20 entry fee). See website for more details.

Eastland Press

PO Box 99749
Seattle, WA 98139
Tel: +1 (206) 217-0204
Fax: +1 (206) 217-0205
Email: info@eastlandpress.com
Website: http://www.eastlandpress.com

Publishes: Nonfiction; *Areas:* Health; Medicine; *Markets:* Professional

Publishes textbooks for practitioners of Chinese medicine, osteopathy, and other forms of bodywork.

EDCON Publishing Group

30 Montauk Boulevard
Oakdale, NY 11769-1399
Tel: +1 (631) 567-7227
Fax: +1 (631) 567-8745
Email: edcon@EDCONPublishing.com
Website: https://www.edconpublishing.com

Publishes: Fiction; Nonfiction; *Markets:* Children's

Publishes educational nonfiction, fiction, and puzzles for children. Particularly maths, science, reading and social studies. For fiction, send query with SASE, synopsis, and one sample chapter.

Edupress, Inc.

PO Box 8610
Madison, WI 53708-8610
Tel: +1 (800) 694-5827
Email: lbowie@highsmith.com
Website: http://www.edupressinc.com

Publishes: Nonfiction; *Markets:* Professional

Publishes original curriculum resources for PreK through to eighth grade, designed to aid teachers in helping students reach current assessment standards. Mostly written by authors in the educational field. See website for full guidelines.

EMIS Inc. Medical Publishers
PO Box 270666
Fort Collins, CO 80527-0666
Tel: +1 (214) 349-0077
Fax: +1 (970) 672-8606
Website: http://www.emispub.com

Publishes: Nonfiction; Reference; *Areas:* Health; Medicine; Psychology; *Markets:* Professional

Publishes medical books for physicians. Send query with three sample chapters and SASE.

ETC Publications
1456 Rodeo Road
Palm Springs, CA 92262
Tel: +1 (760) 316-9695
Fax: +1 (760) 316-9681
Website: http://www.etcpublications.com

Publishes: Nonfiction; *Areas:* Business; Historical; Military; Religious; Sociology; Sport; Travel; *Markets:* Academic; Adult; Professional

Primarily concerned with publishing nonfiction works that are interesting and useful to the reader. Prefers books for schools (students, teachers, staff, and administrators) but will consider and publish other nonfiction types as well. Send complete ms with SASE.

Faery Rose
Email: queryus@thewildrosepress.com
Website: http://wildrosepress.us

Publishes: Fiction; *Areas:* Fantasy; Romance; Sci-Fi; *Markets:* Adult

Publisher of fantasy romance. Stories may include fantasticaly creatures (dragons, elves, etc.), time travel, futuristic worlds, etc. but must be primarily romances. Send queries by email only, with synopsis, personal information, and word count in the body of the email. No attachments. See website for full details.

Farcountry Press
Acquisitions
Farcountry Press
PO Box 5630
Helena, MT 59604
Email: editor@farcountrypress.com
Website: http://www.farcountrypress.com

Publishes: Nonfiction; *Areas:* Cookery; Historical; Nature; Photography; *Markets:* Adult; Children's

Publishes photography, nature, and history books for adults and children, as well as guidebooks and cookery titles. No fiction or poetry. Send query with SASE, sample chapters, and sample table of contents. See website for full submission guidelines.

Florida Academic Press
PO Box 357425
Gainesville, FL 32635
Tel: +1 (352) 332-5104
Fax: +1 (352) 331-6003
Email: FAPress@gmail.com
Website:
http://www.floridaacademicpress.com

Publishes: Fiction; Nonfiction; *Areas:* Historical; Politics; Sociology; *Markets:* Academic; Adult

Publishes mainly nonfiction and scholarly books, however also publishes fiction. Particularly interested in the history and politics of the Third World (Africa, Middle East, Asia) and books on the social sciences in general. Do not send query letter. Send complete ms with SASE. See website for full guidelines.

48fourteen
Email: query@48fourteen.com
Website: http://www.48fourteen.com

Publishes: Fiction; *Areas:* Fantasy; Horror; Humour; Romance; Sci-Fi; Thrillers; Women's Interests; *Markets:* Adult; Children's; Youth

Publishes all genres, including science fiction, fantasy, urban fantasy, cyber/steam punk, thrillers, horror, romance, women's fiction, comedy, young adult/children's, and graphic novels/comics. Send query with synopsis, bio, and first three chapters in the body of an email (no attachments). Alternatively, send query and synopsis only using online form. See website for full details.

Four Way Books

P.O. Box 535, Village Station
New York, NY 10014
Tel: +1 (212) 334-5430
Email: editors@fourwaybooks.com
Website: http://www.fourwaybooks.com

Publishes: Fiction; Poetry; *Areas:* Short Stories; *Markets:* Adult

Not-for-profit literary press publishing poetry and short fiction by both established and emerging writers. Prefers to receive contributions during specific reading periods (see website), but may consider work outside of these periods – send query by email to ask if this is acceptable. See website for full details.

Fox Chapel Publishing

1970 Broad Street
East Petersburg, PA 17520
Tel: +1 (800) 457-9112
Fax: +1 (717) 560-4702
Email:
acquisitions@foxchapelpublishing.com
Website:
http://www.foxchapelpublishing.com

Publishes: Nonfiction; Reference; *Areas:* Arts; Cookery; Crafts; Design; Gardening; How-to; Nature; Photography; Sport; Travel; *Markets:* Adult; Professional

Contact: Book Acquisition Editor

Publishes books on woodworking, crafting, gardening, do-it-yourself projects, cooking, and other similar topics. See website for full submission guidelines and FAQ.

Frederic C. Beil, Publisher

609 Whitaker Street
Savannah, GA 31401
Tel: +1 (912) 233-2446
Email: editor@beil.com
Website: http://www.beil.com

Publishes: Fiction; Nonfiction; *Areas:* Biography; Historical; *Markets:* Adult

Publishes general trade books in the fields of history, biography, and fiction. Will respond to email queries, but prefers queries by post with SASE. No unsolicited mss.

Freya's Bower

PO Box 4897
Culver City, CA 90231-4897
Tel: +1 (424) 258-0897
Email: submit@freyasbower.com
Website: http://www.freyasbower.com

Publishes: Fiction; *Areas:* Erotic; Romance; Short Stories; *Markets:* Adult

Publishes romance and erotica. Send query with synopsis and first chapter in the body of an email, including details about the book and a marketing plan. See website for full details.

Fulcrum Publishing

4690 Table Mountain Drive, Suite 100
Golden, Colorado 80403
Tel: +1 (800) 992-2908
Fax: +1 (800) 726-7112
Email: acquisitions@fulcrumbooks.com
Website: http://www.fulcrum-books.com

Publishes: Nonfiction; *Areas:* Culture; Gardening; Historical; Nature; Politics; *Markets:* Adult; Children's

Publishes nonfiction exploring Western Culture and History (adult and children's), Native American Culture and History (adult and children's), Environment and Nature (adult and children's), Public Policy, and Western Gardening. No fiction or memoirs. Accepts queries by email only. See website for full guidelines.

Gauthier Publications

PO Box 806241
Saint Clair Shores, MI 48080
Email:
Submissions@Gauthierpublications.com
Website:
http://www.gauthierpublications.com

Publishes: Fiction; Nonfiction; *Areas:*
Adventure; Culture; Fantasy; Historical;
Horror; Humour; Military; Mystery;
Photography; Religious; Romance; Self-
Help; Short Stories; Suspense; Thrillers;
Translations; *Markets:* Adult; Children's;
Youth; *Treatments:* Contemporary; Literary;
Mainstream

No unsolicited mss. Send query by post with
SASE or by email. Send outline and sample
chapters only if requested. Postal queries
without SASE will be destroyed without
reply if not interested. See website for more
information.

Gem Guides Book Co.

1275 West 9th Street
Upland, CA 91786
Email: info@gemguidesbooks.com
Website: http://www.gemguidesbooks.com

Publishes: Nonfiction; *Areas:* Crafts; How-
to; New Age; Science; Travel; *Markets:*
Adult

Publishes how-to and where-to books on
Rocks, Minerals, Gems; Field Guides for
Rock and Fossil Collectors; Lapidary Work
or Jewellery Crafts; New Age Related to
Crystals and Gems; Gold Prospecting /
Treasure Hunting; Travel, Hiking, and
Outdoor Guides of the West/Southwest.
Accepts submissions of proposals or
unsolicited mss by post. Include SASE if
return of material required. See website for
full details.

Geostar Publishing & Services LLC

6423 Woodbine Court
St. Louis, MO 63109
Tel: +1 (314) 260-9978
Email:
opportunities@geostarpublishing.com

Website: http://www.geostarpublishing.com/
opportunities.htm

Publishes: Nonfiction; Reference; *Areas:*
Adventure; Anthropology; Antiques;
Archaeology; Architecture; Arts;
Autobiography; Beauty and Fashion;
Biography; Business; Cookery; Crafts;
Crime; Criticism; Culture; Current Affairs;
Design; Drama; Entertainment; Erotic;
Fantasy; Film; Finance; Gardening; Gothic;
Health; Historical; Hobbies; Horror; How-to;
Humour; Legal; Leisure; Lifestyle;
Literature; Media; Medicine; Men's
Interests; Military; Music; Mystery; Nature;
New Age; Philosophy; Photography;
Politics; Psychology; Radio; Religious;
Romance; Science; Sci-Fi; Self-Help; Short
Stories; Sociology; Spiritual; Sport;
Suspense; Technology; Theatre; Thrillers;
Translations; Travel; TV; Westerns;
Women's Interests; *Markets:* Academic;
Adult; Children's; Family; Professional;
Youth; *Treatments:* Commercial;
Contemporary; Cynical; Dark; Experimental;
In-depth; Light; Mainstream; Niche;
Popular; Positive; Progressive; Satirical;
Serious; Traditional

Contact: Richard J. Runion

We invite SMEs (Subject Matter Experts),
Small Businesspersons and Niche Service
Providers to visit our site.

We market your services, worldwide!
Absolutely Free!!
...And Pay You Too!!!

How Can Anyone Do That?
Sounds Too Good To Be True?
Is Geostar A Charity?
Is There A Catch?
...Read On!

We are a UNIQUE Publisher. Unlike Any
Other! We're like Venture Capital Investor
of the Publishing Industry. We publish
eBooks on topics people are desperately
looking for. We don't publish on a topic just
because we can find writers. We do
extensive & intensive research, secondary &
primary, on every topic we publish on. Our
customers for eBooks (like the ones on
Waste Water Treatment and Content

Management Systems) are more than eBook buyers; many of them are actively looking for a product/ service/ help from experts: some are looking for Consultancy, some for services, even on a long term basis.

We have evolved business models that will work like a charm for you, fetching you pre-qualified business leads, at no cost to you, from across the globe. (Or locally if you so prefer.)

If you want to work with us, please fill in the form on our site, or contact us thru email/ phone.

Glass Page Books
PO Box 333
Signal Mountain, TN 37377
Email: glasspage@epbfi.com
Website: http://www.glasspagebooks.com

Publishes: Fiction; *Areas:* Drama; Short Stories; *Markets:* Adult

Accepts submissions for dramatic literature via literary agents only. No agent is required for submissions of short stories for anthologies. See submissions section of website for current calls and details on submitting.

Glenbridge Publishing Ltd
19923 East Long Avenue
Centennial, CO 80016
Tel: +1 (800) 986-4135
Email: glenbridge@qwestoffice.net
Website:
http://www.glenbridgepublishing.com

Publishes: Fiction; Nonfiction; *Areas:* Business; Cookery; Film; Finance; Historical; Humour; Lifestyle; Literature; Medicine; Music; Nature; Politics; Self-Help; Theatre; *Markets:* Adult

Send query by email, including outline or synopsis and sample chapters.

The Glencannon Press
P.O. Box 1428
El Cerrito, CA 94530

Tel: +1 (510) 528-4216
Fax: +1 (510) 528-3194
Email: info@glencannon.com
Website: http://www.glencannon.com

Publishes: Fiction; Nonfiction; *Areas:* Adventure; Military; Travel; *Markets:* Adult; Children's

Publishes nonfiction and fiction about ships and the sea; including World War I and II, steamships, battleships, sailing ships, and true adventure.

Golden West Books
PO Box 80250
San Marino CA 91118
Tel: +1 (626) 458-8148
Fax: +1 (626) 458-8148
Email: trainbook@earthlink.net
Website: http://www.goldenwestbooks.com

Publishes: Nonfiction; *Areas:* Historical; Travel; *Markets:* Adult

Publishes books on railroad history. Send query in first instance, via online form on website or by post with SASE.

Grand Canyon Association
PO Box 399
Grand Canyon, AZ 86023
Tel: +1 (928) 638-2481
Fax: +1 (928) 638-2484
Email: gcassociation@grandcanyon.org
Website: http://www.grandcanyon.org

Publishes: Fiction; Nonfiction; *Areas:* Anthropology; Archaeology; Architecture; Historical; Leisure; Nature; Photography; Science; Sport; Travel; *Markets:* Adult; Children's

Publishes nonfiction and children's fiction and nonfiction relating to the Grand Canyon only. Send query with SASE, outline, details of previous publishing credits, and either 3-4 sample chapters or complete ms.

Gulf Publishing Company
2 Greenway Plaza, Suite 1020
Houston, Texas 77046

Tel: +1 (713) 529-4301
Fax: +1 (713) 520-4433
Email: store@gulfpub.com
Website: http://www.gulfpub.com

Publishes: Nonfiction; *Areas:* Design;
Science; Technology; *Markets:* Academic;
Professional

Oil and gas industry publisher, producing
books for engineers, students, well
managers, academics, etc. Submit outline
with 1-2 sample chapters, or complete ms.

Heritage Books, Inc.
5810 Ruatan Street
Berwyn Heights, MD 20740
Tel: +1 (800) 876-6103
Fax: +1 (410) 558-6574
Email: submissions@HeritageBooks.com
Website: http://www.heritagebooks.com

Publishes: Fiction; Nonfiction; Reference;
Areas: Autobiography; Historical; Military;
Markets: Academic; Adult

Publishes nonfiction in genealogy, history,
military history, historical fiction, and
memoirs. Also some fact-rich historical
novels. Send query with SASE or submit
outline by email.

The Habit of Rainy Nights Press
Oregon
Email: editors@rainynightspress.org
Website: http://rainynightspress.org

Publishes: Fiction; Nonfiction; Poetry;
Markets: Adult; *Treatments:* Literary

Contact: Duane Poncy, Fiction Editor;
Patricia McLean, Nonfiction Editor; Ger
Killeen, Poetry Editor

A very small micro-press publishing 2-3
print books and half a dozen ebooks a year.
Accepts submissions for ebooks all year, but
submission window for print books is
January 1 – May 31 only. Emphasises
unknown or under-appreciated authors
whose work has depth and social importance,
as well as under-represented voices:

immigrants, persons of colour, and Native
American voices, in particular. Looks for
strong narrative in both fiction and poetry.
No romance, erotica, Christian, New Age,
vampires, zombies, or superheroes. Submit
via online submission system only (see
website).

Hadley Rille Books
PO Box 25466
Overland Park KS 66225
Email: subs@hadleyrillebooks.com
Website: http://www.hadleyrillebooks.com

Publishes: Fiction; *Areas:* Archaeology;
Fantasy; Historical; Sci-Fi; *Markets:* Adult

Contact: Eric T. Reynolds, Editor/Publisher

Publishes Science Fiction stories with an
emphasis on space, archaeology, climate and
other science-related topics. Opens to
submissions in specific months. See website
for details.

Harry N. Abrams, Inc.
115 West 18th Street
New York, NY 10011
Tel: +1 (212) 206-7715
Fax: +1 (212) 519-1210
Email: abrams@abramsbooks.com
Website: http://www.abramsbooks.com

Publishes: Fiction; Nonfiction; Reference;
Areas: Architecture; Arts; Beauty and
Fashion; Crafts; Culture; Design;
Entertainment; Film; Gardening; Hobbies;
Humour; Leisure; Lifestyle; Music; Nature;
Photography; Religious; Science; Sport;
Markets: Adult; Children's; Youth

In general, does not accept unsolicited
manuscripts or book proposals without a
literary agent, except for two imprints: one
of comic art and one of crafts. Email
approaches accepted only by crafts imprint.
See website for full details.

The Harvard Common Press
535 Albany Street
Boston, MA 02118
Tel: +1 (617) 423-5803

Fax: +1 (617) 695-9794
Email: editorial@harvardcommonpress.com
Website:
http://www.harvardcommonpress.com

Publishes: Nonfiction; *Areas:* Cookery;
Lifestyle; *Markets:* Adult

Independent publisher of books on cookery
and parenting. See website for full guidelines
on submitting a proposal. No phone calls.
Postal submissions cannot be returned.

Hayes School Publishing Co., Inc.

321 Pennwood Avenue
Pittsburgh, PA 15221

Tel: +1 (800) 245-6234
Email: chayes@hayespub.com
Website: http://www.hayespub.com

Publishes: Nonfiction; *Markets:* Academic;
Children's

Publishes school books for children.
Welcomes manuscripts and ideas for new
products. Send query by email to receive a
copy of the author's guide.

Hearts 'N Tummies Cookbook Co. / Quixote Press

3544 Blakslee Street
Wever, IA 52658
Tel: +1 (800) 571 2665
Website: http://www.heartsntummies.com

Publishes: Fiction; Nonfiction; *Areas:*
Cookery; Humour; Short Stories; Markets

Publishes books on cookery, ghosts, humour,
and folklore. Send query with SASE. Also
offers services for which writers are charged.

High-Lonesome

P. O. Box 878
Silver City, NM 88062
Tel: +1 (575) 388-3763
Fax: +1 (575) 388-5705
Email: Orders@High-LonesomeBooks.com
Website: http://www.high-
lonesomebooks.com/cgi-bin/hlb/index.html

Publishes: Fiction; Nonfiction; *Areas:*
Adventure; Anthropology; Archaeology;
Biography; Crime; Historical; Westerns;
Markets: Academic; Adult; *Treatments:*
Experimental; Niche; Traditional

Contact: Cherie and M. H. Salmon

Specializes in topics dealing with NM, AZ,
TX, wilderness, history, fishing,
environment, western americana.

Founded by a writer, publisher, former
newspaperman in 1986.

Query by email.

Highland Press

Submissions Department
PO Box 2292
High Springs, FL 32655
Email: Submissions.hp@gmail.com
Website: http://www.highlandpress.org

Publishes: Fiction; Nonfiction; Reference;
Areas: Fantasy; Historical; Mystery;
Romance; Suspense; *Markets:* Adult;
Children's; Youth; *Treatments:*
Contemporary

Has previously focused on publishing
historical fictions, but currently open to all
genres except erotic. Particularly interested
in both contemporary and historical Christian
/ Inspirational / family. Accepts queries by
post and email, but any approaches not
adhering to the submission guidelines will be
discarded. See website for full submission
guidelines.

Homestead Publishing

Acquisitions
Box 193
Moose, Wyoming 83012
Tel: +1 (307) 733-6248
Fax: +1 (307) 733-6248
Email: homesteadpublishing@mac.com
Website:
http://www.homesteadpublishing.net

Publishes: Fiction; Nonfiction; *Areas:*
Architecture; Arts; Biography; Cookery;
Design; Literature; Nature; Photography;

Travel; *Markets:* Adult; *Treatments:* Literary

Publishes fine art, design, photography, and architecture; full-color nature books; national park guide books: cookbooks; biographies and literary fiction; Western Americana; regional and international travel guides, including Yellowstone, Grand Teton, Glacier-Waterton and Banff-Jasper national parks. Particularly interested in outdoor guide—hiking, climbing, bicycling, canoeing, mountaineering—and travel books. Accepts queries with samples. See website for full submission guidelines.

Hopewell Publications
PO Box 11
Titusville, NJ 08560-0011
Tel: +1 (609) 818-1049
Fax: +1 (609) 964-1718
Email: submissions@hopepubs.com
Website: http://www.hopepubs.com

Publishes: Fiction; Nonfiction; *Markets:* Adult; Youth

Publishes fiction and nonfiction. Specialises in classic reprints but also considers new titles. See website for submission guidelines. Queries which do not follow them will be deleted unread.

Humanics Publishing Group
12 S. Dixie Hwy, Ste. 203
Lake Worth, FL 33460
Tel: +1 (800) 874-8844
Fax: +1 (888) 874-8844
Email: humanics@mindspring.com
Website: http://www.humanicspub.com

Publishes: Nonfiction; Finance; How-to; New Age; Religious; Science; Self-Help; *Markets:* Adult; Children's

Contact: W. Arthur Bligh, Acquisitions Editor

Started in 1969, in response to the need from the education community for quality classroom materials to support parents as the prime educators of their children. In 1984 launched a New Age imprint. Accepts

unsolicited mss by post with SASE. See website for full submission guidelines.

Ideals Publications
2630 Elm Hill Pike, Suite 100
Nashville, TN 37214
Tel: +1 (615) 781-1451
Email: kwest@guideposts.org
Website: http://www.idealsbooks.com

Publishes: Fiction; Nonfiction; *Markets:* Children's

Publishes fiction and nonfiction picture books for children aged 4-8 (up to 800 words), and board and novelty books for children 2-5 (up to 250 words). Subjects include holiday, inspirational, and patriotic themes; relationships and values; and general fiction. Submit complete mss only – no queries or proposals. No submissions by email or computer disk. See website for full guidelines.

Ignatius Press
1348 10th Avenue
San Francisco, CA 94122
Email: info@ignatius.com
Website: http://www.ignatius.com

Publishes: Nonfiction; *Areas:* Religious; *Markets:* Adult

Christian publisher. Submit complete ms. No phone calls or emails. See webite for full submission guidelines.

The Ilium Press
Tel: +1 (509) 928-7950
Email: submissions@iliumpress.com
Website: http://www.iliumpress.com

Publishes: Fiction; Nonfiction; Poetry; *Areas:* Biography; Crime; Historical; Music; *Markets:* Adult; *Treatments:* Literary

Contact: John Lemon

Publishes epic poetry, literary fiction, books on music (both fiction and nonfiction), crime novels, historical fiction, and dystopian speculative fiction. Send query by email with summary, two or three sample chapters (up to 50 pages), bio and list of previous publications, and contact information. See website for full guidelines.

Image Comics
Submissions
c/o Image Comics
2134 Allston Way, 2nd Floor
Berkeley, CA 94704
Email: submissions@imagecomics.com
Website: http://www.imagecomics.com

Publishes: Fiction; *Markets:* Adult; Youth

Third largest comic book publisher in the United States. Publishes comics and graphic novels. Only interested in creator-owned comics. Does not acquire any rights. Looking for comics that are well written and well drawn, by people who are dedicated and can meet deadlines, not any specific genre or type of comic book. See website for full submission guidelines.

ImaJinn Books
Tel: +1 (623) 236-3361
Email: editors@imajinnbooks.com
Website: http://www.imajinnbooks.com

Publishes: Fiction; *Areas:* Erotic; Fantasy; Horror; Mystery; Romance; Sci-Fi; *Markets:* Adult

Print-on-demand publisher also offering ebooks. No unsolicited mss. Send query in first instance by email only, including synopsis up to six double-spaced pages long. Prefers shorter works (as small as 30,000 words) and does not publish books over 90,000 words. See website for more details.

Immedium
PO Box 31846
San Francisco, CA 94131

Email: submissions@immedium.com
Website: http://www.immedium.com

Publishes: Fiction; Nonfiction; *Areas:* Arts; Culture; *Markets:* Children's

Publishes children's picture books, Asian-America, and Arts and Culture. Send query with SASE, CV, and full manuscript (picture books) or one-page summary and two sample chapters (50 pages total). See website for full guidelines.

Impact Books
F+W Media, Inc.
10151 Carver Road, Suite 200
Blue Ash, OH 45242
Email: Pam.wissman@fwpubs.com
Website: http://www.impact-books.com

Publishes: Nonfiction; Reference; *Areas:* Arts; How-to; *Markets:* Adult

Contact: Pamela Wissman, Acquisitions Editor

Publishes books to assist artists drawing comics, superheroes, Japanese-style manga, fantasy, creatures, action, caricature, anime, etc.

Ingalls Publishing Group, Inc.
PO Box 2500
Banner Elk, NC 28604
Tel: +1 (828) 297-6884
Fax: +1 (828) 297-6880
Email: editor@ingallspublishinggroup.com
Website:
http://www.ingallspublishinggroup.com

Publishes: Fiction; Nonfiction; *Areas:* Adventure; Autobiography; Crime; Historical; Humour; Mystery; Romance; *Markets:* Adult

Publishes memoirs and fiction with authors and settings in North Carolina, South Carolina, Virginia, Florida, Tennessee or Georgia. Fiction must involve adventure, murder, mystery, humour, romance, or historical events. 50,000 – 100,000 words. Prefers queries by email, with synopsis up to a maximum of two pages. Include link to your website if available.

International Press
PO Box 43502
Somerville, MA 02143

Tel: +1 (617) 623-3855
Fax: +1 (617) 623-3101
Email: ipb-info@intlpress.com
Website: http://www.intlpress.com

Publishes: Nonfiction; Science; *Markets:* Academic

Contact: Mr Lixin Qin

Academic publisher of high-level mathematics and mathematical physics book titles, including monographs, textbooks, and more.

Ion Imagination Entertainment, Inc.
PO Box 210943
Nashville, TN 37221-0943
Tel: +1 (615) 646-6276
Email: ionimagin@aol.com
Website: http://www.flumpa.com

Publishes: Fiction; *Areas:* Science; *Markets:* Children's

Publishes science-related fiction for children. Send query with SASE, bio, and publishing history. No unsolicited mss.

Itoh Press
535 Moats Lane
Bowling Green, KY 42103
Fax: +1 (270) 783-0888
Email: carolitoh@itohpress.com
Website: http://www.itohpress.com

Publishes: Fiction; Nonfiction; *Areas:* Adventure; Autobiography; Beauty and Fashion; Crime; Culture; Current Affairs; Drama; Entertainment; Erotic; Fantasy; Film; Gothic; Historical; Horror; Humour; Leisure; Lifestyle; Literature; Music; New Age; Philosophy; Politics; Religious; Romance; Sci-Fi; Sociology; Spiritual; Suspense; Theatre; TV; Westerns; Women's Interests; *Markets:* Adult; Youth; *Treatments:* Contemporary; Dark; Light; Literary; Mainstream; Niche; Popular; Positive; Satirical

Contact: Carol Itoh

We are dedicated to women writers and the southern voice. We welcome all submissions and we never charge authors any fees. We are committed to providing the highest standard in literaure to our readers. In an effort to green we only accept electronic queries and submissions.

Jewish Lights Publishing
Sunset Farm Offices
Route 4, PO Box 237
Woodstock, VT 05091
Tel: +1 (802) 457-4000
Fax: +1 (802) 457-4004
Email: editorial@jewishlights.com
Website: http://jewishlights.com

Publishes: Fiction; Nonfiction; *Areas:* Crime; Historical; Men's Interests; Mystery; Philosophy; Religious; Sci-Fi; Spiritual; Women's Interests; *Markets:* Adult; Children's; Youth

Publishes books for people of all faiths and backgrounds, drawing on the Jewish wisdom tradition. Books are almost exclusively nonfiction, covering topics such as religion, Jewish life cycle, theology, philosophy, history, and spirituality, however does publish some fiction, including children's books and graphic novels. No biography, haggadot, or poetry. Send proposal by post only – no email submissions or unsolicited mss. See website for full details.

John F. Blair, Publisher
1406 Plaza Drive
Winston-Salem, NC 27103
Tel: +1 (800) 222-9796
Fax: +1 (336) 768-9194
Email: kirk@blairpub.com
Website: http://www.blairpub.com

Publishes: Fiction; Nonfiction; *Areas:* Biography; Historical; Travel; *Markets:* Adult

Contact: Steve Kirk, Editor-in-Chief

Publishes regional books relating to the Southeast of the United States. Publishes mainly nonfiction in areas such as history, travel, folklore, and biography, but also one or two works of fiction each year which are connected to the Southeast either by setting or by the author's background. No children's books, poetry, or category fiction such as romances, science fiction, or spy thrillers; collections of short stories, essays, or newspaper columns. No electronic or fax proposals. SASE required for response / return of materials. See website for full submission guidelines.

Jonathan David Publishers, Inc.

68-22 Eliot Avenue
Middle Village, NY 11379-1194
Email: submissions@JDBooks.com
Website: http://www.jdbooks.com

Publishes: Nonfiction; Reference; *Areas:* Cookery; Culture; Humour; Religious; Sport; *Markets:* Adult; *Treatments:* Popular

New York-based nonfiction trade book publisher specialising in sports, biography, reference, and popular Judaica. Send query by post only with SASE, brief synopsis, table of contents, sample chapter, and résumé. No multiple submissions, or submissions by email.

Jones & Bartlett Learning

5 Wall Street
Burlington, MA 01803
Tel: +1 (978) 443-5000
Fax: +1 (978) 443-8000
Email: info@jblearning.com
Website: http://www.jblearning.com

Publishes: Nonfiction; *Areas:* Health; Legal; Medicine; Science; Technology; *Markets:* Academic; Professional

Publisher of educational and professional material. See website for full list of editorial contacts.

Jupiter Gardens Press

Email: submissions@jupitergardens.com
Website: http://jupitergardenspress.com

Publishes: Fiction; Nonfiction; *Areas:* Erotic; Fantasy; New Age; Romance; Sci-Fi;

Short Stories; *Markets:* Adult; Children's; Youth

Send query by email with 2-4 pages synopsis, author bio, and first three chapters as .DOC or .RTF attachments.

Just Us Books

Submissions Manager
Just Us Books
356 Glenwood Avenue
East Orange, NJ 07017
Tel: +1 (973) 672-7701
Fax: +1 (973) 677-7570
Email: cheryl_hudson@justusbooks.com
Website: http://justusbooks.com

Publishes: Fiction; Nonfiction; Poetry; *Markets:* Children's; Youth

Publishes Black-interest books for young people, including picture books, chapter books for middle readers, poetry, nonfiction series, biographies and young adult fiction. Currently accepting queries for young adult titles only. Send query with SAE, author bio, 1-2 page synopsis, and 3-5 page sample. See website for full submission guidelines.

Kalmbach Publishing Co.

21027 Crossroads Circle
PO Box 1612
Waukesha, WI 53187-1612
Tel: +1 (262) 796-8776 Ext. 421
Fax: +1 (262) 796-1615
Email: books@kalmbach.com
Website: http://www.kalmbach.com

Publishes: Nonfiction; Reference; *Areas:* Crafts; Hobbies; How-to; *Markets:* Adult

Publishes books on arts and crafts, model-making, jewellery-making, toy trains, etc. Send query with 2-3 page outline, plus sample chapter with photos.

Kamehameha Publishing

567 South King Street, Suite 118
Honolulu, HI 96813
Tel: +1 (808) 523-6200
Email: publishing@ksbe.edu

Website:
http://www.kamehamehapublishing.org

Publishes: Fiction; Nonfiction; *Areas:*
Biography; Culture; Historical; *Markets:*
Academic; Adult; Children's; Youth

Publishes books on Hawaiian language,
culture, history, and community, for
children, young people, and adults. See
website for full details and submission
guidelines.

Kane Miller Books

4901 Morena Boulevard, Ste 213
San Diego, CA 92117
Tel: +1 (800) 475-4522
Email: submissions@kanemiller.com
Website: http://www.kanemiller.com

Publishes: Fiction; *Areas:* Adventure;
Fantasy; Historical; Mystery; *Markets:*
Children's; Youth

This publisher is committed to expanding
their picture book, chapter book, and middle-
grade fiction lists. Particularly interested in
engaging characters and American subjects.
Send query by email with complete ms
(picture books) or synopsis and two sample
chapters in the body of the email. No
attachments or links to websites.

Kearney Street Books

PO Box 2021
Bellingham, WA 98227
Tel: +1 (360) 738-1355
Email: garyrmc@mac.com
Website: http://kearneystreetbooks.com

Publishes: Fiction; *Areas:* Music; *Markets:*
Adult; *Treatments:* Niche

Publishes fiction by or about musicians or
music. Publishes very few titles a year. Send
query by email or send complete ms by post
with SASE for reply only.

Kelly Point Publishing LLC

Martin Sisters Publishing LLC
PO Box 1154
Barbourville, KY 40906

Email:
submissions@kellypointpublishing.com
Website:
http://www.kellypointpublishing.com

Publishes: Fiction; *Areas:* Adventure;
Fantasy; Historical; Humour; Mystery;
Religious; Romance; Sci-Fi; Short Stories;
Spiritual; Sport; Westerns; Women's
Interests; *Markets:* Adult; Children's; Youth;
Treatments: Contemporary; Literary;
Mainstream

Open to all genres of fiction. No nonfiction
or poetry. Send query by email, with
marketing plan and first three chapters
pasted into the body of the email. No
attachments. See website for full guidelines.

Kind of a Hurricane Press

Email: kindofahurricanepress@yahoo.com
Website:
http://www.kindofahurricanepress.com

Publishes: Fiction; Poetry; *Areas:* Short
Stories; *Markets:* Adult

Eclectic small press publishing anthologies
of poetry and flash fiction. See website for
calls for current anthologies and submission
guidelines.

Knox Robinson Publishing (US)

244 5th Avenue, Suite 1861
New York, NY 10001
Tel: +1 (646) 652-6980
Email: subs@knoxrobinsonpublishing.com
Website:
http://www.knoxrobinsonpublishing.com

Publishes: Fiction; *Areas:* Fantasy;
Historical; Romance; *Markets:* Adult

Publishes historical fiction, historical
romance (pre-1960), and medieval fantasy.
No science fiction, time travel, or fantasy
with children and/or animal protagonists.
Send query by email only, with detailed
synopsis and the first three chapters. No
approaches by fax or post. See website for
full details.

Legacy Press

Rainbow Publishers
PO Box 261129
San Diego, CA 92196
Tel: +1 (800) 638-4428
Fax: +1 (800) 331-0297
Email:
john.gregory@rainbowpublishers.com
Website: http://www.legacypresskids.com

Publishes: Fiction; Nonfiction; *Areas:*
Religious; *Markets:* Children's

Publishes devotions, instructional books, and
faith-based fiction for kids. See website for
submission guidelines.

Lawyers & Judges Publishing Co.

917 N Swan, Suite 300
Tucson, AZ 85711
Tel: +1 (520) 323-1500
Fax: +1 (520) 323-0055
Email: steve@lawyersandjudges.com
Website: http://www.lawyersandjudges.com

Publishes: Nonfiction; Reference; *Areas:*
Legal; Medicine; *Markets:* Professional

Contact: Steve Weintraub

Publishes legal and medical books for
professionals. See website for submission
guidelines.

Leapfrog Press

PO Box 505
Fredonia, NY 14063
Email: acquisitions@leapfrogpress.com
Website: http://www.leapfrogpress.com

Publishes: Fiction; Nonfiction; Poetry;
Markets: Adult; Children's; *Treatments:*
Literary

Publisher with an eclectic list of fiction,
poetry, and nonfiction, including paperback
originals of adult and middle-grade fiction
and nonfiction. Closed to submissions
between January 15 and May each year.
Accepts queries by email only: send query
letter and short sample within the email

itself. No attachments. See website for full
guidelines.

Ledge Hill Publishing

PO Box 337
Alton, NH 03809
Tel: +1 (603) 998-6801
Email: info@ledgehillpublishing.com
Website:
http://www.ledgehillpublishing.com

Publishes: Fiction; Nonfiction; Poetry;
Areas: Short Stories; *Markets:* Adult

Publishes short fiction, poetry, and creative
nonfiction. Electronic approaches only. Send
short query via webform on website, or send
complete ms with covering letter by email.
See website for full details.

Les Figues Press

PO Box 7736
Los Angeles, CA 90007
Tel: +1 (323) 734-4732
Email: info@lesfigues.com
Website: http://www.lesfigues.com

Publishes: Fiction; Poetry; *Areas:* Short
Stories; *Markets:* Adult

Publishes fiction and poetry. Accepts
submissions through its annual contest only
($25 entry fee). Accepts poetry, novellas,
innovative novels, anti-novels, short story
collections, lyric essays, hybrids, and all
forms not otherwise specified. Submit via
form on website.

Lethe Press

Email: editor@lethepressbooks.com
Website: http://www.lethepressbooks.com

Publishes: Fiction; Nonfiction; Poetry;
Markets: Adult

Small press publisher of gay and lesbian
fiction, nonfiction, and poetry. Send query
by email in first instance.

Lillenas Drama Resources

PO Box 419527
Kansas City, MO 64141

Tel: +1 (800) 877-0700
Fax: +1 (816) 412-8390
Email: drama@lillenas.com
Website: http://www.lillenas.com

Publishes: Scripts; *Areas:* Religious;
Markets: Adult; Children's; Family; Youth

Accepts creatively conceived and practically
producible resources for church and school
programs. Not currently accepting full-length
plays. See website for more details.

Linden Publishing

2006 South Mary
Fresno, CA 93721
Tel: +1 (559) 233-6633
Fax: +1 (559) 233-6933
Email: richard@lindenpub.com
Website: http://www.lindenpub.com

Publishes: Nonfiction; *Areas:* Arts; Crafts;
Historical; Hobbies; How-to; *Markets:* Adult

Publishes books on woodworking. Send
email for full submission guidelines.

Liquid Silver Books

10509 Sedgegrass Drive
Indianapolis, IN 46235
Email: submissions@liquidsilverbooks.com
Website: http://www.lsbooks.com

Publishes: Fiction; *Areas:* Romance;
Markets: Adult

Considers all romance genres and romance
subgenres. Send query by email with
complete ms as a .doc, .docx, or .rtf
attachment. Manuscripts must be at least
15,000 words. See website for full
guidelines.

Listen & Live Audio, Inc.

PO Box 817
Roseland, New Jersey 07068
Tel: +1 (201) 558-9000
Fax: +1 (201) 558-9800
Email: alisa@listenandlive.com
Website: http://www.listenandlive.com

Publishes: Fiction; Nonfiction; *Areas:*

Adventure; Autobiography; Biography;
Culture; Fantasy; Health; Humour; Lifestyle;
Military; Mystery; Politics; Religious;
Romance; Sci-Fi; Self-Help; Sport; *Markets:*
Adult; Children's; Youth

Independent audiobook publisher based in
Roseland, New Jersey. Describes itself as
"the premier independent audiobook
publishing company in the US."

Local Gems Poetry Press

Email: localgemspoetrypress@gmail.com
Website:
http://www.localgemspoetrypress.com

Publishes: Poetry; *Areas:* Humour; *Markets:*
Family; Professional; Youth; *Treatments:*
Contemporary; Experimental; Mainstream;
Niche

Contact: Ishwa

A Long Island based poetry press
specializing in anthologies with creative
themes. Best method of approach for authors
looking to publish full length books with us
is to submit to our anthologies first so we
become familiar with their material. We are
open to all forms of poetry and like to use
poetry for social change.

Loose Id

Email: submissions@loose-id.com
Website: http://www.loose-id.com

Publishes: Fiction; *Areas:* Erotic; Fantasy;
Historical; Mystery; Romance; Sci-Fi;
Suspense; Westerns; *Markets:* Adult;
Treatments: Contemporary

Publisher of erotic romance ebooks, which
are occasionally also released in print. Send
query by email with synopsis and first three
chapters as RTF attachments only (no .doc
files or submissions in the body of the
email). See website for full guidelines.

Lucent Books

Attn: Publisher – Lucent Books
27500 Drake Road
Farmington Hills, MI 48331

Email: betz.deschenes@cengage.com
Website:
http://www.gale.cengage.com/greenhaven

Publishes: Nonfiction; *Markets:* Academic;
Children's

Publishes educational, nonfiction books that
support middle school curriculum and
national standards. Send query by email with
CV and list of previous publications.

Lucky Marble Books

Email: yaeditor@pagespringpublishing.com
Website: http://luckymarblebooks.com

Publishes: Fiction; *Areas:* Adventure;
Culture; Fantasy; Historical; Humour;
Mystery; Romance; Sci-Fi; Sport; Suspense;
Markets: Children's; Youth; *Treatments:*
Contemporary; Literary; Mainstream

Publishes Young Adult and Middle Grade
novels. All material must be age appropriate
and avoid content that might put off schools.
No nonfiction. Send query by email with
synopsis and first thirty pages in the body of
the email, and the word "SUBMISSION"
and the title of your book in the subject line.
See website for full details.

M P Publishing USA

6 Petaluma Blvd N, Suite 6
Petaluma, CA
94952
Email: msatris@mppublishingusa.com
Website: http://mppublishingusa.com

Publishes: Fiction; Nonfiction; *Areas:*
Adventure; Crime; Fantasy; Gothic;
Literature; Mystery; Romance; Sci-Fi; Short
Stories; Suspense; Thrillers; Women's
Interests; *Markets:* Adult; Youth;
Treatments: Commercial; Contemporary;
Dark; Experimental; In-depth; Light;
Literary; Mainstream; Niche; Popular;
Progressive; Satirical; Serious; Traditional

Contact: Marthine Satris

Founded on the Isle of Man in 2008 as an
aggregator to small and mid-size publishers
wishing to enter the world of electronic
books. After acquiring and distributing more
than four hundred e-book titles, the publisher
decided to turn an eye to launching original
titles both in electronic format and by
conventional means. In 2010, released its
first original title, a SIBA award finalist.
Following in its wake, 2011 marks the
company's first full list of original titles and
paperback reprints. With offices and
distribution both in the U.S. and U.K., the
publishing house is rapidly expanding and
looking forward to launching great new
books throughout the world for years to
come.

Looking for a range of genres -- the only
thing we insist on is excellent, fresh writing.
We publish thriller and mystery novels,
young adult novels, experimental fiction, and
literary fiction. We believe in publishing the
author, not just the manuscript, and in
building a close and fruitful relationship
between our authors and our editors. Because
agents reject books for the wrong reasons,
we encourage authors to submit manuscripts
directly to our editors for review, and we will
deliver thoughtful, substantive responses to
all submissions within 30 days.

Submit via form on website.

Magination Press

American Psychological Association
750 First Street, NE
Washington, DC 20002-4242
Email: magination@apa.org
Website: http://www.apa.org

Publishes: Fiction; Nonfiction; *Areas:*
Psychology; *Markets:* Children's; Youth

Publishes psychology-based books covering
a broad range of topics of concern to
children and teens, including everyday
situations, such as starting school and the
growing family, and more serious
psychological, clinical, or medical problems,
such as divorce, depression, anxiety, asthma,
attention disorders, bullying, death, etc. Most
books written by PhD psychologists, school
counselors, mental health professionals, and
MD physicians. Doctorate-level credentials
are not a requirement, but the author should
have expertise in the topic area. See website

for full submission guidelines. No submissions by email or on disk.

Mandala Earth
10 Paul Drive
San Rafael CA 94903
Tel: +1 (415) 526-1370
Email: info@mandalapublishing.com
Website:
http://www.mandalaeartheditions.com

Publishes: Fiction; Nonfiction; *Areas:* Arts; Culture; Nature; Philosophy; Photography; Spiritual; Travel; *Markets:* Adult; Children's

Publisher aiming to "bring to its readers authentic and accessible renderings of thousands of years of wisdom and philosophy" from the culture of the East. Publishes adult nonfiction and fiction for children. Send query with SASE.

Martin Sisters Publishing
Email:
submissions@martinsisterspublishing.com
Website:
http://www.martinsisterspublishing.com

Publishes: Fiction; Nonfiction; *Areas:* Fantasy; Religious; Sci-Fi; Self-Help; Short Stories; *Markets:* Adult; Children's; Family; Youth

Accepts queries for all genres of fiction, including science fiction and fantasy, and nonfiction, including self-help. Submissions may include Christian fiction, inspirational, collections of stories. Send query by email with marketing plan and (for fiction) 5-10 pages in the body of the email. No attachments. See website for full guidelines.

Master Books
PO Box 726
Green Forest, AR 72638
Tel: +1 (800) 999-3777
Email: nlp@newleafpress.net
Website: http://www.masterbooks.net

Publishes: Nonfiction; *Areas:* Religious; *Markets:* Adult; Children's; Family; Youth

Publishes Christian and creation-based books.

Maverick Duck Press
Email: maverickduckpress@yahoo.com
Website:
http://www.maverickduckpress.com

Publishes: Poetry; *Markets:* Adult; *Treatments:* Literary

Contact: Kendall A. Bell

Publishes poetry chapbooks of 18-24 pages. Submit by email only.

Medallion Media Group
100 S. River Street
Aurora, IL 60506
Tel: +1 (630) 513-8316
Fax: +1 (630) 513-8362
Email:
submissions@medallionmediagroup.com
Website: http://medallionmediagroup.com

Publishes: Fiction; Nonfiction; *Areas:* Arts; Autobiography; Biography; Design; Fantasy; Health; Historical; Horror; Mystery; Religious; Romance; Sci-Fi; Suspense; Thrillers; *Markets:* Adult; Youth; *Treatments:* Literary; Mainstream

Contact: Emily Steele

Publishes fiction and nonfiction for adults and young adults. No children's books, short stories, or erotica. Accepts nonfiction proposals through agents only. Submit via submission form on website. No hard copy submissions.

Medical Group Management Association (MGMA)
104 Inverness Terrace East
Englewood, CO 80112-5306
Tel: +1 (303) 799-1111
Email: support@mgma.com
Website: http://www.mgma.com

Publishes: Nonfiction; *Areas:* Business; Medicine; *Markets:* Professional

Publishes books for professionals, aimed at the business side of medicine. Submit complete ms, or proposal including outline and three sample chapters.

Messianic Jewish Publishers

6120 Day Long Lane
Clarksville, MD 21029
Tel: +1 (410) 531-6644
Email: editor@messianicjewish.net
Website: http://www.messianicjewish.net

Publishes: Fiction; Nonfiction; *Areas:* Religious; *Markets:* Adult

Publishes books which address Jewish evangelism; the Jewish roots of Christianity; Messianic Judaism; Israel; the Jewish People. Publishes mainly nonfiction, but some fiction. See website for full submission guidelines.

Moon Tide Press

PO Box 27182
Anaheim, CA 92809
Website: http://www.moontidepress.com

Publishes: Poetry; *Markets:* Adult

Publisher dedicated to showcasing the finest poets in Southern California. Send query with sample poems, bio, and details of any previous publishing credits.

Moonshadow Press

Email: submissions@wakestonepress.com
Website: http://www.wakestonepress.com

Publishes: Fiction; *Areas:* Adventure; Fantasy; Horror; *Markets:* Children's; Youth

Imprint publishing fiction, fantasy, young adult stories, and stories for boys. Send submissions by email. See website for more information.

Morgan Kaufmann Publishers

30 Corporate Drive, Suite 400
Burlington, MA 01803-4252
Tel: +1 (781) 663-5200
Email: a.dierna@elsevier.com
Website: http://mkp.com

Publishes: Nonfiction; *Areas:* Science; Technology; *Markets:* Professional

Publishes books for the computer science community. Complete New Book Proposal Questionnaire (available on website) and send it by email to the appropriate editor (list available on website).

Mountain Press Publishing Company

PO Box 2399
Missoula, MT 59806
Tel: +1 (406) 728-1900
Email: Info@mtnpress.com
Website: http://mountain-press.com

Publishes: Nonfiction; *Areas:* Historical; Nature; Science; *Markets:* Adult; Children's

Publishes books on natural history, western US history, and earth science. Send query by post only, with proposal including outline or table of contents and sample (one or two chapters). See website for full submission guidelines.

My Pouty Lips

Email: angelicka@mypoutylips.com
Website: http://www.mypoutylips.com

Publishes: Fiction; Nonfiction; Reference; *Areas:* Erotic; How-to; Men's Interests; Romance; Self-Help; Short Stories; Women's Interests; *Markets:* Adult; *Treatments:* Contemporary; Dark; Experimental; In-depth; Light; Literary; Mainstream; Niche; Popular; Positive; Progressive; Traditional

Contact: Angelicka Wallows

Publishing Erotica Authors.

I am happy to announce that I have started publishing erotica authors to help them make their name out there, or widen their distribution network. Basically what I do is editing and publishing (entirely free of charge) erotica stories, novels, anthologies, guides and how-tos both in eBook and paperback formats. EBooks are distributed via the major online retailers such as Apple,

Sony, Barnes & Noble, Amazon, Kobo and more. Paperback versions are distributed via Amazon. An author contract is signed between us and you will be getting royalties on the profits made with the books.

If you are interested, please use the submission form at the bottom of the page to send us your text to publish. Please note that we will need more than just your text though, so get everything ready before submitting it to us. Here is what we will need:

Your complete manuscript (in word format – .doc – please do not format your text with bold, italic, tabs, colors or anything like that. We need to remove all formatting before we can start publishing and reformatting it in our system. Make sure you have your text checked again for typos, grammar, style, spelling, punctuation. Your minimum word count should be 10,000 or above. The best size for erotica eBooks is around 60,000 words. Please note that we publish only text, so don't send photos to illustrate your pages!)
A photo of you (it could be a drawing, an illustration, a picture. Just make sure it is high resolution, clear, and clean)
Your biography (in less than half a page, tell us about you as an author, your background and inspiration, if you have published books already, etc). Feel free to include some links like social media, your blog, twitter, etc.
A short description of your work (It will be used to market your book on our site, and shared with some retailers. Please no email, hyperlink, or promotion. Your description should be a single paragraph in complete sentences, limited to 400 characters or less).
A long presentation of your work (An extended version of the above, needed for promotion purpose. Again, no email, hyperlink, or promotion. Try to raise the curiosity of the reader and want to learn more about your book. Minimum 600 characters, maximum 4,000)
Your Paypal email (we need to update our files with your payment info. Also you will be automatically opted in to our Authors newsletter to keep you in the loop about what is going on on our side. Please do not opt out as this method will be used to send you important information)

Once you have all these files ready, please do double check them again for typos, grammar, style, spelling, punctuation... The better the files you send, the better your final book will be. If you are 100% confident that they are OK, visit the website to start the submission of your files.

New Libri
Email: query@newlibri.com
Website: http://www.newlibri.com

Publishes: Fiction; Nonfiction; *Areas:* Fantasy; Literature; Sci-Fi; Technology; *Markets:* Adult; *Treatments:* Literary

Contact: Stanislav Fritz; Michael Muller

Send query by email with complete ms or at least 50 pages as Word or PDF format file. Include synopsis, word count, and genre/target market. No vampire stories. See website for full guidelines.

NavPress
PO Box 35002
Colorado Springs, CO 80935
Tel: +1 (800) 366-7788
Fax: +1 (800) 343-3902
Email: CustomerService@NavPress.com
Website: http://www.navpress.com

Publishes: Nonfiction; *Areas:* Culture; How-to; Lifestyle; Religious; Sociology; Spiritual; *Markets:* Adult

Christian publisher based in Colorado Springs. Aims to publish products that are biblically rooted, culturally relevant, and highly practical.

NBM
160 Broadway, Suite 700 East Wing
New York, NY 10038
Email: tnantier@nbmpub.com
Website: http://nbmpub.com

Publishes: Fiction; *Areas:* Erotic; Fantasy; Horror; Humour; Mystery; Sci-Fi; *Markets:* Adult; Youth; *Treatments:* Satirical

Contact: Terry Nantier

Publisher of graphic novels, interested in general fiction, humour, satire of fantasy and horror, erotica, and mystery. No superheroes. Accepting approaches from previously published authors only (including those with proven success in online comics). No submissions from authors outside North America, except for adult. See website for full submission guidelines.

New Issues Poetry & Prose
1903 West Michigan Avenue
Kalamazoo, MI 49008-5463
Email: new-issues@wmich.edu
Website: http://wmich.edu/newissues

Publishes: Poetry; *Markets:* Adult

Publishes poetry books submitted through its poetry contests only – entry fee of $20-$25 applies. Submit by post or via online submission system. See website for more details.

New Native Press
Post Office Box 661
Cullowhee, North Carolina 28723
Tel: +1 (828) 293-9237
Email: NewNativePress@hotmail.com
Website: http://www.newnativepress.com

Publishes: Poetry; *Areas:* Translations; *Markets:* Adult

Contact: Thomas Rain Crowe

Publishes bilingual books by authors writing poetry in marginalised languages, translated into English. Send query with bio, publishing credits, and ten sample poems.

New Rivers Press
Minnesota State University Moorhead
1104 7th Ave South
Moorhead, MN 56563
Tel: +1 (800) 593-7246
Email: davisa@mnstate.edu
Website: http://www.newriverspress.com

Publishes: Fiction; Nonfiction; Poetry; *Areas:* Autobiography; Short Stories; *Markets:* Adult; *Treatments:* Literary

Contact: Alan Davis; Suzzanne Kelley

Reads general book-length submissions in April and May. Also runs fiction and poetry contests at other times of the year. See website for full details.

New Victoria Publishers
P.O. Box 13173
Chicago, IL 60613-0173
Tel: +1 (773) 793-2244
Email: newvictoriapub@att.net
Website: http://www.newvictoria.com

Publishes: Fiction; Nonfiction; Poetry; Reference; *Areas:* Biography; Cookery; Crime; Fantasy; Humour; Mystery; New Age; Politics; Religious; Romance; Sci-Fi; Short Stories; Thrillers; Travel; Women's Interests; *Markets:* Adult

Publishes lesbian feminist fiction, nonfiction, and poetry. Accepts unsolicited mss, but prefers query in first instance with synopsis and sample up to 50 pages. No queries by email.

Nicolas Hays Publishers
PO Box 540206
Lake Worth, FL 33454-0206
Email: info@nicolas hays.com
Website: http://www.nicolashays.com

Publishes: Nonfiction; *Areas:* Biography; Health; Historical; Mystery; Politics; Psychology; Religious; Self-Help; *Markets:* Adult

Publishes books on topics such as Eastern and Western mysteries, magick and occultism, alchemy, astrology, etc. See website for more details.

The Ninety-Six Press
Department of English
Furman University
3300 Poinsett Highway
Greenville, SC 29613
Tel: +1 (864) 294-3152
Email: gil.allen@furman.edu
Website: http://library.furman.edu/specialcollections/96Press

Publishes: Poetry; *Markets:* Adult

Contact: Gilbert Allen

Focuses on publishing collections of poetry by poets from South Carolina. Accepts submissions by invitation only – see website for any current calls.

Nortia Press
Tel: +1 (800) 283-3572
Fax: +1 (800) 351-5073
Email: acquisitions@nortiapress.com
Website: http://nortiapress.com

Publishes: Fiction; Nonfiction; *Areas:* Current Affairs; *Markets:* Adult; *Treatments:* Literary

Publishes literary fiction and nonfiction with a global affairs bent. Send queries for fiction and proposals for nonfiction by email. See website for more details.

Nova Press
9058 Lloyd P,ace
West Hollywood CA 90069
Email: sales@novapress.net
Website: http://novapress.net

Publishes: Nonfiction; Reference; *Markets:* Academic

Publishes test prep books for college entrance exams, and related reference books.

Oceanview Publishing
CEO Center at Mediterranean Plaza
595 Bay Isles Road, Suite 120-G
Longboat Key, FL 34228
Tel: +1 (941) 387-8500
Fax: +1 (941) 387-0039
Email: submissions@oceanviewpub.com
Website: http://oceanviewpub.com

Publishes: Fiction; *Areas:* Mystery; Thrillers; *Markets:* Adult

Publishes adult fiction, with a primary interest in the mystery/thriller genre. No children's or young adult literature, poetry, memoirs, cookbooks, technical manuals, or short stories. Accepts submissions only from authors who either have a literary agent; have been previously published by a traditional publishing house; or have been specifically invited to submit by a representative or author of the publishing house. See website for more details.

Ooligan Press
369 Neuberger Hall
724 SW Harrison Street
Portland, Oregon 97201
Tel: +1 (503) 725-9748
Fax: +1 (503) 725-3561
Email: acquisitions@ooliganpress.pdx.edu
Website: http://www.ooliganpress.pdx.edu

Publishes: Fiction; Nonfiction; Poetry; *Areas:* Historical; Sociology; *Markets:* Adult; Youth; *Treatments:* Literary

Publishes works of historical and social value, or significance to the Pacific Northwest region (Northern California, Oregon, Idaho, Washington, British Columbia, and Alaska). Accepts queries by email and proposals via onlnie submission system. See website for full details.

Open Court Publishing Company
Attn: Acquisitions Editor
70 East Lake Street, Suite 300
Chicago, IL 60601
Tel: +1 (800) 815-2280
Fax: +1 (312) 701-1728
Email: opencourt@caruspub.com
Website: http://www.opencourtbooks.com

Publishes: Nonfiction; *Areas:* Culture; Philosophy; *Markets:* Adult; *Treatments:* Popular

Accepts approaches for its Popular Culture and Philosophy series only. Send query by post only, with SASE, outline, and sample chapter. No approaches by fax or email. See website for full guidelines.

Open Idea Publishing, LLC
PO Box 1060
Owings Mills, MD 21117

Tel: +1 (410) 356-7014
Email: editors@openideapublishing.com
Website:
http://www.openideapublishing.com

Publishes: Fiction; Poetry; *Areas:*
Adventure; Arts; Drama; Erotic; Fantasy;
Leisure; Literature; Mystery; Romance;
Short Stories; Theatre; *Markets:* Adult;
Family; Youth; *Treatments:* Contemporary;
Literary; Popular; Positive; Progressive;
Satirical; Traditional

Contact: K Jones

Publishing company founded in 2012 whose
mission is to get talented writers successfully
published. There is no specialty at this time.
Mainly interested in true life emotions and
events.

The Overlook Press
141 Wooster Street
New York, NY 10012
Tel: +1 (212) 673-2210
Fax: +1 (212) 673-2296
Email: sales@overlookny.com
Website: http://www.overlookpress.com

Publishes: Fiction; Nonfiction; *Areas:*
Architecture; Arts; Current Affairs; Design;
Film; Health; Historical; How-to; Lifestyle;
Theatre; Translations; *Markets:* Adult;
Treatments: Commercial; Literary

Independent general-interest publisher.
Eclectic list, with areas of strength in fiction,
history, biography, drama, design, and other
visual media. Submissions via literary agents
only.

P&R Publishing
PO Box 817
Phillipsburg, NJ 08865-0817
Tel: +1 (908) 454-0505
Fax: +1 (908) 859-2390
Email: editorial@prpbooks.com
Website: http://www.prpbooks.com

Publishes: Fiction; Nonfiction; *Areas:*
Biography; Historical; Lifestyle; Religious;
Women's Interests; *Markets:* Academic;

Adult; Children's; Youth; *Treatments:*
Popular

Publishes books that promote biblical
understanding and godly living, ranging
from books aimed at the popular market to
academic works that advance biblical and
theological scholarship. Submit 2-3 chapters
as Word or .rtf files by email, along with
completed submission form (available from
website).

Parenting Press, Inc.
PO Box 75267
Seattle, WA 98175-0267
Tel: +1 (206) 364-2900
Fax: +1 (206) 364-0702
Website: http://www.parentingpress.com

Publishes: Nonfiction; *Areas:* How-to;
Lifestyle; *Markets:* Adult; Children's

Contact: Carolyn Threadgill, Acquisitions

Publishes books that teach practical life
skills to parents, children, and the people
who care for them. No fiction or poetry. See
website for submission guidelines.

Pants On Fire Press
13750 West Colonial Dr., Suite 350
Winter Garden, FL 34787
Tel: +1 (863) 546-0760
Email: editor@pantsonfirepress.com
Website: http://www.pantsonfirepress.com

Publishes: Fiction; Nonfiction; *Areas:*
Adventure; Crime; Culture; Drama;
Entertainment; Fantasy; Health; Historical;
Horror; Military; Nature; Romance; Sci-Fi;
Sport; Suspense; Technology; Thrillers;
Westerns; *Markets:* Children's; Youth;
Treatments: Commercial; Mainstream;
Popular; Traditional

Contact: Becca Goldman

A children's book publisher. We publish
popular genre fiction and select nonfiction
children's books, picture books and young
adult books for children and discerning
adults. We are carefully building the brand.
Being deeply entrenched in Disney values, as

it is our heritage, we strive to follow a high standard of excellence while maintaining high-quality standards. Titles we publish will tell timeless and engaging stories that delight and inspire. At this press, entertainment is about hope, aspiration and positive resolutions. We seek our audiences trust. Our fun is about laughing at our experiences and ourselves.

Manuscript Submissions

Attention picture book authors: Thank you for all the picture book submissions. We have enjoyed reading them. Please note that we have selected the picture books for our 2013 catalog, hence we are no longer accepting unsolicited picture book queries. We are still open to YA and Middle Grade submissions.

We are one of a few children's book publishers accepting unsolicited manuscripts. Please note that we are not interested in evaluating scripts simultaneously submitted to, or under consideration by, another publisher unless you are prepared to accept an offer from us within eight weeks. We are acquiring Children's Picture Books, Chapter Books, Middle-grade and Young Adult fiction. We are looking for strong writers who are excited about marketing their stories and building a following of readers. For novels, the body of the email should include your query and the first three chapters along with:

A synopsis
The genre of the book
Approximate word count
A short pitch
Writing credentials
Your contact info
If the work is agented, agent info
Complete bio
List of any and all previous titles with sales history

For illustrations, send three sample illustrations. Paste the query letter and chapters in the body of the e-mail and send by email. Text attachments will be deleted. Art may be attached.

Quick Guide

0-2,000 words for picture books
10,000-35,000 for middle-grade fiction
40,000-80,000 for young adult
always include a synopsis which includes the ending
allow 8-12 weeks for response

Picture Books
We're looking for author/illustrators who have the ability to use language and art to inspire the imagination, and:

0-2,000 words
a clear and fantastic theme
strong storytelling
beautiful artwork

Middle-grade Fiction
Our readers want to relate to the characters and the world they live in, so we're looking of authors who have:

10,000-35,000 words
an exciting plot
strong voices and edited scripts
developed characters
strong storytelling

Young Adult Fiction
We are looking for strong writers whose books have something fresh to offer the growing Young Adult audience.

40,000-80,000 words
A real voice for the readers
A new premise with a marketing hook that can be conveyed in 2-3 sentences
Protagonists who are 15-19
Powerful, believable world-building
An age-appropriate romantic element is a plus even if it's not the center of the story
Memorable characters readers care about and can relate to one way or another

Please allow 8-12 weeks for a response.

Note that we do not accept unsolicited novel-length manuscripts. So do not send them! And never send us your original work or art. And finally, we will contact you if we are interested.

We do not assume responsibility for any unsolicited manuscripts which we may receive. Further, in receiving a submission, we do not assume any duty not to publish a book based on a similar idea, concept or story. All submissions are recycled.

One more thing to note. We actively blog. In sending your submission you acknowledge that we may post any or all of your correspondence with us on our blog.

Papercutz

160 Broadway, Suite 700E
New York, NY 10038
Tel: +1 (646) 559-4681
Email: nantier@papercutz.com
Website: http://www.papercutz.com

Publishes: Fiction; *Areas:* Adventure; Horror; Humour; Mystery; *Markets:* Children's; Youth

Publisher dedicated to graphic novels for children, tweens, and teens. Publishes a wide range of genres, including humour, action adventure, mystery, horror, and favourite characters.

Paul Dry Books, Inc.

1700 Sansom Street, Suite 700
Philadelphia, PA 19103
Tel: +1 (215) 231-9939
Fax: +1 (215) 231-9942
Email: editor@pauldrybooks.com
Website: http://pauldrybooks.com

Publishes: Fiction; Nonfiction; Poetry; *Areas:* Architecture; Autobiography; Biography; Criticism; Culture; Historical; Philosophy; Science; Short Stories; Translations; Travel; *Markets:* Adult; Youth; *Treatments:* Contemporary; Literary

Publisher with the aim to publish lively books "to awaken, delight, and educate"—and to spark conversation. Publishes fiction, including both novels and short stories; and nonfiction, including biography, memoirs, history, and essays.

Pauline Books and Media

50 St Paul's Avenue
Boston, MA 02130
Tel: +1 (617) 522-8911

Email: editorial@paulinemedia.com
Website: http://www.pauline.org

Publishes: Fiction; Nonfiction; *Areas:* Biography; Religious; Self-Help; Spiritual; *Markets:* Adult; Children's; Family; Youth

Catholic publisher, publishing nonfiction for children and adults of all ages, as well as fiction for children and teens only. Send complete manuscript or table of contents with sample chapter by email or by post. See website for full guidelines.

Peachtree Publishers

1700 Chattahoochee Avenue
Atlanta, GA 30318-2112
Tel: +1 (404) 876-8761
Fax: +1 (404) 875-2578
Email: hello@peachtree-online.com
Website: http://peachtree-online.com

Publishes: Fiction; Nonfiction; *Areas:* Autobiography; Biography; Health; Historical; Lifestyle; Nature; Science; Self-Help; Sport; *Markets:* Adult; Children's; Youth

Contact: Helen Harriss, Acquisitions Editor

Publishes children's fiction and nonfiction picture books, chapter books, middle readers, and young adult books, as well as education, parenting, self-help, and health books of interest to the general trade. All submissions must include complete ms or sample chapters, and must be made by post. No submissions by fax or email. See website for full guidelines.

PennWell Books

1421 South Sheridan
Tulsa, OK 74112
Tel: +1 (918) 831-9421
Fax: +1 (918) 831-9555
Email: BookProposals@pennwell.com
Website: http://www.pennwellbooks.com

Publishes: Nonfiction; *Areas:* How-to; Technology; *Markets:* Professional

Publishes practical books that would be of immediate use to practitioners in the following industries:

Petroleum
Energy
Electric Utility
Fire Service and Training
Controls and Instrumentation

Accepts proposals by email. See website for full guidelines.

Penny-Farthing Press

2000 West Sam Houston Parkway South,
Suite 550
Houston, Texas 77042
Tel: +1 (713) 780-0300
Fax: +1 (713) 780-4004
Email: corp@pfpress.com
Website: http://www.pfpress.com

Publishes: Fiction; *Markets:* Adult;
Children's

Award-winning publisher of comics and children's books. Send query with synopsis by post only. If submitting one single-issue story (standard 32 pp.), include full script. If submitting a story for a series or graphic novel send only first chapter. No submissions by fax or email. See website for full guidelines.

Persea Books

277 Broadway, Suite 708
New York, NY 10007
Tel: +1 (212) 260-9256
Fax: +1 (212) 267-3165
Email: info@perseabooks.com
Website: http://www.perseabooks.com

Publishes: Fiction; Nonfiction; Poetry;
Areas: Autobiography; Biography;
Criticism; Short Stories; Translations;
Markets: Adult; Youth; *Treatments:* Literary

Publishes literary fiction and nonfiction manuscripts, including novels, novellas, short story collections, biography, essays, literary criticism, literature in translation, memoir. Encourages submissions to growing YA list in nonfiction, fiction, and poetry, aimed at the literary reader. No social science, psychology, self-help, textbooks, or

children's books. Accepts submissions by post or by email. See website for full guidelines. For poetry, query by email in first instance.

Peter Lang Publishing, Inc.

29 Broadway
New York, NY 10006
Tel: +1 (212) 647-7706
Fax: +1 (212) 647-7707
Email: CustomerService@plang.com
Website: http://www.peterlang.com

Publishes: Nonfiction; *Markets:* Academic

International academic publisher. Submit query via web form.

Piano Press

P.O. Box 85
Del Mar, CA 92014-0085
Tel: +1 (619) 884-1401
Fax: +1 (858) 755-1104
Email: pianopress@pianopress.com

Publishes: Fiction; Nonfiction; Poetry;
Areas: Music; *Markets:* Children's; Youth

Publishes books related to music for young readers, middle readers and young adults. Includes fiction, nonfiction, poetry, colouring books, and songbooks. Send query by email only.

Picador USA

175 Fifth Avenue
New York, NY 10010
Tel: +1 (646) 307-5421
Fax: +1 (212) 388-9065
Email: publicity@picadorusa.com
Website: http://www.picadorusa.com

Publishes: Fiction; Nonfiction; *Markets:*
Adult; *Treatments:* Literary

Publishes literary fiction and nonfiction. Submissions via a literary agent only.

Piccadilly Books Ltd

PO Box 25203
Colorado Springs, CO 80936
Tel: +1 (719) 550-9887

Fax: +1 (719) 550-8810
Email: info@piccadillybooks.com
Website: http://www.piccadillybooks.com

Publishes: Nonfiction; *Areas:* Cookery;
Health; Nature; *Markets:* Adult

Publishes books on natural health, nutrition,
diet, physical fitness, and related topics.
Send query with a minimum of three sample
chapters, however prefers to see complete
ms. Include cover letter with overview of the
book and market, and your qualifications in
writing the book. Pitches accepted by email.
See website for full guidelines.

Plan B Press
PO Box 4067
Alexandria, VA 22303
Tel: +1 (215) 732-2663
Email: planbpress@gmail.com
Website: http://www.planbpress.com

Publishes: Poetry; *Markets:* Adult;
Treatments: Literary

Small, independent publishing company
primarily producing limited-run poetry
chapbooks. Send 20-30 poems between June
1 and November 30, only, by post or by
email. See website for full guidelines.

Possibility Press
One Oakglade circle
Hummelstown, PA 17036
Tel: +1 (717) 566-0468
Fax: +1 (717) 566-6423
Email: info@possibilitypress.com
Website: http://www.possibilitypress.com

Publishes: Fiction; Nonfiction; *Areas:*
Business; Finance; Health; How-to;
Lifestyle; Psychology; Religious; Self-Help;
Spiritual; Technology; *Markets:* Adult

Contact: Mike Markowski; Marjie
Markowski

Publishes mainly nonfiction books on
personal improvement, covering finances,
religion, relationships, self-esteem, public
speaking, leadership, etc. Also considers
fiction that teaches lessons about life and

success. See website for detailed guide on
preparing a submission.

Presa Press
PO Box 792
Rockford, MI 49341
Email: presapress@aol.com
Website: http://www.presapress.com

Publishes: Nonfiction; Poetry; *Areas:*
Criticism; Literature; *Markets:* Adult;
Treatments: Literary

Publishes poetry paperbacks and literary
magazine, including poetry, reviews, essays,
and criticism. Query for guidelines.

Press 53
411 West Fourth Street, Suite 101A
Winston-Salem, NC 27101
Tel: +1 (336) 770-5353
Email: kevin@press53.com
Website: http://www.press53.com

Publishes: Fiction; Poetry; *Areas:* Short
Stories; *Markets:* Adult; *Treatments:*
Literary

Contact: Kevin Morgan Watson

Publishes collections of poetry and short
stories. No novels or book length fiction.
Finds authors through its competitions, and
through writers being active in the literary
community and literary magazines.

Pressgang
4600 Sunset Ave
Jordan Hall, Eng. Dept.
Indianapolis, IN 46208
Email: pressgang@butler.edu
Website: http://blogs.butler.edu/pressgang

Publishes: Fiction; Nonfiction; *Areas:*
Autobiography; Drama; Horror; Humour;
Literature; Mystery; Short Stories; Suspense;
Markets: Academic; Adult; *Treatments:*
Commercial; Contemporary; Literary;
Popular; Satirical

Contact: Bryan Furuness

Who We Are

A small press affiliated with the MFA Program in Creative Writing at a University. Founded in 2012, our mission is to publish full-length books of fiction, creative nonfiction, graphic novels, and, in the future, poetry.

What We Like

Literary heft and helium. Seriousness of purpose, surprising execution, the well-wrought joke, the well-crafted sentence. The blurring of boundaries. Think Vonnegut meets Saunders meets Poe. Think Byron meets Bulgakov, Gogol, Nabokov. Think Kafka and Beckett. Think Lorrie Moore, think Laurie Anderson, think Lemony Snickett. Think Dorothy Parker mixed with Edward Gorey meets Steven Millhauser meets Dickens with a word limit.

Princeton University Press
41 William Street
Princeton, NJ 08540
Tel: +1 (609) 258-4900
Fax: +1 (609) 258-6305
Email: front_desk@press.princeton.edu
Website: http://press.princeton.edu

Publishes: Nonfiction; Poetry; Reference; *Areas:* Anthropology; Archaeology; Architecture; Arts; Film; Finance; Historical; Legal; Literature; Medicine; Music; Nature; Philosophy; Photography; Politics; Psychology; Religious; Science; Self-Help; Sociology; Spiritual; Technology; *Markets:* Academic

Scholarly publisher. Send brief proposals fitting the scholarly profile and the composition of their current lists, 1-2 pages maximum. No unsolicited mss.

Pro Lingua Associates ESL
PO Box 1348
Brattleboro, VT 05302-1348
Tel: +1 (802) 257-7779
Fax: +1 (802) 257-5117
Email: Ray@ProLinguaAssociates.com
Website:
http://www.prolinguaassociates.com

Publishes: Nonfiction; *Markets:* Academic

Contact: Raymond C. Clark, Senior Editor

Small publisher dedicated to producing "superior language teaching materials". Will respond to enquiries made by email, but no proposals by email. See website for full submission guidelines.

Quarto Publishing Group USA
400 First Avenue North, Suite 400
Minneapolis, MN 55401
Tel: +1 (612) 344-8100
Fax: +1 (612) 344-8691
Website: http://www.quartous.com

Publishes: Nonfiction; Reference; *Areas:* Arts; Cookery; Crafts; Current Affairs; Design; Health; Historical; Hobbies; How-to; Military; Music; Politics; Science; Self-Help; Sport; Technology; Travel; *Markets:* Adult

Nonfiction publisher with offices in the US and UK. See website for specific interests and guidelines for different imprints.

Quest Books
306 West Geneva Road
PO Box 270
Wheaton, IL 60187-0270
Tel: +1 (630) 665-0130
Email: submissions@questbooks.net
Website: http://www.questbooks.net

Publishes: Nonfiction; *Areas:* Arts; Health; Music; Mystery; Philosophy; Psychology; Religious; Science; Self-Help; Spiritual; *Markets:* Adult

Contact: Submissions Department

Publishes books of intelligence, readability, and insight for the contemporary spiritual seeker, exploring ancient wisdom, modern science, world religions, philosophy, the arts, and the inner meaning of life to "provide dynamic tools for spiritual healing and self-transformation". See website for full submission guidelines.

Ragged Sky Press

PO Box 312
Annandale, NJ 08801
Email: info@raggedsky.com
Website: http://www.raggedsky.com

Publishes: Poetry; *Areas:* Women's
Interests; *Markets:* Adult; *Treatments:*
Literary

Small and selective co-operative press
publishing collections of poetry. Has
historically focused on mature voices,
overlooked poets, and women's perspectives.
Does no accept unsolicited mss. Poets are
encouraged to join the community.
Submissions by invitation.

Rainbow Books, Inc.

PO Box 430
Highland City, FL 33846-0430
Tel: +1 (863) 648-4420
Email:
Submissions@RainbowBooksInc.com
Website: http://www.rainbowbooksinc.com

Publishes: Fiction; Nonfiction; *Areas:* How-
to; Mystery; Self-Help; *Markets:* Adult

Publishes self-help, how-to, and cozy murder
mysteries. Send query by post with SASE,
one-page synopsis, up to three sample
chapters, outline, details of any photos or
illustrations, author background and
credentials, and your email address. Queries
may also be sent by email, however
attachments will not be opened. See website
for full guidelines.

RainTown Press

1111 E. Burnside St. #309
Portland, OR 97214
Email: submissions@raintownpress.com
Website: http://raintownpress.com

Publishes: Fiction; *Markets:* Children's;
Youth

Independent press dedicated to publishing
literature for middle grade and young adults
in any genre. No short stories or novellas –
young adult novels should be at least 60,000
words and Middle Grade novels should be at

least 45,000 words. No poems or poetry
chapbooks; picture books; memoirs;
nonfiction; or incomplete manuscripts. See
website for full submission guidelines.

Reading Harbor

Lansdale, PA
Email: ReadingHarborCo@gmail.com
Website: http://www.readingharbor.com

Publishes: Fiction; Nonfiction; *Areas:*
Autobiography; Culture; Current Affairs;
Entertainment; Literature; Philosophy;
Psychology; Self-Help; Short Stories;
Women's Interests; *Markets:* Adult; Family;
Youth; *Treatments:* Commercial; Literary;
Mainstream; Niche; Popular; Positive

Contact: Grace C

An American-based Publication Company,
founded in 2014. Our goal is to bring quality
literature to the public. Reading should be a
passtime that not only informs the mind but
stirs the spirit and inspires the heart. A good
book is a treasured find. We want to provide
you memories you will share.

Regnery Publishing, Inc.

One Massachusetts Avenue, NW
Washington, DC 20001
Tel: +1 (202) 216-0600
Fax: +1 (202) 216-0612
Email: editorial@regnery.com
Website: http://www.regnery.com

Publishes: Nonfiction; *Areas:* Historical;
Military; Politics; Science; *Markets:* Adult;
Children's

Publisher of conservative books. Accepts
submissions via agents only.

Renaissance House

465 Westview Avenue
Englewood, NY 07631
Tel: +1 (201) 408-4048
Email: info@renaissancehouse.net
Website: http://renaissancehouse.net

Publishes: Fiction; Nonfiction; *Markets:*
Adult; Children's

Creates books in English and in Spanish. Offers c-publishing. Send ideas by email.

Richard C. Owen Publishers, Inc.

PO Box 585
Katonah, NY 10536
Tel: +1 (914) 232-3903
Fax: +1 (914) 232-3977
Email: richardowen@rcowen.com
Website: http://www.rcowen.com

Publishes: Nonfiction; *Markets:* Academic; Children's; Professional

Publishes books on literacy education, including classroom materials for for grades PK-8, and books for teachers and administrators.

Rio Nuevo Publishers

PO Box 5250
Tucson, AZ 85703
Tel: +1 (520) 623-9558
Fax: +1 (520) 624-5888
Email: info@rionuevo.com
Website: http://www.rionuevo.com

Publishes: Fiction; Nonfiction; *Areas:* Architecture; Arts; Autobiography; Biography; Cookery; Culture; Design; Gardening; Historical; Nature; Photography; Spiritual; Travel; *Markets:* Adult; Children's

Publishes books for adults and children relating to the West and Southwest. Publishes only nonfiction for adults. Publishes fiction and nonfiction for children, via imprint. Send query and proposal by post or by email for adult titles; for children's books submit complete ms by email to address provided on website. See website for full submission guidelines.

Ripple Grove Press

PO Box 491
Hubbardston, MA 01452
Email: submit@ripplegrovepress.com
Website: http://www.ripplegrovepress.com

Publishes: Fiction; *Markets:* Children's

Publishes picture-driven stories for children aged 2-6. No early readers, middle grade, young adult, religious, or holiday-themed stories. Send submissions by post with SASE or by email, including cover letter with summary; age range of audience; brief bio; contact info; and full ms (as a PDF attachment if submitting by email). See website for full guidelines.

Rose Alley Press

4203 Brooklyn Avenue NE, #103A, Seattle, WA 98105-5911
Tel: +1 (206) 633-2725
Email: rosealleypress@juno.com
Website: http://www.rosealleypress.com

Publishes: Poetry; *Markets:* Adult

Contact: David D. Horowitz, Publisher

Publisher contacts authors whose work he wants to publish. Does not accept or consider unsolicited mss.

Rowman & Littlefield Publishing Group

4501 Forbes Boulevard, Suite 200
Lanham, MD 20706
Tel: +1 (301) 459-3366
Fax: +1 (301) 429-5748
Email: jsisk@rowmanlittlefield.com
Website: https://rowman.com

Publishes: Nonfiction; *Areas:* Crime; Health; Historical; Legal; Nature; Philosophy; Politics; Psychology; Religious; Sociology; *Markets:* Academic; Adult; Professional

Publishes books on subjects throughout the humanities and social sciences, both for general readers and professional and scholarly titles. See website for submission guidelines.

Ruka Press

PO Box 1409
Washington, DC 20013
Tel: +1 (202) 546-8049
Email: submissions@rukapress.com
Website: http://www.rukapress.com

Publishes: Nonfiction; *Areas:* Finance; Nature; Science; *Markets:* Adult

Publishes books on economics, science, nature, climate change and sustainability. No fiction or poetry. Send query by post or email. See website for full guidelines.

Shelfstealers

220 N. Zapata Hwy, #11
Laredo, TX 78043
Tel: +1 (210) 399-9013
Email: shelfstealers@shelfstealers.com
Website: http://www.shelfstealers.com

Publishes: Fiction; Nonfiction; *Areas:* Adventure; Anthropology; Architecture; Arts; Autobiography; Beauty and Fashion; Biography; Business; Cookery; Crime; Criticism; Culture; Current Affairs; Fantasy; Finance; Health; Historical; Hobbies; Horror; How-to; Humour; Legal; Leisure; Lifestyle; Literature; Men's Interests; Military; Mystery; Nature; Philosophy; Politics; Psychology; Romance; Science; Sci-Fi; Self-Help; Short Stories; Sociology; Spiritual; Suspense; Technology; Thrillers; Travel; Westerns; Women's Interests; *Markets:* Adult; Children's; Family; Professional; Youth

Contact: Sheryl J. Dunn

A royalty publisher, not a self-publisher. We edit, produce the covers and do all the layout work, market our books and help our authors to market them, and we care about quality writing beyond any other factor.

Best to submit using the online form.

We don't pay advances, but we offer a 50/50 split on ebooks, POD books, and audio books.

Our existing authors would be pleased to be contacted about us.

Skinner House Books

25 Beacon Street
Boston, MA 02108
Email: bookproposals@uua.org

Website: http://www.uua.org/publications/skinnerhouse/

Publishes: Nonfiction; *Areas:* Religious; Spiritual; *Markets:* Adult

Contact: Betsy Martin

Book publisher of the Unitarian Universalist faith. See website for current requirements and details on how to approach.

St Augustine's Press

PO Box 2285
South Bend, IN 46680-2285
Tel: +1 (574) 291-3500
Email: bruce@staugustine.net
Website: http://www.staugustine.net

Publishes: Nonfiction; *Areas:* Culture; Historical; Philosophy; Religious; *Markets:* Academic

Contact: Bruce Fingerhut

Publishes scholarly works in the fields of philosophy, theology, and cultural and intellectual history. Send query by post or electronically; see website for full guidelines. No unsolicited mss.

Stemmer House Publishers

PO Box 89
4 White Brook Road
Gilsum, NH 03448
Tel: +1 (603) 357-0236
Fax: +1 (603) 357-2073
Email: pbs@pathwaybook.com
Website: http://www.stemmer.com

Publishes: Fiction; Nonfiction; Poetry; Reference; *Areas:* Arts; Culture; Hobbies; Nature; Science; Short Stories; *Markets:* Adult; Children's

Publishes nonfiction and reference for adults and children on nature, science, hobbies, culture, and arts. Also publishes stories and poetry for children. Send query with SASE in first instance.

Sunbury Press

PO BOX 548
Boiling Springs, PA 17007
Tel: +1 (855) 338-8359
Fax: +1 (855) 338-8359
Email: proposals@sunburypress.com
Website: http://www.sunburypress.com

Publishes: Fiction; Nonfiction; Reference;
Areas: Arts; Current Affairs; Historical;
Humour; Religious; Science; *Markets:*
Adult; Children's

Rapidly growing publisher, actively seeking
new material. Receives about 1,000
manuscripts a year, and publishes around 70.
No hard copy submissions or phone calls.
Submit using form on website.

Tantor Audio

2 Business Park Road
Old Saybrook, CT 06475
Tel: +1 (860) 395-1155
Fax: +1 (888) 782-7821
Email: rights@tantor.com
Website: http://www.tantor.com

Publishes: Fiction; Nonfiction; *Areas:*
Adventure; Anthropology; Autobiography;
Biography; Business; Cookery; Criticism;
Culture; Current Affairs; Entertainment;
Erotic; Fantasy; Finance; Gothic; Health;
Historical; Horror; How-to; Humour; Legal;
Leisure; Lifestyle; Military; Music; Mystery;
Nature; New Age; Philosophy; Politics;
Psychology; Religious; Romance; Science;
Self-Help; Short Stories; Sociology;
Spiritual; Sport; Suspense; Westerns;
Women's Interests; *Markets:* Academic;
Adult; Youth; *Treatments:* Contemporary;
Experimental; Literary; Mainstream

Publisher of fiction and nonfiction
audiobooks. Send query by post with SASE,
or submit proposal with three sample
chapters, plus synopsis for fiction.

Texas Tech University Press

Box 41037
Lubbock, TX 79409-1037
Tel: +1 (806) 742-2982
Fax: +1 (806) 742-2979
Email: ttup@ttu.edu

Website: http://universitypress.
texastechprintanddesign.com

Publishes: Fiction; Nonfiction; Poetry;
Areas: Autobiography; Biography; Culture;
Historical; Legal; Literature; Nature;
Technology; *Markets:* Academic; Adult

University press, publishing all subject areas
relating to Texas, the Great Plains, and the
American West, particularly history,
biography, and memoir; American and
European history; American Indian studies;
American legal studies; Costume and textile
history; Environmental studies and literature
of place; Fiction rooted in the American
West and Southwest; and Jewish literature,
culture, and history. Also publishes an
invited first book of poetry each year, but no
unsolicited submissions of poetry. See
website for full details.

•Latin American and Latino fiction, in
translation or English
•Natural history and natural science
•Sport in the American West
•Technical communication and rhetoric
•Vietnam and Southeast Asia, particularly
during and after the Vietnam War

The Poisoned Pencil

6962 E. First Avenue, Suite 103
Scottsdale, AZ 85251
Tel: +1 (480) 945-3375
Email: ellen@thepoisonedpencil.com
Website: http://thepoisonedpencil.com

Publishes: Fiction; *Areas:* Mystery;
Markets: Youth

Publishes young adult mystery by authors
from the US and Canada. Avoid serial
killers, excessive gore or horror, or heavy
SF, supernatural, or fantasy content. No short
story collections or middle grade fiction.
Submit online via submission manager on
website.

Tor/Forge

Tom Doherty Associates, LLC
175 Fifth Avenue
New York, NY 10010

Website:
http://us.macmillan.com/TorForge.aspx

Publishes: Fiction; Nonfiction; *Areas:*
Fantasy; Historical; Horror; Mystery; Sci-Fi;
Suspense; Women's Interests; *Markets:*
Adult

Particular emphasis on science fiction,
fantasy, and horror. Open submissions
policy. Send query with synopsis, first three
chapters, and SASE for response. See
website for full submission guidelines.

Tristan Publishing

2355 Louisiana Avenue North
Golden Valley, MN 55427
Tel: +1 (763) 545-1383
Fax: +1 (763) 545-1387
Email: manuscripts@tristanpublishing.com
Website: http://www.tristanpublishing.com

Publishes: Fiction; Nonfiction; *Areas:*
Lifestyle; Self-Help; Short Stories; *Markets:*
Adult; Children's; *Treatments:* Positive

Contact: Brett Waldman; Sheila Waldman

Publishes uplifting, inspirational gift books
of typically 36-42 pages and up to 1,000
words. Books should take readers fewer than
10 minutes to read, but should leave a lasting
message of hope. Send submissions by email
or by post. See website for full details.

Tsaba House

2252 12th Street
Reedley, CA 93654
Tel: +1 (559) 643-8575
Fax: +1 (559) 638-2640
Website: http://www.TsabaHouse.com

Publishes: Fiction; Nonfiction; *Areas:*
Adventure; Autobiography; Beauty and
Fashion; Biography; Current Affairs;
Fantasy; Finance; How-to; Leisure;
Lifestyle; Literature; Men's Interests;
Mystery; Nature; Psychology; Religious;
Romance; Science; Self-Help; Spiritual;
Suspense; Thrillers; Women's Interests;
Markets: Adult; Family; Youth; *Treatments:*
Contemporary; Mainstream; Positive

Contact: Corrie Schwagerl

Dedicated to promoting the Gospel through
the written word by producing quality,
family friendly literature that covers a
myriad of topics ranging from educational
nonfiction to entertaining fiction and
providing Christian based reading
entertainment for all ages.
We accept unsolicited submissions once a
year during the month of January ONLY.
Full Submission guidelines are on our
website. We are not a subsidy publisher and
take full financial responsibility for
publishing and marketing but we do require
that our authors be willing to do a book tour
and be actively involved in our Marketing
Plan.

Tuttle Publishing

Airport Business Part
364 Innovation Drive
North Clarendon, VT 05759-9436
Tel: +1 (800) 526-2778
Fax: +1 (800) 329-8885
Email: submissions@tuttlepublishing.com
Website: http://www.tuttlepublishing.com

Publishes: Fiction; Nonfiction; *Areas:*
Architecture; Arts; Business; Cookery;
Culture; Design; Gardening; Health;
Historical; Literature; Nature; Religious;
Spiritual; Sport; Travel; *Markets:* Adult;
Children's

Publishes books on Asian cultures, Language
and Martial Arts, including graphic novels.
Accepts queries by post or by email, but
prefers email approaches. See website for
full submission guidelines.

University of Nebraska Press

1111 Lincoln Mall
Lincoln NE 68588-0630
Tel: +1 (402) 472-3581
Fax: +1 (402) 472-6214
Email: pressmail@unl.edu
Website: http://nebraskapress.unl.edu

Publishes: Fiction; Nonfiction; Poetry;
Translations; *Markets:* Academic; Adult;
Treatments: Contemporary; Literary; Serious

Primarily publishes serious nonfiction books and scholarly journals. Publishes a few titles of regional poetry and prose each season, and occasional reprints of fiction with an established reputation. Also publishes literary woks in translation. Submit proposal in first instance. See website for more details.

University of Tampa Press
401 W. Kennedy Blvd
Tampa, FL 33606
Tel: +1 (813) 253-6266
Fax: +1 (813) 258-7593
Email: utpress@ut.edu
Website: http://www.ut.edu/tampapress/pressmain.aspx

Publishes: Fiction; Nonfiction; Poetry; *Areas:* Arts; Historical; *Markets:* Academic; Adult; *Treatments:* Literary

Has been dedicated to the publication of books and periodicals featuring poetry, fiction and nonfiction from Florida and around the globe for more than 50 years. Publishes poetry, Florida history, supernatural literature, book arts, and other titles. Also publishes literary journal and runs annual poetry and fiction competitions.

Vanderbilt University Press
Vanderbilt University
PMB 351813 2301 Vanderbilt Place
Nashville, TN 37235-1813
Tel: +1 (615) 322-3585
Email: vupress@vanderbilt.edu
Website:
http://www.vanderbilt.edu/university-press/

Publishes: Nonfiction; *Areas:* Anthropology; Archaeology; Culture; Health; Historical; Literature; Medicine; Music; Nature; Philosophy; Politics; Women's Interests; *Markets:* Academic; Adult

Contact: Michael Ames, Director

Publishes books in most areas of the humanities and social sciences, as well as health care and education. See website for full submission guidelines.

Voyageur Press
Book Proposals—Voyageur Press
Quayside Publishing Group
400 First Avenue North, Suite 300
Minneapolis, MN 55401
Tel: +1 (800) 458-0454
Fax: +1 (612) 344-8691
Email: customerservice@quaysidepub.com
Website: http://www.voyageurpress.com

Publishes: Nonfiction; *Areas:* Culture; Historical; Lifestyle; Music; Nature; Photography; Travel; *Markets:* Adult

Publishes books on nature and the environment; country living and farming heritage; regional and cultural history; music; travel and photography. See website for full submission guidelines.

Waveland Press, Inc.
4180 IL Route 83, Suite 101
Long Grove, Illinois 60047
Tel: +1 (847) 634-0081
Fax: +1 (847) 634-9501
Email: info@waveland.com
Website: http://www.waveland.com

Publishes: Nonfiction; *Areas:* Anthropology; Archaeology; Architecture; Arts; Business; Design; Finance; Health; Historical; Legal; Literature; Music; Nature; Philosophy; Politics; Psychology; Religious; Science; Sociology; Technology; Theatre; Women's Interests; *Markets:* Academic

Publisher of college textbooks and supplements, providing reasonably priced teaching materials for the classroom. See website for submission guidelines.

Westminster John Knox Press (WJK)
100 Witherspoon Street
Louisville, KY 40202-1396
Tel: +1 (800) 523-1631
Fax: +1 (800) 541-5113
Email: submissions@wjkbooks.com
Website: http://www.wjkbooks.com

Publishes: Nonfiction; *Areas:* Culture; Religious; Spiritual; *Markets:* Academic; Adult; Professional

Publishes books specifically related to the Presbyterian Church (USA), including theology, biblical studies, preaching, worship, ethics, religion and culture, and other related fields. Serves four main markets: scholars and students in colleges, universities, seminaries, and divinity schools; preachers, educators, and counselors working in churches; members of mainline Protestant congregations; and general readers. See website for detailed submission guidelines.

The Wild Rose Press

PO Box 708
Adam's Basin NY 14410
Email: queryus@thewildrosepress.com
Website: http://www.thewildrosepress.com

Publishes: Fiction; *Areas:* Romance; *Markets:* Adult

Publishes romance only. Send query by email with synopsis in the body of the email. No attachments. See website for full submission guidelines.

Williamson Books

2630 Elm Hill Pike, Suite 100
Nashville, TN 37214
Tel: +1 (615) 781-1451
Email: kwest@guideposts.org

Publishes: Nonfiction; Arts; Cookery; Crafts; Historical; Hobbies; Science; *Markets:* Children's

Publishes nonfiction titles for children aged 3 to 12 that emphasise hands-on learning through crafts and activities. Subject matter ranges from maths and science to geography, history, art, and cooking. Send query with SASE for guidelines.

The Zharmae Publishing Press

1827 W Shannon Ave
Spokane, WA 99205
Tel: +1 (206) 383-5776
Email: tgrundy@zharmae.com

Website: http://www.zharmae.com

Publishes: Fiction; Nonfiction; *Areas:* Adventure; Crime; Erotic; Fantasy; Horror; Literature; Men's Interests; Romance; Sci-Fi; Suspense; Thrillers; Women's Interests; *Markets:* Adult; Children's; Youth; *Treatments:* Commercial; Contemporary; Cynical; Dark; Experimental; In-depth; Light; Literary; Mainstream; Niche; Popular; Progressive; Serious

Contact: Travis Grundy

A Pacific Northwest based Independent Publisher, dedicated to producing the best genre fiction from around the universe. A living, breathing idea of what the future of book publishing can and should be. Devoted to literary works of depth and detail as well as the broader knowledge and exchange of ideals that can be conveyed from the reading and analysis of fiction. Created with the notion that publishing can and should be hip, youthful, and accessible; as well as focused on author development with regards to both the art and science of writing, this is the result of this ongoing effort.

Our focuse is on category fiction with a heavy emphasis on artistry through prose, while staying true to the formulaic, sensationalistic, melodramatic, and sentimental nature normally exhibited in such types of fiction. We are committed to producing work featuring elevated, poetic, and idiosyncratic prose that defy reader expectations, or which go beyond the normal plot scope.

Though some might categorize us as a small independent press (and be correct), we see our size as our main strength. This is what allows us to focus our energies on developing fantastic writers into brilliant authors. Our purpose, as with all businesses, is the bottom line; however, we are not out to produce cookie cutter books – the simple reason for our existence is to produce magnificent novels, period.

UK Publishers

For the most up-to-date listings of these and hundreds of other publishers, visit http://www.firstwriter.com/publishers

*To claim your **free** access to the site, please see the back of this book.*

AA Publishing
The Automobile Association
Fanum House
Basingstoke
RG21 4EA
Tel: +44 (0) 1256 491524
Fax: +44 (0) 1614 887544
Email: AAPublish@TheAA.com
Website: http://www.theAA.com

Publishes: Nonfiction; Reference; *Areas:* Leisure; Travel; *Markets:* Adult

Contact: David Watchus

Publishes motoring and travel books including maps, guidebooks and atlases etc.

Absolute Press
Scarborough House
29 James Street West
Bath
BA1 2BT
Tel: +44 (0) 1225 316013
Fax: +44 (0) 1225 445836
Email: info@absolutepress.co.uk
Website: http://www.absolutepress.co.uk

Publishes: Nonfiction; *Areas:* Cookery; *Markets:* Adult

Contact: Jon Croft (Managing Director); Meg Avent (Commissioning Editor)

Publishes book relating to food and wine. No unsolicited MSS, but accepts synopses and ideas.

Alastair Sawday Publishing Co. Ltd
The Old Farmyard
Yanley Lane
Long Ashton
Bristol
BS41 9LR
Tel: +44 (0) 1275 395430
Email: specialplaces@sawdays.co.uk
Website: http://www.sawdays.co.uk

Publishes: Nonfiction; *Areas:* Nature; Travel; *Markets:* Adult

Publishes guidebooks and books on environmental topics.

Ian Allan Publishing Ltd
Riverdene Business Park
Molesey Road
Hersham
KT12 4RG
Tel: +44 (0) 1932 266600
Fax: +44 (0) 1932 266601
Email: info@ianallanpublishing.co.uk
Website: http://www.ianallanpublishing.com

Publishes: Nonfiction; Reference; *Areas:* Historical; Hobbies; Military; Travel; *Markets:* Adult

Publishes nonfiction and reference books relating to transport, including aviation, military, road, rail, maps, and atalases. Also modelling, including railway modelling. Send query with SAE, synopsis, and sample chapter.

Alma Books Ltd
London House
243-253 Lower Mortlake Road
Richmond
Surrey
TW9 2LL
Tel: +44 (0) 20 8948 9550
Fax: +44 (0) 20 8948 5599
Email: info@almabooks.com
Website: http://www.almabooks.co.uk

Publishes: Fiction; Nonfiction; *Areas:* Historical; Literature; *Markets:* Adult; *Treatments:* Contemporary; Literary

Publishes literary fiction and a small number of nonfiction titles with a strong literary or historical connotation. No children's books, poetry, academic works, science fiction, horror, or fantasy. Accepts unsolicited MSS by post with synopsis, two sample chapters, and SAE if return of material required. No submissions by email, or submissions from outside the UK. Submissions received from outside the UK will not receive a response.

Amberley Publishing
The Hill
Stroud
Gloucestershire
GL5 4EP
Tel: +44 (0) 1453 847800
Fax: +44 (0) 1453 847820
Email: submissions@amberley-books.com
Website: http://www.amberleybooks.com

Publishes: Nonfiction; *Areas:* Archaeology; Biography; Crime; Historical; Military; Sociology; Sport; Travel; *Markets:* Adult

Publishes local interest and niche history. Send query by email or by post, with one-page proposal describing the book; reason for writing the book; proposed word count; proposed number of images; and any other relevant information.

Ammonite Press
166 High Street
Lewes
East Sussex
BN7 1XU
Tel: +44 (0) 1273 488006
Fax: +44 (0) 1273 472418
Email: richard.wiles@ammonitepress.com
Website: http://www.ammonitepress.com

Publishes: Nonfiction; *Areas:* Historical; Photography; Sociology; *Markets:* Adult

Contact: Richard Wiles (Managing Editor)

Publishes books on photography, social history, and also gift books.

Andersen Press Ltd
20 Vauxhall Bridge Road
London
SW1V 2SA
Tel: +44 (0) 20 7840 8701
Fax: +44 (0) 20 7233 6263
Email: anderseneditorial@randomhouse.co.uk
Website: http://www.andersenpress.co.uk

Publishes: Fiction; *Markets:* Children's

Publishes picture books and longer children's fiction up to 75,000 words. Publishes rhyming stories, but no poetry, adult fiction, nonfiction, or short story collections. Send query with synopsis and first three chapters.

Antique Collectors' Club Ltd
Sandy Lane
Old Martlesham
Woodbridge
Suffolk
IP12 4SD
Tel: +44 (0) 1394 389950
Fax: +44 (0) 1394 389999
Email: submissions@antique-acc.com
Website: http://www.antiquecollectorsclub.com

Publishes: Nonfiction; *Areas:* Antiques; Architecture; Arts; Beauty and Fashion; Business; Crafts; Design; Gardening;

Historical; Photography; Travel; *Markets:* Adult; Children's

Publishes books on antiques and decorative arts. Send queries or submit manuscripts by post or by email.

Arc Publications

Nanholme Mill
Shaw Wood Road
Todmorden
Lancs
OL14 6DA
Tel: +44 (0) 1706 812338
Fax: +44 (0) 1706 818948
Email: info@arcpublications.co.uk
Website: http://www.arcpublications.co.uk/submissions

Publishes: Poetry; *Areas:* Music; Translations; *Markets:* Adult; *Treatments:* Contemporary

Send 16-24 poems by email as a Word / PDF attachment, maximum one poem per page. Submissions from outside the UK and Ireland should be sent to specific address for international submissions, available on website. Cover letter should include short bio and details of the contemporary poets you read.

The Armchair Traveller at the bookHaus

Editorial Submissions
Haus Publishing Ltd
70 Cadogan Place
London
SW1X 9AH
Tel: +44 (0) 20 7838 9055
Email: info@hauspublishing.com
Website: http://www.thearmchairtraveller.com

Publishes: Nonfiction; *Areas:* Travel; *Markets:* Adult

Publishes travel writing. Send query with book proposal, sample three chapters if book has already been written, and SAE if return of manuscript is required. No submissions by email.

Ashgate Publishing Limited

Wey Court East
Union Road
Farnham
Surrey
GU9 7PT
Tel: +44 (0) 1252 736600
Fax: +44 (0) 1252 736736
Email: info@ashgatepublishing.com
Website: http://www.ashgate.com

Publishes: Nonfiction; *Areas:* Architecture; Arts; Business; Culture; Historical; Legal; Literature; Music; Philosophy; Politics; Religious; Sociology; *Markets:* Academic; Professional

Actively seeking new book proposals. See website for appropriate submission guidelines.

Ashmolean Museum Publications

Ashmolean Museum
Beaumont Street
Oxford
OX1 2PH
Tel: +44 (0) 1865 278010
Fax: +44 (0) 1865 278018
Email: publications@ashmus.ox.ac.uk
Website: http://www.ashmolean.org

Publishes: Nonfiction; *Areas:* Archaeology; Arts; Historical; *Markets:* Adult; Children's

Contact: Declan McCarthy

Publications mainly based on in-house collections. Publishes both adult and Children's on the subjects of European archeology and ancient history, European and Oriental arts, Egyptology and numismatics. No fiction, African / American / modern art, post-medieval history, ethnography, or unsolicited MSS.

Aureus Publishing Limited

Email: info@aureus.co.uk
Website: http://www.aureus.co.uk

Publishes: Nonfiction; *Areas:* Autobiography; Biography; Music; Sport; *Markets:* Adult

Publishes books on music and sport. Not accepting new material as at August 2014.

Aurora Metro Press

67 Grove Avenue
Twickenham
TW1 4HX
Tel: +44 (0) 20 3261 0000
Fax: +44 (0) 20 8898 0735
Email: submissions@aurorametro.com
Website: http://www.aurorametro.com

Publishes: Fiction; Nonfiction; Scripts; *Areas:* Arts; Biography; Cookery; Drama; Humour; Short Stories; Theatre; Translations; Women's Interests; *Markets:* Adult; Children's; Youth

Contact: Neil Gregory (Submissions Manager)

Publisher set up to promote new writing by women. Specialises in anthologising new drama, fiction, and work in translation. Send synopsis and three chapters of the finished book by post or by email. For play submissions, if a production is scheduled then the full script must be sent at least 6 weeks before opening night.

Aurum Press Ltd

74-77 White Lion Street
London
N1 9PF
Tel: +44 (0) 20 7284 9300
Fax: +44 (0) 20 7485 0490
Email: sales@aurumpress.co.uk
Website: http://www.aurumpress.co.uk

Publishes: Nonfiction; *Areas:* Arts; Biography; Crafts; Current Affairs; Film; Historical; Lifestyle; Military; Music; Photography; Sport; Travel; *Markets:* Adult

Publishes adult nonfiction in the above areas, both illustrated and not.

Award Publications Limited

The Old Riding School
The Welbeck Estate
Worksop
Nottinghamshire
S80 3LR
Tel: +44 (0) 1909 478170
Fax: +44 (0) 1909 484632
Email: info@awardpublications.co.uk
Website:
http://www.awardpublications.co.uk

Publishes: Fiction; Nonfiction; Reference; *Markets:* Children's

Publishes children's fiction, nonfiction, and reference. Not currently accepting unsolicited mss, but always on the lookout for illustrators and designers. Send samples by email.

Barrington Stoke

18 Walker Street
Edinburgh
EH3 7LP
Tel: +44 (0) 131 225 4113
Fax: +44 (0) 131 225 4140
Email: info@barringtonstoke.co.uk
Website: http://www.barringtonstoke.co.uk

Publishes: Fiction; Nonfiction; Reference; *Markets:* Children's; Professional

Commissions books via literary agents only. No unsolicited material. Publishes books for "reluctant, dyslexic, disenchanted and under-confident" readers and their teachers.

BFI Publishing

Palgrave Macmillan Ltd
Houndmills
Basingstoke
Hampshire
RG21 6XS
Tel: +44 (0) 1256 302994
Fax: +44 (0) 1256 479476
Email: j.burnell@palgrave.com
Website: http://www.palgrave.com/bfi

Publishes: Nonfiction; Reference; *Areas:* Film; Media; TV; *Markets:* Academic

Contact: Jenni Burnell, Commissioning Editor: BFI and Theatre & Performance

Welcomes book proposals. Publishes film and television-related books and resources, both for schools and academic readerships, and more generally. See website for publishing proposal forms, and lists of editorial contacts to submit them to.

BHW Publishing House

Email: bhwpublishinghouse@live.com
Website:
http://www.bhwpublishinghouse.co.uk

Publishes: Fiction; *Areas:* Adventure; Biography; Crime; Erotic; Fantasy; Horror; Lifestyle; Romance; Sci-Fi; Short Stories; Spiritual; Thrillers; Travel; Women's Interests; *Markets:* Adult; Family; Professional; Youth; *Treatments:* Experimental; In-depth; Niche

Contact: Caroline Williams

We are looking for authors to submit unsolicited manuscripts today. We are accepting any genre. Please ensure you follow our submission guidelines highlighted on our website.

Black & White Publishing Ltd

29 Ocean Drive
Edinburgh
EH6 6JL
Tel: +44 (0) 01316 254500
Email: mail@blackandwhitepublishing.com
Website:
http://www.blackandwhitepublishing.com

Publishes: Fiction; Nonfiction; *Areas:* Autobiography; Biography; Cookery; Crime; Humour; Romance; Sport; *Markets:* Academic; Adult; Children's; Youth

Contact: Campbell Brown; Alison McBride

Publisher of general fiction and nonfiction. See website for an idea of the kind of books normally published. Send query with brief synopsis and sample chapters up to 30 pages, in a single Word file by email.

Blackline Press

15 Lister Road
Ipswich
IP1 5EQ
Email: author@blacklinepress.com

Website: http://www.blacklinepress.com

Publishes: Nonfiction; *Areas:* Sport; *Markets:* Adult

Publishes books about football. Particularly interested in groundhopping tours and challenges, club histories and non-league autobiographies, but welcomes all ideas. Actively seeking new authors. Send query by email.

Blackstaff Press Ltd

4D Weavers Court Business Park
Linfield Road
Belfast
BT12 5GH
Tel: +44 (0) 28 9034 7510
Fax: +44 (0) 28 9034 7508
Email: info@blackstaffpress.com
Website: http://www.blackstaffpress.com

Publishes: Fiction; Nonfiction; Poetry; *Areas:* Autobiography; Biography; Cookery; Historical; Humour; Nature; Politics; Short Stories; Sport; Travel; *Markets:* Adult

Contact: Patsy Horton

Publishes full length fiction and nonfiction, plus one or two collections of short stories and poetry per year. Send query with SAE, synopsis, and three sample chapters in first instance. For nonfiction, include market information. No unsolicited MSS or electronic submissions. Only considers submissions of Northern Ireland/Irish interest. Queries or submissions without SAE will not be considered.

John Blake Publishing

3 Bramber Court
2 Bramber Road
London
W14 9PB
Tel: +44 (0) 20 7381 0666
Fax: +44 (0) 20 7381 6868
Email: words@blake.co.uk
Website: http://www.blake.co.uk

Publishes: Fiction; Nonfiction; *Areas:* Autobiography; Biography; Cookery; Crime; Health; Legal; Military; Music; Politics;

Self-Help; Sport; *Markets:* Adult;
Treatments: Commercial; Mainstream

Welcomes synopses and ideas for nonfiction.
Send query with chapter-by-chapter
synopsis, personal details, publishing
history, sample chapters, and SAE for
response. Always looking for
inspiring/shocking real life stories from
ordinary people. Not currently accepting
fiction. No unsolicited MSS. If submitting by
email, attachments should be no larger than
1MB and be saved in .rtf format. See website
for full submission guidelines..

Bloodaxe Books Ltd

Highgreen
Tarset
Northumberland
NE48 1RP
Tel: +44 (0) 1434 240500
Fax: +44 (0) 1434 240505
Email: editor@bloodaxebooks.com
Website: http://www.bloodaxebooks.com

Publishes: Nonfiction; Poetry; *Areas:*
Criticism; Literature; *Markets:* Adult

Contact: Neil Astley, Managing/Editorial
Director

Submit poetry only if you have a track
record of publication in magazines. If so,
send sample of up to a dozen poems with
SAE or IRCs. No submissions by email or
on disk. Poems sent without return postage
will be recycled unread. Will not respond to
postal submissions by email. As at December
2013, closed to submissions from American
poets as American list is full for the
foreseeable future. Check website for current
situation.

Bloomsbury Publishing Plc

50 Bedford Square
London
WC1B 3DP
Tel: +44 (0) 20 7631 5600
Fax: +44 (0) 20 7631 5800
Email: enquiries@bloomsbury.com
Website: http://www.bloomsbury.com

Publishes: Fiction; Nonfiction; Reference;

Areas: Arts; Historical; Hobbies; Music;
Nature; Sport; *Markets:* Academic; Adult;
Children's; Professional

No longer accepting submissions of fiction,
or nonfiction other than in the following
areas: Education, Music, Natural History,
Nautical, Sport, Visual Arts, Writing and
Yearbooks. See website for full submission
guidelines.

Bloomsbury Spark

Email:
BloomsburySparkUK@bloomsbury.com
Website: http://www.bloomsbury.com/spark

Publishes: Fiction; *Areas:* Historical;
Mystery; Romance; Sci-Fi; Thrillers;
Markets: Adult; Children's; Youth;
Treatments: Contemporary

Global, digital imprint from a major
international publisher. Publishes ebooks for
teen, young adult, and new adult readers.
Willing to consider all genres, including
romance, contemporary, dystopian,
paranormal, sci-fi, mystery, and thrillers.
Accepts unsolicited mss between 25,000 and
60,000 words. Submit by email (see website
for specific email addresses for different
geographic locations) along with query and
author bio. See website for full details.

Blue Guides Limited

27 John Street
London
WC1N 2BX
Email: editorial@blueguides.com
Website: http://blueguides.com

Publishes: Nonfiction; *Areas:* Culture;
Travel; *Markets:* Adult

Publishes travel guides. Always on the
lookout for new authors. Contact by email in
first instance, giving an indication of your
areas of interest.

Boathook Books

Email: query@boathookbooks.com

Publishes: Fiction; Nonfiction; Reference;

Areas: Adventure; Entertainment; Hobbies; How-to; Literature; Nature; Short Stories; Sport; Travel; *Markets:* Adult; Children's; Family; Youth

Imprint designed to serve the boating community – from blue water sailing to canal boats, barges, riverboats, etc.

We are a small traditional publisher, but because it's our money we're putting out there, we have to truly love your book to take it on for our list. And because boating books are a niche market, we will discuss with you the best sort of print runs to produce, depending on the book itself. If we love your book but can't take it on in the traditional way, we'll talk to you about alternatives.

bookouture

23 Sussex Road
Uxbridge
UB10 8PN
Email: oliver@bookouture.com
Website: http://www.bookouture.com

Publishes: Fiction; *Areas:* Crime; Erotic; Fantasy; Historical; Mystery; Romance; Sci-Fi; Suspense; Thrillers; *Markets:* Adult; *Treatments:* Commercial; Contemporary; Light; Mainstream; Popular; Positive

Contact: Oliver Rhodes

A digital first publisher of entertaining women's fiction – anything from contemporary romance to paranormal.

For most authors outside the bestseller lists, traditional publishers simply aren't adding enough value to justify low royalty rates. And because authors aren't all experts in editing, design, or marketing, self-publishing doesn't get the most out of their books or time. Digital publishing offers incredible opportunities to connect with readers all over the world – but finding the help you need to make the most of them can be tricky.

That's why we bring both big publisher experience and small team creativity. We genuinely understand and invest in brands – developing long-term strategies, marketing

plans and websites for each of our authors.

And we work with the most brilliant editorial, design and marketing professionals in the business to make sure that everything we do is perfectly tailored to you and ridiculously good.

Combine all of that with an incredible 45% royalty rate we think we're simply the perfect combination of high returns and inspirational publishing.

Booth-Clibborn Editions

Studio 83
235 Earls Court Road
London
SW5 9FE
Tel: +44 (0) 20 7565 0688
Fax: +44 (0) 20 7244 1018
Email: info@booth-clibborn.com
Website: http://www.booth-clibborn.com

Publishes: Nonfiction; *Areas:* Arts; Culture; Design; Media; Photography; *Markets:* Adult

Publishes books on the fine, media, and decorative arts.

Bowker (UK) Ltd

St Andrew's House
18-20 St Andrew Street
London
EC4A 3AG
Tel: +44 (0) 20 7832 1770
Fax: +44 (0) 20 7832 1710
Email: sales@bowker.co.uk
Website: http://www.bowker.co.uk

Publishes: Reference; *Areas:* Biography; Business; *Markets:* Academic; Professional

No unsolicited material will be read. Publishes reference books; professional and business directories; bibliographies and biographies.

Brown, Son & Ferguson, Ltd

4-10 Darnley Street
Glasgow
G41 2SD

Tel: +44 (0) 141 429 1234
Fax: +44 (0) 141 420 1694
Email: info@skipper.co.uk
Website: http://www.skipper.co.uk

Publishes: Nonfiction; Reference; *Areas:*
Crafts; Historical; Hobbies; Technology;
Markets: Adult; Professional

Nautical publishers, printers and ships'
stationers since 1850. Publishes technical
and non-technical nautical textbooks, books
about the sea, historical books, information
on old sailing ships and how to build model
ships. Welcomes ideas, synopses, and
unsolicited MSS.

Canongate Books
14 High Street
Edinburgh
EH1 1TE
Tel: +44 (0) 1315 575111
Fax: +44 (0) 1315 575211
Email: info@canongate.co.uk
Website: http://www.canongate.net

Publishes: Fiction; Nonfiction; *Areas:*
Autobiography; Biography; Culture;
Historical; Humour; Politics; Science;
Translations; Travel; *Markets:* Adult;
Treatments: Literary

Contact: Jamie Byng, Publisher

Publisher of a wide range of literary fiction
and nonfiction, with a traditionally Scottish
slant but becoming increasingly
international. Publishes fiction in translation
under its international imprint. No children's
books, poetry, or drama. Send synopsis with
three sample chapters and info about
yourself. No submissions by fax, email or on
disk.

Canopus Publishing Ltd
15 Nelson Parade
Bdeminster
Bristol
BS3 4HY
Email: robin@canopusbooks.com
Website: http://www.canopusbooks.com

Publishes: Nonfiction; *Areas:* Science;

Markets: Academic; Adult; *Treatments:*
Popular

Welcomes book proposals for both academic
and popular branches of physics and
astronomy. Send query by email with author
bio, two-page summary outlining concept,
coverage, and readership level. See website
for more details.

Chapman Publishing
4 Broughton Place
Edinburgh
EH1 3RX
Tel: +44 (0) 131 557 2207
Fax: +44 (0) 131 556 9565
Email: chapman-pub@blueyonder.co.uk
Website: http://www.chapman-pub.co.uk

Publishes: Fiction; Poetry; Scripts; *Areas:*
Drama; Short Stories; *Markets:* Adult;
Treatments: Literary

**Note: No new books being undertaken as
at January 2014. Check website for
current status.**

Publishes one or two books of short stories,
drama, and (mainly) poetry by established
and rising Scottish writers per year. Only
considers writers who have previously been
published in the press's magazine (see entry
in magazines database). Only publishes plays
that have been previously performed. No
unsolicited MSS.

Chartered Institute of Personnel and Development (CIPD) Publishing
151 The Broadway
London
SW19 1JQ
Tel: +44 (0) 20 8612 6202
Fax: +44 (0) 20 8612 6201
Email: publish@cipd.co.uk
Website: http://www.cipd.co.uk

Publishes: Nonfiction; Reference; *Areas:*
Business; How-to; *Markets:* Academic;
Professional

Contact: Stephen Dunn, Head of Publishing

Publishes professional and academic books, looseleafs, and online subscription products, covering topics relating to personnel, training, and management. Submit proposal by email or by post.

Christian Focus Publications

Geanies House
Fearn by Tain
Ross-shire
IV20 1TW
Tel: +44 (0) 1862 871011
Fax: +44 (0) 1862 871699
Email: info@christianfocus.com
Website: http://www.christianfocus.com

Publishes: Fiction; Nonfiction; *Areas:* Biography; Current Affairs; Historical; Lifestyle; Religious; *Markets:* Academic; Adult; Children's; Professional

Send query with a synopsis, contents page, two sample chapters, your CV, detailing your own religious background, a completed Author Information Sheet and a completed Book Information Sheet (both available at website). For children's fiction send synopsis, chapter headings, three sameple chapters, and Author Information Sheet. Publishes religious fiction and nonfiction for children, and nonfiction for adults. No poetry or adult fiction. See website for full details.

Classical Comics Limited

PO Box 16310
Birmingham
B30 9EL
Tel: +44 (0) 845 812 3000
Fax: +44 (0) 845 812 3005
Email: info@classicalcomics.com
Website: http://www.classicalcomics.com

Publishes: Fiction; *Areas:* Literature; *Markets:* Children's

Publishes graphic novel adaptations of classical literature.

CN Writers

6 Fox Close
Chipping Norton
Oxfordshire

OX7 5BY
Email: cnwriters@btinternet.com
Website: http://www.cnwriters.webs.com

Publishes: Fiction; *Areas:* Adventure; Crime; Fantasy; Gothic; Horror; Humour; Mystery; Short Stories; *Markets:* Adult; Youth; *Treatments:* Dark; Experimental; Mainstream; Popular; Traditional

Contact: Andy Hesford

Looking for authors of short stories who wish to be published in our first ever anthology of short stories. We do favour Ghost stories but we do accept various genres, We do not accept poetry or non fiction in any way, shape or form.

We usually publish via eBooks but we do sometimes publish paper copies so we prefer to receive submission's via email. All submissions have to be sent via email, MS word/word pad documents only in Dot, Doc or txt format only. Please put your contact details in the body of the email also enclosing your stories title, whilst the document itself needs to be attached.

Please make sure that your submission is thoroughly spell-checked and must be in English. Any submissions that do not meet this criteria will be rejected.

Co & Bear Productions

63 Edith Grove
London
SW10 0LB
Email: info@cobear.co.uk
Website: http://www.scriptumeditions.co.uk

Publishes: Nonfiction; *Areas:* Arts; Beauty and Fashion; Design; Lifestyle; Nature; Photography; *Markets:* Adult

Publishes illustrated books on interior design, fashion and photography, botanical art, natural history and exploration.

Colin Smythe Ltd

38 Mill Lane
Gerrards Cross
Buckinghamshire

SL9 8BA
Tel: +44 (0) 1753 886000
Fax: +44 (0) 1753 886469
Email: cpsmythe@aol.com
Website: http://www.colinsmythe.co.uk

Publishes: Fiction; Nonfiction; Poetry;
Scripts; *Areas:* Biography; Criticism;
Drama; Fantasy; Historical; Hobbies;
Literature; Sci-Fi; Theatre; *Markets:* Adult

Contact: Colin Smythe

Publishes fiction, nonfiction, drama, and
poetry. Particular interest in Irish literature.
No unsolicited MSS.

Compelling Books
Compelling Ideas Ltd
Basepoint Centre
Metcalf Way
RH11 7XX
Email: info@compellingbooks.com
Website: http://www.compellingbooks

Publishes: Fiction; Nonfiction; *Areas:*
Adventure; Autobiography; Biography;
Crime; Culture; Fantasy; Gothic; Historical;
Horror; How-to; Humour; Literature;
Mystery; Philosophy; Psychology; Science;
Sci-Fi; Short Stories; Technology;
Translations; *Markets:* Adult; Youth;
Treatments: Commercial; Contemporary;
Cynical; Dark; Light; Literary; Mainstream;
Niche; Popular; Progressive; Serious;
Traditional

Contact: Peter J Allen

Innovative independent publisher of
compelling new fiction and non-fiction
across all genres. Offers groundbreaking
support for authors, with creative marketing,
international scope, excellent royalty rates
and uniquely ethical contracts.

We welcome new material – send a synopsis
and first chapter via the submissions page of
our website. (Hardcopy/print mss are NOT
accepted.)

Constable & Robinson Ltd
55-56 Russell Square

London
WC1B 4HP
Tel: +44 (0) 20 7268 9700
Email: reader@constablerobinson.com
Website: http://www.constablerobinson.com

Publishes: Fiction; Nonfiction; Reference;
Areas: Arts; Autobiography; Biography;
Cookery; Crime; Current Affairs; Erotic;
Fantasy; Gardening; Health; Historical;
Horror; Humour; Leisure; Lifestyle;
Military; Mystery; Photography;
Psychology; Romance; Science; Sci-Fi; Self-
Help; Sport; Travel; *Markets:* Adult;
Children's; Youth; *Treatments:* Commercial;
Contemporary; Literary

Welcomes synopses and ideas for books by
post with SASE only. Send query outlining
targetted readership, previous experience,
expertise, etc. plus one-page synopsis and
one sample chapter. No unsolicited MSS or
email or fax submissions.

Crescent Moon Publishing
PO Box 393
Maidstone
Kent
ME14 5XU
Tel: +44 (0) 1622 729593
Email: cresmopub@yahoo.co.uk
Website: http://www.crescentmoon.org.uk

Publishes: Fiction; Nonfiction; Poetry;
Areas: Arts; Criticism; Culture; Film;
Literature; Media; Music; Philosophy;
Politics; Women's Interests; *Markets:* Adult;
Treatments: Contemporary; Literary

Contact: Jeremy Robinson

Publishes nonfiction on literature, culture,
media, and the arts; as well as poetry and
some fiction. Non-rhyming poetry is
preferred. Send query with one or two
sample chapters or up to six poems, with
author bio and appropriate return postage for
response. Material is only returned if
requested and if adequate postage is
provided.

Cressrelles Publishing Co. Ltd
10 Station Road Industrial Estate

Colwall
Malvern
WR13 6RN
Tel: +44 (0) 1684 540154
Fax: +44 (0) 1684 540154
Email: simon@cressrelles.co.uk

Publishes: Nonfiction; Scripts; *Areas:*
Drama; *Markets:* Academic; Adult

Welcomes submissions. Publishes plays,
theatre and drama textbooks, and local
interest books.

The Crowood Press

The Stable Block
Crowood Lane
Ramsbury
Marlborough
Wiltshire
SN8 2HR
Tel: +44 (0) 1672 520320
Fax: +44 (0) 1672 520280
Email: enquiries@crowood.com
Website: http://www.crowood.com

Publishes: Nonfiction; Reference; *Areas:*
Architecture; Arts; Crafts; Film; Gardening;
Health; Historical; Hobbies; Leisure;
Military; Nature; Photography; Sport;
Theatre; Travel; *Markets:* Adult;
Professional

Publishes instructional books on sports,
crafts, gardening and DIY; information and
reference books on motoring, aviation and
military history; animal care and husbandry.
Books are aimed at hobbyists, enthusiasts
and professionals. Send query by email, fax,
or post. No unsolicited mss.

Dagda Publishing

Email: dagdapublishing@hotmail.co.uk
Website:
http://www.dagdapublishing.wordpress.com

Publishes: Poetry; *Areas:* Criticism; Culture;
Current Affairs; Drama; Entertainment;
Fantasy; Gothic; Horror; Humour;
Philosophy; Psychology; Sci-Fi; Suspense;
Markets: Adult; *Treatments:* Contemporary;
Dark; Experimental; Literary; Niche;
Progressive; Satirical

Contact: R Davey

Poetry site actively seeking new writers and
unsolicited MSS. We put out a few
anthologies a year, and will feature new
writers on the site on a regular frequency
(every 1-2 weeks).

Please send submissions/ MSS in either the
body of an email or as an attachment (.Doc
.txt or .odt preferred).

Sorry, we cannot enter into correspondence
with unsuccessful authors or provide
criticism if unsuccessful.

DC Thomson

2 Albert Square
Dundee
DD1 9QJ
Tel: +44 (0) 1382 223131
Email: innovation@dcthomson.co.uk
Website: http://www.dcthomson.co.uk

Publishes: Fiction; Nonfiction; *Markets:*
Adult; Children's

Publisher of newspapers, magazines, comics,
and books, with offices in Dundee,
Aberdeen, Glasgow, and London. For fiction
guidelines send large SAE marked for the
attention of the Central Fiction Department.

Dedalus Ltd

Langford Lodge
St Judith's Lane
Sawtry
PE28 5XE
Tel: +44 (0) 1487 832382
Fax: +44 (0) 1487 832382
Email: info@dedalusbooks.com
Website: http://www.dedalusbooks.com

Publishes: Fiction; *Areas:* Literature;
Translations; *Markets:* Adult; *Treatments:*
Contemporary; Literary

Send query letter describing yourself along
with SAE, synopsis, three sample chapters,
and explanation of why you think this
publisher in particular is right for you –
essential to be familiar with and have read
other books on this publisher's list before

submitting, as most material received is entirely inappropriate. Welcomes submissions of suitable original fiction and is particularly interested in intellectually clever and unusual fiction. No email or disk submissions, or collections of short stories by unknown authors. Novels should be over 40,000 words – ideally over 50,000. Most books are translations.

Dovecote Press

Stanbridge
Wimborne Minster
Dorset
BH21 4JD
Tel: +44 (0) 1258 840549
Email: online@dovecotepress.com
Website: http://www.dovecotepress.com

Publishes: Nonfiction; *Areas:* Architecture; Biography; Historical; Nature; *Markets:* Adult

Contact: David Burnett

Publishes books on architecture, local history, and natural history. List is expanding; welcomes ideas for new titles. Prefers to be approached at an early stage of the project. Send query by post with SAE and detailed synopsis or outline. Offers small advance.

Duckworth Publishers

Editorial Submissions
Duckworth General
Duckworth Publishers
First Floor, East Wing
90-93 Cowcross Street
London
EC1M 6BF
Tel: +44 (0) 20 7490 7300
Fax: +44 (0) 20 7490 0080
Email: info@duckworth-publishers.co.uk
Website: http://www.ducknet.co.uk

Publishes: Fiction; Nonfiction; *Areas:* Archaeology; Biography; Historical; Philosophy; Translations; *Markets:* Academic; Adult; *Treatments:* Commercial; Literary

Independent publisher with a general trade

and academic list. Publishes literary and commercial fiction and nonfiction, including history, biography and memoir. Academic imprint features important new scholarly monographs and series in Archaeology, Classics, Ancient History and Ancient Philosophy. Backlist includes school and student texts in Latin, Greek, Russian, French, German and Spanish language and literature. Also has a list of Russian literature in translation.

Not accepting fiction queries. Send nonfiction queries with SASE and three sample chapters by post only. No response without SASE. For academic submissions, approaches are preferred by email to address given on website. See website for full submission guidelines.

Egmont UK Ltd

3rd Floor, Beaumont House
Kensington Village
Avonmore Road
London
W14 6TS
Tel: +44 (0) 20 7605 6600
Fax: +44 (0) 20 7605 6601
Email: childrensreader@euk.egmont.com
Website: http://www.egmont.co.uk

Publishes: Fiction; *Markets:* Children's

Publishes picture books and children's fiction. Submit by email only; any hard copy submissions will be recycled. Send query with synopsis and first three chapters as attachments, or for picture books submit complete MS.

Eleusinian Press

34A Norton Terrace
Newhaven
BN9 0BT
Email: alastair.kemp@yahoo.co.uk
Website: http://www.eleusinianpress.co.uk

Publishes: Fiction; Nonfiction; Poetry; Reference; *Areas:* Anthropology; Archaeology; Architecture; Arts; Autobiography; Biography; Criticism; Culture; Current Affairs; Drama; Fantasy; Film; Health; Historical; Horror; Legal;

Literature; Media; Medicine; Men's Interests; Music; Philosophy; Photography; Politics; Psychology; Science; Sci-Fi; Self-Help; Short Stories; Sociology; Spiritual; Theatre; Thrillers; Translations; Travel; Women's Interests; *Markets:* Academic; Adult; Professional; *Treatments:* Contemporary; Cynical; Dark; Experimental; In-depth; Literary; Niche; Progressive; Satirical; Serious

Contact: Alastair Kemp

A small publisher specialising in madness, music and radical politics. It has a flagship series of edited volumes, for which we accept fiction and non-fiction of 4000 words plus.
We also are looking for longer book-length monologues for 2013 and 2014.

Emissary Publishing

PO Box 33
Bicester
OX26 2BU
Tel: +44 (0) 1869 323447
Fax: +44 (0) 1869 322552
Email: books@emissary-publishing.com
Website: http://www.emissary-publishing.com

Publishes: Fiction; Nonfiction; *Areas:* Humour; Thrillers; *Markets:* Adult

Contact: Val Miller

Publisher based in Bicester, originally set up to reprint a range of humour books only available in hardback from libraries as new paperbacks. Now also diversifying into other genres such as nonfiction and thrillers.

Enitharmon Press

10 Bury Place
London
WC1A 2JL
Tel: +44 (0) 20 7430 0844
Email: info@enitharmon.co.uk
Website: http://www.enitharmon.co.uk

Publishes: Fiction; Poetry; *Areas:* Arts; Criticism; Photography; *Markets:* Adult; *Treatments:* Literary

One of Britain's leading literary publishers, specialising in poetry and in high-quality artists' books and original prints. It is divided into two companies: the press, which publishes poetry and general literature in small-format volumes and anthologies, and the editions, which produces de luxe artists' books in the tradition of the livre d'artiste. Send a preliminary enquiry to the editor before submitting material.

Erotic Review (ER) Books

Email: submissions@erbooks.org
Website: http://erbooks.org

Publishes: Fiction; Nonfiction; *Areas:* Arts; Erotic; Literature; Photography; Short Stories; *Markets:* Adult

Send query including biographical information by email with synopsis and two sample chapters / stories. See website for more details.

Euromonitor

60-61 Britton Street
London
EC1M 5UX
Tel: +44 (0) 20 7251 8024
Fax: +44 (0) 20 7608 3149
Email: info@euromonitor.com
Website: http://www.euromonitor.com

Publishes: Nonfiction; Reference; *Areas:* Business; *Markets:* Professional

International publisher of business reference and nonfiction, including market reports, directories, etc. for the professional market.

Evans Brothers Ltd

2A Portman Mansions
Chiltern Street
London
W1U 6NR
Tel: +44 (0) 20 7487 0920
Fax: +44 (0) 20 7487 0921
Email: sales@evansbrothers.co.uk
Website: http://www.evansbooks.co.uk

Publishes: Fiction; Nonfiction; Poetry; *Areas:* Arts; Design; Drama; Historical;

Media; Music; Religious; Science; Sociology; Technology; *Markets:* Children's; Professional

Publishes children's fiction, poetry, and nonfiction; educational books; as well as teacher resources, etc. Strong connections in Africa. Welcomes submissions but no response unless interested.

Ex-L-Ence Publishing

Deepfurrow Bungalow
Main Road
Minsterworth
Gloucestershire
GL2 8JH
Tel: +44 (0) 1452 751 276
Email: robert@winghigh.co.uk
Website: http://www.kindlebook.me

Publishes: Fiction; Nonfiction; Poetry; Reference; *Areas:* Adventure; Anthropology; Antiques; Archaeology; Architecture; Arts; Autobiography; Beauty and Fashion; Biography; Business; Cookery; Crafts; Crime; Criticism; Culture; Current Affairs; Design; Drama; Entertainment; Fantasy; Film; Finance; Gardening; Gothic; Health; Historical; Hobbies; How-to; Humour; Leisure; Lifestyle; Literature; Media; Medicine; Men's Interests; Military; Music; Mystery; Nature; New Age; Philosophy; Photography; Politics; Psychology; Religious; Romance; Science; Sci-Fi; Self-Help; Short Stories; Sociology; Spiritual; Sport; Suspense; Technology; Theatre; Thrillers; Travel; TV; Westerns; Women's Interests; *Markets:* Family; Professional; *Treatments:* Commercial; Contemporary; Experimental; In-depth; Light; Literary; Mainstream; Niche; Popular; Positive; Progressive; Satirical; Serious; Traditional

Contact: Robert Agar-Hutton

We get your manuscript ready for publication without it costing you any money, and then we pay you 50% of net royalties. Please visit our website then call or email to discuss how we can work together.

F&W Media International Ltd

Brunel House
Forde Close
Newton Abbot
TQ12 4PU
Tel: +44 (0) 1626 323200
Fax: +44 (0) 1626 323319
Email: ali.myer@fwmedia.com
Website: http://fwmedia.co.uk

Publishes: Nonfiction; *Areas:* Arts; Business; Crafts; Gardening; Historical; Hobbies; Humour; Lifestyle; Military; Nature; Photography; Travel; *Markets:* Adult

Contact: Ali Myer (Editorial and Design)

Publishes books for hobbyists and enthusiasts.

Faber & Faber Ltd

Bloomsbury House
74-77 Great Russell Street
London
WC1B 3DA
Tel: +44 (0) 20 7927 3800
Fax: +44 (0) 20 7927 3801
Website: http://www.faber.co.uk

Publishes: Fiction; Nonfiction; Poetry; Scripts; *Areas:* Biography; Drama; Film; Music; Politics; Theatre; *Markets:* Adult; Children's

Originally published poetry and plays but has expanded into other areas. Has published some of the most prominent writers of the twentieth century, including several poet laureates. No longer accepting unsolicited MSS in any areas other than poetry. Submit 6 poems in first instance, with adequate return postage. Submissions of material other than poetry will neither be read nor returned. No submissions by email, fax, or on disk.

Fingerpress UK

Email: firstwriter@fingerpress.co.uk
Website: http://www.fingerpress.co.uk

Publishes: Fiction; Nonfiction; *Areas:* Adventure; Crime; Culture; Entertainment; Erotic; Fantasy; Gothic; Historical; Horror; How-to; Humour; Men's Interests; Military; Photography; Science; Sci-Fi; Suspense; Technology; Thrillers; Travel; Women's

Interests; *Markets:* Adult; Youth;
Treatments: Commercial; Contemporary;
Cynical; Dark; Experimental; Mainstream;
Niche; Popular; Positive; Progressive;
Satirical; Serious; Traditional

Only open to submissions at certain times.
Check website for current status. When open
to submissions, this will be announced on the
publisher's Facebook page.

We're an independent publisher based in
London. We're building a range of savvy,
entertaining titles that are both thought-
provoking and a good read. The ideal novel
will have memorable characters with good
plot development and pacing.

We look for:

* high-quality travel writing for inclusion in
iBooks-based travel guides

* books on IT/software development

* submissions of completed, professionally
edited, commercial-grade novels

Please read the submissions page on the
website before submitting anything.

Fitzrovia Press Limited

10 Grafton Mews
London
W1T 5JG
Tel: +44 (0) 20 7380 0749
Email: info@fitzroviapress.co.uk
Website: http://www.fitzroviapress.com

Publishes: Fiction; Nonfiction; *Areas:*
Philosophy; Spiritual; *Markets:* Adult

Contact: Ranchor Prime

Publishes fiction and nonfiction on
Hinduism, spirituality, and Eastern
philosophy. No unsolicited mss. Send query
with outline and sample chapter.

Flame Lily Books

13 Stapleton Road
Meole Brace
Shrewsbury

Shropshire
SY3 9LY
Tel: +44 (0) 1743 245969
Email: timpagden@flamelilybooks.co.uk
Website: http://www.flamelilybooks.co.uk

Publishes: Fiction; Nonfiction; *Areas:*
Adventure; Archaeology; Biography;
Business; Cookery; Crafts; Crime; Design;
Drama; Fantasy; Film; Gardening;
Historical; Hobbies; How-to; Humour;
Leisure; Literature; Military; Music;
Mystery; Nature; Religious; Romance;
Science; Sci-Fi; Short Stories; Suspense;
Technology; Thrillers; Travel; Westerns;
Markets: Adult; Children's; Youth;
Treatments: Commercial; In-depth; Light;
Literary; Mainstream; Niche; Popular;
Positive; Traditional

Contact: Tim Pagden

We accept submissions from unpublished
writers.

Of particular interest are new and different
books aimed at children and early teens,
especially science fiction and fantasy, but not
exclusively. We will, however, read
submissions in almost any genre and aimed
at any age group.

We are also interested in non-fiction books
on any subject. For example "How to ..."
books again aimed at the younger generation.
And finally we would welcome books with a
Christian theme.

There are some subjects and genres which
we will not publish and we don't accept
printed manuscripts. For these reasons, and
so as not too waste our time and yours,
please read the submissions page before
sending any work to us.

Flame Tree Publishing

Crabtree Hall
Crabtree Lane
London
SW6 6TY
Tel: +44 (0) 20 7386 4700
Fax: +44 (0) 20 7386 4701
Email: info@flametreepublishing.com

Website:
http://www.flametreepublishing.com

Publishes: Nonfiction; *Areas:* Cookery;
Culture; Lifestyle; Music; *Markets:* Adult;
Treatments: Popular

Publihses practical cookbooks, music,
popular culture and lifestyle books. Very
rarely accepts unsolicited mss or book
proposals.

Floris Books
15 Harrison Gardens
Edinburgh
EH11 1SH
Tel: +44 (0) 1313 372372
Fax: +44 (0) 1313 479919
Email: floris@florisbooks.co.uk
Website: http://www.florisbooks.co.uk

Publishes: Fiction; Nonfiction; *Areas:*
Architecture; Arts; Biography; Crafts;
Health; Historical; Literature; Philosophy;
Religious; Science; Self-Help; Sociology;
Spiritual; *Markets:* Adult; Children's; Youth

Publishes a wide range of books including
adult nonfiction, picture books and
children's novels. No poetry or verse, fiction
for people over the age of 15, or
autobiography, unless it specifically relates
to a relevant nonfiction subject area. No
submissions by email. See website for full
details of areas covered and submission
guidelines.

George Ronald Publisher
3 Rosecroft Lane
Welwyn
Herts
AL6 0UB
Tel: +44 (0) 1438 716062
Email: sales@grbooks.com
Website: http://grbooks.com

Publishes: Nonfiction; *Areas:* Religious;
Markets: Adult

Religious publisher, concentrating solely on
books of interest to Bahá'ís. Send email for
copy of submission guidelines.

Geddes & Grosset
144 Port Dundas Road
Glasgow
G4 0HZ
Tel: +44 (0) 1415 672830
Fax: +44 (0) 1415 672831
Website: http://www.geddesandgrosset.co.uk

Publishes: Fiction; Nonfiction; Reference;
Areas: Cookery; Historical; Humour;
Markets: Adult; Children's

Contact: Ron Grosset; R. Michael Miller

Publishes Children's and reference books.
Unsolicited MSS, and synopses and ideas for
books are welcomed, but adult fiction is not
accepted.

Ghostwoods Books
Email: ghostwoodsbooks@gmail.com
Website: http://www.gwdbooks.com

Publishes: Fiction; *Areas:* Crime; Fantasy;
Gothic; Historical; Horror; Romance; Sci-Fi;
Short Stories; Thrillers; Women's Interests;
Markets: Adult; *Treatments:* Dark

Contact: Tim Dedopulos; Salome Jones

In the process of expanding. In order to do
that we need to publish good books that
attract readers. Providing information about
your target market is helpful in your
approach.

From personal interest, we like smart, funny,
or dark fiction. Answering one of our
specific calls for submissions, especially for
an anthology, is a good way to get in.

Gibson Square Books Ltd
47 Lonsdale Square
London
N1 1EW
Tel: +44 (0) 20 7096 1100
Fax: +44 (0) 20 7993 2214
Email: info@gibsonsquare.com
Website: http://www.gibsonsquare.com

Publishes: Fiction; Nonfiction; *Areas:* Arts;
Biography; Criticism; Culture; Current
Affairs; Historical; Philosophy; Politics;

Psychology; Travel; Women's Interests; *Markets:* Adult

Synopses, and ideas welcomed. Send query by email only. Publishes books which contribute to a general debate. Almost exclusively nonfiction, but does publish a small amount of fiction. See website for full guidelines.

Glastonbury Publishing
Mirador
Wearne Lane
Langport
TA109HB
Tel: +44 (0) 845 519 7471
Email: sarah@glastonburypublishing.com
Website:
http://www.glastonburypublishing.com

Publishes: Fiction; *Areas:* Adventure; Crime; Drama; Erotic; Fantasy; Gothic; Historical; Horror; Humour; Men's Interests; Mystery; New Age; Romance; Sci-Fi; Suspense; Thrillers; Women's Interests; *Markets:* Adult; *Treatments:* Contemporary; Dark; Mainstream; Niche; Popular

Contact: Sarah Luddington

After many years as a successful author I have decided to give something back and help a few new writers on the road to success.

I select a very few titles each year with which I feel I can work. I will then guide you, the author, to polish your work up to the required standard and together we will bring your book to the market.

Gomer Press
Llandysul Enterprise Park
Llandysul
Ceredigion
SA44 4JL
Tel: +44 (0) 1559 362371
Fax: +44 (0) 1559 363758
Email: gwasg@gomer.co.uk
Website: http://www.gomer.co.uk

Publishes: Fiction; Nonfiction; Poetry; Reference; Scripts; *Areas:* Arts;

Autobiography; Biography; Culture; Drama; Historical; Leisure; Literature; Music; Nature; Religious; Sport; Theatre; Travel; *Markets:* Academic; Adult; Children's

Publishes fiction, nonfiction, plays, poetry, language books, and educational material, for adults and children, in English and in Welsh. See website for contact details of editors and query appropriate editor with sample chapter, synopsis, CV, and sales strengths of your proposal. Do not send complete MS in first instance.

Goss & Crested China Club
62 Murray Road
Horndean
Waterlooville
PO8 9JL
Tel: +44 (0) 23 9259 7440
Fax: +44 (0) 23 9259 7440
Email: info@gosschinaclub.co.uk
Website: http://www.gosschinaclub.co.uk

Publishes: Nonfiction; Reference; *Areas:* Antiques; *Markets:* Adult; Professional

Publishes books on crested heraldic china and antique porcelain.

Grey Hen Press
PO Box 450
Keighley
West Yorkshire
BD22 9WS
Email: contact@greyhenpress.com
Website: http://www.greyhenpress.com

Publishes: Poetry; *Markets:* Adult

Publishes anthologies of poetry by women over 60. Aims to give less well-known poets the opportunity of having their work published alongside that of established writers.

Grub Street Publishing
4 Rainham Close
London
SW11 6SS
Tel: +44 (0) 20 7924 3966 / 20 7738 1008
Fax: +44 (0) 20 7738 1009

Email: post@grubstreet.co.uk
Website: http://www.grubstreet.co.uk

Publishes: Nonfiction; Reference; *Areas:* Cookery; Health; Historical; Military; *Markets:* Adult

Contact: John Davies (Military); Anne Dolamore (Cookery)

Publishes books on cookery and military aviation history only. No fiction or poetry. Accepts synopses and unsolicited MSS by post only with SASE. No email queries or submissions. See website for full submission guidelines.

Guild of Master Craftsman (GMC) Publications Ltd
166 High Street
Lewes
BN7 1XU
Tel: +44 (0) 1273 477374
Fax: +44 (0) 1273 402866
Email: pubs@thegmcgroup.com

Publishes: Nonfiction; Reference; *Areas:* Architecture; Arts; Cookery; Crafts; Film; Gardening; Hobbies; How-to; Humour; Photography; TV; *Markets:* Adult; Children's

Welcomes ideas, synopses, and unsolicited MSS. Publishes books on the above topics, plus woodworking, dolls houses, and miniatures. Also publishes magazines and videos. No fiction.

Gullane Children's Books
185 Fleet Street
London
EC4A 2HS
Tel: +44 (0) 20 7400 1037
Fax: +44 (0) 20 7400 1084
Email: stories@gullanebooks.com
Website: http://www.gullanebooks.com

Publishes: Fiction; *Markets:* Children's

Contact: Submissions Editor

Publishes picture books for children up to 500 words. Send submissions by post or

email. Response only if interested. Include SAE if return of manuscript required. Submissions from outside the UK cannot be returned under any circumstances.

Hachette Children's Books
338 Euston Road
London
NW1 3BH
Tel: +44 (0) 20 7873 6000
Fax: +44 (0) 20 7873 6024
Email: ad@hachettechildrens.co.uk
Website: http://www.hachettechildrens.co.uk

Publishes: Fiction; Nonfiction; Reference; *Markets:* Children's

Large publisher of fiction, nonfiction, reference, picture books, audio books, and novelty books, for children. No unsolicited mss.

Hachette UK
338 Euston Road
London
NW1 3BH
Tel: +44 (0) 20 7873 6000
Fax: +44 (0) 20 7873 6024
Website: http://www.hachette.co.uk

Publishes: Fiction; Nonfiction; *Markets:* Adult

Describes itself as the largest and one of the most diversified book publishers in the UK. Accepts submissions via literary agents only.

Halban Publishers
22 Golden Square
London
W1F 9JW
Tel: +44 (0) 20 7437 9300
Fax: +44 (0) 20 7437 9512
Email: books@halbanpublishers.com
Website: http://www.halbanpublishers.com

Publishes: Fiction; Nonfiction; *Areas:* Autobiography; Biography; Criticism; Historical; Literature; Philosophy; Politics; Religious; *Markets:* Adult

Contact: Peter Halban; Martine Halban

Independent publisher of fiction, memoirs, history, biography, and books of Jewish interest. Send query by post or by email. No unsolicited MSS. Unsolicited emails deleted unread.

Halsgrove

Halsgrove House
Ryelands Business Park
Bagley Road
Wellington
Somerset
TA21 9PZ
Tel: +44 (0) 1823 653777
Fax: +44 (0) 1823 216796
Email: sales@halsgrove.com
Website: http://www.halsgrove.com

Publishes: Nonfiction; *Areas:* Arts; Biography; Historical; Photography; *Markets:* Adult

Publishes regional material covering various regions in the areas of history, biography, photography, and art. No fiction or poetry. Send query by email with brief synopsis in first instance.

Harlequin Mills & Boon Ltd

Eton House
18-24 Paradise Road
Richmond
Surrey
TW9 1SR
Tel: +44 (0) 20 8288 2800
Fax: +44 (0) 20 8288 2899
Email: submissions@hqnuk.co.uk
Website: http://www.millsandboon.co.uk

Publishes: Fiction; *Areas:* Crime; Historical; Romance; *Markets:* Adult; *Treatments:* Commercial; Contemporary

Major publisher with extensive romance list and various romance imprints. Send synopsis and three sample chapters in one Word document by email. See website for full submission guidelines.

Also includes digital imprint accepting submissions in any genre, and particularly interested in authors from rapidly expanding

digital markets in the UK, Ireland, South Africa and India. See website for separate submission guidelines and specific email address for this imprint. Commercial fiction and crim imprint accepts submissions via literary agents only.

Hawthorn Press

1 Lansdown Lane
Stroud
Gloucestershire
GL5 1BJ
Tel: +44 (0) 1453 757040
Fax: +44 (0) 1453 751138
Email: info@hawthornpress.com
Website: http://www.hawthornpress.com

Publishes: Nonfiction; *Areas:* Lifestyle; Self-Help; *Markets:* Adult

Publisher aiming to contribute to a more creative, peaceful and sustainable world through its publishing. Publishes mainly commissioned work, but will consider approaches. Send first two chapters with introduction, full table of contents/book plan, brief author biography and/or CV, and SAE. Allow at least 2–4 months for response. Accepts email enquiries, but full submissions should be made by post.

Headland Publications

38 York Avenue
West Kirby
Wirral
CH48 3JF
Tel: +44 (0) 01516 259128
Email: headlandpublications@hotmail.co.uk
Website:
http://www.headlandpublications.co.uk

Publishes: Fiction; Nonfiction; Poetry; *Areas:* Biography; Short Stories; *Markets:* Adult

Specialises in poetry, but has expanded scope to include short stories and biography.

Honno Welsh Women's Press

Honno
Unit 14, Creative Units
Aberystwyth Arts Centre

Aberystwyth
Ceredigion
SY23 3GL
Tel: +44 (0) 1970 623150
Fax: +44 (0) 1970 623150
Email: post@honno.co.uk
Website: http://www.honno.co.uk

Publishes: Fiction; Nonfiction; Poetry;
Areas: Autobiography; Short Stories;
Women's Interests; *Markets:* Adult;
Children's; Youth

Contact: Caroline Oakley

Welcomes MSS and ideas for books from
women born in, living in, or significantly
connected to Wales, only. Publishes fiction,
autobiographical writing and reprints of
classic titles in English and Welsh, as well as
anthologies of poetry and short stories. All
submissions must be sent as hard copy; no
email submissions. Send query with synopsis
and first 50 pages. Not currently accepting
children/teenage novels or poetry or short
story collections by a single author.

House of Lochar

Isle of Colonsay
PA61 7YR
Tel: +44 (0) 1951 200232
Fax: +44 (0) 1951 200232
Email: Lochar@colonsay.org.uk
Website: http://www.houseoflochar.com

Publishes: Fiction; Nonfiction; *Areas:*
Biography; Historical; Literature; Travel;
Markets: Adult; Children's

Welcomes unsolicited MSS for fiction and
nonfiction related to Scotland and / or Celtic
themes, including history, fiction, transport,
maritime, genealogy, Gaelic, and books for
children. No poetry or books unrelated to
Scottish or Celtic themes.

Icon Books Ltd

Omnibus Business Centre
39-41 North Road
London
N7 9DP
Tel: +44 (0) 20 7697 9695
Fax: +44 (0) 20 7697 9501

Email: submissions@iconbooks.net
Website: http://www.iconbooks.co.uk

Publishes: Nonfiction; *Areas:* Arts;
Historical; Humour; Philosophy; Politics;
Psychology; Religious; Science; Sport;
Markets: Adult; *Treatments:* Popular

Submit by email only. See website for full
guidelines. Has in the past tended to publish
series of books, including an ongoing series
of graphic introductions to key figure and
ideas in history, science, psychology,
philosophy, religion, and the arts, but
increasingly publishing individual nonfiction
titles in such areas as politics, popular
philosophy and psychology, history, sport,
humour and, especially, popular science.

Igloo Books Limited

Cottage Farm
Mears Ashby Road
Sywell
Northants
NN6 0BJ
Tel: +44 (0) 1604 741116
Fax: +44 (0) 1604 670495
Email: customerservice@igloobooks.com
Website: http://igloobooks.com

Publishes: Fiction; Nonfiction; Reference;
Areas: Cookery; Hobbies; *Markets:* Adult;
Children's

Publishes nonfiction and gift and puzzle
books for adults, and fiction, nonfiction, and
novelty books for children.

The Ilex Press

Tel: +44 (0) 1273 403124
Email: jones@ilex-press.com
Website: http://www.ilex-press.com

Publishes: Nonfiction; Reference; *Areas:*
Arts; Culture; Photography; *Markets:* Adult

Contact: Nick Jones

Publishes high quality illustrated reference
books which cover all aspects of creativity
and popular culture. Send query by email in
first instance.

Impress Books Limited

Innovation Centre
Rennes Drive
University of Exeter
Devon
EX4 4RN
Tel: +44 (0) 1392 262301
Fax: +44 (0) 1392 262303
Email: enquiries@impress-books.co.uk
Website: http://www.impress-books.co.uk

Publishes: Fiction; Nonfiction; *Markets:*
Adult

Interested in quality, thought-provoking titles
for the enquiring general reader. Send query
by post or by email, or via form on website.

Indigo Dreams Publishing

132 Hinckley Road
Stoney Stanton
Leics
LE9 4LN
Tel: +44 (0) 1455 272861
Email: publishing@indigodreams.co.uk
Website: http://www.indigodreams.co.uk

Publishes: Fiction; Nonfiction; Poetry;
Areas: Adventure; Antiques; Arts;
Autobiography; Biography; Crime;
Entertainment; Erotic; Fantasy; Film;
Gothic; Historical; Hobbies; Horror; How-to;
Humour; Leisure; Lifestyle; Literature;
Media; Men's Interests; Music; Mystery;
Nature; New Age; Photography; Romance;
Science; Sci-Fi; Spiritual; Sport; Suspense;
Theatre; Thrillers; Translations; Travel;
Westerns; Women's Interests; *Markets:*
Adult; Family; Professional; *Treatments:*
Commercial; Contemporary; Cynical; Dark;
Experimental; In-depth; Light; Literary;
Mainstream; Niche; Popular; Positive;
Progressive; Satirical; Serious; Traditional

Contact: Ronnie Goodyer

Note: Closed to poetry submissions until
2013. Check website for latest information.

IDP are an independant publisher of fiction
and poetry but are also looking to the nonfiction market. They have a speedy decision
process through frequent Acquisition
Meetings and an established method of
approach, initially via a form on their
website. Interesting proposals are then
contacted for complete manuscripts in a
second stage process and these are read and
considered at the relevant Acquisitions
Meetings. Books are distributed through
Central Books, London. IDP are free to
choose whatever material they wish as they
have independant finance and no restrictions
other than those which are self-imposed.

Jo Fletcher Books

55 Baker Street
7th Floor
South Block
London
W1U 8EW
Tel: +44 (0) 20 7291 7200
Email: submissions@jofletcherbooks.co.uk
Website: http://www.jofletcherbooks.com

Publishes: Fiction; *Areas:* Fantasy; Horror;
Sci-Fi; *Markets:* Adult

Contact: Nicola Budd

Specialist science fiction, fantasy and horror
imprint. Send query by email with synopsis
and first three chapters or first 10,000 words.

Kindred Rainbow Publishing

Tel: +44 (0) 20 8133 3751
Email: submissions@kindredrainbow.com
Website: http://kindredrainbow.com

Publishes: Fiction; Nonfiction; *Areas:*
Adventure; Entertainment; Fantasy; Humour;
Mystery; Science; Sci-Fi; *Markets:*
Children's; Youth; *Treatments:* Commercial;
Contemporary; Experimental; Light; Niche;
Popular; Positive

Contact: Alexandra Mercury

We look for picture books, fiction, nonfiction and illustration for children of aged
three to eight approx. We will consider
books of all genres. It's all about the story,
and if we feel that it is amazing and catchy
we will consider for publishing.

What works best:
- Stories that are very visual with robust

characterisations – not too long-winded
- Humorous plots
- Scary parts – not too scary though!
- Stories with a message – but not too moralistic
- Unusual styles to non-fiction material
- Diverse themes

Knox Robinson Publishing (UK)

34 New House
67-68 Hatton Garden
London
EC1N 8JY
Tel: +44 (0) 20 8816 8630
Fax: +44 (0) 20 8711 2334
Email: subs@knoxrobinsonpublishing.com
Website:
http://www.knoxrobinsonpublishing.com

Publishes: Fiction; *Areas:* Fantasy;
Historical; Romance; *Markets:* Adult

Publishes historical fiction, historical romance (pre-1960), and medieval fantasy. No science fiction, time travel, or fantasy with children and/or animal protagonists. Send query by email only, with detailed synopsis and the first three chapters. No approaches by fax or post. See website for full details.

Kyle Books

192-198 Vauxhall Bridge Road
London
SW1V 1DX
Tel: +44 (0) 20 7692 7215
Email: general.enquiries@kylebooks.com
Website: http://www.kylebooks.com

Publishes: Nonfiction; *Areas:* Cookery;
Gardening; Health; Lifestyle; *Markets:* Adult

Describes itself as "one of the UK's leading publishers in the areas of cookery, health, lifestyle and gardening."

Legend Press

2 London Wall Buildings
London
EC2M 5UU
Tel: +44 (0) 20 7448 5137

Email: submissions@legend-paperbooks.co.uk
Website: http://www.legendpress.co.uk

Publishes: Fiction; *Markets:* Adult;
Treatments: Contemporary; Mainstream

Contact: Tom Chalmers

Publishes a diverse list of contemporary adult novels. Send query by email, including synopsis, and first three chapters as attachments. No hard copy submissions.

Frances Lincoln Ltd

4 Torriano Mews
Torriano Avenue
London
NW5 2RZ
Tel: +44 (0) 20 7284 4009
Fax: +44 (0) 20 7485 0490
Email: fl@frances-lincoln.com
Website: http://www.franceslincoln.com

Publishes: Fiction; Nonfiction; *Areas:*
Architecture; Arts; Design; Gardening;
Leisure; Lifestyle; Travel; *Markets:* Adult;
Children's

Publishers of illustrated nonfiction books for adults, particularly on gardening, walking and the outdoors, art, architecture, design and landscape. In the area of children's fiction, accepts picture books only. See website for full submission guidelines and specific email addresses for adult/children submissions.

Little Tiger Press

1 The Coda Centre
189 Munster Road
London
SW6 6AW
Tel: +44 (0) 20 7385 6333
Fax: +44 (0) 20 7385 7333
Email: info@littletiger.co.uk
Website: http://www.littletigerpress.com

Publishes: Fiction; *Markets:* Children's

Contact: Mara Alperin, Submissions Editor

Accepts unsolicited MSS up to 750 words. If

inside UK include SAE for response (no postage vouchers/coupons); if from outside the UK include email address for response (no material returned). See website for full guidelines. No submissions by email or on disc.

Logaston Press

Little Logaston
Woonton
Almeley
Herefordshire
HR3 6QH
Tel: +44 (0) 1544 327344
Email: logastonpress@phonecoop.coop
Website: http://www.logastonpress.co.uk

Publishes: Nonfiction; *Areas:* Archaeology; Biography; Historical; Sociology; Travel; *Markets:* Adult

Contact: Andy and Karen Johnson

Publishes biographies and books on the rural West Midlands and mid and South Wales. Welcomes ideas: submit synopsis in first instance.

Lost Tower Publications

Email: rainbowme@rocketmail.com
Website:
http://losttowerpublications.jigsy.com

Publishes: Fiction; Poetry; *Areas:* Adventure; Autobiography; Crime; Fantasy; Gothic; Horror; Leisure; Lifestyle; Mystery; Sci-Fi; Spiritual; Suspense; Thrillers; Women's Interests; *Markets:* Adult; Children's; Family; Youth; *Treatments:* Contemporary; Dark; Experimental; Niche; Positive; Progressive

Contact: Harry Yang

Formed in 2011 as part of a poetry book publishing campaign to promote poetry world wide as an attractive and entertaining art form for the twenty first century. We print 3-4 books a year collecting the best photographs and poetry from around the world, to produce high quality books for people to enjoy. Our books are available to buy worldwide either from Amazon or to order through your local bookshop.

In March 2013 we published a journey of hope through poems and photographs which have been collected from around the world. The work in this anthology has been collected from every continent of our planet and illustrates ideas of hope from many of the world religions; looks at the different forms hope can take and how hope can always be found if you look carefully into the world which surrounds you.

Luath Press Ltd

543/2 Castlehill
The Royal Mile
Edinburgh
EH1 2ND
Tel: +44 (0) 131 225 4326
Fax: +44 (0) 131 225 4324
Email: submissions@luath.co.uk
Website: http://www.luath.co.uk

Publishes: Fiction; Nonfiction; Poetry; *Areas:* Arts; Beauty and Fashion; Biography; Crime; Current Affairs; Drama; Historical; Leisure; Lifestyle; Nature; Photography; Politics; Sociology; Sport; Thrillers; Travel; *Markets:* Adult; Children's; Youth

Contact: G.H. MacDougall, Managing Editor

Publishes a range of books, usually with a Scottish connection. Check upcoming publishing schedule on website, and – if you think your book fits – send query with SAE, synopsis, manuscript or sample chapters, author bio, and any other relevant material. See website FAQ for full submission guidelines.

Mainstream Publishing Co. (Edinburgh) Ltd

7 Albany Street
Edinburgh
EH1 3UG
Tel: +44 (0) 131 557 2959
Fax: +44 (0) 131 556 8720
Email: admin@mainstreampublishing.com
Website:
http://www.mainstreampublishing.com

Publishes: Nonfiction; *Areas:* Arts;
Autobiography; Biography; Culture; Current
Affairs; Health; Historical; Politics; Sport;
Markets: Adult

Nonfiction publisher based in Scotland, with
particular emphasis on biography, history,
politics, art, popular culture, sport, health
and current affairs.

Management Books 2000 Ltd

Forge House
Limes Road
Kemble
Cirencester
Gloucestershire
GL7 6AD
Tel: +44 (0) 1285 771 441
Fax: +44 (0) 1285 771 055
Email: info@mb2000.com
Website: http://www.mb2000.com

Publishes: Nonfiction; *Areas:* Business;
Finance; Lifestyle; Self-Help; *Markets:*
Adult

Send outline of book, including why it was
written, where it would be sold and read, etc.
synopsis or detailed contents page, and a
couple of sample chapters. Publishes books
on management, business, finance, and
related topics. Welcomes new ideas.

Mandrake of Oxford

PO Box 250
Oxford
OX1 1AP
Email: mandrake@mandrake.uk.net
Website: http://mandrake.uk.net

Publishes: Fiction; Nonfiction; *Areas:* Arts;
Crime; Culture; Erotic; Health; Horror;
Lifestyle; Mystery; Philosophy; Self-Help;
Spiritual; *Markets:* Adult

Send query by post or by email. May also
include synopsis. See website for full
guidelines, and for examples of the kind of
material published.

Mango Publishing

PO Box 13378
London
SE27 0ZN
Tel: +44 (0) 20 8480 7771
Fax: +44 (0) 20 8480 7771
Email: info@mangoprint.com
Website: http://www.mangoprint.com

Publishes: Fiction; Nonfiction; Poetry;
Areas: Autobiography; Literature; Short
Stories; Translations; *Markets:* Adult;
Treatments: Literary

Small press publishing literary works by
writers from British, Caribbean, and Latin
American literary traditions, including short
story anthologies, poetry, novels,
autobiographical work, and translations into
English.

Mantra Lingua Ltd

Global House
303 Ballards Lane
London
N12 8NP
Tel: +44 (0) 20 8445 5123
Fax: +44 (0) 20 8446 7745
Email: editor@mantralingua.com
Website: http://www.mantralingua.com

Publishes: Fiction; Nonfiction; *Areas:*
Translations; *Markets:* Children's

Multilingual educational publishers of
nonfiction and picture books for children up
to 12 years. 1,400 words maximum (800 for
children up to 7). Send submissions by
email. See website for more details.

Kevin Mayhew Publishers

Buxhall
Stowmarket
Suffolk
IP14 3BW
Tel: +44 (0) 845 3881634
Fax: +44 (0) 1449 737834
Email: info@kevinmayhew.com
Website: http://www.kevinmayhew.com

Publishes: Nonfiction; *Areas:* Music;
Religious; Spiritual; *Markets:* Academic;
Adult; Children's

Contact: Manuscript Submissions
Department

Publishes books relating to Christiantity and music, for adults, children, schools, etc. Send query with synopsis and one or two sample chapters. No approaches by telephone. See website for full guidelines.

Meadowside Children's Books
185 Fleet Street
London
EC4A 2HS
Tel: +44 (0) 20 7400 1084
Fax: +44 (0) 20 7400 1037
Email: queries@dctbooks.co.uk
Website: http://www.meadowsidebooks.com

Publishes: Fiction; *Markets:* Children's; Youth

Contact: Submissions Editor

Publishes picture and novelty books, and junior fiction. Send complete MS with cover letter, and SAE if return of samples required. Prefers to receive material digitally, but do also send a printed copy of the story. Only replies to successful submissions.

The Merlin Press
99b Wallis Road
London
E9 5LN
Tel: +44 (0) 20 8533 5800
Email: info@merlinpress.co.uk
Website: http://www.merlinpress.co.uk

Publishes: Nonfiction; *Areas:* Historical; Philosophy; Politics; *Markets:* Adult

Publisher based in London specialising in history, philosophy, and politics.

Methuen Publishing Ltd
35 Hospital Fields Road
York
YO10 4DZ
Tel: +44 (0) 1904 624730
Fax: +44 (0) 1904 624733
Email: editorial@methuen.co.uk
Website: http://www.methuen.co.uk

Publishes: Fiction; Nonfiction; Poetry; Scripts; *Areas:* Architecture; Autobiography; Biography; Culture; Current Affairs; Film; Historical; Hobbies; How-to; Humour; Literature; Military; Philosophy; Politics; Sport; Theatre; Travel; *Markets:* Adult

No unsolicited submissions. Send query by email for information about manuscript submission policy. No children's books.

Michelin Maps and Guides
Hannay House
39 Clarendon Road
Watford
Hertfordshire
WD17 1JA
Tel: +44 (0) 1923 205247
Email: themichelinguide-gbirl@uk.michelin.com
Website: http://travel.michelin.co.uk

Publishes: Nonfiction; Reference; *Areas:* Travel; *Markets:* Adult

Publishes travel guides; maps; atlases; and hotel and restaurant guides.

Motor Racing Publications
PO Box 1318
Croydon
CR9 5YP
Tel: +44 (0) 20 8654 2711
Fax: +44 (0) 20 8407 0339
Email: john@mrpbooks.co.uk
Website:
http://www.motorracingpublications.co.uk

Publishes: Nonfiction; *Areas:* Historical; Sport; *Markets:* Adult

Contact: John Blunsden (Chairman / Editorial Head)

Send synopses and ideas for books on motor sport history, race track driving, off-road driving, collection and restoration of classic and performance cars, etc.

Myriad Editions
59 Lansdowne Place
Brighton

BN3 1FL
Tel: +44 (0) 1273 720000
Fax: +44 (0) 1273 720000
Email: info@MyriadEditions.com
Website: http://www.myriadeditions.com

Publishes: Fiction; Nonfiction; Reference;
Markets: Adult

Contact: Vicky Blunden

Publishes atlases, works or graphical
nonfiction, and fiction. Send synopsis and
first three chapters by post only. No email
approaches. Include SASE if return required.
No short stories, poetry, plays, children's
books, teenage/young adult fiction or general
nonfiction.

New Dawn Publishers Ltd

292 Rochfords Gardens
Slough, Berkshire
SL2 5XW
Tel: +44 (0) 1753 822557
Email: newdawnpublishersltd@gmail.com
Website:
http://www.newdawnpublishersltd.co.uk

Publishes: Fiction; *Areas:* Adventure;
Crime; Current Affairs; Drama;
Entertainment; Fantasy; Gothic; Horror;
Humour; Literature; Mystery; Romance; Sci-
Fi; Short Stories; Suspense; Thrillers;
Westerns; *Markets:* Adult; Children's;
Family; Youth; *Treatments:* Commercial;
Contemporary; Dark; Light; Literary;
Mainstream; Popular; Progressive; Satirical;
Serious

Contact: Sundeep S. Parhar

A young fiction publishing house which
focuses on giving student and graduate
authors the opportunity they deserve.

Here it isn't the soliciting of a manuscript by
literary agents that matters to us. Instead, we
only accept submissions from those who
have the qualifications, or those working
towards acquiring them. As the only
publisher in the UK to implement such a
policy, we believe that the investment of

time and effort to further one's self and
improve the standard of one's work deserves
to be rewarded.

After all, Creative Writing degrees have been
offered at several institutions across the UK
for so long now, but when it comes down to
it, the wider publishing industry still seems
to perceive these qualifications to be barely
worth the paper that the award certificates
are printed on. Not any more. Here we give
these qualifications the credit they deserve.

So, whether you're a university student or
graduate with ambitions of becoming a
professional fiction author, an institute of
higher education or book retailer who may
be interested in getting involved, or just
someone who wants to take a look at what
today's emerging literary talent has to offer,
then --- is here for YOU.

We accept fiction of all genres and all
lengths- full length novels, novellas and
short stories*. In responding to submissions
we make an effort to supply constructive
feedback whenever possible, citing the key
reasons for our decision and outlining the
strengths and weaknesses of your work. And
if we do decide to take your work on, we'll
be here for you, ready to give you our
support and guidance whenever you need it,
working closely with you at every stage of
the editing process to make your work the
best it can be.

To submit your work to us, simply send up
to three sample chapters and a one -
paragraph blurb, together with a brief section
(no more than 600 word s long) outlining
your credentials and explaining why you and
your work deserve to get published, to us by
email. And until the 13th May 2012, unless
you let us know that you don't want them to
be, any submissions will also be entered into
our competition, with the opportunity to get
your work published in an anthology and win
a cash prize!

*-those submitting short stories will need to
send the entirety of the work, along with a
full synopsis instead of a blurb.

Neil Wilson Publishing Ltd
G/R 19 Netherton Avenue
Glasgow
G13 1BQ
Tel: +44 (0) 1419 548007
Fax: +44 (0) 5601 504806
Email: submissions@nwp.co.uk
Website: http://www.nwp.co.uk

Publishes: Nonfiction; Reference; *Areas:*
Biography; Cookery; Crime; Culture;
Historical; Humour; Music; Nature; Travel;
Markets: Adult

Welcomes approaches by email only.
Publishes books of Scottish interest through
a variety of imprints, including history, hill-
walking, humour, food and drink (including
whisky), biography, true crime, and
reference. Has published fiction in the past,
but longer does so. No academic, political,
fiction, or technical. See website for full
guidelines.

Netherworld Books
Wearne Lane
Langport
Tel: +44 (0) 845 519 7471
Email: claire@netherworldbooks.com
Website: http://www.netherworldbooks.com

Publishes: Fiction; *Areas:* Adventure;
Erotic; Fantasy; Gothic; Horror; Humour;
Mystery; New Age; Religious; Romance;
Science; Sci-Fi; Spiritual; Suspense;
Thrillers; *Markets:* Adult; Family;
Treatments: Commercial; Contemporary;
Dark; Light; Mainstream; Niche; Popular;
Satirical

Contact: Claire Edwards

We are a traditional publisher looking to
support new talent in the specific genres of
Horror, Science Fiction, Fantasy,
Supernatural Romance and Historical
Fantasy. We prefer email submissions and
will not accept novels of over 100k words
for first time novelists.

New Beacon Books, Ltd
76 Stroud Green Road
Finsbury Park

London
N4 3EN
Tel: +44 (0) 20 7272 4889
Fax: +44 (0) 20 7281 4662
Email: newbeaconbooks@btconnect.com

Publishes: Fiction; Nonfiction; Poetry;
Areas: Culture; Historical; Politics; *Markets:*
Adult

Publishes a range of fiction, nonfiction, and
poetry, all concerning black people. No
unsolicited MSS.

New Cavendish Books
3 Denbigh Road
London
W11 2SJ
Tel: +44 (0) 20 7229 6765
Fax: +44 (0) 20 7792 0027
Email: sales@newcavendishbooks.co.uk
Website:
http://www.newcavendishbooks.co.uk

Publishes: Nonfiction; Reference; *Areas:*
Antiques; Arts; Hobbies; *Markets:* Adult

Independent publisher publishing books on
collectable items.

The New Curiosity Shop
Edinburgh
Tel: +44 (0) 1312 081900
Email: contact@newcurioshop.com
Website: http://www.newcurioshop.com

Publishes: Nonfiction; Reference; *Areas:*
Adventure; Anthropology; Antiques;
Archaeology; Architecture; Arts; Beauty and
Fashion; Biography; Business; Cookery;
Crafts; Crime; Criticism; Culture; Current
Affairs; Design; Drama; Fantasy; Film;
Gardening; Gothic; Historical; Hobbies;
Horror; Humour; Literature; Medicine;
Men's Interests; Military; Music; Mystery;
Nature; Philosophy; Photography; Politics;
Psychology; Radio; Religious; Science; Sci-
Fi; Sociology; Sport; Technology; Theatre;
Travel; Women's Interests; *Markets:*
Academic; Adult; Professional; *Treatments:*
Commercial; Contemporary; Mainstream;
Niche; Positive; Progressive; Traditional

Contact: Noel Chidwick

We're looking for informative and entertaining ebooks on topics you know and love well. We're not looking for dry and dusty, we're looking for nonfiction page turners to grab your readers; leave them wanting more. Above all, bring your subject screaming to life. Your ebook will be between 13,000 to 17,000 words in length, just right for someone with a Kindle tucked into their travel bag.

Full information available on the website

Queries by email, initial submissions preferred via form on website.

Nick Hern Books Ltd
The Glasshouse
49a Goldhawk Road
London
W12 8QP
Tel: +44 (0) 20 8749 4953
Fax: +44 (0) 20 8735 0250
Email: matt@nickhernbooks.co.uk
Website: http://www.nickhernbooks.co.uk

Publishes: Nonfiction; Scripts; *Areas:* Film; Theatre; *Markets:* Adult; Professional

Contact: Matt Applewhite, Commissioning Editor

Publishes plays attached to significant professional productions in major theatres only. No unsolicited scripts. Also publishes books by theatre practitioners and for theatre practitioners. No critical, analytical or historical studies.

Nightingale Press
Manning Partnership
7 Green Park Station
Green Park Road
Bath
BA1 1JB
Tel: +44 (0) 1225 478444
Fax: +44 (0) 1225 478440
Email: karen@manning-partnership.co.uk
Website: http://www.manning-partnership.co.uk

Publishes: Nonfiction; *Areas:* Humour; Lifestyle; *Markets:* Adult

Contact: Karen Twissell

Publishes health, lifestyle, humour, gift, and language and learning.

Northumbria University Press
Trinity Building
Northumbria University
Newcastle upon Tyne
NE1 8ST
Tel: +44 (0) 1912 274603
Email: andrew.peden-smith@northumbria.ac.uk
Website: http://www.northumbria.ac.uk/sd/central/its/uni_press/

Publishes: Nonfiction; *Areas:* Arts; Biography; Culture; Leisure; Music; Nature; Photography; Sport; *Markets:* Adult

Contact: Andrew Peden Smith

Emphasis on popular culture. Send query with up to three sample chapters and completed Initial Author Questionnaire (available to download from website).

Not Your Eyes
Email: notyoureyes@gmail.com
Website: http://www.notyoureyes.com

Publishes: Fiction; Nonfiction; Poetry; *Areas:* Adventure; Anthropology; Antiques; Archaeology; Architecture; Arts; Autobiography; Beauty and Fashion; Biography; Business; Cookery; Crafts; Crime; Criticism; Culture; Current Affairs; Design; Drama; Entertainment; Erotic; Fantasy; Film; Finance; Gardening; Gothic; Health; Historical; Hobbies; Horror; How-to; Humour; Legal; Leisure; Lifestyle; Literature; Media; Medicine; Men's Interests; Military; Music; Mystery; Nature; New Age; Philosophy; Photography; Politics; Psychology; Radio; Religious; Romance; Science; Sci-Fi; Self-Help; Short Stories; Sociology; Spiritual; Sport; Suspense; Technology; Theatre; Thrillers; Translations; Travel; TV; Westerns;

Women's Interests; *Markets:* Adult; Youth; *Treatments:* Contemporary; Cynical; Dark; Experimental; In-depth; Light; Literary; Niche; Positive; Progressive; Satirical; Serious

Contact: Victor Rohm

A publishing house established in 2013. Content is mainly published online but will also find its way into annual, biannual or quarterly print anthologies, depending on how much time, money and energy are available.

We publish short works of fiction and nonfiction which let you escape your daily routine. There are no particular submission criteria for fiction. For nonfiction, a strong personal dimension to the prose is important. The reader must be given the chance to see the world through the eyes of the author.

Submissions need to be in English but do not need to be unpublished. However, please respect any exclusivity arrangements you might be engaged in.

This publisher is non-profit and any money that might (miraculously) be made through the sale of print anthologies will contribute to the production of subsequent issues.

When it comes to format, anything goes. We welcome good old-fashioned structures such as the essay or the short story. But we also feel very positive about anything that challenges conventions, such as maybe a collection of Twitter or Facebook posts or a WhatsApp conversation.

The publisher is currently working in publishing in London, holds an MSc in Political Theory and sleeps in a bed at night.

Michael O'Mara Books Ltd
9 Lion Yard
Tremadoc Road
London
SW4 7NQ
Tel: +44 (0) 20 7720 8643
Fax: +44 (0) 20 7627 4900
Email: enquiries@mombooks.com

Website: http://www.mombooks.com
Publishes: Nonfiction; *Areas:* Biography; Historical; Humour; *Markets:* Adult; Children's

Independent publisher dealing in general nonfiction, royal and celebrity biographies, humour, and anthologies, and books for children through its imprint (including quirky nonfiction, humour, novelty, picture, and board books). Welcomes ideas, and prefers synopses and sample text to unsolicited mss. No fiction. See website for full details.

Oberon Books
521 Caledonian Road
London
N7 9RH
Tel: +44 (0) 20 7607 3637
Fax: +44 (0) 20 7607 3629
Email: andrew@oberonbooks.com
Website: http://www.oberonbooks.com

Publishes: Nonfiction; Scripts; *Areas:* Drama; Theatre; *Markets:* Adult

Contact: Andrew Walby, Senior Editor

Publishes play texts, and books on dance and theatre. Specialises in translations of European classics and contemporary plays, though also publishes edited performance versions of classics including Shakespeare. Play texts are usually published in conjunction with a production.

Octopus Publishing Group Limited
Endeavour House
189 Shaftesbury Avenue
London
WC2H 8JY
Tel: +44 (0) 20 7632 5400
Fax: +44 (0) 20 7632 5405
Email: publisher@octopus-publishing.co.uk
Website: http://www.octopus-publishing.co.uk

Publishes: Nonfiction; Reference; *Areas:* Antiques; Architecture; Arts; Cookery; Crafts; Culture; Design; Film; Gardening;

Health; Historical; Humour; Lifestyle; Music; Psychology; Spiritual; Sport; Travel; *Markets:* Adult

Publisher with wide range of imprints dealing with a variety of nonfiction and reference subjects. See website for specific email addresses dedicated to each individual imprint.

Omnibus Press

14/15 Berners Street
London
W1T 3LJ
Tel: +44 (0) 20 7612 7400
Fax: +44 (0) 20 7612 7545
Email: info@omnibuspress.com
Website: http://www.omnibuspress.com

Publishes: Nonfiction; *Areas:* Biography; Music; *Markets:* Adult

Contact: Chris Charlesworth

Publisher of music books, including song sheets and rock and pop biographies. Welcomes ideas, synopses, and unsolicited MSS for appropriate books.

Oneworld Publications

10 Bloomsbury Street
London
WC1B 3SR
Tel: +44 (0) 20 7307 8900
Email: submissions@oneworld-publications.com
Website: http://www.oneworld-publications.com

Publishes: Fiction; Nonfiction; *Areas:* Biography; Business; Current Affairs; Historical; Philosophy; Politics; Psychology; Religious; Science; Self-Help; *Markets:* Adult; *Treatments:* Commercial; Literary

Nonfiction authors must be academics and/or experts in their field. Approaches for fiction must provide a clear and concise synopsis, outlining the novel's main themes. See website for full submission guidelines, and forms for fiction and nonfiction, which may be submitted by email.

Onlywomen Press Ltd

40d St Lawrence Terrace
London
W10 5ST
Tel: +44 (0) 20 8354 0796
Fax: +44 (0) 20 8960 2817
Email: onlywomenpress@btconnect.com
Website: http://onlywomenpress.com

Publishes: Fiction; Nonfiction; Poetry; *Areas:* Women's Interests; *Markets:* Adult; *Treatments:* Literary

Send query with SASE, author bio, intended market, and synopsis. Not currently accepting poetry. Prose writers should send only the first 60 pages of novels or of non-fiction. Queries accepted by email, but no electronic submissions, by email, disk, or other (hard copy MSS only).

Publishes consistent with a feminist perpective: feminist fiction, nonfiction and poetry. Priority given to lesbian authors.

Open Gate Press

51 Achilles Road
London
NW6 1DZ
Tel: +44 (0) 20 7431 4391
Fax: +44 (0) 20 7431 5129
Email: books@opengatepress.co.uk
Website: http://www.opengatepress.co.uk

Publishes: Nonfiction; *Areas:* Culture; Literature; Nature; Philosophy; Politics; Psychology; Religious; Sociology; *Markets:* Adult

Aims to provide a forum for psychoanalytic social studies. Publishes books on psychoanalysis, philosophy, social sciences, politics, literature, religion, and environment.

The Orion Publishing Group Limited

Orion House
5 Upper Saint Martin's Lane
London
WC2H 9EA
Tel: +44 (0) 20 7240 3444
Fax: +44 (0) 20 7240 4822
Website: http://www.orionbooks.co.uk

Publishes: Fiction; Nonfiction; Reference; *Areas:* Adventure; Archaeology; Arts; Autobiography; Beauty and Fashion; Biography; Cookery; Culture; Current Affairs; Design; Fantasy; Gardening; Health; Historical; Lifestyle; Literature; Military; Nature; Sci-Fi; Sport; Travel; *Markets:* Adult; Children's; Youth; *Treatments:* Commercial

One of the UK's leading commercial publishers. Accepts approaches through agents only.

Osprey Publishing Ltd

Commissioning Editor
Editorial Department
Osprey Publishing
Kemp House
Chawley Park
Cumnor Hill
Oxford
OX2 9PH
Tel: +44 (0) 1865 757022
Fax: +44 (0) 1865 242009
Email: editorial@ospreypublishing.com
Website: http://www.ospreypublishing.com

Publishes: Nonfiction; *Areas:* Historical; Military; *Markets:* Adult

Publishes illustrated books on military history and aviation. Welcomes synopses and ideas for books by post or by email, but no unsolicited MSS. See website for full guidelines.

Oversteps Books

6 Halwell House
South Pool
Nr Kingsbridge
Devon
TQ7 2RX
Email: alwynmarriage@overstepsbooks.com
Website: http://www.overstepsbooks.com

Publishes: Poetry; *Markets:* Adult

Poetry publisher. Send email with copies of three poems that have been published in magazines or won competitions, along with details of dates or issue numbers and email addresses of the editors. Include poems and information in the body of your email.

Peter Owen Publishers

20 Holland Park Avenue
London
W11 3QU
Tel: +44 (0) 20 8350 1775
Fax: +44 (0) 20 8340 9488
Email: admin@peterowen.com
Website: http://www.peterowen.com

Publishes: Fiction; Nonfiction; *Areas:* Arts; Biography; Criticism; Historical; Literature; Translations; *Markets:* Adult; *Treatments:* Literary

Contact: Antonia Owen (Editorial Director)

Publishes general nonfiction and international literary fiction. No first novels, short stories, poetry, plays, sport, spirituality, self-help, or children's or genre fiction. Prefers query by email or alternatively by post with return postage, including cover letter, synopsis, and one or two sample chapters. Prefers fiction to come from an agent or translator as appropriate.

Oxford University Press

Great Clarendon Street
Oxford
OX2 6DP
Tel: +44 (0) 1865 556767
Fax: +44 (0) 1865 556646
Email: webenquiry.uk@oup.com
Website: http://www.oup.com

Publishes: Fiction; Nonfiction; Reference; *Areas:* Current Affairs; Drama; Finance; Historical; Legal; Literature; Medicine; Music; Philosophy; Politics; Religious; Science; Sociology; *Markets:* Academic; Adult; Children's; Professional

Publishes academic works including journals, schoolbooks, dictionaries, reference works, classics, and children's fiction, and nonfiction. Email addresses for editorial available on website.

Pavilion Publishing

Rayford House
School Road
Hove
East Sussex
BN3 5HX
Tel: +44 (0) 1273 434943
Fax: +44 (0) 1273 227308
Email: info@pavpub.com
Website: http://www.pavpub.com

Publishes: Nonfiction; Reference; *Areas:*
Health; Sociology; *Markets:* Professional

Publishes books and resources for public,
private and voluntary workers in the health,
social care, education and community safety
sectors.

Pearson UK

Edinburgh Gate
Harlow
CM20 2JE
Tel: +44 (0) 845 313 6666
Fax: +44 (0) 845 313 7777
Website: http://www.pearsoned.co.uk

Publishes: Nonfiction; *Markets:* Academic;
Professional

World's largest publisher of educational
material, inclusing books for primary school
pupils through to professionals. See website
for appropriate imprint to approach, and
specific submission guidelines.

Pen & Sword Books Ltd

47 Church Street
Barnsley
South Yorkshire
S70 2AS
Tel: +44 (0) 1226 734555
Fax: +44 (0) 1226 734438
Email: editorialoffice@pen-and-sword.co.uk
Website: http://www.pen-and-sword.co.uk

Publishes: Fiction; Nonfiction; *Areas:*
Adventure; Archaeology; Autobiography;
Biography; Crime; Historical; Military;
Sociology; Travel; *Markets:* Adult

Submissions of unsolicited synopses and
ideas welcomed, but no unsolicited MSS.

Publishes across a number of areas including
military, aviation, maritime, family, local,
true crime and transport history. Also
launching historical fiction, adventure and
discovery, archaeology and social history
imprints. Send query by email with synopsis
and sample chapter.

Pennant Books Ltd

PO Box 5675
London
W1A 3FB
Tel: +44 (0) 20 7387 6400
Email: editor@pennantbooks.com
Website: http://www.pennantbooks.com

Publishes: Nonfiction; *Areas:* Biography;
Crime; Culture; Sport; *Markets:* Adult

Contact: Paul A Woods, Editor

Send initial query by email. No fiction,
unsolicited MSS, or books for children. See
website for full submission guidelines.

Persephone Books

59 Lamb's Conduit Street
London
WC1N 3NB
Tel: +44 (0) 20 7242 9292
Fax: +44 (0) 20 7242 9272
Email: info@persephonebooks.co.uk
Website: http://www.persephonebooks.co.uk

Publishes: Fiction; Nonfiction; *Areas:*
Women's Interests; *Markets:* Adult

Publishes mainly forgotten fiction and nonfiction by women, for women and about
women. Publishes reprints, so no unsolicited
material.

Phaidon Press Limited

Regent's Wharf
All Saints Street
London
N1 9PA
Tel: +44 (0) 20 7843 1000
Fax: +44 (0) 20 7843 1010
Email: submissions@phaidon.com
Website: http://www.phaidon.com

Publishes: Nonfiction; *Areas:* Architecture; Arts; Beauty and Fashion; Cookery; Culture; Design; Film; Historical; Music; Photography; Travel; *Markets:* Academic; Adult; Children's

Publishes books in the areas of art, architecture, design, photography, film, fashion, contemporary culture, decorative arts, music, performing arts, cultural history, food and cookery, travel and books for children. No fiction or approaches by post. Send query by email only, with CV and short description of the project.

Phoenix Yard Books

65 King's Cross Road
London
WC1X 9LW
Tel: +44 (0) 20 7239 4968
Email: submissions@phoenixyardbooks.com
Website: http://www.phoenixyardbooks.com

Publishes: Fiction; Nonfiction; Poetry; *Markets:* Children's; Youth; *Treatments:* Literary

Contact: Emma Langley

Publishes picture books, fiction, poetry, nonfiction and illustration for children aged around three to thirteen. Considers books of all genres, but leans more towards the literary and of the fiction spectrum. Particularly interested in character-based series, and fiction appealing to boys aged 6-9. Does not concentrate on young adult fiction, but will consider older fiction as part of epic series, sagas or trilogies. Send query by post with SAE or by email, with synopsis and three sample chapters. See website for full submission guidelines. Replies to email queries only if interested.

Piatkus Books

Piatkus Submissions
Little, Brown Book Group
100 Victoria Embankment
London
EC4Y 0DY
Tel: +44 (0) 20 7911 8030
Fax: +44 (0) 20 7911 8100
Email: info@littlebrown.co.uk

Website: http://www.piatkus.co.uk

Publishes: Fiction; Nonfiction; *Areas:* Autobiography; Biography; Business; Crime; Health; Historical; Humour; Lifestyle; Psychology; Self-Help; Spiritual; Thrillers; *Markets:* Adult; *Treatments:* Light; Popular; Serious

Contact: Gill Bailey (Nonfiction); Emma Beswetherick (Fiction)

No longer accepts unsolicited submissions. Accepts material through a literary agent only.

Piccadilly Press

5 Castle Road
London
NW1 8PR
Tel: +44 (0) 20 7267 4492
Fax: +44 (0) 20 7267 4493
Email: books@piccadillypress.co.uk
Website: http://www.piccadillypress.co.uk

Publishes: Fiction; Nonfiction; *Areas:* Humour; *Markets:* Children's; Youth; *Treatments:* Contemporary; Light

Publishes a range of titles, including parental books, but for new titles focuses on three main areas: picture books for children aged 2 to 5; teen fiction; and teen nonfiction.

Picture books should be character led and between 500 and 1,000 words. No novelty books. Prefers authors to be familiar with other books published before submitting – a catalogue is available upon request.

Publishes teen fiction and nonfiction which is contemporary, humorous, and deals with the issues faced by teenagers. Usually 25,000-35,000 words.

Send letter with SAE and entire MS for picture books, or synopsis and a couple of chapters for longer books, double-spaced. Do not send disks. No submissions by email.

Plexus Publishing Limited

25 Mallinson Road
London

SW11 1BW
Tel: +44 (0) 20 7924 4662
Fax: +44 (0) 20 7924 5096
Email: info@plexusuk.demon.co.uk
Website: http://www.plexusbooks.com

Publishes: Nonfiction; *Areas:* Biography;
Culture; Film; Music; *Markets:* Adult;
Treatments: Popular

Publishes illustrated nonfiction books
specialising in biography, popular culture,
movies and music.

Pluto Publishing Ltd

345 Archway Road
London
N6 5AA
Tel: +44 (0) 20 8348 2724
Fax: +44 (0) 20 8340 8252
Email: pluto@plutobooks.com
Website: http://www.plutobooks.com

Publishes: Nonfiction; *Areas:* Anthropology;
Culture; Current Affairs; Finance; Historical;
Legal; Media; Nature; Politics; Sociology;
Markets: Academic

Contact: Anne Beech; David Castle; David
Shulman

Academic press publishing books for
students and academics in higher education.
Consult website for appropriate
commissioning editor to submit your
proposal to, then contact by email giving
outline of book, synopsis and table of
contents, format and delivery estimate, plus
market info (see website for more
information).

Pocket Mountains

Jenny Wren
Holm Street
Moffat
Dumfries and Gallloway
DG10 9EB
Tel: +44 (0) 1683 221641
Email: info@pocketmountains.com
Website: http://www.pocketmountains.com

Publishes: Nonfiction; *Areas:* Adventure;
Leisure; Nature; Travel; *Markets:* Adult

Contact: Robbie Porteous; April Simmons

Publisher of outdoor books, including guides
on mountaineering, walking, and cycling in
Scotland and Europe, plus wildlife books.
Send query by email or by post with SAE,
including outline, draft couple of pages (up
to about 1,000 words), and author info and
experience.

The Policy Press

University of Bristol
Fourth Floor
Beacon House
Queen's Road
Bristol
BS8 1QU
Tel: +44 (0) 117 331 4054
Fax: +44 (0) 117 331 4093
Email: tpp-info@bristol.ac.uk
Website: http://www.policypress.co.uk

Publishes: Nonfiction; *Areas:* Sociology;
Markets: Academic; Professional

Publishes monographs, texts and journals for
scholars internationally; reports for policy
makers, professionals and researchers; and
practice guides for practitioners and user
groups. Aims to publish the latest policy
research for the whole policy studies
community, including academics, policy
makers, practitioners and students.
Welcomes proposals for books, reports,
guides or journals. Author guidelines
available on website.

Portland Press Ltd

Third floor
Charles Darwin House
12 Roger Street
London
WC1N 2JU
Tel: +44 (0) 20 7685 2410
Fax: +44 (0) 20 7685 2469
Email: editorial@portlandpress.com
Website: http://www.portlandpress.com

Publishes: Nonfiction; *Areas:* Medicine;
Science; *Markets:* Academic; Adult

Publisher of books on biochemistry and
medicine, mainly for graduate, post-

graduate, and research students, but
increasingly also for schools and general
readership. Welcomes synopses, ideas, and
unsolicited MSS. No fiction.

Prestel Publishing Ltd
4 Bloomsbury Place
London
WC1A 2QA
Tel: +44 (0) 20 7323 5004
Fax: +44 (0) 20 7636 8004
Email: sales@prestel-uk.co.uk
Website: http://www.prestel.com

Publishes: Nonfiction; *Areas:* Architecture;
Arts; Beauty and Fashion; Design;
Photography; *Markets:* Adult; Children's

German publisher of art, architecture,
photography, design, cultural history, and
ethnography, with offices in the UK and
USA. Welcomes unsolicited MSS and
synopses by post or email.

Princeton University Press Europe
3 Market Place
Woodstock
Oxfordshire
OX20 1SY
Tel: +44 (0) 1993 814500
Fax: +44 (0) 1993 814504
Email: admin@pupress.co.uk
Website: http://www.pupress.co.uk

Publishes: Nonfiction; Reference; *Areas:*
Anthropology; Archaeology; Architecture;
Arts; Film; Finance; Historical; Legal;
Literature; Media; Medicine; Music; Nature;
Philosophy; Photography; Politics;
Religious; Science; Self-Help; Sociology;
Markets: Academic

Contact: Richard Baggaley, Publishing
Director, Europe

European office of US academic publisher.

Profile Books
3A Exmouth House
Pine Street
Exmouth Market

London
EC1R OJH
Tel: +44 (0) 20 7841 6300
Fax: +44 (0) 20 7833 3969
Email: info@profilebooks.co.uk
Website: http://www.profilebooks.co.uk

Publishes: Nonfiction; *Areas:* Biography;
Business; Culture; Current Affairs; Finance;
Historical; Humour; Politics; Psychology;
Science; *Markets:* Adult

Award-winning small publisher noted for
author-friendly relations. Published the
number-one Christmas bestseller in 2003.
Recommends approaches be through a
literary agent.

Psychology Press
27 Church Road
Hove
East Sussex
BN3 2FA
Tel: +44 (0) 20 7017 7747
Fax: +44 (0) 20 7017 6717
Website: http://www.psypress.com

Publishes: Nonfiction; *Areas:* Psychology;
Markets: Academic; Professional

Publishes academic and professional books
and journals on psychology. Use book
proposal submission form on website, or
send hard copy submission following
guidelines on website.

Quarto Publishing Group UK
The Old Brewery
6 Blundell Street
London
N7 9BH
Tel: +44 (0) 20 7700 6700
Fax: +44 (0) 20 7700 8066
Email: info@quarto.com
Website: http://www.quarto.com

Publishes: Nonfiction; *Areas:* Arts; Beauty
and Fashion; Cookery; Crafts; Design;
Entertainment; Gardening; Health;
Historical; Hobbies; How-to; Lifestyle;
Sport; *Markets:* Adult; Children's

Publisher of illustrated nonfiction books for adults and children.

Quercus Books

55 Baker Street, 7th Floor
South Block
London
W1U 8EW
Tel: +44 (0) 20 7291 7200
Email: enquiries@quercusbooks.co.uk
Website: http://www.quercusbooks.co.uk

Publishes: Fiction; Nonfiction; *Areas:* Crime; Fantasy; Sci-Fi; *Markets:* Adult; Children's

Publishes fiction and nonfiction. Does not accept unsolicited submissions at this time.

Quiller Publishing Ltd

Wykey House
Wykey
Shrewsbury
Shropshire
SY4 1JA
Tel: +44 (0) 1939 261616
Fax: +44 (0) 1939 261606
Email: admin@quillerbooks.com
Website:
http://www.countrybooksdirect.com

Publishes: Nonfiction; Reference; *Areas:* Architecture; Biography; Business; Cookery; Gardening; Humour; Sport; Travel; *Markets:* Adult

Contact: John Beaton

Publishes books for all lovers of fishing, shooting, equestrian and country pursuits. Accepts unsolicited MSS from authors. Send submissions as hard copy only, with email address for reply or SAE if return of ms is required.

Radcliffe Publishing Ltd

Unit C5, Sunningdale House,
Caldecotte Lake Business Park,
43 Caldecotte Lake Drive,
Milton Keynes
MK7 8LF
Tel: +44 (0) 1908 277177

Fax: +44 (0) 1908 278297
Email:
gillian.nineham@radcliffepublishing.com
Website: http://www.radcliffe-oxford.com

Publishes: Nonfiction; *Areas:* Health; Medicine; *Markets:* Professional

Contact: Gillian Nineham (Editorial Director)

Publishes books on medicine, including health care policy and management, and also training materials. Welcomes synopses, ideas, and unsolicited MSS.

Ragged Bears Limited

Unit 14A
Bennett's Field Trading Estate
Southgate Road
Wincanton
Somerset
BA9 9DT
Tel: +44 (0) 1963 34300
Email: info@raggedbears.co.uk
Website: http://www.raggedbears.co.uk

Publishes: Fiction; *Markets:* Children's; Youth

Publishes picture books and novelty books, up to young teen fiction. Accepts submissions by post with SAE (no original artwork), but prefers submissions by email.

Ramsay Publishing

17 Castle Heather Drive
Inverness
Email: submissions@ramsaypublishing.com

Publishes: Fiction; *Areas:* Adventure; Entertainment; Humour; Sci-Fi; Short Stories; *Markets:* Children's; Family; *Treatments:* Mainstream; Popular

Contact: Aaron Ramsay

Brand new publisher starting up dealing solely with electronic media. Please note, we do not publish printed books in any form.

Specifically looking for new children's books, pictures books and any books rich in graphics and media. Our new cutting edge service turns standard print books into fully interactive digital products which can be sold for laptops/computer, android phones and pads, iPhones and iPads, Meego, Blackberry and more.

All conversion is done by us – submission need only be artwork with accompanying stories. Full voice over service available. Complete projects are fully interactive and read aloud the book with rich graphics, interactive animation, sounds and even questions/activities about page content.

Books will never die, but we aim to help bring them back into the current generation.

Note, you must own all the rights to your work for publication, however existing print publications are acceptable if this criteria is met.

Ransom Publishing Ltd
Radley House
8 St Cross Road
Winchester
Hampshire
SO23 9HX
Tel: +44 (0) 1962 862307
Fax: +44 (0) 5601 148881
Email: ransom@ransom.co.uk
Website: http://www.ransom.co.uk

Publishes: Fiction; Nonfiction; *Markets:* Adult; Children's; Professional; Youth

An independent specialist publisher of high quality, inspirational books that encourage and help children, young adults, and adults to develop their reading skills. Books are intended to have content which is age appropriate and engaging, but reading levels that would normally be appropriate for younger readers. Also publishes resources for both the library and classroom. Will consider unsolicited mss. Email in first instance.

Reed Business Information (RBI)
Tel: +44 (0) 20 8652 3500
Email: webmaster@rbi.co.uk

Website: http://www.reedbusiness.com

Publishes: Nonfiction; *Areas:* Business; Culture; Current Affairs; Entertainment; Finance; Media; Politics; Science; Travel; *Markets:* Professional

Publishes a range of information and data services for professionals in a range of sectors.

Rivers Oram Press
144 Hemingford Road
London
N1 1DE
Tel: +44 (0) 20 7607 0823
Fax: +44 (0) 20 7609 2776
Email: ro@riversoram.com
Website: http://www.riversoram.com

Publishes: Nonfiction; *Areas:* Culture; Current Affairs; Historical; Politics; Sociology; Women's Interests; *Markets:* Adult

Publisher of social and political sciences, including sexual politics, gender studies, social history, cultural studies, and current affairs.

Robert Hale Publishers
Clerkenwell House
45-47 Clerkenwell Green
London
EC1R 0HT
Tel: +44 (0) 20 7251 2661
Fax: +44 (0) 20 7490 4958
Email: submissions@halebooks.com
Website: http://www.halebooks.com

Publishes: Fiction; Nonfiction; Reference; *Areas:* Arts; Autobiography; Biography; Cookery; Crime; Historical; Hobbies; Humour; Leisure; Military; Spiritual; Westerns; *Markets:* Adult

See website for full submission guidelines, and list of material not currently being accepted. Send query with synopsis and three sample chapters.

Sage Publications

1 Oliver's Yard
55 City Road
London
EC1Y 1SP
Tel: +44 (0) 20 7324 8500
Fax: +44 (0) 20 7324 8600
Email: info@sagepub.co.uk
Website: http://www.sagepub.co.uk

Publishes: Nonfiction; *Areas:* Anthropology;
Archaeology; Arts; Business; Crime;
Finance; Health; Historical; Media;
Medicine; Politics; Psychology; Religious;
Science; Sociology; Technology; *Markets:*
Academic; Professional

Publishes academic books and journals. See
website for guides for authors and making
submissions, etc.

SalGad Publishing Group

Redditch
Worcestershire
Email: info@salgad.com
Website: http://www.salgadpublishing.com

Publishes: Fiction; *Areas:* Crime; Drama;
Horror; Mystery; Romance; Thrillers;
Markets: Adult; Youth; *Treatments:*
Commercial; Contemporary; Dark; Light;
Mainstream; Popular

Contact: Sally Stote

A publisher dedicated to 'helping writers
make a living'.

We are a group of young and enthusiastic
people that understand the current
generation's reliance upon technology and
"social media". While older publishers are
struggling to adapt their old ways and
outdated methods, we are fully prepared for
the digital revolution of the book industry.

One of our founding members is an already-
established writer that has found great
success himself through the sale of his
ebooks and by exploiting social media's
marketing prowess. Our other members
include a world-class artist, a successful
businesswoman, and several other people
directly involved in publishing.

Please see our why choose us page on our
website.

Salt Publishing Ltd

12 Norwich Road
CROMER
Norfolk
NR27 0AX
Tel: +44 (0) 1263 511011
Email: submissions@saltpublishing.com
Website: http://www.saltpublishing.com

Publishes: Fiction; *Areas:* Crime; Gothic;
Literature; Thrillers; *Markets:* Adult;
Treatments: Dark; Literary; Mainstream;
Traditional

Must be in English and aimed at a British
market, and should be under 80,000 words.
Not currently accepting short stories, poetry,
fantasy or memoirs. Send query by email
with biographical note up to 80 words,
exciting 250 word description, and six bullet
points up to 15 words each explaining why
British booksellers would want to sell your
novel. Full submission guidelines on
website.

Samuel French Ltd

Performing Rights Department
52 Fitzroy Street
London
W1T 5JR
Tel: +44 (0) 20 7387 9373
Fax: +44 (0) 20 7387 2161
Email: submissions@samuelfrench-
london.co.uk
Website: http://www.samuelfrench-
london.co.uk

Publishes: Scripts; *Areas:* Drama; *Markets:*
Adult

Publishes plays only. Send query by email
only, following the guidelines in the FAQ
section of the website. No unsolicited MSS.

Science Navigation Group

Middlesex House
34-42 Cleveland Street
London
W1T 4LB

Tel: +44 (0) 20 7323 0323
Fax: +44 (0) 20 7580 1938
Email: info@sciencenavigation.com
Website: http://www.sciencenavigation.com

Publishes: Nonfiction; *Areas:* Medicine;
Science; *Markets:* Academic; Adult;
Professional

Publishes material for the biomedical
community, aimed at physicians, scientists,
pharmaceutical companies, patients, students
and the general public.

SCM-Canterbury Press
Hymns Ancient and Modern Ltd
3rd Floor
Invicta House
108-114 Golden Lane
London
EC1Y 0TG
Tel: +44 (0) 20 7776 7540
Fax: +44 (0) 20 7776 7556
Email: christine@hymnsam.co.uk
Website: http://www.canterburypress.co.uk

Publishes: Nonfiction; Reference; *Areas:*
Philosophy; Religious; Spiritual; *Markets:*
Adult

Publisher of religious nonfiction and
reference. No dissertations, fiction, poetry,
drama, children's books, books of specialist
local interest, or (as a general rule) multi-
authored collections of essays or symposium
papers.

Seafarer Books
102 Redwald Road
Rendlesham
Woodbridge
Suffolk
IP12 2TE
Tel: +44 (0) 1394 420789
Fax: +44 (0) 1394 461314
Email: info@seafarerbooks.com
Website: http://www.seafarerbooks.com

Publishes: Fiction; Nonfiction; *Areas:* Arts;
Crafts; Historical; How-to; Military; Music;
Travel; *Markets:* Adult; *Treatments:*
Traditional

Contact: Patricia Eve

Publishes fiction and nonfiction books on
sailing, including maritime history, practical
seamanship and boatbuilding, etc. Also
music CDs, cards, and calendars. No
unsolicited MSS. Send query in first
instance.

Seren
57 Nolton Street
Bridgend
Wales
CF31 3AE
Tel: +44 (0) 1656 663018
Fax: +44 (0) 1656 649226
Email: Info@SerenBooks.com
Website: http://www.serenbooks.com

Publishes: Fiction; Nonfiction; Poetry;
Areas: Anthropology; Arts; Biography;
Criticism; Current Affairs; Drama;
Historical; Music; Photography; Politics;
Sport; Translations; Travel; *Markets:* Adult;
Children's; *Treatments:* Literary

Unsolicited MSS, synopses, and ideas
welcomed. Specialises in English-language
writing from Wales and aims to bring Welsh
culture, art, literature, and politics to a wider
audience. Accepts nonfiction submissions
only by email; no poetry or fiction
submissions by email. See website for
complete submission guidelines.

Shearsman Books
50 Westons Hill Drive
Emersons Green
Bristol
BS16 7DF
Tel: +44 (0) 1179 572957
Email: editor@shearsman.com
Website: http://www.shearsman.com

Publishes: Nonfiction; Poetry; *Areas:*
Autobiography; Criticism; Literature;
Translations; *Markets:* Adult

Contact: Tony Frazer

Publishes poetry books of 70-72 A5 pages.
Publishes mainly poetry by British, Irish,
North American and Australian/New

Zealand poets, plus poetry in translation from any language—although particular interest in German, Spanish and Latin American poetry.

Submit only if MS is of appropriate length and most of it has already appeared in UK or US magazines of some repute. Send selection of 10 poems or 10 pages (whichever is shorter) by post with SASE or by email with material embedded in the text or as PDF attachment. No other kind of attachments accepted.

Also sometimes publishes literary criticism on poetry, and essays or memoirs by poets.

Sheldrake Press

188 Cavendish Road
London
SW12 0DA
Tel: +44 (0) 20 8675 1767
Fax: +44 (0) 20 8675 7736
Email: enquiries@sheldrakepress.co.uk
Website: http://www.sheldrakepress.co.uk

Publishes: Nonfiction; *Areas:* Architecture; Cookery; Design; Historical; Travel; *Markets:* Adult

Contact: Simon Rigge, Publisher

Publisher of illustrated nonfiction titles covering travel, history, cookery, and stationery. Ideas and synopses welcome. No fiction.

Shepheard-Walwyn (Publishers) Ltd

107 Parkway House
Sheen Lane
London
SW14 8LS
Tel: +44 (0) 20 8241 5927
Email: books@shepheard-walwyn.co.uk
Website: http://www.shepheard-walwyn.co.uk

Publishes: Nonfiction; Poetry; *Areas:* Biography; Finance; Historical; Philosophy; Politics; *Markets:* Adult

Publishes mainly nonfiction, particularly the

areas listed above and also books of Scottish interest, and gift books in calligraphy and / or illustrated. Also some poetry.

Short Books

3A Exmouth House
Pine St
London
EC1R 0JH
Tel: +44 (0) 20 7833 9429
Email: info@shortbooks.co.uk
Website: http://shortbooks.co.uk

Publishes: Fiction; Nonfiction; *Markets:* Adult

Cannot guarantee that all unsolicited submissions will be read, so recommends approach via literary agent. Will accept direct submissions, however. Send cover letter with synopsis and first three chapters / roughly 30 pages by post. Include email address or SAE for response, however response not guaranteed.

Society of Genealogists

14 Charterhouse Buildings
Goswell Road
London
EC1M 7BA
Tel: +44 (0) 20 7251 8799
Fax: +44 (0) 20 7250 1800
Email: sales@sog.org.uk
Website: http://sog.org.uk

Publishes: Nonfiction; *Areas:* Historical; *Markets:* Adult

Publishes books, magazines, and software on local and family history.

SportsBooks Limited

1 Evelyn Court
Malvern Road
Cheltenham
GL50 2JR
Tel: +44 (0) 1242 256755
Fax: +44 (0) 0560 310 8126
Email: info@sportsbooks.ltd.uk
Website: http://www.sportsbooks.ltd.uk

Publishes: Nonfiction; *Areas:* Biography;

Sport; *Markets:* Adult

Welcomes submissions by hard copy or email as .txt or .rtf attachments. Send query with synopsis and up to three sample chapters, plus information on market and marketing. No fiction.

Stacey International

128 Kensington Church Street
London
W8 4BH
Tel: +44 (0) 20 7221 7166
Fax: +44 (0) 20 7792 9288
Email: editorial@stacey-international.co.uk
Website: http://www.stacey-international.co.uk

Publishes: Fiction; Nonfiction; Poetry; Reference; *Areas:* Archaeology; Historical; Literature; Nature; Photography; Travel; *Markets:* Adult; Children's

Publishes nonfiction, fiction, and poetry, for adults and children. Submit manuscripts and proposals by email. See website for more information.

Stairwell Books

Email: rose@stairwellbooks.com
Website: http://www.stairwellbooks.co.uk

Publishes: Fiction; Poetry; *Areas:* Short Stories; *Markets:* Adult

Contact: Rose Drew

Small press publisher specialising in poetry anthologies, short stories, and novels from new writers. Send query by email. See website for full details.

Sunberry Books

10 Aspen Close
Harriseahead
Staffordshire
ST5 9PL
Tel: +44 (0) 1692 678832
Email: query@sunpenny.com
Website: http://www.sunberrybooks.com

Publishes: Fiction; *Areas:* Adventure;

Entertainment; Literature; Mystery; Religious; *Markets:* Children's; Youth; *Treatments:* Literary

We believe that while we are going to be spending a lot of time and effort getting your book into shape for publication, and on follow-through afterwards, it's still your book – you provide the manuscript, we publish at our expense, and do what marketing we can while you do your bit too.

Sunflower Books

Commissioning Editor
Sunflower Books
PO Box 36160
London
SW7 3HG
Email: mail@sunflowerbooks.co.uk
Website: http://www.sunflowerbooks.co.uk

Publishes: Nonfiction; *Areas:* Leisure; Travel; *Markets:* Adult

Publishes walking guides only. Authors are advised to submit a proposal (hard copy by post only) before starting work on a book, as the format must match that of existing titles. No proposals by email.

Sussex Academic Press

PO Box 139
Eastbourne
East Sussex
BN24 9BP
Tel: +44 (0) 1323 479220
Fax: +44 (0) 1323 478185
Email: edit@sussex-academic.com
Website: http://www.sussex-academic.com

Publishes: Nonfiction; *Areas:* Anthropology; Archaeology; Arts; Biography; Criticism; Culture; Drama; Finance; Historical; Literature; Media; Music; Nature; Philosophy; Politics; Psychology; Religious; Sociology; Theatre; Women's Interests; *Markets:* Academic

Contact: Anthony V. P. Grahame, Editorial Director

Academic publisher. Send query by post.

Book proposal form available on website. No unsolicited MSS.

Sweet Cherry Publishing
Unit E Vulcan Business Complex
Vulcan Road
Leicester
LE5 3EB
Email: info@sweetcherrypublishing.com
Website:
http://www.sweetcherrypublishing.com

Publishes: Fiction; *Markets:* Children's; Youth

Contact: Abdul Thadha

Publishes books for children aged 5 to young adult. Currently considering submissions from the UK only. Send query by post with SAE, including details about you and your writing, synopsis, and first three chapters. Email queries will receive a response, but no submissions by email. See website for full guidelines.

TSO (The Stationery Office)
St Crispins
Duke Street
Norwich
NR3 1PD
Tel: +44 (0) 1603 622211
Email: customer.services@tso.co.uk
Website: http://www.tso.co.uk

Publishes: Nonfiction; Reference; *Areas:* Business; Current Affairs; Medicine; *Markets:* Professional

One of the largest publishers by volume in the UK, publishing more than 9,000 titles a year in print and digital formats.

Tango Books Ltd
PO Box 32595
London
W4 5YD
Tel: +44 (0) 20 8996 9970
Fax: +44 (0) 20 8996 9977
Email: info@tangobooks.co.uk
Website: http://www.tangobooks.co.uk

Publishes: Fiction; Nonfiction; *Markets:* Children's

Contact: David Fielder; Sheri Safran

Publisher of children's fiction (ages 1-8), nonfiction (ages 1-15), and novelty books, up to 1,000 words. Send query by email or by post with complete text, bio, and SAE. No poetry or verse, or texts that are very British in content or style. See website for complete guidelines.

Taylor & Francis Books
4 Park Square
Milton Park
Abingdon
Oxfordshire
OX14 4RN
Tel: +44 (0) 20 7017 6000
Fax: +44 (0) 20 7017 6336
Email: info@tandf.co.uk
Website:
http://www.taylorandfrancisgroup.com

Publishes: Nonfiction; *Markets:* Academic

Publishes everything from core text books to research monographs, mainly at university level.

The Templar Company Limited
Deepdene Lodge
Deepdene Avenue
Dorking
Surrey
RH5 4AT
Tel: +44 (0) 1306 876361
Fax: +44 (0) 1306 889097
Email: clare.kuzimski@templarco.co.uk
Website: http://www.templarco.co.uk

Publishes: Fiction; Nonfiction; *Markets:* Children's

Contact: Clare Kuzimski

Publisher of children's fiction and illustrated nonfiction for ages 8-12. Particularly interested in picture book MSS and ideas for new novelty concepts. Welcomes ideas and synopses. Send query by post only with synopsis and first three chapters, or complete ms for picture and novelty books. Include SAE if return required. No submissions by email.

Thames and Hudson Ltd
181A High Holborn
London
WC1V 7QX
Tel: +44 (0) 20 7845 5000
Fax: +44 (0) 20 7845 5050
Email: editorial@thameshudson.co.uk
Website: http://www.thamesandhudson.com

Publishes: Nonfiction; Reference; *Areas:* Archaeology; Architecture; Arts; Beauty and Fashion; Biography; Culture; Design; Gardening; Historical; Photography; Religious; Travel; *Markets:* Adult

Publishes illustrated nonfiction only. No fiction. Send query by email with short outline and CV in the body of the email. No attachments.

Tiger of the Stripe
50 Albert Road
Richmond
Surrey
TW10 6DP
Tel: +44 (0) 20 8940 8087
Email: peter@tigerofthestripe.co.uk
Website: http://www.tigerofthestripe.co.uk

Publishes: Fiction; Nonfiction; Poetry; *Areas:* Antiques; Archaeology; Architecture; Arts; Autobiography; Biography; Business; Cookery; Crafts; Crime; Criticism; Culture; Current Affairs; Design; Drama; Entertainment; Film; Finance; Gardening; Health; Historical; Hobbies; How-to; Humour; Legal; Leisure; Lifestyle; Literature; Media; Medicine; Military; Music; Mystery; Nature; Photography; Politics; Psychology; Radio; Religious; Romance; Science; Self-Help; Short Stories; Suspense; Technology; Theatre; Thrillers; Translations; Travel; *Markets:* Academic; Adult; Professional; *Treatments:* In-depth; Literary; Popular; Serious; Traditional

Contact: Peter Danckwerts

Eclectic but with an emphasis on well-researched academic or semi-academic works. Also interested in biographies, history, language textbooks, cookbooks, typography.

Titan Books
Titan House
144 Southwark Street
London
SE1 0UP
Tel: +44 (0) 20 7620 0200
Fax: +44 (0) 20 7620 0032
Email: editorial@titanemail.com
Website: http://www.titanbooks.com

Publishes: Fiction; Nonfiction; *Areas:* Entertainment; Film; Humour; Sci-Fi; Short Stories; TV; *Markets:* Adult; Youth

Contact: Commissioning Editor

Publisher of graphic novels, particularly with film or television tie-ins, and books related to film and TV. No unsolicited fiction or books for children, but will consider ideas for licensed projects they have already contracted. Send query with synopsis by post only. No email submissions.

Top That! Publishing
Marine House
Tide Mill Way
Woodbridge
Suffolk
IP12 1AP
Tel: +44 (0) 1394 386651
Email: dan@topthatpublishing.com
Website: http://topthatpublishing.com

Publishes: Fiction; Nonfiction; Reference; *Areas:* Cookery; Humour; *Markets:* Adult; Children's

Contact: Dan Graham, Editorial Director

Publishes Activity Books, Character Books, Cookery Books, Felt Books, Fiction, Humour, Magnetic Books, Novelty Books, Phonics Books, Picture Storybooks, Pop-Up Books, Press Out & Play, Reference Books, and Sticker Books. Does not currently publish "regular" children's or adults fiction.

See online book catalogue for the kinds of books published. If suitable for the list, send submissions by email (preferred) or by post (mss not returned). See website for full guidelines. Responds within 8 weeks if interested. No simultaneous submissions.

Trentham Books Limited

28 Hillside Gardens
Highgate
London
N6 5ST
Tel: +44 (0) 1782 745567
Fax: +44 (0) 1782 745553
Email: Gillian@trentham-books.co.uk
Website: http://www.trentham-books.co.uk

Publishes: Nonfiction; *Areas:* Culture; Humour; Legal; Sociology; Women's Interests; *Markets:* Academic; Professional

Contact: Dr Gillian Klein

Publishes academic and professional books. No fiction, biography, or poetry. No unsolicited MSS, but accepts queries by post with SASE, or by email with your name in the subject line. See website for full guidelines.

Ulric Publishing

PO Box 55
Church Stretton
Shropshire
SY6 6WR
Tel: +44 (0) 1694 781354
Email: enquiries@ulricpublishing.com
Website: http://www.ulricpublishing.com

Publishes: Nonfiction; *Areas:* Military; Technology; Travel; *Markets:* Adult

Publishes military and motoring history.

Unicorn Press Ltd

66 Charlotte Street
LONDON
W1T 4QE
Tel: +44 (0) 7836 633377
Email: ian@unicornpress.org
Website: http://unicornpress.org

Publishes: Nonfiction; Reference; *Areas:* Architecture; Arts; Biography; Historical; *Markets:* Adult

Contact: Ian Strathcarron (Publisher)

Works with artists, authors, museums, and galleries to publish high-quality fine and decorative art reference books, guides and monographs.

University of Wales Press

10 Columbus Walk
Brigantine Place
Cardiff
CF10 4UP
Tel: +44 (0) 29 2049 6899
Fax: +44 (0) 29 2049 6108
Email: press@press.wales.ac.uk
Website: http://www.uwp.co.uk

Publishes: Nonfiction; *Areas:* Culture; Historical; Literature; Media; Nature; Philosophy; Politics; Religious; Sociology; *Markets:* Academic

Submit proposal by email at an early stage – preferably before book is written.

Unthank Books

PO Box 3506
Norwich
Norfolk
NR7 7QP
Tel: +44 (0) 1603 471300
Email: robin.jones@unthankbooks.com
Website: http://www.unthankbooks.com

Publishes: Fiction; Nonfiction; *Markets:* Adult; *Treatments:* Literary

Contact: Robin Jones (Publisher); Ashley Stokes (Editorial Director)

Publishes adult literary fiction and nonfiction. Send query with SAE, synopsis, and 50 double spaced pages.

Usborne Publishing

83-85 Saffron Hill
London
EC1N 8RT

Tel: +44 (0) 20 7430 2800
Fax: +44 (0) 20 7430 1562
Email: mail@usborne.co.uk
Website: http://www.usborne.co.uk

Publishes: Fiction; Nonfiction; Reference;
Markets: Children's

Publisher of children's reference now
expanding into children's fiction. All
nonfiction written in-house and fiction
submissions accepted via literary agents
only.

Wooden Books
8A Market Place
Glastonbury
BA6 8LT
Email: info@woodenbooks.com
Website: http://www.woodenbooks.com

Publishes: Nonfiction; *Areas:* Historical;
Science; Spiritual; *Markets:* Adult

Publishes illustration-heavy books on such
topics as ancient sciences, magic,
mathematics, etc. Prospective authors will
need to provide high quality illustrations.
Essential to query before commencing work.
Send query by email or by post. See website
for full details.

Wallflower Press
4 Eastern Terrace Mews
Brighton
BN2 1EP
Email: yoram@wallflowerpress.co.uk
Website: http://www.wallflowerpress.co.uk

Publishes: Nonfiction; *Areas:* Culture;
Entertainment; Film; Media; *Markets:*
Academic; Adult

Contact: Yoram Allon, Consulting Editor to
Columbia

Publisher of books relating to film, plus
related media and culture, for both popular
and academic markets. Contact by email in
first instance. No fiction, or academic
nonfiction which is not related to the moving
image.

Acquired by a US publisher in 2011, the
previous editorial and pre-production team
continue to work directly with authors as an
imprint of the US firm.

Welsh Academic Press
PO Box 733,
Caerdydd
Cardiff
CF14 7ZY
Tel: +44 (0) 29 2021 8187
Email: post@welsh-academic-press.com
Website: http://www.welsh-academic-press.com

Publishes: Nonfiction; *Areas:* Historical;
Politics; *Markets:* Academic

Publishes academic monographs, reference
works, text books and popular scholarly titles
in the fields of education, history, political
studies, Scandinavian and Baltic studies,
contemporary work and employment, and
medieval Wales. Complete questionnaire
available on website.

Which? Books
2 Marylebone Road
London
NW1 4DF
Tel: +44 (0) 20 7770 7000
Fax: +44 (0) 20 7770 7600
Email: which@which.co.uk
Website: http://www.which.net

Publishes: Nonfiction; Reference; *Areas:*
Finance; Gardening; Health; Legal;
Lifestyle; Technology; *Markets:* Adult

Publishes books on consumer issues. Send
query with outline of idea or synopsis. No
unsolicited MSS.

Whittet Books Ltd
1 St John's Lane
Stansted
Essex
CM24 8JU
Tel: +44 (0) 1279 815871
Fax: +44 (0) 1279 647564
Email: mail@whittetbooks.com
Website: http://www.whittetbooks.com

Publishes: Nonfiction; *Areas:* Nature; *Markets:* Adult

Publishes books of rural interest, including horses, pets, poultry, livestock, horticulture, natural history, etc. Send query with outline in first instance; preferably by email.

William Reed Business Media

Broadfield Park
Crawley
West Sussex
RH11 9RT
Tel: +44 (0) 1293 613400
Website: http://www.william-reed.com

Publishes: Nonfiction; Reference; *Areas:* Business; *Markets:* Professional

Publishes business to business directories and reports.

Wolters Kluwer (UK) Ltd

145 London Road
Kingston upon Thames
Surrey
KT2 6SR
Tel: +44 (0) 20 8547 3333
Fax: +44 (0) 20 8547 2637
Email: info@croner.co.uk
Website: http://www.wolterskluwer.co.uk

Publishes: Nonfiction; Reference; *Areas:* Business; Finance; Legal; *Markets:* Professional

Publishes books, looseleafs, and online services for professionals. Areas of expertise include: Human Resources, Health and Safety, Tax and Accountancy, Education and Healthcare, Manufacturing and Construction.

The X Press

PO Box 25694
London
N17 6FP
Tel: +44 (0) 20 8801 2100
Fax: +44 (0) 20 8885 1322
Email: vibes@xpress.co.uk
Website: http://www.xpress.co.uk

Publishes: Fiction; *Areas:* Culture; *Markets:* Adult; Children's; *Treatments:* Contemporary; Literary; Popular

Contact: Dotun Adebayo (Editorial Director); Steve Pope (Marketing Director)

Europe's largest publisher of Black interest books. Publishes popular contemporary fiction, children's fiction, and black classics, though scope is expanding. Send SAE with MS, rather than synopses or ideas. No poetry.

Zero to Ten Limited

327 High Street
Slough
Berkshire
SL1 1TX
Tel: +44 (0) 1753 578 499
Email: annamcquinn@zerototen.co.uk

Publishes: Nonfiction; *Markets:* Children's

Contact: Anna McQuinn

Publishes nonfiction for children up to 10 years old, including board books and toddler books. Welcomes submissions, but responds only if interested.

ZigZag Education

Unit 3
Greenway Business Centre
Doncaster Road
Bristol
BS10 5PY
Tel: +44 (0) 1179 503199
Fax: +44 (0) 1179 591695
Email: support@PublishMeNow.co.uk
Website: http://www.zigzageducation.co.uk

Publishes: Nonfiction; *Areas:* Arts; Business; Design; Drama; Finance; Health; Historical; Legal; Leisure; Media; Music; Philosophy; Politics; Psychology; Religious; Science; Sociology; Sport; Technology; Travel; *Markets:* Academic; Children's; Professional; Youth

Educational publisher publishing

photocopiable and digital teaching resources for schools and colleges. Register on publisher's author support website if

interested in writing or contributing to resources.

Canadian Publishers

For the most up-to-date listings of these and hundreds of other publishers, visit http://www.firstwriter.com/publishers

*To claim your **free** access to the site, please see the back of this book.*

Annick Press

15 Patricia Avenue
Toronto, ON
M2M 1H9
Email: annickpress@annickpress.com
Website: http://www.annickpress.com

Publishes: Fiction; Nonfiction; *Markets:* Children's; Youth

Canadian publisher committed to publishing Canadian authors. Publishes fiction and nonfiction for children aged six months to twelve years and young adults. Not currently accepting picture book submissions. No submissions by fax or email. See website for full submission guidelines.

Brighter Books Publishing House

4825 Fairbrook Cresc.
Nanaimo, B.C. V9T 6M6
Tel: +1 (250) 585-7372
Email: info@brighterbooks.com
Website: http://www.brighterbooks.com

Publishes: Fiction; Nonfiction; *Areas:* Fantasy; How-to; Sci-Fi; *Markets:* Children's; Youth

Canadian publisher with a focus on children's books and educational books. See website for full guidelines and online submission system.

Brine Books Publishing

Email: Help@BrineBooks.com
Website: http://BrineBooks.com

Publishes: Fiction; Nonfiction; Poetry; *Areas:* Adventure; Arts; Crime; Criticism; Culture; Current Affairs; Drama; Entertainment; Fantasy; Historical; Horror; Humour; Literature; Men's Interests; Military; Mystery; New Age; Philosophy; Photography; Politics; Psychology; Religious; Romance; Sci-Fi; Short Stories; Sociology; Spiritual; Suspense; Thrillers; Translations; Westerns; Women's Interests; *Markets:* Adult; *Treatments:* Commercial; Contemporary; Cynical; Dark; Experimental; In-depth; Light; Literary; Mainstream; Niche; Popular; Positive; Progressive; Satirical; Serious; Traditional

Contact: Chris Brine and Olga Brine

We are an activist publishing house trying to raise awareness for human rights issues from all around the world. In doing so, we also will donate a fair portion of our earnings to these causes. Our hopes are to create a steady stream of funds to numerous human rights problems from human trafficking to domestic violence to racial or LGBT equality and many more. We will depend on our writers and readers to make this happen.

The Brucedale Press

Box 2259
Port Elgin, Ontario N0H 2C0
Tel: +1 (519) 832-6025
Email: info@brucedalepress.ca
Website: http://www.brucedalepress.ca

Publishes: Fiction; Nonfiction; *Areas:*
Historical; *Markets:* Adult; *Treatments:*
Literary

Publishes literary, historical, and pictorial
works focusing on the Bruce Peninsula and
Queen's Bush area of Ontario. Publishes
books by Canadian authors only. Query by
post in first instance. See website for full
details.

Central Avenue Publishing

Delta, British Columbia
Email:
meghan@centralavenuepublishing.com
Website:
http://www.centralavenuepublishing.com

Publishes: Fiction; Poetry; *Areas:*
Adventure; Arts; Autobiography; Beauty and
Fashion; Biography; Crime; Culture; Current
Affairs; Drama; Entertainment; Erotic;
Fantasy; Gothic; Historical; Horror;
Humour; Leisure; Lifestyle; Literature;
Media; Men's Interests; Military; Music;
Mystery; Nature; New Age; Philosophy;
Photography; Politics; Psychology;
Religious; Romance; Science; Sci-Fi; Self-
Help; Short Stories; Sociology; Spiritual;
Sport; Suspense; Technology; Theatre;
Thrillers; Translations; Travel; Westerns;
Women's Interests; *Markets:* Adult;
Children's; Family; Youth; *Treatments:*
Commercial; Contemporary; Cynical; Dark;
Experimental; In-depth; Light; Literary;
Mainstream; Niche; Popular; Positive;
Progressive; Satirical; Serious; Traditional

Contact: Michelle Halket

Press specialising in electronic books (with
select books going into print). Fiction,
poetry, short stories. Email with query, agent
not necessary.

Coastal West Publishing

324-1755 Robson Street
Vancouver, British Columbia
Fax: +1 (604) 677-6651
Email: info@coastalwest.ca
Website: http://coastalwest.ca

Publishes: Nonfiction; *Areas:* Biography;
Crime; Culture; Historical; Legal; Media;
Short Stories; Spiritual; *Markets:* Adult;
Family; Professional; *Treatments:* In-depth;
Literary; Niche; Positive; Progressive;
Serious

It is our goal to both educate and entertain
our readers with stories that have an
emphasis in and around the justice system
and all of its participants. Was founded on
and for the purpose of truth, encouragement,
education through books.

If you have a manuscript and would like us
to review it, make sure it falls into one of the
following categories:

Organized Crime
Law and Policing
The Criminal Court System
The Prison System
The Parole System
Youth Gangs
Testimonials of change in any of these
systems

Accepts manuscripts by snail mail, email and
fax.

Has won an award of Excellence Graphic
Design.

We do not accept books that are fictional or
that glorify crime, criminal behaviour or
illegal activities.

Submissions do not have a length required,
and do not need to be passed though a
literary agent.

Our staff is happy to answer any questions
you may have.

Everheart Books

Email:
meghan@centralavenuepublishing.com

Website: http://www.everheartbooks.com

Publishes: Fiction; Poetry; *Areas:* Erotic; Romance; *Markets:* Adult; Family; *Treatments:* Commercial; Contemporary; Cynical; Dark; Experimental; In-depth; Light; Literary; Mainstream; Niche; Popular; Positive; Progressive; Satirical; Serious; Traditional

Contact: Meg

We publish erotica and all subgenres of romance. Send us your query and first three chapters of your story. We pay royalties quarterly. We handle everything from cover design to distribution. We'd love to take a look at your romance or erotic novel.

Fifth House Publishers

Fitzhenry & Whiteside Limited
195 Allstate Parkway
Markham, Ontario L3R 4T8
Tel: +1 (800) 387-9776
Fax: +1 (800) 260-9777
Email: stewart@fifthhousepublishers.ca
Website: http://www.fifthhousepublishers.ca

Publishes: Nonfiction; *Areas:* Culture; Historical; Nature; *Markets:* Adult

Contact: Tracey Dettman

Publishes books on Canadian history, culture, and environment, particularly focusing on the west. See website for more details.

House of Anansi Press

110 Spadina Ave., Suite 801
Toronto, ON
M5V 2K4
Tel: +1 (416) 363-4343
Fax: +1 (416) 363-1017
Email: customerservice@houseofanansi.com
Website: http://www.houseofanansi.com

Publishes: Fiction; Nonfiction; Poetry; *Markets:* Adult; *Treatments:* Literary; Serious

Publishes literary fiction, poetry, and serious nonfiction. Particular interest in Canadian

writers; attitude towards international writers seems potentially contradictory:

"publishes Canadian and international writers..."

Yet further down the same page of their website:

"does not accept unsolicited materials from non-Canadian writers."

Kindred Productions

1310 Taylor Avenue
Winnipeg, MB R3M 3Z6
Tel: +1 (204) 669-6575
Fax: +1 (204) 654-1865
Email: custserv@kindredproductions.com
Website: https://www.kindredproductions.com

Publishes: Nonfiction; *Areas:* Historical; Religious; *Markets:* Adult; Children's; Youth

Religious book publisher. Send query by email for a copy of the full submission guidelines. See website for more details.

Kids Can Press

Corus Quay
25 Dockside Drive
Toronto, Ontario
M5A 0B5
Tel: +1 (416) 479-7000
Fax: +1 (416) 960-5437
Email: customerservice@kidscan.com
Website: http://www.kidscanpress.com

Publishes: Fiction; Nonfiction; *Markets:* Children's

Publishes quality picture books and nonfiction manuscripts for children, as well as chapter books for ages 7–10. No young adult fiction or fantasy novels for any age. No unsolicited manuscripts from children or teenagers, or from authors outside of Canada. No submissions by disk, fax, or email.

Magenta Publishing for the Arts
151 Winchester Street
Toronto, Ontario
M4X 1B5
Email: info@magentafoundation.org
Website: http://www.magentafoundation.org

Publishes: Nonfiction; *Areas:* Arts;
Photography; *Markets:* Adult

Established to publish works of art by
Canadian and International artists.

Manor House Publishing
452 Cottingham Crescent
Ancaster ON L9G 3V6
Email: mbdavie@manor-house.biz
Website: http://manor-house.biz

Publishes: Fiction; Nonfiction; Poetry;
Areas: Biography; Business; Fantasy; New
Age; Politics; Short Stories; *Markets:* Adult;
Youth

Send query by email only. See website for
full guidelines. Response only if interested.

MBooks of BC (Multicultural Books of British Columbia)
307 Birchwood Court
6311 Gilbert Road
Richmond, B.C.
V7C 3V7
Tel: +1 (604) 447-0979
Email: jrmbooks@hotmail.com
Website: http://www.mbooksofbc.com

Publishes: Fiction; Nonfiction; Poetry;
Markets: Adult; Children's; *Treatments:*
Literary

Contact: Joe M. Ruggier B.A.; Mr. Basil
Nainan

Small press publishing mainly poetry and
related literature. Also offers publishing
services. Send query with sample or
complete ms in first instance. See website for
more information.

Moose Hide Books
684 Walls Road
Sault Ste. Marie
Ontario
P6A 5K6
Tel: +1 (705) 779-3331
Fax: +1 (705) 779-3331
Email: ealcid@moosehidebooks.com
Website: http://www.moosehidebooks.com

Publishes: Fiction; Nonfiction; Poetry;
Areas: Adventure; Biography; Culture;
Drama; Fantasy; Historical; Humour;
Mystery; Short Stories; Suspense; Theatre;
Markets: Adult; Children's; Youth

Contact: Edmond Alcid (Editor)

Publishes novels, short story collections,
nonfiction, narrative verse, and theatrical
plays for age groups children to adult. Query
in first instance. See website for full details.

NeWest Press
Attn: Acquisitions
#201 8540 – 109 Street
Edmonton, Alberta T6G 1E6
Website: http://www.newestpress.com

Publishes: Fiction; Nonfiction; Poetry;
Scripts; *Areas:* Drama; Historical; Literature;
Nature; Politics; *Markets:* Adult;
Treatments: Literary

Publishes fiction, poetry, drama, and
nonfiction works with literary merit by
established and emerging Canadian authors.
Not considering poetry, mystery, or short
fiction manuscripts as at May 2012 (check
website for latest information). See website
for submission guidelines.

Pedlar Press
113 Bond Street
St John's NL
A1C 1T6
Email: feralgrl@interlog.com
Website: http://www.pedlarpress.com

Publishes: Fiction; Poetry; *Markets:* Adult;
Treatments: Contemporary; Experimental;
Literary

Publishes innovative contemporary Canadian poetry and fiction. Particularly interested in work that preserves and extends the literary tradition that values experimentation in style and form. Send query by email in first instance. No attachments.

Red Deer Press

195 Allstate Parkway
Markham, Ontario
L3R 4T8
Tel: +1 (905) 477-9700
Fax: +1 (905) 477-9179
Email: rdp@reddeerpress.com
Website: http://www.reddeerpress.com

Publishes: Fiction; Nonfiction; *Areas:* Biography; Drama; Fantasy; Historical; Sci-Fi; *Markets:* Adult; Children's; Youth; *Treatments:* Contemporary

Publishes fiction and nonfiction for adults and children of all ages, though currently less interested in picture books and more interested in middle grade and young adult fiction. See website for full submission guidelines.

Ronsdale Press

3350 West 21st Avenue
Vancouver, B.C.
V6S 1G7
Tel: +1 (604) 738-4688
Fax: +1 (604) 731-4548
Email: ronsdale@shaw.ca
Website: http://www.ronsdalepress.com

Publishes: Fiction; Nonfiction; Poetry; *Areas:* Biography; Historical; Short Stories; Theatre; *Markets:* Adult; Children's; *Treatments:* Literary

Contact: Ronald B. Hatch (General

Acquisition Editor); Veronica Hatch (Children's Acquisition Editor)

Literary publishing house, publishing fiction, poetry, biography, regional history, and children's literature. Particularly interested in young adult historical novels. No mass-market, pulp, mystery stories, or fiction that is entirely plot-driven. MSS considered only from writers who have had work published in literary magazines. See website for full submission guidelines.

All prospective authors are encouraged to familiarise themselves with the list (perusing the catalogue; reading published titles) to assess suitability before submitting. Send query with sample or full MS with SASE for response, with brief bio and list of writing credits (if any).

Second Story Press

20 Maud Street, Suite 401
Toronto ON
M5V 2M5
Tel: +1 (416) 537-7850
Fax: +1 (416) 537-0588
Email: info@secondstorypress.ca
Website: http://secondstorypress.ca

Publishes: Fiction; Nonfiction; *Areas:* Women's Interests; *Markets:* Adult; Children's

Canadian feminist press publishing fiction, nonfiction and children's books of special interest to women. Tries to focus on Canadian authors. No poetry, rhyming picture books, or books with anthropomorphised animals. Send query by post with SASE, synopsis, and up to three chapters. No submissions on disk or by email. See website for full guidelines.

Irish Publishers

For the most up-to-date listings of these and hundreds of other publishers, visit http://www.firstwriter.com/publishers

To claim your free access to the site, please see the back of this book.

Cork University Press

Tel: +353 (0) 21 490 2980
Email: corkuniversitypress@ucc.ie
Website:
http://www.corkuniversitypress.com

Publishes: Nonfiction; *Areas:* Architecture;
Arts; Cookery; Culture; Current Affairs;
Film; Historical; Legal; Literature; Music;
Philosophy; Politics; Travel; Women's
Interests; *Markets:* Academic

Publishes distinctive and distinguished
scholarship in the broad field of Irish
Cultural Studies.

The Educational Company of Ireland

Ballymount Road
Walkinstown
Dublin 12
Email: amulloy@edco.ie
Website: http://www.edco.ie

Publishes: Nonfiction; *Markets:* Academic;
Adult; Children's; Professional

Contact: Áine Mulloy

Publishes textbooks and ancillary
educational materials for the Primary and
Post-Primary markets. Submit proposals by
post or by email. See website for full
guidelines.

The Gallery Press

Loughcrew
Oldcastle
County Meath
Tel: +353 (0) 49 8541779
Fax: +353 (0) 49 8541779
Email: gallery@indigo.ie
Website: http://www.gallerypress.com

Publishes: Fiction; Nonfiction; Poetry;
Scripts; *Areas:* Theatre; *Markets:* Adult;
Treatments: Literary

Contact: Peter Fallon

Publishes poetry, drama, and prose by
Ireland's leading contemporary writers. See
website for submission guidelines. No
submissions by fax or email.

Institute of Public Administration (IPA)

57-61 Lansdowne Road
Ballsbridge
Dublin 4
Tel: +353 1 240 3600
Fax: +353 1 668 9135
Email: information@ipa.ie

Publishes: Nonfiction; *Areas:* Current
Affairs; Finance; Health; Legal; Politics;
Sociology; *Markets:* Academic; Professional

Irish publisher specialising in texts on public service administration and management.

John Lynch Digital Publishing House

Email:
sian@johnlynchdigitalpublishinghouse.com
Website: http://www.johnlynchdigital
publishinghouse.com

Publishes: Fiction; *Areas:* Romance; Sci-Fi; *Markets:* Adult; *Treatments:* Contemporary; Literary

Looking for novel-length literary or contemporary fiction (between 70,000 and 120,000 words). Will consider sub-genres within contemporary fiction (e.g. contemporary romance or science fiction), provided that they provide a compelling storyline and strong characters. Send query by email with synopsis and first three chapters. See website for full guidelines.

The Lilliput Press

62-63 Sitric Road
Arbour Hill
Dublin 7
Tel: +353 (01) 671 16 47
Fax: +353 (01) 671 12 33
Email: info@lilliputpress.ie
Website: http://www.lilliputpress.ie

Publishes: Fiction; Nonfiction; Poetry; Reference; Scripts; *Areas:* Architecture; Arts; Autobiography; Biography; Business; Cookery; Criticism; Culture; Current Affairs; Drama; Historical; Literature; Music; Nature; Philosophy; Photography; Politics; Sociology; Sport; Travel; *Markets:* Adult; *Treatments:* Literary; Popular

Publishes books broadly focused on Irish themes.

Mentor Books

43 Furze Road
Sandyford Industrial Estate
Dublin 18
Tel: 01 2952112
Fax: 01 295 2114
Email: admin@mentorbooks.ie

Website: http://www.mentorbooks.ie

Publishes: Nonfiction; *Areas:* Biography; Business; Crime; Historical; Humour; Politics; Science; Sport; *Markets:* Academic; Adult

Publishes educational books and general nonfiction of Irish interest.

Mercier Press

Unit 3b
Oak House
Bessboro Road
Blackrock
Cork
Tel: +353 21-4614700
Email: commissioning@mercierpress.ie
Website: http://www.mercierpress.ie

Publishes: Fiction; Nonfiction; *Areas:* Autobiography; Biography; Business; Cookery; Current Affairs; Health; Historical; Humour; Lifestyle; Military; Politics; Religious; Sport; *Markets:* Adult; Children's

Contact: Mary Feehan

Publishes Irish-interest fiction and nonfiction for adults and children. Prefers approaches by email. See website for full submission guidelines.

New Island

New Island
2 Brookside
Dundrum Road
Dublin 14
Tel: 00 353 1 2989937 / 2983411
Fax: 00 353 1 2982783
Email: editor@newisland.ie
Website: http://www.newisland.ie

Publishes: Fiction; Nonfiction; Poetry; Scripts; *Areas:* Biography; Criticism; Current Affairs; Drama; Historical; Humour; Literature; Politics; Sociology; Travel; Women's Interests; *Markets:* Adult; *Treatments:* Literary; Popular

Contact: Editorial Manager

Committed to literature and literary

---

publishing. Publishes in all literary areas, from fiction to drama to poetry. Also publishes nonfiction of Irish interest, especially social affairs and biographies. No children's books. Accepts submissions by email only. Send query with one-page synopsis and sample of the text as Word .doc or .docx attachments. Include details of any previous publications. No submissions by post. See website for full details.

The O'Brien Press

12 Terenure Road East
Rathgar
Dublin 6
Tel: +353-1-4923333
Fax: +353-1-4922777
Email: books@obrien.ie
Website: http://www.obrien.ie

Publishes: Fiction; Nonfiction; Poetry; Reference; *Areas:* Architecture; Arts; Autobiography; Biography; Business; Cookery; Crafts; Crime; Drama; Historical; Humour; Lifestyle; Literature; Music; Nature; Photography; Politics; Religious; Sport; Travel; *Markets:* Adult; Children's; Youth

Mainly publishes children's fiction, children's nonfiction and adult nonfiction. Generally doesn't publish poetry, academic works or adult fiction. Send synopsis and two or three sample chapters. If fewer than 1,000 words, send complete ms. See website for full guidelines.

Onstream Publications Ltd

Currabaha
Cloghroe
Blarney
Co. Cork
Tel: +353 21 4385798
Email: info@onstream.ie
Website: http://www.onstream.ie

Publishes: Fiction; Nonfiction; *Areas:* Cookery; Historical; Travel; *Markets:* Academic; Adult

Publisher of mainly nonfiction, although some fiction published. Also offers services to authors.

Poolbeg

123 Grange Hill
Baldoyle Industrial Estate
Baldoyle
Dublin 13
Tel: +353 1 832 1477
Email: info@poolbeg.com
Website: http://www.poolbeg.com

Publishes: Fiction; Nonfiction; *Areas:* Cookery; Gardening; Travel; *Markets:* Adult; Children's

Contact: Paula Campbell, publisher

Accepts submissions of nonfiction, and fiction up to 100,000 words. Send query by post with SASE, CV, short bio, first six chapters in hard copy, and full ms as Word file on CD. See website for full submission guidelines.

Somerville Press

Dromore
Bantry
Co. Cork
Tel: 353 (0) 28 32873
Fax: 353 (0) 28 328
Email: somervillepress@eircom.net
Website: http://www.somervillepress.com

Publishes: Fiction; Nonfiction; *Markets:* Adult

Publishes fiction and nonfiction of Irish interest.

Tirgearr Publishing

Email: info@tirgearrpublishing.com
Website: http://www.tirgearrpublishing.com

Publishes: Fiction; *Areas:* Adventure; Anthropology; Biography; Business; Cookery; Crafts; Crime; Culture; Current Affairs; Drama; Entertainment; Erotic; Fantasy; Film; Gothic; Health; Historical; Hobbies; Horror; How-to; Humour; Legal; Leisure; Lifestyle; Literature; Media; Men's Interests; Military; Nature; New Age; Romance; Science; Sci-Fi; Self-Help; Suspense; Technology; Thrillers; Westerns; Women's Interests; *Markets:* Adult; Family; Commercial; Contemporary; Popular

Contact: Kemberlee Shortland

A small independently-owned digital-only publishing company of adult genre fiction.

They offer full-circle services, working with authors on a one-on-one basis to ensure each book we publish is of the highest quality.

Australian Publishers

For the most up-to-date listings of these and hundreds of other publishers, visit http://www.firstwriter.com/publishers

*To claim your **free** access to the site, please see the back of this book.*

Hinkler Books
45-55 Fairchild Street
Heatherton
Victoria 3202
Tel: +61 (0) 3 9552 1333
Fax: +61 (0) 3 9558 2566
Email: editor@hinkler.com.au
Website: http://www.hinklerbooks.com

Publishes: Nonfiction; Reference; *Areas:* Cookery; Crafts; Health; Humour; Lifestyle; Music; Spiritual; Sport; *Markets:* Adult; Children's; Family

Book publisher and packager – creates and produces books for publishers and consumers around the world. Specialises in nonfiction for adults and children. Send one-page query by fax, post, or email in first instance. No unsolicited mss. See website for full details.

Publishers Subject Index

This section lists publishers by their subject matter, with directions to the section of the book where the full listing can be found.

You can create your own customised lists of publishers using different combinations of these subject areas, plus over a dozen other criteria, instantly online at http://www.firstwriter.com.

To claim your **free** access to the site, please see the back of this book.

Adventure
Anaiah Press, LLC (*US*)
Arcade Publishing (*US*)
Aurora Publishing, Inc (*US*)
BHW Publishing House (*UK*)
Blurbeo (*US*)
Boathook Books (*UK*)
Bold Strokes Books (*US*)
Brine Books Publishing (*Can*)
Burford Books (*US*)
Central Avenue Publishing (*Can*)
Changeling Press LLC (*US*)
CN Writers (*UK*)
Compelling Books (*UK*)
Ex-L-Ence Publishing (*UK*)
Fingerpress UK (*UK*)
Flame Lily Books (*UK*)
Gauthier Publications (*US*)
Geostar Publishing & Services LLC (*US*)
Glastonbury Publishing (*UK*)
The Glencannon Press (*US*)
High-Lonesome (*US*)
Indigo Dreams Publishing (*UK*)
Ingalls Publishing Group, Inc. (*US*)
Itoh Press (*US*)
Kane Miller Books (*US*)
Kelly Point Publishing LLC (*US*)
Kindred Rainbow Publishing (*UK*)
Listen & Live Audio, Inc. (*US*)
Lost Tower Publications (*UK*)
Lucky Marble Books (*US*)
M P Publishing USA (*US*)
Moonshadow Press (*US*)
Moose Hide Books (*Can*)
New Dawn Publishers Ltd (*UK*)
Netherworld Books (*UK*)
The New Curiosity Shop (*UK*)
Not Your Eyes (*UK*)
Open Idea Publishing, LLC (*US*)
The Orion Publishing Group Limited (*UK*)
Pants On Fire Press (*US*)
Papercutz (*US*)
Pen & Sword Books Ltd (*UK*)
Pocket Mountains (*UK*)
Ramsay Publishing (*UK*)
Shelfstealers (*US*)
Sunberry Books (*UK*)
Tirgearr Publishing (*Ire*)
Tantor Audio (*US*)
Tsaba House (*US*)
The Zharmae Publishing Press (*US*)

Anthropology
Alondra Press (*US*)
American Press (*US*)
Baywood Publishing Company, Inc. (*US*)
Blurbeo (*US*)
Eleusinian Press (*UK*)
Ex-L-Ence Publishing (*UK*)
Geostar Publishing & Services LLC (*US*)
Grand Canyon Association (*US*)
High-Lonesome (*US*)
The New Curiosity Shop (*UK*)
Not Your Eyes (*UK*)
Pluto Publishing Ltd (*UK*)
Princeton University Press (*US*)
Princeton University Press Europe (*UK*)
Sage Publications (*UK*)
Seren (*UK*)

Shelfstealers (*US*)
Sussex Academic Press (*UK*)
Tirgearr Publishing (*Ire*)
Tantor Audio (*US*)
Vanderbilt University Press (*US*)
Waveland Press, Inc. (*US*)

Antiques

Antique Collectors' Club Ltd (*UK*)
Dover Publications, Inc. (*US*)
Ex-L-Ence Publishing (*UK*)
Geostar Publishing & Services LLC (*US*)
Goss & Crested China Club (*UK*)
Indigo Dreams Publishing (*UK*)
New Cavendish Books (*UK*)
The New Curiosity Shop (*UK*)
Not Your Eyes (*UK*)
Octopus Publishing Group Limited (*UK*)
Tiger of the Stripe (*UK*)

Archaeology

Alondra Press (*US*)
Amberley Publishing (*UK*)
Ashmolean Museum Publications (*UK*)
Baywood Publishing Company, Inc. (*US*)
Duckworth Publishers (*UK*)
Eleusinian Press (*UK*)
Ex-L-Ence Publishing (*UK*)
Flame Lily Books (*UK*)
Geostar Publishing & Services LLC (*US*)
Grand Canyon Association (*US*)
Hadley Rille Books (*US*)
High-Lonesome (*US*)
Logaston Press (*UK*)
The New Curiosity Shop (*UK*)
Not Your Eyes (*UK*)
The Orion Publishing Group Limited (*UK*)
Pen & Sword Books Ltd (*UK*)
Princeton University Press (*US*)
Princeton University Press Europe (*UK*)
Sage Publications (*UK*)
Stacey International (*UK*)
Sussex Academic Press (*UK*)
Thames and Hudson Ltd (*UK*)
Tiger of the Stripe (*UK*)
Vanderbilt University Press (*US*)
Waveland Press, Inc. (*US*)

Architecture

American Press (*US*)
Antique Collectors' Club Ltd (*UK*)
Ashgate Publishing Limited (*UK*)
Betterway Home Books (*US*)
Cork University Press (*Ire*)
The Crowood Press (*UK*)
Dovecote Press (*UK*)
Dover Publications, Inc. (*US*)
Eleusinian Press (*UK*)
Ex-L-Ence Publishing (*UK*)
Floris Books (*UK*)
Geostar Publishing & Services LLC (*US*)
Grand Canyon Association (*US*)
Guild of Master Craftsman (GMC) Publications
Ltd (*UK*)
Harry N. Abrams, Inc. (*US*)
Homestead Publishing (*US*)

The Lilliput Press (*Ire*)
Frances Lincoln Ltd (*UK*)
Methuen Publishing Ltd (*UK*)
The New Curiosity Shop (*UK*)
Not Your Eyes (*UK*)
The O'Brien Press (*Ire*)
Octopus Publishing Group Limited (*UK*)
The Overlook Press (*US*)
Paul Dry Books, Inc. (*US*)
Phaidon Press Limited (*UK*)
Prestel Publishing Ltd (*UK*)
Princeton University Press (*US*)
Princeton University Press Europe (*UK*)
Quiller Publishing Ltd (*UK*)
Rio Nuevo Publishers (*US*)
Sheldrake Press (*UK*)
Shelfstealers (*US*)
Thames and Hudson Ltd (*UK*)
Tiger of the Stripe (*UK*)
Tuttle Publishing (*US*)
Unicorn Press Ltd (*UK*)
Waveland Press, Inc. (*US*)

Arts

American Press (*US*)
Antique Collectors' Club Ltd (*UK*)
Arcade Publishing (*US*)
Ashgate Publishing Limited (*UK*)
Ashmolean Museum Publications (*UK*)
Aurora Metro Press (*UK*)
Aurum Press Ltd (*UK*)
Bick Publishing House (*US*)
Bloomsbury Publishing Plc (*UK*)
Booth-Clibborn Editions (*UK*)
Brine Books Publishing (*Can*)
Central Avenue Publishing (*Can*)
Co & Bear Productions (*UK*)
Constable & Robinson Ltd (*UK*)
Cork University Press (*Ire*)
The Creative Company (*US*)
Crescent Moon Publishing (*UK*)
The Crowood Press (*UK*)
Dover Publications, Inc. (*US*)
Eleusinian Press (*UK*)
Enitharmon Press (*UK*)
Erotic Review (ER) Books (*UK*)
Evans Brothers Ltd (*UK*)
Ex-L-Ence Publishing (*UK*)
F&W Media International Ltd (*UK*)
Floris Books (*UK*)
Fox Chapel Publishing (*US*)
Geostar Publishing & Services LLC (*US*)
Gibson Square Books Ltd (*UK*)
Gomer Press (*UK*)
Guild of Master Craftsman (GMC) Publications
Ltd (*UK*)
Halsgrove (*UK*)
Harry N. Abrams, Inc. (*US*)
Homestead Publishing (*US*)
Icon Books Ltd (*UK*)
The Ilex Press (*UK*)
Immedium (*US*)
Impact Books (*US*)
Indigo Dreams Publishing (*UK*)

The Lilliput Press (*Ire*)
Frances Lincoln Ltd (*UK*)
Linden Publishing (*US*)
Luath Press Ltd (*UK*)
Magenta Publishing for the Arts (*Can*)
Mainstream Publishing Co. (Edinburgh) Ltd (*UK*)
Mandala Earth (*US*)
Mandrake of Oxford (*UK*)
Medallion Media Group (*US*)
New Cavendish Books (*UK*)
The New Curiosity Shop (*UK*)
Northumbria University Press (*UK*)
Not Your Eyes (*UK*)
The O'Brien Press (*Ire*)
Octopus Publishing Group Limited (*UK*)
Open Idea Publishing, LLC (*US*)
The Orion Publishing Group Limited (*UK*)
The Overlook Press (*US*)
Peter Owen Publishers (*UK*)
Phaidon Press Limited (*UK*)
Prestel Publishing Ltd (*UK*)
Princeton University Press (*US*)
Princeton University Press Europe (*UK*)
Quarto Publishing Group UK (*UK*)
Quarto Publishing Group USA (*US*)
Quest Books (*US*)
Rio Nuevo Publishers (*US*)
Robert Hale Publishers (*UK*)
Sage Publications (*UK*)
Seafarer Books (*UK*)
Seren (*UK*)
Shelfstealers (*US*)
Stemmer House Publishers (*US*)
Sunbury Press (*US*)
Sussex Academic Press (*UK*)
Thames and Hudson Ltd (*UK*)
Tiger of the Stripe (*UK*)
Tuttle Publishing (*US*)
Unicorn Press Ltd (*UK*)
University of Tampa Press (*US*)
Waveland Press, Inc. (*US*)
Williamson Books (*US*)
ZigZag Education (*UK*)
Autobiography
Arcade Publishing (*US*)
Aureus Publishing Limited (*UK*)
Black & White Publishing Ltd (*UK*)
Black Lawrence Press (*US*)
Blackstaff Press Ltd (*UK*)
John Blake Publishing (*UK*)
Cadence Jazz Books (*US*)
Canongate Books (*UK*)
Canterbury House Publishing, Ltd (*US*)
Central Avenue Publishing (*Can*)
Chicago Review Press (*US*)
City Lights Publishers (*US*)
Coffee House Press (*US*)
Compelling Books (*UK*)
Constable & Robinson Ltd (*UK*)
The Countryman Press (*US*)
Cross-Cultural Communications Publications (*US*)

Eleusinian Press (*UK*)
Ex-L-Ence Publishing (*UK*)
Geostar Publishing & Services LLC (*US*)
Gomer Press (*UK*)
Heritage Books, Inc. (*US*)
Halban Publishers (*UK*)
Honno Welsh Women's Press (*UK*)
Indigo Dreams Publishing (*UK*)
Ingalls Publishing Group, Inc. (*US*)
Itoh Press (*US*)
The Lilliput Press (*Ire*)
Listen & Live Audio, Inc. (*US*)
Lost Tower Publications (*UK*)
Mainstream Publishing Co. (Edinburgh) Ltd (*UK*)
Mango Publishing (*UK*)
Medallion Media Group (*US*)
Mercier Press (*Ire*)
Methuen Publishing Ltd (*UK*)
New Rivers Press (*US*)
Not Your Eyes (*UK*)
The O'Brien Press (*Ire*)
The Orion Publishing Group Limited (*UK*)
Paul Dry Books, Inc. (*US*)
Peachtree Publishers (*US*)
Pen & Sword Books Ltd (*UK*)
Persea Books (*US*)
Piatkus Books (*UK*)
Pressgang (*US*)
Reading Harbor (*US*)
Rio Nuevo Publishers (*US*)
Robert Hale Publishers (*UK*)
Shearsman Books (*UK*)
Shelfstealers (*US*)
Tantor Audio (*US*)
Texas Tech University Press (*US*)
Tiger of the Stripe (*UK*)
Tsaba House (*US*)
Beauty and Fashion
Antique Collectors' Club Ltd (*UK*)
Central Avenue Publishing (*Can*)
Co & Bear Productions (*UK*)
Ex-L-Ence Publishing (*UK*)
Geostar Publishing & Services LLC (*US*)
Harry N. Abrams, Inc. (*US*)
Itoh Press (*US*)
Luath Press Ltd (*UK*)
The New Curiosity Shop (*UK*)
Not Your Eyes (*UK*)
The Orion Publishing Group Limited (*UK*)
Phaidon Press Limited (*UK*)
Prestel Publishing Ltd (*UK*)
Quarto Publishing Group UK (*UK*)
Shelfstealers (*US*)
Thames and Hudson Ltd (*UK*)
Tsaba House (*US*)
Biography
ABC-CLIO / Greenwood (*US*)
Amberley Publishing (*UK*)
Aureus Publishing Limited (*UK*)
Aurora Metro Press (*UK*)
Aurum Press Ltd (*UK*)
BHW Publishing House (*UK*)

Black & White Publishing Ltd (*UK*)
Black Lawrence Press (*US*)
Blackstaff Press Ltd (*UK*)
John Blake Publishing (*UK*)
Blue Dolphin Publishing (*US*)
Bowker (UK) Ltd (*UK*)
Cadence Jazz Books (*US*)
Canongate Books (*UK*)
Centerstream Publishing (*US*)
Central Avenue Publishing (*Can*)
Chicago Review Press (*US*)
Christian Focus Publications (*UK*)
Coastal West Publishing (*Can*)
Colin Smythe Ltd (*UK*)
Compelling Books (*UK*)
Constable & Robinson Ltd (*UK*)
The Creative Company (*US*)
Dovecote Press (*UK*)
Duckworth Publishers (*UK*)
Eleusinian Press (*UK*)
Ex-L-Ence Publishing (*UK*)
Faber & Faber Ltd (*UK*)
Flame Lily Books (*UK*)
Floris Books (*UK*)
Frederic C. Beil, Publisher (*US*)
Geostar Publishing & Services LLC (*US*)
Gibson Square Books Ltd (*UK*)
Gomer Press (*UK*)
Halban Publishers (*UK*)
Halsgrove (*UK*)
Headland Publications (*UK*)
High-Lonesome (*US*)
Homestead Publishing (*US*)
House of Lochar (*UK*)
The Ilium Press (*US*)
Indigo Dreams Publishing (*UK*)
John F. Blair, Publisher (*US*)
Kamehameha Publishing (*US*)
The Lilliput Press (*Ire*)
Listen & Live Audio, Inc. (*US*)
Logaston Press (*UK*)
Luath Press Ltd (*UK*)
Mainstream Publishing Co. (Edinburgh) Ltd (*UK*)
Manor House Publishing (*Can*)
Medallion Media Group (*US*)
Mentor Books (*Ire*)
Mercier Press (*Ire*)
Methuen Publishing Ltd (*UK*)
Moose Hide Books (*Can*)
Neil Wilson Publishing Ltd (*UK*)
The New Curiosity Shop (*UK*)
New Island (*Ire*)
New Victoria Publishers (*US*)
Nicolas Hays Publishers (*US*)
Northumbria University Press (*UK*)
Not Your Eyes (*UK*)
The O'Brien Press (*Ire*)
Michael O'Mara Books Ltd (*UK*)
Omnibus Press (*UK*)
Oneworld Publications (*UK*)
The Orion Publishing Group Limited (*UK*)
Peter Owen Publishers (*UK*)

P&R Publishing (*US*)
Paul Dry Books, Inc. (*US*)
Pauline Books and Media (*US*)
Peachtree Publishers (*US*)
Pen & Sword Books Ltd (*UK*)
Pennant Books Ltd (*UK*)
Persea Books (*US*)
Piatkus Books (*UK*)
Plexus Publishing Limited (*UK*)
Profile Books (*UK*)
Quiller Publishing Ltd (*UK*)
Red Deer Press (*Can*)
Rio Nuevo Publishers (*US*)
Robert Hale Publishers (*UK*)
Ronsdale Press (*Can*)
Seren (*UK*)
Shelfstealers (*US*)
Shepheard-Walwyn (Publishers) Ltd (*UK*)
SportsBooks Limited (*UK*)
Sussex Academic Press (*UK*)
Tirgearr Publishing (*Ire*)
Tantor Audio (*US*)
Texas Tech University Press (*US*)
Thames and Hudson Ltd (*UK*)
Tiger of the Stripe (*UK*)
Tsaba House (*US*)
Unicorn Press Ltd (*UK*)
Business
Alexander Hamilton Institute (*US*)
American Press (*US*)
Antique Collectors' Club Ltd (*UK*)
Arcade Publishing (*US*)
Ashgate Publishing Limited (*UK*)
Bowker (UK) Ltd (*UK*)
Chartered Institute of Personnel and Development (CIPD) Publishing (*UK*)
Chemical Publishing Company (*US*)
ETC Publications (*US*)
Euromonitor (*UK*)
Ex-L-Ence Publishing (*UK*)
F&W Media International Ltd (*UK*)
Flame Lily Books (*UK*)
Geostar Publishing & Services LLC (*US*)
Glenbridge Publishing Ltd (*US*)
The Lilliput Press (*Ire*)
Management Books 2000 Ltd (*UK*)
Manor House Publishing (*Can*)
Medical Group Management Association (MGMA) (*US*)
Mentor Books (*Ire*)
Mercier Press (*Ire*)
The New Curiosity Shop (*UK*)
Not Your Eyes (*UK*)
The O'Brien Press (*Ire*)
Oneworld Publications (*UK*)
Piatkus Books (*UK*)
Possibility Press (*US*)
Profile Books (*UK*)
Quiller Publishing Ltd (*UK*)
Reed Business Information (RBI) (*UK*)
Sage Publications (*UK*)
Shelfstealers (*US*)
TSO (The Stationery Office) (*UK*)

Tirgearr Publishing (*Ire*)
Tantor Audio (*US*)
Tiger of the Stripe (*UK*)
Tuttle Publishing (*US*)
Waveland Press, Inc. (*US*)
William Reed Business Media (*UK*)
Wolters Kluwer (UK) Ltd (*UK*)
ZigZag Education (*UK*)

Cookery
Absolute Press (*UK*)
Arcade Publishing (*US*)
Aurora Metro Press (*UK*)
Black & White Publishing Ltd (*UK*)
Blackstaff Press Ltd (*UK*)
John Blake Publishing (*UK*)
Bristol Publishing Enterprises (*US*)
Burford Books (*US*)
Clear Light Books (*US*)
Constable & Robinson Ltd (*UK*)
Cork University Press (*Ire*)
The Countryman Press (*US*)
Ex-L-Ence Publishing (*UK*)
Farcountry Press (*US*)
Flame Lily Books (*UK*)
Flame Tree Publishing (*UK*)
Fox Chapel Publishing (*US*)
Geddes & Grosset (*UK*)
Geostar Publishing & Services LLC (*US*)
Glenbridge Publishing Ltd (*US*)
Grub Street Publishing (*UK*)
Guild of Master Craftsman (GMC) Publications
Ltd (*UK*)
The Harvard Common Press (*US*)
Hearts 'N Tummies Cookbook Co. / Quixote
Press (*US*)
Hinkler Books (*Aus*)
Homestead Publishing (*US*)
Igloo Books Limited (*UK*)
Jonathan David Publishers, Inc. (*US*)
Kyle Books (*UK*)
The Lilliput Press (*Ire*)
Mercier Press (*Ire*)
Neil Wilson Publishing Ltd (*UK*)
The New Curiosity Shop (*UK*)
New Victoria Publishers (*US*)
Not Your Eyes (*UK*)
The O'Brien Press (*Ire*)
Octopus Publishing Group Limited (*UK*)
Onstream Publications Ltd (*Ire*)
The Orion Publishing Group Limited (*UK*)
Phaidon Press Limited (*UK*)
Piccadilly Books Ltd (*US*)
Poolbeg (*Ire*)
Quarto Publishing Group UK (*UK*)
Quarto Publishing Group USA (*US*)
Quiller Publishing Ltd (*UK*)
Rio Nuevo Publishers (*US*)
Robert Hale Publishers (*UK*)
Sheldrake Press (*UK*)
Shelfstealers (*US*)
Tirgearr Publishing (*Ire*)
Tantor Audio (*US*)
Tiger of the Stripe (*UK*)

Top That! Publishing (*UK*)
Tuttle Publishing (*US*)
Williamson Books (*US*)

Crafts
Antique Collectors' Club Ltd (*UK*)
Aurum Press Ltd (*UK*)
Brown, Son & Ferguson, Ltd (*UK*)
Chicago Review Press (*US*)
The Countryman Press (*US*)
The Creative Company (*US*)
The Crowood Press (*UK*)
Divertir Publishing LLC (*US*)
Dover Publications, Inc. (*US*)
Ex-L-Ence Publishing (*UK*)
F&W Media International Ltd (*UK*)
Flame Lily Books (*UK*)
Floris Books (*UK*)
Fox Chapel Publishing (*US*)
Gem Guides Book Co. (*US*)
Geostar Publishing & Services LLC (*US*)
Guild of Master Craftsman (GMC) Publications
Ltd (*UK*)
Harry N. Abrams, Inc. (*US*)
Hinkler Books (*Aus*)
Kalmbach Publishing Co. (*US*)
Linden Publishing (*US*)
The New Curiosity Shop (*UK*)
Not Your Eyes (*UK*)
The O'Brien Press (*Ire*)
Octopus Publishing Group Limited (*UK*)
Quarto Publishing Group UK (*UK*)
Quarto Publishing Group USA (*US*)
Seafarer Books (*UK*)
Tirgearr Publishing (*Ire*)
Tiger of the Stripe (*UK*)
Williamson Books (*US*)

Crime
Amberley Publishing (*UK*)
BHW Publishing House (*UK*)
Black & White Publishing Ltd (*UK*)
John Blake Publishing (*UK*)
Blurbeo (*US*)
Bold Strokes Books (*US*)
bookouture (*UK*)
Brine Books Publishing (*Can*)
Central Avenue Publishing (*Can*)
CN Writers (*UK*)
Coastal West Publishing (*Can*)
Compelling Books (*UK*)
Constable & Robinson Ltd (*UK*)
Ex-L-Ence Publishing (*UK*)
Fingerpress UK (*UK*)
Flame Lily Books (*UK*)
Geostar Publishing & Services LLC (*US*)
Ghostwoods Books (*UK*)
Glastonbury Publishing (*UK*)
Harlequin Mills & Boon Ltd (*UK*)
High-Lonesome (*US*)
The Ilium Press (*US*)
Indigo Dreams Publishing (*UK*)
Ingalls Publishing Group, Inc. (*US*)
Itoh Press (*US*)
Jewish Lights Publishing (*US*)

Thames and Hudson Ltd (*UK*)
Tiger of the Stripe (*UK*)
Trentham Books Limited (*UK*)
Tuttle Publishing (*US*)
University of Wales Press (*UK*)
Vanderbilt University Press (*US*)
Voyageur Press (*US*)
Wallflower Press (*UK*)
Westminster John Knox Press (WJK) (*US*)
The X Press (*UK*)

Current Affairs
Arcade Publishing (*US*)
Aurum Press Ltd (*UK*)
Brine Books Publishing (*Can*)
Central Avenue Publishing (*Can*)
Christian Focus Publications (*UK*)
Constable & Robinson Ltd (*UK*)
Cork University Press (*Ire*)
Dagda Publishing (*UK*)
Divertir Publishing LLC (*US*)
Eleusinian Press (*UK*)
Ex-L-Ence Publishing (*UK*)
Geostar Publishing & Services LLC (*US*)
Gibson Square Books Ltd (*UK*)
Institute of Public Administration (IPA) (*Ire*)
Itoh Press (*US*)
The Lilliput Press (*Ire*)
Luath Press Ltd (*UK*)
Mainstream Publishing Co. (Edinburgh) Ltd (*UK*)
Mercier Press (*Ire*)
Methuen Publishing Ltd (*UK*)
New Dawn Publishers Ltd (*UK*)
The New Curiosity Shop (*UK*)
New Island (*Ire*)
Nortia Press (*US*)
Not Your Eyes (*UK*)
Oneworld Publications (*UK*)
The Orion Publishing Group Limited (*UK*)
The Overlook Press (*US*)
Oxford University Press (*UK*)
Pluto Publishing Ltd (*UK*)
Profile Books (*UK*)
Quarto Publishing Group USA (*US*)
Reading Harbor (*US*)
Reed Business Information (RBI) (*UK*)
Rivers Oram Press (*UK*)
Seren (*UK*)
Shelfstealers (*US*)
Sunbury Press (*US*)
TSO (The Stationery Office) (*UK*)
Tirgearr Publishing (*Ire*)
Tantor Audio (*US*)
Tiger of the Stripe (*UK*)
Tsaba House (*US*)

Design
Antique Collectors' Club Ltd (*UK*)
Betterway Home Books (*US*)
Booth-Clibborn Editions (*UK*)
Co & Bear Productions (*UK*)
Evans Brothers Ltd (*UK*)
Ex-L-Ence Publishing (*UK*)
Flame Lily Books (*UK*)

Fox Chapel Publishing (*US*)
Geostar Publishing & Services LLC (*US*)
Gulf Publishing Company (*US*)
Harry N. Abrams, Inc. (*US*)
Homestead Publishing (*US*)
Frances Lincoln Ltd (*UK*)
Medallion Media Group (*US*)
The New Curiosity Shop (*UK*)
Not Your Eyes (*UK*)
Octopus Publishing Group Limited (*UK*)
The Orion Publishing Group Limited (*UK*)
The Overlook Press (*US*)
Phaidon Press Limited (*UK*)
Prestel Publishing Ltd (*UK*)
Quarto Publishing Group UK (*UK*)
Quarto Publishing Group USA (*US*)
Rio Nuevo Publishers (*US*)
Sheldrake Press (*UK*)
Thames and Hudson Ltd (*UK*)
Tiger of the Stripe (*UK*)
Tuttle Publishing (*US*)
Waveland Press, Inc. (*US*)
ZigZag Education (*UK*)

Drama
American Press (*US*)
Anaiah Press, LLC (*US*)
Aurora Metro Press (*UK*)
Blurbeo (*US*)
Brine Books Publishing (*Can*)
Bronze Man Books (*US*)
Central Avenue Publishing (*Can*)
Chapman Publishing (*UK*)
Colin Smythe Ltd (*UK*)
Cressrelles Publishing Co. Ltd (*UK*)
Dagda Publishing (*UK*)
Eleusinian Press (*UK*)
Evans Brothers Ltd (*UK*)
Ex-L-Ence Publishing (*UK*)
Faber & Faber Ltd (*UK*)
Flame Lily Books (*UK*)
Geostar Publishing & Services LLC (*US*)
Glass Page Books (*US*)
Glastonbury Publishing (*UK*)
Gomer Press (*UK*)
Itoh Press (*US*)
The Lilliput Press (*Ire*)
Luath Press Ltd (*UK*)
Moose Hide Books (*Can*)
New Dawn Publishers Ltd (*UK*)
The New Curiosity Shop (*UK*)
New Island (*Ire*)
NeWest Press (*Can*)
Not Your Eyes (*UK*)
The O'Brien Press (*Ire*)
Oberon Books (*UK*)
Open Idea Publishing, LLC (*US*)
Oxford University Press (*UK*)
Pants On Fire Press (*US*)
Pressgang (*US*)
Red Deer Press (*Can*)
SalGad Publishing Group (*UK*)
Samuel French Ltd (*UK*)
Seren (*UK*)

Fiction

Alma Books Ltd (*UK*)
Alondra Press (*US*)
Anaiah Press, LLC (*US*)
Andersen Press Ltd (*UK*)
Annick Press (*Can*)
Arcade Publishing (*US*)
Aunt Lute Books (*US*)
Aurora Metro Press (*UK*)
Aurora Publishing, Inc (*US*)
Award Publications Limited (*UK*)
Azro Press (*US*)
Barrington Stoke (*UK*)
BHW Publishing House (*UK*)
Bick Publishing House (*US*)
Black & White Publishing Ltd (*UK*)
Black Lawrence Press (*US*)
Blackstaff Press Ltd (*UK*)
John Blake Publishing (*UK*)
Blind Eye Books (*US*)
Bloomsbury Publishing Plc (*UK*)
Bloomsbury Spark (*UK*)
Blue Dolphin Publishing (*US*)
Blurbeo (*US*)
Boathook Books (*UK*)
Bold Strokes Books (*US*)
bookouture (*UK*)
Bracket Books (*US*)
Brighter Books Publishing House (*Can*)
Brine Books Publishing (*Can*)
Bronze Man Books (*US*)
The Brucedale Press (*Can*)
Bullitt Publishing (*US*)
By Light Unseen Media (*US*)
Canongate Books (*UK*)
Canterbury House Publishing, Ltd (*US*)
Cedar Fort (*US*)
Central Avenue Publishing (*Can*)
Changeling Press LLC (*US*)
Chapman Publishing (*UK*)
Chicago Review Press (*US*)
Christian Focus Publications (*UK*)
City Lights Publishers (*US*)
Classical Comics Limited (*UK*)
CN Writers (*UK*)
Coffee House Press (*US*)
Colin Smythe Ltd (*UK*)
Compelling Books (*UK*)
Constable & Robinson Ltd (*UK*)
The Creative Company (*US*)
Crescent Moon Publishing (*UK*)
Cross-Cultural Communications Publications (*US*)
Cup of Tea Books (*US*)
DC Thomson (*UK*)
Dedalus Ltd (*UK*)
Digital Manga, Inc. (*US*)
Divertir Publishing LLC (*US*)
Down East Books (*US*)
Down The Shore Publishing (*US*)
Dragonfairy Press (*US*)
Duckworth Publishers (*UK*)
Dzanc Books (*US*)

EDCON Publishing Group (*US*)
Egmont UK Ltd (*UK*)
Eleusinian Press (*UK*)
Emissary Publishing (*UK*)
Enitharmon Press (*UK*)
Erotic Review (ER) Books (*UK*)
Evans Brothers Ltd (*UK*)
Everheart Books (*Can*)
Ex-L-Ence Publishing (*UK*)
Faber & Faber Ltd (*UK*)
Faery Rose (*US*)
Fingerpress UK (*UK*)
Fitzrovia Press Limited (*UK*)
Flame Lily Books (*UK*)
Florida Academic Press (*US*)
Floris Books (*UK*)
48fourteen (*US*)
Four Way Books (*US*)
Frederic C. Beil, Publisher (*US*)
Freya's Bower (*US*)
The Gallery Press (*Ire*)
Gauthier Publications (*US*)
Geddes & Grosset (*UK*)
Ghostwoods Books (*UK*)
Gibson Square Books Ltd (*UK*)
Glass Page Books (*US*)
Glastonbury Publishing (*UK*)
Glenbridge Publishing Ltd (*US*)
The Glencannon Press (*US*)
Gomer Press (*UK*)
Grand Canyon Association (*US*)
Gullane Children's Books (*UK*)
Heritage Books, Inc. (*US*)
The Habit of Rainy Nights Press (*US*)
Hachette Children's Books (*UK*)
Hachette UK (*UK*)
Hadley Rille Books (*US*)
Halban Publishers (*UK*)
Harlequin Mills & Boon Ltd (*UK*)
Harry N. Abrams, Inc. (*US*)
Headland Publications (*UK*)
Hearts 'N Tummies Cookbook Co. / Quixote Press (*US*)
High-Lonesome (*US*)
Highland Press (*US*)
Homestead Publishing (*US*)
Honno Welsh Women's Press (*UK*)
Hopewell Publications (*US*)
House of Anansi Press (*Can*)
House of Lochar (*UK*)
Ideals Publications (*US*)
Igloo Books Limited (*UK*)
The Ilium Press (*US*)
Image Comics (*US*)
ImaJinn Books (*US*)
Immedium (*US*)
Impress Books Limited (*UK*)
Indigo Dreams Publishing (*UK*)
Ingalls Publishing Group, Inc. (*US*)
Ion Imagination Entertainment, Inc. (*US*)
Itoh Press (*US*)
Jewish Lights Publishing (*US*)
Jo Fletcher Books (*UK*)

Tristan Publishing (*US*)
Tsaba House (*US*)
Tuttle Publishing (*US*)
University of Nebraska Press (*US*)
University of Tampa Press (*US*)
Unthank Books (*UK*)
Usborne Publishing (*UK*)
The Wild Rose Press (*US*)
The X Press (*UK*)
The Zharmae Publishing Press (*US*)
Film
Aurum Press Ltd (*UK*)
BFI Publishing (*UK*)
Chicago Review Press (*US*)
Cork University Press (*Ire*)
Crescent Moon Publishing (*UK*)
The Crowood Press (*UK*)
Eleusinian Press (*UK*)
Ex-L-Ence Publishing (*UK*)
Faber & Faber Ltd (*UK*)
Flame Lily Books (*UK*)
Geostar Publishing & Services LLC (*US*)
Glenbridge Publishing Ltd (*US*)
Guild of Master Craftsman (GMC) Publications Ltd (*UK*)
Harry N. Abrams, Inc. (*US*)
Indigo Dreams Publishing (*UK*)
Itoh Press (*US*)
Methuen Publishing Ltd (*UK*)
The New Curiosity Shop (*UK*)
Nick Hern Books Ltd (*UK*)
Not Your Eyes (*UK*)
Octopus Publishing Group Limited (*UK*)
The Overlook Press (*US*)
Phaidon Press Limited (*UK*)
Plexus Publishing Limited (*UK*)
Princeton University Press (*US*)
Princeton University Press Europe (*UK*)
Tirgearr Publishing (*Ire*)
Tiger of the Stripe (*UK*)
Titan Books (*UK*)
Wallflower Press (*UK*)
Finance
American Press (*US*)
Ex-L-Ence Publishing (*UK*)
Geostar Publishing & Services LLC (*US*)
Glenbridge Publishing Ltd (*US*)
Humanics Publishing Group (*US*)
Institute of Public Administration (IPA) (*Ire*)
Management Books 2000 Ltd (*UK*)
Not Your Eyes (*UK*)
Oxford University Press (*UK*)
Pluto Publishing Ltd (*UK*)
Possibility Press (*US*)
Princeton University Press (*US*)
Princeton University Press Europe (*UK*)
Profile Books (*UK*)
Reed Business Information (RBI) (*UK*)
Ruka Press (*US*)
Sage Publications (*UK*)
Shelfstealers (*US*)
Shepheard-Walwyn (Publishers) Ltd (*UK*)
Sussex Academic Press (*UK*)

Tantor Audio (*US*)
Tiger of the Stripe (*UK*)
Tsaba House (*US*)
Waveland Press, Inc. (*US*)
Which? Books (*UK*)
Wolters Kluwer (UK) Ltd (*UK*)
ZigZag Education (*UK*)
Gardening
Antique Collectors' Club Ltd (*UK*)
Burford Books (*US*)
Chicago Review Press (*US*)
Constable & Robinson Ltd (*UK*)
The Crowood Press (*UK*)
Ex-L-Ence Publishing (*UK*)
F&W Media International Ltd (*UK*)
Flame Lily Books (*UK*)
Fox Chapel Publishing (*US*)
Fulcrum Publishing (*US*)
Geostar Publishing & Services LLC (*US*)
Guild of Master Craftsman (GMC) Publications Ltd (*UK*)
Harry N. Abrams, Inc. (*US*)
Kyle Books (*UK*)
Frances Lincoln Ltd (*UK*)
The New Curiosity Shop (*UK*)
Not Your Eyes (*UK*)
Octopus Publishing Group Limited (*UK*)
The Orion Publishing Group Limited (*UK*)
Poolbeg (*Ire*)
Quarto Publishing Group UK (*UK*)
Quiller Publishing Ltd (*UK*)
Rio Nuevo Publishers (*US*)
Thames and Hudson Ltd (*UK*)
Tiger of the Stripe (*UK*)
Tuttle Publishing (*US*)
Which? Books (*UK*)
Gothic
Central Avenue Publishing (*Can*)
CN Writers (*UK*)
Compelling Books (*UK*)
Dagda Publishing (*UK*)
Ex-L-Ence Publishing (*UK*)
Fingerpress UK (*UK*)
Geostar Publishing & Services LLC (*US*)
Ghostwoods Books (*UK*)
Glastonbury Publishing (*UK*)
Indigo Dreams Publishing (*UK*)
Itoh Press (*US*)
Lost Tower Publications (*UK*)
M P Publishing USA (*US*)
New Dawn Publishers Ltd (*UK*)
Netherworld Books (*UK*)
The New Curiosity Shop (*UK*)
Not Your Eyes (*UK*)
Salt Publishing Ltd (*UK*)
Tirgearr Publishing (*Ire*)
Tantor Audio (*US*)
Health
American Press (*US*)
Baywood Publishing Company, Inc. (*US*)
Bick Publishing House (*US*)
John Blake Publishing (*UK*)
Blue Dolphin Publishing (*US*)

Constable & Robinson Ltd (*UK*)
The Creative Company (*US*)
The Crowood Press (*UK*)
Eastland Press (*US*)
Eleusinian Press (*UK*)
EMIS Inc. Medical Publishers (*US*)
Ex-L-Ence Publishing (*UK*)
Floris Books (*UK*)
Geostar Publishing & Services LLC (*US*)
Grub Street Publishing (*UK*)
Hinkler Books (*Aus*)
Institute of Public Administration (IPA) (*Ire*)
Jones & Bartlett Learning (*US*)
Kyle Books (*UK*)
Listen & Live Audio, Inc. (*US*)
Mainstream Publishing Co. (Edinburgh) Ltd (*UK*)
Mandrake of Oxford (*UK*)
Medallion Media Group (*US*)
Mercier Press (*Ire*)
Nicolas Hays Publishers (*US*)
Not Your Eyes (*UK*)
Octopus Publishing Group Limited (*UK*)
The Orion Publishing Group Limited (*UK*)
The Overlook Press (*US*)
Pants On Fire Press (*US*)
Pavilion Publishing (*UK*)
Peachtree Publishers (*US*)
Piatkus Books (*UK*)
Piccadilly Books Ltd (*US*)
Possibility Press (*US*)
Quarto Publishing Group UK (*UK*)
Quarto Publishing Group USA (*US*)
Quest Books (*US*)
Radcliffe Publishing Ltd (*UK*)
Rowman & Littlefield Publishing Group (*US*)
Sage Publications (*UK*)
Shelfstealers (*US*)
Tirgearr Publishing (*Ire*)
Tantor Audio (*US*)
Tiger of the Stripe (*UK*)
Tuttle Publishing (*US*)
Vanderbilt University Press (*US*)
Waveland Press, Inc. (*US*)
Which? Books (*UK*)
ZigZag Education (*UK*)
Historical
ABC-CLIO / Greenwood (*US*)
Ian Allan Publishing Ltd (*UK*)
Alma Books Ltd (*UK*)
Alondra Press (*US*)
Amberley Publishing (*UK*)
American Press (*US*)
Ammonite Press (*UK*)
Anaiah Press, LLC (*US*)
Antique Collectors' Club Ltd (*UK*)
Arcade Publishing (*US*)
Ashgate Publishing Limited (*UK*)
Ashmolean Museum Publications (*UK*)
Aurum Press Ltd (*UK*)
Behrman House (*US*)
Blackstaff Press Ltd (*UK*)
Bloomsbury Publishing Plc (*UK*)

Bloomsbury Spark (*UK*)
Bold Strokes Books (*US*)
bookouture (*UK*)
Brine Books Publishing (*Can*)
Brown, Son & Ferguson, Ltd (*UK*)
The Brucedale Press (*Can*)
By Light Unseen Media (*US*)
Canongate Books (*UK*)
The Catholic University of America Press (*US*)
Cedar Fort (*US*)
Central Avenue Publishing (*Can*)
Chicago Review Press (*US*)
Christian Focus Publications (*UK*)
Clear Light Books (*US*)
Coastal West Publishing (*Can*)
Colin Smythe Ltd (*UK*)
Compelling Books (*UK*)
Constable & Robinson Ltd (*UK*)
Cork University Press (*Ire*)
The Countryman Press (*US*)
The Creative Company (*US*)
Cross-Cultural Communications Publications (*US*)
The Crowood Press (*UK*)
Divertir Publishing LLC (*US*)
Dovecote Press (*UK*)
Down East Books (*US*)
Down The Shore Publishing (*US*)
Duckworth Publishers (*UK*)
Eleusinian Press (*UK*)
ETC Publications (*US*)
Evans Brothers Ltd (*UK*)
Ex-L-Ence Publishing (*UK*)
F&W Media International Ltd (*UK*)
Farcountry Press (*US*)
Fifth House Publishers (*Can*)
Fingerpress UK (*UK*)
Flame Lily Books (*UK*)
Florida Academic Press (*US*)
Floris Books (*UK*)
Frederic C. Beil, Publisher (*US*)
Fulcrum Publishing (*US*)
Gauthier Publications (*US*)
Geddes & Grosset (*UK*)
Geostar Publishing & Services LLC (*US*)
Ghostwoods Books (*UK*)
Gibson Square Books Ltd (*UK*)
Glastonbury Publishing (*UK*)
Glenbridge Publishing Ltd (*US*)
Golden West Books (*US*)
Gomer Press (*UK*)
Grand Canyon Association (*US*)
Grub Street Publishing (*UK*)
Heritage Books, Inc. (*US*)
Hadley Rille Books (*US*)
Halban Publishers (*UK*)
Halsgrove (*UK*)
Harlequin Mills & Boon Ltd (*UK*)
High-Lonesome (*US*)
Highland Press (*US*)
House of Lochar (*UK*)
Icon Books Ltd (*UK*)
The Ilium Press (*US*)

Indigo Dreams Publishing (*UK*)
Ingalls Publishing Group, Inc. (*US*)
Itoh Press (*US*)
Jewish Lights Publishing (*US*)
John F. Blair, Publisher (*US*)
Kindred Productions (*Can*)
Kamehameha Publishing (*US*)
Kane Miller Books (*US*)
Kelly Point Publishing LLC (*US*)
Knox Robinson Publishing (UK) (*UK*)
Knox Robinson Publishing (US) (*US*)
The Lilliput Press (*Ire*)
Linden Publishing (*US*)
Logaston Press (*UK*)
Loose Id (*US*)
Luath Press Ltd (*UK*)
Lucky Marble Books (*US*)
Mainstream Publishing Co. (Edinburgh) Ltd (*UK*)
Medallion Media Group (*US*)
Mentor Books (*Ire*)
Mercier Press (*Ire*)
The Merlin Press (*UK*)
Methuen Publishing Ltd (*UK*)
Moose Hide Books (*Can*)
Motor Racing Publications (*UK*)
Mountain Press Publishing Company (*US*)
Neil Wilson Publishing Ltd (*UK*)
New Beacon Books, Ltd (*UK*)
The New Curiosity Shop (*UK*)
New Island (*Ire*)
NeWest Press (*Can*)
Nicolas Hays Publishers (*US*)
Not Your Eyes (*UK*)
The O'Brien Press (*Ire*)
Michael O'Mara Books Ltd (*UK*)
Octopus Publishing Group Limited (*UK*)
Oneworld Publications (*UK*)
Onstream Publications Ltd (*Ire*)
Ooligan Press (*US*)
The Orion Publishing Group Limited (*UK*)
Osprey Publishing Ltd (*UK*)
The Overlook Press (*US*)
Peter Owen Publishers (*UK*)
Oxford University Press (*UK*)
P&R Publishing (*US*)
Pants On Fire Press (*US*)
Paul Dry Books, Inc. (*US*)
Peachtree Publishers (*US*)
Pen & Sword Books Ltd (*UK*)
Phaidon Press Limited (*UK*)
Piatkus Books (*UK*)
Pluto Publishing Ltd (*UK*)
Princeton University Press (*US*)
Princeton University Press Europe (*UK*)
Profile Books (*UK*)
Quarto Publishing Group UK (*UK*)
Quarto Publishing Group USA (*US*)
Red Deer Press (*Can*)
Regnery Publishing, Inc. (*US*)
Rio Nuevo Publishers (*US*)
Rivers Oram Press (*UK*)
Robert Hale Publishers (*UK*)

Ronsdale Press (*Can*)
Rowman & Littlefield Publishing Group (*US*)
Sage Publications (*UK*)
Seafarer Books (*UK*)
Seren (*UK*)
Sheldrake Press (*UK*)
Shelfstealers (*US*)
Shepheard-Walwyn (Publishers) Ltd (*UK*)
Society of Genealogists (*UK*)
St Augustine's Press (*US*)
Stacey International (*UK*)
Sunbury Press (*US*)
Sussex Academic Press (*UK*)
Tirgearr Publishing (*Ire*)
Tantor Audio (*US*)
Texas Tech University Press (*US*)
Thames and Hudson Ltd (*UK*)
Tiger of the Stripe (*UK*)
Tor/Forge (*US*)
Tuttle Publishing (*US*)
Unicorn Press Ltd (*UK*)
University of Tampa Press (*US*)
University of Wales Press (*UK*)
Vanderbilt University Press (*US*)
Voyageur Press (*US*)
Wooden Books (*UK*)
Waveland Press, Inc. (*US*)
Welsh Academic Press (*UK*)
Williamson Books (*US*)
ZigZag Education (*UK*)
Hobbies
Ian Allan Publishing Ltd (*UK*)
Bloomsbury Publishing Plc (*UK*)
Boathook Books (*UK*)
Bristol Publishing Enterprises (*US*)
Brown, Son & Ferguson, Ltd (*UK*)
Cardoza Publishing (*US*)
Carstens Publications, Inc. (*US*)
Colin Smythe Ltd (*UK*)
The Countryman Press (*US*)
The Creative Company (*US*)
The Crowood Press (*UK*)
Cycle Publishing / Van der Plas Publications (*US*)
Divertir Publishing LLC (*US*)
Ex-L-Ence Publishing (*UK*)
F&W Media International Ltd (*UK*)
Flame Lily Books (*UK*)
Geostar Publishing & Services LLC (*US*)
Guild of Master Craftsman (GMC) Publications Ltd (*UK*)
Harry N. Abrams, Inc. (*US*)
Igloo Books Limited (*UK*)
Indigo Dreams Publishing (*UK*)
Kalmbach Publishing Co. (*US*)
Linden Publishing (*US*)
Methuen Publishing Ltd (*UK*)
New Cavendish Books (*UK*)
The New Curiosity Shop (*UK*)
Not Your Eyes (*UK*)
Quarto Publishing Group UK (*UK*)
Quarto Publishing Group USA (*US*)
Robert Hale Publishers (*UK*)

Shelfstealers (*US*)
Stemmer House Publishers (*US*)
Tirgearr Publishing (*Ire*)
Tiger of the Stripe (*UK*)
Williamson Books (*US*)

Horror
Anaiah Press, LLC (*US*)
BHW Publishing House (*UK*)
Blurbeo (*US*)
Bold Strokes Books (*US*)
Brine Books Publishing (*Can*)
By Light Unseen Media (*US*)
Central Avenue Publishing (*Can*)
CN Writers (*UK*)
Compelling Books (*UK*)
Constable & Robinson Ltd (*UK*)
Dagda Publishing (*UK*)
Eleusinian Press (*UK*)
Fingerpress UK (*UK*)
48fourteen (*US*)
Gauthier Publications (*US*)
Geostar Publishing & Services LLC (*US*)
Ghostwoods Books (*UK*)
Glastonbury Publishing (*UK*)
ImaJinn Books (*US*)
Indigo Dreams Publishing (*UK*)
Itoh Press (*US*)
Jo Fletcher Books (*UK*)
Lost Tower Publications (*UK*)
Mandrake of Oxford (*UK*)
Medallion Media Group (*US*)
Moonshadow Press (*US*)
New Dawn Publishers Ltd (*UK*)
NBM (*US*)
Netherworld Books (*UK*)
The New Curiosity Shop (*UK*)
Not Your Eyes (*UK*)
Pants On Fire Press (*US*)
Papercutz (*US*)
Pressgang (*US*)
SalGad Publishing Group (*UK*)
Shelfstealers (*US*)
Tirgearr Publishing (*Ire*)
Tantor Audio (*US*)
Tor/Forge (*US*)
The Zharmae Publishing Press (*US*)

How-to
Betterway Home Books (*US*)
Boathook Books (*UK*)
The Bold Strummer Ltd (*US*)
Brighter Books Publishing House (*Can*)
Carstens Publications, Inc. (*US*)
Centerstream Publishing (*US*)
Chartered Institute of Personnel and
Development (CIPD) Publishing (*UK*)
Church Growth Institute (*US*)
The College Board (*US*)
Compelling Books (*UK*)
Ex-L-Ence Publishing (*UK*)
Fingerpress UK (*UK*)
Flame Lily Books (*UK*)
Fox Chapel Publishing (*US*)
Gem Guides Book Co. (*US*)

Geostar Publishing & Services LLC (*US*)
Guild of Master Craftsman (GMC) Publications
Ltd (*UK*)
Humanics Publishing Group (*US*)
Impact Books (*US*)
Indigo Dreams Publishing (*UK*)
Kalmbach Publishing Co. (*US*)
Linden Publishing (*US*)
Methuen Publishing Ltd (*UK*)
My Pouty Lips (*US*)
NavPress (*US*)
Not Your Eyes (*UK*)
The Overlook Press (*US*)
Parenting Press, Inc. (*US*)
PennWell Books (*US*)
Possibility Press (*US*)
Quarto Publishing Group UK (*UK*)
Quarto Publishing Group USA (*US*)
Rainbow Books, Inc. (*US*)
Seafarer Books (*UK*)
Shelfstealers (*US*)
Tirgearr Publishing (*Ire*)
Tantor Audio (*US*)
Tiger of the Stripe (*UK*)
Tsaba House (*US*)

Humour
Anaiah Press, LLC (*US*)
Aurora Metro Press (*UK*)
Black & White Publishing Ltd (*UK*)
Blackstaff Press Ltd (*UK*)
Blurbeo (*US*)
Brine Books Publishing (*Can*)
Canongate Books (*UK*)
Central Avenue Publishing (*Can*)
CN Writers (*UK*)
Compelling Books (*UK*)
Constable & Robinson Ltd (*UK*)
Dagda Publishing (*UK*)
Divertir Publishing LLC (*US*)
Emissary Publishing (*UK*)
Ex-L-Ence Publishing (*UK*)
F&W Media International Ltd (*UK*)
Fingerpress UK (*UK*)
Flame Lily Books (*UK*)
48fourteen (*US*)
Gauthier Publications (*US*)
Geddes & Grosset (*UK*)
Geostar Publishing & Services LLC (*US*)
Glastonbury Publishing (*UK*)
Glenbridge Publishing Ltd (*US*)
Guild of Master Craftsman (GMC) Publications
Ltd (*UK*)
Harry N. Abrams, Inc. (*US*)
Hearts 'N Tummies Cookbook Co. / Quixote
Press (*US*)
Hinkler Books (*Aus*)
Icon Books Ltd (*UK*)
Indigo Dreams Publishing (*UK*)
Ingalls Publishing Group, Inc. (*US*)
Itoh Press (*US*)
Jonathan David Publishers, Inc. (*US*)
Kelly Point Publishing LLC (*US*)
Kindred Rainbow Publishing (*UK*)

Listen & Live Audio, Inc. (*US*)
Local Gems Poetry Press (*US*)
Lucky Marble Books (*US*)
Mentor Books (*Ire*)
Mercier Press (*Ire*)
Methuen Publishing Ltd (*UK*)
Moose Hide Books (*Can*)
New Dawn Publishers Ltd (*UK*)
NBM (*US*)
Neil Wilson Publishing Ltd (*UK*)
Netherworld Books (*UK*)
The New Curiosity Shop (*UK*)
New Island (*Ire*)
New Victoria Publishers (*US*)
Nightingale Press (*UK*)
Not Your Eyes (*UK*)
The O'Brien Press (*Ire*)
Michael O'Mara Books Ltd (*UK*)
Octopus Publishing Group Limited (*UK*)
Papercutz (*US*)
Piatkus Books (*UK*)
Piccadilly Press (*UK*)
Pressgang (*US*)
Profile Books (*UK*)
Quiller Publishing Ltd (*UK*)
Ramsay Publishing (*UK*)
Robert Hale Publishers (*UK*)
Shelfstealers (*US*)
Sunbury Press (*US*)
Tirgearr Publishing (*Ire*)
Tantor Audio (*US*)
Tiger of the Stripe (*UK*)
Titan Books (*UK*)
Top That! Publishing (*UK*)
Trentham Books Limited (*UK*)
Legal
Alexander Hamilton Institute (*US*)
American Press (*US*)
Ashgate Publishing Limited (*UK*)
John Blake Publishing (*UK*)
Coastal West Publishing (*Can*)
Cork University Press (*Ire*)
Eleusinian Press (*UK*)
Geostar Publishing & Services LLC (*US*)
Institute of Public Administration (IPA) (*Ire*)
Jones & Bartlett Learning (*US*)
Lawyers & Judges Publishing Co. (*US*)
Not Your Eyes (*UK*)
Oxford University Press (*UK*)
Pluto Publishing Ltd (*UK*)
Princeton University Press (*US*)
Princeton University Press Europe (*UK*)
Rowman & Littlefield Publishing Group (*US*)
Shelfstealers (*US*)
Tirgearr Publishing (*Ire*)
Tantor Audio (*US*)
Texas Tech University Press (*US*)
Tiger of the Stripe (*UK*)
Trentham Books Limited (*UK*)
Waveland Press, Inc. (*US*)
Which? Books (*UK*)
Wolters Kluwer (UK) Ltd (*UK*)
ZigZag Education (*UK*)

Leisure
AA Publishing (*UK*)
Burford Books (*US*)
Cardoza Publishing (*US*)
Central Avenue Publishing (*Can*)
Constable & Robinson Ltd (*UK*)
The Countryman Press (*US*)
The Crowood Press (*UK*)
Cycle Publishing / Van der Plas Publications (*US*)
Down East Books (*US*)
Ex-L-Ence Publishing (*UK*)
Flame Lily Books (*UK*)
Geostar Publishing & Services LLC (*US*)
Gomer Press (*UK*)
Grand Canyon Association (*US*)
Harry N. Abrams, Inc. (*US*)
Indigo Dreams Publishing (*UK*)
Itoh Press (*US*)
Frances Lincoln Ltd (*UK*)
Lost Tower Publications (*UK*)
Luath Press Ltd (*UK*)
Northumbria University Press (*UK*)
Not Your Eyes (*UK*)
Open Idea Publishing, LLC (*US*)
Pocket Mountains (*UK*)
Robert Hale Publishers (*UK*)
Shelfstealers (*US*)
Sunflower Books (*UK*)
Tirgearr Publishing (*Ire*)
Tantor Audio (*US*)
Tiger of the Stripe (*UK*)
Tsaba House (*US*)
ZigZag Education (*UK*)
Lifestyle
Anaiah Press, LLC (*US*)
Aurum Press Ltd (*UK*)
Betterway Home Books (*US*)
BHW Publishing House (*UK*)
Blue Dolphin Publishing (*US*)
Blurbeo (*US*)
Central Avenue Publishing (*Can*)
Chicago Review Press (*US*)
Christian Focus Publications (*UK*)
Co & Bear Productions (*UK*)
Constable & Robinson Ltd (*UK*)
The Countryman Press (*US*)
Ex-L-Ence Publishing (*UK*)
F&W Media International Ltd (*UK*)
Flame Tree Publishing (*UK*)
Geostar Publishing & Services LLC (*US*)
Glenbridge Publishing Ltd (*US*)
Harry N. Abrams, Inc. (*US*)
The Harvard Common Press (*US*)
Hawthorn Press (*UK*)
Hinkler Books (*Aus*)
Indigo Dreams Publishing (*UK*)
Itoh Press (*US*)
Kyle Books (*UK*)
Frances Lincoln Ltd (*UK*)
Listen & Live Audio, Inc. (*US*)
Lost Tower Publications (*UK*)
Luath Press Ltd (*UK*)

Management Books 2000 Ltd (*UK*)
Mandrake of Oxford (*UK*)
Mercier Press (*Ire*)
NavPress (*US*)
Nightingale Press (*UK*)
Not Your Eyes (*UK*)
The O'Brien Press (*Ire*)
Octopus Publishing Group Limited (*UK*)
The Orion Publishing Group Limited (*UK*)
The Overlook Press (*US*)
P&R Publishing (*US*)
Parenting Press, Inc. (*US*)
Peachtree Publishers (*US*)
Piatkus Books (*UK*)
Possibility Press (*US*)
Quarto Publishing Group UK (*UK*)
Shelfstealers (*US*)
Tirgearr Publishing (*Ire*)
Tantor Audio (*US*)
Tiger of the Stripe (*UK*)
Tristan Publishing (*US*)
Tsaba House (*US*)
Voyageur Press (*US*)
Which? Books (*UK*)

Literature
Alma Books Ltd (*UK*)
Anaiah Press, LLC (*US*)
Ashgate Publishing Limited (*UK*)
Black Lawrence Press (*US*)
Bloodaxe Books Ltd (*UK*)
Blurbeo (*US*)
Boathook Books (*UK*)
Brine Books Publishing (*Can*)
The Catholic University of America Press (*US*)
Central Avenue Publishing (*Can*)
Classical Comics Limited (*UK*)
Colin Smythe Ltd (*UK*)
Compelling Books (*UK*)
Cork University Press (*Ire*)
Corwin (*US*)
Crescent Moon Publishing (*UK*)
Cross-Cultural Communications Publications (*US*)
Dedalus Ltd (*UK*)
Dover Publications, Inc. (*US*)
Dzanc Books (*US*)
Eleusinian Press (*UK*)
Erotic Review (ER) Books (*UK*)
Ex-L-Ence Publishing (*UK*)
Flame Lily Books (*UK*)
Floris Books (*UK*)
Geostar Publishing & Services LLC (*US*)
Glenbridge Publishing Ltd (*US*)
Gomer Press (*UK*)
Halban Publishers (*UK*)
Homestead Publishing (*US*)
House of Lochar (*UK*)
Indigo Dreams Publishing (*UK*)
Itoh Press (*US*)
The Lilliput Press (*Ire*)
M P Publishing USA (*US*)
Mango Publishing (*UK*)
Methuen Publishing Ltd (*UK*)

New Dawn Publishers Ltd (*UK*)
New Libri (*US*)
The New Curiosity Shop (*UK*)
New Island (*Ire*)
NeWest Press (*Can*)
Not Your Eyes (*UK*)
The O'Brien Press (*Ire*)
Open Gate Press (*UK*)
Open Idea Publishing, LLC (*US*)
The Orion Publishing Group Limited (*UK*)
Peter Owen Publishers (*UK*)
Oxford University Press (*UK*)
Presa Press (*US*)
Pressgang (*US*)
Princeton University Press (*US*)
Princeton University Press Europe (*UK*)
Reading Harbor (*US*)
Salt Publishing Ltd (*UK*)
Shearsman Books (*UK*)
Shelfstealers (*US*)
Stacey International (*UK*)
Sunberry Books (*UK*)
Sussex Academic Press (*UK*)
Tirgearr Publishing (*Ire*)
Texas Tech University Press (*US*)
Tiger of the Stripe (*UK*)
Tsaba House (*US*)
Tuttle Publishing (*US*)
University of Wales Press (*UK*)
Vanderbilt University Press (*US*)
Waveland Press, Inc. (*US*)
The Zharmae Publishing Press (*US*)

Media
BFI Publishing (*UK*)
Booth-Clibborn Editions (*UK*)
Central Avenue Publishing (*Can*)
Coastal West Publishing (*Can*)
Crescent Moon Publishing (*UK*)
Eleusinian Press (*UK*)
Evans Brothers Ltd (*UK*)
Ex-L-Ence Publishing (*UK*)
Geostar Publishing & Services LLC (*US*)
Indigo Dreams Publishing (*UK*)
Not Your Eyes (*UK*)
Pluto Publishing Ltd (*UK*)
Princeton University Press Europe (*UK*)
Reed Business Information (RBI) (*UK*)
Sage Publications (*UK*)
Sussex Academic Press (*UK*)
Tirgearr Publishing (*Ire*)
Tiger of the Stripe (*UK*)
University of Wales Press (*UK*)
Wallflower Press (*UK*)
ZigZag Education (*UK*)

Medicine
Chemical Publishing Company (*US*)
Eastland Press (*US*)
Eleusinian Press (*UK*)
EMIS Inc. Medical Publishers (*US*)
Ex-L-Ence Publishing (*UK*)
Geostar Publishing & Services LLC (*US*)
Glenbridge Publishing Ltd (*US*)
Jones & Bartlett Learning (*US*)

Lawyers & Judges Publishing Co. (*US*)
Medical Group Management Association
(MGMA) (*US*)
The New Curiosity Shop (*UK*)
Not Your Eyes (*UK*)
Oxford University Press (*UK*)
Portland Press Ltd (*UK*)
Princeton University Press (*US*)
Princeton University Press Europe (*UK*)
Radcliffe Publishing Ltd (*UK*)
Sage Publications (*UK*)
Science Navigation Group (*UK*)
TSO (The Stationery Office) (*UK*)
Tiger of the Stripe (*UK*)
Vanderbilt University Press (*US*)

Men's Interests
Blurbeo (*US*)
Brine Books Publishing (*Can*)
Central Avenue Publishing (*Can*)
Eleusinian Press (*UK*)
Ex-L-Ence Publishing (*UK*)
Fingerpress UK (*UK*)
Geostar Publishing & Services LLC (*US*)
Glastonbury Publishing (*UK*)
Indigo Dreams Publishing (*UK*)
Jewish Lights Publishing (*US*)
My Pouty Lips (*US*)
The New Curiosity Shop (*UK*)
Not Your Eyes (*UK*)
Shelfstealers (*US*)
Tirgearr Publishing (*Ire*)
Tsaba House (*US*)
The Zharmae Publishing Press (*US*)

Military
ABC-CLIO / Greenwood (*US*)
Ian Allan Publishing Ltd (*UK*)
Amberley Publishing (*UK*)
Arcade Publishing (*US*)
Aurum Press Ltd (*UK*)
John Blake Publishing (*UK*)
Blurbeo (*US*)
Brine Books Publishing (*Can*)
Burford Books (*US*)
Central Avenue Publishing (*Can*)
Constable & Robinson Ltd (*UK*)
The Crowood Press (*UK*)
ETC Publications (*US*)
Ex-L-Ence Publishing (*UK*)
F&W Media International Ltd (*UK*)
Fingerpress UK (*UK*)
Flame Lily Books (*UK*)
Gauthier Publications (*US*)
Geostar Publishing & Services LLC (*US*)
The Glencannon Press (*US*)
Grub Street Publishing (*UK*)
Heritage Books, Inc. (*US*)
Listen & Live Audio, Inc. (*US*)
Mercier Press (*Ire*)
Methuen Publishing Ltd (*UK*)
The New Curiosity Shop (*UK*)
Not Your Eyes (*UK*)
The Orion Publishing Group Limited (*UK*)
Osprey Publishing Ltd (*UK*)

Pants On Fire Press (*US*)
Pen & Sword Books Ltd (*UK*)
Quarto Publishing Group USA (*US*)
Regnery Publishing, Inc. (*US*)
Robert Hale Publishers (*UK*)
Seafarer Books (*UK*)
Shelfstealers (*US*)
Tirgearr Publishing (*Ire*)
Tantor Audio (*US*)
Tiger of the Stripe (*UK*)
Ulric Publishing (*UK*)

Music
Amadeus Press (*US*)
American Press (*US*)
Arc Publications (*UK*)
Ashgate Publishing Limited (*UK*)
Aureus Publishing Limited (*UK*)
Aurum Press Ltd (*UK*)
John Blake Publishing (*UK*)
Bloomsbury Publishing Plc (*UK*)
The Bold Strummer Ltd (*US*)
Cadence Jazz Books (*US*)
Centerstream Publishing (*US*)
Central Avenue Publishing (*Can*)
Chicago Review Press (*US*)
Consortium Publishing (*US*)
Cork University Press (*Ire*)
The Creative Company (*US*)
Crescent Moon Publishing (*UK*)
Dover Publications, Inc. (*US*)
Eleusinian Press (*UK*)
Evans Brothers Ltd (*UK*)
Ex-L-Ence Publishing (*UK*)
Faber & Faber Ltd (*UK*)
Flame Lily Books (*UK*)
Flame Tree Publishing (*UK*)
Geostar Publishing & Services LLC (*US*)
Glenbridge Publishing Ltd (*US*)
Gomer Press (*UK*)
Harry N. Abrams, Inc. (*US*)
Hinkler Books (*Aus*)
The Ilium Press (*US*)
Indigo Dreams Publishing (*UK*)
Itoh Press (*US*)
Kearney Street Books (*US*)
The Lilliput Press (*Ire*)
Kevin Mayhew Publishers (*UK*)
Neil Wilson Publishing Ltd (*UK*)
The New Curiosity Shop (*UK*)
Northumbria University Press (*UK*)
Not Your Eyes (*UK*)
The O'Brien Press (*Ire*)
Octopus Publishing Group Limited (*UK*)
Omnibus Press (*UK*)
Oxford University Press (*UK*)
Phaidon Press Limited (*UK*)
Piano Press (*US*)
Plexus Publishing Limited (*UK*)
Princeton University Press (*US*)
Princeton University Press Europe (*UK*)
Quarto Publishing Group USA (*US*)
Quest Books (*US*)
Seafarer Books (*UK*)

Seren (*UK*)
Sussex Academic Press (*UK*)
Tantor Audio (*US*)
Tiger of the Stripe (*UK*)
Vanderbilt University Press (*US*)
Voyageur Press (*US*)
Waveland Press, Inc. (*US*)
ZigZag Education (*UK*)

Mystery

Anaiah Press, LLC (*US*)
Bloomsbury Spark (*UK*)
Blurbeo (*US*)
Bold Strokes Books (*US*)
bookouture (*UK*)
Brine Books Publishing (*Can*)
Canterbury House Publishing, Ltd (*US*)
Central Avenue Publishing (*Can*)
CN Writers (*UK*)
Compelling Books (*UK*)
Constable & Robinson Ltd (*UK*)
The Countryman Press (*US*)
Cup of Tea Books (*US*)
Divertir Publishing LLC (*US*)
Ex-L-Ence Publishing (*UK*)
Flame Lily Books (*UK*)
Gauthier Publications (*US*)
Geostar Publishing & Services LLC (*US*)
Glastonbury Publishing (*UK*)
Highland Press (*US*)
ImaJinn Books (*US*)
Indigo Dreams Publishing (*UK*)
Ingalls Publishing Group, Inc. (*US*)
Jewish Lights Publishing (*US*)
Kane Miller Books (*US*)
Kelly Point Publishing LLC (*US*)
Kindred Rainbow Publishing (*UK*)
Listen & Live Audio, Inc. (*US*)
Loose Id (*US*)
Lost Tower Publications (*UK*)
Lucky Marble Books (*US*)
M P Publishing USA (*US*)
Mandrake of Oxford (*UK*)
Medallion Media Group (*US*)
Moose Hide Books (*Can*)
New Dawn Publishers Ltd (*UK*)
NBM (*US*)
Netherworld Books (*UK*)
The New Curiosity Shop (*UK*)
New Victoria Publishers (*US*)
Nicolas Hays Books (*US*)
Not Your Eyes (*UK*)
Oceanview Publishing (*US*)
Open Idea Publishing, LLC (*US*)
Papercutz (*US*)
Pressgang (*US*)
Quest Books (*US*)
Rainbow Books, Inc. (*US*)
SalGad Publishing Group (*UK*)
Shelfstealers (*US*)
Sunberry Books (*UK*)
Tantor Audio (*US*)
The Poisoned Pencil (*US*)
Tiger of the Stripe (*UK*)

Tor/Forge (*US*)
Tsaba House (*US*)

Nature

Alastair Sawday Publishing Co. Ltd (*UK*)
Arcade Publishing (*US*)
Baywood Publishing Company, Inc. (*US*)
Birdsong Books (*US*)
Blackstaff Press Ltd (*UK*)
Bloomsbury Publishing Plc (*UK*)
Boathook Books (*UK*)
Burford Books (*US*)
Central Avenue Publishing (*Can*)
Co & Bear Productions (*UK*)
The Countryman Press (*US*)
The Creative Company (*US*)
The Crowood Press (*UK*)
Dovecote Press (*UK*)
Down East Books (*US*)
Down The Shore Publishing (*US*)
Ex-L-Ence Publishing (*UK*)
F&W Media International Ltd (*UK*)
Farcountry Press (*US*)
Fifth House Publishers (*Can*)
Flame Lily Books (*UK*)
Fox Chapel Publishing (*US*)
Fulcrum Publishing (*US*)
Geostar Publishing & Services LLC (*US*)
Glenbridge Publishing Ltd (*US*)
Gomer Press (*UK*)
Grand Canyon Association (*US*)
Harry N. Abrams, Inc. (*US*)
Homestead Publishing (*US*)
Indigo Dreams Publishing (*UK*)
The Lilliput Press (*Ire*)
Luath Press Ltd (*UK*)
Mandala Earth (*US*)
Mountain Press Publishing Company (*US*)
Neil Wilson Publishing Ltd (*UK*)
The New Curiosity Shop (*UK*)
NeWest Press (*Can*)
Northumbria University Press (*UK*)
Not Your Eyes (*UK*)
The O'Brien Press (*Ire*)
Open Gate Press (*UK*)
The Orion Publishing Group Limited (*UK*)
Pants On Fire Press (*US*)
Peachtree Publishers (*US*)
Piccadilly Books Ltd (*US*)
Pluto Publishing Ltd (*UK*)
Pocket Mountains (*UK*)
Princeton University Press (*US*)
Princeton University Press Europe (*UK*)
Rio Nuevo Publishers (*US*)
Rowman & Littlefield Publishing Group (*US*)
Ruka Press (*US*)
Shelfstealers (*US*)
Stacey International (*UK*)
Stemmer House Publishers (*US*)
Sussex Academic Press (*UK*)
Tirgearr Publishing (*Ire*)
Tantor Audio (*US*)
Texas Tech University Press (*US*)
Tiger of the Stripe (*UK*)

EDCON Publishing Group (*US*)
The Educational Company of Ireland (*Ire*)
Edupress, Inc. (*US*)
Eleusinian Press (*UK*)
EMIS Inc. Medical Publishers (*US*)
Emissary Publishing (*UK*)
Erotic Review (ER) Books (*UK*)
ETC Publications (*US*)
Euromonitor (*UK*)
Evans Brothers Ltd (*UK*)
Ex-L-Ence Publishing (*UK*)
F&W Media International Ltd (*UK*)
Faber & Faber Ltd (*UK*)
Farcountry Press (*US*)
Fifth House Publishers (*Can*)
Fingerpress UK (*UK*)
Fitzrovia Press Limited (*UK*)
Flame Lily Books (*UK*)
Flame Tree Publishing (*UK*)
Florida Academic Press (*US*)
Floris Books (*UK*)
Fox Chapel Publishing (*US*)
Frederic C. Beil, Publisher (*US*)
Fulcrum Publishing (*US*)
George Ronald Publisher (*UK*)
The Gallery Press (*Ire*)
Gauthier Publications (*US*)
Geddes & Grosset (*UK*)
Gem Guides Book Co. (*US*)
Geostar Publishing & Services LLC (*US*)
Gibson Square Books Ltd (*UK*)
Glenbridge Publishing Ltd (*US*)
The Glencannon Press (*US*)
Golden West Books (*US*)
Gomer Press (*UK*)
Goss & Crested China Club (*UK*)
Grand Canyon Association (*US*)
Grub Street Publishing (*UK*)
Guild of Master Craftsman (GMC) Publications Ltd (*UK*)
Gulf Publishing Company (*US*)
Heritage Books, Inc. (*US*)
The Habit of Rainy Nights Press (*US*)
Hachette Children's Books (*UK*)
Hachette UK (*UK*)
Halban Publishers (*UK*)
Halsgrove (*UK*)
Harry N. Abrams, Inc. (*US*)
The Harvard Common Press (*US*)
Hawthorn Press (*UK*)
Hayes School Publishing Co., Inc. (*US*)
Headland Publications (*UK*)
Hearts 'N Tummies Cookbook Co. / Quixote Press (*US*)
High-Lonesome (*US*)
Highland Press (*US*)
Hinkler Books (*Aus*)
Homestead Publishing (*US*)
Honno Welsh Women's Press (*UK*)
Hopewell Publications (*US*)
House of Anansi Press (*Can*)
House of Lochar (*UK*)
Humanics Publishing Group (*US*)

Icon Books Ltd (*UK*)
Ideals Publications (*US*)
Igloo Books Limited (*UK*)
Ignatius Press (*US*)
The Ilex Press (*UK*)
The Ilium Press (*US*)
Immedium (*US*)
Impact Books (*US*)
Impress Books Limited (*UK*)
Indigo Dreams Publishing (*UK*)
Ingalls Publishing Group, Inc. (*US*)
Institute of Public Administration (IPA) (*Ire*)
International Press (*US*)
Itoh Press (*US*)
Jewish Lights Publishing (*US*)
John F. Blair, Publisher (*US*)
Jonathan David Publishers, Inc. (*US*)
Jones & Bartlett Learning (*US*)
Jupiter Gardens Press (*US*)
Just Us Books (*US*)
Kindred Productions (*Can*)
Kalmbach Publishing Co. (*US*)
Kamehameha Publishing (*US*)
Kids Can Press (*Can*)
Kindred Rainbow Publishing (*UK*)
Kyle Books (*UK*)
Legacy Press (*US*)
Lawyers & Judges Publishing Co. (*US*)
Leapfrog Press (*US*)
Ledge Hill Publishing (*US*)
Lethe Press (*US*)
The Lilliput Press (*Ire*)
Frances Lincoln Ltd (*UK*)
Linden Publishing (*US*)
Listen & Live Audio, Inc. (*US*)
Logaston Press (*UK*)
Luath Press Ltd (*UK*)
Lucent Books (*US*)
M P Publishing USA (*US*)
Magenta Publishing for the Arts (*Can*)
Magination Press (*US*)
Mainstream Publishing Co. (Edinburgh) Ltd (*UK*)
Management Books 2000 Ltd (*UK*)
Mandala Earth (*US*)
Mandrake of Oxford (*UK*)
Mango Publishing (*UK*)
Manor House Publishing (*Can*)
Mantra Lingua Ltd (*UK*)
Martin Sisters Publishing (*US*)
Master Books (*US*)
Kevin Mayhew Publishers (*UK*)
MBooks of BC (Multicultural Books of British Columbia) (*Can*)
Medallion Media Group (*US*)
Medical Group Management Association (MGMA) (*US*)
Mentor Books (*Ire*)
Mercier Press (*Ire*)
The Merlin Press (*UK*)
Messianic Jewish Publishers (*US*)
Methuen Publishing Ltd (*UK*)
Michelin Maps and Guides (*UK*)

Moose Hide Books (*Can*)
Morgan Kaufmann Publishers (*US*)
Motor Racing Publications (*UK*)
Mountain Press Publishing Company (*US*)
My Pouty Lips (*US*)
Myriad Editions (*UK*)
New Libri (*US*)
NavPress (*US*)
Neil Wilson Publishing Ltd (*UK*)
New Beacon Books, Ltd (*UK*)
New Cavendish Books (*UK*)
The New Curiosity Shop (*UK*)
New Island (*Ire*)
New Rivers Press (*US*)
New Victoria Publishers (*US*)
NeWest Press (*Can*)
Nick Hern Books Ltd (*UK*)
Nicolas Hays Publishers (*US*)
Nightingale Press (*UK*)
Northumbria University Press (*UK*)
Nortia Press (*US*)
Not Your Eyes (*UK*)
Nova Press (*US*)
The O'Brien Press (*Ire*)
Michael O'Mara Books Ltd (*UK*)
Oberon Books (*UK*)
Octopus Publishing Group Limited (*UK*)
Omnibus Press (*UK*)
Oneworld Publications (*UK*)
Onlywomen Press Ltd (*UK*)
Onstream Publications Ltd (*Ire*)
Ooligan Press (*US*)
Open Court Publishing Company (*US*)
Open Gate Press (*UK*)
The Orion Publishing Group Limited (*UK*)
Osprey Publishing Ltd (*UK*)
The Overlook Press (*US*)
Peter Owen Publishers (*UK*)
Oxford University Press (*UK*)
P&R Publishing (*US*)
Parenting Press, Inc. (*US*)
Pants On Fire Press (*US*)
Paul Dry Books, Inc. (*US*)
Pauline Books and Media (*US*)
Pavilion Publishing (*UK*)
Peachtree Publishers (*US*)
Pearson UK (*UK*)
Pen & Sword Books Ltd (*UK*)
Pennant Books Ltd (*UK*)
PennWell Books (*US*)
Persea Books (*US*)
Persephone Books (*UK*)
Peter Lang Publishing, Inc. (*US*)
Phaidon Press Limited (*UK*)
Phoenix Yard Books (*UK*)
Piano Press (*US*)
Piatkus Books (*UK*)
Picador USA (*US*)
Piccadilly Books Ltd (*US*)
Piccadilly Press (*UK*)
Plexus Publishing Limited (*UK*)
Pluto Publishing Ltd (*UK*)
Pocket Mountains (*UK*)

The Policy Press (*UK*)
Poolbeg (*Ire*)
Portland Press Ltd (*UK*)
Possibility Press (*US*)
Presa Press (*US*)
Pressgang (*US*)
Prestel Publishing Ltd (*UK*)
Princeton University Press (*US*)
Princeton University Press Europe (*UK*)
Pro Lingua Associates ESL (*US*)
Profile Books (*UK*)
Psychology Press (*UK*)
Quarto Publishing Group UK (*UK*)
Quarto Publishing Group USA (*US*)
Quercus Books (*UK*)
Quest Books (*US*)
Quiller Publishing Ltd (*UK*)
Radcliffe Publishing Ltd (*UK*)
Rainbow Books, Inc. (*US*)
Ransom Publishing Ltd (*UK*)
Reading Harbor (*US*)
Red Deer Press (*Can*)
Reed Business Information (RBI) (*UK*)
Regnery Publishing, Inc. (*US*)
Renaissance House (*US*)
Richard C. Owen Publishers, Inc. (*US*)
Rio Nuevo Publishers (*US*)
Rivers Oram Press (*UK*)
Robert Hale Publishers (*UK*)
Ronsdale Press (*Can*)
Rowman & Littlefield Publishing Group (*US*)
Ruka Press (*US*)
Sage Publications (*UK*)
Science Navigation Group (*UK*)
SCM-Canterbury Press (*UK*)
Seafarer Books (*UK*)
Second Story Press (*Can*)
Seren (*UK*)
Shearsman Books (*UK*)
Sheldrake Press (*UK*)
Shelfstealers (*US*)
Shepheard-Walwyn (Publishers) Ltd (*UK*)
Short Books (*UK*)
Skinner House Books (*US*)
Society of Genealogists (*UK*)
Somerville Press (*Ire*)
SportsBooks Limited (*UK*)
St Augustine's Press (*US*)
Stacey International (*UK*)
Stemmer House Publishers (*US*)
Sunbury Press (*US*)
Sunflower Books (*UK*)
Sussex Academic Press (*UK*)
TSO (The Stationery Office) (*UK*)
Tango Books Ltd (*UK*)
Tantor Audio (*US*)
Taylor & Francis Books (*UK*)
The Templar Company Limited (*UK*)
Texas Tech University Press (*US*)
Thames and Hudson Ltd (*UK*)
Tiger of the Stripe (*UK*)
Titan Books (*UK*)
Top That! Publishing (*UK*)

Tor/Forge (*US*)
Trentham Books Limited (*UK*)
Tristan Publishing (*US*)
Tsaba House (*US*)
Tuttle Publishing (*US*)
Ulric Publishing (*UK*)
Unicorn Press Ltd (*UK*)
University of Nebraska Press (*US*)
University of Tampa Press (*US*)
University of Wales Press (*UK*)
Unthank Books (*UK*)
Usborne Publishing (*UK*)
Vanderbilt University Press (*US*)
Voyageur Press (*US*)
Wooden Books (*UK*)
Wallflower Press (*UK*)
Waveland Press, Inc. (*US*)
Welsh Academic Press (*UK*)
Westminster John Knox Press (WJK) (*US*)
Which? Books (*UK*)
Whittet Books Ltd (*UK*)
William Reed Business Media (*UK*)
Williamson Books (*US*)
Wolters Kluwer (UK) Ltd (*UK*)
Zero to Ten Limited (*UK*)
The Zharmae Publishing Press (*US*)
ZigZag Education (*UK*)

Philosophy
Alondra Press (*US*)
American Press (*US*)
Ashgate Publishing Limited (*UK*)
Behrman House (*US*)
Bick Publishing House (*US*)
Blue Dolphin Publishing (*US*)
Brine Books Publishing (*Can*)
The Catholic University of America Press (*US*)
Central Avenue Publishing (*Can*)
Clear Light Books (*US*)
Compelling Books (*UK*)
Cork University Press (*Ire*)
Crescent Moon Publishing (*UK*)
Dagda Publishing (*UK*)
Duckworth Publishers (*UK*)
Eleusinian Press (*UK*)
Ex-L-Ence Publishing (*UK*)
Fitzrovia Press Limited (*UK*)
Floris Books (*UK*)
Geostar Publishing & Services LLC (*US*)
Gibson Square Books Ltd (*UK*)
Halban Publishers (*UK*)
Icon Books Ltd (*UK*)
Itoh Press (*US*)
Jewish Lights Publishing (*US*)
The Lilliput Press (*Ire*)
Mandala Earth (*US*)
Mandrake of Oxford (*UK*)
The Merlin Press (*UK*)
Methuen Publishing Ltd (*UK*)
The New Curiosity Shop (*UK*)
Not Your Eyes (*UK*)
Oneworld Publications (*UK*)
Open Court Publishing Company (*US*)
Open Gate Press (*UK*)

Oxford University Press (*UK*)
Paul Dry Books, Inc. (*US*)
Princeton University Press (*US*)
Princeton University Press Europe (*UK*)
Quest Books (*US*)
Reading Harbor (*US*)
Rowman & Littlefield Publishing Group (*US*)
SCM-Canterbury Press (*UK*)
Shelfstealers (*US*)
Shepheard-Walwyn (Publishers) Ltd (*UK*)
St Augustine's Press (*US*)
Sussex Academic Press (*UK*)
Tantor Audio (*US*)
University of Wales Press (*UK*)
Vanderbilt University Press (*US*)
Waveland Press, Inc. (*US*)
ZigZag Education (*UK*)

Photography
Ammonite Press (*UK*)
Antique Collectors' Club Ltd (*UK*)
Aurum Press Ltd (*UK*)
Booth-Clibborn Editions (*UK*)
Bracket Books (*US*)
Brine Books Publishing (*Can*)
Carstens Publications, Inc. (*US*)
Central Avenue Publishing (*Can*)
Co & Bear Productions (*UK*)
Constable & Robinson Ltd (*UK*)
The Countryman Press (*US*)
The Crowood Press (*UK*)
Eleusinian Press (*UK*)
Enitharmon Press (*UK*)
Erotic Review (ER) Books (*UK*)
Ex-L-Ence Publishing (*UK*)
F&W Media International Ltd (*UK*)
Farcountry Press (*US*)
Fingerpress UK (*UK*)
Fox Chapel Publishing (*US*)
Gauthier Publications (*US*)
Geostar Publishing & Services LLC (*US*)
Grand Canyon Association (*US*)
Guild of Master Craftsman (GMC) Publications Ltd (*UK*)
Halsgrove (*UK*)
Harry N. Abrams, Inc. (*US*)
Homestead Publishing (*US*)
The Ilex Press (*UK*)
Indigo Dreams Publishing (*UK*)
The Lilliput Press (*Ire*)
Luath Press Ltd (*UK*)
Magenta Publishing for the Arts (*Can*)
Mandala Earth (*US*)
The New Curiosity Shop (*UK*)
Northumbria University Press (*UK*)
Not Your Eyes (*UK*)
The O'Brien Press (*Ire*)
Phaidon Press Limited (*UK*)
Prestel Publishing Ltd (*UK*)
Princeton University Press (*US*)
Princeton University Press Europe (*UK*)
Rio Nuevo Publishers (*US*)
Seren (*UK*)
Stacey International (*UK*)

Thames and Hudson Ltd (*UK*)
Tiger of the Stripe (*UK*)
Voyageur Press (*US*)
Poetry
Alice James Books (*US*)
Arc Publications (*UK*)
Aunt Lute Books (*US*)
Black Lawrence Press (*US*)
Blackstaff Press Ltd (*UK*)
Bloodaxe Books Ltd (*UK*)
Blue Dolphin Publishing (*US*)
Brine Books Publishing (*Can*)
Bronze Man Books (*US*)
Central Avenue Publishing (*Can*)
Chapman Publishing (*UK*)
City Lights Publishers (*US*)
Coffee House Press (*US*)
Colin Smythe Ltd (*UK*)
Crescent Moon Publishing (*UK*)
Cross-Cultural Communications Publications (*US*)
Dagda Publishing (*UK*)
Divertir Publishing LLC (*US*)
Down The Shore Publishing (*US*)
Eleusinian Press (*UK*)
Enitharmon Press (*UK*)
Evans Brothers Ltd (*UK*)
Everheart Books (*Can*)
Ex-L-Ence Publishing (*UK*)
Faber & Faber Ltd (*UK*)
Four Way Books (*US*)
The Gallery Press (*Ire*)
Gomer Press (*UK*)
Grey Hen Press (*UK*)
The Habit of Rainy Nights Press (*US*)
Headland Publications (*UK*)
Honno Welsh Women's Press (*UK*)
House of Anansi Press (*Can*)
The Ilium Press (*US*)
Indigo Dreams Publishing (*UK*)
Just Us Books (*US*)
Kind of a Hurricane Press (*US*)
Leapfrog Press (*US*)
Ledge Hill Publishing (*US*)
Les Figues Press (*US*)
Lethe Press (*US*)
The Lilliput Press (*Ire*)
Local Gems Poetry Press (*US*)
Lost Tower Publications (*UK*)
Luath Press Ltd (*UK*)
Mango Publishing (*UK*)
Manor House Publishing (*Can*)
Maverick Duck Press (*US*)
MBooks of BC (Multicultural Books of British Columbia) (*Can*)
Methuen Publishing Ltd (*UK*)
Moon Tide Press (*US*)
Moose Hide Books (*Can*)
New Beacon Books, Ltd (*UK*)
New Island (*Ire*)
New Issues Poetry & Prose (*US*)
New Native Press (*US*)
New Rivers Press (*US*)

New Victoria Publishers (*US*)
NeWest Press (*Can*)
The Ninety-Six Press (*US*)
Not Your Eyes (*UK*)
The O'Brien Press (*Ire*)
Onlywomen Press Ltd (*UK*)
Ooligan Press (*US*)
Open Idea Publishing, LLC (*US*)
Oversteps Books (*UK*)
Paul Dry Books, Inc. (*US*)
Pedlar Press (*Can*)
Persea Books (*US*)
Phoenix Yard Books (*UK*)
Piano Press (*US*)
Plan B Press (*US*)
Presa Press (*US*)
Press 53 (*US*)
Princeton University Press (*US*)
Ragged Sky Press (*US*)
Ronsdale Press (*Can*)
Rose Alley Press (*US*)
Seren (*UK*)
Shearsman Books (*UK*)
Shepheard-Walwyn (Publishers) Ltd (*UK*)
Stacey International (*UK*)
Stairwell Books (*UK*)
Stemmer House Publishers (*US*)
Texas Tech University Press (*US*)
Tiger of the Stripe (*UK*)
University of Nebraska Press (*US*)
University of Tampa Press (*US*)
Politics
American Press (*US*)
Ashgate Publishing Limited (*UK*)
Blackstaff Press Ltd (*UK*)
John Blake Publishing (*UK*)
Blue Dolphin Publishing (*US*)
Brine Books Publishing (*Can*)
Canongate Books (*UK*)
The Catholic University of America Press (*US*)
Central Avenue Publishing (*Can*)
Chicago Review Press (*US*)
City Lights Publishers (*US*)
Cork University Press (*Ire*)
Crescent Moon Publishing (*UK*)
Divertir Publishing LLC (*US*)
Eleusinian Press (*UK*)
Ex-L-Ence Publishing (*UK*)
Faber & Faber Ltd (*UK*)
Florida Academic Press (*US*)
Fulcrum Publishing (*US*)
Geostar Publishing & Services LLC (*US*)
Gibson Square Books Ltd (*UK*)
Glenbridge Publishing Ltd (*US*)
Halban Publishers (*UK*)
Icon Books Ltd (*UK*)
Institute of Public Administration (IPA) (*Ire*)
Itoh Press (*US*)
The Lilliput Press (*Ire*)
Listen & Live Audio, Inc. (*US*)
Luath Press Ltd (*UK*)
Mainstream Publishing Co. (Edinburgh) Ltd (*UK*)

Manor House Publishing (*Can*)
Mentor Books (*Ire*)
Mercier Press (*Ire*)
The Merlin Press (*UK*)
Methuen Publishing Ltd (*UK*)
New Beacon Books, Ltd (*UK*)
The New Curiosity Shop (*UK*)
New Island (*Ire*)
New Victoria Publishers (*US*)
NeWest Press (*Can*)
Nicolas Hays Publishers (*US*)
Not Your Eyes (*UK*)
The O'Brien Press (*Ire*)
Oneworld Publications (*UK*)
Open Gate Press (*UK*)
Oxford University Press (*UK*)
Pluto Publishing Ltd (*UK*)
Princeton University Press (*US*)
Princeton University Press Europe (*UK*)
Profile Books (*UK*)
Quarto Publishing Group USA (*US*)
Reed Business Information (RBI) (*UK*)
Regnery Publishing, Inc. (*US*)
Rivers Oram Press (*UK*)
Rowman & Littlefield Publishing Group (*US*)
Sage Publications (*UK*)
Seren (*UK*)
Shelfstealers (*US*)
Shepheard-Walwyn (Publishers) Ltd (*UK*)
Sussex Academic Press (*UK*)
Tantor Audio (*US*)
Tiger of the Stripe (*UK*)
University of Wales Press (*UK*)
Vanderbilt University Press (*US*)
Waveland Press, Inc. (*US*)
Welsh Academic Press (*UK*)
ZigZag Education (*UK*)
Psychology
Alondra Press (*US*)
American Press (*US*)
Baywood Publishing Company, Inc. (*US*)
Bick Publishing House (*US*)
Blue Dolphin Publishing (*US*)
Brine Books Publishing (*Can*)
Central Avenue Publishing (*Can*)
Compelling Books (*UK*)
Consortium Publishing (*US*)
Constable & Robinson Ltd (*UK*)
Dagda Publishing (*UK*)
Eleusinian Press (*UK*)
EMIS Inc. Medical Publishers (*US*)
Ex-L-Ence Publishing (*UK*)
Geostar Publishing & Services LLC (*US*)
Gibson Square Books Ltd (*UK*)
Icon Books Ltd (*UK*)
Magination Press (*US*)
The New Curiosity Shop (*UK*)
Nicolas Hays Publishers (*US*)
Not Your Eyes (*UK*)
Octopus Publishing Group Limited (*UK*)
Oneworld Publications (*UK*)
Open Gate Press (*UK*)
Piatkus Books (*UK*)

Possibility Press (*US*)
Princeton University Press (*US*)
Profile Books (*UK*)
Psychology Press (*UK*)
Quest Books (*US*)
Reading Harbor (*US*)
Rowman & Littlefield Publishing Group (*US*)
Sage Publications (*UK*)
Shelfstealers (*US*)
Sussex Academic Press (*UK*)
Tantor Audio (*US*)
Tiger of the Stripe (*UK*)
Tsaba House (*US*)
Waveland Press, Inc. (*US*)
ZigZag Education (*UK*)
Radio
Geostar Publishing & Services LLC (*US*)
The New Curiosity Shop (*UK*)
Not Your Eyes (*UK*)
Tiger of the Stripe (*UK*)
Reference
AA Publishing (*UK*)
ABC-CLIO / Greenwood (*US*)
Ian Allan Publishing Ltd (*UK*)
Award Publications Limited (*UK*)
Barrington Stoke (*UK*)
BFI Publishing (*UK*)
Bloomsbury Publishing Plc (*UK*)
Boathook Books (*UK*)
Bowker (UK) Ltd (*UK*)
Brown, Son & Ferguson, Ltd (*UK*)
Cadence Jazz Books (*US*)
Centerstream Publishing (*US*)
Chartered Institute of Personnel and
Development (CIPD) Publishing (*UK*)
Chemical Publishing Company (*US*)
Constable & Robinson Ltd (*UK*)
The Crowood Press (*UK*)
Eleusinian Press (*UK*)
EMIS Inc. Medical Publishers (*US*)
Euromonitor (*UK*)
Ex-L-Ence Publishing (*UK*)
Fox Chapel Publishing (*US*)
Geddes & Grosset (*UK*)
Geostar Publishing & Services LLC (*US*)
Gomer Press (*UK*)
Goss & Crested China Club (*UK*)
Grub Street Publishing (*UK*)
Guild of Master Craftsman (GMC) Publications
Ltd (*UK*)
Heritage Books, Inc. (*US*)
Hachette Children's Books (*UK*)
Harry N. Abrams, Inc. (*US*)
Highland Press (*US*)
Hinkler Books (*Aus*)
Igloo Books Limited (*UK*)
The Ilex Press (*UK*)
Impact Books (*US*)
Jonathan David Publishers, Inc. (*US*)
Kalmbach Publishing Co. (*US*)
Lawyers & Judges Publishing Co. (*US*)
The Lilliput Press (*Ire*)
Michelin Maps and Guides (*UK*)

My Pouty Lips (*US*)
Myriad Editions (*UK*)
Neil Wilson Publishing Ltd (*UK*)
New Cavendish Books (*UK*)
The New Curiosity Shop (*UK*)
New Victoria Publishers (*US*)
Nova Press (*US*)
The O'Brien Press (*Ire*)
Octopus Publishing Group Limited (*UK*)
The Orion Publishing Group Limited (*UK*)
Oxford University Press (*UK*)
Pavilion Publishing (*UK*)
Princeton University Press (*US*)
Princeton University Press Europe (*UK*)
Quarto Publishing Group USA (*US*)
Quiller Publishing Ltd (*UK*)
Robert Hale Publishers (*UK*)
SCM-Canterbury Press (*UK*)
Stacey International (*UK*)
Stemmer House Publishers (*US*)
Sunbury Press (*US*)
TSO (The Stationery Office) (*UK*)
Thames and Hudson Ltd (*UK*)
Top That! Publishing (*UK*)
Unicorn Press Ltd (*UK*)
Usborne Publishing (*UK*)
Which? Books (*UK*)
William Reed Business Media (*UK*)
Wolters Kluwer (UK) Ltd (*UK*)

Religious
ABC-CLIO / Greenwood (*US*)
American Press (*US*)
Anaiah Press, LLC (*US*)
Ashgate Publishing Limited (*UK*)
Behrman House (*US*)
Blue Dolphin Publishing (*US*)
Blurbeo (*US*)
Brine Books Publishing (*Can*)
The Catholic University of America Press (*US*)
Cedar Fort (*US*)
Central Avenue Publishing (*Can*)
Christian Focus Publications (*UK*)
Church Growth Institute (*US*)
Clear Light Books (*US*)
The Creative Company (*US*)
Crossway (*US*)
Divertir Publishing LLC (*US*)
ETC Publications (*US*)
Evans Brothers Ltd (*UK*)
Ex-L-Ence Publishing (*UK*)
Flame Lily Books (*UK*)
Floris Books (*UK*)
George Ronald Publisher (*UK*)
Gauthier Publications (*US*)
Geostar Publishing & Services LLC (*US*)
Gomer Press (*UK*)
Halban Publishers (*UK*)
Harry N. Abrams, Inc. (*US*)
Humanics Publishing Group (*US*)
Icon Books Ltd (*UK*)
Ignatius Press (*US*)
Itoh Press (*US*)
Jewish Lights Publishing (*US*)

Jonathan David Publishers, Inc. (*US*)
Kindred Productions (*Can*)
Kelly Point Publishing LLC (*US*)
Legacy Press (*US*)
Lillenas Drama Resources (*US*)
Listen & Live Audio, Inc. (*US*)
Martin Sisters Publishing (*US*)
Master Books (*US*)
Kevin Mayhew Publishers (*UK*)
Medallion Media Group (*US*)
Mercier Press (*Ire*)
Messianic Jewish Publishers (*US*)
NavPress (*US*)
Netherworld Books (*UK*)
The New Curiosity Shop (*UK*)
New Victoria Publishers (*US*)
Nicolas Hays Publishers (*US*)
Not Your Eyes (*UK*)
The O'Brien Press (*Ire*)
Oneworld Publications (*UK*)
Open Gate Press (*UK*)
Oxford University Press (*UK*)
P&R Publishing (*US*)
Pauline Books and Media (*US*)
Possibility Press (*US*)
Princeton University Press (*US*)
Princeton University Press Europe (*UK*)
Quest Books (*US*)
Rowman & Littlefield Publishing Group (*US*)
Sage Publications (*UK*)
SCM-Canterbury Press (*UK*)
Skinner House Books (*US*)
St Augustine's Press (*US*)
Sunberry Books (*UK*)
Sunbury Press (*US*)
Sussex Academic Press (*UK*)
Tantor Audio (*US*)
Thames and Hudson Ltd (*UK*)
Tiger of the Stripe (*UK*)
Tsaba House (*US*)
Tuttle Publishing (*US*)
University of Wales Press (*UK*)
Waveland Press, Inc. (*US*)
Westminster John Knox Press (WJK) (*US*)
ZigZag Education (*UK*)

Romance
Anaiah Press, LLC (*US*)
BHW Publishing House (*UK*)
Black & White Publishing Ltd (*UK*)
Blind Eye Books (*US*)
Bloomsbury Spark (*UK*)
Blurbeo (*US*)
Bold Strokes Books (*US*)
bookouture (*UK*)
Brine Books Publishing (*Can*)
Bullitt Publishing (*US*)
Canterbury House Publishing, Ltd (*US*)
Central Avenue Publishing (*Can*)
Changeling Press LLC (*US*)
Constable & Robinson Ltd (*UK*)
Cup of Tea Books (*US*)
Divertir Publishing LLC (*US*)
Dragonfairy Press (*US*)

Everheart Books (*Can*)
Ex-L-Ence Publishing (*UK*)
Faery Rose (*US*)
Flame Lily Books (*UK*)
48fourteen (*US*)
Freya's Bower (*US*)
Gauthier Publications (*US*)
Geostar Publishing & Services LLC (*US*)
Ghostwoods Books (*UK*)
Glastonbury Publishing (*UK*)
Harlequin Mills & Boon Ltd (*UK*)
Highland Press (*US*)
ImaJinn Books (*US*)
Indigo Dreams Publishing (*UK*)
Ingalls Publishing Group, Inc. (*US*)
Itoh Press (*US*)
John Lynch Digital Publishing House (*Ire*)
Jupiter Gardens Press (*US*)
Kelly Point Publishing LLC (*US*)
Knox Robinson Publishing (UK) (*UK*)
Knox Robinson Publishing (US) (*US*)
Liquid Silver Books (*US*)
Listen & Live Audio, Inc. (*US*)
Loose Id (*US*)
Lucky Marble Books (*US*)
M P Publishing USA (*US*)
Medallion Media Group (*US*)
My Pouty Lips (*US*)
New Dawn Publishers Ltd (*UK*)
Netherworld Books (*UK*)
New Victoria Publishers (*US*)
Not Your Eyes (*UK*)
Open Idea Publishing, LLC (*US*)
Pants On Fire Press (*US*)
SalGad Publishing Group (*UK*)
Shelfstealers (*US*)
Tirgearr Publishing (*Ire*)
Tantor Audio (*US*)
Tiger of the Stripe (*UK*)
Tsaba House (*US*)
The Wild Rose Press (*US*)
The Zharmae Publishing Press (*US*)

Science
American Press (*US*)
Anaiah Press, LLC (*US*)
Arcade Publishing (*US*)
Baywood Publishing Company, Inc. (*US*)
Bick Publishing House (*US*)
Birdsong Books (*US*)
Canongate Books (*UK*)
Canopus Publishing Ltd (*UK*)
Central Avenue Publishing (*Can*)
Chemical Publishing Company (*US*)
Chicago Review Press (*US*)
Compelling Books (*UK*)
Consortium Publishing (*US*)
Constable & Robinson Ltd (*UK*)
Corwin (*US*)
The Creative Company (*US*)
Dover Publications, Inc. (*US*)
Eleusinian Press (*UK*)
Evans Brothers Ltd (*UK*)
Ex-L-Ence Publishing (*UK*)

Fingerpress UK (*UK*)
Flame Lily Books (*UK*)
Floris Books (*UK*)
Gem Guides Book Co. (*US*)
Geostar Publishing & Services LLC (*US*)
Grand Canyon Association (*US*)
Gulf Publishing Company (*US*)
Harry N. Abrams, Inc. (*US*)
Humanics Publishing Group (*US*)
Icon Books Ltd (*UK*)
Indigo Dreams Publishing (*UK*)
International Press (*US*)
Ion Imagination Entertainment, Inc. (*US*)
Jones & Bartlett Learning (*US*)
Kindred Rainbow Publishing (*UK*)
Mentor Books (*Ire*)
Morgan Kaufmann Publishers (*US*)
Mountain Press Publishing Company (*US*)
Netherworld Books (*UK*)
The New Curiosity Shop (*UK*)
Not Your Eyes (*UK*)
Oneworld Publications (*UK*)
Oxford University Press (*UK*)
Paul Dry Books, Inc. (*US*)
Peachtree Publishers (*US*)
Portland Press Ltd (*UK*)
Princeton University Press (*US*)
Princeton University Press Europe (*UK*)
Profile Books (*UK*)
Quarto Publishing Group USA (*US*)
Quest Books (*US*)
Reed Business Information (RBI) (*UK*)
Regnery Publishing, Inc. (*US*)
Ruka Press (*US*)
Sage Publications (*UK*)
Science Navigation Group (*UK*)
Shelfstealers (*US*)
Stemmer House Publishers (*US*)
Sunbury Press (*US*)
Tirgearr Publishing (*Ire*)
Tantor Audio (*US*)
Tiger of the Stripe (*UK*)
Tsaba House (*US*)
Wooden Books (*UK*)
Waveland Press, Inc. (*US*)
Williamson Books (*US*)
ZigZag Education (*UK*)

Sci-Fi
Anaiah Press, LLC (*US*)
BHW Publishing House (*UK*)
Bick Publishing House (*US*)
Blind Eye Books (*US*)
Bloomsbury Spark (*UK*)
Blurbeo (*US*)
Bold Strokes Books (*US*)
bookouture (*UK*)
Brighter Books Publishing House (*Can*)
Brine Books Publishing (*Can*)
By Light Unseen Media (*US*)
Central Avenue Publishing (*Can*)
Changeling Press LLC (*US*)
Colin Smythe Ltd (*UK*)
Compelling Books (*UK*)

Constable & Robinson Ltd (*UK*)
Dagda Publishing (*UK*)
Divertir Publishing LLC (*US*)
Dragonfairy Press (*US*)
Eleusinian Press (*UK*)
Ex-L-Ence Publishing (*UK*)
Faery Rose (*US*)
Fingerpress UK (*UK*)
Flame Lily Books (*UK*)
48fourteen (*US*)
Geostar Publishing & Services LLC (*US*)
Ghostwoods Books (*UK*)
Glastonbury Publishing (*UK*)
Hadley Rille Books (*US*)
ImaJinn Books (*US*)
Indigo Dreams Publishing (*UK*)
Itoh Press (*US*)
Jewish Lights Publishing (*US*)
Jo Fletcher Books (*UK*)
John Lynch Digital Publishing House (*Ire*)
Jupiter Gardens Press (*US*)
Kelly Point Publishing LLC (*US*)
Kindred Rainbow Publishing (*UK*)
Listen & Live Audio, Inc. (*US*)
Loose Id (*US*)
Lost Tower Publications (*UK*)
Lucky Marble Books (*US*)
M P Publishing USA (*US*)
Martin Sisters Publishing (*US*)
Medallion Media Group (*US*)
New Dawn Publishers Ltd (*UK*)
New Libri (*US*)
NBM (*US*)
Netherworld Books (*UK*)
The New Curiosity Shop (*UK*)
New Victoria Publishers (*US*)
Not Your Eyes (*UK*)
The Orion Publishing Group Limited (*UK*)
Pants On Fire Press (*US*)
Quercus Books (*UK*)
Ramsay Publishing (*UK*)
Red Deer Press (*Can*)
Shelfstealers (*US*)
Tirgearr Publishing (*Ire*)
Titan Books (*UK*)
Tor/Forge (*US*)
The Zharmae Publishing Press (*US*)
Scripts
Aurora Metro Press (*UK*)
Bronze Man Books (*US*)
Chapman Publishing (*UK*)
Colin Smythe Ltd (*UK*)
Cressrelles Publishing Co. Ltd (*UK*)
Faber & Faber Ltd (*UK*)
The Gallery Press (*Ire*)
Gomer Press (*UK*)
Lillenas Drama Resources (*US*)
The Lilliput Press (*Ire*)
Methuen Publishing Ltd (*UK*)
New Island (*Ire*)
NeWest Press (*Can*)
Nick Hern Books Ltd (*UK*)
Oberon Books (*UK*)

Samuel French Ltd (*UK*)
Self-Help
Bick Publishing House (*US*)
John Blake Publishing (*UK*)
Blue Dolphin Publishing (*US*)
Cedar Fort (*US*)
Central Avenue Publishing (*Can*)
Consortium Publishing (*US*)
Constable & Robinson Ltd (*UK*)
Divertir Publishing LLC (*US*)
Eleusinian Press (*UK*)
Ex-L-Ence Publishing (*UK*)
Floris Books (*UK*)
Gauthier Publications (*US*)
Geostar Publishing & Services LLC (*US*)
Glenbridge Publishing Ltd (*US*)
Hawthorn Press (*UK*)
Humanics Publishing Group (*US*)
Listen & Live Audio, Inc. (*US*)
Management Books 2000 Ltd (*UK*)
Mandrake of Oxford (*UK*)
Martin Sisters Publishing (*US*)
My Pouty Lips (*US*)
Nicolas Hays Publishers (*US*)
Not Your Eyes (*UK*)
Oneworld Publications (*UK*)
Pauline Books and Media (*US*)
Peachtree Publishers (*US*)
Piatkus Books (*UK*)
Possibility Press (*US*)
Princeton University Press (*US*)
Princeton University Press Europe (*UK*)
Quarto Publishing Group USA (*US*)
Quest Books (*US*)
Rainbow Books, Inc. (*US*)
Reading Harbor (*US*)
Shelfstealers (*US*)
Tirgearr Publishing (*Ire*)
Tantor Audio (*US*)
Tiger of the Stripe (*UK*)
Tristan Publishing (*US*)
Tsaba House (*US*)
Short Stories
Aurora Metro Press (*UK*)
BHW Publishing House (*UK*)
Black Lawrence Press (*US*)
Blackstaff Press Ltd (*UK*)
Blurbeo (*US*)
Boathook Books (*UK*)
Brine Books Publishing (*Can*)
Bronze Man Books (*US*)
Cedar Fort (*US*)
Central Avenue Publishing (*Can*)
Chapman Publishing (*UK*)
CN Writers (*UK*)
Coastal West Publishing (*Can*)
Coffee House Press (*US*)
Compelling Books (*US*)
Divertir Publishing LLC (*US*)
Down The Shore Publishing (*US*)
Dzanc Books (*US*)
Eleusinian Press (*UK*)
Erotic Review (ER) Books (*UK*)

Ex-L-Ence Publishing (*UK*)
Flame Lily Books (*UK*)
Four Way Books (*US*)
Freya's Bower (*US*)
Gauthier Publications (*US*)
Geostar Publishing & Services LLC (*US*)
Ghostwoods Books (*UK*)
Glass Page Books (*US*)
Headland Publications (*UK*)
Hearts 'N Tummies Cookbook Co. / Quixote Press (*US*)
Honno Welsh Women's Press (*UK*)
Jupiter Gardens Press (*US*)
Kelly Point Publishing LLC (*US*)
Kind of a Hurricane Press (*US*)
Ledge Hill Publishing (*US*)
Les Figues Press (*US*)
M P Publishing USA (*US*)
Mango Publishing (*UK*)
Manor House Publishing (*Can*)
Martin Sisters Publishing (*US*)
Moose Hide Books (*Can*)
My Pouty Lips (*US*)
New Dawn Publishers Ltd (*UK*)
New Rivers Press (*US*)
New Victoria Publishers (*US*)
Not Your Eyes (*UK*)
Open Idea Publishing, LLC (*US*)
Paul Dry Books, Inc. (*US*)
Persea Books (*US*)
Press 53 (*US*)
Pressgang (*US*)
Ramsay Publishing (*UK*)
Reading Harbor (*US*)
Ronsdale Press (*Can*)
Shelfstealers (*US*)
Stairwell Books (*UK*)
Stemmer House Publishers (*US*)
Tantor Audio (*US*)
Tiger of the Stripe (*UK*)
Titan Books (*UK*)
Tristan Publishing (*US*)

Sociology
ABC-CLIO / Greenwood (*US*)
Amberley Publishing (*UK*)
American Press (*US*)
Ammonite Press (*UK*)
Ashgate Publishing Limited (*UK*)
Baywood Publishing Company, Inc. (*US*)
Blue Dolphin Publishing (*US*)
Brine Books Publishing (*Can*)
The Catholic University of America Press (*US*)
Central Avenue Publishing (*Can*)
City Lights Publishers (*US*)
The Creative Company (*US*)
Eleusinian Press (*UK*)
ETC Publications (*US*)
Evans Brothers Ltd (*UK*)
Ex-L-Ence Publishing (*UK*)
Florida Academic Press (*US*)
Floris Books (*UK*)
Geostar Publishing & Services LLC (*US*)
Institute of Public Administration (IPA) (*Ire*)

Itoh Press (*US*)
The Lilliput Press (*Ire*)
Logaston Press (*UK*)
Luath Press Ltd (*UK*)
NavPress (*US*)
The New Curiosity Shop (*UK*)
New Island (*Ire*)
Not Your Eyes (*UK*)
Ooligan Press (*US*)
Open Gate Press (*UK*)
Oxford University Press (*UK*)
Pavilion Publishing (*UK*)
Pen & Sword Books Ltd (*UK*)
Pluto Publishing Ltd (*UK*)
The Policy Press (*UK*)
Princeton University Press (*US*)
Princeton University Press Europe (*UK*)
Rivers Oram Press (*UK*)
Rowman & Littlefield Publishing Group (*US*)
Sage Publications (*UK*)
Shelfstealers (*US*)
Sussex Academic Press (*UK*)
Tantor Audio (*US*)
Trentham Books Limited (*UK*)
University of Wales Press (*UK*)
Waveland Press, Inc. (*US*)
ZigZag Education (*UK*)

Spiritual
Anaiah Press, LLC (*US*)
BHW Publishing House (*UK*)
Blue Dolphin Publishing (*US*)
Blurbeo (*US*)
Brine Books Publishing (*Can*)
Cedar Fort (*US*)
Central Avenue Publishing (*Can*)
Coastal West Publishing (*Can*)
Divertir Publishing LLC (*US*)
Eleusinian Press (*UK*)
Ex-L-Ence Publishing (*UK*)
Fitzrovia Press Limited (*UK*)
Floris Books (*UK*)
Geostar Publishing & Services LLC (*US*)
Hinkler Books (*Aus*)
Indigo Dreams Publishing (*UK*)
Itoh Press (*US*)
Jewish Lights Publishing (*US*)
Kelly Point Publishing LLC (*US*)
Lost Tower Publications (*UK*)
Mandala Earth (*US*)
Mandrake of Oxford (*UK*)
Kevin Mayhew Publishers (*UK*)
NavPress (*US*)
Netherworld Books (*UK*)
Not Your Eyes (*UK*)
Octopus Publishing Group Limited (*UK*)
Pauline Books and Media (*US*)
Piatkus Books (*US*)
Possibility Press (*US*)
Princeton University Press (*US*)
Quest Books (*US*)
Rio Nuevo Publishers (*US*)
Robert Hale Publishers (*UK*)
SCM-Canterbury Press (*UK*)

Shelfstealers (*US*)
Skinner House Books (*US*)
Tantor Audio (*US*)
Tsaba House (*US*)
Tuttle Publishing (*US*)
Wooden Books (*UK*)
Westminster John Knox Press (WJK) (*US*)
Sport
Amberley Publishing (*UK*)
American Press (*US*)
Aureus Publishing Limited (*UK*)
Aurum Press Ltd (*UK*)
Black & White Publishing Ltd (*UK*)
Blackline Press (*UK*)
Blackstaff Press Ltd (*UK*)
John Blake Publishing (*UK*)
Bloomsbury Publishing Plc (*UK*)
Boathook Books (*UK*)
Burford Books (*US*)
Central Avenue Publishing (*Can*)
Chicago Review Press (*US*)
Constable & Robinson Ltd (*UK*)
The Creative Company (*US*)
The Crowood Press (*UK*)
Cycle Publishing / Van der Plas Publications (*US*)
Down East Books (*US*)
ETC Publications (*US*)
Ex-L-Ence Publishing (*UK*)
Fox Chapel Publishing (*US*)
Geostar Publishing & Services LLC (*US*)
Gomer Press (*UK*)
Grand Canyon Association (*US*)
Harry N. Abrams, Inc. (*US*)
Hinkler Books (*Aus*)
Icon Books Ltd (*UK*)
Indigo Dreams Publishing (*UK*)
Jonathan David Publishers, Inc. (*US*)
Kelly Point Publishing LLC (*US*)
The Lilliput Press (*Ire*)
Listen & Live Audio, Inc. (*US*)
Luath Press Ltd (*UK*)
Lucky Marble Books (*US*)
Mainstream Publishing Co. (Edinburgh) Ltd (*UK*)
Mentor Books (*Ire*)
Mercier Press (*Ire*)
Methuen Publishing Ltd (*UK*)
Motor Racing Publications (*UK*)
The New Curiosity Shop (*UK*)
Not Your Eyes (*UK*)
The O'Brien Press (*Ire*)
Octopus Publishing Group Limited (*UK*)
The Orion Publishing Group Limited (*UK*)
Pants On Fire Press (*US*)
Peachtree Publishers (*US*)
Pennant Books Ltd (*UK*)
Quarto Publishing Group UK (*UK*)
Quarto Publishing Group USA (*US*)
Quiller Publishing Ltd (*UK*)
Seren (*UK*)
SportsBooks Limited (*UK*)

Tantor Audio (*US*)
Tuttle Publishing (*US*)
ZigZag Education (*UK*)
Suspense
Anaiah Press, LLC (*US*)
Blurbeo (*US*)
bookouture (*UK*)
Brine Books Publishing (*Can*)
Canterbury House Publishing, Ltd (*US*)
Central Avenue Publishing (*Can*)
Dagda Publishing (*UK*)
Divertir Publishing LLC (*US*)
Ex-L-Ence Publishing (*UK*)
Fingerpress UK (*UK*)
Flame Lily Books (*UK*)
Gauthier Publications (*US*)
Geostar Publishing & Services LLC (*US*)
Glastonbury Publishing (*UK*)
Highland Press (*US*)
Indigo Dreams Publishing (*UK*)
Itoh Press (*US*)
Loose Id (*US*)
Lost Tower Publications (*UK*)
Lucky Marble Books (*US*)
M P Publishing USA (*US*)
Medallion Media Group (*US*)
Moose Hide Books (*Can*)
New Dawn Publishers Ltd (*UK*)
Netherworld Books (*UK*)
Not Your Eyes (*UK*)
Pants On Fire Press (*US*)
Pressgang (*US*)
Shelfstealers (*US*)
Tirgearr Publishing (*Ire*)
Tantor Audio (*US*)
Tiger of the Stripe (*UK*)
Tor/Forge (*US*)
Tsaba House (*US*)
The Zharmae Publishing Press (*US*)
Technology
American Press (*US*)
Baywood Publishing Company, Inc. (*US*)
Brown, Son & Ferguson, Ltd (*UK*)
Central Avenue Publishing (*Can*)
Chemical Publishing Company (*US*)
Compelling Books (*UK*)
Corwin (*US*)
Evans Brothers Ltd (*UK*)
Ex-L-Ence Publishing (*UK*)
Fingerpress UK (*UK*)
Flame Lily Books (*UK*)
Geostar Publishing & Services LLC (*US*)
Gulf Publishing Company (*US*)
Jones & Bartlett Learning (*US*)
Morgan Kaufmann Publishers (*US*)
New Libri (*US*)
The New Curiosity Shop (*UK*)
Not Your Eyes (*UK*)
Pants On Fire Press (*US*)
PennWell Books (*US*)
Possibility Press (*US*)
Princeton University Press (*US*)
Quarto Publishing Group USA (*US*)

Sage Publications (*UK*)
Shelfstealers (*US*)
Tirgearr Publishing (*Ire*)
Texas Tech University Press (*US*)
Tiger of the Stripe (*UK*)
Ulric Publishing (*UK*)
Waveland Press, Inc. (*US*)
Which? Books (*UK*)
ZigZag Education (*UK*)

Theatre
American Press (*US*)
Aurora Metro Press (*UK*)
Central Avenue Publishing (*Can*)
Colin Smythe Ltd (*UK*)
The Crowood Press (*UK*)
Eleusinian Press (*UK*)
Ex-L-Ence Publishing (*UK*)
Faber & Faber Ltd (*UK*)
The Gallery Press (*Ire*)
Geostar Publishing & Services LLC (*US*)
Glenbridge Publishing Ltd (*US*)
Gomer Press (*UK*)
Indigo Dreams Publishing (*UK*)
Itoh Press (*US*)
Methuen Publishing Ltd (*UK*)
Moose Hide Books (*Can*)
The New Curiosity Shop (*UK*)
Nick Hern Books Ltd (*UK*)
Not Your Eyes (*UK*)
Oberon Books (*UK*)
Open Idea Publishing, LLC (*US*)
The Overlook Press (*US*)
Ronsdale Press (*Can*)
Sussex Academic Press (*UK*)
Tiger of the Stripe (*UK*)
Waveland Press, Inc. (*US*)

Thrillers
Anaiah Press, LLC (*US*)
BHW Publishing House (*UK*)
Bloomsbury Spark (*UK*)
Blurbeo (*US*)
bookouture (*UK*)
Brine Books Publishing (*Can*)
Central Avenue Publishing (*Can*)
Eleusinian Press (*UK*)
Emissary Publishing (*UK*)
Ex-L-Ence Publishing (*UK*)
Fingerpress UK (*UK*)
Flame Lily Books (*UK*)
48fourteen (*US*)
Gauthier Publications (*US*)
Geostar Publishing & Services LLC (*US*)
Ghostwoods Books (*UK*)
Glastonbury Publishing (*UK*)
Indigo Dreams Publishing (*UK*)
Lost Tower Publications (*UK*)
Luath Press Ltd (*UK*)
M P Publishing USA (*US*)
Medallion Media Group (*US*)
New Dawn Publishers Ltd (*UK*)
Netherworld Books (*UK*)
New Victoria Publishers (*US*)
Not Your Eyes (*UK*)

Oceanview Publishing (*US*)
Pants On Fire Press (*US*)
Piatkus Books (*UK*)
SalGad Publishing Group (*UK*)
Salt Publishing Ltd (*UK*)
Shelfstealers (*US*)
Tirgearr Publishing (*Ire*)
Tiger of the Stripe (*UK*)
Tsaba House (*US*)
The Zharmae Publishing Press (*US*)

Translations
Alondra Press (*US*)
Arc Publications (*UK*)
Aurora Metro Press (*UK*)
Aurora Publishing, Inc (*US*)
Black Lawrence Press (*US*)
Brine Books Publishing (*Can*)
Canongate Books (*UK*)
Central Avenue Publishing (*Can*)
City Lights Publishers (*US*)
Compelling Books (*UK*)
Cross-Cultural Communications Publications (*US*)
Dedalus Ltd (*UK*)
Duckworth Publishers (*UK*)
Eleusinian Press (*UK*)
Gauthier Publications (*US*)
Geostar Publishing & Services LLC (*US*)
Indigo Dreams Publishing (*UK*)
Mango Publishing (*UK*)
Mantra Lingua Ltd (*UK*)
New Native Press (*US*)
Not Your Eyes (*UK*)
The Overlook Press (*US*)
Peter Owen Publishers (*UK*)
Paul Dry Books, Inc. (*US*)
Persea Books (*US*)
Seren (*UK*)
Shearsman Books (*UK*)
Tiger of the Stripe (*UK*)
University of Nebraska Press (*US*)

Travel
AA Publishing (*UK*)
Alastair Sawday Publishing Co. Ltd (*UK*)
Ian Allan Publishing Ltd (*UK*)
Amberley Publishing (*UK*)
Antique Collectors' Club Ltd (*UK*)
Arcade Publishing (*US*)
The Armchair Traveller at the bookHaus (*UK*)
Aurum Press Ltd (*UK*)
BHW Publishing House (*UK*)
Blackstaff Press Ltd (*UK*)
Blue Guides Limited (*UK*)
Boathook Books (*UK*)
Burford Books (*US*)
Canongate Books (*UK*)
Central Avenue Publishing (*Can*)
Channel Lake, Inc. (*US*)
Chicago Review Press (*US*)
Constable & Robinson Ltd (*UK*)
Cork University Press (*Ire*)
The Countryman Press (*US*)
The Crowood Press (*UK*)

US Magazines

For the most up-to-date listings of these and hundreds of other magazines, visit http://www.firstwriter.com/magazines

*To claim your **free** access to the site, please see the back of this book.*

American Indian Art Magazine
7314 East Osborn Drive
Scottsdale, AZ 85251
Tel: +1 (480) 994-5445
Fax: +1 (480) 945-9533
Email: editorial@aiamagazine.com
Website: http://www.aiamagazine.com

Publishes: Articles; Nonfiction; *Areas:* Arts; *Markets:* Adult; Professional

Publishes articles covering the art of all native Americans. Articles should be of interest to both casual readers and professionals. See website for full guidelines.

Adventure Cyclist
150 East Pine Street
Missoula, MT 59802
Tel: +1 (406) 532-2762
Email: mdeme@adventurecycling.org
Website: http://www.adventurecycling.org/adventure-cyclist

Publishes: Articles; Essays; Features; Nonfiction; *Areas:* How-to; Technology; Travel; *Markets:* Adult

Editors: Mike Deme

Magazine dedicated to bicycle travel and adventure. See website for full submission guidelines, and submit using online submission system.

African-American Career World
Equal Opportunity Publications, Inc.
445 Broad Hollow Road, Suite 425
Melville, NY 11747
Tel: +1 (631) 421-9421
Fax: +1 (631) 421-1352
Email: info@eop.com
Website: http://www.eop.com

Publishes: Articles; Nonfiction; Reference; *Areas:* How-to; Self-Help; *Markets:* Adult; Professional

Careers magazine aimed at African Americans.

Akron Life
1653 Merriman Road, Suite 116
Akron OH 44313
Tel: +1 (330) 253-0056
Fax: +1 (330) 253-5868
Email: editor@bakermediagroup.com
Website: http://www.akronlife.com

Publishes: Articles; Features; Interviews; Nonfiction; *Areas:* Arts; Beauty and Fashion; Culture; Entertainment; Gardening; Health; Historical; How-to; Humour; Leisure; Lifestyle; Travel; *Markets:* Adult

Editors: Abby Cymerman

Monthly regional lifestyle publication committed to providing information that enhances and enriches the experience of living in or visiting Akron and the surrounding region of Summit, Portage, Medina and Stark Counties.

Alimentum
PO Box 210028
Nashville, TN 37221
Email: editor@alimentumjournal.com
Website: http://www.alimentumjournal.com

Publishes: Essays; Fiction; Nonfiction; Poetry; Reviews; *Areas:* Cookery; Short Stories; *Markets:* Adult; *Treatments:* Literary

Editors: Peter Selgin, fiction and nonfiction editor; Cortney Davis, poetry editor

Publishes poetry, fiction, creative nonfiction, book reviews, and art, related to food. Send submissions by post with SAE in specific submission windows. See website for more details.

American Careers
6701 West 64th Street, Suite 210
Overland Park, KS 66202
Tel: +1 (800) 669-7795
Email: ccinfo@carcom.com
Website: http://www.carcom.com

Publishes: Articles; Nonfiction; *Areas:* How-to; Self-Help; *Markets:* Children's

Publishes career information for middle and high school students. Send query with sample and CV in first instance.

American Turf Monthly
747 Middle Neck Road
Great Neck, NY 11024
Tel: +1 (516) 773-4075
Fax: +1 (516) 773-2944
Email: editor@americanturf.com
Website: http://www.americanturf.com

Publishes: Articles; Nonfiction; *Areas:*

Sport; *Markets:* Adult

Editors: Joe Girardi

Horse racing magazine aimed at horseplayers, focusing on handicapping and wagering. Not aimed at owners or breeders. Send query in first instance.

Amulet
PO Box 761495
San Antonio, CA 78245

or

PO Box 884223
San Francisco, CA 94188-4223
Email: amulet20032003@yahoo.com
Website:
https://sites.google.com/site/conceitmagazine/home/amulet

Publishes: Poetry; *Markets:* Adult

Editors: Perry Terrell

Publishes 16 writers each month – both new and established writers. Unsolicited, simultaneous, and previously published manuscripts are welcomed. No reading fee. Submit by post or by email.

Angus Beef Bulletin
3201 Frederick Avenue
St Joseph, MO 64506-2997
Tel: +1 (816) 383-5270
Email: shermel@angusjournal.com
Website: http://www.angusbeefbulletin.com

Publishes: Articles; Interviews; Nonfiction; *Areas:* Business; How-to; Nature; Technology; *Markets:* Professional; *Treatments:* Commercial

Editors: Shauna Rose Hermel

Publishes material aimed at commercial cattle owners of Angus bulls.

Aquatics International
6222 Wilshire Boulevard, Suite 600
Los Angeles, CA 90048

Tel: +1 (972) 536-6439
Email: etaylor@hanleywood.com
Website: http://www.aquaticsintl.com

Publishes: Articles; Interviews; Nonfiction;
Areas: Business; How-to; Technology;
Theatre; *Markets:* Professional

Editors: Erika Taylor, Editorial Director

Magazine aimed at professionals in the
commercial and public swimming pool
industries. Send query with published clips.

Arms Control Today
1313 L Street, NW, Suite 130
Washington, DC 20005
Tel: +1 (202) 463-8270
Fax: +1 (202) 463-8273
Email: aca@armscontrol.org
Website: https://www.armscontrol.org

Publishes: Articles; Nonfiction; *Areas:*
Military; *Markets:* Adult; Professional

Publishes articles providing information and
ideas to solve global nuclear, biological,
chemical, and conventional weapons-related
security challenges. Articles should be aimed
at both experts and non-experts. Send query
with outline in first instance.

Asheville Poetry Review
PO Box 7086
Asheville, NC 28802
Email: editor@ashevillepoetryreview.com
Website:
http://www.ashevillepoetryreview.com

Publishes: Essays; Interviews; Nonfiction;
Poetry; Reviews; *Areas:* Translations;
Markets: Adult; *Treatments:* Literary

Editors: Keith Flynn

Accepts regular submissions between
January 15 and July 15 each year. Send 3-6
poems of any length or style, with SASE.
Between July 15 and January 15 each year,
accepts submissions through its annual
poetry competition: $1,000 prize and $20
entry fee. No submissions by email.

Astronomy
Kalmbach Publishing
21027 Crossroads Circle
PO Box 1612
Waukesha, WI 53187-1612
Tel: +1 (800) 533-6644
Fax: +1 (262) 798-6468
Website: http://www.astronomy.com

Publishes: Articles; *Areas:* Hobbies; How-
to; Science; *Markets:* Adult

Magazine publishing articles on the science
and hobby of astronomy. Send query by post
or via form on website.

ATV Rider Magazine
GrindMedia, LLC
1733 Alton Parkway
Irvine, CA 92606
Tel: +1 (763) 383-4499
Website: http://www.atvrider.com

Publishes: Articles; Features; Interviews;
Nonfiction; *Areas:* Hobbies; Technology;
Travel; *Markets:* Adult

Editors: John Prusak

Magazine for all-terain vehicle enthusiasts.
Send query with published clips.

Big Fiction
Email: info@bigfictionmagazine.com
Website:
http://www.bigfictionmagazine.com

Publishes: Fiction; *Areas:* Short Stories;
Markets: Adult; *Treatments:* Literary

Literary magazine devoted to longer short
fiction, between 7,500 and 30,000 words.
Accepts submissions online via competition
($20 entry fee).

Black Heart Magazine
Email: laura@blackheartmagazine.com
Website: http://blackheartmagazine.com

Publishes: Fiction; Interviews; Nonfiction;
Poetry; Reviews; *Areas:* Arts; Crime;
Criticism; Fantasy; Humour; Literature;

Mystery; Philosophy; Sci-Fi; Short Stories; Suspense; *Markets:* Adult; *Treatments:* Contemporary; Cynical; Dark; Experimental; Light; Literary; Positive; Progressive; Satirical

Editors: Laura Roberts

An independent online literary magazine, transmitting our tenacious texts around the world at the speed of wifi. Tthe site has been combating clichés and berating boring wordslinging since 2004. Our objective can be summarised in three short words:

Reading. Writing. Rebellion.

That's LITERARY rebellion, so ease off the trigger there, tiger.

In brief, we publish fiction that breaks the rules. Join us, if you dare.

Burnside Review
Portland, Oregon
Email: sid@burnsidereview.org
Website: http://burnsidereview.org

Publishes: Fiction; Poetry; *Areas:* Short Stories; *Markets:* Adult

Editors: Sid Miller

Publishes poetry and fiction. Send 3-5 poems and brief bio, or fiction up to 5,000 words (can be collections of flash fiction or a single story), using online submission system only. $3 fee.

Carve Magazine
PO Box 701510
Dallas, TX 75370
Email: managingeditor@carvezine.com
Website: http://carvezine.com

Publishes: Fiction; *Areas:* Short Stories; *Markets:* Adult; *Treatments:* Literary

Editors: Kristin S. vanNamen, PhD

Publishes literary fiction up to 10,000 words, and poetry/fiction crossovers: poetry that tells a story; or flash fiction that has a lyrical

feel, etc. No genre fiction or previously published fiction. Submit by post for free, or via online submission system for $3. See website for full guidelines.

China Grove
Website: http://www.chinagrovepress.com

Publishes: Essays; Fiction; Nonfiction; Poetry; *Areas:* Short Stories; *Markets:* Adult; *Treatments:* Literary

Literary journal publishing fiction, poetry, and essays. Submit via online submission system only – small fee ($2-$3) to cover expenses. Also offers prizes.

Christian Home & School
3350 East Paris Ave. S.E.
Grand Rapids, MI 49512
Tel: +1 (800) 635-8288
Fax: +1 (616) 957-5022
Email: Rheyboer@CSIonline.org

Publishes: Articles; Nonfiction; *Areas:* Lifestyle; Religious; *Markets:* Adult

Editors: Rachael Heyboer

Magazine for parents who send their children to Christian schools. Promotes Christian education and addresses a wide range of parenting topics. Send complete ms. See website for full guidelines.

Cigar Aficionado
M. Shanken Communications, Inc.,
387 Park Avenue, South, 8th Floor
New York, NY 10016
Tel: +1 (212) 684-4224
Fax: +1 (212) 684-5424
Website: http://www.cigaraficionado.com

Publishes: Articles; Features; Nonfiction; *Areas:* Hobbies; *Markets:* Adult

Magazine covering cigar smoking. Query in the first instance.

Classic Toy Trains
To the Editor, CLASSIC TOY TRAINS
Kalmbach Publishing Co.

PO Box 1612
21027 Crossroads Cir.
Waukesha, WI 53187-1612
Tel: +1 (262) 796-8776, ext. 524
Fax: +1 (262) 796-1142
Email: manuscripts@classictoytrains.com
Website: http://ctt.trains.com

Publishes: Articles; Nonfiction; *Areas:*
Historical; Hobbies; How-to; *Markets:* Adult

Magazine publishing articles on toy trains:
how-to guides and articles on their history.
Accepts submissions by post and by email –
see website for detailed submission
guidelines.

Club Management

Finan Publishing Co.
107 West Pacific Avenue
St Louis, MO 63119
Tel: +1 (314) 961-6644
Fax: +1 (314) 961-4809
Email: clubs@theYGSgroup.com
Website: http://www.club-mgmt.com

Publishes: Articles; Nonfiction; *Areas:*
Business; Leisure; *Markets:* Professional

Magazine for hospitality industry
professionals, covering the private club
industry and club management. Send query
with published clips.

Colorado Homes & Lifestyles

1777 S. Harrison Street Suite 903
Denver, CO 80210
Tel: +1 (303) 248-2060
Fax: +1 (303) 248-2066
Email: mabel@coloradohomesmag.com
Website:
http://www.coloradohomesmag.com

Publishes: Articles; Nonfiction; *Areas:*
Architecture; Design; Gardening; Lifestyle;
Markets: Adult

Magazine of homes, gardening, and lifestyles
in Colorado. Send query with published clips
in the first instance.

Common Ground Review

H-5132
Western New England University
1215 Wilbraham Road, Springfield, MA
01119
Tel: +1 (413) 782-1729
Email: submissions@cgreview.org
Website: http://www.cgreview.org

Publishes: Fiction; Nonfiction; Poetry;
Areas: Short Stories; *Markets:* Adult;
Treatments: Literary

Editors: Janet Bowdan

Publishes two issues a year, with deadlines
of August 31 and March 31. Submit up to
three poems per issue. Publishes one piece of
creative nonfiction in the Autumn/Winter
issue, and one short story in the
Spring/Summer issue. Prose may be up to 12
double-spaced pages. Accepts submissions
by post or by email. See website for full
guidelines.

Conceit Magazine

PO Box 761495
San Antonio, CA 78245

or

PO Box 884223
San Francisco, CA 94188-4223
Email: Conceitmagazine2007@yahoo.com
Website:
https://sites.google.com/site/conceitmagazine
/

Publishes: Articles; Essays; Fiction; News;
Nonfiction; Poetry; *Areas:* Short Stories;
Markets: Adult; *Treatments:* Literary

Editors: Perry Terrell

Publishes poetry, short stories, articles,
essays, and new book and magazine
announcements. Material must be family-
friendly. Submit by post or by email. See
website for more details.

Concrete Homes Magazine

Publications and Communications, Inc.
13581 Pond Springs Road, Suite 450

Austin, TX 78729
Fax: +1 (512) 331-3950
Email: homes@pcinews.com
Website: http://concretehomesmagazine.com

Publishes: Articles; News; Nonfiction;
Areas: Architecture; Design; How-to;
Markets: Adult; Professional

Publishes news and articles on concrete
homes. Aimed at both consumers and
professionals (builders / architects, etc.).
Send query with published clips.

The Conium Review
Portland, OR
Email: coniumreview@gmail.com
Website: http://www.coniumreview.com

Publishes: Fiction; Poetry; *Areas:* Arts;
Culture; Drama; Fantasy; Lifestyle;
Literature; Philosophy; Photography;
Markets: Academic; Adult; *Treatments:*
Contemporary; Experimental; Literary;
Niche; Progressive; Satirical

Editors: James R. Gapinski, Uma Sankaram,
Tristan Beach, and Susan Lynch

A print-based publication. We seek eclectic,
eccentric, and idiosyncratic writing from
new and established, authors. Visit our
website to order an issue, submit your
creative writing, listen to our free podcast, or
read our editorial reviews.

Consumers Digest
Consumers Digest Communications, LLC
520 Lake Cook Road
Suite 500
Deerfield, IL 60015
Email: editor@consumersdigest.com
Website: http://www.consumersdigest.com

Publishes: Articles; Nonfiction; *Areas:*
Finance; Gardening; Health; Leisure;
Lifestyle; Technology; Travel; *Markets:*
Adult

Magazine consumer issues / items of interest
to consumers / new products, etc. Send query
in first instance.

Crain's Detroit Business
Crain Communications, Inc.
1155 Gratiot
Detroit, MI 48207
Tel: +1 (313) 446-0419
Fax: +1 (313) 446-1687
Email: kcrain@crain.com
Website: http://www.crainsdetroit.com

Publishes: Articles; News; Nonfiction;
Areas: Business; *Markets:* Adult;
Professional

Editors: Keith Crain

Magazine covering business in the Detroit
metropolitan area. Local topics only. Send
query with published clips.

Currents
Marine Technology Society
5565 Sterrett Place, Suite 108
Columbia, MD 21044
Email: publications@mtsociety.org
Website:
https://www.mtsociety.org/publications/

Publishes: Articles; News; Nonfiction;
Areas: Science; Technology; *Markets:*
Academic; Professional

Bimonthly newsletter of marine technology.
Send query in first instance.

DASH Journal
Department of English and Comparative
Literature
California State University Fullerton
800 North State College Boulevard
Fullerton, CA 92831
Email: DASHLiteraryJournal@gmail.com
Website: http://dashliteraryjournal.com

Publishes: Essays; Fiction; Nonfiction;
Poetry; *Areas:* Criticism; Short Stories;
Markets: Adult; *Treatments:* Literary

Submit one piece of prose or up to five
poems, between January 1 and March 1
annually. Prefers email submissions. Any
submissions not conforming to the guidelines
will be immediately discarded. See website
for full details.

Delaware Today

3301 Lancaster Pike, Suite 5C
Wilmington, DE 19805
Tel: +1 (302) 656-1809
Email: editors@delawaretoday.com

Publishes: Articles; Features; Interviews;
News; Nonfiction; *Areas:* Business; Health;
Historical; *Markets:* Adult

All material must be of genuine interest to
residents of Delaware. No national topics
dressed up as having a Delaware slant. Send
query with published clips.

Diabetes Self-Management

R.A. Rapaport Publishing, Inc.
150 West 22nd Street, Suite 800
New York, NY 10011
Tel: +1 (212) 989-0200
Fax: +1 (212) 989-4786
Email: editor@diabetes-self-mgmt.com
Website:
http://www.diabetesselfmanagement.com

Publishes: Articles; Reviews; *Areas:* Health;
Medicine; Self-Help; *Markets:* Adult;
Treatments: Positive

Magazine for people with diabetes who want
to know more about controlling and
managing their diabetes. Articles must
address the day-to-day and long-term
concerns of readers in a positive and upbeat
manner. Queries accepted by email. See
website for more details.

Discover Maine Magazine

10 Exchange St. Suite 208
Portland, ME 04101
Tel: +1 (800) 753-8684
Email: info@discovermainemagazine.com
Website:
http://www.discovermainemagazine.com

Publishes: Articles; Nonfiction; *Areas:*
Historical; Leisure; Nature; Sport; *Markets:*
Adult

Regional magazine publishing articles on the
history of Maine, as well as its hunting,
fishing, and sports. Submit stories via
website.

The Doctor T. J. Eckleburg Review

The Johns Hopkins University
1717 Massachusetts Avenue, NW Suite 101
Washington, DC 20036
Tel: +1 (202) 452-1927
Fax: +1 (202) 452-8713
Website:
http://thedoctortjeckleburgreview.com

Publishes: Fiction; Poetry; Reviews; *Areas:*
Arts; Short Stories; *Markets: Treatments:*
Experimental; Literary; Mainstream

Magazine describing itself as eclectic,
literary mainstream to experimental.
Publishes poetry, fiction, creative nonfiction,
and reviews. Submit 1-5 poems or one piece
of prose up to 8,000 words. No multiple
submissions. Simultaneous submissions are
accepted if immediate notification of
publication elsewhere is provided. See
website for full guidelines, and for link to
online submission system.

Draft

Draft Publishing
4742 North 24th Street, Suite 210
Phoenix, AZ 85016
Tel: +1 (888) 806-4677
Email: jessica.daynor@draftmag.com
Website: http://draftmag.com

Publishes: Articles; News; Nonfiction;
Areas: Cookery; Hobbies; Leisure; Sport;
Travel; *Markets:* Adult

Beer magazine, also publishing articles on
food, sports (both professional and leisure),
travel, and many other topics. Beer articles
should concentrate on beer and brewery
news, rather than the technical aspects of
brewing. No pre-written stories. Send query
by email with pitch. See website for full
guidelines.

Eclectica Magazine

Email: submissions@eclectica.org
Website: http://www.eclectica.org

Publishes: Essays; Fiction; Interviews;
Nonfiction; Poetry; Reviews; Scripts; *Areas:*
Drama; Film; Humour; Literature; Travel;

Markets: Adult; *Treatments:* Experimental; Literary; Satirical

Editors: Tom Dooley (fiction); Colleen Mondor (reviews); Elizabeth P. Glixman (interviews); Jennifer Finstrom (poetry)

Online magazine. Send a maximum of five poems or three pieces of fiction per submission period. Submissions should be sent by email as plain text or an attachment in a popular word processing package. Microsoft Word is preferred. See website for full details.

EcoHome

Hanley Wood Business Media
One Thomas Circle, NW
Suite 600
Washington, DC 20005
Tel: +1 (202) 452-0800
Fax: +1 (202) 785-1974
Email: cserlin@hanleywood.com
Website: http://www.hanleywood.com

Publishes: Articles; Features; Nonfiction; *Areas:* Business; How-to; Technology; *Markets:* Professional

Editors: Christine Serlin

Magazine covering environmentally friendly building practices and trends. Send query with published clips in first instance.

18 Wheels & Heels

Email: Photos@18wheelsandheels.com
Website: http://18wheelsandheelsmagazine.com

Publishes: Articles; Interviews; Nonfiction; Poetry; *Areas:* Beauty and Fashion; Business; Cookery; Culture; Hobbies; How-to; Leisure; Lifestyle; Men's Interests; Music; *Markets:* Adult; Family; *Treatments:* Contemporary; Niche; Positive

Editors: Tina Foca

Female truckers magazine. Articles and stories are related to the trucking industry. Product reviews have to be for products or services for people on the go. Music reviews are for driving conditions.

Employee Assistance Report

Impact Publications, Inc.
PO Box 322
Waupaca, WI 54981
Tel: +1 (715) 258-2448
Fax: +1 (715) 258-9048
Email: mike.jacquart@impacttrainingcenter.net
Website: http://www.impact-publications.com

Publishes: Articles; Interviews; News; Nonfiction; *Areas:* How-to; Legal; *Markets:* Professional

Editors: Mike Jacquart

Monthly newlsetter for employee assistance professionals. Query in the first instance.

Enchanted Conversation

Email: ENCHANTED CONVERSATION@GMAIL.com
Website: http://www.fairytalemagazine.com

Publishes: Essays; Fiction; Nonfiction; Poetry; *Areas:* Fantasy; *Markets:* Adult

Editors: Kate Wolford

Magazine for lovers of fairy tales. Publishes fiction, poetry, and scholarly essays. Each issue has a theme and a specific submission window. See website for details. Send complete MS by email only as an attachment, with the title of the work and your name in the subject line. Include brief bio and PayPal address for payment. Considers work up to 2,500 words but prefers up to 1,500. Aimed at adults but should not be unsuitable for children.

Equus Magazine

656 Quince Orchard Road, Suite 600
Gaithersburg, MD 20878-1409
Fax: +1 (301) 990-9015
Email: EEQEletters@equinetwork.com
Website: http://www.equisearch.com/magazines/equus

Publishes: Articles; News; Nonfiction; *Areas:* Business; Hobbies; How-to; Medicine; Nature; Sport; *Markets:* Adult; Professional

Magazine covering horse care, behaviour, treatment, medicine, etc. Send complete MS.

Escapees Magazine
100 Rainbow Drive
Livingston, TX 77351
Tel: +1 (888) 757-2582
Fax: +1 (936) 327-4388
Email: editor@escapees.com
Website: http://escapees.com

Publishes: Articles; Nonfiction; *Areas:* Lifestyle; Travel; *Markets:* Adult

Editors: Allyssa Dyson

Magazine covering the RV community and lifestyle.

Evening Street Review
7652 Sawmill Road, #352
Dublin, Ohio 43016-9296
Email: editor@eveningstreetpress.com
Website: http://www.eveningstreetpress.com

Publishes: Essays; Fiction; Nonfiction; Poetry; *Areas:* Short Stories; *Markets:* Adult; *Treatments:* Literary

Editors: Gordon Grigsby

Publishes poetry, short stories, essays, and creative nonfiction. Prefers to receive submissions by email as a single Word or .rtf file attachment. See website for full guidelines.

Evidence Technology Magazine
PO Box 555
Kearney, MO 64060
Email: kmayo@evidencemagazine.com
Website: http://www.evidencemagazine.com

Publishes: Articles; News; Nonfiction; *Areas:* Crime; Science; Technology; *Markets:* Professional

Editors: Kristi Mayo

Magazine publishing news and articles covering evidence collection, processing, and preservation. Articles should: be understandable to every reader with any level of knowledge and experience; and provide useful information to every reader with any level of knowledge and experience. Send query by email in first instance. See website for full guidelines.

Faith & Form
47 Grandview Terrace
Essex, CT 06426
Tel: +1 (860) 575-4702
Email: mcrosbie@faithandform.com
Website: http://www.faithandform.com/magazine

Publishes: Articles; Nonfiction; *Areas:* Architecture; Arts; Religious; *Markets:* Adult; Professional

Editors: Michael J. Crosbie, Ph.D., FAIA

Magazine for professionals and lay people concerned with environments for worship, and religious arts and architecture. Accepts electronic submissions only, either by post on CD or other storage medium, or via form on website. See website for full submission guidelines.

Fence
Science Library 320
University at Albany
1400 Washington Avenue
Albany, NY 12222
Tel: +1 (518) 591-8162
Email: peter.n.fence@gmail.com
Website: http://www.fenceportal.org

Publishes: Fiction; Nonfiction; Poetry; *Areas:* Arts; Criticism; Literature; Short Stories; *Markets:* Adult; *Treatments:* Literary

Biannual journal of poetry, fiction, art, and criticism. Submit online using web-based submission system. Submit no more than five poems at any one time, and up to twenty-five pages of fiction.

FIDO Friendly

PO Box 160
Marsing, ID 83639
Tel: +1 (800) 896-0976
Email: fieldeditor@fidofriendly.com
Website: http://www.fidofriendly.com

Publishes: Articles; Essays; Interviews;
Nonfiction; *Areas:* How-to; Humour; Short
Stories; Travel; *Markets:* Adult

Magazine on travel with your dog. Send
query with published clips.

Forum

1384 Broadway (38th Street), 11th Floor
New York, NY 10018
Tel: +1 (212) 686-4412
Fax: +1 (212) 686-6821
Email: stunifoo@busjour.com
Website:
http://www.busjour.com/forum.html

Publishes: Articles; Interviews; Nonfiction;
Areas: Beauty and Fashion; Hobbies;
Leisure; Lifestyle; Sport; Travel; *Markets:*
Adult

Fashion and lifestyle magazine for upscale
readers. Send query in the first instance.

Ingram's Magazine

Show-Me Publishing, Inc.
P.O. Box 411356
Kansas City, Missouri 64141-1356
Tel: +1 (816) 842-9994
Fax: +1 (816) 474-1111
Email: editorial@ingramsonline.com
Website: http://www.ingramsonline.com

Publishes: Articles; Interviews; News;
Nonfiction; *Areas:* Business; Finance;
Markets: Adult

Magazine covering business and economics
in Kansas City. Local writers familiar with
the magazine only. Send query by email.

International Bluegrass

2 Music Circle South, Suite 100
Nashville, TN 37203
Tel: +1 (615) 256-3222

Fax: +1 (615) 256-0450
Email: info@ibma.org
Website: http://ibma.org

Publishes: Articles; Features; News;
Nonfiction; *Areas:* Business; Music;
Markets: Professional

Professional publication of the bluegrass
music business. Send query in first instance.

Islands

Bonnier Corporation
460 North Orlando Avenue, Suite 200
Winter Park, FL 32789
Tel: +1 (407) 628-4802
Email: editor@islands.com
Website: http://www.islands.com

Publishes: Articles; Essays; Features;
Interviews; News; Nonfiction; *Areas:*
Travel; *Markets:* Adult

Publishes material relating to islands. Send
complete ms.

Journal of Emergency Medical Services (JEMS)

Elsevier Public Safety
525 B Street, Suite 1900
San Diego, CA 92101
Fax: +1 (619) 699-6396
Email: jems.editor@elsevier.com
Website: http://ees.elsevier.com/jems/

Publishes: Articles; Essays; Interviews;
News; Nonfiction; *Areas:* Medicine;
Markets: Professional

Medical journal for the emergency services.
Submit queries via website submission
system only.

Junior Baseball

JSAN Publishing LLC
14 Woodway Lane
Wilton, CT 06897
Tel: +1 (203) 210-5726
Email: publisher@juniorbaseball.com
Website: http://www.juniorbaseball.com

Publishes: Articles; Features; Interviews;

Nonfiction; *Areas:* How-to; Sport; *Markets:* Adult; Children's; Youth

Magazine for baseball players aged 7-17, their coaches and their parents. No fiction, poetry, or first-person articles about your own child. Send query in first instance.

Kalyani Magazine.
Email: info@kalyanimagazine.com
Website: http://kalyanimagazine.com

Publishes: Articles; Essays; Fiction; Nonfiction; Poetry; Scripts; *Areas:* Autobiography; Culture; Short Stories; Women's Interests; *Markets:* Adult; *Treatments:* Experimental; Literary

Editors: Shubha Bala

Publishes work by women of colour. Publishes poetry, prose, lyrical prose, scripts, essays, experimental, flash fiction, investigative reporting, fiction, non-fiction, memoir, and cross-genre. Each issue is on a different theme. See website for next theme and full submission guidelines.

Kids' Ministry Ideas
55 West Oak Ridge Drive
Hagerstown, MD 21740
Email: KidsMin@rhpa.org
Website: http://www.kidsministryideas.com

Publishes: Articles; Features; Nonfiction; *Areas:* Religious; *Markets:* Professional

Magazine geared towards those who provide spiritual nurturing to children in a local church. Send complete ms by post or email. See website for full guidelines.

LabTalk
PO Box 1945
Big Bear Lake, CA 92315
Tel: +1 (909) 547-2234
Email: cwalker@jobson.com
Website: http://www.labtalkonline.com

Publishes: Articles; Features; News; Nonfiction; *Areas:* Business; How-to; Technology; *Markets:* Professional;

Treatments: In-depth

Editors: Christie Walker

Magazine for optical laboratory managers, supervisors, and owners.

Launch Pad: Where Young Authors and Illustrators Take Off!
PO Box 80578
Baton Rouge, LA 70898
Email: editor@launchpadmag.com
Website: http://www.launchpadmag.com

Publishes: Articles; Fiction; Nonfiction; Poetry; Reviews; *Areas:* Adventure; Arts; Fantasy; Sci-Fi; *Markets:* Children's; *Treatments:* Niche; Positive

Editors: Paul Kelsey

An online magazine that publishes fiction, nonfiction, poetry, book reviews, and art by kids ages 6 through 14. Founded by a librarian, has been recognised by the American Library Association with the Scholastic Library Publishing Award.

Law Enforcement Technology Magazine
Cygnus Business Media
1233 Janesville Avenue
Fort Atkinson, WI 53538
Tel: +1 (800) 547-7377
Email: officer@corp.officer.com
Website: http://www.officer.com

Publishes: Articles; Features; News; Nonfiction; *Areas:* Legal; Technology; *Markets:* Professional

Magazine aimed at law enforcement agencies, covering technology and management.

The Living Church
PO Box 514036
Milwaukee, WI 53203-3436
Tel: +1 (414) 276-5420
Fax: +1 (414) 276-7483

Email: tlc@livingchurch.org
Website: http://www.livingchurch.org

Publishes: Articles; Essays; Features; News; Nonfiction; Reviews; *Areas:* Religious; Spiritual; *Markets:* Adult

Editors: John Schuessler

Publishes material of relevance to the Episcopal Church and the wider Anglican Communion. Send complete ms.

LONE STARS Magazine

4219 Flinthill
San Antonio, TX 78230
Email: lonestarsmagazine@yahoo.com

Publishes: Poetry; *Areas:* Arts; Culture; Current Affairs; Fantasy; Literature; Music; *Markets:* Adult; *Treatments:* Commercial; Contemporary; In-depth; Literary; Mainstream; Popular; Progressive; Serious; Traditional

Editors: Milo Rosebud

8 1/2 x 11, 25+ pages, Saddle stapled. Graphic Art accepted for Cover and Illustration. Authors retain All Rights. Limit 5 poems per submission. Single spaced Camera ready, the way you want to see it in print.

Lummox

c/o PO Box 5301
San Pedro, CA 90733-5301
Email: poetraindog@gmail.com
Website: http://www.lummoxpress.com

Publishes: Articles; Essays; Fiction; Interviews; Nonfiction; Poetry; *Areas:* Biography; Literature; Short Stories; *Markets:* Adult; *Treatments:* Literary

Annual poetry magazine publishing micro and flash fiction; essays on poetics, biographies, and the craft of writing; along with "well written rants", topical articles, and interviews. Submissions will be accepted between March 31 and August 31 each year, pasted into the body of an email (no

attachments), or by snail mail if necessary. See website for full guidelines.

MyBusiness Magazine

600 West Fulton Street, Suite 600
Chicago, IL 60661
Tel: +1 (615) 872-5800
Email: nfib@imaginepub.com
Website: http://www.mybusinessmag.com

Publishes: Articles; Nonfiction; *Areas:* Business; How-to; *Markets:* Professional

Publishes articles of interest to small business owners. Send query with author CV and two published clips in first instance.

Machine Design

1300 East Ninth Street
Cleveland, OH 44114
Tel: +1 (216) 931-9221
Fax: +1 (216) 621-8469
Email: leland.teschler@penton.com
Website: http://machinedesign.com

Publishes: Articles; News; Nonfiction; *Areas:* Design; How-to; Technology; *Markets:* Professional

Editors: Leland Teschler

Magazine covering design engineering of manufactured products. Send complete ms by post or email.

The Maine Sportsman

183 State Street
Augusta, ME 04330
Tel: +1 (207) 622-4242
Fax: +1 (207) 622-4255
Email: info@mainesportsman.com
Website: http://www.mainesportsman.com

Publishes: Articles; Features; News; Nonfiction; *Areas:* Hobbies; Leisure; Nature; Sport; *Markets:* Adult

Monthly outdoors / hunting magazine. Send query or complete ms by email.

Massage Magazine

5150 Palm Valley Road, Suite 103

Ponte Vedra Beach, FL 32082
Tel: +1 (904) 285-6020
Fax: +1 (904) 285-9944
Email: kmenahan@massagemag.com
Website: http://www.massagemag.com

Publishes: Articles; Features; Interviews;
News; Nonfiction; *Areas:* Health; How-to;
Markets: Professional

Publishes articles of interest to professionals
providing massage and other touch therapies.
Trade magazine not accepting articles aimed
at the general public.

Message of the Open Bible
2020 Bell Avenue
Des Moines, IA 50315-1096
Tel: +1 (515) 288-6761
Email: info@openbible.org
Website:
http://www.openbible.org/publications_mess
age.aspx

Publishes: Articles; Essays; Interviews;
News; Nonfiction; *Areas:* Religious;
Markets: Adult

Religious magazine providing news about
ministries, testimonies of God's miracles and
power, inspirational stories and features, and
biblical insight on contemporary issues. No
sermons. Send complete ms.

Midwest Living
Meredith Corporation
1716 Locust Street
Des Moines, IA 50309
Tel: +1 (515) 284-3000
Fax: +1 (515) 284-3836
Email: midwestliving@meredith.com
Website: http://www.midwestliving.com

Publishes: Articles; Interviews; Nonfiction;
Areas: Historical; Lifestyle; Travel;
Markets: Adult; Family

Lifestyle magazine aimed at Midwest
families. All stories must have direct
relevance to a Midwest audience.

Milwaukee Magazine
126 North Jefferson Street, Suite 100
Milwaukee, WI 53202
Tel: +1 (414) 273-1101
Fax: +1 (414) 287-4373
Email: milmag@milwaukeemagazine.com
Website: http://www.milwaukeemag.com

Publishes: Articles; Essays; Interviews;
News; Nonfiction; *Areas:* Arts; Business;
Current Affairs; Historical; Lifestyle;
Politics; Travel; *Markets:* Adult

Editors: Cristina Daglas

All material must have a strong Milwaukee
or Wisconsin angle. Send query with
published clips.

Model Cars Magazine
2403 Champa Street
Denver, CO 80205
Tel: +1 (303) 296-1600
Email: gregg@modelcarsmag.com
Website: http://www.modelcarsmag.com

Publishes: Articles; Nonfiction; *Areas:*
Hobbies; How-to; *Markets:* Adult

Publishes how-to articles for model car
enthusiasts. Query by post or by email.

Montana Magazine
PO Box 4249
Helena, MT 59604
Tel: +1 (888) 666-8624
Email: editor@montanamagazine.com
Website: http://www.montanamagazine.com

Publishes: Articles; Features; Nonfiction;
Areas: Current Affairs; Historical; Lifestyle;
Nature; Travel; *Markets:* Adult

Editors: Butch Larcombe

Publishes well-written, well-researched
articles and features on issues, interesting
people, and life in Montana. Send query by
post or by email. No queries by phone. See
website for full details.

MSW Management

Forester Media Inc.
PO Box 3100
Santa Barbara, CA 93130
Tel: +1 (805) 682-1300
Fax: +1 (805) 682-0200
Email: jtrotti@forester.net
Website: http://www.mswmanagement.com

Publishes: Articles; Interviews; Nonfiction;
Markets: Professional

Editors: John Trotti

Magazine aimed at municipal solid waste
professionals in the public sector. Query in
first instance.

Native Max

Roth Park
1401 West 85th Avenue
Unit A-103
Federal Heights, CO 80260
Email: talent@native-max.com
Website: http://www.native-max.com

Publishes: Articles; Nonfiction; *Areas:*
Beauty and Fashion; Culture; Men's
Interests; Women's Interests; *Markets:*
Adult; *Treatments:* Contemporary

Fashion magazine geared toward Native
American men and women and non-Native
Americans who want to learn about the
culture.

National Parks Magazine

777 6th Street, NW, Suite 700 Washington,
DC 20001-3723
Tel: +1 (800) 628-7275
Email: npmag@npca.org
Website:
http://www.npca.org/news/magazine/

Publishes: Articles; Features; News;
Nonfiction; *Areas:* Nature; *Markets:* Adult

Publishes articles about areas in the National
Park System, proposed new areas, threats to
parks or park wildlife, scientific discoveries,
legislative issues, and endangered species of
plants or animals relevant to national parks.
No general environmental pieces, fiction,

poetry, or "my trip to" pieces. Query in the
first instance with published clips. See
website for full details.

Netsagas.com

Vesturberg 78
Email: netsagas@gmail.com
Website: http://www.netsagas.com

Publishes: Articles; Essays; Fiction;
Nonfiction; Poetry; *Areas:* Adventure;
Anthropology; Antiques; Archaeology;
Architecture; Arts; Autobiography; Beauty
and Fashion; Biography; Business; Cookery;
Crafts; Crime; Criticism; Culture; Current
Affairs; Design; Drama; Entertainment;
Fantasy; Film; Finance; Gardening; Gothic;
Health; Historical; Hobbies; Horror; How-to;
Humour; Legal; Leisure; Lifestyle;
Literature; Media; Medicine; Men's
Interests; Military; Music; Mystery; Nature;
New Age; Philosophy; Photography;
Politics; Psychology; Radio; Religious;
Romance; Science; Sci-Fi; Self-Help; Short
Stories; Sociology; Spiritual; Sport;
Suspense; Technology; Theatre; Thrillers;
Translations; Travel; TV; Westerns;
Women's Interests; *Markets:* Adult;
Children's; Family; Youth; *Treatments:*
Commercial; Contemporary; Cynical; Dark;
Experimental; In-depth; Light; Literary;
Mainstream; Niche; Popular; Positive;
Progressive; Satirical; Serious; Traditional

Editors: Olithor Eiriks

Publishes free stories, poems, articles,
videos, pics and music.

New Jersey Monthly

55 Park Place
PO Box 920
Morristown, NJ 07963-0920
Tel: +1 (973) 539-8230
Fax: +1 (973) 538-2953
Email: kschlager@njmonthly.com
Website: http://njmonthly.com

Publishes: Articles; Essays; Features;
Nonfiction; Reviews; *Areas:* Arts; Beauty
and Fashion; Business; Culture; Current
Affairs; Gardening; Health; Historical;
Leisure; Lifestyle; Music; Nature; Politics;

Science; Technology; *Markets:* Adult

Publishes material relating directly to New Jersey only. Send query by email with published clips in first instance. No unsolicited mss. Phone queries are discouraged.

New York
Editorial Submissions
New York Media
75 Varick Street
New York, NY 10013
Email: editorialsubmissions@nymag.com
Website: http://nymag.com

Publishes: Articles; Features; News; Nonfiction; *Areas:* Beauty and Fashion; Design; Entertainment; Lifestyle; Travel; *Markets:* Adult

Magazine covering the New York metropolitan area. Send query by email describing the topic of your email in the first instance.

NextStepU Magazine
Next Step Publishing Inc.
2 W. Main St., Suite 200
Victor, NY 14564
Tel: +1 (800) 771-3117
Email: info@NextStepU.com
Website: http://www.nextstepu.com

Publishes: Articles; Features; Interviews; Nonfiction; *Areas:* Finance; How-to; Self-Help; Travel; *Markets:* Youth

Magazine aimed at preparing students for life after school; covering careers, college, finance, etc. Send query by email.

Northern Woodlands
1776 Center Road
PO Box 471
Corinth, Vermont 05039
Tel: +1 (802) 439-6292
Fax: +1 (802) 368-1053
Email: mail@northernwoodlands.org
Website: http://northernwoodlands.org

Publishes: Articles; Nonfiction; *Areas:*

Nature; *Markets:* Adult

Publishes nonfiction relating to natural history, conservation, and forest management. Send query with published clips.

O&A (Oil & Automotive Service) Marketing News
KAL Publications, Inc.
559 South Harbor Boulevard, Suite A
Anaheim, CA 92805-4525
Tel: +1 (714) 563-9300
Fax: +1 (714) 563-9310
Email: kathy@kalpub.com
Website: http://www.kalpub.com

Publishes: Articles; Features; Interviews; News; Nonfiction; *Areas:* Business; *Markets:* Professional

Trade magazine covering the petroleum marketing industry in the 13 Western states.

One
Catholic Near East Welfare Association
1011 First Avenue
New York, NY 10022
Tel: +1 (212) 826-1480
Fax: +1 (212) 838-1344
Email: cnewa@cnewa.org
Website: http://www.cnewa.org

Publishes: Articles; News; Nonfiction; *Areas:* Culture; Current Affairs; Politics; Religious; *Markets:* Adult

Catholic magazine covering political, cultural, and religious affairs in the Near East. Send query by fax or by post.

Overdrive
Randall-Reilly Publishing
3200 Rice Mine Road NE
Tuscaloosa, AL 35406
Tel: +1 (205) 349-2990
Fax: +1 (205) 750-8070
Email: mheine@randallreilly.com
Website: http://www.overdriveonline.com

Publishes: Essays; Features; Interviews; Nonfiction; *Areas:* Business; How-to;

Technology; Travel; *Markets:* Professional

Editors: Max Heine, Editorial Director

Magazine for self-employed truck drivers. Send complete ms.

PMS poemmemoirstory

HB 217
1530 3rd Avenue South
Birmingham, AL 35294–1260
Tel: +1 (205) 934-2641
Fax: +1 (205) 975-8125
Email: poememoirstory@gmail.com
Website: http://pms-journal.org

Publishes: Essays; Fiction; Nonfiction; Poetry; *Areas:* Autobiography; Short Stories; Women's Interests; *Markets:* Adult; *Treatments:* Literary

Editors: Kerry Madden

Journal of exclusively women's writing, on any subject. Publishes poetry, fiction, and personal experience. Send up to five poems, or up to 15 pages of prose up to 4,300 words total, between January 1 and March 1 annually. See website for full submission guidelines.

Pulse

International SPA Association
2365 Harrodsburg Road, Suite A325
Lexington, KY 40504
Tel: +1 (859) 226-4326
Fax: +1 (859) 226-4445
Email: mae.manacap-
johnson@ispastaff.com
Website: http://www.experienceispa.com/
media/pulse-magazine

Publishes: Articles; News; Nonfiction; *Areas:* Business; *Markets:* Professional

Magazine for spa professionals. Send query with published clips.

PRISM Magazine

PO Box 367
Wayne PA 19087
Email: kkomarni@eastern.edu

Website: http://prismmagazine.org

Publishes: Articles; Essays; Features; Interviews; Nonfiction; Reviews; *Areas:* Religious; *Markets:* Adult

Editors: Kristyn Komarnicki

Evangelical magazine. Aims to be a prophetic, consistently biblical voice in the North American church. Submit by post or by email, with email address or SAE for response. See website for full guidelines.

Pakn Treger

The Yiddish Book Center
Harry and Jeanette Weinberg Building
1021 West Street
Amherst, MA 01002
Tel: +1 (413) 256-4900
Fax: +1 (413) 256-4700
Email: pt@bikher.org
Website: http://www.yiddishbookcenter.org

Publishes: Articles; Essays; Features; Fiction; Interviews; Nonfiction; *Areas:* Culture; Historical; Humour; Literature; Mystery; Religious; Travel; *Markets:* Adult

Publishes fiction and nonfiction for a secular audience interested in Yiddish and Jewish history, literature, and culture. Send query by email in first instance.

Pallet Enterprise

Industrial Reporting, Inc.
10244 Timber Ridge Dr.
Ashland, VA 23005
Tel: +1 (804) 550-0323
Fax: +1 (804) 550-2181
Email: edb@ireporting.com
Website: http://www.palletenterprise.com

Publishes: Articles; Interviews; Nonfiction; *Areas:* Business; How-to; Nature; Technology; *Markets:* Professional

Editors: Edward C. Brindley, Jr., Ph.D.

Describes itself as the leading pallet and sawmill magazine in America. Send query with published clips.

The Paterson Literary Review

Passaic County Community College
One College Blvd, Paterson, NJ 07505-1179
Tel: +1 (973) 684-6555
Email: mGillan@pccc.edu
Website:
http://www.pccc.edu/home/cultural-affairs/poetry-center/publications

Publishes: Fiction; Poetry; *Areas:* Short
Stories; *Markets:* Adult; *Treatments:*
Literary

Publishes high quality poetry and fiction;
any style, but no formula stories. Send up to
five poems or no more than one story with
SASE.

The Paumanok Review

Email: submissions@paumanokreview.com
Website: http://www.paumanokreview.com

Publishes: Essays; Fiction; Nonfiction;
Poetry; *Areas:* Historical; Horror; Mystery;
Politics; Sci-Fi; Short Stories; Westerns;
Markets: Adult; *Treatments:* Experimental;
Mainstream; Satirical

Online English-language magazine, neither
US or UK specific. Accepting short short
stories up to 1,000 words, short stories
between 1,000 and 6,000 words (or over),
poetry up to 100 lines (submit up to 5 poems
per submission) and essays up to 6,000
words. Submit by email only, with
submission(s) as WORD, RTF, HTML,
TEXT, or in the body of an email. See
website for full details.

The Pedestal Magazine

6815 Honors Court
Charlotte, NC 28210
Tel: +1 (704) 643-0244
Email: pedmagazine@carolina.rr.com
Website:
http://www.thepedestalmagazine.com

Publishes: Fiction; Interviews; Nonfiction;
Poetry; Reviews; *Areas:* Short Stories;
Markets: Adult

Online magazine publishing fiction, poetry,

book reviews, and interviews. Previously
unpublished material only. All submissions
must be sent via the online form. Guidelines
change each issue so consult website before
submitting.

Pembroke Magazine

P.O. Box 1510
Pembroke, N.C. 28372-1510
Tel: +1 (910) 521-6358
Fax: +1 (910) 775-4092
Email: pembrokemagazine@uncp.edu
Website:
http://www.uncp.edu/pembrokemagazine

Publishes: Essays; Fiction; Interviews;
Nonfiction; Poetry; Reviews; *Areas:*
Translations; *Markets:* Adult

Accepts unsolicited poetry, fiction,
translations, and essays. For book reviews or
interviews query in first instance.

Pennsylvania English

Penn State DuBois
College Place
DuBois, PA 15801-3199
Tel: +1 (814) 375-4785
Fax: +1 (814) 375-4785
Email: ajv2@psu.edu
Website: http://www.english.iup.edu/
pcea/publications.htm

Publishes: Essays; Fiction; Poetry; *Areas:*
Criticism; Literature; Short Stories; *Markets:*
Adult; *Treatments:* Contemporary; Literary;
Mainstream

Editors: Antonio Vallone

For a complete set of editorial guidelines
send SASE by post. No electronic
submissions accepted.

Pennsylvania Heritage

The Pennsylvania Heritage Society
Commonwealth Keystone Building
400 North Street
Harrisburg, PA 17120
Tel: +1 (717) 787-2407
Fax: +1 (717) 346-9099
Email: miomalley@state.pa.us

Website: http://www.paheritage.org/pa-magazine.html

Publishes: Articles; Essays; Interviews; Nonfiction; *Areas:* Culture; Historical; *Markets:* Adult

Editors: Michael J. O'Malley III

Publishes material relating to Pennsylvania history and/or culture. Send query by email.

Peregrine

Amherst Writers & Artists Press
PO Box 1076
Amherst, MA 01004
Tel: +1 (413) 253-3307
Fax: +1 (413) 253-7764
Email: peregrinetwo@mac.com
Website:
http://www.amherstwriters.com/awa-press/peregrine/guidelines.html

Publishes: Fiction; Poetry; *Areas:* Short Stories; *Markets:* Adult

Editors: Nancy Rose

Accepts submissions between March 15 and May 15 only. Send one story or 3-5 poems with cover letter and author bio up to 40 words. No inspirational poetry, greeting-card verse, religious tirades, or nostalgia. Shorter stories stand a better chance of acceptance. See website for full guidelines.

Permafrost

University of Alaska Fairbanks
Department of English
P.O. Box 755720
Fairbanks, AK 99775-0640
Tel: +1 (907) 474-5074
Email: editor@permafrostmag.com
Website: http://permafrostmag.com

Publishes: Fiction; Nonfiction; Poetry; *Areas:* Short Stories; *Markets:* Adult; *Treatments:* Literary

Submit by post with SASE or through online submission system ($3 charge per online entry). No submissions directly by email. Submit up to five poems of any length, or

prose of up to 8,000 words. See website for more details.

Persimmon Tree

Email: Submissions@persimmontree.org
Website: http://www.persimmontree.org

Publishes: Fiction; Nonfiction; *Areas:* Short Stories; Women's Interests; *Markets:* Adult

Online magazine publishing fiction and nonfiction by women over 60. See website for full details.

Philadelphia Stories

93 Old York Road, Ste 1/#1-753
Jenkintown, PA 19046
Email: christine@philadelphiastories.org
Website: http://www.philadelphiastories.org

Publishes: Essays; Fiction; Nonfiction; Poetry; *Markets:* Adult

Publishes fiction, poetry, and essays by authors living in, or originally from, Pennsylvania, Delaware, or New Jersey. Submit via online submission form only. No postal submissions.

The Photo Review

140 East Richardson Avenue, Suite 301,
Langhorne, PA 19047-2824
Email: info@photoreview.org
Website: http://www.photoreview.org

Publishes: Essays; Interviews; Nonfiction; Reviews; *Areas:* Criticism; Photography; *Markets:* Adult

Photography magazine publishing critical reviews, essays, and interviews. No how-to or technical. Submit complete ms.

Pilgrimage

Box 9110
Pueblo, CO 81008
Email: editor@pilgrimagepress.org

Publishes: Fiction; Nonfiction; Poetry; *Areas:* Short Stories; Spiritual; Translations; *Markets:* Adult; *Treatments:* Literary

Editors: Maria Melendez

Publishes literary nonfiction, poetry, and fiction relating to soul, spirit, place, and social justice. Accepts unsolicited poetry and nonfiction, but fiction by solicitation only. See website for full details.

Pink Chameleon

Email: dpfreda@juno.com
Website: http://www.thepinkchameleon.com

Publishes: Articles; Fiction; Nonfiction; Poetry; *Areas:* Short Stories; *Markets:* Adult; Family; *Treatments:* Positive

Editors: Dorothy Paula Freda

Publishes upbeat stories, touching emotional pieces, short stories, poetry, short anecdotes, articles, and words of wisdom. Any genre as long as the material submitted is in good taste (family orientated) and gives hope for the future, even in sadness. Reading periods are January 1 to April 30, and September 1 to October 31. Send complete MS by email only, pasted into the body of the email. No email attachments or postal submissions. See website for full guidelines.

Pinyon

Languages, Literature and Mass Communication
Colorado Mesa University
1100 North Avenue
Grand Junction, CO 81501-3122
Email: pinyonpoetry@hotmail.com
Website:
http://www.coloradomesa.edu/english/public ations.html

Publishes: Fiction; Nonfiction; Poetry; *Areas:* Short Stories; *Markets:* Adult; *Treatments:* Literary

Send 3-5 poems, or one piece of fiction or creative nonfiction by post with SASE only. Submissions without an SASE will be recycled without notification. No electronic submissions. Reading period from August 1 to December 1. See website for full guidelines.

Pipeline & Gas Journal

Oildom Publishing Company of Texas, Inc.
PO Box 941669
Houston, TX 77094-8669
Tel: +1 (281) 558-6930, ext. 218
Email: jshare@oildompublishing.com
Website: http://www.pgjonline.com

Publishes: Articles; Features; Nonfiction; *Areas:* Business; Design; Technology; *Markets:* Professional

Editors: Jeff Share

Publishes articles and features relating to the pipeline business: natural gas, crude oil, or products. See website for full submission guidelines.

Pisgah Review

Division of Humanities, Brevard College
400 North Broad Street
Brevard, NC 28712
Tel: +1 (828) 884-8349
Email: tinerjj@brevard.edu
Website: http://www.pisgahreview.com

Publishes: Fiction; Nonfiction; Poetry; *Areas:* Short Stories; *Markets:* Adult; *Treatments:* Literary

Editors: Jubal Tiner

Literary journal publishing short fiction, creative nonfiction, and poetry. Submit via online submission system on website.

Plain Spoke

Amsterdam Press
6199 Steubenville Road SE
Amsterdam, Ohio 43903
Email: plainspoke@gmail.com
Website: http://www.plainspoke.net

Publishes: Fiction; Poetry; *Areas:* Short Stories; *Markets:* Adult; *Treatments:* Literary

Editors: Cindy M. Kelly (poetry); Shaun M. Barcalow (fiction)

Quarterly literary magazine accepting work which can be described as: specific; honest;

well-crafted with a strong sense of clarity; wise; quiet; gritty; surprising, true. Prefers email submissions but will also accept submissions by post. No specific reading periods. Material must be unpublished, but may be submitted elsewhere simultaneously provided immediate notification is given of acceptance elsewhere.

Pockets

PO Box 340004
Nashville, TN 37203-0004
Email: pockets@upperroom.org
Website: http://pockets.upperroom.org

Publishes: Articles; Fiction; Nonfiction; Poetry; *Areas:* Cookery; Hobbies; Leisure; Religious; Short Stories; *Markets:* Children's

Magazine for 6 to 12-year-olds, offering wholesome devotional readings that teach about God's love and presence in life. Submissions do not need to be overtly religious, but must support the purpose of the magazine to help children grow in their faith. Welcomes submissions of stories, poems, recipes, puzzles, games, and activities. No email submissions. See website for full guidelines.

Poetry International

Department of English and Comparative Literature
San Diego State University
5500 Campanile Drive
San Diego, CA 92182-6020
Tel: +1 (619) 594-1522
Fax: +1 (619) 594-4998
Email: poetry.international@yahoo.com
Website: http://poetryinternational.sdsu.edu

Publishes: Essays; Nonfiction; Poetry; Reviews; *Areas:* Criticism; Literature; Translations; *Markets:* Adult

Publishes new poetry as well as commentary, criticism, and reviews of poetry. Open to submissions from Autumn 2012.

Pointe Magazine

333 7th Avenue, 11th Floor
New York, NY 10001

Tel: +1 (212) 979-4862
Fax: +1 (646) 459-4848
Email: pointe@dancemedia.com
Website: http://www.pointemagazine.com

Publishes: Articles; Features; Interviews; News; Nonfiction; *Areas:* Drama; Historical; How-to; Music; *Markets:* Adult; Professional

Editors: Amy Cogan, Vice President and Group Publisher

Ballet magazine. Send query with published clips.

Popular Woodworking Magazine

F+W Media, Inc.
8469 Blue Ash Road, Suite 100
Cincinnati, OH 45236
Email: popwood@fwmedia.com
Website: http://www.popularwoodworking.com

Publishes: Articles; Nonfiction; *Areas:* Crafts; Design; Hobbies; How-to; Humour; Technology; *Markets:* Adult; Professional

Editors: Megan Fitzpatrick

Publishes articles on woodworking as a profession and as a hobby, including how-to and technical guides. Also publishes relevant humour. Does not consider reviews of tools. Send complete ms.

Portland Magazine

165 State
Portland, ME 04101
Tel: +1 (207) 775-4339
Fax: +1 (207) 775-2334
Email: staff@portlandmonthly.com
Website: http://www.portlandmonthly.com

Publishes: Articles; Features; Fiction; Interviews; Nonfiction; *Areas:* Arts; Beauty and Fashion; Business; Cookery; Leisure; Lifestyle; Short Stories; *Markets:* Adult

Editors: Colin Sargent

Regional magazine of Portland / Maine,

publishing nonfiction and fiction. Send query by post or by email, with clips and bio if available. See website for full submission guidelines.

The Portland Review

Portland State University
PO Box 347
Portland, OR 97207-0347
Tel: +1 (503) 725-4533
Email: theportlandreview@gmail.com
Website: http://portlandreview.tumblr.com

Publishes: Fiction; Poetry; *Areas:* Short Stories; *Markets:* Adult

Publishes quality fiction, poetry, and art, which is previously unpublished. Submit up to ten poems or one piece of prose via online submission system only.

Post Road

PO Box 600725
Newtown, MA 02460
Email: postroad@bc.edu
Website: http://www.postroadmag.com

Publishes: Essays; Fiction; Interviews; Nonfiction; Poetry; *Areas:* Criticism; Literature; Short Stories; Translations; *Markets:* Adult; *Treatments:* Literary

Nationally distributed literary magazine based out of New York and Boston. Submit online via website.

Potomac Review

Montgomery College
51 Mannakee Street, MT/212
Rockville, MD 20850
Email: zachary.benavidez@montgomerycollege.edu
Website: http://www.montgomerycollege.edu/potomacreview

Publishes: Fiction; Poetry; *Areas:* Short Stories; *Markets:* Adult; *Treatments:* Literary

Editors: Zachary Benavidez

Send up to three poems / five pages, or fiction up to 5,000 words. Submit electronically via website, or by post with SASE, brief bio, and email address. Simultaneous submissions are accepted if identified as such. See website for more details.

Prairie Schooner

123 Andrews Hall
University of Nebraska–Lincoln
Lincoln, NE 68588-0334
Tel: +1 (402) 472-0911
Fax: +1 (402) 472-1817
Email: PrairieSchooner@unl.edu
Website: http://prairieschooner.unl.edu

Publishes: Essays; Fiction; Interviews; Nonfiction; Poetry; Reviews; *Areas:* Literature; Short Stories; *Markets:* Adult; *Treatments:* Literary

Publishes short stories, poems, interviews, imaginative essays of general interest, and reviews of current books of poetry and fiction. Does not publish scholarly articles requiring footnote references. Submit one piece of prose or 5-7 poems at a time by post or using online submission system. See website for more details.

Prairie Winds

Dakota Wesleyan University
1200 West University Avenue
Box 536
Mitchell, SD 57301
Email: prairiewinds@dwu.edu
Website: http://www.dwu.edu/prairiewinds

Publishes: Essays; Nonfiction; Poetry; *Markets:* Adult; *Treatments:* Literary

Welcomes poetry, essay, and photography. Send complete ms, typed, with SASE, short biography, and email address (where available).

Produce Business

5400 Broken Sound Boulevard NW, Suite 400
Boca Raton, FL 33487
Tel: +1 (561) 994-1118

Fax: +1 (561) 994-1610
Email: info@producebusiness.com
Website: http://www.producebusiness.com

Publishes: Nonfiction; *Areas:* Business;
Markets: Professional

Trade magazine concentrating on the buying
end of the produce/floral industry.

Promo

Tel: +1 (203) 899-8442
Email: podell@accessintel.com
Website:
http://www.chiefmarketer.com/promotional-marketing

Publishes: Articles; Interviews; Nonfiction;
Areas: Business; How-to; *Markets:*
Professional

Editors: Patty Odell, Senior Editor

Magazine for marketing professionals. Send
query with published clips.

Provincetown Arts

650 Commercial Street
Provincetown, MA 02657
Tel: +1 (508) 487-3167
Email: cbusa@comcast.net
Website: http://provincetownarts.org

Publishes: Articles; Essays; Features;
Fiction; Interviews; Nonfiction; Reviews;
Areas: Arts; Literature; Short Stories;
Theatre; *Markets:* Adult; *Treatments:*
Literary

Editors: CHRISTOPHER BUSA

Welcomes unsolicited manuscripts between
September and December. Send by email as
Word file attachment (no PDFs) with short
bio. See website for full submission
guidelines.

Pseudopod

Escape Artists, Inc.
PO Box 965609
Marietta, GA 30066
Email: submit@pseudopod.org

Website: http://pseudopod.org

Publishes: Fiction; *Areas:* Crime; Fantasy;
Horror; Short Stories; *Markets:* Adult;
Treatments: Dark; Literary; Mainstream;
Popular

Audio podcast, therefore stories must
translate well into the spoken word. Seeks
dark horror short stories up to 6,000 words,
or flash up to 1,500 words. Most material
published is not suitable for children. Happy
to consider both genre horror and literary
horror. Send complete ms by email. Accepts
simultaneous submissions but no multiple
submissions. See website for full guidelines.

Puckerbrush Review

Email: sanphip@aol.com
Website: http://puckerbrushreview.com

Publishes: Essays; Fiction; Poetry; Reviews;
Areas: Short Stories; *Markets:* Adult;
Treatments: Literary

Editors: Sanford Phippen

Publishes poetry, short stories, literary essays
and reviews. Submit complete ms by email
only. No hard copy submissions.

Quiddity

Benedictine University at Springfield
1500 North Fifth Street
Springfield, IL 62702
Website:
http://www1.ben.edu/springfield/quiddity/

Publishes: Fiction; Nonfiction; Poetry;
Areas: Short Stories; *Markets:* Adult;
Treatments: Experimental; Literary;
Mainstream

Publishes creative nonfiction and fiction
(including novel extracts) up to 5,000 words.
Send one piece of prose or up to five poems
(up to ten pages maximum) by post with
SASE, or via website with $3.50 submission
charge. See website for full details.

Quilter's World

306 E PARR RD

BERNE, IN 46711
Email: Editor@QuiltersWorld.com
Website: http://www.quiltersworld.com

Publishes: Articles; Features; Interviews;
Nonfiction; *Areas:* Crafts; Hobbies; How-to;
Markets: Adult

Magazine covering quilting. Send query or
manuscript by post or email.

Romance Flash

Email: submissions@romanceflash.com
Website: http://www.romanceflash.com

Publishes: Fiction; *Areas:* Romance; Short
Stories; *Markets:* Adult

Editors: Kat de Falla; Rachel Green

Publishes romance flash fiction up to 1,000
words. No heavy erotica or postal
submissions. Submit by email or through
form on website only.

Radix Magazine

PO Box 4307
Berkeley, CA 94704
Tel: +1 (510) 548-5329
Email: Radixmag@aol.com
Website: http://www.radixmagazine.com

Publishes: Articles; Nonfiction; Poetry;
Areas: Arts; Culture; Finance; Health;
Literature; Media; Religious; *Markets:*
Adult; *Treatments:* Contemporary

Christian magazine focusing on the interface
between faith and contemporary culture.
Submit 1-4 poems at a time, or query with
ideas for articles.

Railroad Evangelist Magazine

PO Box 5026
Vancouver, WA 98668
Email: REA@comcast.net
Website: http://www.railroadevangelist.com

Publishes: Articles; Essays; Fiction;
Interviews; Nonfiction; Poetry; *Areas:*
Historical; Hobbies; Religious; Short Stories;
Travel; *Markets:* Adult; Children's; Youth

Evangelistic magazine the entire railroad
community worldwide, including the railroad
industry, the model railroad hobbyist and the
rail fan enthusiast. All material must be
railroad related. Prose should be between
300 and 800 words. See website for full
details.

RealPoetik

Email: realpoetikblog@gmail.com
Website: http://www.realpoetik.org

Publishes: Poetry; *Markets:* Adult;
Treatments: Contemporary; Experimental;
Literary; Progressive

Editors: Lily Brown; Claire Becker

Send query by email in first instance.

The Red Clay Review

c/o Jim Elledge, Director, MA in
Professional Writing Program
Department of English, Kennesaw State
University
1000 Chastain Road, #2701
Kennesaw, GA 30144-5591
Email: redclay2013@gmail.com
Website: http://redclayreview.com

Publishes: Fiction; Nonfiction; Poetry;
Areas: Short Stories; *Markets:* Adult;
Treatments: Literary

Publishes poetry, fiction, and creative
nonfiction by graduate writing students only.
See website for more details, and to submit
via online submission system.

Red Rock Review

Email: RedRockReview@csn.edu
Website:
http://sites.csn.edu/english/redrockreview/

Publishes: Essays; Fiction; Nonfiction;
Poetry; Reviews; *Areas:* Literature; *Markets:*
Adult; *Treatments:* Contemporary; Literary

Accepts submissions by email only. Send all
submissions as MS Word, RTF, or PDF file
attachments. No postal submissions. Closed

to submissions in June, July, August, and December. See website for full guidelines.

Redactions: Poetry, Poetics, & Prose

604 North 31st Avenue, Apt. D-2
Hattiesburg, MS 39401
Email: redactionspoetry@yahoo.com
Website: http://www.redactions.com

Publishes: Fiction; Nonfiction; Poetry; *Areas:* Short Stories; *Markets:* Adult; *Treatments:* Literary

Editors: Tom Holmes

Accepts submissions by email only. Send 3-5 poems, a single piece of fiction or creative nonfiction up to 2,500 words, or up to three flash fictions, in a single file as an attachment, or in the body of an email.

Reed Magazine

San Jose State University
English Department
One Washington Square
San Jose, CA 95192-0090
Email: reed@email.sjsu.edu
Website: http://www.reedmag.org

Publishes: Essays; Fiction; Nonfiction; Poetry; *Areas:* Short Stories; *Markets:* Adult; *Treatments:* Literary

Submit up to five poems, or as many stories or essays as you like. Work must be sent as .doc or .rtf formats. No paper submissions. Accepts work between June 1 and November 1, only. See website for full submission guidelines.

Rhino Poetry

PO Box 591
Evanston, IL 60204
Email: editors@rhinopoetry.org
Website: http://rhinopoetry.org

Publishes: Fiction; Poetry; *Areas:* Short Stories; Translations; *Markets:* Adult; *Treatments:* Literary

Accepts submissions between April 1 and

October 1 annually. Publishes poetry, poetry translations, and flash fiction up to 1,000 words. Submissions accepted via online submissions manager, or by post with SASE. See website for full guidelines.

Road King

Parthenon Publishing
102 Woodmont Boulevard, Suite 450
Nashville, TN 37205
Website: http://roadking.com

Publishes: Articles; Nonfiction; *Areas:* Business; Travel; *Markets:* Professional

Magazine publishing articles of interest to those in the trucking industry. Send query with published clips.

The Rockford Review

Rockford Writers' Guild
Attn: Connie Kuntz
PO Box 858
Rockford, IL 61105
Email: editor@rockfordwritersguild.com
Website:
http://www.rockfordwritersguild.com

Publishes: Fiction; Poetry; *Areas:* Short Stories; *Markets:* Adult; *Treatments:* Literary

Publishes two issues per year: one is open to submissions from members only, the other is open to submissions from all writers. Publishes poetry up to 50 lines and prose up to 1,300 words which express fresh insights into the human condition.

RTJ's Creative Catechist

PO Box 6015
New London, CT 06320
Tel: +1 (800) 321-0411
Email:
creativesubs@rtjscreativecatechist.com
Website:
http://www.rtjscreativecatechist.com

Publishes: Articles; Nonfiction; *Areas:* How-to; Religious; *Markets:* Professional

Magazine for Catholic Directors of Religious

Education. Send complete ms. No response without SASE.

The Rusty Nail

Email: rustynailmag@gmail.com
Website: http://www.rustynailmag.com

Publishes: Essays; Fiction; Nonfiction; Poetry; Reviews; *Areas:* Adventure; Arts; Crime; Culture; Horror; Literature; Mystery; Sci-Fi; Short Stories; Suspense; Thrillers; Westerns; *Markets:* Adult; *Treatments:* Contemporary; Cynical; Dark; Literary; Mainstream; Niche; Popular

Our goal is to join the growing community of Internet-based English types who not only love literature and the written word, but are enamored with the future of both. We believe that the Internet has given authors and poets the opportunity to share and get recognition for their work without having to sell their soul to "The Man." This preserves artistic dignity and lets the reader see the writer's thoughts and soul without the often numbing influence of industry "professionals."

We'd love to have you join us on this journey. If you have work to share, visit the Submissions page to learn how to submit your writing. Otherwise, you can help by being a enthusiastic reader and sharing our page with your friends.

Thanks and we hope you enjoy.

RV Business

2901 E. Bristol Street, Suite B
Elkhart, IN 46514
Tel: +1 (800) 831-1076
Fax: +1 (574) 266-7984
Email: bhampson@rvbusiness.com
Website: http://www.rvbusiness.com

Publishes: Articles; News; Nonfiction; *Areas:* Business; Design; Finance; Technology; Travel; *Markets:* Professional

Editors: Bruce Hampson

Magazine for professionals in the recreational vehicle industry. Send query with published clips.

Symphony

33 West 60th Street, Fifth Floor
New York, NY 10023
Tel: +1 (212) 262-5161
Fax: +1 (212) 262-5198
Email: clane@americanorchestras.org
Website: http://www.symphony.org

Publishes: Articles; Essays; Features; Nonfiction; *Areas:* Historical; Music; *Markets:* Adult; Professional

Editors: Chester Lane

Magazine publishing items reflecting the concerns and interests of the orchestra field. General interest classical-music subjects may also be of interest. Prefers to receive queries rather than completed articles. See website for full guidelines.

Salmagundi Magazine

Skidmore College
815 North Broadway
Saratoga Springs, NY 12866
Tel: +1 (518) 580-5000
Email: salsubmit@skidmore.edu
Website:
http://cms.skidmore.edu/salmagundi/

Publishes: Essays; Fiction; Nonfiction; Reviews; *Areas:* Criticism; Culture; *Markets:* Adult

Publishes poetry, fiction, personal essays, cultural criticism, and book reviews. Submit five or six poems or up to 12,000 words of prose as an attachment to an email only. Book reviews generally by commission only. No hard copy submissions. See website for dates of reading periods.

Salt Hill Journal

Creative Writing Program, Syracuse University
English Deptartment
401 Hall of Languages, Syracuse University
Syracuse, NY 13244
Email: salthilljournal@gmail.com

Website: http://www.salthilljournal.com

Publishes: Essays; Fiction; Interviews; Nonfiction; Poetry; Reviews; *Areas:* Short Stories; Translations; *Markets:* Adult; *Treatments:* Literary

Reads submissions for the magazine between August 1 and April 1 of each year and for the Poetry Award between May 15 and August 1. Send up to five poems or up to 30 pages of prose. No submissions by email – submit via online submission system.

Salt Water Sportsman
Email: Editor@saltwatersportsman.com
Website: http://www.saltwatersportsman.com

Publishes: Articles; Nonfiction; *Areas:* Leisure; Sport; *Markets:* Adult

Editors: John Brownlee

Magazine for serious marine sport fishermen. Send articles etc. by email.

Sandy River Review
111 South Street
Farmington, ME 04938
Tel: +1 (207) 778-7000
Fax: +1 (207) 778-7000
Email: SRReview@gmail.com
Website: http://sandyriverreview.umf.maine.edu

Publishes: Fiction; Nonfiction; Poetry; *Areas:* Short Stories; *Markets:* Adult; *Treatments:* Literary

Publishes poetry, literary fiction, and nonfiction. No horror, fantasy, sci-fi, or romance. Submit up to five poems or up to three pieces of prose, by email, as Word attachments. See website for full guidelines.

Santa Clara Review
PO Box 3212
500 El Camino Real
Santa Clara, CA 95053-3212
Tel: +1 (408) 554-4484
Email: santaclarareview@gmail.com

Website: http://www.santaclarareview.com

Publishes: Essays; Fiction; Nonfiction; Poetry; Scripts; *Areas:* Drama; Short Stories; *Markets:* Adult; *Treatments:* Literary

For poetry send up to three poems, up to ten pages in length. Fiction, nonfiction, and scripts should be less than 5,000 words. 2,000-4,000 is more normal. Accepts submissions by post, but prefers electronic submissions.

Santa Monica Review
Santa Monica College
1900 Pico Boulevard
Santa Monica, CA 90405
Website: http://www2.smc.edu/sm_review

Publishes: Essays; Fiction; Interviews; Nonfiction; *Areas:* Short Stories; *Markets:* Adult; *Treatments:* Literary

Publishes literary short stories, essays and interviews by established and emerging writers. Makes a special effort to present and promote writers from Southern California. Include SASE with submissions.

Saranac Review
CVH, Dept of English
SUNY Plattsburgh
101 Broad Street
Plattsburgh, NY 12901
Email: saranacreview@plattsburgh.edu
Website: http://research.plattsburgh.edu/saranacreview

Publishes: Essays; Fiction; Nonfiction; Poetry; *Areas:* Short Stories; Translations; *Markets:* Adult; *Treatments:* Literary

Publishes poetry and literary fiction and nonfiction. Accepts submissions between September 1 and May 15 each year. Submit one story or essay, or 3-5 poems by post only with SASE. No genre fiction (science fiction, etc.) or light verse. See website for full submission guidelines.

The Saturday Evening Post
1100 Waterway Boulevard

Indianapolis, IN 46202
Tel: +1 (317) 634-1100
Email: editor@saturdayeveningpost.com
Website:
http://www.saturdayeveningpost.com

Publishes: Articles; Features; Fiction;
Interviews; Nonfiction; *Areas:* Beauty and
Fashion; Entertainment; Finance; Gardening;
Health; How-to; Humour; Lifestyle;
Medicine; Short Stories; Technology;
Travel; *Markets:* Adult; *Treatments:* Light

Publishes articles, features, and new fiction
with a light, humorous touch. Send complete
ms with SASE for return or response. See
website for full details.

Scary Monsters Magazine
Email: Scaremail@aol.com
Website:
http://www.scarymonstersmagazine.com

Publishes: Fiction; *Areas:* Horror; Short
Stories; *Markets:* Adult

Horror magazine focusing on monsters. Send
query in first instance.

School Nurse News
Franklin Communications, Inc.
71 Redner Road
Morristown, NJ 07960
Tel: +1 (973) 644-4003
Fax: +1 (973) 644-4062
Email: editor@schoolnursenews.org
Website: http://www.schoolnursenews.org

Publishes: Articles; Interviews; News;
Nonfiction; *Areas:* Medicine; *Markets:*
Professional

Editors: Deb Ilardi, RN, BSN

Magazine aimed at school nurses and other
healthcare professionals serving children.
Send query by email.

Sea Magazine
17782 Cowan, Suite C
Irvine, CA 92614
Tel: +1 (949) 660-6150

Fax: +1 (949) 660-6172
Email: editorial@seamagazine.com
Website: http://www.seamag.com

Publishes: Articles; Features; Nonfiction;
Areas: How-to; Technology; Travel;
Markets: Adult

Describes itself as "America's western
boating magazine". Aims to provide up-to-
date information on boating trends, new boat
and equipment reports and new product
news; electronics, accessory and gear
features; maintenance tips and how-to
project ideas; anchorages, places to fish, and
cruising destinations. Regional editions for
California and the Pacific Northwest.

Seek
Standard Publishing
8805 Governor's Hill Drive, Suite 400
Cincinnati, OH 45249
Tel: +1 (800) 543-1353
Email: seek@standardpub.com
Website: http://www.standardpub.com

Publishes: Articles; Fiction; Nonfiction;
Areas: Religious; Short Stories; *Markets:*
Adult

Publishes religious articles and short stories
for adults. See website for list of upcoming
topics and submit complete ms by email.

Sequestrum
Email: sequr.info@gmail.com
Website: http://www.sequestrum.org

Publishes: Articles; Essays; Features;
Fiction; Nonfiction; Poetry; *Areas:* Arts;
Criticism; Culture; Drama; Fantasy; Horror;
Literature; Mystery; Philosophy; Sci-Fi;
Short Stories; *Markets:* Adult; Youth;
Treatments: Commercial; Contemporary;
Literary; Mainstream; Progressive; Satirical

Editors: Ralph Cooper

Founded by graduates of creative writing
programs. This magazine has faithfully
published award-winning writers and new
voices alike for its 1,000+ monthly
readership since its advent.

We accept and publish manuscripts on a rolling basis, and maintain our archives for the public free of charge. We only accept submissions through our online submission system. Hard copy or otherwise emailed submissions will not be read.

Sew News

Creative Crafts Group
741 Corporate Circle, Suite A
Golden, CO 80401
Tel: +1 (303) 215-5600
Fax: +1 (303) 215-5601
Email: sewnews@sewnews.com
Website: http://www.sewnews.com

Publishes: Articles; Features; News; Nonfiction; *Areas:* Crafts; Hobbies; *Markets:* Adult; Professional

Sewing magazine for amateurs and professionals. Send query with published clips.

The Sewanee Review

University of the South
735 University Avenue
Sewanee, TN 37383-1000
Email: Lcouch@sewanee.edu
Website:
http://www.sewanee.edu/sewanee_review

Publishes: Articles; Essays; Fiction; Nonfiction; Poetry; Reviews; *Areas:* Short Stories; *Markets:* Adult; *Treatments:* Literary

Editors: George Core

For fiction and poetry send complete ms with SASE for response. Stories should be at least 3,500 words. Submit a maximum of six poems per submission. For reviews, query first; for essays a query is acceptable, but the complete ms preferred. No submissions between June 1 and August 31. See website for full guidelines.

Shadows Express

Email:
managingeditor@shadowexpress.com
Website: http://www.shadowexpress.com

Publishes: Articles; Essays; Fiction; Nonfiction; Poetry; *Areas:* Short Stories; *Markets:* Adult; *Treatments:* Literary

Online literary magazine publishing short stories, novel excerpts, poetry, and articles. Submit complete ms by email to specific addresses listed on website if under 2,500 words. For works over 2,500 words, query. See website for full guidelines.

Short Story America

2121 Boundary Street, Suite 204
Beaufort, SC 29902
Tel: +1 (843) 597-3220
Email: editors@shortstoryamerica.com
Website: http://www.shortstoryamerica.com

Publishes: Fiction; *Areas:* Short Stories; *Markets:* Adult; *Treatments:* Literary

Editors: Tim Johnston

Online magazine. Submit short stories and flash fiction using form on website only.

The Sierra Nevada Review

999 Tahoe Boulevard
Incline Village, NV 89451
Tel: +1 (775) 831-1314
Email: sncreview@sierranevada.edu
Website:
http://www.sierranevada.edu/academics/hum anities-social-sciences/english/the-sierra-nevada-review/

Publishes: Fiction; Poetry; *Markets:* Adult; *Treatments:* Literary

Submit up to five poems or fiction up to ten pages at a time. Particularly interested in flash fiction. Accepts submissions between September 1 and March 1 annually. Use submission manager on website to submit.

Sign Builder Illustrated

Simmons-Boardman Publishing Corporation
55 Broad Street, 26th floor
New York, NY 10004
Tel: +1 (212) 620-7200
Fax: +1 (212) 633-1863
Email: jwooten@sbpub.com

Website: http://www.signshop.com

Publishes: Articles; Features; Interviews; Nonfiction; *Areas:* Design; How-to; Technology; *Markets:* Professional

Editors: Jeff Wooten

Magazine aimed at professionals in the signage industry. Query in first instance.

Skin Deep
Associated Skin Care Professionals
25188 Genesee Trail Road, Suite 200
Golden, CO 80401
Tel: +1 (800) 789-0411
Fax: +1 (800) 790-0299
Email: getconnected@ascpskincare.com
Website: http://www.ascpskincare.com

Publishes: Articles; Nonfiction; *Areas:* Beauty and Fashion; Business; Health; *Markets:* Professional

Industry magazine for professional skin care practitioners. Query in first instance.

Skipping Stones
PO BOX 3939
Eugene, OR 97403-0939
Email: editor@skippingstones.org

Publishes: Articles; Essays; Features; Fiction; Interviews; Nonfiction; Poetry; *Areas:* Biography; Cookery; Culture; Historical; Humour; Nature; Sociology; Sport; Travel; *Markets:* Children's

Aimed at children aged 7-17 from diverse cultural and socioeconomic backgrounds. Publishes creative informational stories by adults, and fiction, poetry, and nonfiction from children.

Slate & Style
National Federation of the Blind Writers' Division
504 South 57th Street
Omaha, Nebraska 68106-1202
Tel: +1 (402) 556-3216
Email: newmanrl@cox.net
Website: http://www.nfb-writers-

division.net/slate_style/slate_style.cfm

Publishes: Articles; Essays; Fiction; Nonfiction; Poetry; Reviews; *Areas:* Autobiography; Literature; Short Stories; *Markets:* Adult; *Treatments:* Literary

Magazine aimed at visually impaired writers. Publishes fiction, poetry, and nonfiction related to writing. Send submissions by email between January 1 and September 1 only, as Word or .rtf attachments. Do not include submissions within the body of the email.

Slow Trains
Email: editor@slowtrains.com
Website: http://www.slowtrains.com

Publishes: Essays; Fiction; Nonfiction; Poetry; *Markets:* Adult; *Treatments:* Literary

Publishes fiction, essays, and poetry reflecting the spirit of adventure, the exploration of the soul, the energies of imagination, and the experience of Big Fun. Music, travel, sex, humour, love, loss, art, spirituality, childhood/coming of age, baseball, and dreams. No sci-fi, erotica, horror, or romance. Email submissions only. Prefers material pasted into the body of the email, but will accept .rtf attachments. See website for full details.

Smithsonian Magazine
Capital Gallery, Suite 6001
MRC 513, PO Box 37012
Washington, DC 20013
Tel: +1 (202) 275-2000
Email: smithsonianmagazine@si.edu
Website: http://www.smithsonianmag.com

Publishes: Articles; Nonfiction; *Areas:* Anthropology; Archaeology; Arts; Culture; Historical; Lifestyle; Nature; Science; Technology; *Markets:* Adult

Publishes articles on archaeology, arts, different lifestyles, cultures and peoples, nature, science and technology. Submit proposal through online form on website.

Snowy Egret

PO Box 9265
Terre Haute, IN 47808
Website: http://www.snowyegret.net

Publishes: Articles; Essays; Fiction;
Nonfiction; Poetry; Reviews; *Areas:* Nature;
Short Stories; *Markets:* Adult

Publishes fiction, nonfiction, and poetry,
relating to the natural world and human
interactions with it. Submit by post only.

Sorry We're Booked

8 Ogden Avenue
White Plains, NY 10605
Tel: +1 (914) 610-0132
Fax: +1 (914) 610-0132
Email: swbooked@gmail.com
Website: http://www.sorrywerebooked.com

Publishes: Essays; Fiction; Nonfiction;
Poetry; Reviews; *Areas:* Arts;
Autobiography; Biography; Criticism;
Culture; Entertainment; Historical;
Literature; Philosophy; Politics; Short
Stories; Theatre; Women's Interests;
Markets: Adult; Children's; Family; Youth;
Treatments: Contemporary; Literary;
Positive; Satirical; Serious

Editors: Zach Borenstein; Dagny Leonard

There are three things we know to be true:

(1) All people are writers. It isn't even that
all people have the ability to be writers; all
acting humans influence each other, shape
each others' consciousness, leave their lives
written upon the world.

For those that are writers in the more literal
sense, we present another chance to have
your words reach a wider audience. Writing
is a form of expression that helps us to
understand the human condition; so, as a
human, you have a right (a write! -- we like
puns) to be a writer; the term "humanities" is
not so accidental. So, send us anything
you've written, and we'll put forth an honest
effort to publish it.

(2) All people are readers, influenced by
world around them. Everything is free, not

only because it would be unfeasible to
charge access, but also because of a hazy
moral line from which we are choosing to
steer clear. If someone were to have written
something that could be of dire importance
to the greater world, would it not be our
obligation to make it accessible to as many
people as possible?

(3) Language is metaphorical -- nonexistent
ideas being rearranged and restructured to
convey meaning. You might even say that all
writing is playing around with words. The
term "wordplay" is also not so accidental,
and we hope you'll contribute to what we
hope will be the greatest list of puns ever
assembled.

Now, for the five Ws, or four Ws and an H,
or really, two Ws, an H, and then another
two Ws.

What we publish: Poetry, fiction, nonfiction,
reviews -- respecting the work we did not
personally make vailable -- original book
cover designs, and puns. We're also open to
new ideas, so if there is a form of expression
relevant to the literary world that we do not
yet accommodate here, please let us know.

Why we publish: In addition to our
ideological quest to support all we know this
may just be a place where we publish our
own work, our friends' work, and where only
the parents of each individual author actually
read the content. We're cool with that. We
also may have hidden aspirations to publish
anthologies of this work, and lay a
foundation for further literary ambitions we
may have down the road.

How we publish: You may have noticed that
we're not using a blog CMS, the most
common online publishing format. We
wanted a little more creative control, to keep
the site clean, and honor the idea of the
permanence of the written word. Perhaps you
can think of this as a repository of
expression, knowledge, inquisition.

Where we belong: The community will
decide what literary works are of importance,
and we're comfortable with having just a
small say (for now). Your humble editors are
aware that our contributions pale in

comparison to the works of greater minds, or of those privy to as yet under-appreciated human experiences; those who have something greater to offer should receive greater attention. But every writer deserves some attention, some care, some love.

Who we are: We have used strong language to convey a moral basis for this site's existence, but we are, largely, deplorable people. While the written word can have a positive impact on the globe, we could spend time trying to more directly engage the world in efforts to fix it. We'll get on that eventually, but until then, sorry, we're booked.

South Carolina Review

Clemson University
Strode Tower Room 611, Box 340522
Clemson SC 29634-0522
Tel: +1 (864) 656-5399
Fax: +1 (864) 656-1345
Email: cwayne@clemson.edu
Website: http://www.clemson.edu/
cedp/cudp/journals.htm

Publishes: Essays; Fiction; Nonfiction; Poetry; Reviews; *Areas:* Literature; Short Stories; *Markets:* Adult; *Treatments:* Literary; Mainstream

Editors: Wayne Chapman

Publishes fiction, poetry, essays, and reviews. No previously published or simultaneous submissions. Submit 3-10 poems at a time. No submissions accepted in December or June to August.

South Dakota Review

The University of South Dakota
Department of English
414 East Clark Street
Vermillion, SD 57069
Email: sdreview@usd.edu
Website: http://southdakotareview.com

Publishes: Essays; Fiction; Interviews; Nonfiction; Poetry; Reviews; *Areas:* Short Stories; Translations; *Markets:* Adult; *Treatments:* Literary

Publishes fiction, poetry, essays (and mixed/hybrid-genre work), literary reviews, interviews, and translations. Accepts submission by post, or online via form on website (no submissions by email). No length limits, but prose is generally no longer than 6,000 words. Accepts simultaneous submissions, provided notification is given. See website for full guidelines.

South Florida Parenting

1701 Green Road, Suite B
Deerfield Beach, FL 33064
Tel: +1 (954) 698-6397
Fax: +1 (954) 421-9002
Email: klcamarena@tribune.com
Website: http://www.sun-sentinel.com

Publishes: Articles; Essays; Features; News; Nonfiction; *Markets:* Adult

Editors: Kyara Lomer-Camarena

Magazine aimed at parents living in the South of Florida, publishing features on topics of interest to local families, including personal essays, advice (maternity, baby, toddler/preschool, child and preteen), local news, deals, travel, and health and safety. Send queries by email. Preference given to local writers.

Southeast Review

Email: southeastreview@gmail.com
Website: http://southeastreview.org

Publishes: Essays; Fiction; Interviews; Nonfiction; Poetry; Reviews; *Areas:* Autobiography; Short Stories; Travel; *Markets:* Adult; *Treatments:* Literary

Editors: Katie Cortese

Publishes poetry, literary fiction, creative nonfiction (including personal essays, autobiography, and travel writing), book reviews, interviews, and art. Accepts submissions via online web system only. See website for more details. For interviews, query by email in first instance.

Southern California Review

Master of Professional Writing Program
University of Southern California
3501 Trousdale Parkway
Mark Taper Hall of Humanities, THH 355J
Los Angeles, CA 90089-0355
Email: scr@dornsife.usc.edu
Website: http://southerncaliforniareview.
wordpress.com

Publishes: Essays; Fiction; Nonfiction;
Poetry; Scripts; *Areas:* Drama; Short Stories;
Markets: Adult; *Treatments:* Literary

Literary magazine, publishing fiction, poetry,
nonfiction, and dramatic forms. See website
for more details and to submit via online
submissions manager. Also accepts
submissions by post. Only open to
submissions between September 1 and
December 1.

Southwestern American Literature

Center for the Study of the Southwest
Texas State University
Brazos Hall
601 University Drive
San Marcos, TX 78666-4616
Tel: +1 (512) 245-2224
Fax: +1 (512) 245-7462
Email: swpublications@txstate.edu
Website: http://www.txstate.edu/
cssw/publications/sal.html

Publishes: Fiction; Nonfiction; Poetry;
Reviews; *Areas:* Criticism; Short Stories;
Markets: Adult; *Treatments:* Literary

Scholarly journal publishing literary
criticism, fiction, poetry, and book reviews
concerning the Greater Southwest. Submit
online via online submission system.

Sou'wester

Department of English
Box 1438
Southern Illinois University Edwardsville
Edwardsville, IL 62026-1438
Website: http://souwester.org

Publishes: Fiction; Poetry; *Areas:* Short
Stories; *Markets:* Adult; Literary

Submit up to five poems, or one piece of
prose (or up to three pieces of flash fiction)
via submission system on website. No
submissions by post.

SpeciaLiving magazine

PO Box 1000
Bloomington, IL 61702-1000
Tel: +1 (309) 962-2003
Email: gareeb@aol.com
Website: http://www.specialiving.com

Publishes: Articles; Interviews; Nonfiction;
Reviews; *Areas:* How-to; Humour; Lifestyle;
Technology; Travel; *Markets:* Adult

Online magazine publishing articles,
interviews, and product reviews etc. of
interest to the physically disabled / mobility
impaired.

Spider

Submissions Editor
Spider
Carus Publishing
70 E. Lake Street, Suite 800
Chicago, IL 60601
Tel: +1 (800) 821-0115
Email: customerservice@caruspub.com
Website: http://www.cricketmag.com

Publishes: Articles; Fiction; Nonfiction;
Poetry; *Areas:* Nature; Science; Short
Stories; *Markets:* Children's

Magazine for children aged 6-9. Publishes
fiction, poetry, and articles on such topics as
animals, cool scientific discoveries, and kids
of the reader's own age doing amazing
things. See website for full details. Submit
by post with SASE, or using online web
submission system. No submissions in
emails.

Springs

2001 Midwest Road, Suite 106
Oak Brook, IL 60523-1335
Tel: +1 (630) 495-8588
Fax: +1 (630) 495-8595
Email: lynne@smihq.org
Website: http://www.smihq.org

Publishes: Articles; Interviews; Nonfiction; *Areas:* How-to; Technology; *Markets:* Professional

Editors: Lynne Carr

Magazine for spring manufacturers.

Steamboat Magazine

Ski Town Publications, Inc.
1120 South Lincoln Avenue, Suite F
Steamboat Springs, CO 80487
Tel: +1 (970) 871-9413
Fax: +1 (970) 871-1922
Email: info@steamboatmagazine.com
Website:
http://www.steamboatmagazine.com

Publishes: Articles; Essays; Interviews; Nonfiction; *Areas:* Historical; Humour; Leisure; Lifestyle; Travel; *Markets:* Adult

Magazine covering Steamboat Springs and the Yampa Valley. Send query with published clips.

Stirring : A Literary Collection

Email: eesmith81@gmail.com
Website: http://www.sundress
publications.com/stirring/

Publishes: Fiction; Nonfiction; Poetry; Reviews; *Areas:* Short Stories; *Markets:* Adult; *Treatments:* Literary

Editors: Erin Elizabeth Smith (Poetry); Josh Webster (fiction)

Describes itself as one of the oldest continuously publishing journals on the internet. Publishes poetry, short fiction, creative nonfiction, book reviews, and photography. Submit by email. See website for more details.

Stone Canoe

700 University Avenue, Suite 326
Syracuse, NY 13244-2530
Tel: +1 (315) 443-4165
Fax: +1 (315) 443-4174
Email: stonecanoe@syr.edu
Website: http://www.stonecanoejournal.org

Publishes: Features; Fiction; Nonfiction; Poetry; Scripts; *Areas:* Drama; Literature; Music; Short Stories; Technology; *Markets:* Adult; *Treatments:* Literary

Editors: Robert Colley (Editor); Allison Vincent (Assistant Editor)

Magazine publishing previously unpublished works of short fiction, creative nonfiction, technical writing, short plays, poems, and works of visual art created by people who live or have lived in Upstate New York (not New York City). Submit up to five poems or prose up to 10,000 words. See website for details and for online submission system.

storySouth

Email: terry@storysouth.com
Website: http://www.storysouth.com

Publishes: Essays; Fiction; Nonfiction; Poetry; *Markets:* Adult; *Treatments:* Experimental; Literary

Editors: Terry Kennedy

Publishes poetry, fiction, and creative nonfiction from the "new south". The exact definition of "new south" varies from person to person, but if you can make a case for why you consider yourself part of the new south, then you can submit. Accepts work March 15 to June 15, and September 15 to December 15. Submit 3-5 poems or one piece of fiction or nonfiction. No length limits and longer pieces are encouraged. See website for more details.

The Stray Branch

Email: thestraybranchlitmag@yahoo.com
Website: http://www.thestraybranch.org

Publishes: Fiction; Poetry; *Areas:* Short Stories; Suspense; *Markets:* Adult; *Treatments:* Dark; Literary

Editors: Debbie Berk

Submit up to 6 poems or up to 2 pieces of fiction up to two and a half pages each. Shorter pieces stand a better chance of publication. Looking for edgy, dark, suspense, and anything on the paranormal or after life. Topics include depression, mental illness, loss, sorrow, addiction, recovery, abuse, survival, daily existence, self struggles and discovery through words. No stories by or for children. Submissions by email only. See website for full submission guidelines.

Straylight

English Department
University of Wisconsin-Parkside
900 Wood Road
Kenosha, WI 53141
Email: submissions@straylightmag.com
Website: http://www.straylightmag.com

Publishes: Fiction; Poetry; *Areas:* Short Stories; *Markets:* Adult; *Treatments:* Literary

Literary magazine with separate print and online editions, with different content. Accepts stories of 1,000-5,000 words for the print edition (but prefers 1,500-3,000), and up to 1,000 for online. Also publishes novellas up to 45,000 words online only. Poems may be submitted for both print and online editions. See website for specific submission guidelines.

Struggle

Box 28536
Detroit, MI 48228
Email: timhall11@yahoo.com
Website: http://www.strugglemagazine.net

Publishes: Fiction; Poetry; Scripts; *Areas:* Drama; Politics; Short Stories; *Markets:* Adult; *Treatments:* Literary; Progressive

Magazine publishing progressive and revolutionary literature and art expressing the "anti-establishment struggles of the working class and oppressed people in the U.S. and worldwide". Publishes poems, songs, stories, short plays, drawings, cartoons. See website for full details.

The Summerset Review

25 Summerset Drive
Smithtown, New York 11787

Email: editor@summersetreview.org
Website: http://www.summersetreview.org

Publishes: Essays; Fiction; Nonfiction; Poetry; *Areas:* Short Stories; *Markets:* Adult; *Treatments:* Literary

Editors: Joseph Levens

Submit literary fiction and nonfiction up to 8,000 words or up to five poems. Prefers to receive submissions by email. Will accept prose by post but no hard copy poetry submissions. See website for full details.

The Sun

107 N. Roberson Street
Chapel Hill, NC 27516
Tel: +1 (919) 942-5282
Fax: +1 (919) 932-3101
Website: http://thesunmagazine.org

Publishes: Essays; Fiction; Interviews; Nonfiction; Poetry; *Areas:* Culture; Philosophy; Politics; Short Stories; *Markets:* Adult; *Treatments:* Literary

Publishes essays, interviews, fiction, and poetry. Favours personal writing, but also looking for thoughtful, well-written essays on political, cultural, and philosophical themes. No journalistic features, academic works, or opinion pieces.

Sun Valley Magazine

111 1st Avenue North #1M,
Meriwether Building
Hailey, ID 83333
Tel: +1 (208) 788-0770
Fax: +1 (208) 788-3881
Email: michael@sunvalleymag.com
Website: http://www.sunvalleymag.com

Publishes: Articles; Features; Interviews; News; Nonfiction; *Areas:* Arts; Culture; Historical; Leisure; Travel; *Markets:* Adult

Editors: Mike McKenna

Regional magazine covering the Sun Valley area and the Wood River Valley. Send query with published clips.

Suspense Magazine

26500 Agoura Road, #102-474
Calabasas, CA 91302
Email: editor@suspensemagazine.com
Website: http://www.suspensemagazine.com

Publishes: Fiction; Nonfiction; Reviews;
Areas: Horror; Mystery; Short Stories;
Suspense; Thrillers; *Markets:* Adult

Magazine of suspense, mystery, horror, and
thriller fiction. Send stories up to 5,000
words in the body of an email. No
attachments. Response not guaranteed unless
story is accepted.

T. Gene Davis's Speculative Blog

Email: tgenedavis@gmail.com
Website: http://tgenedavis.com/submission-guidelines/

Publishes: Fiction; *Areas:* Fantasy; Gothic;
Horror; Sci-Fi; Short Stories; *Markets:*
Adult; Family; *Treatments:* Dark;
Experimental; Light; Literary; Mainstream;
Popular; Satirical; Serious

Editors: T. Gene Davis

A web-based magazine releasing a family-
friendly speculative story every Monday,
mostly by guest authors. Speculative stories
include horror, fantasy, science fiction and
other related genres.

The stories accepted are for adults with
mature themes, but safe to read out loud with
children in the room. All stories MUST be
written so that adults will enjoy them.

Stories can be of any length. This includes
flash fiction, short stories, novelettes, and
novellas. Preference is given to flash fiction
and short stories. Formatting should be in
standard manuscript format.

Payment for accepted stories is made upon
my receipt of the signed author agreement.

Tales of the Talisman

Hadrosaur Productions
PO Box 2194
Mesilla Park, NM 88047-2194
Email: hadrosaur@zianet.com
Website: http://www.talesofthetalisman.com

Publishes: Fiction; Poetry; *Areas:* Fantasy;
Horror; Sci-Fi; Short Stories; *Markets:* Adult

Editors: David L. Summers

Publishes Science Fiction, fantasy, and
horror short stories up to 6,000 words and
poems up to 50 lines. Accepts submissions
by post and by email. See website for full
guidelines.

Talking River

Lewis-Clark State College
500 8th Avenue
Lewiston, ID 83501
Email: talkingriver@lcmail.lcsc.edu
Website: http://www.lcsc.edu/talking-river/

Publishes: Fiction; Nonfiction; Poetry;
Reviews; *Areas:* Short Stories; *Markets:*
Adult; *Treatments:* Literary

Submit fiction or creative nonfiction up to
4,000 words, or up to five poems at a time.
Also publishes reviews between 500 and
1,000 words. Accepts submissions between
August 1 and April 1. Include cover letter,
email address for correspondence, and SASE
for return of material. See website for full
guidelines.

Tattoo Highway

Email: submissions@tattoohighway.org
Website: http://www.tattoohighway.org

Publishes: Fiction; Poetry; *Areas:* Short
Stories; *Markets:* Adult; *Treatments:*
Literary

Online magazine publishing fiction and
poetry. Submit by email as RTF attachments,
or as plain text in the body of your email.

The Teacher's Voice

PO Box 150384
Kew Gardens, NY 11415
Email: editor@the-teachers-voice.org
Website: http://www.the-teachers-voice.org

Publishes: Fiction; Nonfiction; Poetry; Scripts; *Areas:* Drama; Short Stories; *Markets:* Professional; *Treatments:* Experimental; Literary

Litetary magazine for poets and writers in education. Publishes poems, flash fiction, flash creative nonfiction, flash plays, and flash experimental. Simultaneous submissions accepted if immediate notification of acceptance elsewhere is given. Send query with up to 5 pages of poetry, or prose pieces no longer than 1,500 words. Prefers shorter work. See website for full submission guidelines, and/or to submit using online submission system.

Teaching Music

National Association for Music Education
1806 Robert Fulton Drive
Reston, VA 20191
Tel: +1 (703) 860-4000
Fax: +1 (703) 860-1531
Email: lindab@nafme.org
Website: http://www.nafme.org

Publishes: Articles; Nonfiction; *Areas:* How-to; Music; *Markets:* Academic; Professional

Publishes articles aimed at music teachers. Send complete ms.

Telluride Magazine

PO Box 3488
Telluride, CO 81435
Tel: +1 (970) 728-4245
Fax: +1 (866) 936-8406
Email: deb@telluridemagazine.com
Website: http://www.telluridemagazine.com

Publishes: Articles; Nonfiction; *Areas:* Historical; Humour; Leisure; Lifestyle; Nature; Travel; *Markets:* Adult

Editors: Deb Dion Kees

Magazine publishing material relating to the immediate surrounding area and mountain life in general. Send query with published clips.

Textile World

2100 RiverEdge Parkway, Suite 1200
Atlanta, Georgia 30328
Tel: +1 (678) 569-4876
Fax: +1 (770) 952-0669
Email: editor@textileworld.com
Website: http://www.textileworld.com

Publishes: Articles; Nonfiction; *Areas:* Business; Crafts; Design; Technology; *Markets:* Professional

Magazine for the textile industry, covering manufacturing processes, products, technology, etc. Query in first instance.

The Rejected Quarterly

PO Box 1351
Cobb, CA 95426
Email: bplankton@yahoo.com
Website: http://www.rejectedq.com

Publishes: Features; Fiction; Nonfiction; Poetry; Reviews; *Areas:* Humour; Short Stories; *Markets:* Adult

Editors: Daniel Weiss, Jeff Ludecke

Magazine publishing fiction that has been rejected at least 5 times elsewhere, poetry about rejection, plus humour, opinions, and reviews. See website for full submission guidelines.

The Vehicle

600 Lincoln Avenue
Charleston, IL
Email: vehicleeiu@gmail.com
Website: http://www.thevehiclemagazine.com

Publishes: Essays; Fiction; Interviews; Nonfiction; Poetry; Scripts; *Areas:* Adventure; Arts; Crime; Drama; Fantasy; Gothic; Historical; Horror; Humour; Literature; Mystery; Photography; Romance; Sci-Fi; Short Stories; Suspense; Theatre; Thrillers; Westerns; *Markets:* Adult

Editors: Hannah Green

A biannual literary magazine produced by students. Since 1959, the magazine has been

---

publishing poetry, short stories, creative nonfiction, and artwork by the university's students but now has opened its doors to submissions from anyone, anywhere, and has moved online to facilitate the transition.

34th Parallel

Email: 34thParallel@gmail.com
Website: http://www.34thparallel.net

Publishes: Essays; Fiction; Nonfiction; Poetry; Scripts; *Areas:* Short Stories; *Markets:* Adult; *Treatments:* Literary

Editors: Tracey Boone Swan; Martin Chipperfield

Publishes fiction, creative nonfiction, essays, scripts, poetry, and artwork. Submit via online submission system. $6 fee includes download of latest digital edition.

Timber

Email: timberjournal@gmail.com
Website: http://www.timberjournal.com

Publishes: Fiction; Nonfiction; Poetry; *Areas:* Short Stories; *Markets:* Adult; *Treatments:* Literary

Editors: Matthew Treon

Publishes innovative fiction, flash fiction, poetry, nonfiction, visual art and webcomics. Accepts prose up to 5,000 words and 3-5 poems. One submission per reading period (August to March) only. Submit using submission system on website.

TimberLine

10244 Timber Ridge Drive
Ashland, VA 23005
Tel: +1 (804) 550-0323
Fax: +1 (804) 550-2181
Email: edb@ireporting.com
Website: http://www.timberlinemag.com

Publishes: Articles; News; Nonfiction; *Areas:* Business; How-to; Technology; *Markets:* Professional

Editors: Edward C. Brindley, Jr., Ph.D

Online newspaper for the forest products industry including loggers, sawmills, remanufacturers and secondary wood processors. Send query with published clips.

Timeline

1982 Velma Avenue
Columbus, Ohio 43211-2497
Tel: +1 (614) 297-2360
Fax: +1 (614) 297-2367
Email: timeline@ohiohistory.org
Website: http://ww2.ohiohistory.org/resource/publicat/timeline/

Publishes: Articles; Features; Nonfiction; *Areas:* Anthropology; Archaeology; Architecture; Arts; Biography; Finance; Historical; Military; Nature; Politics; Science; Sociology; Technology; *Markets:* Adult

Publishes historical articles and features, particularly focusing on Ohio, but also willing to consider pieces of regional or national relevance. Suitable topics include the traditional fields of political, economic, military, and social history; biography; the history of science and technology; archaeology and anthropology; architecture; the fine and decorative arts; and the natural sciences including botany, geology, zoology, ecology, and paleontology. If unsure of suitability, send query in first instance.

Toledo Area Parent

1120 Adams Street
Toledo, OH 43604
Tel: +1 (419) 244-9859
Fax: +1 (419) 244-9871
Email: cjacobs@toledocitypaper.com
Website: http://www.toledoparent.com

Publishes: Articles; Features; Interviews; News; Nonfiction; *Areas:* How-to; Humour; Lifestyle; *Markets:* Adult

Editors: Collette Jacobs, Editor in Chief

Magazine aimed at parents living in Northwest Ohio/Southeast Michigan. Send queries by email, post, or fax.

Tradicion Revista Magazine
925 Salamanca NW
Los Ranchos de ABQ, NM 87107-5647
Tel: +1 (505) 344-9382
Fax: +1 (505) 345-5129
Email: LPDPress@q.com
Website. http://www.LPDPress.com

Publishes: Articles; Essays; Features;
Nonfiction; *Areas:* Arts; Culture; Historical;
Travel; *Markets:* Adult

Editors: Barbe Awalt and Paul Rhetts

Magazine with a focus on the art and culture
of the American Southwest. Query in first
instance.

Trajectory
PO Box 655
Frankfort, KY 40602
Tel: +1 (502) 330-4746
Email: adobechris@hotmail.com
Website: http://www.trajectoryjournal.com

Publishes: Fiction; Interviews; Nonfiction;
Poetry; Reviews; *Areas:* Autobiography;
Short Stories; *Markets:* Adult; Literary

Editors: Chris Helvey

Publishes fiction, poetry, creative nonfiction,
memoirs, book reviews, and author
interviews. No fiction or poetry for young
children, young adult, fantasy, romance, sci-
fi, or horror. Send submissions by post with
SASE and 25-75 word bio. No electronic
submissions.

Traverse
Prism Publications / MyNorth Media
148 East Front Street
Traverse City, MI 49684
Tel: +1 (231) 941-8174
Email: smith@traversemagazine.com
Website: http://www.mynorth.com

Publishes: Articles; Essays; Nonfiction;
Areas: Arts; Crafts; Culture; Gardening;
Historical; Leisure; Lifestyle; Nature; Sport;
Markets: Adult

Editors: Jeff Smith

Regional magazine for Northern Michigan.
Prefers submissions by email. See website
for full guidelines.

True West
PO Box 8008
Cave Creek, AZ 85327
Tel: +1 (888) 687-1881
Fax: +1 (480) 575-1903
Email: editor@twmag.com
Website: http://www.truewestmagazine.com

Publishes: Articles; Features; Nonfiction;
Areas: Historical; Westerns; *Markets:* Adult

Editors: Meghan Saar

Magazine covering the history of the
American West. Send query with hard copy
ms and copy on CD or DVD. See website for
more details.

Ultimate MMA
Beckett Media, LLC
22840 Savi Ranch Parkway, Suite 200
Yorba Linda, CA 92887
Tel: +1 (714) 200-1930
Fax: +1 (714) 456-0146
Email: DJeffrey@Beckett.com
Website: http://www.ultimatemmamag.com

Publishes: Articles; Nonfiction; *Areas:*
Men's Interests; Sport; *Markets:* Adult

Editors: Doug Jeffrey

Magazine covering mixed martial arts
fighting. Query in first instance.

Validation Times
19-B Wirt Street SW
Leesburg, VA 20175
Email: publisher@FDAINFO.com
Website: http://www.fdainfo.com

Publishes: Articles; News; Nonfiction;
Areas: Business; Legal; Medicine;
Technology; *Markets:* Professional

Newsletter covering the regulation of
medical and pharmaceutical devices. Send
query by post in first instance.

Vanillerotica

Email:
talentdripseroticpublishing@yahoo.com
Website:
http://eroticatalentdrips.wordpress.com

Publishes: Fiction; *Areas:* Erotic; Romance;
Markets: Adult

Editors: Kimberly Steele

Print and electronic magazine publishing
erotic and romantic short fiction between
10,000 and 15,000 words, plus poetry up to
30 lines.

Verbatim

PO Box 597302
Chicago, IL 60659
Tel: +1 (800) 897-3006
Email: editor@verbatimmag.com
Website: http://www.verbatimmag.com

Publishes: Articles; Nonfiction; *Areas:*
Humour; *Markets:* Adult; *Treatments:*
Popular

Publishes articles on English and other
languages, focusing on amusing and
interesting features of language. Authors are
advised to query editor in advance regarding
subject matter. No fiction. Submit via online
submission system. No hard copy
approaches.

Veterinary Economics

Advanstar Communications, Veterinary
Group
8033 Flint
Lenexa, KS 66214

Tel: +1 (800) 255-6864
Fax: +1 (913) 871-3808
Email: ve@advanstar.com
Website:
http://veterinarybusiness.dvm360.com

Publishes: Articles; Interviews; Nonfiction;
Areas: Business; Finance; How-to;
Medicine; *Markets:* Professional

Magazine for vets, focusing on the business
side of managing a practice.

VMSD

ST Media Group International
11262 Cornell Park Drive
Cincinnati, OH 45242
Tel: +1 (513) 263-9386
Email: robin.donovan@stmediagroup.com
Website: http://vmsd.com

Publishes: Articles; Nonfiction; *Areas:*
Business; Design; *Markets:* Professional

Editors: Robin Donovan

Magazine covering retail store design. Query
editor by email with details of your project in
first instance. See website for full guidelines.

Wild Violet

P.O. Box 39706
Philadelphia, PA 19106-9706
Email: wildvioletmagazine@yahoo.com
Website: http://www.wildviolet.net

Publishes: Essays; Fiction; Interviews;
Nonfiction; Poetry; Reviews; *Areas:* Culture;
Humour; Politics; Short Stories; *Markets:*
Adult; *Treatments:* Literary

Quarterly online literary magazine designed
to challenge and uplift the reader. Publishes
poetry, fiction, and creative nonfiction. See
website for full guidelines. Submissions
accepted by post or by email.

Wag's Revue

Email: editors@wagsrevue.com
Website: http://www.wagsrevue.com

Publishes: Essays; Fiction; Interviews;
Nonfiction; Poetry; *Markets:* Adult

Reading periods run from the beginning of
March to the end of May, and from the start
of September to the end of November. In
addition to these reading periods, accepts
submissions via competitions, for which
there is a reading fee and a prize of $1,000.
See website for full details. All submissions
to made via system on website.

Water-Stone Review

The Creative Writing Programs at Hamline

University
MS-A1730
1536 Hewitt Avenue
St Paul, MN 55104-1284
Email: water-stone@hamline.edu
Website: http://www.waterstonereview.com

Publishes: Essays; Fiction; Interviews;
Nonfiction; Poetry; Reviews; *Areas:* Short
Stories; *Markets:* Adult; *Treatments:*
Literary

Publishes poetry, fiction, and creative
nonfiction in all genres as well as
essays/reviews and writers' interviews.
Accepts work between October 1 and
December 1 only. No electronic submissions.
See website for full details.

Wesleyan Life

PO Box 50434
Indianapolis, IN 46250
Tel: +1 (317) 774-7900
Email: info@wesleyan.org
Website: http://www.wesleyanlifeonline.com

Publishes: Articles; Nonfiction; *Areas:*
Religious; *Markets:* Adult

Magazine publishing inspirational and
religious articles. No poetry. Send complete
ms.

Whole Life Times

Whole Life Media, LLC
23705 Vanowen Street, #306
West Hills, CA 91307
Tel: +1 (877) 807-2599
Fax: +1 (310) 933-1693
Email: abigail@wholelifemagazine.com
Website: http://www.wholelifemagazine.com

Publishes: Articles; Interviews; Nonfiction;
Areas: Finance; Health; Lifestyle; Medicine;
Nature; New Age; Sociology; Spiritual;
Markets: Adult

Publishes stories that deal with a progressive,
healthy lifestyle, including stories on natural
health, alternative healing, green living,
sustainable and local food, social
responsibility, conscious business, the
environment, spirituality and personal

growth. Relies heavily on freelances. See
website for full submission guidelines.

Wine Press Northwest

333 West Canal Drive
Kennewick, WA 99336
Tel: +1 (509) 582-1443
Email: gmcconnell@winepressnw.com
Website: http://www.winepressnw.com

Publishes: Articles; Features; Interviews;
Nonfiction; *Areas:* Historical; Travel;
Markets: Adult

Editors: Gregg McConnell

Wine magazine focusing on wines of
Washington, Oregon, Idaho and British
Columbia.

Wine Spectator

M. Shanken Communications
387 Park Avenue South
New York, NY 10016
Tel: +1 (212) 684-4224
Email: wsonline@mshanken.com
Website: http://www.winespectator.com

Publishes: Articles; Features; Interviews;
News; Nonfiction; *Areas:* Hobbies; Travel;
Markets: Adult

Consumer magazine publishing news,
interviews, features, and articles aimed at
wine enthusiasts. Send query in first
instance.

Woodshop News

10 Bokum Road
Essex, CT 06426
Tel: +1 (860) 767-8227
Fax: +1 (860) 767-1048
Email: editorial@woodshopnews.com
Website: http://www.woodshopnews.com

Publishes: Articles; Features; Interviews;
News; Nonfiction; *Areas:* Business; Crafts;
How-to; *Markets:* Professional

Magazine for professional woodworkers.
Send query or complete ms.

The Writing Disorder

PO Box 93613
Los Angeles, CA 90093-0613
Email: submit@thewritingdisorder.com
Website: http://www.thewritingdisorder.com

Publishes: Articles; Nonfiction; Poetry;
Reviews; *Areas:* Short Stories; *Markets:*
Adult; *Treatments:* Experimental; Literary;
Traditional

Editors: C.E. Lukather

Publishes: Fiction, Poetry, Nonfiction, Art,
Reviews, Comic Art, Experimental. Send
prose or poetry to appropriate email
addresses (see website) as MS Word
attachments, or submit by post or via online
form. No specific guidelines regarding
subject matter, and no length limits.
Traditional accepted as well as experimental.

Written By

7000 West Third Street
Los Angeles, CA 90048
Tel: +1 (323) 782-4699
Website: http://www.wga.org/
writtenby/writtenby.aspx

Publishes: Articles; Essays; Features;
Interviews; Nonfiction; *Areas:* Business;
Film; TV; *Markets:* Professional

Magazine for screen and TV writers, aimed
at those already inside the industry rather
than those trying to break in.

Yachting Magazine

55 Hammarlund Way
Middletown, RI 02842
Fax: +1 (401) 845-5180
Email: letters@yachtingmagazine.com
Website: http://www.yachtingmagazine.com

Publishes: Articles; Nonfiction; *Areas:*
Hobbies; Travel; *Markets:* Adult

Magazine on yachting, aimed at an
experienced and knowledgeable audience.

Send query with published clips in first
instance.

The Yes Factory

169 Rogers Ave #1A
Brooklyn, NY 11216
Tel: +1 (201) 665-3243
Email: submit@theyesfactory.org
Website: http://www.theyesfactory.org

Publishes: Fiction; Poetry; *Areas:*
Adventure; Arts; Crime; Drama;
Entertainment; Fantasy; Gothic; Horror;
Humour; Military; Mystery; Philosophy;
Photography; Politics; Romance; Science;
Sci-Fi; Short Stories; Spiritual; Thrillers;
Westerns; *Markets:* Adult; *Treatments:*
Contemporary; Experimental; Literary;
Positive; Progressive

Editors: Christa Pagliei

Seeks to publish outstanding and innovative
poetry, art, and literary fiction. Our aim is to
help new, emerging, and established artists
reach a wider audience through a variety of
mediums: print, online, e-readers, and live
events.

The work we're looking to see is thoughtful,
positive, sometimes conceptual, and always
honest. We strive to answer each submission
individually and offer notes whenever we
can.

Zink

Email: fashion@zinkmediagroup.com
Website: http://www.zinkmagazine.com

Publishes: Articles; Features; Nonfiction;
Areas: Beauty and Fashion; *Markets:* Adult

Editors: Leila Cole; Jennifer Stevens

Fashion magazine. Like edgy material.
Submission must be in line with the theme of
the issue. See website for upcoming themes
and detailed submission guidelines.

UK Magazines

For the most up-to-date listings of these and hundreds of other magazines, visit http://www.firstwriter.com/magazines

To claim your **free** access to the site, please see the back of this book.

Accountancy Age
Incisive Media
32-34 Broadwick Street
London
W1A 2HG
Tel: +44 (0) 20 7316 9000
Fax: +44 (0) 20 7316 9250
Email: kevin.reed@incisivemedia.com
Website: http://www.accountancyage.com

Publishes: Articles; Features; News; Nonfiction; *Areas:* Business; Finance; *Markets:* Professional

Editors: Kevin Reed

Weekly magazine publishing articles on accountancy, business, and the financial world. Unsolicited MSS welcome; outline ideas in writing.

Accounting and Business
ACCA
29 Lincoln's Inn Fields
London
WC2A 3EE
Tel: +44 (0) 20 7059 5000
Fax: +44 (0) 20 7059 5050
Email: chris.quick@accaglobal.com
Website:
http://www.accaglobal.com/en/member/acco
unting-business.html

Publishes: Articles; Nonfiction; *Areas:* Business; Finance; *Markets:* Professional

Editors: Chris Quick

Magazine aimed at accountants and finance directors.

Acumen
6 The Mount
Higher Furzeham
Brixham
South Devon
TQ5 8QY
Tel: +44 (0) 1803 851098
Email: patriciaoxley6@gmail.com
Website: http://www.acumen-poetry.co.uk

Publishes: Articles; Features; Interviews; Nonfiction; Poetry; Reviews; *Areas:* Criticism; Literature; *Markets:* Adult; *Treatments:* Literary

Editors: Patricia Oxley

Magazine publishing poetry and articles, features, and reviews connected to poetry. Send submissions with SAE and author details on each page, or submit by email as Word attachment. See website for full submission guidelines.

Aesthetica: A Review of Contemporary Artists
PO Box 371

York
YO23 1WL
Tel: +44 (0) 1904 629137
Email: info@aestheticamagazine.com
Website:
http://www.aestheticamagazine.com

Publishes: Articles; Essays; Features;
Fiction; Interviews; News; Nonfiction;
Poetry; Reviews; *Areas:* Arts; Culture;
Current Affairs; Drama; Film; Humour;
Literature; Music; Short Stories; Theatre;
Women's Interests; *Markets:* Adult;
Treatments: Literary

Editors: Cherie Federico

I am the founder and editor of a literary and
arts magazine that I actually began with my
MA fee money (I eventually paid the fees
and received my MA). I started the magazine
because I believe that there are too many
closed doors in the literary and art world. I
believe in making the arts accessible and
available for all. My convictions are deep
because I believe that in this modern, some
say, post-modern world that we live in it is
important to remember the essentials about
being human. There are too many reality TV
shows that mock existence. As a culture we
are slipping away from the arts. Writing has
too many stigmas attached and people
believe that there are too many rules. My aim
was to bring a magazine to life that would
challenge some of these notions and make a
difference.

This writing and artistic platform is
spreading across the UK and making it to
places like Israel, Italy, Ireland, New
Zealand, Australia, America, Canada,
Bulgaria, and Switzerland. We started in
York and are now selling at Borders in York,
Leeds, Brighton, Islington, and Oxford Street
as well as in some local York bookshops and
direct either from the website or by post.

I believe that art and literature is something
that is found within all of us. We need to
believe in ourselves and see the beauty of the
moment to take this concept further. With
my literary magazine I have created a space
for new ideas and fresh opinions. I believe in
creativity, diversity, and equality.

Agenda

The Wheelwrights
Fletching Street
Mayfield
East Sussex
TN20 6TL
Tel: +44 (0) 1435 873703
Email: submissions@agendapoetry.co.uk
Website: http://www.agendapoetry.co.uk

Publishes: Essays; Poetry; Reviews; *Areas:*
Criticism; Literature; *Markets:* Adult;
Treatments: Literary

Editors: Patricia McCarthy

Publishes poems, critical essays, and
reviews. Send up to five poems or up to two
essays / reviews with email address, age, and
short bio. No previously published material.
Submit by email only, with each piece in a
separate Word attachment. Accepts work
only during specific submission windows –
see website for current status.

Amateur Photographer

Blue Fin Building
110 Southwark Street
London
SE1 0SU
Tel: +44 (0) 20 3148 4118
Email: amateurphotographer@ipcmedia.com
Website:
http://www.amateurphotographer.co.uk

Publishes: Articles; Features; News;
Nonfiction; Reviews; *Areas:* How-to;
Photography; Technology; *Markets:* Adult;
Professional

The world's oldest consumer weekly
photographic magazine, first published in
October 1884. Accepts work from
freelances, but generally requires images to
be provided to accompany the text.

Ambit

Staithe House
Main Road
Brancaster Staithe
Norfolk
PE31 8BP
Tel: +44 (0) 7503 633601

Email: info@ambitmagazine.co.uk
Website: http://ambitmagazine.co.uk

Publishes: Fiction; Poetry; *Areas:* Arts;
Short Stories; *Markets:* Adult; *Treatments:*
Literary

An international magazine. Potential
contributors are advised to read a copy
before submitting work to us. Send 3-6
poems, a story up to 5,000 words, or flash
fiction up to 1,000 words. Submit via online
portal on website, or by post (see website for
full details). No submissions by email.

Angling Times
1 Lincoln Court
Lincoln Road
Peterborough
PE1 2RF
Tel: +44 (0) 1733 395097
Email: steve.fitzpatrick@bauermedia.co.uk
Website:
http://www.gofishing.co.uk/Angling-Times

Publishes: Articles; News; Nonfiction;
Areas: Hobbies; Nature; Sport; *Markets:*
Adult

Editors: Steve Fitzpatrick

Magazine for fishing enthusiasts.

Animals and You
PO Box 305
London
NW1 1TX
Email: animalsandyou@dcthomson.co.uk
Website: http://www.animalsandyou.co.uk

Publishes: Articles; Features; Nonfiction;
Areas: How-to; Nature; *Markets:* Children's

Magazine for girls who love animals. Most
material generated in-house, but will
consider short features with photos or good
illustrations. Send query by email in the first
instance.

Aquila
Studio 2
67A Willowfield Road
Eastbourne
East Sussex
BN22 8AP
Tel: +44 (0) 1323 431313
Fax: +44 (0) 1323 731136
Email: info@aquila.co.uk
Website: https://www.aquila.co.uk

Publishes: Features; Fiction; Nonfiction;
Areas: Short Stories; *Markets:* Children's

Magazine for children aged 8-13. Publishes
fiction 1,000-1,150 words; serials 1,050-
1,150 words per episode; and features
between 600 and 800 words. See website for
full submission guidelines.

Arc
c/o New Scientist
Lacon House
84 Theobald's Road
London
WC1X 8NS
Tel: +44 (0) 20 7611 1205
Email: simon.ings@arcfinity.org
Website: http://www.arcfinity.org

Publishes: Essays; Features; Fiction;
Nonfiction; *Areas:* Science; Sci-Fi; Short
Stories; *Markets:* Adult

Editors: Simon Ings

"Journal of the future". Publishes features,
essays, and speculative fiction about the
world to come. Most work is commissioned.

Areopagus Magazine
48 Cornwood Road
Plympton
Plymouth
PL7 1AL
Fax: +44 (0) 870 1346384
Email: editor@areopagus.org.uk
Website: http://www.areopagus.org.uk

Publishes: Articles; Fiction; Poetry;
Reviews; *Areas:* Religious; Short Stories;
Markets: Adult

Editors: Julian Barritt

A Christian-based arena for creative writers.

A forum for debate on contemporary issues relating to Christianity and wider issues. A chance for new writers to have their work published for the first time. Writers' workshop's and market news also help inform both new and established writers. This press produce a range of small publications and have recently produced their first royalty-paying book. We can only consider MSS which are submitted by subscribers to the magazine however. Subscribers may submit by email.

Areté

8 New College Lane
Oxford
OX1 3BN
Tel: +44 (0) 1865 289193
Fax: +44 (0) 1865 289194
Email: craigraine@aretemagazine.co.uk
Website: http://www.aretemagazine.com

Publishes: Fiction; Poetry; Reviews; *Areas:* Drama; Short Stories; *Markets:* Adult

Editors: Craig Raine

Arts magazine publishing fiction, poetry, reportage, and reviews. Previous contributors have included TS Eliot, William Golding, Harold Pinter, Ian McEwan, Martin Amis, Simon Armitage, Rosemary Hill, Ralph Fiennes, and many more.

Send hard copy only. Unsolicited MSS should be accompanied by an SAE or email address for response. No International Reply Coupons, and no submissions by email.

Art Business Today

16-18 Empress Place
London
SW6 1TT
Tel: +44 (0) 20 7381 6616
Email: info@fineart.co.uk
Website: http://www.fineart.co.uk

Publishes: Articles; News; Nonfiction; *Areas:* Arts; Business; Technology; *Markets:* Professional

Magazine aimed at professionals in the fine art and framing industries.

The Art Newspaper

Third Floor
70 South Lambeth Road
London
SW8 1RL
Tel: +44 (0) 20 3416 9000
Fax: +44 (0) 20 7735 3332
Email: contact@theartnewspaper.com
Website: http://www.theartnewspaper.com

Publishes: Articles; News; Nonfiction; *Areas:* Arts; *Markets:* Adult

Editors: Jane Morris

Tabloid-format monthly arts publication. No unsolicited mss. Send ideas in writing in first instance.

Assent

Room E701
Kedelston Road
University of Derby
Derby
DE22 1GB
Email: editorassent@gmail.com
Website: http://assentpoetry.com

Publishes: Essays; Interviews; Nonfiction; Poetry; Reviews; *Areas:* Criticism; Literature; *Markets:* Adult; *Treatments:* Literary

Editors: Julia Gaze

A leading small press magazine with a world wide circulation and readership. Publishes poetry, critical essays, interviews and reviews of contemporary collections.

Athletics Weekly

Athletics Weekly Limited
PO Box 614
Farnham
Surrey
GU9 1GR
Tel: +44 (0) 1733 808531
Fax: +44 (0) 1733 808530
Email: jason.henderson@athleticsweekly.com
Website: http://www.athletics-weekly.com

Publishes: Features; News; Nonfiction;

Areas: Sport; *Markets:* Adult

Editors: Jason Henderson

Publishes features, news, and fixtures relating to track and field, race walking, sport politics, etc. Send query in writing in first instance.

Autocar
Tel: +44 (0) 20 8267 5630
Email: autocar@haymarket.com
Website: http://www.autocar.co.uk

Publishes: Articles; Features; Interviews; News; Nonfiction; Reviews; *Areas:* Technology; Travel; *Markets:* Adult

Weekly car magazine publishing reviews, news, interviews, etc. Welcomes relevant contributions.

Awen
Atlantean Publishing
4 Pierrot Steps
71 Kursaal Way
Southend-on-Sea
Essex
SS1 2UY
Email: atlanteanpublishing@hotmail.com
Website: http://atlanteanpublishing. wikia.com/wiki/Awen

Publishes: Fiction; Poetry; *Areas:* Short Stories; *Markets:* Adult

Editors: David-John Tyrer

Mostly around four sides in length, this magazine manages to cram in a surprising amount of poetry and two or three Vignette length pieces of prose. Something for everyone and everyone welcomed!

Email submissions must be pasted into the body of the email. No attachments.

BackTrack
PO Box No.3
Easingwold
York
YO61 3YS

Tel: +44 (0) 1347 824397
Email: pendragonpublishing@btinternet.com
Website: http://www.pendragonpublishing.co.uk

Publishes: Articles; Features; Nonfiction; *Areas:* Historical; Travel; *Markets:* Adult

Editors: Michael Blakemore

Publishes articles on British railway history. See website for full guidelines.

Baptist Times
Baptist House
PO Box 44
129 Broadway
Didcot
Oxon
OX11 8RT
Email: editor@baptisttimes.co.uk
Website: http://www.baptisttimes.co.uk

Publishes: Articles; Features; News; Nonfiction; Reviews; *Areas:* Religious; *Markets:* Adult

Religious magazine. Welcomes direct submissions. Approach via contact form on website.

Bard
Atlantean Publishing
4 Pierrot Steps
71 Kursaal Way
Southend-on-Sea
Essex
SS1 2UY
Email: atlanteanpublishing@hotmail.com
Website: http://atlanteanpublishing. wikia.com/wiki/Bard

Publishes: Poetry; *Markets:* Adult

Flyer-style broadsheet of poetry released roughly monthly and available for free to subscribers of the publisher's magazines. Occasionally runs themed issues but generally open to any and all poetry.

Submissions by email must be pasted into the text of the email. No attachments. See website for full submission guidelines.

Best of British

The Clock Tower
6 Market Gate
Market Deeping
Lincolnshire
PE6 8DL
Tel: +44 (0) 20 8752 8181
Email:
chris.peachment@bestofbritishmag.co.uk
Website: http://www.bestofbritishmag.co.uk

Publishes: Articles; Nonfiction; *Areas:*
Historical; *Markets:* Adult

Editors: Chris Peachment

Welcomes contributions of articles
celebrating all things British, both past and
present. Emphasis placed on nostalgia and
memories from the 40s, 50s, and 60s, but
will consider things up to the 70s and even
80s. Potential contributors should study a
copy of the magazine before submitting.
Submissions may be sent by email or by
post. See website for more details.

The Big Issue in the North

10 Swan Street
Manchester
M4 5JN
Tel: +44 (0) 1618 315563
Email: kevin.gopal@bigissuenorth.co.uk
Website: http://www.bigissueinthenorth.com

Publishes: Articles; Features; News;
Nonfiction; *Areas:* Arts; Sociology;
Markets: Adult

Publishes general interest articles,
particularly on social issues. Also news and
arts features covering the North of England.
Query with ideas in first instance.

Bird Watching

Media House
Lynch Wood
Peterborough
PE2 6EA
Tel: +44 (0) 1733 468000
Email: birdwatching@bauermedia.co.uk
Website: http://www.birdwatching.co.uk

Publishes: Articles; Features; Nonfiction;

Reviews; *Areas:* Hobbies; Nature; *Markets:*
Adult

Editors: Matthew Merritt

Magazine publishing articles, features,
photography and reviews relating to birds.
Send query with synopsis in first instance.

Black Static

TTA Press
5 Martins Lane
Witcham
Ely
Cambs
CB6 2LB
Website: http://ttapress.com

Publishes: Fiction; *Areas:* Fantasy; Horror;
Short Stories; *Markets:* Adult; *Treatments:*
Dark

Editors: Andy Cox

Publishes short stories of horror and dark
fantasy. See website for full guidelines.

bliss Magazine

Panini UK Ltd
Brockbourne House
77 Mount Ephraim
Tunbridge Wells
Kent
TN4 8BS
Tel: +44 (0) 1892 500100
Fax: +44 (0) 1892 545666
Email: bliss@panini.co.uk
Website: http://www.mybliss.co.uk

Publishes: Articles; Features; News;
Nonfiction; *Areas:* Beauty and Fashion;
Lifestyle; Women's Interests; *Markets:*
Youth

Editors: Leslie Sinoway; Angeli Milburn
(Features Editor): amilburn@panini.co.uk

Lifestyle magazine for teenage girls,
publishing teenage news articles from around
the world up to 200 words, plus true life
features and items tackling teenage issues up
to 1,500 words. Send query by email and
follow up by telephone.

BMA News

BMA House
Tavistock Square
London
WC1H 9JP
Tel: +44 (0) 20 7387 4499
Email: bmanews@bma.org.uk
Website: http://bma.org.uk

Publishes: Features; News; Nonfiction;
Areas: Medicine; *Markets:* Professional

Publishes medical news and analysis.

Bowls International

Key Publishing Ltd
PO BOX 100
Stamford
PE9 1XQ
Tel: +44 (0) 1780 755131
Fax: +44 (0) 1780 751323
Email: patrick.hulbert@keypublishing.com
Website: http://www.bowlsinternational.com

Publishes: Articles; Features; News;
Nonfiction; *Areas:* Hobbies; Leisure; Sport;
Markets: Adult

Editors: Patrick Hulbert

Magazine covering the sport of bowls. See
website for more information.

British Journal of Photography

Apptitude Media Ltd
Unit A, Zetland House
5-25 Scrutton Street
Shoreditch
London
EC2A 4HJ
Tel: +44 (0) 20 8123 6873
Email: bjp.editor@bjphoto.co.uk
Website: http://www.bjp-online.com

Publishes: Articles; News; Nonfiction;
Reviews; *Areas:* Arts; Beauty and Fashion;
Photography; Technology; *Markets:*
Professional

Editors: Simon Bainbridge

Magazine for professional photographers,
publishing articles and reviews.

British Woodworking

Freshwood Publishing
The Hope Workshops
Ampney St Peter
Cirencester
Glos
GL7 5SH
Tel: +44 (0) 1285 850481
Email: bw@freshwoodpublishing.com
Website:
http://www.britishwoodworking.com

Publishes: Articles; Features; News;
Nonfiction; *Areas:* Hobbies; *Markets:* Adult

Magazine publishing articles, features, and
news of interest to woodworking hobbyists.

Brittle Star

PO Box 56108
London
E17 0AY
Tel: +44 (0) 20 8802 1507
Email: post@brittlestar.org.uk
Website: http://www.brittlestar.org.uk

Publishes: Fiction; Poetry; *Areas:* Short
Stories; *Markets:* Adult

Editors: Louise Hooper

Publishes original and unpublished poetry
and short stories. Send 1-4 poems or 1-2
stories of up to 2,000 words each. Include
short bio of up to 40 words. No simultaneous
submissions.

Buses

PO Box 14644
Leven
KY9 1WX
Tel: +44 (0) 1780 755131
Fax: +44 (0) 1780 751323
Email: buseseditor@btconnect.com
Website: http://www.busesmag.com

Publishes: Articles; Nonfiction; *Areas:*
Travel; *Markets:* Adult; Professional

Editors: Alan Millar

The UK's highest circulation magazine covering the bus and coach industries. Aimed at both industry professionals and interested enthusiasts. Query in first instance.

Candelabrum Poetry Magazine

The Red Candle Press
Rose Cottage
Main Road Threeholes
WISBECH
PE14 9JR
Email: rcp@poetry7.fsnet.co.uk
Website: http://www.members.tripod.com/redcandlepress/Magazine.htm

Publishes: Poetry; *Markets:* Adult; *Treatments:* Literary; Traditional

Editors: Leonard McCarthy

Poetry: traditionalist metrical and rhymed preferred, but good quality free verse not excluded – 5/7/5 haiku accepted. Advise study of the magazine before submitting work.

Sexist, racist, ageist matter is not accepted. CPM is a magazine for people who like their poetry rhythmic and shapely.

No submissions by email. See website for full guidelines.

Car Magazine

Bauer Automotive
Media House
Lynchwood
Peterborough
Cambridgeshire
PE2 6EA
Tel: +44 (0) 1733 468485
Fax: +44 (0) 1733 468660
Email: car@bauermedia.co.uk
Website: http://www.carmagazine.co.uk

Publishes: Articles; Features; News; Nonfiction; *Areas:* Technology; Travel; *Markets:* Adult

Car magazine with sister publications around the world.

Caravan Magazine

Warners Group Publications
The Maltings
Bourne
Lincs
PE10 9PH
Tel: +44 (0) 1778 392450
Email: johns@warnersgroup.co.uk
Website: http://www.caravanmagazine.co.uk

Publishes: Articles; Nonfiction; *Areas:* Hobbies; Leisure; Travel; *Markets:* Adult

Editors: John Sootheran

Magazine for those interested in caravanning.

Carillon Magazine

19 Godric Drive
Brinsworth
Rotherham
South Yorkshire
S60 5AN
Email: editor@carillonmag.org.uk
Website: http://www.carillonmag.org.uk

Publishes: Articles; Fiction; Nonfiction; Poetry; Reviews; *Areas:* Adventure; Crime; Criticism; Drama; Entertainment; Fantasy; Humour; Literature; Mystery; Sci-Fi; Short Stories; Suspense; *Markets:* Adult; *Treatments:* Contemporary

Editors: Graham Rippon

Perfect-bound paperback,usually with 84 pages.

An eclecic mix of poetry and prose, with a small reward for published pieces.

No "Bad" or discriminatory language.

Accepts email submissions from contributors outside the UK only.

Caterer and Hotelkeeper

Reed Business Information Ltd

Quadrant House
The Quadrant
Sutton
Surrey
SM2 5AS
Tel: +44 (0) 20 8652 3656
Email: info@catererandhotelkeeper.com
Website:
http://www.catererandhotelkeeper.com

Publishes: Articles; Nonfiction; *Areas:*
Business; Leisure; Travel; *Markets:*
Professional

Editors: Mark Lewis
(mark.lewis@rbi.co.uk)

Magazine for the hotel and catering
industries.

Ceramic Review

63 Great Russell Street
London
WC1B 3BF
Tel: +44 (0) 20 7183 5583
Fax: +44 (0) 20 3137 0924
Email: editorial@ceramicreview.com
Website: http://www.ceramicreview.com

Publishes: Articles; Features; Nonfiction;
Reviews; *Areas:* Crafts; *Markets:* Adult

Magazine covering ceramics and clay art.
See website for full submission guidelines.

Chapman

4 Broughton Place
Edinburgh
EH1 3RX
Tel: +44 (0) 131 557 2207
Email: chapman-pub@blueyonder.co.uk
Website: http://www.chapman-pub.co.uk

Publishes: Articles; Essays; Features;
Fiction; Nonfiction; Poetry; Reviews; *Areas:*
Arts; Criticism; Culture; Literature; Short
Stories; Theatre; *Markets:* Adult;
Treatments: Literary

Editors: Joy Hendry

Describes itself as Scotland's leading literary
magazine, publishing new creative writing –

poetry, fiction, discussion of cultural affairs,
theatre, reviews and the arts in general, plus
critical essays. It publishes international as
well as Scottish writers and is a dynamic
force for artistic and cultural change and
development. Always open to new writers
and ideas.

Fiction may be of any length, but average is
around 3,000 words. Send one piece at a
time. Poetry submissions should contain
between four and ten poems. Single poems
are not usually published.

Articles and reviews are usually
commissioned and ideas should be discussed
with the editor in advance.

All submissions must include an SAE or
IRCs or email address for response. No
submissions by email.

Church Times

3rd Floor
Invicta House
108-114 Golden Lane
London
EC1Y 0TG
Tel: +44 (0) 20 7776 1060
Email: editor@churchtimes.co.uk
Website: http://www.churchtimes.co.uk

Publishes: Articles; News; Nonfiction;
Areas: Religious; *Markets:* Adult

Editors: Paul Handley

Describes itself as the world's leading
Anglican newspaper. Publishes news and
articles on religious topics. No poetry or
fiction.

Classic Boat

The Chelsea Magazine Company
Jubilee House
2 Jubilee Place
London
SW3 3TQ
Tel: +44 (0) 20 7349 3700
Fax: +44 (0) 20 7349 3701
Email:
Dan.Houston@chelseamagazines.com
Website: http://www.classicboat.co.uk

Publishes: Articles; Features; News; Nonfiction; Reviews; *Areas:* Crafts; Historical; Hobbies; Travel; *Markets:* Adult

Editors: Dan Houston

Showcases classic yachts and traditionally designed workboats, plus news, opinions and reviews. Read at least three previous issues then query for guidelines if appropriate.

Classical Music

241 Shaftesbury Avenue
London
WC2H 8TF
Tel: +44 (0) 20 7333 1742
Fax: +44 (0) 20 7333 1769
Email: classical.music@rhinegold.co.uk
Website: http://www.rhinegold.co.uk

Publishes: Features; News; *Areas:* Business; Music; *Markets:* Adult; Professional

Editors: Keith Clarke

Magazine for the classical music profession. Focuses on musicians, venue managers, agents, composers, festival directors, and marketing and public relations experts. Publishes news, previews and features to inform, stimulate and amuse anyone who works in the classical music business in any capacity. Offers music lovers a behind-the-scenes view, which gives them a more realistic take on the business than is offered by consumer magazines and newspapers. Includes job listings in all areas of the music industry including performing, management, teaching and marketing. Most material is commissioned, but ideas from freelances considered. Approach in writing after familiarisation with the magazine's style and content.

Commando

185 Fleet Street
London
EC4A 2HS
Email: webmaster@commandocomics.com
Website: http://www.commandocomics.com

Publishes: Fiction; *Areas:* Adventure;

Military; Short Stories; *Markets:* Adult; Children's; Youth

Publishes stories of action and adventure set in times of war, told in graphic novel format. May be wars of the modern age or ancient wars, or even occasionally wars of the future. Encourages new writers. Send synopsis in first instance.

Computer Weekly

1st Floor
3-4a Little Portland Street
London
W1W 7JB
Tel: +44 (0) 20 7186 1400
Email: cw-news@computerweekly.com

Publishes: Articles; News; Nonfiction; *Areas:* Technology; *Markets:* Professional

Publishes news and articles relating to IT for business users.

The Countryman

Country Publications Ltd
The Water Mill, Broughton Hall
Skipton
North Yorkshire
BD23 3AG
Tel: +44 (0) 1756 701381
Fax: +44 (0) 1756 701326
Email: editorial@thecountryman.co.uk
Website:
http://www.countrymanmagazine.co.uk

Publishes: Articles; Features; News; Nonfiction; *Areas:* Nature; *Markets:* Adult

Long-running magazine for the countryside. Send news, letters, and feature ideas by email.

Crafts

44a Pentonville Road
Islington
N1 9BY
Tel: +44 (0) 20 7806 2538
Email: editorial@craftscouncil.org.uk
Website: http://www.craftsmagazine.org.uk

Publishes: Articles; Features; News;
Nonfiction; Reviews; *Areas:* Crafts;
Markets: Adult

Magazine covering crafts. Send query by
email with brief outline and example of
previous work. Response not guaranteed.

Criminal Law & Justice Weekly (Incorporating Justice of the Peace)

Halsbury House
35 Chancery Lane
London
WC2A 1EL
Tel: +44 (0) 20 7400 2828
Email: diana.rose@lexisnexis.co.uk
Website:
http://www.criminallawandjustice.co.uk

Publishes: Articles; Nonfiction; *Areas:*
Legal; *Markets:* Professional

Editors: Diana Rose

Weekly magazine covering key
developments in criminal law, plus practice
and procedure across the whole criminal
court system. Includes licensing and the
coroners' court. Send complete ms or précis
by email. See website for full details.

Crystal Magazine

3 Bowness Avenue
Prenton
Birkenhead
CH43 0SD
Tel: +44 (0) 1516 089736
Email: christinecrystal@hotmail.com
Website:
http://www.christinecrystal.blogspot.com

Publishes: Articles; Fiction; Nonfiction;
Poetry; *Areas:* Fantasy; Humour; Literature;
Mystery; Nature; Sci-Fi; Short Stories;
Suspense; Thrillers; Travel; Westerns;
Markets: Adult; *Treatments:* Light; Literary;
Mainstream; Popular; Positive; Traditional

Editors: Christine Carr

Your Poems, Your Stories, Your Articles
and More.

40-page A4 bi-monthly for creative writers.
It is for subscribers only. Contributions
required are poems, stories (true and fiction)
and articles. Where room permits, work is
enhanced with colour photos/graphics. Your
submissions can be any length and theme
except erotica. You can send your work by
email (either in the body of the email or as
attachment) or by post. Handwritten material
is acceptable. If sent by snail mail, and you
wish your work returned, a stamp would be
appreciated. Under normal circumstances,
you will not have to wait weeks and weeks
for a reply.

Usually contains pages and pages of
Readers' Letters. The subscriber mentioned
the most times will receive £10.

Should you have been successful with
writing elsewhere, you would be welcome to
share your achievements in Subscribers'
News.

A regular feature every issue is
Wordsmithing – Titters, Tips, Titillations.
This is an amusing and informative look into
the world of writers and writing.

"Valleys of the Wye", a new addition, is a
series of short fictional stories touching upon
real focal points in the upper and then lower
valleys of the river on its journey to merge
with the River Severn into the Bristol
Channel.

I also run a free pen-friend service enabling
subscribers to get in touch with each other by
email.

I have received a lot of positive feedback
over the years. Here are just two comments:

"The magazine is good value for money and
worth every penny."

"Thanks for providing us with such a great
and friendly magazine."

Cycle Sport

IPC Focus Network
Leon House
233 High Street
Croydon

CR9 1HZ
Tel: +44 (0) 20 8726 8453
Email: cyclesport@ipcmedia.com
Website: http://www.cyclesportmag.com

Publishes: Articles; Features; Interviews;
News; Nonfiction; *Areas:* Sport; *Markets:*
Adult; Professional

Editors: Robert Garbutt

Magazine on professional cycle racing.
Includes coverage of events such as the Tour
de France, and interviews with the big names
in the field. Most material commissioned,
but will consider unsolicited materia.
Welcomes ideas for articles and features.

Dairy Farmer

PO Box 18
Preston
PR2 9GU
Tel: +44 (0) 1772 799459
Email: FGSupport@farmersguardian.com
Website: http://www.farmersguardian.com

Publishes: Articles; Nonfiction; *Areas:*
Business; Nature; *Markets:* Professional;
Treatments: In-depth

Publishes material of interest to professionals
in the dairy industry, including milk
marketing and farm management.

The Dawntreader

24 Forest Houses
Cookworthy Moor
Halwill
Beaworthy
Devon
EX21 5UU
Email: dawnidp@indigodreams.co.uk
Website: http://www.indigodreams.co.uk

Publishes: Articles; Features; Fiction;
Nonfiction; Poetry; *Areas:* Fantasy; Nature;
Short Stories; *Markets:* Adult

Editors: Ronnie Goodyer

A quarterly publication specialising in the
landscape; myth and legend... nature;

spirituality and pre-history... environment
and ecology... the mystic.

Seeking poetry in all forms and also
welcomes short stories, prose and legend that
follow the themes.

Decanto

PO Box 3257
84 Dinsdale Gardens
Littlehampton
BN16 9AF
Email: masque_pub@btinternet.com
Website:
http://myweb.tiscali.co.uk/masquepublishing

Publishes: Poetry; *Markets:* Adult

Editors: Lisa Stewart

Send up to six original, unpublished poems
by post with SAE or by email in the body of
the message (no attachments). Poems of any
subject or style are considered.

Devon Life

Archant House
Babbage Road
Totnes
TQ9 5JA
Tel: +44 (0) 1803 860910
Fax: +44 (0) 1803 860922
Email: jane.fitzgerald@archant.co.uk
Website: http://devon.greatbritishlife.co.uk

Publishes: Articles; Nonfiction; *Areas:* Arts;
Cookery; Culture; Historical; Lifestyle;
Nature; Travel; *Markets:* Adult

Editors: Jane Fitzgerald

Magazine publishing articles relating to
Devon. Welcomes ideas.

The Dickensian

The School of English
Rutherford College
University of Kent
Canterbury
Kent
CT2 7NX

Email: M.Y.Andrews@kent.ac.uk
Website: http://www.dickensfellowship.org/
dickensian

Publishes: Articles; Nonfiction; *Areas:*
Biography; Criticism; Historical; Literature;
Markets: Adult

Editors: Professor Malcolm Andrews

Publishes articles on the life and works of
Dickens. Send articles as hard copy by post
with SAE and electronic copy in .doc format
(not .docx). See website for full guidelines.

DIY Week

Faversham House Ltd
Windsor Court
Wood Street
East Grinstead
West Sussex
RH19 1UZ
Tel: +44 (0) 1342 332000
Website: http://www.diyweek.net

Publishes: Articles; News; Nonfiction;
Areas: Business; *Markets:* Professional

Editors: Fiona Hodge

Magazine providing news and articles of
interest to retailers and suppliers in the home
improvement market.

Dogs Today

The Old Print House
62 The High Street
Chobham
Surrey
GU24 8AA
Tel: +44 (0) 1276 858880
Fax: +44 (0) 1276 858860
Email: enquiries@dogstodaymagazine.co.uk
Website:
http://www.dogstodaymagazine.co.uk

Publishes: Articles; Features; Interviews;
Nonfiction; *Areas:* Entertainment; Health;
Hobbies; Nature; Travel; *Markets:* Adult

Glossy monthly magazine for dog lovers.
Send submissions by post with SAE, or by

email with "Editorial Submission" in the
subject line.

Dream Catcher

Stairwell Books
161 Lowther Street
York
YO31 7LZ
Tel: +44 (0) 1904 733767
Email: rose@stairwellbooks.com
Website:
http://www.dreamcatchermagazine.co.uk

Publishes: Fiction; Interviews; Nonfiction;
Poetry; Reviews; *Areas:* Short Stories;
Translations; *Markets:* Adult; *Treatments:*
Literary

Editors: Paul Sutherland

Send submissions by post, following
guidelines on website.

Early Music

Faculty of Music
University of Cambridge
11 West Road
Cambridge
CB3 9DP
Tel: +44 (0) 1223 335178
Email: earlymusic@oxfordjournals.org
Website: http://em.oxfordjournals.org

Publishes: Articles; Nonfiction; *Areas:*
Music; *Markets:* Academic; Adult;
Professional

Editors: Francis Knights

Magazine covering early music and how it is
being interpreted today. Aimed at scholars,
professional performers, and enthusiasts. An
excessively academic tone should be
avoided. See website for full submission
guidelines.

East Lothian Life

1 Beveridge Row
Belhaven
Dunbar
East Lothian
EH42 1TP

Tel: +44 (0) 1368 863593
Fax: +44 (0) 1368 863593
Email: info@eastlothianlife.co.uk
Website: http://www.eastlothianlife.co.uk

Publishes: Articles; Features; Nonfiction;
Markets: Adult

Editors: Pauline Jaffray

Publishes articles and features relating to
East Lothian.

The Edge
Unit 138
22 Notting Hill Gate
London
W11 3JE
Tel: +44 (0) 8454 569337
Email: enquiries@theedgemagazine.co.uk
Website: http://www.theedgemagazine.co.uk

Publishes: Features; Fiction; Interviews;
Nonfiction; Reviews; *Areas:* Crime;
Entertainment; Erotic; Fantasy; Gothic;
Horror; Sci-Fi; *Markets:* Adult; *Treatments:*
Contemporary; Experimental

Editors: Dave Clark

Not accepting submissions as at May 2014.
See website for current status.

Education Journal
The Education Publishing Company
Devonia House
4 Union Terrace
Crediton
EX17 3DY
Tel: +44 (0) 1363 774455
Fax: +44 (0) 1363 776592
Email: ejw@educationpublishing.com
Website:
http://www.educationpublishing.com

Publishes: Articles; Features; News;
Nonfiction; *Markets:* Professional

Magazine for education professionals,
including news, features, analysis,
conference and parliamentary reports,
reviews of major documents and research

reports on schools, colleges, universities and
the full range of educational issues.

Electrical Review
St John Patrick Publishers Ltd
6 Laurence Pountney Hill
London
EC4R 0BL
Tel: +44 (0) 20 8319 1807
Email: elinorem@electricalreview.co.uk
Website: http://www.electricalreview.co.uk

Publishes: Articles; Features; News;
Nonfiction; *Areas:* Business; Technology;
Markets: Professional

Electrical journal aimed at electrical
engineers, project managers, consultants and
electrical contractors, and any other key
personnel specifying electrical systems in
public/commercial buildings and industry.

Envoi
Meirion House
Glan yr afon
Tanygrisiau
Blaenau Ffestiniog
LL41 3SU
Tel: +44 (0) 1766 832112
Email: jan@envoipoetry.com
Website:
http://www.cinnamonpress.com/envoi

Publishes: Articles; Nonfiction; Poetry;
Reviews; *Areas:* Literature; Translations;
Markets: Adult; *Treatments:* Literary

Editors: Dr Jan Fortune-Wood

Magazine of poems, poetry sequences,
reviews, and competitions, now more than
50 years old. Occasional poetry related
articles and poetry in translation. Submit up
to 6 poems up to 40 lines each or one or two
longer poems by post or by email (in the
body of the email; attachments will not be
read).

What others say:

"Probably the best poetry magazine currently
available" – The Writers' College

"Without a grant and obviously well read, this poetry magazine excels itself." – Ore

"The policy of giving poets space to show their skills is the right one." – Haiku Quarterly

"Good quality, lots of bounce, poems, comps, reviews, reader comeback" – iota

"If you haven't tried it yet, do so, you'll get your money's worth." – New Hope International

Esquire

Hearst Magazines UK London
72 Broadwick Street
London
W1F 9EP
Tel: +44 (0) 20 7439 5000
Email: alex.bilmes@hearst.co.uk
Website: http://www.esquire.co.uk

Publishes: Articles; Features; Nonfiction; *Areas:* Beauty and Fashion; Culture; Lifestyle; Men's Interests; Technology; *Markets:* Adult

Editors: Alex Bilmes

Men's general interest magazine. Publishes features and articles on style, tech gadgets, food and drink, culture, and women.

Eventing

IPC Media Limited
Blue Fin Building
110 Southwark Street
London
SE1 0SU
Tel: +44 (0) 20 3148 4545
Email: julie_harding@ipcmedia.com
Website: http://www.ipcmedia.com/eventing

Publishes: Articles; Essays; Features; News; Nonfiction; *Areas:* How-to; Sport; *Markets:* Adult

Editors: Julie Harding

Magazine covering the sport of horse trials. Includes news, results, features, opinions and instructional articles. Most material is commissioned, but welcomes ideas.

Family Law Journal

Jordan Publishing Limited
21 St Thomas Street
Bristol
BS1 6JS
Tel: +44 (0) 1179 230600
Fax: +44 (0) 1179 250486
Email: sales@jordanpublishing.co.uk
Website: http://www.jordanpublishing.co.uk

Publishes: Articles; Nonfiction; *Areas:* Legal; *Markets:* Professional

Editors: Elizabeth Walsh

Legal journal publishing articles in the area of family law.

Financial Adviser

Financial Times Business
One Southwark Bridge
London
SE1 9HL
Tel: +44 (0) 20 7775 6639
Email: hal.austin@ft.com
Website: http://www.ftadviser.com

Publishes: Articles; Features; News; Nonfiction; *Areas:* Finance; *Markets:* Adult

Editors: Hal Austin, Senior Editor

Publishes news and features on personal finance.

Fire

Field Cottage
Old Whitehill
Tackley
Kidlington
Oxon
OX5 3AB
Website: http://www.poetical.org

Publishes: Fiction; Poetry; *Areas:* Short Stories; *Markets:* Adult; *Treatments:* Literary

Editors: Jeremy Hilton

A poetry magazine with a big reputation and represents big value for money. It appears twice a year (March, October) and each issue contains 170 pages of poetry (mostly) and some prose. It is radical, multicultural and international in outlook, and publishes a broad range of poetry from around the world. It tends towards the more alternative end of the poetry spectrum, and is interested in poetry with heart, spirit, imagination, innovation, risk-taking, open-endedness, and most of all poems that have something to say. Not neat, tight, closed, clever, cynical, fashionable poems. This magazine exists to promote unknown, little-known, new or unpublished writers and to include features on young writers and poems by children. Although the magazine is on email and has a website (see below), the printed magazine retains its format. ALL submissions must be by snailmail, and must include a stamped addressed envelope. To subscribe (3 issues) please send a cheque or postal order made out to FIRE, for £9.00 to the address below. Single copies cost £5.00. The magazine is available at some specialist libraries and bookshops, and at some poetry festivals, but most copies are sold by mail-order.

Fire Magazine

Ground Floor
Rayford House
School Road
Hove
BN3 5HX
Tel: +44 (0) 1273 434951
Email: andrew.lynch@pavpub.com
Website: http://www.fire-magazine.com

Publishes: Articles; Nonfiction; *Markets:* Professional

Editors: Andrew Lynch

Publishes expert articles and fire fighting and prevention. No unsolicited mss; query in first instance.

FourFourTwo

FREEPOST RSBZ-BKGC-BRLH
PO Box 326
Sittingbourne
Kent

ME9 8FA
Tel: +44 (0) 1795 592979
Email: 442@servicehelpline.co.uk
Website:
http://www.fourfourtwo.magazine.co.uk

Publishes: Articles; Features; Interviews; Nonfiction; *Areas:* Sport; *Markets:* Adult

Describes itself as the only magazine to truly reflect football in all its extremes: spectacular, dramatic, hilarious, opinionated, authoritative, intelligent, quirky.

France

Archant House
3 Oriel Road
Cheltenham
GL50 1BB
Tel: +44 (0) 1242 216050
Email: editorial@francemag.com
Website: http://www.francemag.com

Publishes: Articles; Features; Interviews; Nonfiction; *Areas:* Cookery; Culture; Film; Historical; Literature; Travel; *Markets:* Adult

Editors: Carolyn Boyd

Magazine about France, including articles on weekend getaways, destinations and holiday ideas, food and wine section, history and culture, guide to improving your French, book and film reviews, interviews with A-list French stars and France-loving celebrities.

Freelance Market News

8-10 Dutton Street
Manchester
M3 1LE
Tel: +44 (0) 161 819 9919
Fax: +44 (0) 161 819 2842
Email: fmn@writersbureau.com
Website:
http://www.freelancemarketnews.com

Publishes: Articles; News; Nonfiction; *Markets:* Adult; Professional

Editors: Angela Cox

Publishes well-researched notes for markets

for writers (including the editor's full name with a complete address, telephone and fax number, email address and website, and preferably a quote from the editor or editorial office giving advice to potential contributors) and short articles around 700 words (one page) or 1500 words (two pages). Welcomes unsolicited MSS.

The Frogmore Papers

21 Mildmay Road
Lewes
East Sussex
BN7 1PJ
Email: j.n.page@sussex.ac.uk
Website: http://www.frogmorepress.co.uk

Publishes: Fiction; Nonfiction; Poetry; Reviews; *Areas:* Short Stories; *Markets:* Adult; *Treatments:* Contemporary; Literary

Editors: Jeremy Page

Poetry and prose by new and established authors. There is no house style but the extremes of tradition and experiment are equally unlikely to find favour.

Send between four and six poems, or up to two prose pieces.

Go Girl Magazine

239 Kensington High Street
Kensington
W8 6SA
Email:
GOGIRLMAG@EUK.EGMONT.COM
Website: http://www.gogirlmag.co.uk

Publishes: Articles; Features; Interviews; News; Nonfiction; *Areas:* Beauty and Fashion; Entertainment; Film; Lifestyle; Music; *Markets:* Children's

Magazine for girls aged 7-11, covering beauty, fashion, celebrity news and gossip, friends, pets, etc.

GamesMaster

Future plc
30 Monmouth Street
Bath

BA1 2BW
Tel: +44 (0) 1225 442244
Fax: +44 (0) 1225 446019
Email: gamesmaster@futurenet.co.uk
Website: http://www.futureplc.com

Publishes: Articles; News; Nonfiction; Reviews; *Areas:* Entertainment; Leisure; Technology; *Markets:* Adult; Youth

Editors: Robin Alway

Games magazine, covering all major formats.

Garbaj

Atlantean Publishing
4 Pierrot Steps
71 Kursaal Way
Southend-on-Sea
Essex
SS1 2UY
Email: atlanteanpublishing@hotmail.com
Website: http://atlanteanpublishing.
wikia.com/wiki/Garbaj

Publishes: Fiction; News; Poetry; *Areas:* Humour; Politics; Short Stories; *Markets:* Adult; *Treatments:* Satirical

Editors: David-John Tyrer

Humorous and slightly politically incorrect paper between four and ten pages long. Vignette-length fiction and fake news, etc. Some issues are themed but mostly not too strictly. Something for everyone who likes to laugh.

Gay Times (GT Magazine)

Millivres Prowler Group
Unit M, Spectrum House
32-34 Gordon House Road
London
NW5 1LP
Tel: +44 (0) 20 7424 7400
Email: edit@gaytimes.co.uk
Website: http://www.gaytimes.co.uk

Publishes: Articles; Features; Interviews; Nonfiction; *Areas:* Arts; Beauty and Fashion; Culture; Current Affairs; Entertainment; Film; Health; Lifestyle;

Music; Technology; *Markets:* Adult

Editors: Darren Scott

Lifestyle magazine aimed at gay men.

The Good Book Guide
4A All Hallows Road
Bispham
Blackpool
Lancs
FY2 0AS
Tel: +44 (0) 1213 143539
Fax: +44 (0) 20 3070 0343
Email: enquiries@thegoodbookguide.com
Website: http://www.thegoodbookguide.com

Publishes: Nonfiction; Reviews; *Areas:*
Literature; *Markets:* Adult

Publishes reviews of books published in the
UK.

Greetings Today
1 Churchgates
The Wilderness
Berkhamsted
HP4 2UB
Tel: +44 (0) 1442 289930
Email: tracey@lemapublishing.co.uk
Website: http://www.greetingstoday.co.uk

Publishes: Articles; Features; News;
Nonfiction; Reference; *Areas:* Business;
Markets: Professional

Editors: Tracey Bearton

Trade magazine for the greetings card
industry, publishing articles, features, news,
and a directory for artists seeking publishers.

The Grocer
William Reed Business Media Ltd
Broadfield Park
Crawley
RH11 9RT
Tel: +44 (0) 1293 610263
Email: adam.leyland@wrbm.com
Website: http://www.thegrocer.co.uk

Publishes: Articles; News; Nonfiction;

Areas: Business; *Markets:* Professional

Editors: Adam Leyland

Magazine for professionals in the grocery
trade.

Grow Your Own
25 Phoenix Court
Hawkins Road
Colchester
Essex
CO2 8JY
Tel: +44 (0) 1206 505979
Email: lucy.halsall@aceville.co.uk
Website: http://www.growfruitandveg.co.uk

Publishes: Articles; Features; News;
Nonfiction; *Areas:* Gardening; How-to;
Markets: Adult

Editors: Lucy Halsall

Magazine covering the growing of fruit and
veg.

Health Club Management
The Leisure Media Company Ltd
Portmill House
Portmill Lane
Hitchin
Hertfordshire
SG5 1DJ
Tel: +44 (0) 1462 431385
Fax: +44 (0) 1462 433909
Email: lizterry@leisuremedia.com
Website:
http://www.healthclubmanagement.co.uk

Publishes: Articles; News; Nonfiction;
Areas: Business; Health; Leisure; *Markets:*
Professional

Editors: Liz Terry

Professional magazine for those involved in
the running of health clubs, sports centres,
etc.

Heat
Endeavour House
189 Shaftesbury Avenue

London
WC2H 8JG
Email: heatEd@heatmag.com
Website: http://www.heatworld.com

Publishes: Articles; Features; News;
Nonfiction; *Areas:* Entertainment; *Markets:*
Adult

Publishes news and features on celebrities.

Horse & Hound

IPC Media
Blue Fin Building
110 Southwark Street
SE1 0SU
Tel: +44 (0) 20 3148 4562
Fax: +44 (0) 20 3148 8128
Email: lucy_higginson@ipcmedia.com
Website: http://www.horseandhound.co.uk

Publishes: Articles; News; Nonfiction;
Areas: Sport; *Markets:* Adult

Editors: Lucy Higginson

Weekly magazine publishing news and
articles relating to equestrian sports.

I-70 Review

913 Joseph Drive
Lawrence, KS 66044
Email: i70review@gmail.com

Publishes: Fiction; Poetry; *Areas:* Short
Stories; *Markets:* Adult; *Treatments:*
Literary

Accepts submissions of fiction and flash
fiction or 3-5 poems, by email, during the
reading period that runs from July 1 to
January 31. Maximum one submission per
reading period. Accepts simultaneous
submissions, but no previously published
work. See website for full details.

ICIS Chemical Business Magazine

Reed Business Information
Quadrant House
The Quadrant
Sutton

Surrey
SM2 5AS
Tel: +44 (0) 20 8652 3500
Fax: +44 (0) 20 8652 3375
Email: icbeditorial@icis.com
Website: http://www.icis.com

Publishes: Articles; Features; News;
Nonfiction; *Areas:* Business; Science;
Markets: Professional

Business magazine covering the global
chemical markets.

Inclement (Poetry for the Modern Soul)

White Rose House
8 Newmarket Road
Fordham
Ely
Cambs
CB7 5LL
Email:
inclement_poetry_magazine@hotmail.com
Website:
http://inclementpoetrymagazine.webs.com

Publishes: Poetry; *Markets:* Adult

Editors: Michelle Foster

We are a magazine that considers all forms
and styles of poetry that are submitted. What
is more important is that you believe in your
work. Poetry needs a voice, and through
several superb publications poets all over the
world are finding that voice. Too often,
poetry is sidelined as a specialist genre when
it should be available to everyone. This is
your chance to have your work recognised.

Email submissions are preferred (either in
the body of the email or as a Word file
attachment), but postal submissions are also
accepted – enclose a stamped, self-addressed
envelope. See website for full guidelines.

Intermedia

The International Institute of
Communications
2 Printers Yard
90a Broadway
London

SW19 1RD
Tel: +44 (0) 20 8417 0600
Fax: +44 (0) 20 8417 0800
Email: j.grimshaw@iicom.org
Website: http://www.iicom.org/intermedia

Publishes: Articles; Nonfiction; *Areas:*
Media; Politics; Science; Technology;
Markets: Academic; Professional

Editors: Joanne Grimshaw

Journal on media and telecom policy, aimed
at regulators and policymakers, academics,
lawyers, consultants and service providers
around the world. Send query by email.

The Interpreter's House
9 Glenhurst Road
Mannamead
Plymouth
PL3 5LT
Email: simon@simoncurtis.net
Website:
http://www.interpretershouse.org.uk

Publishes: Fiction; Poetry; *Areas:* Literature;
Short Stories; *Markets:* Adult; *Treatments:*
Contemporary; Experimental; Light;
Literary; Popular; Positive; Progressive;
Serious; Traditional

Editors: Dr Simon Curtis

While this magazine may tend towards the
mainstream, in these days of rap, slams and
performance poetry, it hopes nonetheless to
welcome inventive and imaginative work,
surreal original pieces have been published.
It does warm to economical, concise writing,
is sympathetic to humour, wit and
quirkiness. It seeks the union of simplicity
and mystery which makes writing
memorable.

Iota
PO BOX 7721
Matlock
Derbyshire
DE4 9DD
Tel: +44 (0) 1629 582500
Email: info@iotamagazine.co.uk
Website: http://www.iotapoetry.co.uk

Publishes: Essays; Features; Fiction;
Interviews; Nonfiction; Poetry; Reviews;
Areas: Short Stories; Translations; *Markets:*
Adult

Editors: Nigel McLoughlin

Poetry magazine now also publishing fiction
and nonfiction. Send up to 6 poems by post,
or by email after paying a £1 submission
charge for electronic submissions. For fiction
send stories between 2,000 and 6,000 words
by post or by email. For nonfiction send
proposals up to 150 words by email. See
website for full guidelines and specific email
addresses to use.

The Irish Post
Suite A
1 Lindsey Street
Smithfield
London
EC1A 9HP
Tel: +44 (0) 20 8900 4193
Email: editor@irishpost.co.uk
Website: http://www.irishpost.co.uk

Publishes: Articles; News; Nonfiction;
Areas: Business; Entertainment; Lifestyle;
Politics; Sport; Travel; *Markets:* Adult

Editors: Siobhán Breatnach

Magazine aimed at the Irish community in
Britain, covering social events, sports,
politics, and entertainment.

The Journal
17 High Street
Maryport
Cumbria
CA15 6BQ
Email: smithsssj@aol.com
Website:
http://www.freewebs.com/thesamsmith/

Publishes: Articles; Interviews; Poetry;
Reviews; *Areas:* Translations; *Markets:*
Adult

Editors: Sam Smith

This publication continues to keep up its

Scandinavian connections, especially with the diaspora. Keen to sustain its international flavour, I favour dual text publication where possible. Regards the criteria for acceptance for those poems written in English, I think it best to quote from the editorial for issue 1 – the aim being .... "to publish those poems ... written with thought to what the poem is saying and to how it is being said." The magazine is A4, stapled, about 40 pages long, a third of the pages given over to articles and/or reviews.

Email submissions accepted in the body of the email only, not as attached files. See website for full details.

Junior

Immediate Media Co. Ltd
(Formerly Magicalia Publishing Ltd)
15-18 White Lion Street
London
N1 9PG

Immediate Media Co.
Vineyard House
44 Brook Green
Hammersmith
W6 7BT
Tel: +44 (0) 20 7150 5000
Email: editorial@juniormagazine.co.uk
Website: http://www.juniormagazine.co.uk

Publishes: Articles; Features; Nonfiction; *Areas:* Beauty and Fashion; Cookery; Entertainment; Health; Lifestyle; Travel; *Markets:* Adult; Family

Editors: Catherine O'Dolan

Glossy, family lifestyle magazine aimed at parents of children 0-8, including informative features and expert advice on child development, education and health, as well as children's fashion, inspirational interiors and child-friendly travel suggestions.

Lancashire Magazine

Seasiders Way
Blackpool
Lancashire
FY1 6NZ

Tel: +44 (0) 1253 336588
Fax: +44 (0) 1253 336587
Email: website@lancashiremagazine.co.uk
Website: http://thelancashiremagazine.com

Publishes: Articles; Nonfiction; *Areas:* Leisure; Lifestyle; *Markets:* Adult

Publishes articles relating to Lancashire and the North West.

The List

14 High Street
Edinburgh
EH1 1TE
Tel: +44 (0) 1315 503050
Email: newwriters@list.co.uk
Website: http://www.list.co.uk

Publishes: Articles; Features; Nonfiction; *Areas:* Arts; Entertainment; Film; Literature; Music; Theatre; TV; *Markets:* Adult

Magazine intended to publicise and promote arts, events and entertainment taking place in Scotland.

The London Magazine

11 Queen's Gate
London
SW7 5EL
Tel: +44 (0) 20 7584 5977
Fax: +44 (0) 20 7225 3273
Email: admin@thelondonmagazine.org
Website: http://thelondonmagazine.org

Publishes: Articles; Features; Fiction; Nonfiction; Poetry; Reviews; *Areas:* Arts; Autobiography; Criticism; Literature; Short Stories; *Markets:* Adult; *Treatments:* Literary

Send submissions by post or by email, with the submission in the body of the message as well as an attachment. Does not normally publish science fiction or fantasy writing, or erotica. See website for full guidelines.

London Review of Books

28 Little Russell Street
London
WC1A 2HN

Tel: +44 (0) 20 7209 1101
Fax: +44 (0) 20 7209 1102
Email: edit@lrb.co.uk
Website: http://www.lrb.co.uk

Publishes: Articles; Essays; Nonfiction;
Poetry; Reviews; *Areas:* Arts; Culture;
Literature; Politics; Science; *Markets:* Adult;
Treatments: Literary

Editors: Mary-Kay Wilmers

Contact editor in writing in first instance,
including SAE. Publishes mainly reviews,
essays, and articles, but also publishes
poetry. Welcomes unsolicited contributions
over 2000 words.

Lunar Poetry

Email: editor@lunarpoetry.co.uk
Website: http://www.lunarpoetry.co.uk

Publishes: Articles; Nonfiction; Poetry;
Reviews; *Areas:* Criticism; Literature;
Markets: Adult; *Treatments:* Literary

Publishes poems of any kind or style, articles
on poetry up to 1,000 words, and reviews.
Send up to six poems in the body of an email
or as attachments, with 50-word bio. See
website for full submission guidelines.

Magma

23 Pine Walk
Carshalton
SM5 4ES
Email: contributions@magmapoetry.com
Website: http://www.magmapoetry.com

Publishes: Nonfiction; Poetry; Reviews;
Areas: Literature; *Markets:* Adult;
Treatments: Literary

Editors: Laurie Smith

Prefers submissions by email. Postal
submissions accepted from the UK only, and
must include SAE. Accepts poems and
artwork. Poems are considered for one issue
only – they are not held over from one issue
to the next. Seeks poems that give a direct
sense of what it is to live today – honest

about feelings, alert about world, sometimes
funny, always well crafted. Strongly prefers
poems to be in the body of the email, rather
than an attachment. If, for formatting
reasons, you feel you must use an attachment
include all the poems you are submitting in
one file. Also publishes reviews of books
and pamphlets of poetry. See website for
details and separate contact details.

Market Newsletter

Bureau of Freelance Photographers
Focus House
497 Green Lanes
London
N13 4BP
Tel: +44 (0) 20 8882 3315
Email: info@thebfp.com
Website: http://www.thebfp.com

Publishes: Articles; News; Nonfiction;
Areas: Photography; *Markets:* Professional

Publishes stories and markets of interest to
freelance photographers.

Media Week

Haymarket Publishing Ltd
174 Hammersmith Road
London
W6 7JP
Tel: +44 (0) 20 8267 8024
Email: arif.durrani@haymarket.com
Website: http://www.mediaweek.co.uk

Publishes: Articles; Features; Interviews;
News; Nonfiction; *Areas:* Business; Media;
Markets: Professional

Editors: Arif Durrani

Online magazine for the media industry.

Modern Poetry in Translation

The Queens College
Oxford
OX1 4AW
Tel: +44 (0) 1865 244701
Email: submissions@mptmagazine.com
Website: http://www.mptmagazine.com

Publishes: Essays; Nonfiction; Poetry; *Areas:* Literature; Translations; *Markets:* Adult

Editors: David and Helen Constantine, The Editors

Respected poetry series originally founded by prominent poets in the sixties. New Series continues their editorial policy: translation of good poets by translators who are often themselves poets, fluent in the foreign language, and sometimes working with the original poet. See website for submission guidelines.

Modern Language Review
1 Carlton House Terrace
London
SW1Y 5AF
Email: mlr@mhra.org.uk
Website: http://www.mhra.org.uk/
Publications/Journals/mlr.html

Publishes: Articles; Reviews; *Areas:* Literature; *Markets:* Academic

Publishes scholarly articles and reviews relating to modern languages. See website for full submission guidelines, including specific email addresses for different languages.

Monkey Kettle
Email: monkeykettle@hotmail.com
Website: http://www.monkeykettle.co.uk

Publishes: Articles; Fiction; Nonfiction; Poetry; *Areas:* Humour; Politics; Short Stories; *Markets:* Adult; *Treatments:* Dark; Satirical

Editors: Matthew Taylor

Send up between five and ten poems at a time, or a short story up to 1,500 words. Favours the funny, surreal, dark, poignant, and political. Not interested "whiny" material about no-one understanding you.

Monomyth
Atlantean Publishing

4 Pierrot Steps
71 Kursaal Way
Southend-on-Sea
Essex
SS1 2UY
Email: atlanteanpublishing@hotmail.com
Website: http://atlanteanpublishing.
wikia.com/wiki/Monomyth

Publishes: Fiction; Poetry; *Areas:* Fantasy; Short Stories; *Markets:* Adult

Editors: David-John Tyrer

Publishes longer short stories and long poetry. Submit by post with SASE or by email with your submission in the body of the email (no attachments).

Mslexia
PO Box 656
Newcastle upon Tyne
NE99 1PZ
Tel: +44 (0) 191 2616656
Fax: +44 (0) 191 2616636
Email: submissions@mslexia.co.uk
Website: http://www.mslexia.co.uk

Publishes: Articles; Essays; Features; Fiction; Interviews; News; Nonfiction; Poetry; Reference; Reviews; *Areas:* Autobiography; Short Stories; Women's Interests; *Markets:* Adult

Editors: Daneet Steffens

By women, for women who write, who want to write, who teach creative writing or who have an interest in womens' literature and creativity. It is a mixture of original work, features, news, views, advice and listings. The UK's only magazine devoted to women writers and their writing.

See website for themes of upcoming issues / competitions.

Publishes features, columns, reviews, flash fiction, and literature listings. Email submissions for themed new writing from overseas writers only. Email submissions for other contributions accepted from anywhere. See website for full details.

Music Teacher

Rhinegold House
20 Rugby Street
London
WC1N 3QZ
Tel: +44 (0) 7785 613145
Fax: +44 (0) 20 7333 1736
Email: music.teacher@rhinegold.co.uk
Website: http://www.rhinegold.co.uk

Publishes: Articles; Nonfiction; Reviews;
Areas: How-to; Music; *Markets:*
Professional

Magazine for both private and school music
teachers.

Neon Highway Poetry Magazine

37 Grinshill Close
Liverpool
L8 8LD
Email: neonhighwaypoetry@yahoo.co.uk
Website:
http://neonhighwaypoetry.webstarts.com

Publishes: Poetry; *Markets:* Adult;
Treatments: Literary

Editors: Alice Lenkiewicz

Avant-garde literary journal publishing
poetry and art. Submissions accepted by post
and by email. See website for details.

.net

30 Monmouth Street
Bath
BA1 2BW
Tel: +44 (0) 1225 442244
Fax: +44 (0) 1225 732295
Email: oliver.lindberg@futurenet.com
Website: http://www.netmagazine.com

Publishes: Articles; Features; News;
Nonfiction; *Areas:* Technology; *Markets:*
Professional

Editors: Oliver Lindberg

Magazine for web designers and developers,
publishing articles, features, and news.

The New Accelerator

Email: editors@thenewaccelerator.com
Website: http://thenewaccelerator.com

Publishes: Fiction; *Areas:* Entertainment;
Fantasy; Horror; Religious; Science; Sci-Fi;
Short Stories; Spiritual; Technology;
Thrillers; *Markets:* Adult; *Treatments:*
Commercial; Contemporary; Dark;
Experimental; Literary; Positive;
Progressive; Satirical; Serious; Traditional

Editors: Andy Coughlan and David
Winstanley

A Science Fiction short story anthology.
Published monthly exclusively through
Apple's Newsstand app, the anthology will
be available to over half a billion iOS users
worldwide.

The aim of the anthology is to bring cutting-
edge fiction to an eager and discerning
global Science Fiction audience.

New London Writers

Flat 34
67 Hatton Garden
London
EC1N 8JY
Tel: +44 (0) 07913 373870
Email: publish@newlondonwriters.com
Website: http://newlondonwriters.com

Publishes: Articles; Fiction; Reviews; *Areas:*
Fantasy; Mystery; Philosophy; Sci-Fi; Short
Stories; Suspense; *Markets:* Adult; Youth;
Treatments: Commercial; Contemporary;
Dark; Experimental; Literary; Mainstream;
Niche; Satirical

Editors: Alice Wickham

A platform for new writing. We act as
publisher and literary agent for emerging
novelists. Work is published and promoted to
our network of over 500 literary agents and
publishers in the UK and overseas, mainly
USA. Work published on our site is noticed
by the people who count.

The New Shetlander

Shetland Council of Social Service

Market House
14 Market Street
LERWICK
Shetland
ZE1 0JP
Tel: +44 (0) 1595 743902
Fax: +44 (0) 1595 696787
Email: vas@shetland.org
Website: http://www.shetland-
communities.org.uk/subsites/vas/the-new-
shetlander.htm

Publishes: Articles; Essays; Fiction;
Nonfiction; Poetry; *Areas:* Arts; Criticism;
Historical; Politics; Short Stories; *Markets:*
Adult; *Treatments:* Literary

Editors: Brian Smith; Laureen Johnson

Publishes short stories, poetry, and historical
articles related to Shetland, Scotland, or
Scandinavia. Items should usually be
between 1,000 and 2,000 words, however
longer pieces can be considered.
Contributions and enquiries may be sent by
email.

New Walk Magazine
c/o Nick Everett
School of English
Leicester University
University Road
Leicester
LE1 7RH
Email: newwalkmagazine@gmail.com
Website:
http://newwalkmagazine.wordpress.com

Publishes: Articles; Essays; Features;
Fiction; Interviews; Nonfiction; Poetry;
Reviews; *Areas:* Criticism; Literature; Short
Stories; *Markets:* Adult; *Treatments:*
Experimental; Literary

Editors: Rory Waterman and Nick Everett

Publishes poetry and poetry-related features;
criticism; debate; short fiction; and art. Send
up to six poems or one piece of prose in the
body of an email.

New Welsh Review
PO Box 170

Aberystwyth
SY23 1WZ
Tel: +44 (0) 1970 628410
Email: submissions@newwelshreview.com
Website: http://www.newwelshreview.com

Publishes: Features; Fiction; Nonfiction;
Poetry; Reviews; *Areas:* Short Stories;
Markets: Adult; *Treatments:* Literary

Editors: Kathryn Gray

Focus is on Welsh writing in English, but
has an outlook which is deliberately diverse,
encompassing broader UK and international
contexts. For feature articles, send 300-word
query by email. Submit fiction or up to 6
poems by email or by post with cover letter
and SAE. Full details available on website.

The New Writer
PO Box 60
Cranbrook
Kent
TN17 2ZR
Tel: +44 (0) 1580 212626
Fax: +44 (0) 1580 212041
Email: editor@thenewwriter.com
Website: http://www.thenewwriter.com

Publishes: Articles; Features; Fiction; News;
Nonfiction; Poetry; *Areas:* Short Stories;
Markets: Adult

Editors: Suzanne Ruthven

Short stories by subscribers and prizewinners
only – no unsolicited short stories. Poetry
welcome from all, but must be previously
unpublished. Submit no more than five
poems at once. Also publishes articles and
features on writing and current editorial
practice, but not looking for introspective
pieces. See website for full details.

New Writing Scotland
ASLS
Department of Scottish Literature
7 University Gardens
University of Glasgow
Glasgow
G12 8QH
Tel: +44 (0) 1413 305309

Fax: +44 (0) 1413 305309
Email: nws@asls.org.uk
Website: http://www.asls.org.uk

Publishes: Fiction; Poetry; Scripts; *Areas:* Drama; Short Stories; *Markets:* Adult

Editors: Duncan Jones

Publishes short fiction, poetry, and short drama, in any of the languages of Scotland. Contributors must be Scottish by birth or upbringing, or be resident in Scotland. Send no more than one short story and/or four poems. No full-length plays, novels, or submissions by fax or email. Check website for reading period. Include one SAE for receipt and another for return of ms.

Notes from the Underground
23 Sutherland Square
London
SE17 3EQ
Tel: +44 (0) 20 7701 2777
Email: editors@nftu.co.uk
Website:
http://www.notesfromtheunderground.co.uk

Publishes: Articles; Fiction; Nonfiction; *Areas:* Short Stories; *Markets:* Adult

Editors: Christopher Vernon; Tristan Summerscale

Welcomes unsolicited submissions of fiction and nonfiction. Include word count, description of article or story, and brief personal bio in a short paragraph at the top. Include at least one image or video per 300 words for nonfiction. See website for specific email addresses for submissions.

Now
IPC Media
Blue Fin Building
110 Southwark Street
London
SE1 4SU
Tel: +44 (0) 20 3148 5000
Fax: +44 (0) 20 3148 8110
Email: nowfriends@ipcmedia.com
Website: http://www.nowmagazine.co.uk

Publishes: Articles; Features; News; Nonfiction; *Areas:* Beauty and Fashion; Entertainment; Lifestyle; Media; Women's Interests; *Markets:* Adult

Women's lifestyle magazine, covering celebrity gossip, fashion, news, etc. Most articles are commissioned or originated in-house.

Obsessed with Pipework
Flarestack Publishing
8 Abbot's Way
Pilton
Somerset
BA4 4BN
Tel: +44 (0) 1749 890019
Email: cannula.dementia@virgin.net
Website: http://www.flarestack.co.uk

Publishes: Poetry; *Markets:* Adult; *Treatments:* Experimental; Literary

Editors: Charles Johnson

Submit up to six poems of any length or style. Looking for poems that are original and display an element of creative risk, rather than things that are simply "clever". Nothing predictable or obvious. SAE essential unless submitting by fax or email. Prefers submissions by post, but if you do email your poems send them in the body of an email or in a single attached document.

Other Poetry
10 Prospect Bank Road
Edinburgh
EH6 7NR
Email: editors@otherpoetry.com
Website: http://www.otherpoetry.com

Publishes: Poetry; *Markets:* Adult

Send up to five poems by email, or by post if impossible to send by email. A live email address must be included for a response. No correspondence will be entered into by post and no SAE is required. Submissions should be sent in the body of the email, rather than as attachments. Any emails containing attachments will be deleted unread and without acknowledgement. Do not submit more than twice per calendar year, or within six months of any editorial decision.

Pony Magazine
Headley House
Headley Road
Grayshott
Surrey
GU26 6TU
Tel: +44 (0) 1428 601020
Fax: +44 (0) 1428 601030
Email: pony@djmurphy.co.uk
Website: http://www.ponymag.com

Publishes: Articles; Nonfiction; *Areas:* Hobbies; Nature; Sport; *Markets:* Children's; Youth

Editors: Janet Rising

Magazine for young horse-lovers aged 8-16.

PC Advisor
101 Euston Road
London
NW1 2RA
Tel: +44 (0) 20 7756 2800
Email: matt_egan@idg.co.uk
Website: http://www.pcadvisor.co.uk

Publishes: Articles; Features; Nonfiction; *Areas:* How-to; Technology; *Markets:* Adult

Editors: Matt Egan

PC magazine aimed at proficient users. May consider unsolicited material.

PC Pro
PC Pro Dennis Technology
30 Cleveland Street
London
W1T 4JD
Tel: +44 (0) 20 7907 6000
Fax: +44 (0) 20 7907 6304
Email: editor@pcpro.co.uk
Website: http://www.pcpro.co.uk

Publishes: Articles; Features; News; Nonfiction; Reviews; *Areas:* Technology; *Markets:* Adult; Professional; *Treatments:* In-depth

Editors: Barry Collins

IT magazine for professionals in the IT industry and enthusiasts.

Peace and Freedom
17 Farrow Road
Whaplode Drove
Spalding
Lincs
PE12 0TS
Tel: +44 (0) 1406 330242
Email: p_rance@yahoo.co.uk
Website:
http://pandf.booksmusicfilmstv.com

Publishes: Articles; Fiction; Interviews; Poetry; Reviews; *Areas:* Nature; Short Stories; Sociology; *Markets:* Adult; *Treatments:* Literary

Editors: Paul Rance

Magazine publishing poetry, fiction, and articles, with an emphasis on social, humanitarian and environmental issues. Also publishes interviews of animal welfare/environmental/human rights campaigners, writers, poets, artists, film, music and TV personalities, up to 1,000 words. Reviews of books / records / events etc. up to 50 words also considered. Email submissions accepted for reviews, short stories, and interviews ONLY. Accepts submissions from subscribers only.

The Penniless Press
100 Waterloo Road
Ashton
Preston
PR2 1EP
Tel: +44 (0) 1772 736421
Email: editor@pennilesspress.co.uk
Website: http://www.pennilesspress.co.uk

Publishes: Essays; Fiction; Nonfiction; Poetry; Reviews; *Areas:* Criticism; Literature; Philosophy; Short Stories; Translations; *Markets:* Adult; *Treatments:* Literary

Editors: Alan Dent

Eclectic magazine publishing material on a diverse range of subjects, as well as fiction, poetry, criticism, translations, and reviews. Prose should be restricted to 3,000 words or less. Send contributions with SAE by post or by email.

Pennine Platform

Frizingley Hall
Frizinghall Road
Bradford
BD9 4LD
Tel: +44 (0) 1274 541015
Email: nicholas.bielby@virgin.co.uk
Website: http://www.pennineplatform.co.uk

Publishes: Poetry; *Markets:* Adult

Editors: Nicholas Bielby

The pick of poetry from the Pennines and beyond. Hard copy submissions only.

Performance

Mediscript Ltd
1 Mountview Court
310 Friern Barnett Lane
London
Tel: +44 (0) 20 8369 5382
Fax: +44 (0) 20 8446 8898
Email: Fatima@mediscript.ltd.uk
Website: http://www.performance
sportandfitness.co.uk

Publishes: Articles; Features; Interviews; News; Nonfiction; Reviews; *Areas:* Health; Sport; *Markets:* Academic; Adult; Professional; *Treatments:* Commercial; Contemporary; Popular

Editors: Fatima Patel

A research led magazine for professionals and sport enthusiasts. It is presented in an attractive easy to read style, covering a series of key issues in sport and fitness. These include training, nutrition, injury and rehabilitation. There are features on elite athletes with interviews and commentary on key research papers by our experts. The editorial board comprises sport training professionals and academics.

Planet

PO Box 44
Aberystwyth
Ceredigion
SY23 3ZZ
Tel: +44 (0) 1970 611255
Fax: +44 (0) 1970 611197
Email:
planet.enquiries@planetmagazine.org.uk
Website: http://www.planetmagazine.org.uk

Publishes: Articles; Features; Fiction; Nonfiction; Poetry; Reviews; *Areas:* Arts; Current Affairs; Literature; Music; Politics; Short Stories; Theatre; *Markets:* Adult; *Treatments:* Literary

Editors: Dr Jasmine Donahaye

Publishes one story and between eight and ten poems per issue. A range of styles and themes are accepted, but postal submissions will not be considered unless adequate return postage is provided. Submit 4-6 poems or fiction up to 4,000 words. Submissions are accepted by email.

Most articles, features, and reviews are commissioned, however if you have an idea for a relevant article send a query with brief synopsis.

Poetic Licence

70 Aveling Close
Purley
Surrey
CR8 4DW
Email: poets@poetsanon.org.uk
Website: http://www.poetsanon.org.uk

Publishes: Poetry; *Markets:* Adult

Editors: Peter L. Evans (co-ordinator)

The editing is rotated through the membership to help ensure that each issue does not get stuck in a rut or 'house style'. Submit up to six poems per issue, by email.

The Poetry Church

Eldwick Crag Farm
High Eldwick
Bingley

Yorkshire
BD16 3BB
Email: reavill@globalnet.co.uk
Website: http://www.waddysweb.freeuk.com

Publishes: Poetry; *Areas:* Religious;
Markets: Adult

Editors: Tony Reavill

Ecumenical Christian poetry magazine.
Features the work of international Christian
poets coming from a wide variety of
backgrounds in the mainline churches.

Poetry Cornwall / Bardhonyeth Kernow

11a Penryn Street
Redruth
Cornwall/Kernow
TR15 2SP

1 Station Hill
Redruth
Cornwall
TR15 2PP
Tel: +44 (0) 1209 218209
Email: poetrycornwall@yahoo.com
Website:
http://www.poetrycornwall.freeservers.com

Publishes: Poetry; *Markets:* Adult;
Treatments: Literary

Editors: Les Merton

Publishes poetry from around the world, in
original language (including Kernewek and
Cornish dialect) with English translation.
Send up to three poems by post with SASE,
or (if a subscriber) by email. Non-subscribers
may not submit by email.

Poetry Express

Survivors' Poetry
Studio 11, Bickerton House
25-27 Bickerton Road
Archway
London
N19 5JT
Tel: +44 (0) 20 7281 4654
Fax: +44 (0) 20 7281 7894
Email: info@survivorspoetry.org

Website:
http://www.survivorspoetry.org/the-poetry/publications/poetry-express/

Publishes: Articles; News; Nonfiction;
Poetry; Reviews; *Areas:* Literature; *Markets:*
Adult

Publishes poetry, articles, reviews, and news.
Name and contact details on each sheet of
submission.

Poetry Review

The Poetry Society
22 Betterton Street
London
WC2H 9BX
Tel: +44 (0) 20 7420 9883
Fax: +44 (0) 20 7240 4818
Email: info@poetrysociety.org.uk
Website: http://www.poetrysociety.org.uk

Publishes: Essays; Nonfiction; Poetry;
Reviews; *Markets:* Adult

Editors: Fiona Sampson

Describes itself as "one of the liveliest and
most influential literary magazines in the
world", and has been associated with the rise
of the New Generation of British poets –
Carol Ann Duffy, Simon Armitage, Glyn
Maxwell, Don Paterson... though its scope
extends beyond the UK, with special issues
focusing on poetries from around the world.

Send up to 6 poems with SAE by post only.
No submissions by email.

Poetry Scotland

91-93 Main Street
Callander
FK17 8BQ
Email: sallyevans35@gmail.com
Website: http://www.poetryscotland.co.uk

Publishes: Poetry; *Markets:* Adult

Editors: Sally Evans

Poetry broadsheet with Scottish emphasis.
Considers poetry in English, Gaelic, Scots,

and (on occasions) Welsh. Please see website for submission guidelines.

Poetry Wales
School of English
Bangor University
Gwynedd
LL57 2DG
Tel: +44 (0) 1656 663018
Email: info@poetrywales.co.uk
Website: http://poetrywales.co.uk

Publishes: Poetry; *Markets:* Adult

Editors: Dr Zoë Skoulding

Send up to six poems with SAE or IRCs for response / return of MSS. No handwritten or emailed submissions.

The Political Quarterly
9600 Garsington Road
Oxford
OX4 2DQ
Tel: +44 (0) 1865 776868
Fax: +44 (0) 1865 714591
Website: http://www.wiley.com

Publishes: Articles; Features; Nonfiction; *Areas:* Politics; *Markets:* Adult; *Treatments:* Progressive

Magazine covering national and international politics. Accepts unsolicited articles.

Practical Wireless
PW Publishing Limited
Tayfield House
38 Poole Road
Westbourne
Bournemouth
BH4 9DW
Tel: +44 (0) 845 803 1979
Email: rob@pwpublishing.ltd.uk
Website: http://www.pwpublishing.ltd.uk

Publishes: Articles; Nonfiction; *Areas:* How-to; Technology; *Markets:* Adult

Editors: Rob Mannion

Magazine covering amateur radio and

communications. Send query by email in first instance.

Premonitions
13 Hazely Combe
Arreton
Isle of Wight
PO30 3AJ
Tel: +44 (0) 1983 865668
Email: mail@pigasuspress.co.uk
Website: http://www.pigasuspress.co.uk

Publishes: Fiction; Poetry; *Areas:* Fantasy; Horror; Sci-Fi; *Markets:* Adult

Editors: Tony Lee

Magazine of cutting edge science fiction and fantasy. Also publishes genre poetry, and horror, however this must have an SF element, and must be psychological rather than simply gory. Send submission with cover letter, bio, and publication credits, with SAE. No supernatural fantasy or swords n' sorcery. Study magazine before submitting.

Presence
90 D Fishergate Hill
Preston
PR1 8JD
Email: haikupresence@gmail.com
Website: http://haiku-presence.50wcbs.com/

Publishes: Poetry; *Markets:* Adult

Editors: Martin Lucas; Matthew Paul; Ian Storr

The UK's leading forum for the full range of haiku-related genres. Includes haiku of the highest standard from an international list of contributors, backed by insightful reviews and critical prose. Our mission is to encourage dialogue and build a sense of community among haiku poets – and we're definitely getting there!

See website for different submission addresses for specific forms.

Professional Photographer
Archant House

Oriel Road
Cheltenham
GL50 1BB
Website:
http://www.professionalphotographer.co.uk

Publishes: Articles; Nonfiction; *Areas:*
Photography; Technology; *Markets:*
Professional

Magazine aimed at professional
photographers.

Pulsar Poetry Magazine

34 Lineacre
Grange Park
Swindon
Wiltshire
SN5 6DA
Tel: +44 (0) 1793 875941
Email: pulsar.ed@btopenworld.com
Website: http://www.pulsarpoetry.com

Publishes: Poetry; *Markets:* Adult

Editors: David Pike

From 2010 a webzine only. We seek
interesting and stimulating unpublished work
– thoughts, comments and observations,
genial or sharp. Prefer hard-hitting work. We
welcome poetry and constructive ideas from
all areas of the world. Normal time taken to
reply is no longer than four weeks, include a
stamped addressed return envelope with your
submission, (or include International Reply
Coupons, if from overseas). Send no more
than six poems at a time via conventional
post, or three poems via email: note, email
file attachments will not be read.

If your work is of a high standard it will be
published – may take a few months to
appear, though. Poets retain copyright of
their poems. Poems which are
simultaneously sent to other publications will
not be considered.

Quantum Leap

York House
15 Argyle Terrace
Rothesay
Isle of Bute

PA20 0BD
Tel: +44 (0) 1700 505422
Website: http://www.qqpress.co.uk

Publishes: Poetry; *Markets:* Adult

Editors: Alan J. Carter

A poetry magazine only – no short stories
please! We have a four-page information
leaflet – send SAE or 2 IRCs to 'Guidelines /
Competitions' at the address below. We also
provide a publication service for collections
of people's poetry – send SAE or 2 IRCs to
'Collections' at address below.

We aim to run a 'user-friendly' magazine for
our subscribers / contributors, so don't be
afraid to ask for advice. We also pay for all
poetry we use.

Reach

IDP
24 Forest Houses
Halwill
Beaworthy
Devon
EX21 5UU
Email: publishing@indigodreams.co.uk
Website:
http://www.indigodreams.co.uk/#/reach-
poetry/4536232470

Publishes: Poetry; *Markets:* Adult

Editors: Ronnie Goodyer

Publishes quality poetry from both
experienced and new poets. Formal or free
verse, haiku.. everything is considered.
Subscribers can comment on and vote for
poetry from the previous issue, the winner
receiving £50, plus regular in-house
anthologies and competitions. Receives no
external funding and depends entirely on
subscriptions.

The Reader

Magazine Submissions
The Reader Organisation
The Friary Centre
Bute Street
LIVERPOOL

L5 3LA
Tel: + 44 (0) 1512 077207
Email: magazine@thereader.org.uk
Website: http://www.thereader.org.uk

Publishes: Articles; Essays; Fiction;
Nonfiction; Poetry; Reviews; *Areas:*
Literature; Philosophy; Short Stories;
Markets: Adult; Literary

Publishes poetry, short stories,
recommendations for good reading up to
1,000 words, and articles and essays about
reading. Accepts literary articles and essays,
but not theoretical literary discourses.
Approach in writing in first instance.

Real People

Hearst Magazines UK London
72 Broadwick Street
London
W1F 9EP
Email: samm.taylor@hearst.co.uk
Website: http://www.realpeoplemag.co.uk

Publishes: Nonfiction; *Areas:* Lifestyle;
Women's Interests; *Markets:* Adult

Editors: Samm Taylor

Publishes real life stories. See website for
more details.

The Reater

Wrecking Ball Press
Office 9
Danish Buildings
44-46 High Street
Hull
East Yorkshire
HU1 1PS
Email: editor@wreckingballpress.com
Website: http://www.wreckingballpress.com

Publishes: Fiction; Poetry; *Areas:* Short
Stories; *Markets:* Adult; *Treatments:*
Literary

Editors: Shane Rhodes

Send up to six poems or up to two stories.
Submissions can be digital or on paper. If

submitting by email, include the word
"Submission" in the subject box.

Red Pepper

44-48 Shepherdess Walk
London
N1 7JP
Tel: +44 (0) 20 7324 5068
Email: office@redpepper.org.uk
Website: http://www.redpepper.org.uk

Publishes: Articles; Features; News;
Nonfiction; *Areas:* Politics; *Markets:* Adult

Political magazine aimed at the left and
greens.

Red Poets

7 Stryt Gerallt
Wrecsam
LL11 1EH
Email: info@redpoets.org
Website: http://www.redpoets.org

Publishes: Poetry; *Areas:* Politics; *Markets:*
Adult

Editors: Mike Jenkins; Marc Jones

Magazine of politically left-wing poetry.
Submit poems via submission form on
website or by email.

The Resurrectionist

Email: editorial@resurrectionreview.com
Website: http://www.resurrectionreview.com

Publishes: Essays; Nonfiction; Poetry;
Areas: Arts; Criticism; Humour; Music;
Philosophy; Politics; Psychology; Sociology;
Markets: Academic; Adult; *Treatments:*
Contemporary; Cynical; Dark; Experimental;
Light; Literary; Progressive; Satirical;
Traditional

Editors: Kieran Borsden

A biannual poetry journal dedicated to
modern formalist poetry. By modern we
intend poetry that makes use of
contemporary language and grammar,
experiments with verse forms or that handles

contemporary themes. Submit using online submission system only – no submissions by email.

The Rialto
PO Box 309
Aylsham
Norwich
NR11 6LN
Email: info@therialto.co.uk
Website: http://www.therialto.co.uk

Publishes: Articles; Nonfiction; Poetry; Reviews; *Markets:* Adult

Editors: Michael Mackmin

Send up to six poems with SASE or adequate return postage. Overseas contributors can include an email address for response instead of return postage, but poems must still be sent by post. No submissions online or by email. Reviews and articles commissioned.

Right Start Magazine
PO Box 481
Fleet
GU51 9FA
Tel: +44 (0) 7867 574590
Email: lynette@rightstartmagazine.co.uk
Website:
http://www.rightstartmagazine.co.uk

Publishes: Articles; Nonfiction; *Areas:* Health; Lifestyle; Psychology; *Markets:* Adult

Editors: Lynette Lowthian

Magazine covering pre-school children's health, lifestyle, development, education, etc.

Sable
Email: editorial@sablelitmag.org
Website: http://www.sablelitmag.org

Publishes: Essays; Fiction; Nonfiction; Poetry; Reviews; *Areas:* Autobiography; Historical; Short Stories; Translations; Travel; *Markets:* Adult

A showcase of new creative work by writers

of colour. Submit short stories or a novel excerpt up to 5,000 words; 10-15 pages of poetry; or nonfiction up to 3,000 words, by email. See website for full guidelines.

Sarasvati
24 Forest Houses
Halwill
Beaworthy
Devon
EX21 5UU
Email: dawnidp@indigodreams.co.uk
Website: http://www.indigodreams.co.uk

Publishes: Fiction; Poetry; *Areas:* Short Stories; *Markets:* Adult

Editors: Dawn Bauling

Showcases poetry and prose. Each contributor will have three to four pages available to their poetry, up to 35 lines per page, or prose up to 1,000 words.

The Savage Kick
Murder Slim Press
29 Alpha Road
Gorleston
Norfolk
NR31 0LQ
Email: slim@murderslim.com
Website: http://www.murderslim.com

Publishes: Articles; Fiction; Interviews; Nonfiction; *Areas:* Crime; Literature; Military; Westerns; *Markets:* Adult; *Treatments:* Niche

Accepts only three or four stories per year. Publishes work dealing with any passionately held emotion and/or alternative viewpoints. Sleazy tales are encouraged. Prefers real-life stories. No genre fiction or poetry. See website for full submission guidelines. Also accepts articles and interviews relating to authors on the reading list provided on the website.

Scar Tissue
Pigasus Press
13 Hazely Combe
Arreton

Isle of Wight
PO30 3AJ
Email: mail@pigasuspress.co.uk
Website: http://www.pigasuspress.co.uk

Publishes: Fiction; News; Nonfiction;
Poetry; Reviews; *Areas:* Horror; Humour;
Short Stories; *Markets:* Adult; *Treatments:*
Dark

Editors: Tony Lee

Free-sheet collage of horror and dark
humour, featuring short fiction, genre prose,
poetry, artwork, cartoons, lists, reviews,
news, cuttings, trivia, and adverts.

The School Librarian
7 Clifton Bank
Rotherham
South Yorkshire
S60 2NA
Email: sleditor@sla.org.uk
Website: http://www.sla.org.uk/the-school-
librarian.php

Publishes: Articles; Nonfiction; *Markets:*
Professional

Editors: Steve Hird

Magazine for professionals working in the
libraries of educational facilities from pre-
school to adult.

Scribbler!
Remus House
Coltsfoot Drive
Peterborough
Cambridgeshire
PE2 9BF
Tel: +44 (0) 1733 890066
Email: info@scribblermagazine.com
Website: http://www.scribblermagazine.com

Publishes: Fiction; Poetry; Reviews; *Areas:*
Short Stories; *Markets:* Children's

Educational magazine for 7–11 year-olds,
encouraging them to submit their own
poems, stories, and artwork. Email
submissions accepted.

Sea Angler
Bauer Consumer Media Limited
1 Lincoln Court
Lincoln Road
0Peterborough
PE1 2RF
Tel: +44 (0) 01733 395147
Email: mel.russ@bauermedia.co.uk
Website: http://www.gofishing.co.uk/Sea-
Angler

Publishes: Articles; News; Nonfiction;
Areas: Hobbies; How-to; Sport; Technology;
Markets: Adult

Editors: Mel Russ

Magazine for sea fishing enthusiasts.

The Seventh Quarry Swansea Poetry Magazine
8 Cherry Crescent
Parc Penderri
Penllergaer
Swansea
SA4 9FG
Email: requests@peterthabitjones.com
Website: http://www.peterthabitjones.com

Publishes: Poetry; *Markets:* Adult

Editors: Peter Thabit Jones

Poetry magazine with international outlook,
publishing poems from around the world.
Send up to four poems by email or by post
with SASE.

Shearsman
50 Westons Hill Drive
Emersons Green
Bristol
BS16 7DF
Email: editor@shearsman.com
Website: http://www.shearsman.com

Publishes: Nonfiction; Poetry; Reviews;
Markets: Adult

Editors: Tony Frazer

Now operates two reading windows for
submissions: March and September.

Send submissions with SAE for return. If outside UK please send disposable MS and email address for response. Do not send IRCs. Email submissions accepted if submission is sent in body of email, not as an attachment. Please study magazine or at least website before deciding whether or not to submit your work.

Publishes poetry in the modernist tradition, plus some prose, including reviews. Reviews published on website only.

Ships Monthly Magazine

Kelsey Publishing Group
Cudham Tithe Barn
Berrys Hill
Cudham
Kent
TN16 3AG
Tel: +44 (0) 1959 541444
Email: ships.monthly@btinternet.com
Website: http://www.shipsmonthly.com

Publishes: Articles; News; Nonfiction; *Areas:* Design; Historical; Technology; Travel; *Markets:* Adult; Professional

Editors: Nicholas Leach

Magazine aimed at ship enthusiasts and maritime professionals. Publishes news and illustrated articles related to all kinds of ships. No yachting. Query by phone or email in first instance.

Sight & Sound

21 Stephen Street
London
W1T 1LN
Website:
http://www.bfi.org.uk/sightandsound

Publishes: Articles; Nonfiction; Reviews; *Areas:* Film; *Markets:* Adult

Describes itself as the international film magazine, publishing articles on international cinema and reviews of film, DVD, and book releases. Send query in writing in first instance.

Smoke

MPAC
1-27 Bridport Street
Liverpool
L3 5QF
Tel: +44 (0) 7710 644325
Email: windowsproject@btinternet.com
Website: http://www.windowsproject.net/publish/smoke/wpinfs.htm

Publishes: Poetry; *Markets:* Adult

One of the highest selling small poetry magazines in the country. New writing, poetry and graphics by some of the best established names alongside new work from Merseyside, from all over the country and the world.

Somerset Life

Archant House
Babbage Road
Totnes
TQ9 5JA
Website:
http://somerset.greatbritishlife.co.uk

Publishes: Features; Interviews; Nonfiction; *Areas:* Antiques; Arts; Beauty and Fashion; Business; Cookery; Design; Gardening; Health; Historical; Travel; *Markets:* Adult

Regional magazine covering Somerset. Contact through website in first instance.

South

PO Box 4228
Bracknell
RG42 9PX
Email: south@southpoetry.org
Website: http://www.southpoetry.org

Publishes: Poetry; *Markets:* Adult

Editors: Anne Clegg, Andrew Curtis, Peter Keeble, Patrick Osada, and Chrissie Williams

Submit up to three poems by post (two copies of each), along with submission form available on website. No previously published poems (including poems that have appeared on the internet). Submissions are not returned. See website for full details. No submissions by email.

Stamp Lover
Harvard House
621 London Road
Isleworth
TW7 4ER
Email: stamplover@ukphilately.org.uk
Website:
http://www.ukphilately.org.uk/hmag.htm

Publishes: Articles; News; Nonfiction;
Areas: Hobbies; *Markets:* Adult

Magazine for stamp collectors, publishing news and articles on stamps past and present and on the hobby in general. Send query by email.

Stamp Magazine
MyTimeMedia Ltd
PO Box 718
Orpington
Kent
BR6 1AP
Email: julia.lee@mytimemedia.com
Website: http://www.stampmagazine.co.uk

Publishes: Articles; News; Nonfiction;
Areas: Hobbies; *Markets:* Adult

Magazine publishing news and articles relating to classic stamps from the past and present. Send query in first instance.

The Strad
30 Cannon Street
London
EC4M 6YJ
Email: thestrad@thestrad.com
Website: http://www.thestrad.com

Publishes: Articles; Features; Nonfiction;
Reviews; *Areas:* Music; *Markets:* Adult;
Professional

Magazine for professionals and enthusiasts interested in string instruments, including their makers and their players.

Suffolk Norfolk Life
Email: editor@suffolknorfolklife.com
Website: http://www.suffolknorfolklife.com

Publishes: Articles; Features; Nonfiction;
Areas: Arts; Current Affairs; Historical;
Leisure; *Markets:* Adult

Editors: Richard Bryson

Magazine covering Suffolk and Norfolk. Welcomes ideas and accepts unsolicited mss. Contact by email.

The Tablet
The Tablet Publishing Company Ltd.
1 King Street Cloisters
Clifton Walk
London
W6 0GY
Tel: +44 (0) 20 8748 8484
Fax: +44 (0) 20 8748 1550
Email: thetablet@thetablet.co.uk
Website: http://www.thetablet.co.uk

Publishes: Articles; Nonfiction; *Areas:* Arts;
Literature; Politics; Religious; *Markets:*
Adult

Editors: Catherine Pepinster

Catholic magazine publishing articles by writers of international standing.

Tatler
Vogue House
Hanover Square
London
W1S 1JU
Tel: +44 (0) 20 7499 9080
Fax: +44 (0) 20 7409 0451
Email: Sara.Mccorquodale@condenast.co.uk
Website: http://www.tatler.co.uk

Publishes: Articles; Features; News;
Nonfiction; Reviews; *Areas:* Beauty and
Fashion; Cookery; Lifestyle; Travel;
Women's Interests; *Markets:* Adult

Editors: Sara McCorquodale (Senior Editor)

Up-market glossy. Unlikely to publish unsolicited features, but interested writers should submit a sample of their published or unpublished output and, if taken up, will ask writers to work on specific projects.

Tears in the Fence

Portman Lodge
Durweston
Blandford Forum
Dorset
DT11 0QA
Tel: +44 (0) 7824 618708
Email: tearsinthefence@gmail.com
Website: http://tearsinthefence.com

Publishes: Essays; Fiction; Interviews; Nonfiction; Poetry; Reviews; *Areas:* Short Stories; Translations; *Markets:* Adult; *Treatments:* Literary

Editors: David Caddy

International literary magazine publishing poetry, fiction, prose poems, essays, translations, interviews and reviews. Publishes fiction as short as 100 words or as long as 12,000, plus stories of the more normal 3,500 word length. Maximum 6 poems per poet per issue. No simultaneous submissions or previously published material. Send submissions by post or by email as an attachment and in the body of the email.

Tellus Magazine

Faculty of Classics
University of Cambridge
Sidgwick Avenue
Cambridge
CB3 9DA
Email: poetry@tellusmagazine.co.uk
Website: http://www.tellusmagazine.co.uk

Publishes: Poetry; *Markets:* Adult; *Treatments:* Literary

Editors: Ailsa Hunt

Publishes poems interacting with any aspect of ancient civilisations. Send submissions by email, in the body of the email or as Word attachments. See website for more details.

10th Muse

c/o October Books
243 Portswood Road
Southampton
SO17 2NG
Website:
http://www.nonism.org.uk/muse.html

Publishes: Articles; Nonfiction; Poetry; Humour; *Markets:* Adult; *Treatments:* Literary

Editors: Andrew Jordan

Looking for poetry, prose, and b&w artwork, combining lyrical with pastoral and experimental. Poetry is accepted in any style or form.

The Cricketer

The Cricketer Publishing Ltd
70 Great Portland Street
London
W1W 7UW
Tel: +44 (0) 20 7460 5200
Email: magazine@thecricketer.com
Website: http://www.thecricketer.com

Publishes: Articles; News; Nonfiction; *Areas:* Sport; *Markets:* Adult

Editors: Andrew Miller

The world's biggest-selling cricket magazine. Query in writing in first instance.

The Recusant

Email: therecusant@yahoo.co.uk
Website:
http://www.therecusant.moonfruit.com

Publishes: Articles; Essays; Nonfiction; Poetry; Reviews; *Areas:* Politics; *Markets:* Adult

Editors: Alan Morrison

Online magazine publishing poetry, articles, reviews, and polemic of a left-wing political viewpoint. Send submissions by email.

The Supplement

Atlantean Publishing
4 Pierrot Steps
71 Kursaal Way
Southend-on-Sea
Essex
SS1 2UY
Email: atlanteanpublishing@hotmail.com
Website: http://atlanteanpublishing.
wikia.com/wiki/The_Supplement

Publishes: Articles; Fiction; News;
Nonfiction; Poetry; Reviews; *Areas:*
Literature; Short Stories; *Markets:* Adult;
Treatments: Literary

Editors: DJ Tyrer

Magazine publishing news, reviews, and
guidelines for the small press, plus
competition details, etc. Occasional poem or
very short piece of fiction. Requires news,
reviews, and letters of content. Submissions
by email must be pasted into the body of the
email. No attachments.

The Teacher

NUT
Hamilton House
Mabledon Place
London
WC1H 9BD
Email: teacher@nut.org.uk
Website: http://www.teachers.org.uk/teacher-
online/

Publishes: Articles; Features; News;
Nonfiction; Reviews; *Markets:* Professional

Magazine aimed at teaching professionals.
Submit news items and articles for regular
columns by email. Rarely publishes
unsolicited features, but accepts ideas by
email. See website for full details.

thesnailmagazine

Tel: +44 (0) 1314 415619
Email:
ronfrancis.thesnailmagazine@gmail.com
Website: http://www.thesnailmagazine.com

Publishes: Articles; Essays; Features;
Interviews; Nonfiction; *Areas:* Adventure;

Arts; Business; Criticism; Culture; Current
Affairs; Legal; Literature; Media; Sociology;
Markets: Academic; Adult; Professional;
Treatments: Contemporary; Literary;
Progressive; Serious; Traditional

Editors: Ron Francis

A magazine specialising in longform
narrative journalism. No memoir or family
history. Stories should be fact-based, in-
depth studies of events that will resonate
with the reader. Avoid first-person singular
narrative where possible.

Third Way

3rd Floor, Invicta House
108-114 Golden Lane
London
EC1Y 0TG
Tel: +44 (0) 20 7776 1071
Email: editor@thirdway.org.uk
Website:
http://www.thirdwaymagazine.co.uk

Publishes: Articles; Features; Nonfiction;
Poetry; Reviews; *Areas:* Culture; Finance;
Politics; Religious; Sociology; *Markets:*
Adult

Magazine publishing a Christian perspective
on culture, society, economics and politics.
Also publishes poetry. Prefers to receive
submissions by email.

Time Out

Universal House
251 Tottenham Court Road
London
W1T 7AB
Tel: +44 (0) 20 7813 3000
Fax: +44 (0) 20 7813 6001
Website: http://www.timeout.com

Publishes: Articles; Features; News;
Nonfiction; *Areas:* Arts; Design;
Entertainment; Health; Lifestyle; Travel;
Markets: Adult

Material is normally written by staff, or
commissioned, but accepts ideas if
appropriate to the magazine.

Times Educational Supplement (TES) Scotland
Thistle House
21-23 Thistle Street
Edinburgh
EH2 1DF
Tel: +44 (0) 1316 248332
Fax: +44 (0) 1314 678019
Email: scoted@tes.co.uk
Website: http://www.tes.co.uk/scotland

Publishes: Articles; Features; News; Nonfiction; *Markets:* Professional

News articles and features of interest to Scottish teachers. Welcomes unsolicited mss.

Total Flyfisher
2 Stephenson Close
Daventry
Northants
NN11 8RF
Tel: +44 (0) 1327 311999
Fax: +44 (0) 1327 311190
Email: subscriptions@dhpub.co.uk
Website: http://www.totalflyfisher.com

Publishes: Articles; Features; News; Nonfiction; *Areas:* Hobbies; *Markets:* Adult

Instructional magazine publishing news, features, and articles on fly fishing. Approach by email.

Total Politics
21 Dartmouth Street
Westminster
London
SW1H 9BP
Tel: +44 (0) 20 7 593 5500
Email: sam.macrory@dods.co.uk
Website: http://www.totalpolitics.com

Publishes: Articles; Features; Nonfiction; *Areas:* Politics; *Markets:* Adult; Professional

Editors: Sam Macrory

Political magazine publishing articles and features up to 2,200 words.

Tribune
Woodberry
218 Green Lanes
London
N4 2HB
Tel: +44 (0) 20 8800 4281 ext 244
Email: mail@tribunemagazine.co.uk
Website: http://www.tribunemagazine.co.uk

Publishes: Articles; Features; News; Nonfiction; *Areas:* Arts; Current Affairs; Politics; *Markets:* Adult

Editors: Chris McLaughlin

Independent Labour publication, covering politics, the arts, society, current affairs, trade unions, etc. Approach by phone or by email in first instance.

25 Beautiful Homes
Blue Fin Building
110 Southwark Street
London
SE1 0SU
Tel: +44 (0) 20 3148 7154
Email: 25_beautiful_homes@ipcmedia.com
Website: http://www.housetohome.co.uk/25beautifulhomes

Publishes: Articles; Features; Nonfiction; *Areas:* Design; *Markets:* Adult

Editors: Deborah Barker

Introduces readers to real homes, from apartments to farmhouses, delivering real-life homes that inspire and inform.

20x20 magazine
Email: info@20x20magazine.com
Website: http://www.20x20magazine.com

Publishes: Articles; Essays; Fiction; Nonfiction; Poetry; *Areas:* Arts; Culture; Design; Literature; Music; Photography; Short Stories; *Markets:* Academic; Adult; Youth; *Treatments:* Contemporary; Experimental; Literary

Editors: Francesca Ricci & Giovanna Paternò

A square platform for writings, visuals and cross-bred projects. Rather than on a theme, each issue is assembled around meta-words to be interpreted, researched, illustrated according to a loose, wide and multi-angled perspective. The intent is to create homogeneity of spirit within each issue, without the restrictions of a "theme" as such.

The magazine includes 3 sections:

Words – in the shape of fiction, essays, poetry

Visions – drawings, photography and visual projects

The Blender – where words and visions cross paths

Submissions for the three above-mentioned sections are accepted by email only and in response to the meta-words set for the forthcoming issue. These are announced via our website or by joining our e-mailing list.

Unthology

Unthank Submissions (Unthology)
PO Box 3506
Norwich
NR7 7QP
Email: unthology@unthankbooks.com
Website: http://www.unthankbooks.com

Publishes: Essays; Fiction; Nonfiction; *Areas:* Short Stories; *Markets:* Adult; *Treatments:* Experimental; Literary; Traditional

Publishes the work of new or established writers and can include short stories of any length, reportage, essays or novel extracts from anywhere in the world. Allows space for stories of different styles and subjects to rub up against each other, featuring classic slice-of-life alongside the experimental, the shocking and strange. Submit by post with SAE and personal contact details, or by email.

The Vegan

Donald Watson House
21 Hylton Street

Birmingham
B18 6HJ
Tel: +44 (0) 1215 231730
Email: editor@vegansociety.com
Website: http://www.vegansociety.com

Publishes: Articles; Nonfiction; Health; Lifestyle; *Markets:* Adult

Magazine covering veganism. Welcomes unsolicited articles up to 2,000 words.

Viz

30 Cleveland Street
London
W1T 4JD
Tel: +44 (0) 20 7907 6000
Fax: +44 (0) 20 7907 6020
Email: viz@viz.co.uk
Website: http://www.viz.co.uk

Publishes: Articles; Fiction; *Areas:* Humour; *Markets:* Adult

Editors: Graham Dury; Simon Thorp

Magazine of adult humour, including cartoons, spoof articles, etc.

World Fishing

Mercator Media Ltd
The Old Mill
Lower Quay
Fareham
Hampshire
PO16 0RA
Tel: +44 (0) 1329 825335
Fax: +44 (0) 1329 825330
Email: editor@worldfishing.net
Website: http://www.worldfishing.net

Publishes: Articles; Nonfiction; *Areas:* Business; Nature; Technology; *Markets:* Professional

Magazine for fishing industry professionals. Publishes articles between 500 and 1,500 words.

Wedding Ideas

Herd HQ
Mitre House

Taunton
Somerset
TA1 4BH
Tel: +44 (0) 1823 288344
Email: rachelm@weddingideasmag.com
Website: http://www.weddingideasmag.com

Publishes: Articles; Features; Nonfiction;
Areas: How-to; Women's Interests; *Markets:*
Adult

Editors: Rachel Morgan

Magazine for brides working to a budget.
Potential contributors should familiarise
themselves with the magazine before sending
a query by email.

The War Cry

Salvation Army
101 Newington Causeway
London
SE1 6BN
Email: warcry@salvationarmy.org.uk
Website:
http://www.salvationarmy.org.uk/warcry

Publishes: Articles; Features; News;
Nonfiction; *Areas:* Current Affairs;
Religious; *Markets:* Adult

Editors: Major Nigel Bovey

Magazine of Christian comment. Welcomes
appropriate unsolicited mss. Contact by
email or by phone in first instance. No
fiction or poetry.

Wasafiri

1-11 Hawley Crescent
Camden Town
London
NW1 8NP
Tel: +44 (0) 20 7556 6110
Fax: +44 (0) 20 7556 6187
Email: wasafiri@open.ac.uk
Website: http://www.wasafiri.org

Publishes: Articles; Essays; Fiction;
Interviews; Nonfiction; Poetry; Reviews;
Areas: Criticism; Culture; Literature; Short
Stories; *Markets:* Adult; *Treatments:*
Literary

Editors: Susheila Nasta

The indispensable journal of contemporary
African, Asian Black British, Caribbean and
transnational literatures.

In over fifteen years of publishing, this
magazine has changed the face of
contemporary writing in Britain. As a literary
magazine primarily concerned with new and
postcolonial writers, it continues to stress the
diversity and range of black and diasporic
writers world-wide. It remains committed to
its original aims: to create a definitive forum
for the voices of new writers and to open up
lively spaces for serious critical discussion
not available elsewhere. It is Britain's only
international magazine for Black British,
African, Asian and Caribbean literatures. Get
the whole picture, get the magazine at the
core of contemporary international literature
today.

Wedding

Hubert Burda Media UK
The Tower
Phoenix Square
Colchester
Essex
CO4 9HU
Tel: +44 (0) 1206 851117 ext. 273
Email: emma.vince@burdamagazines.co.uk
Website:
http://www.weddingmagazine.co.uk

Publishes: Articles; Features; Nonfiction;
Areas: Beauty and Fashion; How-to; Travel;
Markets: Adult

Editors: Ciara Elliott; Editorial Contact:
Emma Vince

Magazine aimed at brides, wedding planners
and leading industry figures. Provides
articles on weddings, gift ideas, honeymoon
locations, etc.

Who Do You Think You Are? Magazine

9th Floor
Tower House
Fairfax Street
Bristol

BS1 3BN
Tel: +44 (0) 1173 147400
Email:
WDYTYAeditorial@immediatemedia.co.uk
Website: http://www.whodoyouthinkyouare
magazine.com

Publishes: Articles; Nonfiction; *Areas:*
Historical; Military; Sociology; *Markets:*
Adult

Editors: Sarah Williams

Publishes articles on family history. Send
queries to the editor.

Woman Alive
Christian Publishing and Outreach
Garcia Estate
Canterbury Road
Worthing
West Sussex
BN13 1BW
Tel: +44 (0) 1903 264556
Fax: +44 (0) 1903 830066
Email: womanalive@cpo.org.uk
Website: http://www.womanalive.co.uk

Publishes: Articles; Features; Interviews;
Nonfiction; *Areas:* Beauty and Fashion;
Crafts; Entertainment; Health; Lifestyle;
Religious; Travel; Women's Interests;
Markets: Adult

Editors: Jackie Harris

Monthly lifestyle magazine for Christian
women aged 25 and over. Welcomes
unsolicited mss by post or by email. See
website for full submission guidelines.

Woman's Weekly
IPC Media Ltd
Blue Fin Building
110 Southwark Street
London
SE1 0SU
Tel: +44 (0) 20 3148 5000
Email:
womansweeklypostbag@ipcmedia.com

Publishes: Features; Fiction; News;
Nonfiction; *Areas:* Short Stories; Women's

Interests; *Markets:* Adult; *Treatments:*
Contemporary

Editors: Diane Kenwood; Sue Pilkington
(Features); Gaynor Davies (Fiction)

Publishes features of interest to women over
forty, plus fiction between 1,000 and 2,000
words and serials of 12,000 words. Only uses
experienced journalists for nonfiction. Send
query by email.

The Woodworker
MyHobbyStore Ltd
PO Box 718
Orpington
BR6 1AP
Tel: +44 (0) 1689 869876
Email: mike.lawrence@myhobbystore.com
Website: http://www.getwoodworking.com

Publishes: Articles; Features; Nonfiction;
Areas: Crafts; Hobbies; How-to; *Markets:*
Adult

Editors: Mike Lawrence

Magazine on woodworking, including
articles on tips, new products, tenchiques,
etc. Welcomes unsolicited MSS, but no
fiction. Query with ideas by writing, phone,
or email.

Writers' Forum
Select Publisher Services Ltd
PO box 6337
Bournemouth
Dorset
BH9 1EH
Tel: +44 (0) 1202 586848
Email: editorial@writers-forum.com
Website: http://www.writers-forum.com

Publishes: Articles; Nonfiction; *Areas:*
Hobbies; How-to; Literature; *Markets:* Adult

Editors: Carl Styants

Publishes articles on the craft of writing.
Approach editor in writing in first instance.

The Yellow Room

1 Blake Close
Bilton
Rugby
CV22 7LJ
Tel: +44 (0) 1788 334302
Email: jo.derrick@ntlworld.com
Website: http://www.theyellowroom-
magazine.co.uk

Publishes: Fiction; *Areas:* Short Stories;
Women's Interests; *Markets:* Adult;
Treatments: Literary

Editors: Jo Derrick

Magazine publishing short stories by UK
women, for women. Accepts submissions by
email with story submitted as a Word file
attachment. No poetry or nonfiction. No
multiple submissions. Simultaneous
submissions accepted if notification given.
See website for full details.

Yoga and Health Magazine

PO Box 16969
London
E1W 1FY
Tel: +44 (0) 20 7480 5456
Email: Editor@yogaandhealthmag.co.uk
Website:
http://www.yogaandhealthmag.co.uk

Publishes: Articles; Nonfiction; Reviews;
Areas: Health; Hobbies; How-to; Leisure;
Philosophy; *Markets:* Adult

Editors: Jane Sill

Publishes articles on yoga, Eastern
philosophies, complementary therapies,
healthy eating,vegetarian recipes, new
products, book reviews, courses and classes.

Your Cat

BPG Stamford Ltd
Roebuck House
33 Broad Street
Stamford
Lincolnshire
PE9 1RB
Tel: +44 (0) 1780 766199
Email: sue@yourcat.co.uk

Website: http://www.yourcat.co.uk

Publishes: Articles; Fiction; Nonfiction;
Areas: How-to; Short Stories; *Markets:*
Adult

Editors: Sue Parslow

Practical magazine covering the care of cats
and kittens. No poetry and no articles written
from the cat's viewpoint. Considers fiction
by published novelists only. Send query by
email with outline by post or by email.

Yours

Media House
Peterborough Business Park
Peterborough
PE2 6EA
Tel: +44 (0) 1733 468000
Email: yours@bauermedia.co.uk
Website: http://www.yours.co.uk

Publishes: Articles; Features; Fiction;
Nonfiction; *Areas:* Lifestyle; Short Stories;
Women's Interests; *Markets:* Adult;
Treatments: Positive

Editors: Gemma Toms

Lifestyle magazine aimed at women over 55.
Welcomes nonfiction articles. Uses one or
two pieces of fiction each issue. Send
complete MS with SAE.

Zoo

Bauer Consumer Media
Mapin House
4 Winsley Street
London
W1W 8HF
Email: info@zootoday.com
Website: http://www.zootoday.com

Publishes: News; Nonfiction; *Areas:*
Entertainment; Film; Humour; Lifestyle;
Men's Interests; Sport; Technology;
Markets: Adult

Men's interest magazine featuring girls,
sport, humour, movies, showbiz, games,
gadgets, cars, etc.

Canadian Magazines

For the most up-to-date listings of these and hundreds of other magazines, visit http://www.firstwriter.com/magazines

*To claim your **free** access to the site, please see the back of this book.*

Abilities

c/o Canadian Abilities Foundation
340 College Street, Suite 270
Toronto, Ontario M5T 3A9
Tel: +1 (416) 923-9829
Email: jennifer@abilities.ca
Website: http://abilities.ca

Publishes: Articles; Nonfiction; *Areas:* Health; Lifestyle; Self-Help; Sport; Travel; *Markets:* Adult

Editors: Jennifer Rivkin

Lifestyle magazine for the disabled. Covers areas such as travel, health, careers, education, relationships, parenting, new products, social policy, organisations, events and activities, sports, education, careers and more. No fiction, poetry, cartoons/comics or drama. Send query by email.

Canadian Commerce & Industry

Mercury Publications
1740 Wellington Ave
Winnipeg, Manitoba R3H 0E8
Tel: +1 (800) 337-6372 / (204) 954-2085 ext.207
Fax: +1 (204) 954-2057
Email: editorial@mercury.mb.ca
Website: http://www.commerceindustry.ca

Publishes: Articles; News; Nonfiction; *Areas:* Business; *Markets:* Professional

Business magazine. Send query by post, fax, or email, with clippings and details of previous experience.

Canadian Writer's Journal

Box 1178
New Liskeard, Ontario
P0J 1P0
Tel: +1 (705) 647-5424
Fax: +1 (705) 647-8366
Email: editor@cwj.ca
Website: http://www.cwj.ca

Publishes: Articles; Essays; Features; Nonfiction; Poetry; Reviews; *Areas:* Hobbies; How-to; Literature; *Markets:* Adult; Professional

Magazine aimed at amateur and professional writers, offering how-to articles and publishing poetry. Fiction published via contest only. Also publishes book reviews and opinion pieces. Aims at 90% Canadian material. See website for full details.

Cosmetics Magazine

One Mount Pleasant Road, 8th Floor
Toronto, ON
M4Y 2Y5
Tel: +1 (416) 764-1680
Email: kristen.vinakmens@cosmetics.rogers.com

Website: http://cosmeticsmag.com

Publishes: Articles; Features; Interviews; Nonfiction; *Areas:* Beauty and Fashion; Business; *Markets:* Professional

Editors: Kristen Vinakmens

Magazine for professionals working in the retail sector of the cosmetics industry. Query in first instance.

Geist

Suite 210, 111 West Hastings Street
Vancouver, B.C. V6B 1H4
Tel: +1 (604) 681-9161
Fax: +1 (604) 677-6319
Email: editor@geist.com
Website: http://www.geist.com

Publishes: Essays; Features; Fiction; Nonfiction; Poetry; Reviews; *Areas:* Arts; Culture; Historical; Humour; Literature; Short Stories; *Markets:* Adult; *Treatments:* Literary

Magazine of culture and ideas publishing fiction, nonfiction, poetry, photography, art, reviews, little-known facts of interest, cartography, and crossword puzzles. Submit by post or through online submission system. See website for more details.

Link & Visitor

304 The East Mall
Etobicoke, ON
M9B 6E2
Tel: +1 (416) 651 8967
Email: rsejames@gmail.com
Website:
http://www.baptistwomen.com/link-visitor/online

Publishes: Articles; Interviews; Nonfiction; *Areas:* Religious; Women's Interests; *Markets:* Adult

Editors: Renee James

Magazine for Canadian baptist women, accepting unsolicited mss from Canadian writers only. Email submissions must be in the body of the email – no attachments.

Pacific Yachting

200 West Esplanade, Suite 500
North Vancouver, BC V7M 1A4
Tel: +1 (604) 998-3310
Email: editor@pacificyachting.com
Website: http://www.pacificyachting.com

Publishes: Articles; Features; Nonfiction; *Areas:* How-to; Leisure; Travel; *Markets:* Adult

Editors: Dale Miller

Magazine for powerboaters and sailors sharing a common interest in recreational boating in British Columbia and the Pacific Northwest. Query by email in first instance.

The Prairie Journal

28 Crowfoot Terrace NW
P.O. Box 68073
Calgary, Alberta
T3G 3N8
Email: prairiejournal@yahoo.com
Website: http://prairiejournal.org

Publishes: Fiction; Interviews; Nonfiction; Poetry; Reviews; Scripts; *Areas:* Criticism; Drama; Short Stories; *Markets:* Adult; *Treatments:* Literary

Send submissions by post. See website for detailed requirements. No simultaneous submissions.

Prairie Messenger

100 College Drive
Box 190
MUENSTER, SK S0K 2Y0
Tel: +1 (306) 682-1772
Fax: +1 (306) 682-5285
Email: pm.canadian@stpeterspress.ca
Website: http://www.prairiemessenger.ca

Publishes: Articles; Features; News; Nonfiction; Poetry; *Areas:* Current Affairs; Religious; *Markets:* Adult

Editors: Maureen Weber

16-20-page tabloid newspaper covering local, national and international religious news and current affairs. Send complete ms by post, email, or fax. Responds to postal submissions only if return Canadian postage is provided; responds to fax and email submissions only if interested.

PRISM international
Creative Writing Program, UBC
Buch. E462 – 1866 Main Mall
Vancouver, BC, V6T 1Z1
Tel: +1 (604) 822-2514
Fax: +1 (604) 822-3616
Email: prismfiction@gmail.com
Website: http://prismmagazine.ca

Publishes: Fiction; Nonfiction; Poetry; Scripts; *Areas:* Drama; Translations; *Markets:* Adult; *Treatments:* Literary

Editors: Cara Woodruff (Fiction); Jordan Abel (Poetry)

Submit one piece of fiction, drama, or creative nonfiction, or up to 7 poems at a time. Include cover letter with bio and publications list, plus email address for reply, or SASE with Canadian postage or IRCs. See website for full guidelines.

Resources for Feminist Research
Ontario Institute for Studies in Education/University of Toronto
252 Bloor Street West
Toronto, Ontario
M5S 1V6
Email: rfrdrf@oise.utoronto.ca
Website: http://legacy.oise.utoronto.ca/rfr

Publishes: Articles; Nonfiction; *Areas:* Women's Interests; *Markets:* Academic

Editors: Philinda Masters

Bilingual (English/French) Canadian scholarly journal, covering Canadian and international feminist research, issues, and debates.

Riddle Fence
Email: contact@riddlefence.com
Website: http://www.riddlefence.com

Publishes: Fiction; Nonfiction; Poetry; *Areas:* Arts; Culture; Short Stories; *Markets:* Adult; *Treatments:* Literary

Newfoundland and Labrador-based journal of arts and culture. Publishes fiction, nonfiction, poetry, and artwork. Submit to appropriate email address listed on website.

Room Magazine
P.O. Box 46160, Station D
Vancouver, BC
V6J 5G5
Email: submissions@roommagazine.com
Website: http://www.roommagazine.com

Publishes: Fiction; Nonfiction; Poetry; *Areas:* Women's Interests; *Markets:* Adult; *Treatments:* Literary

Publishes fiction, creative nonfiction, and poetry, for, by, and about women. Submit prose up to 3,500 words or up to 5 poems, with cover letter, via online submission system.

subTerrain Magazine
PO Box 3008, MPO
Vancouver, BC V6B 3X5
Tel: +1 (604) 876-8710
Fax: +1 (604) 879-2667
Email: subter@portal.ca
Website: http://www.subterrain.ca

Publishes: Essays; Fiction; Nonfiction; Poetry; *Areas:* Short Stories; *Markets:* Adult; *Treatments:* Literary

Publishes fiction up to 3,000 words, creative nonfiction and commentary up to 4,000 words, and poetry. Each issue has a theme (see website for details of upcoming themes). Poetry only accepted if it relates directly to the theme, however prose may or may not make use of the theme. See website for full guidelines.

Today's Parent
Rogers Media, Inc.
One Mt Pleasant Road, 8th Floor
Toronto, ON
M4Y 2Y5

Tel: +1 (416) 764-2883
Fax: +1 (416) 764-2894
Email: editors@todaysparent.com
Website: http://www.todaysparent.com

Publishes: Articles; Features; Nonfiction;

Areas: Health; Leisure; Lifestyle; *Markets:* Adult

Magazine aimed at Canadian parents of children aged up to 12. Concentrates on Canadian writers and content.

Irish Magazines

For the most up-to-date listings of these and hundreds of other magazines, visit http://www.firstwriter.com/magazines

*To claim your **free** access to the site, please see the back of this book.*

Africa

St Patrick's
Kiltegan
Co. Wicklow
Tel: +353 (0)59 647-3600
Fax: +353 (0)59 647-3622
Email: africa@spms.org
Website: http://www.spms.org

Publishes: Articles; Nonfiction; *Areas:* Religious; *Markets:* Adult

Editors: Fr. Tim Redmond

Catholic missionary magazine.

Cyphers

3 Selskar Terrace
Ranelagh
Dublin 6
Email: letters@cyphers.ie
Website: http://www.cyphers.ie

Publishes: Fiction; Poetry; *Areas:* Short Stories; Translations; *Markets:* Adult; *Treatments:* Literary

Publishes poetry and fiction in English and Irish, from Ireland and around the world. Translations are welcome. No unsolicited critical articles. Submissions by post only. Attachments sent by email will be deleted. See website for full guidelines.

The Dublin Review

PO Box 7948
Dublin 1
Email: enquiry@thedublinreview.com
Website: http://thedublinreview.com

Publishes: Essays; Fiction; Nonfiction; *Areas:* Criticism; Literature; Short Stories; *Markets:* Adult; *Treatments:* Literary

Publishes essays, criticism, reportage, and fiction for a general, intelligent readership. No poetry. Send submissions by post only with email address for response. Material is not returned, so do not include return postage. No response without email address.

Poetry Ireland Review

Poetry Ireland
32 Kildare Street
Dublin 2
Tel: +353 (0)1 6789815
Fax: +353 (0)1 6789782
Email: info@poetryireland.ie
Website: http://www.poetryireland.ie

Publishes: Articles; Nonfiction; Poetry; Reviews; *Areas:* Literature; *Markets:* Adult

Editors: John F Deane

Send up to 6 poems with SASE / IRCs or email address for response. Poetry is accepted from around the world, but must be previously unpublished. No sexism or racism. No submissions by email. Articles and reviews are generally commissioned, however proposals are welcome. No unsolicited reviews or articles.

THE SHOp
Skeagh
Schull
Co. Cork
Tel: +353 (0) 2828263
Email: THESHOp@THESHOp-Poetry-Magazine.ie
Website: http://www.theshop-poetry-magazine.ie

Publishes: Poetry; *Areas:* Translations; *Markets:* Adult

Editors: John and Hilary Wakeman

Publishes poetry by established and upcoming poets from around the world, but especially Ireland. Publishes at least one Gaelic poem per issue, with English translation. Send up to 6 poems with SAE and Irish stamps, IRCs, or indicate email address for response if no return of MS required.

The Songwriter
International Songwriters Association (1967) Ltd
PO Box 46
Limerick City
Email: jliddane@songwriter.iol.ie
Website: http://www.songwriter.co.uk

Publishes: Articles; Interviews; *Areas:* Music; Markets

Magazine publishing articles and interviews of interest to songwriters.

Southword Journal
The Munster Literature Centre
Frank O'Connor House
84 Douglas Street
Cork
Tel: (353) 021 4312955
Email: munsterlit@eircom.net
Website: http://www.munsterlit.ie

Publishes: Fiction; Nonfiction; Poetry; Reviews; *Areas:* Literature; Short Stories; *Markets:* Adult; *Treatments:* Literary

Send submissions of poetry and fiction by post between January and March 15 or July and September 15. Submit online via website submission system.

The Stinging Fly
PO Box 6016
Dublin 1
Email: stingingfly@gmail.com
Website: http://www.stingingfly.org

Publishes: Essays; Fiction; Interviews; Nonfiction; Poetry; Reviews; *Areas:* Short Stories; *Markets:* Adult; *Treatments:* Literary

Editors: Declan Meade

Send submissions with SAE or international reply coupons sufficient for return of MS. Submit one story or up to four poems at a time. Poems and short stories should be as long or as short as they need to be. Has published stories over 5,000 words and as short as 600. Await response before making further submissions. For reviews, email editor with sample review as attachment. No submissions by email. Accepts submissions during specific months only. See website for details.

Australian Magazines

For the most up-to-date listings of these and hundreds of other magazines, visit http://www.firstwriter.com/magazines

*To claim your **free** access to the site, please see the back of this book.*

Alternative Law Journal

c/- Law Faculty
Monash University
Victoria
3800
Tel: +61 (0) 3 9544 0974
Fax: +61 (0) 3 9905 5305
Email: altlj.org@monash.edu
Website: http://www.altlj.org

Publishes: Articles; Features; Nonfiction;
Areas: Legal; *Markets:* Professional

Legal journal with the following goals:

-promotion of social justice, human rights and law reform issues

-critique of the legal system

-monitoring developments in alternative legal practice

-community legal education.

Beyond the Rainbow

PO Box 2014
NIMBIN 2480
Tel: +61 (0) 2 6689 1182
Email: tamaso@aussieisp.net.au
Website: http://www.nimbinnews.com/beyondtherainbow

Publishes: Essays; Fiction; Nonfiction; Poetry; Reviews; *Areas:* Adventure; Biography; Crime; Culture; Drama; Erotic; Fantasy; Humour; Literature; New Age; Sci-Fi; Short Stories; Spiritual; Suspense; *Markets:* Adult; Youth; *Treatments:* Contemporary; Cynical; Light; Literary; Popular; Satirical; Serious; Traditional

Editors: Tamaso Lonsdale

Publishes mostly short stories and poems but is looking for all types of literary creation including extracts from published books and work in progress. We print a photo and short biography of the author.

Magazines Subject Index

This section lists magazines by their subject matter, with directions to the section of the book where the full listing can be found.

You can create your own customised lists of magazines using different combinations of these subject areas, plus over a dozen other criteria, instantly online at http://www.firstwriter.com.

To claim your **free** access to the site, please see the back of this book.

Suffolk Norfolk Life (*UK*)
Sun Valley Magazine (*US*)
The Tablet (*UK*)
The Vehicle (*US*)
thesnailmagazine (*UK*)
Time Out (*UK*)
Timeline (*US*)
Tradicion Revista Magazine (*US*)
Traverse (*US*)
Tribune (*UK*)
20x20 magazine (*UK*)
The Yes Factory (*US*)
Autobiography
Kalyani Magazine. (*US*)
The London Magazine (*UK*)
Mslexia (*UK*)
Netsagas.com (*US*)
PMS poemmemoirstory (*US*)
Sable (*UK*)
Slate & Style (*US*)
Sorry We're Booked (*US*)
Southeast Review (*US*)
Trajectory (*US*)
Beauty and Fashion
Akron Life (*US*)
bliss Magazine (*UK*)
British Journal of Photography (*UK*)
Cosmetics Magazine (*Can*)
18 Wheels & Heels (*US*)
Esquire (*UK*)
Forum (*US*)
Go Girl Magazine (*UK*)
Gay Times (GT Magazine) (*UK*)
Junior (*UK*)
Native Max (*US*)
Netsagas.com (*US*)
New Jersey Monthly (*US*)
New York (*US*)
Now (*UK*)
Portland Magazine (*US*)
The Saturday Evening Post (*US*)
Skin Deep (*US*)
Somerset Life (*UK*)
Tatler (*UK*)
Wedding (*UK*)
Woman Alive (*UK*)
Zink (*US*)
Biography
Beyond the Rainbow (*Aus*)
The Dickensian (*UK*)
Lummox (*US*)
Netsagas.com (*US*)
Skipping Stones (*US*)
Sorry We're Booked (*US*)
Timeline (*US*)
Business
Accountancy Age (*UK*)
Accounting and Business (*UK*)
Angus Beef Bulletin (*US*)
Aquatics International (*US*)
Art Business Today (*UK*)
Canadian Commerce & Industry (*Can*)
Caterer and Hotelkeeper (*UK*)

Classical Music (*UK*)
Club Management (*US*)
Cosmetics Magazine (*Can*)
Crain's Detroit Business (*US*)
Dairy Farmer (*UK*)
Delaware Today (*US*)
DIY Week (*UK*)
EcoHome (*US*)
18 Wheels & Heels (*US*)
Electrical Review (*UK*)
Equus Magazine (*US*)
Greetings Today (*UK*)
The Grocer (*UK*)
Health Club Management (*UK*)
ICIS Chemical Business Magazine (*UK*)
Ingram's Magazine (*US*)
International Bluegrass (*US*)
The Irish Post (*UK*)
LabTalk (*US*)
MyBusiness Magazine (*US*)
Media Week (*UK*)
Milwaukee Magazine (*US*)
Netsagas.com (*US*)
New Jersey Monthly (*US*)
O&A (Oil & Automotive Service) Marketing
News (*US*)
Overdrive (*US*)
Pulse (*US*)
Pallet Enterprise (*US*)
Pipeline & Gas Journal (*US*)
Portland Magazine (*US*)
Produce Business (*US*)
Promo (*US*)
Road King (*US*)
RV Business (*US*)
Skin Deep (*US*)
Somerset Life (*UK*)
Textile World (*US*)
thesnailmagazine (*UK*)
TimberLine (*US*)
Validation Times (*US*)
Veterinary Economics (*US*)
VMSD (*US*)
World Fishing (*UK*)
Woodshop News (*US*)
Written By (*US*)
Cookery
Alimentum (*US*)
Devon Life (*UK*)
Draft (*US*)
18 Wheels & Heels (*US*)
France (*UK*)
Junior (*UK*)
Netsagas.com (*US*)
Pockets (*US*)
Portland Magazine (*US*)
Skipping Stones (*US*)
Somerset Life (*UK*)
Tatler (*UK*)
Crafts
Ceramic Review (*UK*)
Classic Boat (*UK*)
Crafts (*UK*)

Netsagas.com (*US*)
Popular Woodworking Magazine (*US*)
Quilter's World (*US*)
Sew News (*US*)
Textile World (*US*)
Traverse (*US*)
Woman Alive (*UK*)
Woodshop News (*US*)
The Woodworker (*UK*)
Crime
Beyond the Rainbow (*Aus*)
Black Heart Magazine (*US*)
Carillon Magazine (*UK*)
The Edge (*UK*)
Evidence Technology Magazine (*US*)
Netsagas.com (*US*)
Pseudopod (*US*)
The Rusty Nail (*US*)
The Savage Kick (*UK*)
The Vehicle (*US*)
The Yes Factory (*US*)
Criticism
Acumen (*UK*)
Agenda (*UK*)
Assent (*UK*)
Black Heart Magazine (*US*)
Carillon Magazine (*UK*)
Chapman (*UK*)
DASH Journal (*US*)
The Dickensian (*UK*)
The Dublin Review (*Ire*)
Fence (*US*)
The London Magazine (*UK*)
Lunar Poetry (*UK*)
Netsagas.com (*US*)
The New Shetlander (*UK*)
New Walk Magazine (*UK*)
The Penniless Press (*UK*)
Pennsylvania English (*US*)
The Photo Review (*US*)
Poetry International (*US*)
Post Road (*US*)
The Prairie Journal (*Can*)
The Resurrectionist (*UK*)
Salmagundi Magazine (*US*)
Sequestrum (*US*)
Sorry We're Booked (*US*)
Southwestern American Literature (*US*)
thesnailmagazine (*UK*)
Wasafiri (*UK*)
Culture
Aesthetica: A Review of Contemporary Artists
(*UK*)
Akron Life (*US*)
Beyond the Rainbow (*Aus*)
Chapman (*UK*)
The Conium Review (*US*)
Devon Life (*UK*)
18 Wheels & Heels (*US*)
Esquire (*UK*)
France (*UK*)
Gay Times (GT Magazine) (*UK*)
Geist (*Can*)

Kalyani Magazine. (*US*)
London Review of Books (*UK*)
LONE STARS Magazine (*US*)
Native Max (*US*)
Netsagas.com (*US*)
New Jersey Monthly (*US*)
One (*US*)
Pakn Treger (*US*)
Pennsylvania Heritage (*US*)
Radix Magazine (*US*)
Riddle Fence (*Can*)
The Rusty Nail (*US*)
Salmagundi Magazine (*US*)
Sequestrum (*US*)
Skipping Stones (*US*)
Smithsonian Magazine (*US*)
Sorry We're Booked (*US*)
The Sun (*US*)
Sun Valley Magazine (*US*)
thesnailmagazine (*UK*)
Third Way (*UK*)
Tradicion Revista Magazine (*US*)
Traverse (*US*)
20x20 magazine (*UK*)
Wild Violet (*US*)
Wasafiri (*UK*)
Current Affairs
Aesthetica: A Review of Contemporary Artists
(*UK*)
Gay Times (GT Magazine) (*UK*)
LONE STARS Magazine (*US*)
Milwaukee Magazine (*US*)
Montana Magazine (*US*)
Netsagas.com (*US*)
New Jersey Monthly (*US*)
One (*US*)
Planet (*UK*)
Prairie Messenger (*Can*)
Suffolk Norfolk Life (*UK*)
thesnailmagazine (*UK*)
Tribune (*UK*)
The War Cry (*UK*)
Design
Colorado Homes & Lifestyles (*US*)
Concrete Homes Magazine (*US*)
Machine Design (*US*)
Netsagas.com (*US*)
New York (*US*)
Pipeline & Gas Journal (*US*)
Popular Woodworking Magazine (*US*)
RV Business (*US*)
Ships Monthly Magazine (*UK*)
Sign Builder Illustrated (*US*)
Somerset Life (*UK*)
Textile World (*US*)
Time Out (*UK*)
25 Beautiful Homes (*UK*)
20x20 magazine (*UK*)
VMSD (*US*)
Drama
Aesthetica: A Review of Contemporary Artists
(*UK*)
Areté (*UK*)

Finance
Accountancy Age (*UK*)
Accounting and Business (*UK*)
Consumers Digest (*US*)
Financial Adviser (*UK*)
Ingram's Magazine (*US*)
Netsagas.com (*US*)
NextStepU Magazine (*US*)
Radix Magazine (*US*)
RV Business (*US*)
The Saturday Evening Post (*US*)
Third Way (*UK*)
Timeline (*US*)
Veterinary Economics (*US*)
Whole Life Times (*US*)
Gardening
Akron Life (*US*)
Colorado Homes & Lifestyles (*US*)
Consumers Digest (*US*)
Grow Your Own (*UK*)
Netsagas.com (*US*)
New Jersey Monthly (*US*)
The Saturday Evening Post (*US*)
Somerset Life (*UK*)
Traverse (*US*)
Gothic
The Edge (*UK*)
Netsagas.com (*US*)
T. Gene Davis's Speculative Blog (*US*)
The Vehicle (*US*)
The Yes Factory (*US*)
Health
Abilities (*Can*)
Akron Life (*US*)
Consumers Digest (*US*)
Delaware Today (*US*)
Diabetes Self-Management (*US*)
Dogs Today (*UK*)
Gay Times (GT Magazine) (*UK*)
Health Club Management (*UK*)
Junior (*UK*)
Massage Magazine (*US*)
Netsagas.com (*US*)
New Jersey Monthly (*US*)
Performance (*UK*)
Radix Magazine (*US*)
Right Start Magazine (*UK*)
The Saturday Evening Post (*US*)
Skin Deep (*US*)
Somerset Life (*UK*)
Time Out (*UK*)
Today's Parent (*Can*)
The Vegan (*UK*)
Whole Life Times (*US*)
Woman Alive (*UK*)
Yoga and Health Magazine (*UK*)
Historical
Akron Life (*US*)
BackTrack (*UK*)
Best of British (*UK*)
Classic Boat (*UK*)
Classic Toy Trains (*US*)
Delaware Today (*US*)

Devon Life (*UK*)
The Dickensian (*UK*)
Discover Maine Magazine (*US*)
France (*UK*)
Geist (*Can*)
Midwest Living (*US*)
Milwaukee Magazine (*US*)
Montana Magazine (*US*)
Netsagas.com (*US*)
New Jersey Monthly (*US*)
The New Shetlander (*UK*)
Pakn Treger (*US*)
The Paumanok Review (*US*)
Pennsylvania Heritage (*US*)
Pointe Magazine (*US*)
Railroad Evangelist Magazine (*US*)
Symphony (*US*)
Sable (*UK*)
Ships Monthly Magazine (*UK*)
Skipping Stones (*US*)
Smithsonian Magazine (*US*)
Somerset Life (*UK*)
Sorry We're Booked (*US*)
Steamboat Magazine (*US*)
Suffolk Norfolk Life (*UK*)
Sun Valley Magazine (*US*)
Telluride Magazine (*US*)
The Vehicle (*US*)
Timeline (*US*)
Tradicion Revista Magazine (*US*)
Traverse (*US*)
True West (*US*)
Who Do You Think You Are? Magazine (*UK*)
Wine Press Northwest (*US*)
Hobbies
Angling Times (*UK*)
Astronomy (*US*)
ATV Rider Magazine (*US*)
Bird Watching (*UK*)
Bowls International (*UK*)
British Woodworking (*UK*)
Canadian Writer's Journal (*Can*)
Caravan Magazine (*UK*)
Cigar Aficionado (*US*)
Classic Boat (*UK*)
Classic Toy Trains (*US*)
Dogs Today (*UK*)
Draft (*US*)
18 Wheels & Heels (*US*)
Equus Magazine (*US*)
Forum (*US*)
The Maine Sportsman (*US*)
Model Cars Magazine (*US*)
Netsagas.com (*US*)
Pony Magazine (*UK*)
Pockets (*US*)
Popular Woodworking Magazine (*US*)
Quilter's World (*US*)
Railroad Evangelist Magazine (*US*)
Sea Angler (*UK*)
Sew News (*US*)
Stamp Lover (*UK*)
Stamp Magazine (*UK*)

Club Management (*US*)
Consumers Digest (*US*)
Discover Maine Magazine (*US*)
Draft (*US*)
18 Wheels & Heels (*US*)
Forum (*US*)
GamesMaster (*UK*)
Health Club Management (*UK*)
Lancashire Magazine (*UK*)
The Maine Sportsman (*US*)
Netsagas.com (*US*)
New Jersey Monthly (*US*)
Pacific Yachting (*Can*)
Pockets (*US*)
Portland Magazine (*US*)
Salt Water Sportsman (*US*)
Steamboat Magazine (*US*)
Suffolk Norfolk Life (*UK*)
Sun Valley Magazine (*US*)
Telluride Magazine (*US*)
Today's Parent (*Can*)
Traverse (*US*)
Yoga and Health Magazine (*UK*)
Lifestyle
Abilities (*Can*)
Akron Life (*US*)
bliss Magazine (*UK*)
Christian Home & School (*US*)
Colorado Homes & Lifestyles (*US*)
The Conium Review (*US*)
Consumers Digest (*US*)
Devon Life (*UK*)
18 Wheels & Heels (*US*)
Escapees Magazine (*US*)
Esquire (*UK*)
Forum (*US*)
Go Girl Magazine (*UK*)
Gay Times (GT Magazine) (*UK*)
The Irish Post (*UK*)
Junior (*UK*)
Lancashire Magazine (*UK*)
Midwest Living (*US*)
Milwaukee Magazine (*US*)
Montana Magazine (*US*)
Netsagas.com (*US*)
New Jersey Monthly (*US*)
New York (*US*)
Now (*UK*)
Portland Magazine (*US*)
Real People (*UK*)
Right Start Magazine (*UK*)
The Saturday Evening Post (*US*)
Smithsonian Magazine (*US*)
SpecialLiving magazine (*US*)
Steamboat Magazine (*US*)
Tatler (*UK*)
Telluride Magazine (*US*)
Time Out (*UK*)
Today's Parent (*Can*)
Toledo Area Parent (*US*)
Traverse (*US*)
The Vegan (*UK*)
Whole Life Times (*US*)

Woman Alive (*UK*)
Yours (*UK*)
Zoo (*UK*)
Literature
Acumen (*UK*)
Aesthetica: A Review of Contemporary Artists (*UK*)
Agenda (*UK*)
Assent (*UK*)
Beyond the Rainbow (*Aus*)
Black Heart Magazine (*US*)
Canadian Writer's Journal (*Can*)
Carillon Magazine (*UK*)
Chapman (*UK*)
The Conium Review (*US*)
Crystal Magazine (*UK*)
The Dickensian (*UK*)
The Dublin Review (*Ire*)
Eclectica Magazine (*US*)
Envoi (*UK*)
Fence (*US*)
France (*UK*)
Geist (*Can*)
The Good Book Guide (*UK*)
The Interpreter's House (*UK*)
The List (*UK*)
The London Magazine (*UK*)
London Review of Books (*UK*)
LONE STARS Magazine (*US*)
Lummox (*US*)
Lunar Poetry (*UK*)
Magma (*UK*)
Modern Poetry in Translation (*UK*)
Modern Language Review (*UK*)
Netsagas.com (*US*)
New Walk Magazine (*UK*)
Pakn Treger (*US*)
The Penniless Press (*UK*)
Pennsylvania English (*US*)
Planet (*UK*)
Poetry Express (*UK*)
Poetry International (*US*)
Poetry Ireland Review (*Ire*)
Post Road (*US*)
Prairie Schooner (*US*)
Provincetown Arts (*US*)
Radix Magazine (*US*)
The Reader (*UK*)
Red Rock Review (*US*)
The Rusty Nail (*US*)
The Savage Kick (*UK*)
Sequestrum (*US*)
Slate & Style (*US*)
Sorry We're Booked (*US*)
South Carolina Review (*US*)
Southword Journal (*Ire*)
Stone Canoe (*US*)
The Tablet (*UK*)
The Supplement (*UK*)
The Vehicle (*US*)
thesnailmagazine (*UK*)
20x20 magazine (*UK*)
Wasafiri (*UK*)

Writers' Forum (*UK*)
Media
Intermedia (*UK*)
Media Week (*UK*)
Netsagas.com (*US*)
Now (*UK*)
Radix Magazine (*US*)
thesnailmagazine (*UK*)
Medicine
BMA News (*UK*)
Diabetes Self-Management (*US*)
Equus Magazine (*US*)
Journal of Emergency Medical Services (JEMS)
(*US*)
Netsagas.com (*US*)
The Saturday Evening Post (*US*)
School Nurse News (*US*)
Validation Times (*US*)
Veterinary Economics (*US*)
Whole Life Times (*US*)
Men's Interests
18 Wheels & Heels (*US*)
Esquire (*UK*)
Native Max (*US*)
Netsagas.com (*US*)
Ultimate MMA (*US*)
Zoo (*UK*)
Military
Arms Control Today (*US*)
Commando (*UK*)
Netsagas.com (*US*)
The Savage Kick (*UK*)
Timeline (*US*)
Who Do You Think You Are? Magazine (*UK*)
The Yes Factory (*US*)
Music
Aesthetica: A Review of Contemporary Artists
(*UK*)
Classical Music (*UK*)
Early Music (*UK*)
18 Wheels & Heels (*US*)
Go Girl Magazine (*UK*)
Gay Times (GT Magazine) (*UK*)
International Bluegrass (*US*)
The List (*UK*)
LONE STARS Magazine (*US*)
Music Teacher (*UK*)
Netsagas.com (*US*)
New Jersey Monthly (*US*)
Planet (*UK*)
Pointe Magazine (*US*)
The Resurrectionist (*UK*)
Symphony (*US*)
The Songwriter (*Ire*)
Stone Canoe (*US*)
The Strad (*UK*)
Teaching Music (*US*)
20x20 magazine (*UK*)
Mystery
Black Heart Magazine (*US*)
Carillon Magazine (*UK*)
Crystal Magazine (*UK*)
Netsagas.com (*US*)

New London Writers (*UK*)
Pakn Treger (*US*)
The Paumanok Review (*US*)
The Rusty Nail (*US*)
Sequestrum (*US*)
Suspense Magazine (*US*)
The Vehicle (*US*)
The Yes Factory (*US*)
Nature
Angling Times (*UK*)
Angus Beef Bulletin (*US*)
Animals and You (*UK*)
Bird Watching (*UK*)
The Countryman (*UK*)
Crystal Magazine (*UK*)
Dairy Farmer (*UK*)
The Dawntreader (*UK*)
Devon Life (*UK*)
Discover Maine Magazine (*US*)
Dogs Today (*UK*)
Equus Magazine (*US*)
The Maine Sportsman (*US*)
Montana Magazine (*US*)
National Parks Magazine (*US*)
Netsagas.com (*US*)
New Jersey Monthly (*US*)
Northern Woodlands (*US*)
Pony Magazine (*UK*)
Pallet Enterprise (*US*)
Peace and Freedom (*UK*)
Skipping Stones (*US*)
Smithsonian Magazine (*US*)
Snowy Egret (*US*)
Spider (*US*)
Telluride Magazine (*US*)
Timeline (*US*)
Traverse (*US*)
World Fishing (*UK*)
Whole Life Times (*US*)
New Age
Beyond the Rainbow (*Aus*)
Netsagas.com (*US*)
Whole Life Times (*US*)
Nonfiction
American Indian Art Magazine (*US*)
Abilities (*Can*)
Accountancy Age (*UK*)
Accounting and Business (*UK*)
Acumen (*UK*)
Adventure Cyclist (*US*)
Aesthetica: A Review of Contemporary Artists
(*UK*)
Africa (*Ire*)
African-American Career World (*US*)
Akron Life (*US*)
Alimentum (*US*)
Alternative Law Journal (*Aus*)
Amateur Photographer (*UK*)
American Careers (*US*)
American Turf Monthly (*US*)
Angling Times (*UK*)
Angus Beef Bulletin (*US*)
Animals and You (*UK*)

Aquatics International (*US*)
Aquila (*UK*)
Arc (*UK*)
Arms Control Today (*US*)
Art Business Today (*UK*)
The Art Newspaper (*UK*)
Asheville Poetry Review (*US*)
Assent (*UK*)
Athletics Weekly (*UK*)
ATV Rider Magazine (*US*)
Autocar (*UK*)
BackTrack (*UK*)
Baptist Times (*UK*)
Best of British (*UK*)
Beyond the Rainbow (*Aus*)
The Big Issue in the North (*UK*)
Bird Watching (*UK*)
Black Heart Magazine (*US*)
bliss Magazine (*UK*)
BMA News (*UK*)
Bowls International (*UK*)
British Journal of Photography (*UK*)
British Woodworking (*UK*)
Buses (*UK*)
Canadian Commerce & Industry (*Can*)
Canadian Writer's Journal (*Can*)
Car Magazine (*UK*)
Caravan Magazine (*UK*)
Carillon Magazine (*UK*)
Caterer and Hotelkeeper (*UK*)
Ceramic Review (*UK*)
Chapman (*UK*)
China Grove (*US*)
Christian Home & School (*US*)
Church Times (*UK*)
Cigar Aficionado (*US*)
Classic Boat (*UK*)
Classic Toy Trains (*US*)
Club Management (*US*)
Colorado Homes & Lifestyles (*US*)
Common Ground Review (*US*)
Computer Weekly (*UK*)
Conceit Magazine (*US*)
Concrete Homes Magazine (*US*)
Consumers Digest (*US*)
Cosmetics Magazine (*Can*)
The Countryman (*UK*)
Crafts (*UK*)
Crain's Detroit Business (*US*)
Criminal Law & Justice Weekly (Incorporating
Justice of the Peace) (*UK*)
Crystal Magazine (*UK*)
Currents (*US*)
Cycle Sport (*UK*)
Dairy Farmer (*UK*)
DASH Journal (*US*)
The Dawntreader (*UK*)
Delaware Today (*US*)
Devon Life (*UK*)
The Dickensian (*UK*)
Discover Maine Magazine (*US*)
DIY Week (*UK*)
Dogs Today (*UK*)

Draft (*US*)
Dream Catcher (*UK*)
The Dublin Review (*Ire*)
Early Music (*UK*)
East Lothian Life (*UK*)
Eclectica Magazine (*US*)
EcoHome (*US*)
The Edge (*UK*)
Education Journal (*UK*)
18 Wheels & Heels (*US*)
Electrical Review (*UK*)
Employee Assistance Report (*US*)
Enchanted Conversation (*US*)
Envoi (*UK*)
Equus Magazine (*US*)
Escapees Magazine (*US*)
Esquire (*UK*)
Evening Street Review (*US*)
Eventing (*UK*)
Evidence Technology Magazine (*US*)
Faith & Form (*US*)
Family Law Journal (*UK*)
Fence (*US*)
FIDO Friendly (*US*)
Financial Adviser (*UK*)
Fire Magazine (*UK*)
Forum (*US*)
FourFourTwo (*UK*)
France (*UK*)
Freelance Market News (*UK*)
The Frogmore Papers (*UK*)
Go Girl Magazine (*UK*)
GamesMaster (*UK*)
Gay Times (GT Magazine) (*UK*)
Geist (*Can*)
The Good Book Guide (*UK*)
Greetings Today (*UK*)
The Grocer (*UK*)
Grow Your Own (*UK*)
Health Club Management (*UK*)
Heat (*UK*)
Horse & Hound (*UK*)
ICIS Chemical Business Magazine (*UK*)
Ingram's Magazine (*US*)
Intermedia (*UK*)
International Bluegrass (*US*)
Iota (*UK*)
The Irish Post (*UK*)
Islands (*US*)
Journal of Emergency Medical Services (JEMS)
(*US*)
Junior (*UK*)
Junior Baseball (*US*)
Kalyani Magazine. (*US*)
Kids' Ministry Ideas (*US*)
Lancashire Magazine (*UK*)
LabTalk (*US*)
Launch Pad: Where Young Authors and
Illustrators Take Off! (*US*)
Law Enforcement Technology Magazine (*US*)
Link & Visitor (*Can*)
The List (*UK*)
The Living Church (*US*)

20x20 magazine (*UK*)
The Yes Factory (*US*)
Poetry
Acumen (*UK*)
Aesthetica: A Review of Contemporary Artists (*UK*)
Agenda (*UK*)
Alimentum (*US*)
Ambit (*UK*)
Amulet (*US*)
Areopagus Magazine (*UK*)
Areté (*UK*)
Asheville Poetry Review (*US*)
Assent (*UK*)
Awen (*UK*)
Bard (*UK*)
Beyond the Rainbow (*Aus*)
Black Heart Magazine (*US*)
Brittle Star (*UK*)
Burnside Review (*US*)
Canadian Writer's Journal (*Can*)
Candelabrum Poetry Magazine (*UK*)
Carillon Magazine (*UK*)
Chapman (*UK*)
China Grove (*US*)
Common Ground Review (*US*)
Conceit Magazine (*US*)
The Conium Review (*US*)
Crystal Magazine (*UK*)
Cyphers (*Ire*)
DASH Journal (*US*)
The Dawntreader (*UK*)
Decanto (*UK*)
The Doctor T. J. Eckleburg Review (*US*)
Dream Catcher (*UK*)
Eclectica Magazine (*US*)
18 Wheels & Heels (*US*)
Enchanted Conversation (*US*)
Envoi (*UK*)
Evening Street Review (*US*)
Fence (*US*)
Fire (*UK*)
The Frogmore Papers (*UK*)
Garbaj (*UK*)
Geist (*Can*)
I-70 Review (*UK*)
Inclement (Poetry for the Modern Soul) (*UK*)
The Interpreter's House (*UK*)
Iota (*UK*)
The Journal (*UK*)
Kalyani Magazine. (*US*)
Launch Pad: Where Young Authors and Illustrators Take Off! (*US*)
The London Magazine (*UK*)
London Review of Books (*UK*)
LONE STARS Magazine (*US*)
Lummox (*US*)
Lunar Poetry (*UK*)
Magma (*UK*)
Modern Poetry in Translation (*UK*)
Monkey Kettle (*UK*)
Monomyth (*UK*)
Mslexia (*UK*)

Neon Highway Poetry Magazine (*UK*)
Netsagas.com (*US*)
The New Shetlander (*UK*)
New Walk Magazine (*UK*)
New Welsh Review (*UK*)
The New Writer (*UK*)
New Writing Scotland (*UK*)
Obsessed with Pipework (*UK*)
Other Poetry (*UK*)
PMS poemmemoirstory (*US*)
The Paterson Literary Review (*US*)
The Paumanok Review (*US*)
Peace and Freedom (*UK*)
The Pedestal Magazine (*US*)
Pembroke Magazine (*US*)
The Penniless Press (*UK*)
Pennine Platform (*UK*)
Pennsylvania English (*US*)
Peregrine (*US*)
Permafrost (*US*)
Philadelphia Stories (*US*)
Pilgrimage (*US*)
Pink Chameleon (*US*)
Pinyon (*US*)
Pisgah Review (*US*)
Plain Spoke (*US*)
Planet (*UK*)
Pockets (*US*)
Poetic Licence (*UK*)
The Poetry Church (*UK*)
Poetry Cornwall / Bardhonyeth Kernow (*UK*)
Poetry Express (*UK*)
Poetry International (*US*)
Poetry Ireland Review (*Ire*)
Poetry Review (*UK*)
Poetry Scotland (*UK*)
Poetry Wales (*UK*)
The Portland Review (*US*)
Post Road (*US*)
Potomac Review (*US*)
The Prairie Journal (*Can*)
Prairie Messenger (*Can*)
Prairie Schooner (*US*)
Prairie Winds (*US*)
Premonitions (*UK*)
Presence (*UK*)
PRISM international (*Can*)
Puckerbrush Review (*US*)
Pulsar Poetry Magazine (*UK*)
Quantum Leap (*UK*)
Quiddity (*US*)
Radix Magazine (*US*)
Railroad Evangelist Magazine (*US*)
Reach (*UK*)
The Reader (*UK*)
RealPoetik (*US*)
The Reater (*UK*)
The Red Clay Review (*US*)
Red Poets (*UK*)
Red Rock Review (*US*)
Redactions: Poetry, Poetics, & Prose (*US*)
Reed Magazine (*US*)
The Resurrectionist (*UK*)

Rhino Poetry (*US*)
The Rialto (*UK*)
Riddle Fence (*Can*)
The Rockford Review (*US*)
Room Magazine (*Can*)
The Rusty Nail (*US*)
Sable (*UK*)
Salt Hill Journal (*US*)
Sandy River Review (*US*)
Santa Clara Review (*US*)
Saranac Review (*US*)
Sarasvati (*UK*)
Scar Tissue (*UK*)
Scribbler! (*UK*)
Sequestrum (*US*)
The Seventh Quarry Swansea Poetry Magazine
(*UK*)
The Sewanee Review (*US*)
Shadows Express (*US*)
Shearsman (*UK*)
THE SHOp (*Ire*)
The Sierra Nevada Review (*US*)
Skipping Stones (*US*)
Slate & Style (*US*)
Slow Trains (*US*)
Smoke (*UK*)
Snowy Egret (*US*)
Sorry We're Booked (*US*)
South (*UK*)
South Carolina Review (*US*)
South Dakota Review (*US*)
Southeast Review (*US*)
Southern California Review (*US*)
Southwestern American Literature (*US*)
Southword Journal (*Ire*)
Sou'wester (*US*)
Spider (*US*)
The Stinging Fly (*Ire*)
Stirring : A Literary Collection (*US*)
Stone Canoe (*US*)
storySouth (*US*)
The Stray Branch (*US*)
Straylight (*US*)
Struggle (*US*)
subTerrain Magazine (*Can*)
The Summerset Review (*US*)
The Sun (*US*)
Tales of the Talisman (*US*)
Talking River (*US*)
Tattoo Highway (*US*)
The Teacher's Voice (*US*)
Tears in the Fence (*UK*)
Tellus Magazine (*UK*)
10th Muse (*UK*)
The Recusant (*UK*)
The Rejected Quarterly (*US*)
The Supplement (*UK*)
The Vehicle (*US*)
Third Way (*UK*)
34th Parallel (*US*)
Timber (*US*)
Trajectory (*US*)
20x20 magazine (*UK*)

Wild Violet (*US*)
Wag's Revue (*US*)
Wasafiri (*UK*)
Water-Stone Review (*US*)
The Writing Disorder (*US*)
The Yes Factory (*US*)
Politics
Garbaj (*UK*)
Intermedia (*UK*)
The Irish Post (*UK*)
London Review of Books (*UK*)
Milwaukee Magazine (*US*)
Monkey Kettle (*UK*)
Netsagas.com (*US*)
New Jersey Monthly (*US*)
The New Shetlander (*UK*)
One (*US*)
The Paumanok Review (*US*)
Planet (*UK*)
The Political Quarterly (*UK*)
Red Pepper (*UK*)
Red Poets (*UK*)
The Resurrectionist (*UK*)
Sorry We're Booked (*US*)
Struggle (*US*)
The Sun (*US*)
The Tablet (*UK*)
The Recusant (*UK*)
Third Way (*UK*)
Timeline (*US*)
Total Politics (*UK*)
Tribune (*UK*)
Wild Violet (*US*)
The Yes Factory (*US*)
Psychology
Netsagas.com (*US*)
The Resurrectionist (*UK*)
Right Start Magazine (*UK*)
Radio
Netsagas.com (*US*)
Reference
African-American Career World (*US*)
Greetings Today (*UK*)
Mslexia (*UK*)
Religious
Africa (*Ire*)
Areopagus Magazine (*UK*)
Baptist Times (*UK*)
Christian Home & School (*US*)
Church Times (*UK*)
Faith & Form (*US*)
Kids' Ministry Ideas (*US*)
Link & Visitor (*Can*)
The Living Church (*US*)
Message of the Open Bible (*US*)
Netsagas.com (*US*)
The New Accelerator (*UK*)
One (*US*)
PRISM Magazine (*US*)
Pakn Treger (*US*)
Pockets (*US*)
The Poetry Church (*UK*)
Prairie Messenger (*Can*)

Radix Magazine (*US*)
Railroad Evangelist Magazine (*US*)
RTJ's Creative Catechist (*US*)
Seek (*US*)
The Tablet (*UK*)
Third Way (*UK*)
The War Cry (*UK*)
Wesleyan Life (*US*)
Woman Alive (*UK*)
Romance
Netsagas.com (*US*)
Romance Flash (*US*)
The Vehicle (*US*)
Vanillerotica (*US*)
The Yes Factory (*US*)
Science
Arc (*UK*)
Astronomy (*US*)
Currents (*US*)
Evidence Technology Magazine (*US*)
ICIS Chemical Business Magazine (*UK*)
Intermedia (*UK*)
London Review of Books (*UK*)
Netsagas.com (*US*)
The New Accelerator (*UK*)
New Jersey Monthly (*US*)
Smithsonian Magazine (*US*)
Spider (*US*)
Timeline (*US*)
The Yes Factory (*US*)
Sci-Fi
Arc (*UK*)
Beyond the Rainbow (*Aus*)
Black Heart Magazine (*US*)
Carillon Magazine (*UK*)
Crystal Magazine (*UK*)
The Edge (*UK*)
Launch Pad: Where Young Authors and
Illustrators Take Off! (*US*)
Netsagas.com (*US*)
The New Accelerator (*UK*)
New London Writers (*UK*)
The Paumanok Review (*US*)
Premonitions (*UK*)
The Rusty Nail (*US*)
Sequestrum (*US*)
T. Gene Davis's Speculative Blog (*US*)
Tales of the Talisman (*US*)
The Vehicle (*US*)
The Yes Factory (*US*)
Scripts
Eclectica Magazine (*US*)
Kalyani Magazine. (*US*)
New Writing Scotland (*UK*)
The Prairie Journal (*Can*)
PRISM international (*Can*)
Santa Clara Review (*US*)
Southern California Review (*US*)
Stone Canoe (*US*)
Struggle (*US*)
The Teacher's Voice (*US*)
The Vehicle (*US*)
34th Parallel (*US*)

Self-Help
Abilities (*Can*)
African-American Career World (*US*)
American Careers (*US*)
Diabetes Self-Management (*US*)
Netsagas.com (*US*)
NextStepU Magazine (*US*)
Short Stories
Aesthetica: A Review of Contemporary Artists
(*UK*)
Alimentum (*US*)
Ambit (*UK*)
Aquila (*UK*)
Arc (*UK*)
Areopagus Magazine (*UK*)
Areté (*UK*)
Awen (*UK*)
Beyond the Rainbow (*Aus*)
Big Fiction (*US*)
Black Heart Magazine (*US*)
Black Static (*UK*)
Brittle Star (*UK*)
Burnside Review (*US*)
Carillon Magazine (*UK*)
Carve Magazine (*US*)
Chapman (*UK*)
China Grove (*US*)
Commando (*UK*)
Common Ground Review (*US*)
Conceit Magazine (*US*)
Crystal Magazine (*UK*)
Cyphers (*Ire*)
DASH Journal (*US*)
The Dawntreader (*UK*)
The Doctor T. J. Eckleburg Review (*US*)
Dream Catcher (*UK*)
The Dublin Review (*Ire*)
Evening Street Review (*US*)
Fence (*US*)
FIDO Friendly (*US*)
Fire (*UK*)
The Frogmore Papers (*UK*)
Garbaj (*UK*)
Geist (*Can*)
I-70 Review (*UK*)
The Interpreter's House (*UK*)
Iota (*UK*)
Kalyani Magazine. (*US*)
The London Magazine (*UK*)
Lummox (*US*)
Monkey Kettle (*UK*)
Monomyth (*UK*)
Mslexia (*UK*)
Netsagas.com (*US*)
The New Accelerator (*UK*)
New London Writers (*UK*)
The New Shetlander (*UK*)
New Walk Magazine (*UK*)
New Welsh Review (*UK*)
The New Writer (*UK*)
New Writing Scotland (*UK*)
Notes from the Underground (*UK*)
PMS poemmemoirstory (*US*)

The Paterson Literary Review (*US*)
The Paumanok Review (*US*)
Peace and Freedom (*UK*)
The Pedestal Magazine (*US*)
The Penniless Press (*UK*)
Pennsylvania English (*US*)
Peregrine (*US*)
Permafrost (*US*)
Persimmon Tree (*US*)
Pilgrimage (*US*)
Pink Chameleon (*US*)
Pinyon (*US*)
Pisgah Review (*US*)
Plain Spoke (*US*)
Planet (*UK*)
Pockets (*US*)
Portland Magazine (*US*)
The Portland Review (*US*)
Post Road (*US*)
Potomac Review (*US*)
The Prairie Journal (*Can*)
Prairie Schooner (*US*)
Provincetown Arts (*US*)
Pseudopod (*US*)
Puckerbrush Review (*US*)
Quiddity (*US*)
Romance Flash (*US*)
Railroad Evangelist Magazine (*US*)
The Reader (*UK*)
The Reater (*UK*)
The Red Clay Review (*US*)
Redactions: Poetry, Poetics, & Prose (*US*)
Reed Magazine (*US*)
Rhino Poetry (*US*)
Riddle Fence (*Can*)
The Rockford Review (*US*)
The Rusty Nail (*US*)
Sable (*UK*)
Salt Hill Journal (*US*)
Sandy River Review (*US*)
Santa Clara Review (*US*)
Santa Monica Review (*US*)
Saranac Review (*US*)
Sarasvati (*UK*)
The Saturday Evening Post (*US*)
Scar Tissue (*UK*)
Scary Monsters Magazine (*US*)
Scribbler! (*UK*)
Seek (*US*)
Sequestrum (*US*)
The Sewanee Review (*US*)
Shadows Express (*US*)
Short Story America (*US*)
Slate & Style (*US*)
Snowy Egret (*US*)
Sorry We're Booked (*US*)
South Carolina Review (*US*)
South Dakota Review (*US*)
Southeast Review (*US*)
Southern California Review (*US*)
Southwestern American Literature (*US*)
Southword Journal (*Ire*)
Sou'wester (*US*)

Spider (*US*)
The Stinging Fly (*Ire*)
Stirring : A Literary Collection (*US*)
Stone Canoe (*US*)
The Stray Branch (*US*)
Straylight (*US*)
Struggle (*US*)
subTerrain Magazine (*Can*)
The Summerset Review (*US*)
The Sun (*US*)
Suspense Magazine (*US*)
T. Gene Davis's Speculative Blog (*US*)
Tales of the Talisman (*US*)
Talking River (*US*)
Tattoo Highway (*US*)
The Teacher's Voice (*US*)
Tears in the Fence (*UK*)
The Rejected Quarterly (*US*)
The Supplement (*UK*)
The Vehicle (*US*)
34th Parallel (*US*)
Timber (*US*)
Trajectory (*US*)
20x20 magazine (*UK*)
Unthology (*UK*)
Wild Violet (*US*)
Wasafiri (*UK*)
Water-Stone Review (*US*)
Woman's Weekly (*UK*)
The Writing Disorder (*US*)
The Yellow Room (*UK*)
The Yes Factory (*US*)
Your Cat (*UK*)
Yours (*UK*)
Sociology
The Big Issue in the North (*UK*)
Netsagas.com (*US*)
Peace and Freedom (*UK*)
The Resurrectionist (*UK*)
Skipping Stones (*US*)
thesnailmagazine (*UK*)
Third Way (*UK*)
Timeline (*US*)
Who Do You Think You Are? Magazine (*UK*)
Whole Life Times (*US*)
Spiritual
Beyond the Rainbow (*Aus*)
The Living Church (*US*)
Netsagas.com (*US*)
The New Accelerator (*UK*)
Pilgrimage (*US*)
Whole Life Times (*US*)
The Yes Factory (*US*)
Sport
Abilities (*Can*)
American Turf Monthly (*US*)
Angling Times (*UK*)
Athletics Weekly (*UK*)
Bowls International (*UK*)
Cycle Sport (*UK*)
Discover Maine Magazine (*US*)
Draft (*US*)
Equus Magazine (*US*)

BackTrack (*UK*)
Buses (*UK*)
Car Magazine (*UK*)
Caravan Magazine (*UK*)
Caterer and Hotelkeeper (*UK*)
Classic Boat (*UK*)
Consumers Digest (*US*)
Crystal Magazine (*UK*)
Devon Life (*UK*)
Dogs Today (*UK*)
Draft (*US*)
Eclectica Magazine (*US*)
Escapees Magazine (*US*)
FIDO Friendly (*US*)
Forum (*US*)
France (*UK*)
The Irish Post (*UK*)
Islands (*US*)
Junior (*UK*)
Midwest Living (*US*)
Milwaukee Magazine (*US*)
Montana Magazine (*US*)
Netsagas.com (*US*)
New York (*US*)
NextStepU Magazine (*US*)
Overdrive (*US*)
Pacific Yachting (*Can*)
Pakn Treger (*US*)
Railroad Evangelist Magazine (*US*)
Road King (*US*)
RV Business (*US*)
Sable (*UK*)
The Saturday Evening Post (*US*)
Sea Magazine (*US*)
Ships Monthly Magazine (*UK*)
Skipping Stones (*US*)
Somerset Life (*UK*)
Southeast Review (*US*)
SpecialLiving magazine (*US*)
Steamboat Magazine (*US*)
Sun Valley Magazine (*US*)
Tatler (*UK*)
Telluride Magazine (*US*)

Time Out (*UK*)
Tradicion Revista Magazine (*US*)
Wedding (*UK*)
Wine Press Northwest (*US*)
Wine Spectator (*US*)
Woman Alive (*UK*)
Yachting Magazine (*US*)
TV
The List (*UK*)
Netsagas.com (*US*)
Written By (*US*)
Westerns
Crystal Magazine (*UK*)
Netsagas.com (*US*)
The Paumanok Review (*US*)
The Rusty Nail (*US*)
The Savage Kick (*UK*)
The Vehicle (*US*)
True West (*US*)
The Yes Factory (*US*)
Women's Interests
Aesthetica: A Review of Contemporary Artists (*UK*)
bliss Magazine (*UK*)
Kalyani Magazine. (*US*)
Link & Visitor (*Can*)
Mslexia (*UK*)
Native Max (*US*)
Netsagas.com (*US*)
Now (*UK*)
PMS poemmemoirstory (*US*)
Persimmon Tree (*US*)
Real People (*UK*)
Resources for Feminist Research (*Can*)
Room Magazine (*Can*)
Sorry We're Booked (*US*)
Tatler (*UK*)
Wedding Ideas (*UK*)
Woman Alive (*UK*)
Woman's Weekly (*UK*)
The Yellow Room (*UK*)
Yours (*UK*)

Get Free Access to the firstwriter.com Website

To claim your free access to the firstwriter.com website simply go to the website at http://www.firstwriter.com/subscribe and begin the subscription process as normal. On the second page you will be asked to select your preferred payment processor, but don't worry – this doesn't mean you will have to make any payments!

Select whichever payment processor you prefer (we suggest using WorldPay unless you already have a PayPal account) and then continue to enter the requested details. When you are given the opportunity to enter a voucher / coupon reference number please enter the following promotional code:

- **GX47-S2TP**

This will reduce the cost of creating a subscription by up to $15 / £10 / €15, making it free to create a monthly, quarterly, or combination subscription. Alternatively, you can use the discount to take out an annual or life subscription at a reduced rate.

Select the subscription plan you prefer and proceed to complete the subscription process. Please note that you will need to provide your payment details, even if there is no up-front payment. This is in case you choose to leave your subscription running after the free initial period, but there is no obligation for you to do so.

When you use this code to take out a free subscription you are under no obligation to make any payments whatsoever and you are free to cancel your account before you make any payments if you wish.

If you need any assistance, please email support@firstwriter.com.

If you have found this book useful, please consider leaving a review on the website where you bought it!

What you get

Once you have set up access to ths site you will be able to benefit from all the following features:

Databases

All our databases are updated almost every day, and include powerful search facilities to help you find exactly what you need. Searches that used to take you hours or even days in print books or on search engines can now be done in seconds, and produce more accurate and up-to-date information. Our agents database also includes independent reports from at least three separate sources, showing you which are the top agencies and helping you avoid the scams that are all over the internet. You can try out any of our databases before you subscribe:

- Search **over 850 literary agencies**
- Search **over 1,600 book publishers**
- Search **over 1,800 magazines**
- Search between **100** and **250 current competitions**

PLUS advanced features to help you with your search:

- Save searches and save time – set up to 15 search parameters specific to your work, save them, and then access the search results with a single click whenever you log in. You can even save multiple different searches if you have different types of work you are looking to place.
- Add personal notes to listings, visible only to you and fully searchable – helping you to organise your actions.
- Set reminders on listings to notify you when to submit your work, when to follow up, when to expect a reply, or any other custom action.
- Track which listings you've viewed and when, to help you organise your search – any listings which have changed since you last viewed them will be highlighted for your attention!

Daily email updates

As a subscriber you will be able to take advantage of our email alert service, meaning you can specify your particular interests and we'll send you automatic email updates when we change or add a listing that matches them. So if you're interested in agents dealing in romantic fiction in the United States you can have us send you emails with the latest updates about them – keeping you up to date without even having to log in.

User feedback

Our agent, publisher, and magazine databases all include a user feedback feature that allows our subscribers to leave feedback on each listing – giving you not only the chance to have your say about the markets you contact, but giving a unique authors' perspective on the listings.

Save on copyright protection fees

If you're sending your work away to publishers, competitions, or literary agents, it's vital that you first protect your copyright. As a subscriber to firstwriter.com you can do this through our site and save 10% on the copyright registration fees normally payable for protecting your work internationally through the Intellectual Property Rights Office.

firstwriter.magazine

firstwriter.magazine showcases the best in new poetry and fiction from around the world. If you're interested in writing and want to get published, the most important thing you can do is read contemporary writing that's getting into print now. firstwriter.magazine helps you do that.

Half price competitions

As well as saving money on copyright registration, subscribers to firstwriter.com can also make further savings by entering writing competitions at a special reduced rate. Subscribers can enter the firstwriter.com International Poetry Competition and International Short Story Contest for half price.

Monthly newsletter

When you subscribe to firstwriter.com you also receive our monthly email newsletter – described by one publishing company as "the best in the business" – including articles, news, and interviews for writers. And the best part is that you can continue to receive the newsletter even after you stop your paid subscription – at no cost!

Terms and conditions

The promotional code contained in this publication may be used by the owner of the book only to create one subscription to firstwriter.com at a reduced cost, or for free. It may not be used by or disseminated to third parties. Should the code be misused then the owner of the book will be liable for any costs incurred, including but not limited to payment in full at the standard rate for the subscription in question. The code may be used at any time until the end of the calendar year named in the title of the publication, after which time it will become invalid. The code may be redeemed against the creation of a new account only – it cannot be redeemed against the ongoing costs of keeping a subscription open. In order to create a subscription a method of payment must be provided, but there is no obligation to make any payment. Subscriptions may be cancelled at any time, and if an account is cancelled before any payment becomes due then no payment will be made. Once a subscription has been created, the normal schedule of payments will begin on a monthly, quarterly, or annual basis, unless a life Subscription is selected, or the subscription is cancelled prior to the first payment becoming due. Subscriptions may be cancelled at any time, but if they are left open beyond the date at which the first payment becomes due and is processed then payments will not be refundable.

Claim your FREE access to www.firstwriter.com: See p.379